M

ANN ARBOR DISTRICT LIBRARY
31621012227688

D1560797

Gottfried Semper

ARCHITECT OF THE NINETEENTH CENTURY

W. Ungers, *Gottfried Semper*, 1871. From *Zeitschrift für bildende Kunst*, 1879.

GOTTFRIED SEMPER

Architect of the Nineteenth Century

HARRY FRANCIS MALLGRAVE

Yale University Press
New Haven & London

Designed by Gillian Malpass
Printed in Hong Kong

Library of Congress Cataloging-in-Publication Data

Mallgrave. Harry Francis.
Gottfried Semper: architect of the nineteenth century:
a personal and intellectual biography / Harry Francis Mallgrave.
Includes bibliographical references and index.
ISBN 0-300-06624-4 (cloth: alk. paper)
1. Semper, Gottfried, 1803–1879. 2. Architects – Switzerland – Biography.
I. Title.
NA1353.S45M36 1996
720′.92–dc20
[B] 95-47561
CIP

A catalogue record for this book is available from
The British Library

To the Memory of Anni and Wolfgang Herrmann

Contents

Prologue 1

1 The Despondent Years: 1803–1834 11
- Göttingen, Munich, Regensburg 11
- Paris, Bremerhaven, Paris 18
- The Debate on Polychromy 25
- Italy, Sicily, Greece 38
- Return to Rome 46
- Preliminary Remarks . . . 53

2 Royal Success in Dresden: 1834–1849 67
- Artistic Life in "Florence on the Elbe" 67
- The Crisis of Architectural Historicism in Germany 79
- The Making of an Architect 92
- The Dresden Hoftheater 117
- Setbacks in Hamburg 129
- Assyrian Alabaster 149

3 Refugee in Paris and London: 1849–1855 165
- The "Semper Barricade" 165
- The Four Elements of Architecture 177
- The "Great University of 1851" 189
- The Future of Art in the Industrial Age 200
- Professor at the Department of Practical Art 208
- Greek Tectonics and Ancient Missiles 219

4 The Zurich Years: 1855–1869 229
- A New Start in Switzerland 229
- Richard Wagner and the Munich "Episode" 251
- Prolegomena to a Theory of Style 267
- Theory of Artistic Forms 277
- The Masking of Reality in the Arts 290
- The Third Volume of *Der Stil* 302

5 The Monumental Builder: 1869–1879 309
Overtures from Vienna 309
The Ringstrasse Monuments 321
Semper and the Birth of Tragedy 339

Epilogue 355

Notes 382

Bibliography 420

Index 434

Prologue

Architecture and Theatricality

It was, according to the lone account of one eye-witness, a rather meager procession of "German artists and friends of art" that accompanied the casket containing the remains of Gottfried Semper south toward Rome's Porta San Paolo on a mid-May morning in 1879. The deceased's eldest son, the architect Manfred Semper, had, however, hastened to the Italian capital from the north and arrived just in time to grasp the hand of his dying father. Apparently there was no thought given to shipping the body across the Alps for burial. As the cortege approached the pyramid of Caius Cestius, it turned right along the city wall and entered the poplar-crowded confines of Rome's Protestant cemetery (Pl. 1). It was here that "the mortal remains of one of the greatest and most distinguished men of our century" were prepared to be "delivered to foreign soil, to the classical soil of the Eternal City."[1]

The orations at the cemetery, however, did not pass without incident. As the coffin was positioned above the open grave, a quarrel broke out between the orthodox German pastor conducting the funeral service and a longtime friend of the deceased, the physiologist Jakob Moleschott. The pastor was incensed that this agnostic and notorious philosophical materialist, whose ethical neutrality was presumed to pose a grave threat to theologically sanctioned morality, had prepared a lengthy homily to his dear friend. When both men refused to back down from their respective claims and duties, it was only the quick mediation of Manfred that kept them from actually coming to blows.

If funerals are social symbols designed to proclaim and represent the accomplishments of a life, then this small tense gathering over the cold body of Gottfried Semper was in many respects a fitting conclusion to his life, which was fraught with myriad conflicts and scuffles. But the symbolism of this melodrama can also be extended in another way. Earlier in the century, indeed in many previous centuries, great artists were more typically extolled in death, not unlike heads of state. We need only to recall the last offices of the architect Karl Friedrich Schinkel, whose coffin on one chilly morning in October 1841 was followed through the streets of Berlin by a throng of mourners: "a funeral procession such as the great court had seldom seen."[2] At the city's cemetery, respected figures of every persuasion lined up, one after the other, to deliver their eulogies. The young Prussian monarch, Friedrich Wilhelm IV, on the spot commissioned a marble statue of Schinkel, which was to be placed in the vestibule of the architect's famous museum.

Even though Semper, too, would eventually receive his statue (in 1892), he and the circumstances of his lonely passing were progeny of another, somewhat less temperate era.[3] If it was an age only slightly less ingenuous in its overt decorum, it was a time certainly more brutally complex in its gyrations toward that phenomenon known today simply as

1 Tomb of Gottfried Semper. Institut für Geschichte und Theorie der Architectur, Semper Archiv, ETH-Zurich.

"modernity." The years 1841 and 1879 were in so many ways worlds apart, and the cultural experiences and expectations of their participants were more diverse than the simple notion of a generation would suggest.

Schinkel's prolific career, although delayed in reaching stride, could hardly have been more idyllic, his life more stable. A successful designer of dioramas and stage scenery, a painter, energetic traveler, companion to many of Germany's leading intellectuals, confidant and consultant to various princes and kings – the Prussian architect gained a prominent architectural post within the state bureaucracy just as this northern German power was reversing the gloomy financial fortunes of the Napoleonic years and embarking on a dynamic program of building and expansion. He graced Berlin and nearby Potsdam with a host of urban monuments, royal residences, and smaller commissions, many of which are standing today as a legacy to his refined and elegant Neoclassicism. He ruled the Germanic architectural world with scarcely a competitor or peer; after his passing he was unanimously hailed throughout the still independent German towns and states as the greatest German architect of all time.

Semper's life and practice was in every respect less genial; it was rife with great victories, professional setbacks, legal conflicts, artistic resurrections, and no small measure of humiliation. His initial artistic prosperity in the Saxon capital of Dresden, referred to in the nineteenth century as "Florence on the Elbe," brought him early – and by architectural standards truly precocious – fame. By the mid-1840s he was regarded throughout Germany as perhaps the most talented of the younger generation of architects and as the heir apparent to the numinous mantle of Schinkel. This happy phase of his career was brought to a rude close by the political upheavals of 1848–49, which resulted in Semper's banishment from his homeland, years of poverty and disgrace, intellectual isolation, and intense personal acrimony. The gradual reconstruction of his life and career in London and Zurich was marked more often than not by deeply rooted feelings of hostility and embittered frustration. To all intents and purposes, England remained closed to a refugee's practice of architecture, and German-speaking Switzerland, with its long-standing political liberality and almost compulsive fiscal frugality, afforded the former monumental builder few possibilities of major commissions. Even his most sublime artistic labor during these years – his grandiose designs for the colossal Wagnerian Festspielhaus in Munich – fell victim to personal duplicity and courtly intrigues. And Semper's later monumental contributions to the city of Vienna, carried out under the most difficult personal circumstances, were undertaken when his creative powers were on the wane. The aging master was too frail to attend the opening of his final artistic triumph: his masterful second Hoftheater in Dresden. When he decided in his forced retirement to return south to his artistic wellspring (still in moral exile from Germany, his country of birth) he was a proud yet tired and broken man. In the many biographical accounts written in the first years after his death, he was generally acclaimed by his countrymen simply as Germany's "second greatest" architect.

But even this scarcely maculated architectural reputation, earned at a time when many architects (and Semper in particular) still viewed themselves as spiritual descendants of Bramante and Michelangelo, has suffered in our century. The indisputable merit and grandeur of his monumental creations, so universally heralded in his lifetime, was less appreciated over time, due to changing tastes and more stolid attitudes. His work as a theorist meanwhile gained ascendancy. It can even be said, as indeed it was suggested during his lifetime, that the distinctly "modern" flavor of his critical writings – so enormously influential to the practice of art, architecture, art history, aesthetics, and even the archaeology and anthropology of the second half of the nineteenth century – may have harmed his standing as an architect. Somehow a rift came to be construed between his theory and practice, that is to say, between the always rich and discerning level of his artistic analyses and the comparatively lesser regard for his historicist practice.

But here the historical persona of Semper rubs up against some questionable historical assumptions. Since the first years of the twentieth century the architecture of the nineteenth century has come to be seen as a more or less fickle stylistic masquerade of dubious artistic merit. Already in 1902, Hermann Muthesius could characterize (and therefore summarily dismiss) the artistic labor of the previous 100 years as the "inartistic century."[4] In what would later become the standard version of Adam's Fall, some sinful tendency toward infecundity is presumed to have taken root in the early years of the century, poisoning all subsequent efforts, until the work of a few brave leaders or pioneers stepped forth at the start of the new era to reinvigorate design.

According to Sigfried Giedion's even more inspired account of 1928, *Bauen in Frankreich, Bauen in Eisen, Bauen in Eisenbeton* (Building in France, Building in Iron, Building in Ferroconcrete), the controlling *Zeitgeist* of creativity fled the ateliers of the Ecole des Beaux-Arts around 1830 to haunt the nearby Ecole Polytechnique, thereby instilling this newly created institution with its magisterial spirit of progress and development. This thesis allowed Giedion to define an architectural lineage almost entirely non-architectural in its pedigree: a lineage that ran from the cast-iron framework of Henri Labrouste's

Bibliothèque Ste-Geneviève to the courageous "constructors" (they were no longer architects) Tony Garnier, Auguste Perret, and Le Corbusier – via a score of such intervening French engineers as Gustave Eiffel. Thus at a stroke the once high and mighty art of architecture, in particular that phantom practiced between 1830 and 1900, could seemingly forever be exorcized from historical concern.

If indeed this notion of a "divide" has fallen out of favor in recent times, we must still pose the question of just how such an act of historical suppression (or should it be called repression?) could actually take place. Even today the meaning of historicism in most architectural textbooks is virtually synonymous with the practice of a quaint schematism or sterile imitation. But this is indeed a filter – we must recognize – that we ourselves have imposed on historical investigation. If we choose to view the architecture of the nineteenth century as some kind of Ruskinian stroll down a sentimental (Hinkseyian) bylane (taking flight at the idea that on Monday morning a railway line will be run into town), we should at least acknowledge that this perception is vastly different from the more compelling images painted in the critical literature of the nineteenth century. And whereas we often choose to describe historicism in terms of history's stifling grasp over design, architects of this time were perhaps somewhat more honest in admitting that design can never entirely free itself from the dialectic of historical development – that is, historical analyses can also be powerful agents in crafting a new and more cogent architecture for the present. At the very least, to ignore the critical debate that took place during these productive and unsettled years is to divest the nineteenth century of its legitimate intellectual legacy: from the testing drama of Schinkel's self-acknowledged failing with the functional architecture of "pure radical abstraction" (ca. 1830) to Karl Bötticher rearing back from the precipice – that "colossal emptiness" – of non-historical design (1846).[5]

Semper remains today perhaps the more bewitching example of this failed historicist paradigm. As the most influential German architect of the second half of the nineteenth century (that period in which the principles of modernism were intellectually tested and codified) his ideas, in both word and deed, dominated his culture to an extent that has been matched in few artists since. German architectural practice and thought during the last three decades of the century, in fact, operated almost entirely within the intellectual framework established by Semper. At the same time, his theory and practice necessarily displayed the very same historical incongruities or paradoxes seen in so many of his contemporaries. Because he perceived so early the artistic aspirations and implications of industrialization, because he experienced so keenly the intellectual anxieties of his age, because he understood better than most the historical limitations of his own approach to design, in short, because he was one of the first architects of the nineteenth century to articulate the problem of modernity in so many of its more revolutionary aspects – so the various arguments run – Semper's theory was radically inconsistent with his practice.

Such a conclusion, I think, is grounded in two historical simplifications. The first really derives from the persistent wholesale marketing of Semperian catchphrases: the selective solicitation of remarks so that his views have been made to conform to the premises of materialism, idealism, functionalism, modernism, Romanticism, Marxism, historicism, or whichever "ism" has best suited the leading premise of different authors. Thus a single early statement encouraging the honest display of brick and iron has been proclaimed as the intellectual forebear of a functionalist aesthetic. Thus his occasional musings on the relation of architecture to nature have been decked out with the full metaphysical regalia of a Schelling or a Schlegel. Thus the hesitant use of a single mathematical analogy in his discussion of style – comments that were manipulated and distorted by his son in their translation from English into German – has been accepted as the deterministic core of his materialist architectural credo. This last judgment, first exploited in 1901 by Alois Riegl for his own historical purposes, has dogged Semperian scholarship for nearly a century and demonstrated to what absurd lengths historical generalities can be carried when they are accepted unchallenged. Semper's diffusive style of writing has no doubt contributed to this selective reading of his thought: the fact that his ideas underwent decades of questioning and development, allowing few resting points around which to hang the placard "mature thought."

The second historical barrier interposing itself between Semper's theory and his practice has been a general unwillingness in the twentieth century, and now perhaps an inability too, to understand the principal aims and themes of nineteenth-century architectural practice. This is indeed a difficult task now – even for those willing to make the effort. Accustomed as we are to viewing this century in the superficial terms of its many styles, we seem to have lost sight of the fact that architectural production can be tested in the ideological arena in much more profound ways: as a creative act infused with the most ingenious artistic and technical intentions. If we were to approach this period with less bias, perhaps we would discover that we are dealing with some of the best educated and best trained professionals ever to practice their craft, and that the discrepancy between our earlier assessment of their imaginative powers and the depth of issues raised and debated by them at the time is quite striking.

The last half of the nineteenth century for Germany was above all a time of rapid and profound change. From the diffusion across the country of industrial methods and technologies (bridges, railway stations, arcades, exhibition halls), to the ascendancy of democratic, middle-class values (and with them what Friedrich Nietzsche facetiously termed bourgeois "good taste"),[6] Germany found itself – no less than France or Britain or the United States – radically reconstituted: politically, economically, culturally. If most architects viewed these forces as challenges to their vaunted artistic autonomy, they also saw these same changes, more importantly, as grave threats to the very survival of art. The response, quite naturally, was not to seek the overthrow of the historical or representational systems upon which the profession's artistic education had for centuries been based, but rather to search out some means by which precisely these privileged artistic systems, with all the fine artistic nuances that had accrued during the nineteenth-century discourse, might be transformed into a new and meaningful architecture. The underlying assumption in this process, which in every way presages more recent architectural concerns, was that this enhanced representational system would be superior to any constructional alternative – a tendency even then seen as dehumanizing.

Several excellent studies within the last few decades, both within and without the literature on German architecture, have sought to address these historical shortcomings in general, and the perceived rupture of Semper's theory and practice in particular. Recent and insightful efforts to interpret Semper's practice in light of his theory have included varying views of his designs as expressions of his social and political sensibilities, or as demonstrations of one or more of his "four elements" or of his theory of "dressing" (*Bekleidung*), or as logical explications of his aesthetic "authorities" or "stylistic coefficients."[7] In two highly suggestive analyses of Semper's architecture in this regard, his buildings have been read as elaborately conceived, carefully woven, self-referential panoplies of iconographic and constructional motifs, as "grandiloquent meditations on the history of tectonic expression."[8] Such studies have made many new inroads with regard to Semper, and they have illuminated an often overlooked aspect of historicist aspirations in general: that in addition to invoking architecture's traditional representational languages (styles), many architects of the second half of the century lent increasing emphasis to exploring a suitable representation for architecture's new constructional or tectonic purposes.

Yet beyond architecture's capacity for self-referentiality, this art has traditionally sought expression at a monumental level in other ways. Emphasis on iconographic values, for instance, was also an important cornerstone of Semper's conception of monumentality, and it was posthumously given documentation in 1902 with the publication of his elaborate representational program for his two Vienna museums.[9] Through it, these works could now be read as intricate matrices of themes and sub-themes, horizontally, vertically, and chronologically depicting the history of art and science. Other studies, both in the past and present, have reviewed the equally complex iconography of the Dresden Gallery and the second Dresden Hoftheater.[10] In addition, we now have the very instructive drawings by the hand of Semper himself, most especially his sketches for the Wagnerian or Munich Festspielhaus. These sketches make it clear that Semper took into account the iconographic and allegorical content of his works at the start of his visual studies. The detailing thus composed not so much a scheme to be externally applied as an internal articulation of the work's underlying artistic and cultural content. The importance of such aspirations are historically underscored, for instance, when we consider that Semper's efforts to give thematic precedence to Dionysus over Apollo in the iconography of the second Dresden Hoftheater were made during the very same months that Friedrich Nietzsche was composing *The Birth of Tragedy*. Indeed, as the investigation below hopes to makes clear, their artistic outlooks at this time were more or less identical and this accord was more than simple coincidence or the action of some temporal spirit.

Of course the conception of architecture as an expository discipline in service to some personal, political, religious, or artistic ideal has been an approach to building as old as the first crude huts set up to shelter a sacred flame. What gave this didactic intention new importance in the nineteenth century was the translation of these elocutionary motifs into dressings fitted to the aspiring bourgeois culture – that is, architecture in service less to a military institution or political authority and more to a higher social abstraction. These relatively new building types of public museums, libraries, theaters, and opera halls were certainly intended from the start to entertain, but likewise to school their new class of benefactors into the higher reaches of their cultural heritage. Perhaps the most skillful of the early nineteenth-century architects to conceive of architecture in this manner was Semper's mentor, Karl Friedrich Schinkel, who first cultivated this practice through his designs for dioramas, stage designs, and allegorical paintings. With the creation of his grand processional frescoes for the Berlin Museum in the 1820s and 1830s, which depicted in allegorical cycles the evolutionary course of the heavens, the earth, the human race, and – most importantly – human culture, Schinkel pursued a vision of architecture as urban theater: a monumental stage that through its very urbanity appeals to and fosters the highest human instincts, a place where the new burghers of this young metropolis could come and gain initiation into the mythological and poetic rites of their European legacy.

It is the very same intention that Semper brought to his monumental works, which in their attempted artistic synthesis (again not coincidentally) rivaled the operatic productions of his close friend Richard Wagner. Dazzling and variegated surfaces, exaggerated rustication, spatially audacious public areas, grand palatial or processional entries – all were devices intended specifically to astonish and to make the spectator aware of his presence within a larger communal ritual, as Walter Benjamin has made manifest.[11] Now the anonymous spectator, like his presumed counterpart in classical antiquity, could enjoy the pleasure of performing upon a lavish public stage, in addition to having the thrill of viewing others within the same context. The desire on the part of the architects of this period to enhance this drama led them to ever more intense effects and greater sophistication of detailing. For instance, the cavernous and sumptuous ascension toward the domed inner sanctum of the Vienna Art Museum was a deliberate spatial exercise by Semper of truly grandiose proportions. The famous arcades and exhibition halls, of course, carried this tendency forward along a different but parallel pathway.

We shall describe Semper's understanding of monumental architecture in this regard as his sense for *theatricality*, a term that has been applied to his work on at least one occasion in the past.[12] It is a term that unfortunately also carries with it connotations different from those intended here. Through its more general association with the Baroque period, for example, the term has sometimes been used to signify illusional or staged effects, such as produced by the angled perspectives of stage scenery introduced by the Bibiena family at the start of the eighteenth century. Other, more recent, writers have employed the term to signify a regressive relationship between the art work and the beholder, that is, an intrusive, pandering quality of objecthood foreign to more legitimate modernist sensibilities.[13] In colloquial discourse, the term often also suggests a sense of superficiality or deceit.

These meanings are, for the most part, negative declamations of recent vintage. The nineteenth-century architect Charles Garnier, for instance, defined the "theatrical" as a primeval and innate human sentiment: an impulse that manifests itself whenever two or more people come together in any setting. "To see and be seen, to understand and to make oneself understood," he reasoned, "this is the fatal circle of humanity; to be an actor or a spectator, this is the vital condition of life; this is both the end and the means." Again, "All that happens in the world is, in essence, only theater and representation."[14] Garnier concluded his discursive anthropological preface to his book on the nineteenth-century theater by reducing architecture to two primary building types – the church and the theater – the first conceived for the "divine spectacle," the second for the "human spectacle."[15]

We can, however, employ the term theatrical in a positive way, in the sense of the Greek word *théatron*, meaning "a place to view, to behold." We can also apply the term in a stricter architectural sense: yet one that encompasses both Semper's theory and practice. Although it can be argued that this term possesses a lengthy architectural pedigree, and most especially in the French architectural theory of the eighteenth and early nineteenth centuries, our focus in the present volume will restrict itself to the unique way in which the concept took shape within Semper's own artistic development. It is a concept fully evolved in Schinkel's approach to architectural and urban design, but for Semper the notion also has roots in his youthful fascination with the origin of primordial artistic motives and in his vividly polychrome conception of ancient monuments. Already upon his return from his student tour of Italy, Sicily, and Greece (that is, prior to the practice of his art), he could align the birth of monumental architecture with the creation of the primitive theatrical scaffold (the temple), with the richly outfitted and brilliantly bedecked stage upon which the first communal rituals were enacted.

This was a vision to which he held steadfastly. His quest was then to clothe this primitive artistic instinct for ritual within a suitable theory of representation – a variegated approach to design capable of functioning on multiple levels. It was in every sense an exceedingly broad and far-reaching pursuit.

In his many designs, Semper's sense for theatricality could be manifested as a spatial or scenographic device: the conscious pursuit of drama, of dramatic effects intended to impress, inform, amuse, but above all to sever the viewer's "normal" (as Nietzsche once recorded in his close reading of Semper) or everyday complicity with the world. Semper's sense for theatricality can also be seen in the fleshiness and materiality of his forms, in the raw power of his rustication, in his sense for fine execution and complex detailing, once again in often exaggerated proportions. This same feeling can be found in his allegorical effects, in his mastery at composing an ensemble of forms, and in his unparalleled capacity for situating his buildings for their maximum urban effect. Similar intentions, incidentally, were certainly not unique to Semper and can be found throughout the architecture of the nineteenth century.

What truly makes Semper's sense for theatricality different, however, was his attempt to articulate his conception in theoretical terms. We need not refer at this point to the most obvious passages of Semper dealing quite specifically with the theater and monumentality, with the theme of the theatrical mask (his famous references to the "haze of carnival candles" as the "true atmosphere of art"), but rather to his underlying conception of architecture as something that must appeal to the higher laws of humanity, as something to be directed toward the national consciousness of a people. Richard Wagner's well-known regard for dramatic art as the symbolic reenactment of primeval social rites owes much to the artistic tutelage he received under Semper. Even the much bandied notion of a Wagnerian *Gesamtkunstwerk* (synthesis of the arts) possesses an important, yet so far unacknowledged debt to Semper.

In examining Semper's thought in light of this notion of theatricality, precedence can be given neither to his theory nor to his practice, as each must be viewed as a manifestation of the same artistic vision. His theory drove his practice in the same way that his practice, in ways seldom appreciated, directed his theory. It should also be said that Semper considered himself first and foremost an architect, and only secondarily a theorist: regardless of his historical importance in this last respect. He was perhaps the last major architect to measure himself against the high artistic standards of the Renaissance and its great artists.

Our effort to explore Semper in this way has resulted in something of a hybrid work: part monograph, part critical study, part biography. Such an approach was suggested first of all by the forceful and arresting personality of Semper, toward whom so many of his contemporaries stood in deference (Pl. 2). If in the face of his many personal misfortunes he came to rule the artistic culture of his time, it was only because of his enormous energy and indomitable will. Of medium height and stocky build, he was outgoing in his demeanor and by nature forthright and spirited. Wagner famously records Semper as an iconoclast who could always be counted on to bring instant excitement, if not fisticuffs,

2 Portrait of Gottfried Semper, ca. 1870. Institut für Geschichte und Theorie der Architectur, Semper Archiv, ETH-Zurich.

to any social gathering, with his "peculiar habit of contradicting everyone flatly."[16] From the days of his youth, Semper gave an inordinate amount of his time, as he said, to "love affairs, commerce with jealous asses and scoundrels, and dueling," and in his later years he can also be portrayed as a man in perpetual battle with his century's mores, above all with its social conventions and pretensions. And whereas this anger and impetuousness on several occasions carried him near to and over the brink of personal disaster, it was this same intensity that inspired his art.

A friend reported coming upon Semper, one evening in Dresden, throwing stones at the keystones of the first Hoftheater.[17] It seems that the architect was unhappy with his design or the execution of this particular detail and he was violently enraged to see it (presumably forever) etched in stone. Despite such startling behavior, colleagues were unanimous in their praise of his talent: "He possessed," noted one admirer, "the greatest immediacy to artistic sensitivity and the finest artistic judgment of any man I have ever met."[18] If this uncompromising artistic integrity made him on many occasions exceedingly difficult to work with, this same fire also endeared Semper to many architects of the next generation – for whom his stature assumed heroic proportions.

Another reason why a limited biographical format is called for in the case of Semper, is the importance his theory and built works possess for more broadly based cultural studies. The Semper–Wagner–Nietzsche triangle of ideas alluded to above underscores the centrality of Semper's thought to the nineteenth century, but it is a presence yet to be adequately perceived or assessed. Of the many dozens of biographies devoted to Richard Wagner, to take but one example, only a few have in the smallest way paid homage to the intellectual debt Wagner owed to Semper, while many biographers have scarcely taken the trouble to supply the most cursory biographical detail of this architect who figured so prominently in Wagner's letters, diaries, and autobiography. It is as if architects were somehow historically invisible.

This is not the place to discuss whether the fault for these oversights lies with the inwardly directed compass of architectural historians, or with the rather narrow range of concerns embodied in so many cultural studies. This book seeks to demonstrate, however, that Semper was a major player upon the scene, one who can no longer be overlooked. He was an artist, a social rebel, a political revolutionary, an engaging theorist, a monumental designer, but above all someone who fundamentally reshaped the direction and the character of his time. Like every major thinker whose constructed life becomes an edifice that delineates his contemporary landscape, Semper was in more ways than one an architect of the nineteenth century.

* * *

This book owes a great debt to Werner Oechslin and the staff of the Institut für Geschichte und Theorie at the ETH-Hönggerberg. Professor Oechslin invited me to Zurich to work on Semper for an academic year and graciously allowed me free reign of the institute's archives. Within the institute I wish to thank Therese Schweizer for her many efforts on my behalf, and Axel Langer for his transcriptions of various correspondence. The transcription efforts of earlier visitors to the institute, such as Sophie Gobran, also benefited me greatly.

At various times during the course of planning and writing the book I have been greatly assisted by my discussions with J. Duncan Berry, Heidrun Laudel, Robin Middleton, Sokratis Georgiadis, Margaret Olin, and Michael Conforti. The Graham Foundation provided me with a very important financial grant, which made travel to other libraries and archives in Europe possible. I would also like to express my gratitude to Winfried Nerdinger for his assistance at the Architekturmuseum, Technische Universität Munich, Mattias Griebel at the Stadtmuseum Dresden, and the staffs at the (DDR) Dresden Staatsarchiv (Amtsgericht Dresden, Ministerium für Volksbildung), the Landesamt für Denkmalpflege Sachsen, the Sächsisches Landesbibliothek, the Dresden Staatsbibliothek, the Vienna Akademie der Bildenden Künste, the Museum für Kunst und Gewerbe Hamburg, and the Staatsarchiv of the Senat der freien und Hansestadt Hamburg. In the United States I have had the good fortune in recent years to fall back upon the considerable resources of The Getty Center for the History of Art and Humanities, and I am greatly appreciative of the efforts of Julia Bloomfield, Kurt W. Forster, Benedicte Gilman, and Tyson Gaskill. Special thanks to Gillian Malpass in London. My wife Irene Qualters, and my son, Justin, have always provided me with much support.

1

The Despondent Years 1803–1834

"I am so excited that it is difficult to do the slightest thing."
(Gottfried during the July Revolution in Paris, 28 July 1830)

Göttingen, Munich, Regensburg

Gottfried Semper was born on 29 November 1803, a child conceived in a revolutionary age. His place of birth has been given in different biographical accounts, some by Semper himself, as either Hamburg or Altona: two northern German ports and trading rivals adjoining one another along the river Elbe.[1] Even though Altona was incorporated into the city limits of Hamburg in 1937, the distinction at the start of the nineteenth century carried considerably more political significance. Altona was a town in Schleswig-Holstein and was therefore a German speaking province under Danish rule. Hamburg, by contrast, was one of the founding members of the Hanseatic league and in 1510 was designated a "free imperial city" by the Emperor Maximilian I. It was a city that not only enjoyed political autonomy but was also noted historically for its cosmopolitan airs and liberal convictions. As for the matter of Semper's place of birth, it seems reasonable to follow the earlier accounts of his life, which generally indicate that he was born in Hamburg but baptized a few weeks later in the evangelical reform church in Altona.[2]

Gottfried's mother, Johanna Marie Paap, was descended from a French Huguenot family that had emigrated to Holstein from Holland in the seventeenth century. Her family's wool firm of J. W. Paap was founded in 1651 in Altona and was famed across Europe for its production of fine embroidery, stockings, coats, caps, and gloves. A special agreement with the Danish government eased exportation.[3]

Gottfried's father, Christian Gottfried Emmanuel Semper, had emigrated to Hamburg from Silesia when still a child. After his marriage he took over the direction of the Paap firm in Altona and became a prominent businessman and a regular trader at the Hamburg stock exchange. He had, it seems, considerable political connections. Gottfried was the fifth of eight children, of whom six survived infancy. The eldest son, Johann Carl, who preceded Gottfried by almost eight years, was destined to inherit the family's wool manufacture. The eldest daughter, Elisabeth or Elise, never married and remained at home. Gottfried's brother Wilhelm, older by one year, was the sibling who remained closest to him during later years; he eventually owned a pharmacy in Hamburg. The youngest son, Georg, drowned in a swimming accident in 1829 while attending the University of Jena.

Notwithstanding the family's financial security, Gottfried's childhood was dimmed and in large part conditioned by the Napoleonic wars that overwhelmed Europe between 1805 and 1815. Perhaps because of the outbreak of hostilities between France and Prussia, the Semper family moved to the maternal home in Altona in 1806. The Sempers lived on Prinzenstrasse (destroyed in 1945), high on a bluff overlooking the river. The old town hall was situated one block north; the Paap wool factory was located just below.

Altona, however, was swept into the military conflict in 1810, when Napoleon annexed the wealthy littoral towns of Hamburg, Bremen, and Lübeck to buttress his finances and broaden the frontiers of his campaign against England and Russia. Already suffering from the economic woes of an English blockade, Hamburg and Altona were particularly hard hit as Napoleon's most respected field marshal, Louis Nicolas Davout, occupied the cities and directed the dismantling of local institutions. He was a stern and uncompromising disciplinarian in his military rule. To make matters worse, a typhus outbreak decimated the population, turning the schools into mortuaries. Gottfried, at least for a short period of his childhood, daily witnessed scenes of corpses being stacked into piles for burial.[4] It was no doubt during this time that the future architect also came to acquire what would be his lifetime fascination with military tactics.

Gottfried was soon sent out of the occupied city by his parents to continue his education at a parish school in Barmstedt, a village twenty-five kilometers north of Altona. Letters home, beginning in 1818, depict an energetic and serious student enamored with classical literature, as he chronicled his strides with Caesar, Cicero, Plutarch, and Ovid.[5]

Gottfried remained in Barmstedt until the fall of 1819, at which time he returned to Hamburg to enter the Johanneum, the city's oldest and most respected gymnasium. Here he once again excelled in Greek and Latin. While attending the gymnasium, Semper also cultivated an interest in mathematics. The headmaster of the school, Karl Heinrich Hipp, was himself an accomplished mathematician and seems to have personally guided Semper's march through this field. It was Hipp who directed his promising student to Göttingen University in 1823, to continue his studies under two of Germany's leading mathematicians: Carl Friedrich Gauss and Bernhard Friedrich Thibaut.[6]

It has often been said, beginning with Hans Semper's account of his father's life in 1880, that Gottfried anguished over his course of study at the university: weighing his wish to be an artillery officer against his parents' desire for him to follow a career in law, before eventually following his natural inclination into art. Although copious correspondence from the years 1823–25 supports aspects of this picture, the circumstances surrounding his three-semester stay at Göttingen University, the youngest and most secular of the German universities, were far more complex.

Semper's university years began, at least, on a positive note. In the summer of 1823 he sought opinions as to which school he should attend from several former classmates; at the same time he conveyed his interest in mathematics and his wish to study the military sciences. One friend at Göttingen University responded that an appropriate first course at this university might be Thibaut's lectures on applied mathematics and analysis.[7] Another friend studying law at the University of Leipzig, Eduard Sthamer, discussed his situation with an acquaintance at the Dresden Artillery Academy. The latter recommended his own school and conveyed the cost of tuition and the importance of discipline. He also stressed the need for higher mathematics in order to enter the third or highest division of the school.[8] Yet another former classmate attending Göttingen, Friedrich Heeren (the son of the famous historian on the faculty there), offered in early August to assist Semper in finding a room in this crowded university town. Three weeks later he wrote back announcing that he had found lodging, a room sufficiently spacious to accommodate the setting up of Gottfried's war-game set.[9] This was a board-game of military tactics and maneuvers involving the movement of military figures and artillery pieces; it was played by two or more people, sometimes over days, if not weeks or months. Heeren's letter indicates that he was following a game in which Semper and a mutual friend in Hamburg were engaged for a good part of the summer.

Semper arrived in Göttingen in October 1823, by his own account enthused with the anticipation of learning. In one of his first letters home he noted that he was attending up to six lectures a day, chiefly in mathematics.[10] He later reported that he was taking a course on statistics by Arnold Heeren, Thibaut's course on analysis, and lectures on modern history and physics; in the last he was reading Isaac Newton's *Philosophiae Naturalis Principia Mathematica.* In the following spring he enrolled in five courses, among them lectures in chemistry and practical geometry.[11]

Thibaut and Gauss were his two most impressive teachers. Although it has often been noted otherwise, Semper seems not to have enrolled in Carl Otfried Müller's lectures on classical Greece, even though he may have sat in on some lectures. Gottfried in fact remarked in the summer of 1824 that for the past eighteen months he had concerned himself exclusively with mathematics.[12] This is confirmed by more than a dozen lending cards for books that he borrowed from the university library, all of which related to higher mathematics, mechanics, and military science. The lectures on modern European history, which dealt in part with the Napoleonic period, seem to have been the lone exception to this bent.

Gottfried's first year at Göttingen, however, soon became marked by emotional turmoil, compounded by his own and his family's concern over his choice of career. He very heartily fell in with the more intemperate side of German student life of the 1820s – drinking, gambling, and dueling. In one of his first letters home, written to his brother in December 1823, Gottfried recounted the riotous events of a day in which he had set out to witness a duel.[13] Some weeks later, in February, his sister upbraided him for his "resentful and caustic" remarks about the family's letters, and his infrequent and frivolous responses.[14] Over the Easter break, in April 1824, Semper rented a horse and rode with a friend to the nearby town of Kassel where he spent a good portion of the money that his parents had sent him for the coming semester. This was the beginning of what was to become a rather abiding pattern of debt. Semper deflected the fiscal accounting his father demanded by citing such unforeseen expenses as arrears to his landlord, the usurious practices of "bad Göttingen philistines," the entertaining of visiting students, and the lending of money to a friend from Hamburg.[15]

In the same letter, written in May 1824, Semper also referred angrily to a note he had received from Professor Hipp, in which his former gymnasium principal suggested that he attend a few lectures in law, in addition to those in mathematics. It is likely that Hipp's letter was prompted by a conversation with Gottfried's parents, and it is also apparent from subsequent letters that Semper by this date (that is, by the start of his second semester) had already expressed his unhappiness with life in Göttingen and his desire to make a change. Semper did not respond to Hipp until the middle of the summer, at which time he conveyed his plan to leave the university; he asked Hipp to send him information on the

Ecole Polytechnique in Paris.[16] Semper promised to inform his parents of his intentions when he returned home to Altona at the end of August.

Semper did not return home, but instead wrote them a long letter in which he discussed his future. He acknowledged Hipp's reply to his earlier letter, which advised him against going to Paris. After a year and a half of devoting himself to mathematics (actually only ten months), Gottfried admitted that he no longer had a taste for it, and wanted to pursue more practical endeavors. He reacted strongly against studying law, by declining four more years of university life, denigrating the "bourgeois" style of living that law entailed, and stating in no uncertain terms his great aversion to the subject. Instead, he suggested that he shift his attention to one of the many fields presupposing mathematical knowledge, such as hydraulic engineering. With no specific options at the moment he conceded that there was the "highest probability" of his remaining at Göttingen for one more semester – blaming this reluctant decision, quite unfairly, on Hipp's tardy response to his letter.[17]

Gottfried did stay at Göttingen for another term, although with no great dignity. At the start of the semester he approached Gauss with a request for private tutoring; yet he was turned down, in his words "snubbed." He also suggested to his parents that he leave school at once and take private studies in Hamburg, but they insisted that he remain. His father sent him a stern warning in December to end his moody silence and write home at once. Gottfried responded with an emotional letter written on Christmas Eve, which noted that if his life was not happy it was at least without pain: "I survive, as one cares to call it here, in my stoic pomade." He did not bother to write, he continued, because his life was, in effect, too boring, and after Gauss had rejected his study request he was not learning anything in any case. He then raised again the possibility of going to Paris, promising to spend the first six months there learning the language and biding his time by attending public lectures in mathematics and physics.

Gottfried's sister responded in January, reporting that his decision to go to Paris had created a sensation back home. Shortly thereafter Semper notified his father that he would instead travel to Munich over Easter with some other students to search out prospects there.

Semper soon changed his mind again and came up with a three-part proposal for ending his stay at Göttingen.[18] He would leave at the start of the Easter break and travel to Düsseldorf, where, carrying a letter of recommendation from Thibaut, he would approach a hydraulic engineer in charge of a waterworks project and offer his services in voluntary employment. If this option failed, he would continue on to Delft and seek admission at an institute for hydraulic engineering. The third option was to go to Paris and seek entrance into the Ecole Polytechnique. Both he and his parents had discussed the possibility of his declaring French citizenship, based on Napoleon's hereditary Empire and his mother's French lineage. With his parents' blessing and a "half-empty breast," Gottfried set out in the middle of April 1825 to secure his future as an engineer.

The trip proved disastrous. The engineer in charge of the Düsseldorf project was out of town. The Delft institute turned out to be "merely a military school" for students nineteen years old or younger, with no admissions in any case until the following year. Semper, now emotionally spent, did not venture on to Paris. From Rotterdam he wrote his brother that he had met some German students in Leiden and together they had amused themselves: his fists still groaned from pounding shop windows and street lamps.[19] He had originally planned to travel east from Rotterdam to Cologne to pick up traveling funds sent to a bank by his parents, but he changed his mind and traveled instead to Antwerp and Brussels to satisfy his "passionate desire" to see the battlefield at Waterloo. In Antwerp, in what was perhaps the trip's lone redeeming value, he received his first exposure to the paintings of Peter Paul Rubens; in Brussels he attended a play.

After collecting "three or four musket balls" from Waterloo, Semper next turned back toward Cologne, but when he appeared with empty pockets at the bank to which his parents had sent the monetary draft, the banker, knowing from the cable only the family firm's name of Paap, refused him money. Semper by chance met a former school chum from Hamburg who was studying at the University of Bonn. This friend brought him that night to Bonn, where Semper, because he lacked the proper traveling pass, had to remain incognito on account of the police. From there he pleaded for money from his brother Wilhelm but the latter had none. Semper borrowed money from another friend and traveled to Mainz, once again to engage in riotous activity. Finally on 27 May, six weeks after leaving Göttingen, he wrote to his father from Frankfurt, pointing out that he had enjoyed the Mainz Cathedral and a model of a bridge that Napoleon had proposed across the Rhine, and that – almost as an afterthought – he desperately needed money upon his return to Göttingen. The last town was only a temporary landing station as he had no intention of attending classes.

This restlessness was quite in keeping with the general tenor of German university life in the early nineteenth century. It was in many ways a student era noted for its aversion to social conventions and its impassioned attacks on the oppressive forces of the church and state.[20] For this generation of young men imbued with the ideals of Romanticism, drinking, fighting, and dueling, although frowned upon by the authorities, were semi-acceptable pastimes, in some cases requisite initiations into manhood. The practice of dueling, which had steadily declined in the eighteenth century, made a dramatic comeback with the popularity of the Napoleonic code, and since student duels were often fought with pistols or sabers, results were often bloody and sometimes fatal.

In Semper's case, however, there were also underlying personality problems. Intellectually gifted, outwardly favored by the comfortable financial circumstances that he had now come to disdain, he struggled with defining himself and his future under pressure from the rather prosaic expectations of his parents. As subsequent events showed, he did not easily resolve this conflict. Yet beneath his restive vexation there also appeared a genuine strength of will, however destructive its initial impulses. This same engaging, headstrong personality would, in later years, serve him well.

The summer of 1825 passed much like that of the previous year, with Semper seeking advice on a profession. Inquiries that his family had made concerning the Ecole Polytechnique proved discouraging, although his parents were at least willing to let him go to Paris by this time. Professor Hipp wrote to Semper in August, summarizing the counseling words of someone in Kiel and a conversation he had had with Semper's parents. The person in Kiel related the gloomy prospects for employment in Denmark but recommended to Gottfried the fields of mineralogy, chemistry, and mining. Semper's mother reiterated her preference for law. She also raised with Hipp the possibility of something in the "building trade," but Hipp connected this remark to Semper's interest in hydraulic engineering. Hipp, who for his own part still had his former model student in view, encouraged Semper not to be put off by the dryness and leaner parts of mathematics, but to remain true to Humboldt's spirit and courage (presumably Alexander) and further develop "the mathematical mind of the energetic and sensitive young man." "Above all," Hipp concluded in a rousing manner, "decide quickly and firmly what you want to do. Be it, whatever it may be, only you should not become an ordinary man, for you possess an aptitude for something higher and more noble!"[21]

It was also during this summer of 1825 that Semper raised for the first time the possibility of studying architecture. This can be inferred from an exhortative letter his brother Carl wrote to him toward the end of the summer. Carl, now employed in a supervisory capacity in the family wool firm, concurred with Gottfried's decision to turn down a mining and speculative venture in South America (good advice, it seems, in light of the major economic crash that happened at the end of 1825) in favor of more practical experience. "You write that you want to seize architecture," he noted, "I too believe that the lack of practical knowledge that this field demands will prove a hindrance if you do not compensate for it by working for a period of time as an assistant to an architect."[22]

This prospect may have been what led to Gottfried's decision shortly thereafter to depart Göttingen and pursue his future in Munich. Before leaving he had to clean up some messy details of his ever more reckless life. In September he wrote to Carl in confidence, noting that he had just spent a period in jail for witnessing a duel; he requested a substantial loan of money to settle outstanding debts so that their parents would not feel shame at discovering his "sins."[23] Gottfried also visited his parents in Altona during this month: alarming them with his unhappy and volatile mental outlook. Receiving their best wishes and financial support, however, he set out at the beginning of October for Munich, "to start there the practical studies of a new profession."[24]

What specifically Semper did during his stay in Munich remains a question. It has always been said, beginning with Hans Semper's biography of his father, that he studied architecture under Friedrich Gärtner at the Munich Academy of Fine Arts. More recently, the suggestion has been made that Semper went to Munich not to study architecture but to advance his knowledge of hydraulics under Carl Friedrich Wiebeking.[25] Both explanations now seem implausible, although it is unlikely that the matter will ever be settled in the absence of almost any surviving correspondence from this period – a curious lapse in an otherwise regular string of letters. Much more is known and rumored, however, of Semper's continuing difficulties with the law.

Semper arrived in the Bavarian capital on 13 October 1825, the day on which King Maximilian Josef died. Gottfried was saddened by the King's passing, not just because he was a "very good man" but also because the city's theaters would now be closed "for a whole half-year."[26] On 28 October Semper enrolled at the Academy of Fine Arts in the architecture program, but here knowledge of his activities grows dim.[27]

In November his father noted in a letter to Wilhelm that he had received two letters from Gottfried, both indicating that he was unhappy and much preferred to be in Paris. "It is no student life," his father remarked, "and he must first accustom himself to the bourgeois way of life."[28] This comment suggests that Gottfried was employed at this time, presumably settling down and learning a trade, such as architecture.

In a letter written to his brother in the same month, Gottfried alluded to his status as a beginner or neophyte "in the surroundings of artists and such people who at least appear to be skilled." Semper also reported that his main pleasures were "the beautiful galleries and the sight of some splendid buildings here that I look at daily."[29] On the basis of these remarks, and the friendship he developed during this period with other architects, such as

August Wilhelm Döbner and Eduard Metzger (the latter enrolled at the Academy as a pupil of Gärtner, also in 1825), it seems that Semper did attend some lectures, and may even have been active in a studio for a while – if only a short while. Any significant association with Gärtner, the famed architect of the state library and several other major monuments in Munich, is far more doubtful.[30] Gärtner's name is never raised by Semper at this time.

A different perspective of Semper's stay in Munich and subsequent travels can be obtained from a letter he wrote to Döbner in the summer of 1827, depicting some of his escapades since their separation. Semper reflected on the many "unpleasant memories" of Munich: on the "odious stories," "unworthy shits," and frequent encounters with the Munich police, "who I knew were always at my heels." In any case, as this letter suggests, his stay in Munich was not of long duration. A group of student friends from Hamburg passed through Munich in the spring of 1826 and Semper accompanied them to Heidelberg, on a binge that lasted eight "reeling" weeks: "What friends did I find again, what kind of new acquaintances were hailed? There, new alliances were formed for life. Even the enmities that were sometimes manifested in a bloody result were not permanent. I departed that town especially liked by those who knew me and respected even by my enemies."[31]

After the Heidelberg episode, Semper set out on foot for Regensburg: passing through Weinheim, the Odenwald forest, Würzburg, and Nuremberg. In Regensburg he looked up another old friend from Hamburg, the architect Theodor Bülau, who had also attended the Munich Academy. The latter, together with Justus Popp, was at work on his folio-size, illustrative study *Die Architectur des Mittelalters in Regensburg* (Medieval Architecture in Regensburg), published privately by the two authors in 1834. Semper almost certainly did not work with Bülau on the Regensburg Cathedral, as it is sometimes claimed; he only lived nearby and avidly threw himself into the latter's social circle. In his letter to Döbner, Gottfried reported that he assisted a local architect (in the service of the Prince of Thurn and Taxis) on his inspections of construction sites; he gained by his own admission only little practical experience and then in the areas of statics, hydrostatics, and hydraulics.

What did not suffer in Regensburg, in any case, was his flamboyant social life, which now centered around two daughters of Herr von Thon-Dittmar, who owned an estate near Regensburg. Semper later spoke of this rural setting, combining the friendship of a family with pastoral scenery, in the most glowing terms: "Can a young man of my temperament, in such a position as mine, be blamed when he – for real life – sacrifices so much of what others usually call duty, and what is nothing more than the anxious concern for one's future well-being, for which we so often overlook the present"?[32]

This idyllic situation nevertheless provided only a brief respite from his ebbing personal fortunes, as "new shits, love affairs, commerce with jealous asses and scoundrels, and dueling," conspired to make Semper once again "all too well known to the police." The often recounted story of Semper seriously wounding a scorned rival in a duel may have some truth to it; mournful yet poetic letters from no less than four young women, written within days of his departure from Regensburg, testify to a tapestry of youthful infatuations.[33] But there were certainly other factors contributing to Semper's departure in late October, for in the same letter to Döbner Gottfried also spoke of being compelled by "an iron necessity to apply myself rather diligently to something for once."

The effective cause, in any case, was not so much the duel or his bad conscience but the visit of his Göttingen classmate Friedrich Heeren, who passed through Regensburg on his way from Vienna to Paris. Semper jumped at the opportunity to join him, and the two comrades stopped in Munich only long enough to pick up a few of Gottfried's belongings. Their two-week trek to Paris was arduous: Semper's money was exhausted before crossing the French border but Heeren's purse carried him along. Together they passed under the Porte St. Martin at 5:30 in the evening, 10 December 1826.

Paris, Bremerhaven, Paris

Even though Paris presaged for Semper a new start in his quest to secure his identity and avocation, it represented, at least in its first stage, a change more in scenery than in substantive dialogue. Three days after he arrived in the hustle and bustle of the metropolis he received a much needed sum of money from his parents, enabling him and Heeren to leave behind the "rogues" and "cheats" of the seedier side of town and take a room at the Hôtel de Danemark on the rue Mazarin, not far from the Ecole des Beaux-Arts. After failing in his efforts to locate an architect recommended to him by his employer in Regensburg, Semper soon met, through other new acquaintances, a German-born architect who had recently opened a small school for architectural students. Semper presented himself to this Rhenish architect and was promptly accepted into his studio. "Monday I again begin my trade," he informed his brother Carl on 15 December, "and I am very happy about it."[34]

Franz Christian Gau (1790–1854) came to open his architectural school in Paris via a circuitous route from his native city of Cologne. The west bank of the Rhine had been occupied by revolutionary French armies in the 1790s and the area was officially incorporated into the borders of France (for fourteen years) through the Treaty of Lunéville of 1801. This pact allowed Gau to declare French citizenship, and he, together with his schoolmate Jacques Ignace Hittorff (1792–1867), set out for Paris in 1810. In the following year both were admitted to the Ecole des Beaux-Arts: Gau as a pupil of Louis-Hippolyte Lebas, and later of François Debret. Yet when Gau completed his studies at the Ecole in 1814 (without winning any of the prizes) his timing could not have been more inopportune. Napoleon's surrender at Fontainebleau in April of that year had made working prospects difficult for a German-born architect in a country just occupied by German and Austrian troops.

In 1817 Gau traveled to Italy where he fell in with a group of German students living in Rome. Yet his learning made a good impression on the Prussian ambassador to the Vatican, the noted historian and philologist Barthold Niebuhr. The latter recommended Gau to a Prussian nobleman interested in visiting Egypt. Gau accompanied Baron von Sack to Alexandria but after a personal dispute the two men separated there. Without much in the way of funds, Gau continued alone on a dangerous and difficult journey to explore what he deemed to be the cradle of Egyptian architecture – Nubia, or present-day southern Egypt and northern Sudan. He published the results of his travels in his *Antiquités de la Nubia, ou monuments inédits des Bords du Nil, situés entre la première et la seconde cataracte* (1822–27).

Upon his return to Rome in 1820, Gau continued his archaeological interests and he picked up another major project: the completion of François Mazois's illustrative study,

Ruines de Pompeii. This Roman city had been rediscovered in 1748, although serious excavation did not begin until several decades later. Gau eventually produced the plates for the third and fourth volume of the work, which were published in 1829 and 1838 respectively.

But Gau, when he returned to Paris in 1821, was unable to convert these credentials of potential fame into a successful architectural practice. Even though his folio on Nubia soon earned him praise and admittance to higher learned circles, it was only with great difficulty that he was able by the mid-1820s to obtain the relatively insignificant commissions for the presbytery of the church of St. Severin and the restoration of the small church of St. Julien-le-Pauvre. It is for this reason, it is said, that he opened his school sometime around the middle of the decade.[35] Semper described Gau as an excellent man who made every effort on behalf of his students by introducing them to the glorious examples of works that he had brought back from Italy. The students enrolled in the school in 1827 were mostly German – "from the [Friedrich] Weinbrenner school" in Karlsruhe – with the exception of one student from Holland and one from France.[36] Semper seems to have befriended no one.

Notwithstanding Gau's standing as a scholar and architectural educator – the mental stamina that caused Semper for the first time to feel shame for all of his intellectual "privations" – he was unable on this occasion to focus his new student's attention. After only a few months, Semper once again fell back into moody restiveness. When he wrote to Döbner the following summer, he described the Porte St. Martin through which he had entered the city as the "gate of hell" behind which he had found only "rubbish and pools of whores."

Semper's letter to his Munich friend was written not to reminisce but to test another option for employment that he was intent on pursuing in the summer of 1827. "I have it in my head," he remarked near the end of the letter, "to take the examination in civil engineering, if only to satisfy my wish for compensation and if it would make me useful." Having studied mathematics at Göttingen and hydraulics in Regensburg, Semper now admitted that he was in Paris only "to acquire the necessary knowledge of fine architecture" to accommodate this one section of the engineer's examination. Of greatest concern to him now was that section of the exam dealing with construction. Although he felt he had sufficient time to acquaint himself with the nuances of this field, he was writing Döbner to confirm the date of the examination and to solicit the latter's guidance: "Do you think I can pass the exam?"[37]

Semper left Paris in October 1827, after barely ten months in the city – not to take the civil engineering exam but to accept a job in hydraulic engineering in Bremerhaven. It was a voluntary position that was probably arranged for him by his family. Little is known of his activities during the next two years, although they certainly were not happy years for Semper.

Gottfried, as we might by now expect, did not travel directly north to Bremerhaven from Karlsruhe – as he promised his father – but he first continued across Germany to Regensburg in order to renew old friendships and flames. By mid-December he had only made it as far north as Göttingen, at which stop the repentant son, always in need of purse change, now promised his parents that he would muster his strength and good will so as "not to displease the building inspector too much."[38] One account has him arriving in Bremerhaven only in March 1828.[39] By the following November, however, he had developed a severe case of rheumatism in his right shoulder and was unable to move his arm without considerable pain. It was perhaps shortly thereafter that he returned home to Altona: to recuperate and once again to review his options.

His youthful spirits had by now reached their nadir, both physically and emotionally. Approaching his twenty-fifth birthday, he had found little success in all of his travels and endeavors; his return to Altona, in light of his many years of semi-independence, must have been particularly humiliating. His oldest brother, Carl, was being groomed for the top management position in the family firm. Another brother, Wilhelm, was completing his studies in chemistry and preparing for the pharmaceutical examination. Even his younger brother, Georg, was complying with the family's wishes and was nearing the end of his studies in law. Only Gottfried had failed his early promise and spiritually he felt devastated.

In late March 1829 he wrote to his brother Georg in Jena (a few days before the latter's tragic accident), and informed him that things were going badly and that he was losing weight. He was living off the "breadcrumbs of memories," he said, rather than the "dew of hope," and would soon set out on another excursion, first to Holland and then to Italy.[40] On the same day he wrote to another friend in Regensburg, stating that he would probably travel to Holland and then to France; he would actually prefer to come to Regensburg, he speculated, if he could be promised work as an architect.[41]

Finally, in early July 1829, the crisis that had been fermenting fully erupted. In the course of negotiating his departure, Gottfried had a violent argument with his parents and stormed out of the house with only the clothes on his back. The next day, from Cuxhaven (at the mouth of the Elbe), he wrote a pathetic and self-vilifying letter to his mother, bidding her a permanent farewell: "Now since a terrible lassitude makes it possible to grasp the enormity of my behavior, I shudder before myself: to you the contrite mother, whose tears flowed with my departure, imploring from me only *one* friendly last word, whose great misery can yet only be increased by *this,* yet coldly repelled by me with no tears or handshake for you – my heart is dead. And yet I could not have done otherwise. Had I shown a friendly glance, it would have been a hypocritical glance. Had I wept, it would have been with crocodile tears. Had I kissed, it would have been a kiss of Judas."[42]

Vowing never to return to Altona, Semper awaited the departure of a steamship to Holland. His father, still in mourning over the death of Georg and no doubt fearing a second son irretrievably lost, responded with frantic letters to two locations, trying to set up an irenic meeting. A third letter, wishing him calm from this latest emotional storm was sent ahead to Holland. The meeting did not take place and the father and son never saw each other again.

After making an excursion to Bremerhaven to review prospects for employment there, Semper returned to Cuxhaven and boarded his ship for Amsterdam. He was apparently still intending to pursue a career in hydraulic engineering, as he expected a letter of recommendation from the director of a waterworks project in Bremerhaven. His conciliatory father encouraged him in a letter in late July not to hasten to Paris (apparently a contingency destination on his itinerary) but to stay and gather information "concerning your occupation."[43]

Gottfried responded five days later with a letter from Brussels, which noted that his trip had become an engineering and architectural tour: with stops in Haarlem, The Hague, Rotterdam (where he did not pursue the meeting scheduled with the engineer), and

Antwerp (where he gave a long account of the Cathedral).[44] By the first week of August he was back in Paris, lodged in the Hôtel Bordeaux on the rue Guenegaud.

Semper's attitude toward life now began to change; perhaps the argument with his parents had served as a kind of emotional catharsis. He began to show signs of maturing and of exorcizing some of the demons that had haunted his young manhood. Although this change was gradual, it was certainly manifested in the new seriousness with which he committed himself to his avocation-by-default.

He also returned to Gau, who seemed pleased, if not surprised, to have his recalcitrant student back. Gau had in the interim been named a municipal architect for the city's hospital and prison administration, and therefore had office work on which to employ his student part-time. In addition, Gau also guided him through a series of student design projects in his studio. By the end of August Semper displayed a new-found optimism and sense of responsibility for his future. He reported the assiduity with which he was making himself familiar with the writings of architecture and his enthusiasm at the possibility of having a big job to work on in Gau's office over the next year.[45] In this and subsequent letters, now more regular and happier in tone, he began for the first time to discuss his ideas on architecture: his claim for the superiority of the "functional" (*zweckmässiger*) approach of the French over the more traditional building methods of the Germans.[46]

Even socially, Semper began to partake of the advantages of the great city. Gau had introduced him to Madame Valentin, a banker's wife, who was well known for inviting "all German travelers of importance, artists and intellectuals" into her home for soirées.[47] Semper also became friendly with a family of two artists, Achille and Eugène Devéria. Achille later became a conservator at the Cabinet des Estampes and he gained fame for his engravings of such luminaries as Victor Hugo and Alexandre Dumas; the younger Eugène Devéria achieved prominence as a historical painter.

Semper, in addition to watching closely the deteriorating political situation, also attended the theater and other places of interest, such as the Jardin des Plantes. Only a two-week bout with influenza in early April 1830 put a constraint on his social engagements. He was "cured" by a doctor who had him bled and fed quinine.

Several of Semper's student drawings are preserved from his two stays in Paris, and they depict a quite normal progression in their architectural design: from smaller projects (such as a garden pavilion, fire station, and guardhouse in a Doric style) to larger and more complicated designs, such as for a prison, a mental hospital, and a veterinary school. The last project, in its scale, style, and manner of presentation, reflected the influence of contemporary Beaux-Arts compositions.[48]

A few projects were designed with his native city in mind, even though Gottfried admitted to his father (referring to the men guiding the Hamburg rudder of state) that "it would be a highly thankless task to erect buildings for these fools."[49] One such project (Pl. 3) was a storage facility located along a canal, outfitted with two large booms. The ground floor consisted for the most part of an open arcade enclosing a courtyard. A continuous band of square windows along the upper level provided light. The design is without great charm or interest, even though an open trusswork bridged the street at one end.

Another design problem, the last project on which Semper worked in the turbulent summer of 1830, was a stock exchange for his native city (Pl. 4). The need for a new exchange, which had been under discussion in Hamburg since the Napoleonic occupation, was given a boost in the years 1826–28, when efforts were made to finance a

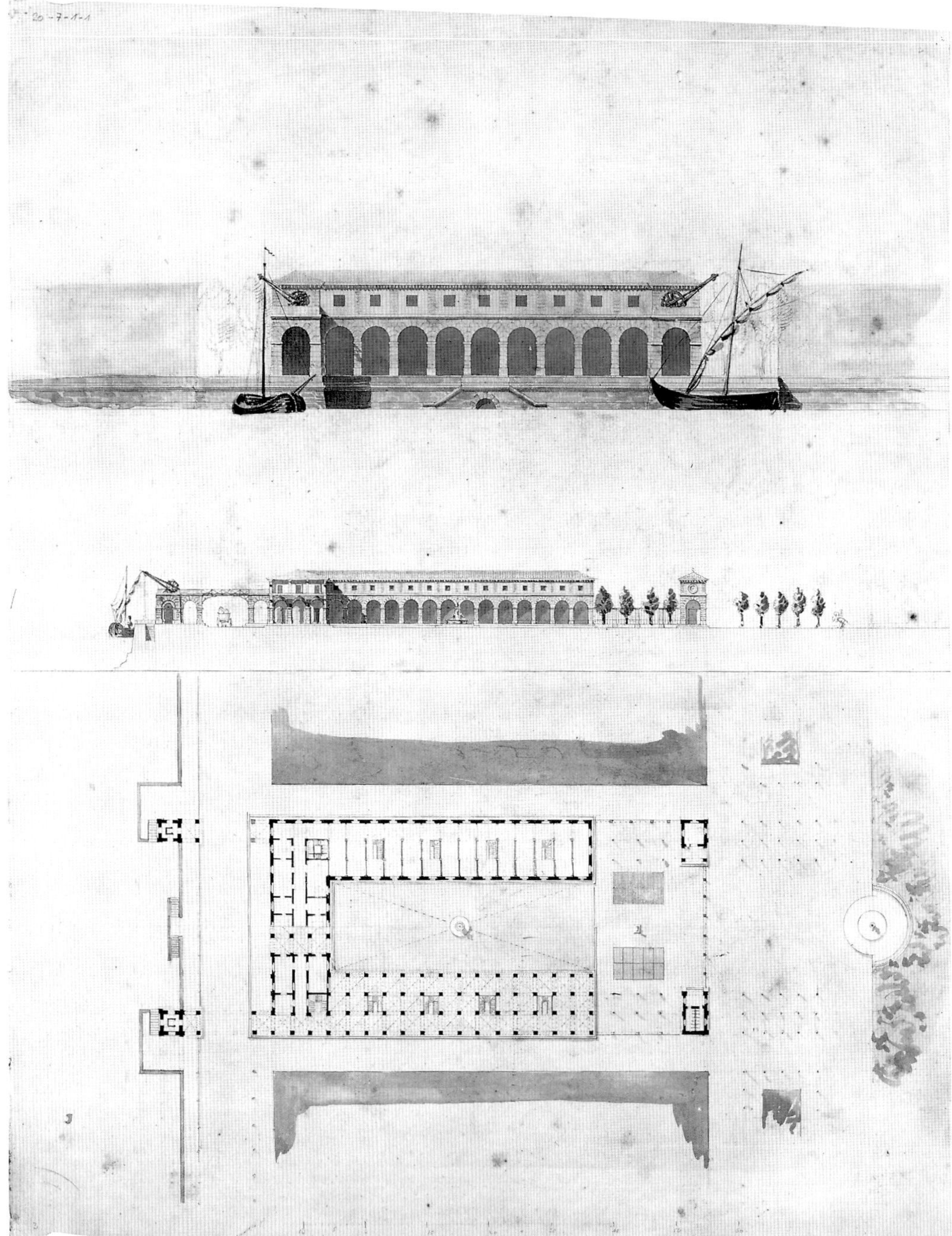

3 Gottfried Semper, student project, storage facility, ca. 1829. Institut für Geschichte und Theorie der Architectur, Semper Archiv, ETH-Zurich.

design by the architect Axel Bundsen.[50] The funding for the project nevertheless failed to pass the Senate and the issue was again thrown open to debate. Semper proposed a two-part plan, consisting of a large porticoed courtyard adjoining an enclosed trading hall. The

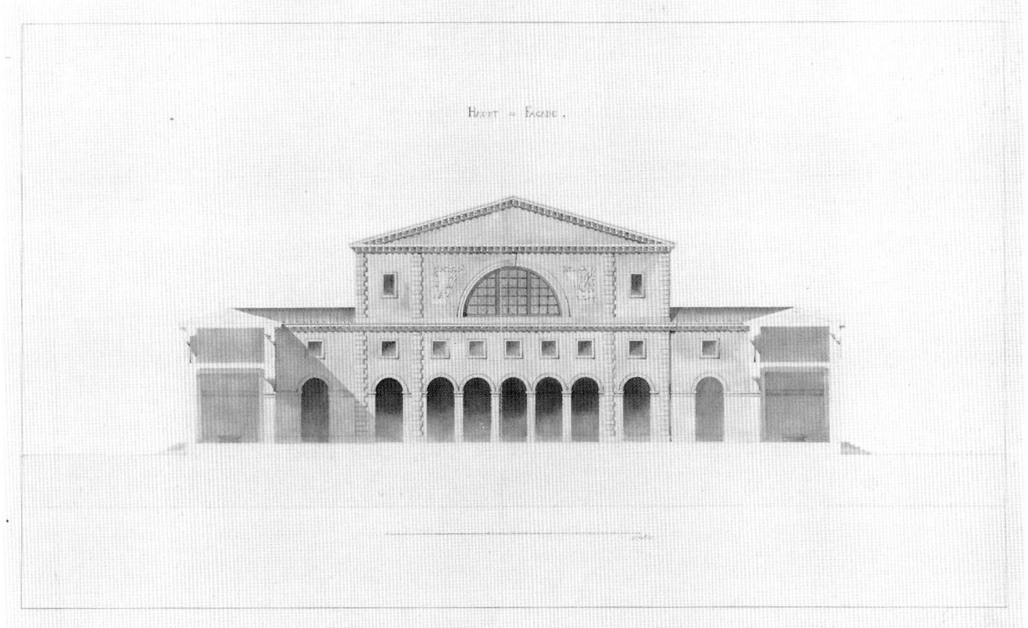

4 Gottfried Semper, student project, Hamburg Exchange, 1830. Institut für Geschichte und Theorie der Architectur, Semper Archiv, ETH-Zurich.

architecture, both inside and outside, is almost Italianate in character and presages Semper's later work only in the plastic reliefs (somewhat awkwardly) placed in the spandrels of the upper story at one end. Semper's father, when he received the packet of drawings in the mail the following winter, proudly put them on display in Hamburg.

Even though Semper's works of his student period display increasing competence and assurance, as well as a growing facility with the pencil, they are by no means exceptional when measured against other student projects from this time. In neither their design nor delineative skill do they suggest the powerful talent that was still to develop. But at this early stage of his artistic evolution Semper was too impatient to allow the maturation process to take its normal course. When he returned to Paris in August 1829, he did so with the intention of working there only until the following summer, at which time he would cap his architectural education with a trip to Italy. He continued with this plan through the following spring, when he noted to his mother that his stay in Paris was drawing to an end and that he was anxiously running about the city with a map in hand, looking at every museum, library, and other building of merit.[51] He hoped to travel in mid-summer to Genoa and Rome by way of Lyon and the Piedmont, that is, until the dramatic political events of July 1830 intervened.

For over a year the increasingly repressive government of Charles X had fallen into an ever more tense working relationship with the representational body of the Chamber of Deputies. In March 1830 the politician and historian François Guizot, heading the liberal reform movement, made a passionate appeal for greater political freedom from the floor of the Chamber. Some weeks later the King, hoping to demonstrate his royalist support, dissolved the troublesome parliamentary house and ordered new elections. They took place in early July but the results only strengthened the republican opposition.

The situation rapidly worsened. On 24 July the King signed secret orders suspending the liberty of the press and the powers of the Chamber of Deputies. When these measures were made known two days later (giving the King time to leave the city), Paris erupted with over 600 barricades and several days of violence. Charles, secluded at his palace in Saint-Cloud, understood neither the intensity of the conflict nor the anger of the people toward his government. Finally, on 7 August, a delegation of deputy members reconvened the assembly, stripped the monarch of his office, and proffered the revoked crown to the Duc d'Orléans, Louis-Philippe. Ten days later the disposed king, hunted by mobs across France, crossed the Channel to safety in England.

Semper's parents watched the events unfolding with increasing concern but Gottfried viewed them with growing enthusiasm. Already in August 1829, Gottfried's father had spoken to his son of his anxiety at the social unrest and advised him to be "prudent in speech and actions," in view of the danger of an uprising.[52] Four months later Gottfried, almost lightly, discussed the possibility of a coup d'état taking place and France being turned into a battlefield.[53] In February 1830, Semper sent his brother newspaper clippings of Guizot's speech with the observations that the situation in France was becoming "very interesting," and that even he was beginning to follow the events closely, "which says a lot."[54]

Semper's animated description of the events of late July depict someone truly swept away by the paroxysm. He recounted in great detail various scenes of fighting, the hoisting of tricolor flags, the redcaps worn by the revolutionary guard, the hesitation of certain regiments to fire on the crowd, and a particular scene in which a lancer was accosted by a crowd in front of the Porte St. Denis and stripped of his orders and weapons. He also reported on canons being placed before the Ministry of Foreign Affairs, the barricades, the arrests, and the many wounded: "I am so excited that it is difficult to do the slightest thing." To ease his parents' concern, he closed with the remark that he was no longer "the old daredevil" that he once was and that he would for now keep his nose out of France's affairs.[55] His commitment to the revolutionary cause, however, could not be disguised; he, like so many students in Paris, fervidly supported the events.[56]

His parents responded in a state of great alarm. A packet of three letters arrived the first week of August, all urging the young architect to depart Paris immediately and proceed to a designated hotel in London, where a letter of credit was also being sent.[57] His father also suggested that he postpone his planned trip to Italy, since Austrian troops were on the move in Lombardy and the border would soon be closed. But Gottfried's response, delayed until the end of August, revealed not only the direction and depth of his political feeling but also his strength of will.

He berated, on one hand, the political slumber of the German people and their seeming inability to take up in earnest the cause of freedom. "What true son of Holstein would think of risking death for the freedom of the press?" he asked sarcastically, and continued: "That would be simple-minded drivel. Freedom allows no man to be complacent and we will remain complacent so long as the Dear Lord allows buckwheat to grow in our fields – assuming that one does not tax us more than three-quarters of the yield."[58]

He reaffirmed, on the other hand, his intention to go to Italy – "It very much astonishes me that you presume with such certainty that I will address my next letter from London" – and then he underscored the urgency of his decision: "I must go to Italy in order to acquire a necessary part of my education and my age permits no delay. In the certain conviction that I was going and could collect examples on the spot, I copied nothing of what others have assembled but rather sought to develop my own ideas. Thus my whole plan of study would be ruined by changing it."[59] The only concession he was willing to make was to bypass Lombardy and sail from Marseille to Genoa.

Responding hastily, Semper's father agreed to the trip but advised his son to choose honest traveling companions, take good roads, and drink much coffee; conversely, to drink little water and Italian wine. He also instructed his intrepid offspring where bank credit would be available in Genoa and Rome. A now determined Gottfried departed for the south in mid-September 1830. The vague hope that he had once expressed to his mother – that his tour of the classical land would be brief and that he would make a speedy return[60] – would soon prove to have been wildly unrealistic.

The Debate on Polychromy

During his two stays in Paris (December 1826–October 1827; August 1829–September 1830), Semper formed a close working relationship and friendship with his teacher Gau, a kinship that would later become very beneficial to his career. Thus the question arises as to how important was Gau's tutelage in leading Semper to some of his basic architectural suppositions; or more generally, in what ways did these twenty-one months of French training prove formative in his architectural development?

It may have had less influence than one might expect; certainly it was different from how it has sometimes been described. Gau's pedagogical approach with respect to Semper, for instance, has been said to be Durandesque in character: an allusion to the typological, modular approach to design taught by Jean-Nicolas-Louis Durand at the Ecole Polytechnique. Yet the architectural character of Semper's projects in Gau's studio – their planning, delineation, and compositional approach – display none of this influence; in fact, they were very much in keeping with the Beaux-Arts training that Gau himself had received. It is difficult to understand why Gau's approach would have been different. We may therefore say, by way of a start, that Semper's training was academic in its broader outlines, although it certainly lacked the formal rigor of the Ecole des Beaux-Arts, a school he never showed any interest in attending.

As a practicing architect, Gau's influence on Semper is difficult to assess, in that Gau had built so little at this stage of his career. Gau's design for the presbytery to the church of St. Severin (1825–27) offers few clues, for it was a piecemeal project and restorative in nature. The fact that it was a Gothic design seems to have had no relevance, and this is also true if we glance at Gau's later works, which Semper always followed. For instance, Gau's design for the church of Ste Clotilde, which formed in the 1840s the principal battleground for the French Gothic Revival movement, was altogether a fiasco. Gau took over a classical design for the church by Jean-Nicolas Huyot in 1838 and was asked by the building committee to transform it into a Gothic work. Gau's design, however, pleased no one: neither the Conseil Général des Bâtiments Civils, which controlled all church building in France, nor the champions of the Gothic Revival, who for tactical reasons were forced to rally around the work. During the early 1840s, Gau was asked to revise his design three times, but to no avail. Only the collapse of the north tower of St. Denis in 1846, which led to the resignation of the key committee member opposing Ste Clotilde, allowed work on this church to go forward. The supervision of construction, however, was taken away from Gau (now nearly deaf and very contentious in his dealings with others) and given to his assistant Théodore Ballu. Gau's design for the church and the controversy it stirred, in the words of Robin Middleton, "forced many admirers of Gothic architecture to consider seriously the merits of a Gothic Revival."[61] By 1846, Semper had come to the same conclusion regarding the Gothic style, even though his view was reached after his own difficulties with a church competition in Hamburg.

The position Gau assumed in 1829 as a municipal architect for the hospital and prison administration of Paris certainly had some bearing on Semper's education, even if it taught him only administrative duties and the preliminary work leading to a design. Shortly after returning to Paris for his second stay, Semper wrote home enthusiastically about how Gau was involving him in the planning of one hospital.[62] He noted a meeting that he had attended with Gau in the office of Dr. Coquirole, the head physician in charge of all mental hospitals in France. The doctor had given them a tour of his facility and had promised to supply them with the plans of the more recent mental institutions in Europe. This administrative position of Gau's was certainly the reason why three of Semper's studio projects over the next year were for a prison, a veterinary school, and a mental hospital.

Gau's architectural influence, however, must be appraised in view of his limitations as a designer. This failing can be seen in his design proposal of 1843 for a guardhouse at the north end of the Place de la Bastille (Pl. 5), opposite the newly erected July Column of Jean-Antoine Alavoine and Louis-Joseph Duc. Although one contemporary German critic praised the scheme for its sensible disposition and detailing, the work does little to fire a designer's imagination.[63] Its Doric forms lack sublety and articulation; the heavy-handed decorative themes in the spandrels lack a sense of restraint. The social message of the building, "Liberté, Ordre Public," literally has to be spelled out in giant letters across the attic balustrade, itself seemingly added as an afterthought. The design is competent but without much appeal. It is decidedly backward-looking in its conception and taste.

Gau's imprint on Semper is perhaps better seen through his role as a scholar and critic. His study of Egyptian architecture and his drawings of Pompeii, for instance, were well known and genuinely admired by the young architect. Pompeii would become an important destination on Semper's itinerary in his travels to the south, and its murals became a source for decorative motifs throughout his career. Similarly, Gau's exploration of Egypt was instructive not only for its archaeology but also for the fact that it challenged many earlier assumptions regarding early Egyptian architecture. Semper, after he had traveled south, would within a few months make plans to emulate Gau's spirit with a folio study of his own. And if he eventually came to reject the leading premise of Gau's Nubian study – that is, that Egyptian architecture developed chronologically from the south to the north – Semper always held this work and its author in high veneration.

Gau was also an outspoken and incisive critic of contemporary trends and his opinions in this regard no doubt helped to shape Semper's initial architectural outlook. A somewhat contentious and choleric personality by nature, Gau's later letters to Semper are riddled with Parisian gossip and his generally negative assessments of the architectural situation in both France and Germany. Gau's failings as a designer perhaps only exacerbated his contempt for those who found some measure of success – in his eyes, those more willing to cater to the dull instincts of popular taste – and this perspective held true for such

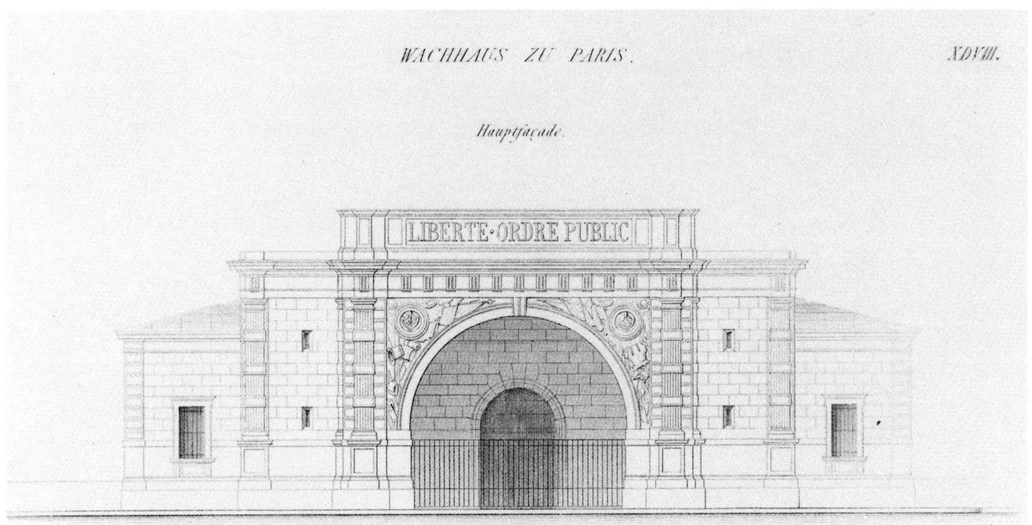

5 Frans Christian Gau, design for a guardhouse, Paris, 1843. From *Allgemeine Bauzeitung*. Courtesy The Getty Center for the History of Art and the Humanities.

leading German architects as Leo von Klenze, Eduard von Gärtner, and even Schinkel. Semper certainly inherited some of this negativity, as his own letters and early writings demonstrate. Gau also took a personal interest in introducing Semper to Parisian intellectual circles and contemporary issues of discussion. The soirées of Madame Valentin, for example, were an important aspect of German intellectual life in this city.

Paris, however, was much larger than Gau and the vibrant architectural life of the city should not be underestimated in its formative affect on Semper. Debates over the structure and curriculum of architectural education at the Ecole des Beaux-Arts grew quite furious in the second half of the 1820s, mirroring in many ways the growing social unrest. This turmoil engaged not only the students and faculty of the school but was also of great interest to architects across Europe, for the institution was still the premier center of artistic learning. Underlying the conflict were the Neoclassical teachings of Antoine-Chrysostome Quatremère de Quincy (1755–1849), the Secrétaire Perpétuel of the Académie des Beaux-Arts from 1816 to 1839. His architectural theory taught first the use of the classical orders within certain proportional guidelines; second the creative adaptation of paradigmatic forms, derived for the most part from the Imperial monuments of Rome.

Indicative of this columnar aesthetic in monumental practice were two gigantic temples imposed upon the Parisian cityscape in the first decades of the century: Alexandre-Théodore Brongniart's Stock Exchange (1807–15) and the "Temple de la Gloire," or church of the Madeleine (1807–45), by Alexandre-Pierre Vignon and Jean-Jacques-Marie Huvé. These vast and costly undertakings – along with the severe idealist aesthetic they embodied – came to be viewed as objects of derision by a highly talented succession of *grand-prix* winners that passed through the Ecole in the mid-1820s, among them Abel Blouet (1795–1853), Félix Duban (1797–1874), Henri Labrouste (1801–75), and Léon Vaudoyer (1803–72). Winning the annual *grand prix* at the Ecole des Beaux-Arts entitled a student to five years of additional study at the French Academy in Rome, during which time he would be required to measure and sketch details mainly of classical Roman works.

In the fourth year the student would undertake an archaeological reconstruction of a classical Roman monument, and in the fifth year he would prepare a design for a contemporary work of national significance. The student was then expected to return home to a prestigious governmental post, in order to apply his exceptionally erudite and exquisitely cultivated artistic sensibilities to the greater glory of France.

It became apparent in the second half of the 1820s, however, that a forceful shift in the students' artistic sensibilities was taking place. Itineraries during student travels in Italy suddenly strayed from the well-known Roman fora to the lesser-known sites of Etruscan, Greek colonial, Latin, medieval, and early Renaissance monuments; fascination at the same time grew with works and periods formerly considered to lie outside the boundaries of classical greatness. Not only did the classical ideal of beauty, so dear to Quatremère de Quincy, now lose much of its former, almost mythical luster, but works of antiquity were also more accurately situated within their localities and conditions of social origin. The heavily proportioned Greek monuments of Paestum and Sicily, the newly discovered Etruscan tomb cities, as well as the very unclassical wall murals at Pompeii – all became requisite student destinations almost overnight.

This new historical awareness was also reflected in the choice of fourth- and fifth-year projects, as *grand-prix* winners no longer selected the highly regarded exemplars of classical greatness or sought to affect classical grandeur. Labrouste, for instance, submitted a small provincial frontier bridge for his fifth-year project of 1829; for his fourth-year archaeological study of 1828, he reconstructed the various Greek temples at Paestum. These he partially painted and endowed with graffiti, and he also inverted their accepted chronology (Pl. 6). He incorrectly argued that the more delicately proportioned temples at Paestum (closer to the classical ideal) preceded in time the squatter, more crudely detailed temples at the same site, and that architects had purposely varied the proportions of the later temples from the presumed classical ideal in response to different materials, social conditions, and *genius loci*.[64] This imaginative reconstruction created an institutional furor when the drawings were put on display in Paris in 1829. The director of the French Academy in Rome, Horace Vernet (himself a liberal and therefore a political adversary to the royalist Quatremère de Quincy), even tendered his resignation during the bureaucratic melee that took place in September 1830.[65]

Still, the contemporary implications of Labrouste's historical thesis was clear to every architectural student in Paris; as Van Zanten has noted: "If Greek colonists at the apogee of Attic art could not meaningfully reproduce the Doric temple form once removed to a foreign place, how could a Frenchman in the nineteenth century hope to do so in Paris?"[66] In March 1830, less than four months before the July Revolution overturned the government, another student in Rome, Léon Vaudoyer, christened this new crusade, spurred on as well by contemporary enthusiasm for Saint-Simonian doctrines, a "little revolution."[67] Labrouste, who was regarded as the leader of this student protest because of his successful defiance of the Academy, was later triumphantly carried on the shoulders of his classmates through the streets of Paris during the political events of the following summer.

Although there is no evidence indicating how closely Semper followed the French architectural developments of 1829 and 1830, it is a fair assumption – given his close relationship with Gau and his own inquisitive and rebellious nature – that he was no passive observer of these generally very public proceedings. It is also likely, particularly

6 H. Labrouste, restoration of the Temple of Neptune, Paestum, 1828 (restoration published later). Courtesy The Getty Center for the History of Art and the Humanities.

during this second stay in Paris, that he would have attended at least a few of the evening lectures and exhibitions at the Ecole des Beaux-Arts, which were free and open to the public. Moreover, whatever details of the uprising he failed to take note of during his stay in Paris, he would have been told of by the various French students of the school with whom he later traveled in Italy.[68] Over his lifetime, in fact, Semper continued to monitor closely all architectural events in Paris, as we learn from reports by Gau and others.[69]

Both framing and supporting these ideological fulminations at the Ecole des Beaux-Arts were the broader debates on classical polychromy of the 1820s and 1830s – discussions that would also dovetail perfectly with Semper's later interests. The problem, of course, is to establish just how much Semper knew of the proceedings during his residence in the city, even though it is often difficult to distinguish this knowledge from what he may have learned immediately thereafter on his travels to the south.

The issue at the center of this controversy over classical polychromy was once again the image of classical greatness, although in this case it was concerned mainly with the marble monuments of Greece during the Periclean age. The so-called rediscovery and recording of Attic works in the 1750s by English and French expeditions not only helped to launch the architectural movement of Neoclassicism, but Greece also provided the new movement with a critical issue to be resolved: determining whether Greek or Roman models best represented the classical ideal to be emulated.

An early and leading advocate of Greek artistic superiority, the influential German historian J. J. Winckelmann (1717–68), even went so far as to codify a Neoplatonic aesthetic for Greek sculptural works, whereby the beauty of a form was made dependent on its degree of whiteness, since the color white best reflected light and thus most sharply defined the contour or its form.[70] This tenet was easily transposed upon the image of the Greek temple: a few bold, pristine masses, preferably of white marble, delicately proportioned and lightly accentuated with decorative reliefs. The antiquarian scholar Christian Ludwig Stieglitz summarized this view in 1801: "Works of architecture receive their beauty as beautiful form, which is evoked in architecture, as in all the fine arts, through order and symmetry, through decorum and good proportions...[To] avoid a facile

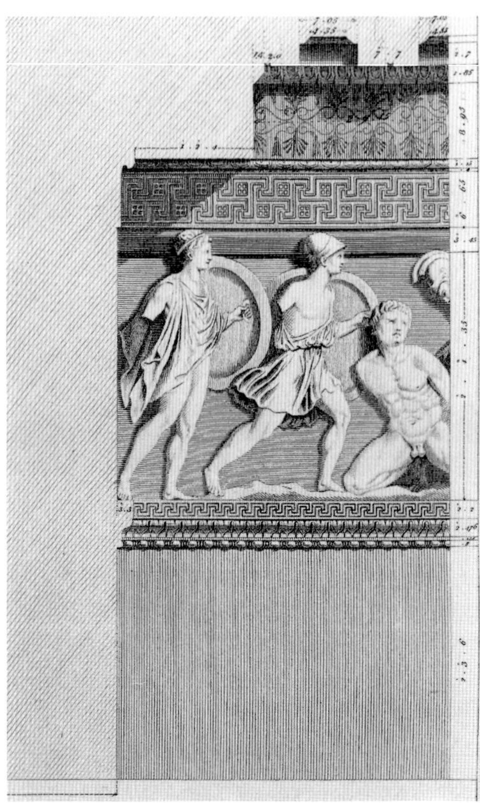

7 Bas-relief from the Temple of Theseus (Hephaesteum). From Stuart and Revett, *The Antiquities of Athens*, vol. I (1762). Courtesy The Getty Center for the History of Art and the Humanities.

monotony and to give the whole a greater multiplicity, elegance should be added through the decoration and embellishment of the essential parts of a building, serving as adornment."[71]

Up until the start of the nineteenth century, both archaeological evidence and philological research tended to support, or at least did not dispute this classical image. The few signs indicating otherwise were always too ambiguous to interpret with confidence. Thus the outlines of painted decorations discovered in Athens on the Temple on the Ilussus and the Temple of Theseus by Stuart and Revett in 1851 (Pl. 7) actually lent credence to this "white" view of classicism, because it demonstrated that the Greeks could tastefully apply small quantities of color to secondary architectural members.[72]

It is true that the classical architect Vitruvius had also referred to a blue color applied to the triglyphs of wooden temples, and Pausanias had mentioned red and green Athenian tribunals, but it was generally assumed that these were simply colorful accents, rather than an indication of a more extensive color scheme.[73] Winckelmann, in fact, provided his later critics with some comfort in this regard, when he argued against a contention of Pliny the Elder and maintained that Greek paintings were executed directly on the walls of temples, not on wooden panels attached to the walls, and by such artists as Polygnotus, Onatus, and Pausias.[74] The interpretation of Pliny's passage was vigorously debated by the classical historians Alois Hirt and Carl August Böttiger in the first decade of the nineteenth century, was raised again by Désiré Raoul-Rochette in Paris in the 1830s, and was still a point of contention for Semper in the 1860s.[75] Evidence of the use of color in non-classical architecture – such as the painted sculpture and bas-reliefs of Egyptian architecture, the brilliant decorations of the Treasury of Atreus at Mycenae, the Etruscan painted tombs at Corneto (Tarquinia) and Vulci, and the colorfully painted walls of Pompeii – again supported the "white" view in that they helped write a theory whereby color could only be associated with periods and places of artistic infancy or provincial decadence. The high art of Pericles, for many, was deemed to have stood apart from other artistic cultures in this regard.

Archaeological evidence gathered shortly after 1800, however, began to undermine this viewpoint. A second contingent of British travelers arrived in Greece around 1800, led by Lord Elgin, William Leake, William Wilkins, and Edward Dodwell – the last three of whom published their findings of traces of paint on Greek monuments. Wilkins detected remnants of paint and gilding in the entablatures of the Propylaea and Temple of Theseus.[76] Leake noted "various colors" applied to the wall surfaces and sculptures of the Parthenon.[77] Dodwell gave perhaps the most extensive accounting: noting remnants of blue, red, and yellow paint that he found on the Parthenon's cornice. As he surmised: "It is difficult to reconcile to our minds the idea of polychrome temples and statues; but it is certain that the practice was familiar to the Greeks in the earliest times, and even in the age of Pericles."[78]

Other investigations carried out at the start of the second decade of the century by another contingent of archaeologists and architects – among them C. R. Cockerell, Carl Haller von Hallerstein, Otto Magnus von Stackelberg, and Peter Oluf Brøndsted – either confirmed these results or shed additional light on them. Still, what was lacking was a theory by which one could appreciate aesthetically these indications of extensive color usage without destabilizing the Greek classical ideal. In effect, a new artistic ideal had to be postulated so that Greek art would not be brought down to the gaudy level of its barbaric counterparts.

Such a theory was proffered, albeit in an indirect way, by none other than Quatremère de Quincy in his masterful philological study, *Le Jupiter olympien, ou l'art de la sculpture antique considéré sous un nouveau point de vue* (1815). The aim of this study, by this self-proclaimed champion of Winckelmann's ideal of beauty, was to reconstruct on the basis of philological evidence the celebrated statues of Zeus and Athena, executed by Phidias in gold and ivory for the major temples at Olympia and Athens (Pl. 8). These colossal works were regarded by several classical authors, by Pausanias especially, as the sculptural masterpieces of antiquity, but such views contrasted sharply with the more hostile reception afforded them by eighteenth-century artists and critics.[79] Quatremère de Quincy listed the complaints most frequently voiced against these works:

1) they were the accidental result of a taste foreign to Greek artistic sensitivity;
2) the mixing of gold and ivory on a statue was aesthetically less pure than executing a work in a single material, especially white marble;
3) the manifest extravagance of gold and ivory falsely swayed antiquity as to their intrinsic artistic value;
4) the combination of gold and ivory in the imitation of cloth and skin violated the essential premise of sculptural works, which was form.[80]

In defense of these works, Quatremère de Quincy argued that the high regard for chryselephantine works in antiquity was due not so much to their material or illusional

8 Phidias, Temple of Athena for the Parthenon, Athens. Reconstruction by A.-C. Quatremère de Quincy in *Le Jupiter Olympien* (1815). Courtesy The Getty Center for the History of Art and the Humanities.

value (that is, their capacity to imitate cloth and skin), but to the fact that they exploited another fundamental element of the Greek artistic psyche, namely, color. Thus what was once regarded as their artistic limitation – their color – was now argued to be their leading and potentially their most sophisticated attribute.

Quatremère de Quincy sought to prove his contention historically by marshaling an impressive body of philological evidence, which chronicled the course of how color came to be applied to sculptural works. He argued, for example, that the earliest models for gold and ivory statuary were the primitive wooden idols of early Greek times – *les statues-mannequins* – painted and dressed with actual materials.[81] These creations led to the development of toreutics, whereby a sculpture was assembled by embossed or chased pieces, in metal, ivory, wood, or other materials. Color, he reasoned, was employed to protect the piece against the effects of the weather and time, to correct material deficiencies, and at a later date to relieve the coldness and monotony of larger surfaces. Thus by the time of Pericles's reign color had become an indigenous part of the Greek artistic consciousness: symbolically consecrated by religious traditions as well as by the nature of this particular sculptural technique. In Quatremère's magnificently rendered polychrome reconstructions of these two works of Phidias, he depicted them with a subtle, almost transparent color sheen, "une sorte de peinture sans être de la couleur, c'est d'être colorés sans avoir été peints, c'est d'offrir enfin l'apparence et non la réalité de l'illusion."[82] In this way he distinguished these works from the more glaring examples of Egyptian or Roman art.

It is fascinating to follow the appropriation of Quatremère de Quincy's thesis by archaeologists and architects over the next decade: as this reasoning came to be applied both to the architectural discoveries made earlier in the decade as well as to the diggings just under way. Four years after the publication of Quatremère de Quincy's study, the English architect C. R. Cockerell described the sculptures that he, together with Haller von Hallerstein, had secretly unearthed and illegally exported from Aegina in 1811 (these eventually went to Munich, even though Cockerell believed he had rigged the auction in favor of the British Museum). He used them as a confirmation "of the practice which prevailed among the Greeks, of painting their sculpture," which he considered a means "of distinguishing the several parts, and heightening the effect by a delicate variety of tones, so as to relieve what might otherwise be inanimate or monotonous." He also suggested that the climate was a reason for this practice: "To paint white marble, or other stone exposed to the open air, appears very singular to us, but there are many considerations not obvious to our northern ideas and prejudices, which must be taken into account. In Greece, the mildness of the climate, and purity of the atmosphere rendered works of finished execution much more secure from degradation; and admitted refinements of sculpture and painting, that would be thrown away and lost in a northern climate."[83]

Cockerell's views were seconded by the Munich architect Leo von Klenze. It was Klenze who in 1816 won the competition design for the Glyptothek, the building designed specifically to house the prize Aeginetan marbles. Klenze proposed as a backdrop to the colored pedimental sculptures (restored in Rome by Bertel Thorwaldsen) a temple facade in plaster relief painted in brilliant colors. Even though he did not visit Sicily until 1823–24 (or Greece until 1834) Klenze set out his views on polychromy in a lecture that he gave, on Etruscan temples, in Munich in March 1821. He began by rebuking

Winckelmann and Caylus for their "dry, cold, and rigid" image of antiquity, and then praised the more recent reassessments of the past by Quatremère de Quincy, Hirt, Böttiger, and Cockerell. In his reconstruction of a wooden Tuscan temple, "whose basic form is opposed to almost every rule of beauty," he noted that its carpentry was "painted with lively colors and decorations:" bold shades of red, blue, green, and yellow.[84]

Another traveler to Greece was the Russian Baron von Stackelberg, who twice nearly died of typhoid, and on another occasion was held for ransom by pirates. In 1812 he led the excavation of the Arcadian temple at Bassae (said to be designed by Ictinus and therefore contemporary with the Parthenon), and in his 1826 presentation of this monument he more broadly applied Quatremère de Quincy's theory to architecture – enhancing it with observations on the picturesque landscape of the region and the ruddy Greek spirit: "The color that even now is indispensable to all southern people to enliven architectural masses was used by the Greeks on the greatest masterworks of the Periclean age, both Doric and Ionic. It can still be seen on the Theseum, the Parthenon, the Temple of Minerva Polias, and the Propylaea, where colors were even applied to the exterior as building decorations... The mild climate favored this use and the Doric temple thereby appeared much more richly decorated than one can imagine."[85]

Yet another group of British travelers – consisting of William Kinnaird, Joseph Woods, T. L. Donaldson, Charles Barry, Charles Eastlake, and William Jenkins – set out for Athens in 1816, with the intention of updating a new edition of Stuart and Revett's *Antiquities of Athens*. Kinnaird recorded their results in his extensive annotations to the second edition of this work, which appeared between 1825 and 1830. His most detailed commentary was reserved for the coloration of the Parthenon, which he claimed to be still "distinctly perceptible." Kinnaird was also the first to suggest that paint may have been used on other than the decorative parts: "The polished columns of white marble with their architrave, triglyphs, and the chief part of the cornice, may therefore have thus been relieved in a manner agreeable to the eye, in so sunny an atmosphere, by the enrichment and combination with colours and gilding judiciously applied." He also adopted Quatremère de Quincy's argument that color was applied first to correct material deficiencies and later became sanctified by tradition, but he extended it one step further: "On that account both polychrome ornaments and gilding may have been therefore introduced on this temple, as well as to cause the edifice to correspond in richness with the gorgeously decorated colossus it enshrined; but here, at this epoch, as in the adoption of every other ancient accessory belonging to the arts and religion of their ancestors, the Athenians were guided by purer principles of design."[86]

The final step in this expanding and ever more dappled saga – the conclusion that color was employed on the walls of the temple cella itself – was taken by the Danish archaeologist P. O. Brøndsted, in his *Reisen und Untersuchungen in Griechenland* (Travels and Investigations in Greece) of 1825–30. Brøndsted went to Greece in 1810 with Haller von Hallerstein, Stackelberg, Cockerell, and Georg Koes. After a stay in Constantinople and a tour of the coast of Turkey with Stackelberg, Brøndsted returned to Aegina in 1811 to join the excavations of Cockerell and Hallerstein. The group then decided to split up but share the proceeds of their excavations. Brøndsted traveled extensively throughout southern and northern Greece, and by the time of his departure from Greece in 1813 he had acquired a very broad perspective of the extent to which the Greeks had resorted to polychromy.

In the section of his grand-folio work devoted to the Parthenon sculptures, he followed the reasoning of Quatremère de Quincy in delineating four stages through which the Greek temple evolved from its wooden prototype, treating color as an attribute that was more fully exploited with each succeeding stage. He also divided the painting of monuments into three categories: 1) the use of color on broad architectural surfaces without the purpose of creating a deception, in order to overcome the plainness and monotony of the stone; 2) the use of color to create an illusion, that is, as a substitute for sculptural effects; and 3) the use of color as a sculptural aid, thereby bringing it into harmony with the architecture.

Although in his study he was mainly concerned with the second and third categories, he nonetheless concluded that "the first kind of color application, namely, that used for actual architectural purposes, was so general in the most beautiful period of Greek architecture that one can, as already noted, confidently assert that all Greek temples were more or less painted."[87] In another conclusion with far-reaching implications, he suggested that these marble monuments had been covered with a stucco coating (a mixture of marble and gypsum), applied so thickly that it would in fact have visually altered the proportions. Stucco, he argued, was used to smooth out the porosity of the stone and to prepare the surface for coats of paint.[88]

Brøndsted's views regarding the use of stucco and paint may well have been inspired by research carried out on the Greek monuments in Sicily, which by the end of the 1820s had become almost synonymous with the controversial claims of J. I. Hittorff.[89] This last architect, of course, was the student who had accompanied Gau to Paris in 1810 to enroll at the Ecole des Beaux-Arts. And whereas Gau's fortunes lagged at the conclusion of his studies, Hittorff, through his connection with the atelier of Charles Percier, had found an important position as an assistant to François-Joseph Bélanger, a decorative architect practicing within aristocratic circles. With the restoration of the Bourbons in 1814, Bélanger resumed his old position as Architecte des Menus-Plaisirs, this time to Louis XVIII. The now elderly designer, however, depended heavily on the younger talents of Hittorff and Joseph Lecointe. Upon Bélanger's death in 1818, Hittorff and Lecointe succeeded him, as Architectes pour les Fêtes et Cérémonies, and were thus able to execute several elaborate decorative schemes for royal events, including the impressive backdrops erected within the cathedral at Rheims for the coronation of Charles X in 1825. By this date Hittorff had become one of the most successful architects in Paris and moved in the highest social circles of France and Germany – a fact that no doubt contributed to his declining friendship with Gau.[90] The latter had by then lost all hope of matching Hittorff's continually expanding and popular architectural practice.

Yet it was Hittorff's reconstruction of a Sicilian temple that would bring him his greatest notoriety. Inspired by Gau's success in Egypt and by the burst of archaeological activity taking place in the early 1820s (in Greece to end in 1821 with the Greek civil war), Hittorff began making preparations for an extended tour of Italy and Sicily, a trip on which he embarked in 1823 with the expectation of making new archaeological findings. In Rome he lived in a room above the studio of Bertel Thorwaldsen (1770–1844), the Danish sculptor who had restored the Aeginetan marbles and who was encouraging his efforts. He was also cheered on by new reports of successful Sicilian diggings at Selinunte (Selinus) by William Harris and Samuel Angell.

Hittorff soon made his way to Palermo, as it turns out, in archaeological competition with the German Leo von Klenze. He caught up with Angell (Harris had just died of malaria) and viewed firsthand the newly discovered painted metopes. After touring Messina and Syracuse, Hittorff commissioned diggings at Agrigento, where he uncovered fragments from various temples, including parts of what he believed to be a female colossus. At Selinunte, however, the team of workmen under his direction made the most important discoveries: numerous fragments encrusted with stucco and paint as well as the partial remains of a small temple (temple B), which he called the "Temple of Empédocles." Hittorff rushed back to Rome and began to plan a publication describing his efforts. What made Hittorff's relatively insignificant discovery unique, however, were his later efforts to circumscribe it within a general theory or "system" of ancient polychromy.

Hittorff outlined aspects of his system while still in Sicily and Rome – to François Gérard, Ludwig von Schorn, and Charles Percier.[91] When he returned to Paris in the spring of 1824, however, he became more reticent: the official memorandum describing his trip, presented to the Académie shortly after his return, scarcely hinted at what was to follow. In the first plates of his folio study, *Architecture antique de la Sicile* (1827–30), only a part of which he was able to finish in his lifetime, he included just three colored examples.[92] In was not until 30 April 1830 (Semper at this time was recovering from his bout with influenza) that he formally read his "system" to the Académie des Beaux-Arts. He accompanied his oral presentation with color drawings of the temple, drawings in which every surface and detail was brilliantly rendered (Pl. 9). It seems certain that Semper, who was concluding his studies with Gau at this time, was not present that evening, and it is now doubtful, in fact, if he saw Hittorff's drawings on display at the Louvre.[93]

The system that Hittorff proposed was in many respects the architectural counterpart to the polychrome explanation of Quatremère de Quincy, in which the painted wooden temple – "comme entièrement identique avec celui de la statuaire coloriée" – transformed itself into an extravagant polychrome production executed in stone, stucco, and marble.[94] Stackelberg's high regard for the climate and landscape was incorporated into this image, as the colorful temples in Hittorff's description formed a harmonious ensemble with the cloudless skies, bright sunlight, and highly variegated landscape of the south. The new theme woven into his narrative, however, was the universality of polychromy: a system employed in antiquity from Selinunte to Athens to Pompeii. Color was the principal variable of the classical decorative system, in contrast to the rather constant use of the orders; color was that attribute which best delineated the particular nuance of character to be sought and therefore was an invaluable component of design. Thus the three orders of Greek architecture remained simple and unchanging, while color was the medium through which the importance of the building could be conveyed.

Still, it was not so much Hittorff's postulation of a "system" of polychromy that so engaged his professional and personal antagonists, a system that was by itself not so far removed from the more scholarly disquisitions of Quatremère de Quincy, Kinnaird, and Brøndsted. Rather, it was the extreme vividness of his polychrome conception. His Sicilian restoration was a stuccoed panoply of richly variegated effects: a temple fully sheathed in brilliant shades of red, blue, ochre, and gold. What is more, with the paucity of actual evidence that he was able to excavate he had to rely quite heavily in his restoration (as he himself candidly admitted) on his own artistic "imagination" in reaching his conclusions. His ornamentation was, in fact, a quiltwork of decorative motifs sewn

9 Reconstruction of "Temple of Empedocles" at Selinunte, 1830. From J.-I. Hittorff, *Restitution du temple d'Empédocle à Sélinonte, ou l'architecture polychrome chez les Grecs*, 1851. Courtesy of Robin Middleton.

together from examples collected from such far-flung places and historical times as Tarquinia, Pompeii, Aegina, and Jerusalem. In short, a very important scientific line had been crossed and the defenders of this new "science" of archaeology were not about to let it pass uncontested.

The showdown fittingly took place during the eventful summer of 1830. Désiré Raoul Rochette, a professor of archaeology at the Bibliothèque Royale and later the successor to Quatremère de Quincy's chair, addressed the Académie and threw down his challenge to the research of Hittorff: by changing his earlier assessment of the restoration from "une restauration satisfaisante" to "une donnée arbitraire ou hypothèque."[95] Thus on the eve of Semper's departure from Paris we have yet another boisterous uprising taking place – the architectural debate over the extent of classical polychromy. Even though the issue of color up to this time had sparked but little opposition, it now exploded into what would shortly become an extremely acrimonious controversy. Hittorff and Raoul Rochette alone, over the next six years, would exchange ever more insulting and personal barbs within this increasingly public debate. Semper, as he was slowly making his way south, could scarcely have had an inkling that he would soon find himself drawn into the center of this discussion.

Italy, Sicily, Greece

Even though we cannot be certain just how familiar Semper was with the exploding polychrome controversy when he left Paris in mid-September 1830, his initial correspondence from Italy seems to suggest that he knew less than has generally been assumed, perhaps little more than the discussion surrounding Hittorff's controversial restoration. He had not yet met Hittorff and it is unlikely that Gau would have privately championed the archaeological claims of his former friend. And Semper's first aim in traveling south was not to survey the monuments of Sicily and Greece but rather to study the better known monuments of classical Roman times and the Renaissance – a tour undertaken by nearly every architectural student of the time who had sufficient resources. The hope that he had expressed to his mother of a short journey seems to have been made in good faith. She and he almost surely believed that he would soon begin his architectural practice: if not in Altona at least in Hamburg.

Semper traveled across France by foot and by carriage, heading first southeast to Burgundy, then down the "splendid Rhone valley" toward Marseille, before turning east along the coast toward Genoa. He arrived in this Italian seaport on 13 October and was immediately overwhelmed by both the artistic treasures of the city and the changes of climate and vegetation, above all by "the pines!" He speculated in his first letter home that he "was actually born a southern man, a grain of seed scattered by the wind into the snowy north."[96] For the next two weeks he studied the famed palaces of Genoa – "architecture that I once viewed only on theatrical decorations" – then followed the coastline south to Massa, Pisa, and Livorno, before turning inland toward Lucca and Florence. In the last city he spent almost three weeks, although he did little sketching in his rush to view as many sights as possible. He hastened to Rome nevertheless, arriving on the outskirts of the city on 30 November.

By this time the gaiety of his mood and the novelty of travel had worn off, and Semper retreated into moroseness. In recounting his first impressions of Rome he refused to wax poetic, he explained, because "the old ill-breeding of my nature" prevents it. "I have never obeyed commands," he continued, "I am so little able to control my emotions . . .

I often become philosophical when others dance, I dance when any danger or important moment presents itself. I am often angry toward people whom I dearly love, and am amiable toward others who do not deserve it."[97]

Gottfried was traveling with a band of students: a Corsican who had attended the Ecole Polytechnique, two Germans (Herr Lüdus and Jtzohon), a Dane (Herr Winter), and an Englishman identified only as having a bad French accent. The Corsican's antics were particularly endearing to Semper; the moment the distant dome of St. Peter's was first sighted the former melodramatically climbed a hill to collect his emotions, then comically fell down and rolled to the bottom.

Semper's sullenness soon gave way as he settled into the city. He took an apartment just off the Spanish steps at Via Gregoriana 17. He therefore resided, like so many students of architecture before him, "near Thorwaldsen and the French Academy."

The now sixty-year-old Thorwaldsen, a native of Denmark, was for some reason known to Semper's father.[98] He was still an active figure within the artistic community, and was still an impassioned exponent of the classical ideal. Much of his best work, however, lay behind him. His controversial restoration of the Aeginetan marbles for the new Glyptothek in Munich had been completed in 1818. His glory-days – first earlier in the century as a member of the Humboldt circle and later, in the early 1820s, at the side of the Bavarian crown-prince Ludwig and other artists, among them Leo von Klenze and Hittorff – had come to an end, although there were always new artists passing through the capital and paying homage to this respected figure. King Ludwig, in fact, returned to Rome for a stay in 1829, after having just purchased the Villa Malta. During Semper's brief tenure in Rome, Thorwaldsen was probably working on his equestrian statue of Maximilian I, a commission that he received from Ludwig in February 1830. From the start Semper felt himself to be a part of this international brotherhood of artists; he preferred to have his letters directed not to his flat but to the Café Greco, because "there all artists take their mail."

By February Semper reported to his father that he was making good use of his time, although a combination of wet weather and bad health (perhaps an occurrence of his chronic asthma) were limiting his effectiveness. In moving about the city he preferred the company of French to German students, but more often than not he worked alone: "My best friends and true godfather are the ruins on which I climb about whenever the weather allows." He noted that they gave him comfort and also served to instruct him when he tried to visualize their original condition, "the first beauty of these solemn remains."[99] He also spoke of making excursions into the surrounding countryside, but it is doubtful that he would have ventured far outside the city at this time.

It was also at the start of February that Semper informed his parents of his intention to travel further south. This decision was very casually put forth at first. In noting his now lazy routine and the bad weather of Rome, he indicated that he was "almost inclined" to follow the advice of his friends and spend the winter in Naples and Pompeii – "in any case, my main place of study."[100] Perhaps uneasy at his father's response, he wrote again some days later, further explaining that his need to go south was due to the French threat of war, the political unrest in Bologna and Ferrara (also threatening Rome), and the fact that working there would please him much. He also once again confessed his "sins," among them exhausting his line of credit. He attributed his prodigality to debts incurred while in Paris, to his excursions to the countryside, and to the need to see so much in such a limited time. His patient father relented, a now familiar pattern. Semper directed his next letter from Naples.

Semper's trip from Rome to Naples was a strenuous hike through difficult mountainous terrain. He left Rome on 18 February 1831, having spent only two and a half months in the Italian capital. The political situation, in some respects arising out of the Paris upheaval, did in fact deteriorate, as foreigners in Rome were occasionally physically assaulted. Gottfried traveled with two companions: the Frenchman Jules Goury and a Swiss sculptor with the last name of Alric. Goury, a former student of Achille Leclère at the Ecole des Beaux-Arts, would prove to be a good friend and constant companion over the next twelve months. He also seems to have exerted a strong influence on Semper's architectural and archaeological development. He unfortunately never returned home as he died of cholera in Granada in 1834.

Together, the three made their way through the Albani and Volscian mountains, visiting various deserted Latin settlements, among them Cora (Cori) and Norba. Near the village of Sonnino, a town once renowned for being the headquarters of bandits, the trio nearly met with disaster. During a heavy evening rainfall the tired and drenched travelers approached a Capuchin monastery for shelter but were greeted with less hospitality than they expected – "We were French and thus in their eyes antichrists and enemies of the Pope."[101] In a fit of rage (brought on, he wrote, by boredom) Semper shoved the head prior hard against the wall and rushed back out into the rain. He eventually made it to the town of Sonnino but the local tavern had no beds. Content to pass the night on a sofa in the bar, he was awakened a few hours later by his two companions, who were accompanied by a half-dozen gendarmes and a crowd of local citizens. The three travelers had their passports carefully scrutinized, their pistols confiscated, and they were invited to spend the night in the brigade armory. In the morning the three hastened out of town toward Terracina.

They arrived in Naples in the first week of March 1831. Semper took a room outside the city in the town of Torre Annunziata, a half-hour walk from Pompeii. Much had changed for him in the past three months; the frivolity he displayed in Rome was now giving way to hard work. Gottfried would awake at seven o'clock in the morning, sketch the whole day in and around Pompeii, then return home at sundown to eat and sleep. "I have buried myself in Pompeii," he informed his mother, "and live off my art and the past."[102] Some of his many sketches of the surrounding countryside may also be from this period (Pl. 10); they document his increasing facility with the pencil.

There can also be little doubt that these were very important weeks in the evolution of Semper's artistic outlook – the stage at which he perhaps first became enamored with the thought of becoming a serious artist. One indication of this change was what must have been a startling letter he sent home in early May, in which he informed his parents of his wish to travel on to Sicily. His parents did not respond soon enough, and the frantic Semper directed another letter home toward the middle of the month: "I am somewhat uneasy, all the more so since I cannot postpone any longer a trip long ago decided upon." Together with Goury, Mathieu Prosper Morey, and four other French students, "we have rented a small boat that will take us to Messina with a stopover in Paestum . . . we sail in an hour."[103]

Semper's first concern, of course, was whether his father would continue to finance his travels. But this decision to venture to Paestum and Sicily – which, as Semper insisted to

10 Gottfried Semper, sketches in vicinity of Naples, 1831 or 1832. Institut für Geschichte und Theorie der Architectur, Semper Archiv, ETH-Zurich.

his parents, was spurred on by the industriousness of the French, "the most active men on the earth" – was indeed a dramatic one. The archaeological findings of others, such as Harris, Angell, and Hittorff, could now be appraised within their proper context, and an effort could be made to chart new terrain (as Morey did with the cathedral at Messina). Perhaps they would even make a new discovery. "We will scour the whole countryside and collect all valuable observations in a portfolio," he informed his father.[104] This collective portfolio has not survived (perhaps lost in part with Goury's papers after his death), but some aspects of the trip are recorded in Semper's "Travel Reminiscences," later published in the *Frankfurt Museum*. Paestum, of all the sites in Italy and Sicily, remained for Semper the most Greek in character: its architectural development, he believed, had become arrested and never moved forward. In Sicily, Semper and his party traveled first along the southern coast, visiting Syracuse, Agrigento, and Selinunte, before turning north to tour Segesta, Monreale, and Palermo. Throughout Sicily, the group observed indications of stucco and paint on many ancient works but, unlike Hittorff, Semper felt the surviving remnants were too few to be assembled into any meaningful system.[105]

Sicily only whetted Semper's archaeological interest, and upon reaching Palermo in early August 1831, his now ravening artistic ambition led him to make what was perhaps the most important decision of his life. His party of seven split up with five members of the group returning to Naples. Semper and Goury, however, remained behind: the former felt driven – as he later explained – "by a feeling of discontent further east, toward Greece."[106]

Hearing that a Greek cutter was anchored in the port of Messina and preparing to sail in mid-August, Semper and Goury raced back across the island. The captain of the ship entertained them in his house for eight windless, anxious days, during which time the travelers frantically searched Messina and the neighboring towns for maps and travel guides to prepare them for this new and unexpected venture. Finally, the wind revived, and – carrying only a French translation of Pausanias, a work by Jean-Jacques Barthélemy (probably an abridged version of *Voyage du Jeune Anacharsis en Grèce*), and William Gell's *The Itinerary of Greece* – the two intrepid artists boarded the ship for their artistic odyssey. Veering out into the Ionian sea, they lost sight of the Sicilian and Calabrian coastlines on the third day. Semper's letter of explanation to his parents, almost certainly a masterpiece in filial diplomacy, has unfortunately been lost. It was not until some months later that he received the news that his father had unexpectedly died of a bleeding ulcer during this time. But it is unlikely that this report would have deterred the young artist from seeking out the "harsh Spinners" of his own artistic fate.

Semper and Goury, it should be emphasized, were altogether ill-prepared for this difficult and dangerous journey. Aside from the risk of catching deadly diseases such as malaria and cholera (the last of which did indeed strike Goury down), travelers to the eastern Mediterranean in the 1830s also had to contend with a host of other inconveniences: among them bandits on land, pirates at sea, and numerous territorial borders. For this reason, archaeological expeditions to these areas often consisted of large parties of people, well financed and with carefully planned itineraries, in some cases years in advance. Yet these two youths made their travel plans on the whim of the moment, taking only letters of passage from consular officials in Palermo. They carried none of the requisite letters of introduction and surely little money in their purses.

There was, however, another and far more deadly obstacle to their plans – a danger that had in fact halted nearly all archaeological activity in Greece for most of a decade. A complex, sometimes fratricidal civil war had engulfed Greece since the early 1820s, one of the bloodiest wars in Greek history. The so-called liberation of Greece from the yoke of Ottoman rule, as European and American public opinion concomitantly liked to portray the conflict, was by no means a simple struggle to understand, and, as history would demonstrate, it scarcely represented a triumph for Western diplomacy.

Turkey had controlled mainland Greece since the fifteenth century, except for a brief period of Venetian rule in the early eighteenth century, shortly after Venetian canons blew up the Parthenon in 1687. Yet the Ottoman Empire was now disintegrating. The French revolutionary war provided the first impetus to the so-called Greek pursuit of liberty, which was manifested in secret societies such as the Philiki Etairia (founded in 1814) and later (in 1821) in an insurgent army under Alexander Ypsilanti. In reality, anarchy had been devouring the country since the start of the century. Philhellenes in both Europe and the United States, however, embraced the liberation of their spiritual homeland; the sensational military expedition led and financed by Lord Byron in 1824 (before he too succumbed to the fever of malaria in Missolonghi) typified the Graecomania that spread across the continent.

Yet the European powers were much too suspicious of each other to pay much attention to the problem and they were also worried about Russian expansion into

Greece. Thus when the Turkish Sultan Mahmud II induced his Egyptian vassal Muhammad Ali to invade the Peloponnese with a large army in 1824, using "scorched earth" tactics, the tide quickly turned against the Greek insurgents. Compounding the violence of the invasion, factions of the Greek revolutionaries were also fighting each other, each seeking covert support from various European governments.

The scale of atrocities eventually forced the three major European powers to intervene. The Treaty of London, signed by Great Britain, Russia, and France in 1827, declared an armistice and promised European mediation for an autonomous but not sovereign state. When Turkey refused the offer, its fleet (by diplomatic mistake, it turns out) was destroyed by a joint Russian, French, and British fleet under Admiral Codrington at Navarino (Pilos) in October of that year. Also in 1827 John Capodistrias was elected president of the new country but he soon compromised his position with autocratic designs. Two London Protocols of 1829 and 1830 further defined Greece as a kingdom and the search was underway in Europe for a prince to install on the Greek throne. This effort was delayed and nearly undermined by the assassination that took place in Nauplion (Návplion) on 9 October 1831. Capodistrias was both stabbed and shot by two brothers of a rival clan, touching off another round of anarchy and bloodletting. Semper and Goury had arrived in the same town only a few days earlier.

The two architects had first sailed to Corfu, an island off the Albanian-Greek coast, then south to Zanthe, where they faced the "tyranny, harassment, and swindling" of British customs officials.[107] They were thoroughly searched, had their weapons temporarily confiscated, and had all letters seized, which they were forced to buy back at two schillings apiece. In addition, each member on board the ship had to post a bond, even though the ship was to remain in port only a few days. From Zanthe they sailed to the coast of Elis and made their way south to Navarino. From the site of the famous naval battle, the two architects turned inland (on foot and part of the way on donkey) to explore the Peloponnese and its classical sites: visiting Messenia, Sparta, Megalopolis, Phigalia, Bassae, Olympia, Pheneos, Orchomenus, Nemea, Argos, Mycenae, and Nauplion.[108]

Semper's "Travel Reminiscences," which were conceived as a series of letters, unfortunately stop at Messenia, but in any case they provide little archaeological detail. Several sketches of the Peloponnese survive but it is certain that many more have been lost (Pl. 11). Travel was indeed perilous, as Semper was quite aware of the hatred and suspicion that was directed toward foreigners and he noted that they were being carefully watched at every step along the way. In one letter home he gave a lengthy account of the political situation in Greece, indicating an almost amazing grasp of all the various persuasions of hostile factions. On the morning of 9 October he was awakened in his hotel by the nearby discharges of the gun that killed Capodistrias. Rushing to the window, he witnessed one of the assassins, in turn, being gunned down by pursuing guards in the street below.

The political situation rapidly deteriorated. The European powers some months later decided to place nominal control of the country in the hands of a triumvirate, composed of Theodor Kolokotronis, John Kolettis, and Agostino Capodistrias, the last the brother of the slain president. This coalition, however, never came to pass in the field, as clan armies representing different interests were already on the march. Shortly after Capodistrias's death, in the besieged town of Nauplion, Semper was unofficially pressed into the diplomatic corps as the personal secretary to Friedrich Theodor Thiersch (1784–1860).

This event in itself, if we knew more of the details, might merit its own book, as

11 Gottfried Semper, sketch of the Apollo Temple at Bassae, 1831. Institut für Geschichte und Theorie der Architectur, Semper Archiv, ETH-Zurich.

Thiersch was one of the more interesting polymaths of the nineteenth century – a famed philologist, pedagogue, and respected art historian. He was a native of Saxony (but resident of Munich), and no doubt had a profound effect on Semper, if only because of his close connection with many of the leading writers and artists of the day, among them Jean Paul, C. A. Böttiger, Heinrich Heine, Wilhelm von Humboldt, Barthold Niebuhr, Ludwig Schorn, Leo von Klenze, and of course Thorwaldsen. Even though his primary avocation was that of a teacher and grammarian of the Greek language, he had turned his attention after 1814 increasingly to archaeology and art, and eventually produced in 1829 his *Ueber die Epochen der bildenden Kunst unter den Griechen* (On the Epochs of Fine Art among the Greeks) – his attempted refinement of Winckelmann's chronology.

Thiersch was traveling in Greece as a private citizen but he was a friend of King Ludwig of Bavaria. In 1830 he had approached Ludwig with a plan to visit Greece and try to mediate the conflict. Ludwig gave him his blessing but no official sanction. Thus, traveling at his own expense, Thiersch sailed from Trieste to Nauplion, arriving in the seaport on 21 September, two weeks before Semper. Thiersch knew Capodistrias personally and thus was emotionally bound to the unfolding events. With his known royal connections, command of the various languages, and excellent historical knowledge of Greece, he was ideally suited after the assassination to negotiate between the various factions, both foreign and national.

Semper seems to have accompanied Thiersch on various of his peacemaking ventures, as well as on at least one archaeological tour. With the ambassadors of the three powers, Thiersch was lobbying for the ascension of Prince Otto, the son of Ludwig, to the Greek throne. In Nauplion, meanwhile, Agostino Capodistrias vainly held onto the remnants of a government that had fallen out of favor with many people. In the fall and winter months of 1831–32 much fighting took place in and around Argos and Megara. In March it became known that the European powers had selected the seventeen-year-old Otto as the new ruler. This announcement, although welcomed by some Greeks, nevertheless brought the conflict to a head.

In the same month Thiersch went to Capodistrias in Nauplion and obtained the release of a rebel leader from prison, thereby warding off a military attack by one faction. He then headed to Megara to meet with another rebel leader, Kolettis, and delay the advance of his army. On his return to Nauplion he eluded, quite by accident, one ambush attempt on his life. By the end of March he had finally succeeded in talking Capodistrias into resigning his position, just as Kolettis's army was approaching the gates of the city. Again Thiersch rushed out and averted bloodshed by speaking with Kolettis, while at the same time having Capodistrias smuggled out of the country during the night.

Semper chronicled these proceedings from Athens in a lengthy letter to his brother, written in April 1832; he also noted that he had just composed, on behalf of Thiersch, the official report to King Ludwig.[109] It was not until the following year, however, that Otto arrived with an army of Bavarian soldiers and administrators and brought some calm to the country. With his scant knowledge of Greece the young king was bound to be ineffective. Only in 1843 did the Greek people succeed in throwing off the Bavarian yoke, as it were, and obtain some semblance of a constitution and national government.

Against the backdrop of these extraordinary events, it is quite remarkable that Semper was still able to pursue substantial archaeological research. He appears to have left Nauplion with Thiersch and Goury in late October 1831, bound for Athens. They stopped along the way to view the theater at Epidaurus and visit the island of Aegina; on the island the three men scaled the hill to view the famous Temple of Aphaia, whose marbles had been in Munich for two decades already. Once in Athens, Semper assiduously set to work studying and recording the city's major monuments. In 1937 Leopold Ettlinger counted 199 drawings by Semper from Athens alone, which ranged from fleeting sketches to pen-and-wash archaeological studies.[110] Semper worked with Goury and the German architectural student Eduard Metzger (1807–94). The latter, who had braved another route to Greece, was known to Semper from his days in Munich.

Semper made detailed studies of the Propylaea, the Erechtheum, the Tower of the Winds, the Choragic Monument of Lysicrates, and the Temple of Theseus or Hephaesteum (Pl. 12). He even unsuccessfully applied to the Turkish governor of the city for permission to excavate on the Acropolis. He devoted most of his attention, however, to the Parthenon, around parts of which he built his own scaffold. Here he felt he had made his most dramatic discovery: "The ancients not only painted the interior of their temples in the most elaborate way but they also richly covered (*bedeckt*) the exteriors. The noblest white marble was dressed (*bekleidet*) with bright colors; even the bas-reliefs were painted."[111]

This burst of archaeological effort, however, was relatively short-lived. In January 1832, Semper, who had just learned of his father's death, was thinking about returning home. He informed his brother that he would shortly set out for Malta with Thiersch. The war and diplomacy intervened and in April, from Nauplion, Semper admitted that he was trapped in Greece because of the hostilities. Still, he hoped to leave within a month, after making another trip to Athens to fill in some details of his studies. He also promised to tour Italy rapidly, "like an Englishman," and return to Germany by early autumn.

But his departure was again delayed, as Thiersch set off on further negotiations in

12 Gottfried Semper, colored reconstruction of the Temple of Theseus (Hephaesteum), 1832. Institut für Geschichte und Theorie der Architectur, Semper Archiv, ETH-Zurich.

Navarino in early May, while Semper remained behind in Nauplion awaiting money for his journey home. It must have been around this time that Semper and Goury split up, with the latter traveling east to Asia Minor, and eventually to Egypt. It was not until the end of the month that Semper left Nauplion for Italy by ship, and then into some difficult weather.

In yet another precarious adventure, his ship at one point on its journey around Greece was stalked for several days by pirates, "circling like cats around their warm gruel." The captain of the ship ordered the passengers to build makeshift ramparts with their mattresses. When the pirates saw that all of the men aboard were "armed to the teeth," as Semper himself phrased it, they dared not come closer.[112] On the last leg of his journey, on 2 July 1832, Semper's vessel anchored at Bari on the Apulian coast of Italy. Swearing off the sea forever, he was ecstatic to be back on *terra firma,* and even did not mind the mandatory fourteen days in medical quarantine.

Return to Rome

Semper's new vow to scurry through Italy and promptly return to Germany again proved ephemeral. He had no sooner arrived in Bari than he began preparing large-scale polychrome reconstructions of Athenian temples. He was already thinking of a publication depicting his findings. "You have no idea of the splendor and opulence of the ancients," he wrote to his brother excitedly.[113]

Once his quarantine in Bari had elapsed, Semper traveled west, back toward Naples and Pompeii, where he sought out further study as well as a chance to enjoy the lush, summer bloom of the southern Italian countryside. His arrival in Naples, as could almost be predicted, coincided with an eruption of Mount Vesuvius. While in the area, he made a foray to Capri and once again sketched natural and architectural features from various other towns around Naples, among them Pozzuoli, Sorrento, and Amalfi. In a passage describing his joy in the south, reminiscent of Goethe's fascination with the climate and vegetation of the region, Semper noted: "How gray will the world appear to me when I am far from this shimmer of colors."[114]

After his relative isolation in Greece, he also reveled in the company of fellow artists, among them the painter Thöming, a native of Hamburg, whom he met in Naples. Gottfried also began to paint the local scenery in an effort, in his words, to understand nature's color scheme and to enhance his skills. By the end of September it was apparent that he was in no rush to pass through Italy at all but would slow down and imbibe the many artistic lessons that the country had to offer. He now wrote to his brother Carl, who had assumed control of the family's finances, and asked for another extension to his line of credit – pointing out that his clothes, now after more than two years of travel, were in tatters.

There was another, more considered reason for his delay: his wish to find employment as a member of Prince Otto's entourage, now preparing to leave for Greece. This must also have been the reason why, while still in Greece, he had hoped to travel back to Germany with Thiersch. When this alignment proved impossible because of the latter's diplomatic obligations, Munich suddenly became an important destination on Semper's itinerary. In his first letter home from Bari, he indicated that he was also writing to the Bavarian prince and in the meantime he had to hurry through Italy because he wished to arrive in Munich before Otto's departure. Yet it must soon have become apparent to Semper that there was no need to travel to Munich at all, since the Prince would need to travel down through Italy.

Prince Otto, accompanied by a host of Bavarian officials and bureaucrats, arrived in Rome in early January 1833. Semper was on hand but was greatly disappointed not to receive an audience. Instead, Semper spoke to one of the aides, General Heidecker, and to other members of the entourage, who indicated that the organization of the new government was going very slowly – too slowly presumably for any decisions regarding employment.[115] It is likely that Semper was seeking a governmental position or some role as the future king's personal architect and artistic advisor.

Semper also revealed his plan for returning to Greece to his former teacher Gau. Although acknowledging the attraction of working and living in Greece, Gau was vehemently opposed to any such decision. He said the idea of a German king in Greece was political nonsense and that the new monarch would not last three years in his position. On a more patriotic note, Gau stressed how much the German fatherland needed a young architect of Semper's great ability and talent. Referring to his own, now painful experience with expatriation, Gau insisted that Semper avoid his mistake: "I preach, dear Semper, and give myself as a bad example; but just for that reason I recognize my guilt and I am deeply angry for it."[116] Gau's advice, written in February 1833, may in fact have

13 Gottfried Semper, colored perspective of the Acropolis, Athens, 1833. Institut für Geschichte und Theorie der Architectur, Semper Archiv, ETH-Zurich.

led his former student to back away from pursuing this matter, although when Semper eventually arrived in Munich much later in the year he did contact Thiersch.

With this plan on hold, Semper fell back to working on the other project that he had been considering for some months – a colored presentation of the results of his archaeological research in Greece. In discussing this project with his brother in the winter of 1833, Semper emphasized that a polychrome study of Greek architecture had never before been attempted: "I have sought to bring it [classical polychromy] into a system, and in order to show the effect I am preparing now a colored restoration of the buildings on the Acropolis."[117] This was no doubt a reference to his now famous bird's-eye perspective of the Acropolis (Pl. 13), in which the entire Parthenon and Propylaea (walls and columns), set against the dark blue sea and almost ominous sky, are rendered in a reddish tone approaching crimson. In a related colored drawing of part of the Parthenon's facade (Pl. 14), probably also done during these months, the red is softened into a more earthy tone, forming a contrasting background to the polychrome egg-and-dart motif of the echinus, the colored frets on the abacus, taenia, mutules, and corona, the green shields and blue triglyphs, and the brilliantly painted anthemion on the cornice.

This was certainly a bold conception of Greek antiquity, particularly in light of the vociferous controversy surrounding polychromy still escalating in Paris. Semper's very use of the word "system" no doubt consciously alluded to Hittorff's use of the term, and his polychrome conception – this time focusing on the acknowledged masterpieces of classical antiquity rather than the minor temples of some provincial outpost – was certainly no less audacious in its attempted reconstruction of the past. Through the archaeological contacts he was now establishing in Rome, Semper was also surely becoming aware of the extent and complexity of the debate over color, not to mention its already lengthy history and

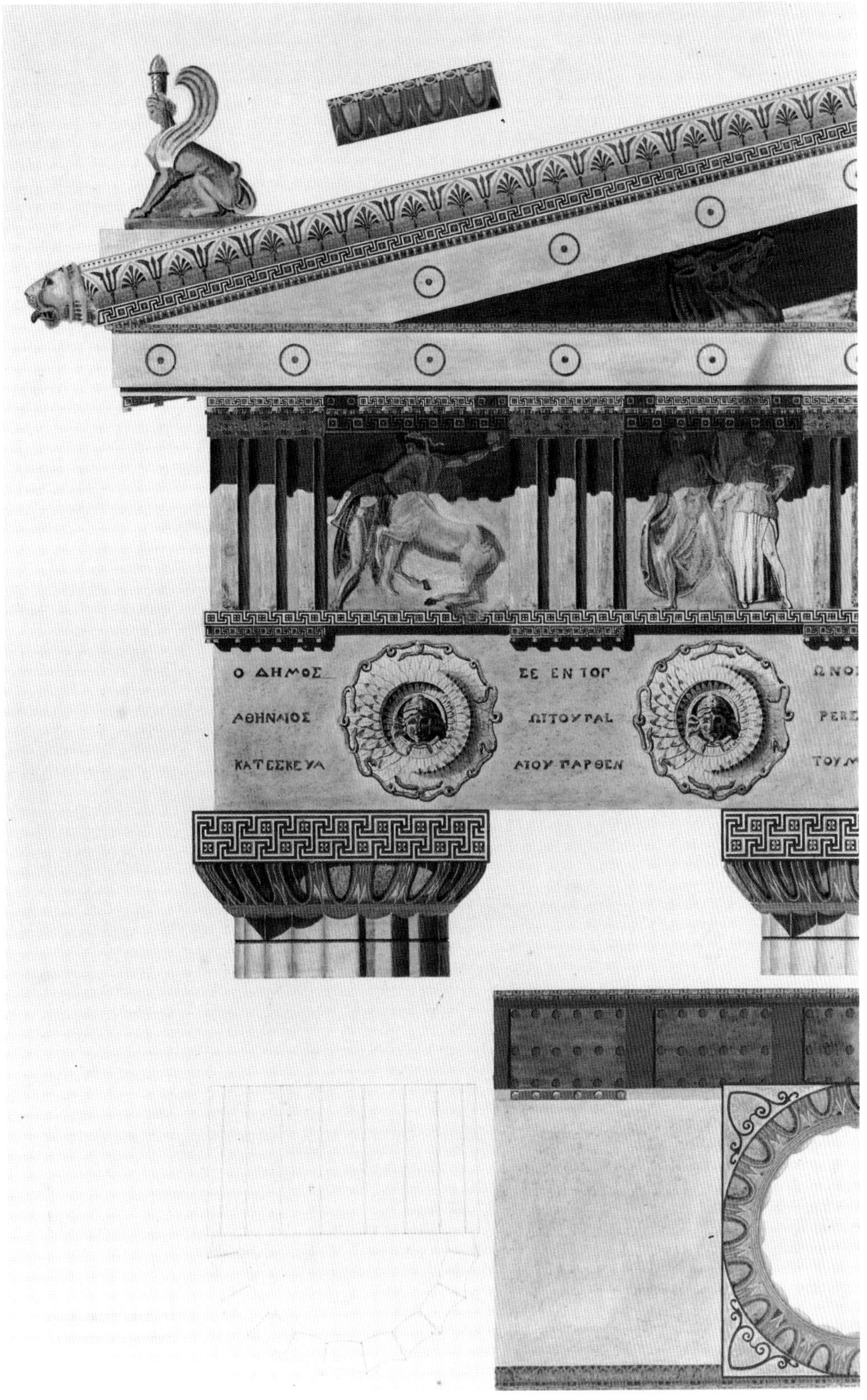

14 Gottfried Semper, colored view of Parthenon entablature, Athens, 1833. Institut für Geschichte und Theorie der Architectur, Semper Archiv, ETH-Zurich.

literature. He even carried with him paint fragments that he had scraped off the Parthenon and the Temple of Theseus, which he hoped his brother Wilhelm, the pharmacist, would be able to analyze for their chemical composition.

Semper discussed at length with Gau the publication of his drawings. Gottfried's first idea was to offer his drawings to the French architect Abel Blouet, who was already at work on a publication on Greece. The latter, a *grand-prix* winner at the Ecole in 1821, had been sent by the French government to the Peloponnese in 1828 to survey all classical buildings; his *L'Expédition scientifique de Morée* appeared in three volumes between 1831 and 1838. Gau rejected this suggestion for three reasons: first because it would not be feasible to add something to a government-sponsored publication thematically related only to southern Greece (Athens was not a part of the Peloponnese), second because of the French tendency to take the credit for all findings, and third because Blouet's work was too small and insignificant in Gau's eyes for what he believed to be Semper's momentous discovery.[118] Gau urged Semper to find a publisher as quickly as possible and again suggested Germany.

Semper remained in Rome working on his drawings through the first part of the summer of 1833. In responding to continuing pressure from his family throughout the year to return home, he defended his delay by pointing out that Christian Bunsen (1791–1860), the former secretary to the Prussian envoy Carsten Niebuhr and the guiding force behind the newly established Istituto di Corrispondenza Archaeologica in Rome (founded in 1829), had encouraged him to stay and finish his work, and had even furthered his endeavors.[119] Bunsen was indeed a persuasive force within Semper's development. He had resided in Rome since 1816, shortly after he had completed his studies at Göttingen at a very early age. In the 1820s his Palazzo Caffarelli had formed another social and physical center for the Capitoline community of German artists living in Rome, a place of discourse for Cornelius, Overbeck, and Thorwaldsen. In 1828 Bunsen drew upon a relationship he had cultivated with Friedrich Wilhelm IV, the Prussian crown prince, and it was the latter's money that had largely funded the new institute.

This connection with the archaeological institute may have helped Semper gain access to various Etruscan grave sites that had recently come to light. Two drawings from this time – of a rock tomb near Viterbo and an Etruscan tomb at Corneto (Pl. 15). – document his research. Semper was not the first to explore them. Stackelberg, together with August Kestner, had permission to explore the Etruscan site at Corneto (now Tarquinia) in 1827, but Stackelberg's declining health forced him to leave Italy the following year. Both Corneto and Viterbo are situated on the opposite side of the trachytic Tolfa hills north of Rome. They were actually under the jurisdiction of Lucien Bonaparte, brother of the deposed French emperor, who in 1803 had married the widow of the King of Etruria. Since 1815 he had resided at the royal estate in Canino, personally supervising the excavations. Corneto is one of the largest and best preserved of the Etruscan cities. Ashlar walls date back to the fourth century BC. The foundations of many buildings, including a major temple that yielded its famed "winged horses," are well preserved. The equally magnificent painted sepulchers of the city, now over sixty identified, were dug out of rock and elaborately furnished, as Semper's polychrome reconstruction suggests.

Another archaeological enterprise that Semper undertook was the examination of Trajan's Column for traces of paint. Taking advantage of a temporary scaffold that had been hung from its top, Semper led a team of ten architects up the column to examine

15 Gottfried Semper, colored sketch of an Etruscan tomb at Corneto, 1833. Institut für Geschichte und Theorie der Architectur, Semper Archiv, ETH-Zurich.

minutely its many crevices. In an article published in the institute's journal in July 1833 (addressed to Olaf Kellermann, the Danish archaeologist and librarian at the institute), Semper noted finding remnants of color on all parts of the column except on the southern side, which had the greatest exposure to harsh weather. He reported seeing traces of red, yellow, and gold paint in the lower parts of the column; he found paint fragments to be even more visible under the abacus, where a red and green enamel, "similar to the bituminous varnish of antique vessels," was still visible. Within the egg-and-dart motif of the echinus, evidence of blue lines were "clearly recognizable." Semper concluded that "originally the whole column was covered in brilliant colors, which, despite the great height, must have splendidly accentuated the beautiful sculptures."[120]

This brief, somewhat controversial article, published in a newly founded scientific journal, nevertheless documents what great strides this young architect had made in the thirty-four months since he had left Paris. No longer the moody, somewhat dazed artistic neophyte haphazardly recording the relics of the past, Gottfried had grown enormously in knowledge, stature, and manly confidence. He had now gained the respect of specialists and had a much clearer vision of what he hoped to achieve in life. At this stage, artistic and intellectual ambition became perhaps his most distinguishing trait.

Semper finally departed Rome in mid-July 1833, a full year after returning to Italy from Greece, for what would become a somewhat leisurely return to the north. He spent ten days in Orvieto admiring and sketching the cathedral. He did not return to Corneto along the way, which wounded the sensitivities of one young woman.[121] He remained about three weeks in Florence, before traveling northward through Bologna, Parma, Milan, and

16 Portrait sketch of Gottfried Semper, 1833. Institut für Denkmalpflege, Dresden.

Como. Approaching the Swiss border he turned southeast to visit Bergamo, Verona, Vicenza, and Venice, the last city "my main point of interest."[122] From Venice he made his way north into the Tyrol, passing through the Brenner Pass and Innsbruck, before arriving in Munich in time for the *Oktoberfest.* The last event – perhaps another sign of his maturity – proved to be a minor disappointment: any Sunday afternoon on the Reeperbahn, he dutifully reported to his mother, was "more jovial."

Semper spent almost six weeks in Munich (Pl. 16). He visited Thiersch and no doubt resumed contacts with several other old acquaintances. He studied the many new buildings that had been built in the decade since his last visit. In a letter to Gau, he made some unflattering remarks concerning the recent architectural work of Klenze and Gärtner, to which Gau nodded his consent.[123] Above all, he searched for a publisher for his planned publication and became especially annoyed after a fruitless meeting with the younger Cotta, who had just inherited his father's (J. F. Cotta's) publishing firm. The house was one of the few in Europe that specialized in the chromolithographic plates so necessary for polychrome texts in art and archaeology.

Throughout his northward trek, Semper fretted over an essay that he had sent to Gau from Rome, which had not arrived. It was by his own description a historical account of the Greek political conflict up to the death of Capodistrias. He also worried over the absence of a chest that he had sent ahead to Munich from Milan, which contained all of his drawings from Italy, Sicily, and Greece. It finally arrived, but not before Gau chastised him for separating himself from his artistic labor.

He left Munich in the third week of November and sought out his old acquaintances in Regensburg. When these reunions proved disappointing, he continued northward to Nuremberg and Bamberg, where he made studies of some Gothic works. After passing through Coburg and Saalfeld, he made a visit to his brother's grave in Jena (Gottfried had earlier designed the tombstone). It was an act that was much appreciated by his mother and sister in Altona. His mother, in particular, had been following his northward trail with growing trepidation because of the bitter circumstances surrounding his departure from home, now over four years ago.

On 22 December 1833 Gottfried passed through the Brandenburg Gate and soon thereafter presented his polychrome drawings to the great Karl Friedrich Schinkel, now approaching the height of his international fame. Friedrich Pecht, in his apotheosizing biography of Semper of 1877, emphasized the importance of this meeting as the symbolic passing of the torch from the aging master to his young successor. Semper's drawings were actually put on display in some kind of public exhibition and their author was asked to give a talk. Pecht also noted the jealousy that Semper's drawings and visit elicited from some of Schinkel's inner circle of admirers, among them the young art historian Franz Kugler.[124]

None of this can be substantiated from Semper's correspondence, but Schinkel, who was himself enthralled during these years with the issue of classical polychromy, received the traveler warmly and invited him into his home for a Christmas Eve dinner.[125] In a letter addressed to Semper in Altona some months later, Schinkel recalled their "most pleasant" personal conversations and concluded that "no one can take a greater interest in all of your worthwhile endeavors" than he himself.[126]

Sometime around the new year of 1834, the now thirty-year-old architect left the Prussian capital by coach for the relatively short trip to his native city of Hamburg. It seems he was successful in forging a reconciliation with his mother, who would now become his closest advisor on his career. His *Wanderjahre,* as he was later fond of calling them, had finally come to an end.

Preliminary Remarks . . .

From Schinkel's letter to Semper, which was dated 19 June 1834, it is apparent that the two men discussed the publication of Semper's findings while the latter was in Berlin. This effort, which had occupied Semper during much of his stay in Rome, was also at the top of his agenda upon his return to Altona in early January. In little more than eight weeks he composed a spirited prelude to the planned folio-size work, carrying the title *Vorläufige Bemerkungen über bemalte Architectur und Plastik bei den Alten* (Preliminary Remarks on Polychrome Architecture and Sculpture in Antiquity). The pamphlet appeared in Altona in the spring of 1834; its preface was dated 10 March.

The Pompeian scaffold (Pl. 17) adorning the front and back covers, within and on which are pasted images of buildings from various historical periods, graphically depicts the work's evolutionary theme. On the front cover are examples of Renaissance and Roman buildings, alluding to their ancestral and spiritual source on the back cover: a resplendent Greek temple in a verdant southern landscape. The youthful inscription beside the sphinx on the back cover – "Gray, dear friend, is all theory, and green the golden tree of life" – is taken from the first part of Goethe's *Faust.* Semper dedicated the forty-nine page pamphlet to "My teacher and friend Herrn Gau." At least one critic, Friedrich Pecht, has aptly termed this short work, "a complete program of the author's artistic and political views."[127]

The larger publication of polychrome plates that *Preliminary Remarks* was intended to

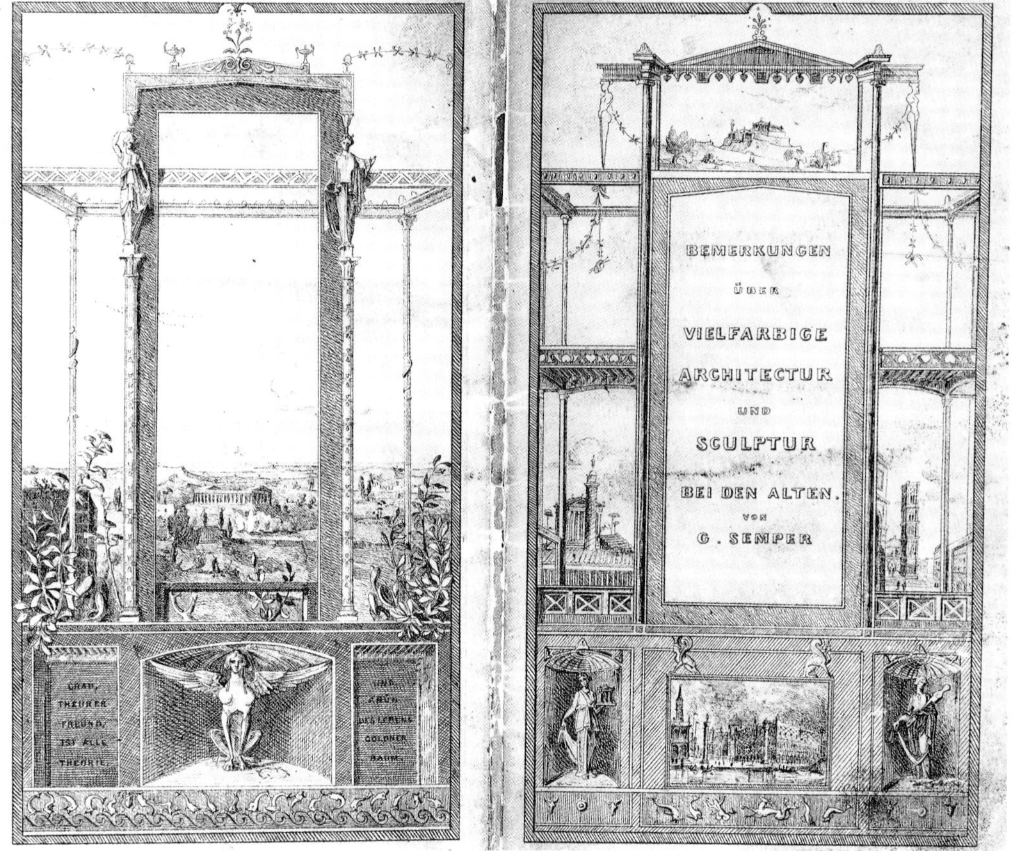

17 Gottfried Semper, front and back covers of *Preliminary Remarks on Polychrome Architecture and Sculpture in Antiquity*, 1834. Institut für Geschichte und Theorie der Architectur, Semper Archiv, ETH-Zurich.

announce, *Die Anwendung der Farben in der Architectur und Plastik* (The Use of Color in Architecture and Sculpture), never appeared. A mere six proof sheets were run off in 1836.[128] Semper envisioned the larger work as an elaborate colored publication issued as fascicles by subscription, with separate numbers devoted to a restoration of the Doric order (Parthenon), the Ionic order (Erechtheum), the Corinthian order (the Choragic Monument of Lysicrates), and selected examples of polychromy in Etruscan, Roman, and Christian times. All were works that he, either alone or with Goury and Metzger, had surveyed; in fact at one point he asked for Metzger's help in completing the project but this was not forthcoming. Of the six proof sheets that were run off two, possibly three, would have appeared in his first volume. These were his color perspective of the Acropolis, and two sheets with details from the Temple of Theseus (Pl. 18).

Preliminary Remarks, for all of its forty-nine printed pages, had a difficult nativity. No less than six working drafts have been preserved, which vary considerably in their underlying conceptions and formats.[129] The first draft apparently was intended in a straightforward way to accompany the first number of Semper's larger work on polychromy. When Semper decided to let these introductory remarks stand on their own, apart from his projected text for the plates, he experimented with the appropriate medium for his ideas. The second draft was conceived as a series of travel reports: letters fictitiously addressed to

Gau. Upon later reflection and on the advice of a family friend, Semper brought together his various polemical remarks concerning contemporary architecture into a short preface. The main body of the text, although at times architectural in its argument, was then given over to the archaeological consideration of classical polychromy.

In more recent times, reviews of the work have focused almost entirely on the preface, in part because its polemics seemed both progressive and "modern" to twentieth-century tastes. Contemporary architecture, Semper announces at the beginning of his work, has fallen into a state of crisis; it is lagging behind the other fine arts in its development and has lost touch with current social needs. In its bankrupt condition it has resorted to issuing two kinds of false paper currencies. The first are represented by Durand's *assignats* or compositional grids, whereby buildings, even cities, almost automatically compose themselves in a very mechanical way. The second false currency is the introduction of tracing paper, which has facilitated eclecticism by its very essence as a tool. Architects employ it to copy historical designs from books, and in their rush to replicate every style from the past they have forgotten in the end to which century they belong. The art of architecture has thus been replaced by blind numbers and rules: "So long as we grasp at every old tatter and our artists sneak off into corners to draw bare subsistence from the moss of the past, there is no prospect for a productive artistic life."[130]

Genuine art, by contrast, can flourish only "on the soil of need and under the sun of freedom."[131] In ancient Greece social needs were "organic," in that they were imbued with the prevailing religious and political sentiments. With the more recent decline of

18 Gottfried Semper, plate from *Die Anwendung der Farben in der Architectur und Plastik*, 1836. Courtesy Victoria and Albert Museum Library, London.

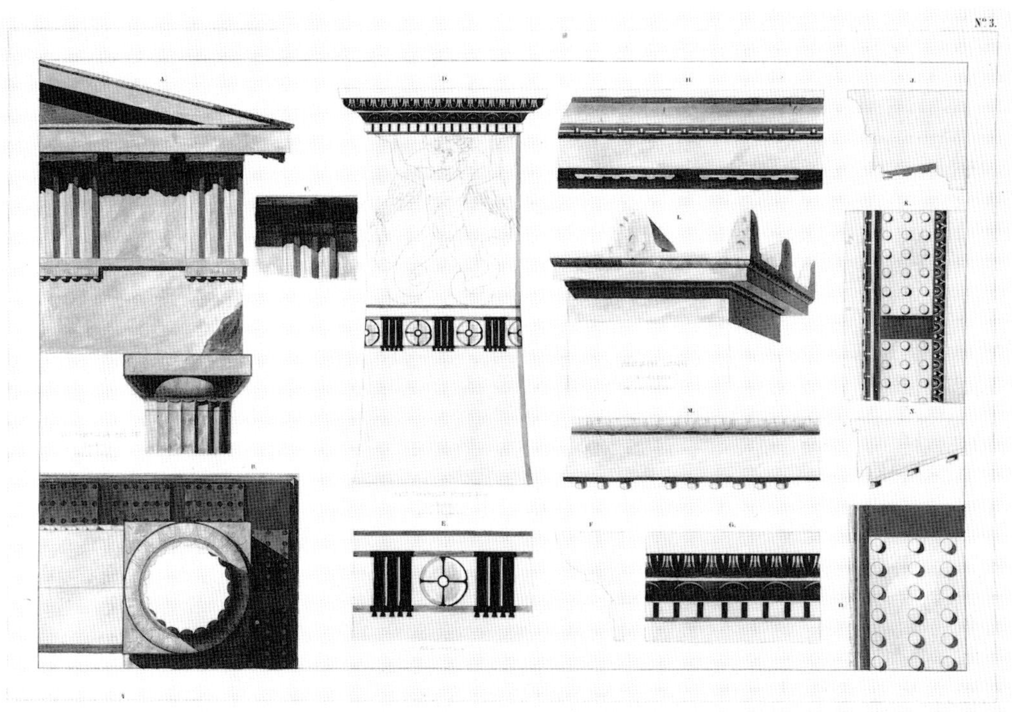

Christianity and with the socially-leveling reforms of nineteenth-century democracy, the reinstated needs of simplicity, comfort, and material honesty have yet to be addressed in a satisfactory way. Miniature palaces are still being constructed by the wealthy and by governments to epitomize the modern sense of selfishness; standing armies are presently draining the country's resources. When buildings dedicated to the public weal are erected, they are often arbitrarily composed according to obsolete laws of symmetry and they lack any human scale.

In a curious twist to his argument – one that quite succinctly presages German polemics of the 1880s – Semper notes that the English with their domestic simplicity and attention to detail are pointing the way to a solution. In an earlier version of the manuscript he makes this point even more cogently; he lists the sense of purpose (*Zweckmässigkeit*), comfort, and elegance of the middle-class home (*Bürgerhauses*) as the most important of the new architectural virtues to be emulated.[132] The issue of polychromy is brought into this discussion only incidentally, in that a pleasant diversity of color is identified as one economical way to overcome the present architectural tedium.

Semper's use of the term "organic" in describing the social, political, and artistic situation of classical Greece certainly suggests his familiarity with Saint-Simonian ideas, so popular in Paris in the late 1820s. The philosopher Claude Henri de Saint-Simon had died in 1825, but his ideas were kept alive, indeed enshrined, in the last half of the decade by a number of followers, led by Père Enfantin. By 1830, as a recent study by Barry Bergdoll has shown, the movement had made its way south to Rome through the efforts of the Beaux-Arts students Albert Lenoir and Alexis Cendrier, and here it also influenced a number of other French architectural students at the Villa Medici.[133] The artistic ideology of the movement was expounded in a lecture given in Paris in 1830 by Emile Barrault (1799-1864), who also published a pamphlet in the same year, *Aux Artistes, du passé et de l'avenir des Beaux-Arts*. The tenor of Semper's preface very much calls to mind Barrault's tract, which begins with the judgment that "The decadence of the arts is obvious," and that it will take more than an aesthetic debate with Aristotle, Boileau, or Schlegel to rectify the situation.[134] What was required, Barrault argued, was a moral revolution following the principles of Saint-Simon, for "the arts are only able to flourish within an organic epoch, and inspiration is only able to be salutary when it is social and religious."[135]

Barrault and the Saint-Simonians viewed history as a continuum of relatively short "organic" epochs followed by much longer "critical" epochs. The epochs were organic when the religious, social, and artistic ideals worked in harmony and mutually advanced one another; they were critical when these same forces competed against one another. Under this scenario, only the early Greek and early medieval periods succeeded in being truly organic epochs, and it was only in the opening stages of a similarly progressing and unified culture that profound and genuine artistic expression could take place. The critical epochs that succeeded the organic epochs, which appeared at times formally and technically more advanced, lacked this essential youthful vigor. The gist of Barrault's optimistic argument was that modern art and architecture were about to enter another organic era. The churches, palaces, assembly halls, and trading exchanges, which up to now had been so lacking in character, would shortly find again that special poetic expression by which truth and beauty would be reconciled.

Whereas Semper's preface almost certainly owes something to the youthful spirit of Barrault's pamphlet, it is also important to note their differences. In a fragment of a draft of a letter to Gau, perhaps written in Rome in 1833, Semper explained that his "bitter scorn" would be directed against two tendencies perpetuating the languid condition of modern art. First there were the twin scourges of antiquarianism and dilettantism, a condition brought on – he felt – by the disorder at the academies of art, which were inundating Europe with talented, yet immature artists. They, in turn, were being exploited by dilettantes and artistic magnates, who excluded everything that was not antique, controlled as they were by the critics of art, aestheticians, and even by the pernicious influence of art galleries. A second reason for art's decline was Protestantism itself, which, thought Semper, had lost its *raison d'être* and sense of community.[136] Protestantism for the Saint-Simonians, on the contrary, was a positive force in that it had advanced critical inquiry in Western thought. In another draft of his essay, Semper traced the same artistic demise to the material extravagance of the "sinister church of Rome."[137] Since his days in Paris, he had felt great contempt for Catholicism, and he denounced it repeatedly in his writings throughout his lifetime.

In his correspondence with Gau, Semper discussed many other aspects of his polemical argument. Gau's responses were also instrumental in establishing the tone of Semper's text. Passages from Gau's letters were even taken over by Semper, some quite literally. For instance, Semper's plea for the "simple" (*einfach*) in architecture, followed by the English word placed in parenthesis, was a rhetorical device borrowed from one of Gau's letters.[138] And Semper's frequently cited remarks concerning eclecticism – which first became fashionable with imitations of the Romantic (Gothic) and Renaissance periods, then advancing to imitations of the Rococo and the Louis XV style, and eventually expiring with the exhaustion of historical possiblities – were also lifted from the same letter with only minor modifications.[139] Klenze, incidentally, was much put off by Semper's reference to his "Walhalla *à la* Parthénon." He first approached Metzger in Munich to voice his anger at Semper's remark; the next spring he wrote to Semper directly and defended himself.[140] Wolfgang Herrmann has speculated that Klenze's argument may have raised doubts in Semper's mind concerning the nature of his sweeping and often facile generalizations.[141]

Both these issues – in particular Gau's role in the formulation of the leading ideas of Semper's preface – call into question the great importance that has been attached to these few pages by more recent critics. Semper's remarks have appealed, on the one hand, to reform-minded architects of the late nineteenth century who sought to appropriate his rationalism for their own purposes. An example of this is Otto Wagner's usurpation of Semper's reference to "need" as the only master of art, which Wagner then converted into his own artistic slogan: "Artis sola domina necessitas."[142] The very same remarks have been invoked, on the other hand, by twentieth-century historians who have viewed these pages as some kind of distant harbinger to modern functionalist thought. Nikolaus Pevsner's influential interpretation of Semper as a proto-functionalist (notwithstanding, in Pevsner's eyes, Semper's unfortunate opposition to Gothic architecture) is a case in point.[143] It would be far better, I think, to take Semper's preface simply for what it is: the animated remarks of a thirty-year-old architect who (fresh from his travels and archaeological pursuits) had yet to erect his first building. Little of his later theory can be gleaned from these introductory remarks.

If we turn to the main body of Semper's essay, however, we find much more that is indicative of Semper's later development, both as an architect and a theorist. The tract's leading theme is the question of why classical polychromy had until recently been so infrequently discussed, that is to say, why it was still considered by many to offend modern artistic ideals. Semper seeks to surmount this problem by interweaving three arguments to buffer his case for ancient and modern polychromy.

First he presents us with the historical argument that great periods of art have always exploited color and that the present-day insensitivity to polychromy was, at heart, a prejudice fostered by Winckelmann's historical conception and the outmoded aesthetics of Neoclassicism. In adapting Quatremère de Quincy's thesis that color became a historically sanctified tradition in Greek art (as well as emending Winckelmann's stylistic scheme that moved from severity, to grandeur, to decline), Semper first considers the historical beginnings of art and argues that in the earliest periods of each culture (for him defined by Nubia in Egypt, Etruria in Italy, and the Mycenaen consciousness of Homer and Hesiod) the use of color was most widespread and luxurious. When Doric art matured color was used in a slightly more sparing way, as it became integrated into a lawful or disciplined system. Appreciation for polychromy, in fact, only began to wane with the advent of the late-Hellenistic age. Here its principles began to be misunderstood and it was in this saturated condition that the Romans inherited and intensified these misunderstandings with their love of mosaics and ostentatious materials.

This great importance now placed on the social and historical roots of architectural polychromy suggests another possible Parisian source for Semper's ideas – the lectures of Jean-Nicolas Huyot (1780–1840). Huyot was a professor of architectural history at the Ecole des Beaux-Arts, having won the *grand prix* there in 1807. Between 1819 and 1822 he had traveled extensively in Egypt and the Middle East, and thereafter he was a close friend of Gau.[144] In the notes that have survived of his lectures given in the 1830s, earlier cycles of which Semper may well have attended in part, Huyot stressed the classical greatness of Greece, but he also gave attention to the origins of classical civilization – in Egypt, the eastern Mediterranean, and Asia Minor, where such ideals were first nurtured and then passed on for subsequent refinement. The nature of the landscape, climate, and cultural institutions also left their mark on each nation's art, which then unfolded in progressive stages as a continual development.

Semper was equally concerned with contemporary conditions and with how the rich polychrome tradition that had been interrupted after the fall of Rome was all but lost except for a brief revival in the Middle Ages. The errors of historians and archaeologists in the eighteenth century (such as Winckelmann, and Stuart and Revett) were both perplexing and grave, Semper felt. They were perplexing because even though traces of color had been noted in Pompeii, Sicily, and Greece, they were either overlooked or ascribed to later, artistically corrupt periods. They were grave because this prejudice against the use of color severely limited the options open to contemporary practice. Thus color, deemed by Semper to be the essence of classical architecture, had been disallowed by Neoclassical theory, which favored instead the imitation of the "wax larvae" of the classical past, that is, the white temple skeletons devoid of their colorful flesh. As Semper phrased it, "The leanness, dryness, severity, and lack of character of modern architectural productions can be explained quite simply by this foolish aping of antique fragments."[145]

Semper buffered his historical argument for polychromy with the environmental contentions of Stackelberg and Hittorff. The sunny climate and variegated landscape of the south made color a necessity: first to mitigate the glaring effects of sunlight (seen at its worst in Milan Cathedral, "a St. Petersburg snow castle transplanted to the sunny, colorful south") and second to harmonize the building with its brilliant surroundings. Primarily on the basis of his studies at Pompeii, Semper argued that the ancients used pure tones side by side to create "impressionistic" effects, whereby color was employed both to soften and to accentuate form. With most Greek temples the porous limestone required first a coating of stucco; with the hard and fine Pentelic marble of the Periclean age, color could be applied directly to the marble. He viewed the "golden crust" of the Parthenon, in fact, as the chemical residue of its former coat of paint.

Yet it was with his third line of reasoning, with what might be called his developmental or evolutionary argument, that Semper broke new ground. At the same time he established an important conceptual underpinning for his later approach to architecture. Underlying this argument – in a way that recalls the liturgical-cosmogonic explanation of ancient architecture of Charles Viel de Saint-Maux in his *Lettres sur l'architecture* (1787) – was Semper's view that the structural members of the primitive temple comprised little more than the basic scaffold, upon which were attached ennobling flowers, festoons, branches, sacrificial animals, implements, shields, and other mystical emblems. These appendages later became typified as symbols and were incorporated into the facade. Even moldings, bead-fillets, egg-and-dart motifs, arabesques, rosettes, meanders, labyrinths, and running palmettes originally had a symbolic meaning, Semper argued, a significance that was now mostly lost. He suggested, for instance, a six-stage depiction of the bead-fillet or pearl molding, which illustrated this gradual process of monumentalization:

1) the hanging of a sacrificial braid made from the wool of the animal;
2) scratching or painting the braid on the wall as a mystical representation;
3) notching the painted string of beads in light relief (soffits of Temple of Theseus);
4) raising the fillet in flat relief and painting on it the pearls (cornice of Propylaea);
5) rounding the painted relief (the antae of the Temple of Theseus);
6) notching the astragal so that it became a string of painted beads (examples everywhere).[146]

Every architectural form, Semper insisted, could be traced through similar stages back to its origin. As a part of this symbolic polyphony, color stands not only in service to the particular symbolic form but it also comes to acquire formal or constructional values – as Ettlinger has noted[147] – such as visually distinguishing the various forms from one another. But it also does more. For now the curvature of a molding or an echinus could be analyzed by examining the painted or carved ornament that generally accompanied it. And from such an analysis arises the possibility of reconstructing the ancient "system."

Semper's conception of the Greek temple, however, differed from that of Viel de Saint-Maux in his interpretation of the end toward which these affects were directed. Whereas Viel de Saint-Maux saw the primitive temple simply as a kind of "speaking poem" enacting the culture's theological and agricultural roots, Semper saw it rather as quasi-theatrical exercise in service to the same communal rituals, but consciously choreographed by the first architects according to higher artistic ideals: "In addition to painting, we should not forget the metal ornaments, gilding, tapestry-like draperies, baldachins, curtains, and movable implements. From the beginning the monuments were designed with all of these things in mind, even for the surroundings – the crowds of people, priests, and the processions. The monuments were the scaffolding intended to bring together these elements on a common stage. The brilliance that fills the imagination when trying to visualize those times makes the imitations that people have since fancied and imposed on us seem pale and stiff."[148]

Here for the first time Semper's image of antique architecture (and indeed for him the genesis of monumental architecture) is linked in its artistic impulse to the inception of the Greek theater. In fact, the Greek temple in Semper's vivid description is little more than a special stage prepared for high sacred drama, the battened-down "improvised scaffolding" complete with scenic props, choral processions, and leading performers. Even the first architects possessed a very special dramatic role within this colorful entourage: "The architect was the choragus, he led them – his name even says it."[149]

It should also be noted that this conception was not an effort by Semper to reduce architecture (ancient or modern) solely to some kind of primitive orphic enterprise; but rather he seems to suggest, in a way that he developed more fully later, that architects and dramatists (for Semper the high drama of Aeschylus, Sophocles, or Euripides) share similar artistic origins, similar artistic themes, and similar artistic instincts, if you will. Their mutual task is the development of a sophisticated festive setting or artistic mask for all kinds of social parables.

This view of classical architecture as dramatic *Gesamtkunstwerk* proved to be a very powerful one in its implications – not just for Semper but also for Richard Wagner. For Semper it provided the basis for his subsequent practice of monumental architecture, which turned almost exclusively on the orchestration of these choral effects. As he himself explained: "Under the architect's supervision the monument became the quintessence of the arts; as a unified work of art, it was defined, developed, and sustained in its details. Architecture as a separate art evolved quite naturally in relation to its sister arts."[150]

The first monumental architect was thus seen by Semper as a grand director, "chosen from among the artists less for his sweeping mastery of all the arts than for his special gift of assessing the situation, allocating the resources, and for having a sharp eye for proportion and economy of means."[151] Although this image of the past can be traced back to some rather well-established models in eighteenth-century European architecture, I would prefer to see it as a vision formed for the most part through Semper's travels to the south. And if the classical architect was the choragus or choral master of artistic effects – it was in just such a light that Semper, like Wagner, would also come to view himself.

For all of its power and rich implications, however, this colorful image of the past became blunted in its first exposition by Semper through his own shortcomings – especially his failings as an archaeologist.[152] Not content to limit his arguments regarding classical polychromy to reporting his own research, Semper peppered his text with a number of rash archaeological statements, which combined to undermine his various insights. With many a rhetorical flourish he noted that all Roman monuments made from white marble or common stone show traces of paint, that the Roman Coliseum was originally painted red, that the color crust on many Greek marble temples was a hard vitreous enamel a half-millimeter thick, and that the present "golden crust" of the Parthenon was a residue of this enamel.[153] No evidence or documentation is supplied, even though Semper did in fact have paint specimens in his possession.

His scholarship on the history of the controversy over polychromy was also basically unsound. He cited as supporting evidence for his theories Stuart and Revett's work, the reports of unnamed English travelers, an unseen book on Cyrene, the travel reports of the

English chemist Humphry Davy, Hittorff's and Brøndsted's investigations, and Domenico Serradifalco's forthcoming *Le antichità siciliane eposte e illustrate* (1835–42). By doing so, however, he exposed at the same time his scholarly shortcomings. Stuart and Revett's remarks concerning polychromy were certainly minimal. The vague allusion to English travelers reveals not only that he was unfamiliar with their writings but also that he had not studied Brøndsted's book carefully, since the latter had given a detailed summary of their findings. The mention of Serradifalco's forthcoming book was even more deleterious to his argument, for the publication of this Palermo nobleman would prove to be a sharp rebuttal to Hittorff's temple restoration, contesting not only the latter's color scheme but also the size and type of temple.[154]

In the addendum to his essay, moreover, Semper acknowledged that he was unfamiliar with the writings of Raoul Rochette, who by 1834 had become, alongside Hittorff, the leading protagonist in the discussion. This unfamiliarity did not deter Semper, somewhat facetiously, from taking the French archaeologist to task for his presumed views on Greek wall painting – an issue that Semper himself was ill-prepared to argue. In short, in his year in Rome he had mastered the spirit but not the important details of the debate over polychromy.

The essay, nevertheless, attracted both admirers and detractors, and gained for Semper his first European exposure. Schinkel praised his courage and cheered his efforts to approach the "spiritual wellspring" of Greek architecture.[155] Gau, on whom Semper's preface had an effect as powerful as a "Beethoven overture," reported that J.-A. Letronne (a friend and defender of Hittorff) had spoken well of it, and that it had even passed muster with Raoul Rochette, who would soon be writing to Semper.[156] He did so later in 1834, expressing his interest in the pamphlet and in Semper's promise to publish a more substantial system, and informing Semper in some detail of his actual views concerning Greek wall painting: no doubt embarrassing the young architect by citing, among other authorities, a conversation he had had with Thiersch.[157]

In a more public review of Semper's essay, published two years later in the *Journal des Savants*, Raoul Rochette was less polite. After noting Semper's skillful and impassioned plea to overturn the coldness of modern architecture, he proceeded to tackle head on Semper's many "déductions aventureuses" – among them his continual lack of documentation, his fixation on color as always indispensable to classical monuments, and his historical account, described as "rapide, vive et irregulière", where one phrase was often used to characterize an entire epoch.[158]

Semper's essay was also reviewed in the *Göttingische gelehrte Anzeigen* by C. O. Müller, the noted Greek historian and archaeologist at Göttingen, whose views Semper had defended in his essay.[159] Müller, who was also familiar with Semper's restoration of the Etruscan tomb at Corneto and his report on Trajan's Column (he praised his intelligence and erudition), argued that the architect in this instance had gone too far in asserting that the marble monuments of the Periclean age had been fully painted. Pointing out that the Greeks had polished their marble in the quarry, he asked: "Should this polishing have been done merely to serve as a base for the paint, which, however thin, would necessarily have denied the shine in every instance?"[160] Not only Müller but also Carl Friedrich Rumohr, a highly respected historian whom Semper had met in Italy, insisted privately that Semper had overstated his case. In a letter to Müller, he dismissed both Brøndsted's and Semper's contentions as "unnecessary."[161]

Yet the most damaging review of Semper's essay was another pamphlet that appeared in 1835, *Über die Polychromie der griechischen Architektur und Sculptür und ihre Grenzen* (On the Polychromy of Greek Architecture and Sculpture and its Limits).[162] Its author was Franz Kugler (1808–58), a twenty-seven-year-old historian and protégé of Schinkel, who was spurred to his task, he noted in his text, by the great interest in ancient polychromy generated by Semper's visit to Berlin. Kugler defined his position as searching for the "proper middle course" – the middle course between those who denied ancient polychromy altogether (parties nonexistent by the 1830s) and those extremists who advocated a full array of color (Semper and Hittorff).

His essay was, in fact, a point-by-point examination of Semper's many contentions, based on his mastery of all philological and archaeological evidence. The task of portraying Semper as an extremist was not difficult in light of his many generalizations, but at issue in Kugler's essay was not so much a denial of classical polychromy as a reaffirmation of the aesthetics of Winckelmann, whereby form and proportion would again be extolled as the essence of classical art. To do so, Kugler prepared his own restoration of the Parthenon, separating the architecture into primary and secondary members: the former (columns, architrave, triglyphs) left in their pristine condition of whiteness; the latter (echinus, mutules, guttae, metopes, and cornice) tastefully painted. The cella walls were white; gold shields were attached to the architrave. It should also be pointed out that Kugler's drawing was entirely speculative, as he had never ventured to Greece.

Nevertheless his rebuttal of Semper was entirely successful, particularly in light of the fact that Semper had published no drawings of his own at this time. Semper's comment several years later that he had been strategically outflanked in the debate was essentially correct. An academic coalition, centered around Kugler in Berlin and Raoul Rochette in Paris, had formed to bring the now somewhat tedious debate over polychromy to a conclusion: less on the basis of specific evidence than with the presumption of judicious moderation.

Thus by the second half of the 1830s (for the time being at least) the debate was at an end. The verdict was rendered by the German historian Carl Schnaase in 1843 in this way: "The temples that were built of a noble material, especially the beautiful Pentelic marble, appeared on the whole and in their essential parts as white. To be sure color was applied to individual smaller members, but never out of a mere desire for variegation, always for the definite reason of accentuating the architectural form or its plastic expression."[163]

Semper was silenced, at least temporarily. The reason that he did not respond to Kugler's onslaught for another seventeen years, however, was not his lack of combativeness or his failing commitment to the ideal of color but rather to the interesting turn his life was taking in other ways in the spring and summer of 1834. Actually two events were coming together to determine his future.

The first was an architectural commission he had received to design a small garden pavilion in Altona for C. H. Donner. Semper first met this wealthy businessman shortly after his return to Rome in the fall of 1832. He reported to his mother at that time that Donner had just paid a huge sum of money for a group of Graces by Thorwaldsen, and that this Altona resident had impressed the artistic community even more with two lavish, truffle-and-champagne Christmas dinners.[164] Donner left Rome in January 1833 for his retreat in Naples, but revisited the city the following June to team up with Semper on some excursions around Italy. Semper also laid out for him his drawings on Greek polychromy at this time.

After returning to Altona late in 1833, Donner inquired after Semper.[165] He must have approached the young architect shortly after the latter's return to discuss his wish for a pavilion on his estate. It was to display his new sculptural acquisitions, as well as to serve as a greenhouse and storage space for wine and fruit. Construction on the complex began in the late spring or early summer of 1834. The building was under roof by November, although work on the elaborate polychrome finishes, both inside and outside, continued through the following summer. The building was eventually completed (it was extensively damaged by bombing in 1942 and demolished after the war), but not before the cost and delay of the enterprise – so trying on Donner's money and patience – caused the interior finishes to be scaled back.[166]

The first conception of the design consisted of a square exhibition hall surmounted by an octagonal drum, attached to which were some storage rooms and an orangery. The hothouse and storage areas were eventually removed to terraces below the complex, but their rectangular form was retained as an extension to the gallery (Pls. 19, 20). Semper's brilliantly colored, interior perspective of this extension shows this room from inside the square hall; the glazed peristyle on the south facade was formed from a series of square and polygonal piers. The color scheme is complicated but is dominated by deep shades of blue and Pompeian red. Donner exhibited his most prized sculptural works in the square hall. Semper concerned himself in particular with its natural lighting, which he filtered through louvers placed in the square windows above. The building as a whole, for all its variegated charm, is not especially refined or articulate in its conception. It is the work of a young architect: overly fussy in its detailing and ponderous in the invocation of classical proportions for what was essentially a garden pavilion.

Semper himself seems to have lost interest in it before its completion, but this was due to yet another stroke of good fortune.[167] In the spring of 1834 Semper had learned through private sources that the Dresden Academy of Fine Arts had him listed as a candidate for the vacant chair caused by the early death of Joseph Thürmer. In the previous fall the Academy had, in fact, approached Schinkel in Berlin, Georg Moller in Darmstadt, and Gau in Paris with offers for the position. All three declined but not without making their own recommendations. Schinkel, a few days before Semper had arrived in Berlin from the south, had proposed his pupil August Soller, who would later become an architect specializing in church design.[168] Moller proposed his nephew Friedrich Hessemer as well as the young architect Rudolf Wiegmann. Gau, of course, championed Semper, whom he characterized as "full of scientific learning and artistic spirit."[169] Other parties were nominated as well, among them Semper's friend Eduard Metzger.

What happened next has only recently been brought to light by the scholarship of Manfred Kobuch.[170] At the instigation of the Saxon Minister of the Interior Prince Vitzthum, information was solicited for each of the proposed candidates. In Semper's case, letters were sent to two prominent men in Hamburg: the businessman Johann Wulsten and a state senator, Christian Pehmöller. Neither knew Semper, but Wulsten invited Semper to dinner in early February. In his report to Dresden he spoke favorably of the architect's demeanor and deportment – his manly appearance, charm with the ladies, and

19 Gottfried Semper, Donner Pavilion, Altona. Plan and Elevation, 1834. Museum für Kunst und Gewerbe, Hamburg.

good manners.[171] Pehmöller collaborated with the attorney Karl Sieveking, a friend of the Semper family, and prepared (with Gottfried's assistance) a much more extensive report conveying information on Semper's lineage, education, drawing skill, travel, architectural activity, and speaking ability.[172]

A formal report addressed to the King and his cabinet concerning the vacancy was prepared by Vitzthum in March 1834.[173] Wiegmann and Metzger were praised, but Semper even more so on account of his period in Paris under Gau's tutelage and particularly for his extensive travels in Italy and Greece. Still, the Saxon bureaucracy moved slowly and in the middle of April an anxious Semper prepared a draft of a formal letter of application for the position, which he was probably advised not to send. Pehmöller interceded instead and in late April sent a copy of Semper's brochure on polychromy to Dresden. This may have accelerated the matter, for on 17 May the Saxon ministry and the King decided in favor of Semper; the letter offering him both the professorship and the directorship of the school was dated 24 May. Semper accepted the position in early June, pledging "to undertake with the best enthusiasm, erudition, and conscience" his new duties and responsibilities.[174]

In late summer 1834 Gottfried turned the supervision of the Donner pavilion over to his friend Franz Georg Stammann, although he continued to send back sketches of various details. Toward the end of September he climbed aboard a coach and departed his native town once more for the south: this time heading to Dresden. Not unlike his first journey, this venture too, in its many gyrations and changes of fortune, turned out to be an eventful odyssey. This time, at least, the citadel of artistic glory would be breached.

20 Gottfried Semper, Donner Pavilion, Altona. Colored interior perspective, 1834. Museum für Kunst und Gewerbe, Hamburg.

2

Royal Success in Dresden 1834–1849

"Art must and should be multifaceted in its appearances; it cannot feign the quiet nativity of a child of nature suckled by graces and muses . . ."
(Gottfried Semper to Ottomar Glöckner, 27 September 1840)

Artistic Life in "Florence on the Elbe"

Semper arrived in Dresden on Thursday evening, 25 September 1834. Early Friday morning he met with Prince Vitzthum, whom he described as a tall, thin man almost completely deaf, therefore difficult to converse with. On Sunday he was introduced to various of his colleagues and given a tour of the city; he then had a brief meeting with the King's chief minister, Bèrnhard August Lindenau. The next day the new professor had a two-hour audience with King Anton and – perplexed with the formality – was glad he did not have to speak. On Tuesday Semper was officially installed in his professorial post and publicly recited his oath of loyalty to the crown and the kingdom of Saxony. He was then told, probably by Lindenau, that the Dresden Academy was undergoing a major reorganization in which he was to play a significant role. Amid the high expectations and responsibilities placed on his inexperienced shoulders, his courage privately began to waver.[1]

Semper had every reason to feel anxious. If his prestigious appointment to the Dresden Academy of Fine Art and his directorship of the architectural program seems somewhat astonishing today, in light of his relatively thin portfolio as an architect or his lack of experience as a pedagogue, it was almost certainly no less so in the 1830s. Moreover, he was assuming a prominent position in a city that during these years was seen as one of Germany's leading cultural centers, in many activities a rival to Berlin and Munich. He was coming into a sophisticated cultural milieu with exacting standards of decorum, cordiality, and high expectations of individual artistic performance.

Situated in southeastern Germany along both banks of the River Elbe, Dresden has a rich and sometimes painful history, spanning many centuries. The medieval settlement burned to the ground in 1491. The rebuilt town returned to political and cultural prosperity in the sixteenth century with the building of fortifications and the Renaissance palace. In the eighteenth century, under the reign of Augustus the Strong (1670–1733) and Augustus III (1696–1763), the city expanded culturally. At that time the Electors of Saxony, that is, Electors of the Holy Roman Empire, also carried the title King of Poland. This political authority was severely delimited by the Seven Years War (1756–63), during

21 Gottfried Semper, Dresden Art Gallery, 1839–55. Photo by author.

which time Saxony was stripped of its kingdom to the east, and Frederick the Great again leveled much of the city.

The city was rebuilt but faced further perils. In 1806 Napoleon transformed the Saxon electorate into a kingdom and incorporated the state into his Confederation of the Rhine. The Emperor and his army occupied the city in 1813 and nearby Napoleon won his last major military victory in Germany. After the Emperor's subsequent defeat at Leipzig and expulsion from Germany, Prussia lobbied heavily for the annexation of Saxony at the Congress of Vienna in 1814, but it had to be content (for the time being) with grabbing only the northern third of its territory.

The two principal Saxon cities in the south, Dresden and Leipzig, nevertheless continued to prosper. Dresden's replay of the July Revolution in Paris – the "September Uprising" of 1830 – induced significant political and social reforms, which made the city and state of Saxony one of the most liberal in Germany. In 1832 the young Prince Friedrich August II was named co-regent with his uncle, King Anton, which he remained until the latter's death in 1836. Lindenau, who was a respected astronomer in addition to being an experienced diplomat, was brought in to become the first cabinet minister. He oversaw the massive reforms of the legal and judicial system, property rights, the military, and education. He urged Saxony to join the German Zollverein, or tariff federation, and helped to write a constitution guaranteeing for the first time political rights to its citizens.

Even earlier, between 1817 and 1831, Dresden had been undergoing a major economic and physical expansion with the dismantling of its old ramparts. A new middle class began to take shape and to compete with the aging aristocracy both politically and culturally. In 1836 a steamship line was inaugurated along the Elbe. Two years later the "Saxonia," Germany's first locomotive (built by the Dresden engineer Andreas Schubert), inaugurated a train service between Dresden and Leipzig. This engine was built thirteen years after George Stephenson's "Locomotion" was built in Yorkshire. The industrial age, although more advanced elsewhere, was nevertheless dawning in Germany.

Throughout its history, however, Dresden had been a city with a thriving artistic life. In the 1830s it was still very much a late-Baroque or Rococo city in its architecture – its major monuments all dating from the first half of the eighteenth century. Whatever Augustus the Strong and Augustus III may have lacked as military strategists, they more than made up for with their love of art and extensive building campaigns. The city's skyline was dominated by two imposing works: the huge cupola (93 meters tall) of Georg Bähr's Frauenkirche (1722–43) and the Rococo tower (90 meters tall) of Gaëtano Chiaveri's Hofkirche (1739–53). The architectural coronet of the city, however, was the Zwinger, the palatial extension (later museum) built by Matthäus Daniel Pöppelmann between 1709 and 1732 (Pl. 22). Its impressive courtyard, which Pöppelmann called a "Roman theater," was designed for hosting tournaments; a new palace (never built) was to be situated along the northern end of the courtyard, connecting it with the Elbe. Adjacent to the Zwinger to the east was the old palace, a complex of odd buildings, some of which dated back to the Middle Ages. Various other villas, palaces, and sumptuous townhouses further defined the character of the city. The nearby scenic river valley was also amply graced with royal palaces and aristocratic estates.

Perhaps even more impressive than its architecture, however, was the city's famed art collections. The Saxon rulers had always been avid collectors, in part because of the natural wealth of southern Saxony with its abundance of silver, tin, iron, copper, cobalt

22 Matthäus Daniel Pöppelmann, Zwinger pavilion and courtyard, 1709–32. Photo by author.

mines, in addition to valuable stones. Royal artifacts and jewelry commissioned by the court – in gold, silver, brass, bronze, ivory, ebony, amber, and glass – formed the stock of the city's famed Grünes Gewölbe (Green Vault), the first museum of its kind laid out by Pöppelmann in 1723. Another specialty of great renown was the region's production of porcelain. The alchemist Johann Friedrich Böttger, virtually held prisoner by Augustus the Strong, accidentally stumbled upon the secret of porcelain making in 1708 and this led, within a decade, to a thriving export industry. The royal operation eventually came to be housed at Meissen Castle, 21 kilometers away, from which the porcelain took its name.

A third area in which Dresden excelled was in the acquisition by its rulers of works of fine art. Augustus the Strong first laid the basis for Dresden's – still today – extraordinary collections, with his extensive purchases of antique works from the Chigi and Albini collections in Rome. In the 1740s Augustus III, with the help of the court painter Anton Raphael Mengs, added hundreds of Dutch, Flemish, and Italian masterpieces, among them paintings by Correggio, Rubens, Vermeer, Titian, Veronese, and (in 1754) Raphael's *Sistine Madonna*. In 1742 Francesco Algarotti drew up a program for publicly displaying these works, which in turn lured numerous visitors to the city. Johann Joachim Winckelmann, for instance, came to Dresden in 1754 as a librarian and tutor of Greek and he left the city one year later to begin his career as a historian of art. In 1763 the Dresden Academy of Fine Arts was founded, further enriching the city's artistic reputation and now supplying it with a community of trained artists. Five years later the prodigy Johann Wolfgang von Goethe came to Dresden from Weimar at his own initiative to see great works of art for the first time.[2]

It was this combination of collections, academic learning, and emphasis on the arts that provided the momentum in Dresden for the intellectual and artistic renaissance that unfolded with the Romantic movement in the first part of the nineteenth century. Much of the movement revolved around the solitary and melancholic figure of Caspar David Friedrich (1774–1840), who settled in Dresden in 1798; he was joined four years later by the painter and theorist Philipp Otto Runge (1777–1810). Runge eventually moved on but Friedrich remained behind and gradually amassed a train of followers who were attracted to the atmospheric symbolism and supernatural imagery of his landscape paintings. Friedrich began teaching at the Dresden Academy in 1816 and was named a professor in 1824. In that year he was joined by another landscape painter of high repute, the Norwegian Johann Christian Dahl (1788–1857).

Another influential member of this romantic contingent was the writer Ludwig Tieck (1772–1853), who lived in the city between 1819 and 1842, while maintaining solid connections with the Berlin circle of Wilhelm Heinrich Wackenroder and the Schlegel brothers. Tieck moved to Dresden at the height of his literary fame. Following the success of his early novel *Franz Sternbalds Wanderungen* (1798) he became increasingly concerned with the theater, and soon made a name for himself as the drama critic for the city's evening newspaper. From his home he gave semi-private dramatic readings, events that for many years were seen as central to Dresden's cultural life.

In 1824 Tieck was named dramaturge to the Dresden Theater, where he joined Carl Maria von Weber (choir and operatic director) and August von Lüttichau (theatrical director) in reshaping the Dresden stage, principally showing the works of Goethe and Shakespeare. The theater and opera company was also enriched by the renowned Devrient family of singers, actors, and directors. Karl August Devrient (1797–1872) was the first actor to arrive in 1821. Although he left following his divorce from Wilhelmine Schröder-Devrient in 1828, his place was filled a few years later by Gustav Emil (1803–72), who was noted in particular for his Shakespearean roles. Eventually joining him was his older brother, Phillip Eduard (1801–77), who served as artistic director of the theater from 1844–46. Wilhelmine Schröder-Devrient, the celebrated soprano and daughter of the actress Sophie Schröder, remained throughout these years as one of the city's most illustrious and compelling personalities.

One offshoot of this artistic activity was the Saxon *Kunstverein* or Artist Association, founded in 1828. It was concerned with advancing the fine arts by hosting regular exhibitions, lectures, and public debates. Nearly everyone connected with the arts in Dresden belonged to this organization; in the 1830s its membership locally exceeded 500 people. Semper joined in 1834 and in 1838 gave a lecture on polychromy in architecture.[3] The two lodestars of the union were Johann Gottlob Quandt (1787–1859) and Carl Gustav Carus (1789–1869). Both were instrumental in shaping the development of the arts in the city.

Quandt, a longtime friend of Goethe and Arthur Schopenhauer (who wrote the first volume of *The World as Will and Representation* while living in Dresden), was born to a wealthy Leipzig family with connections to the tobacco trade. Shortly after his first meeting with Goethe in 1808, he shifted his interest to art. In 1811 he made his first trip south as a connoisseur to study Italian architecture, painting, and sculpture. He returned to Italy in 1819 with a new bride from Dresden and established his villa in Rome as a social center of the German capitoline community. There he assisted poorer artists and purchased numerous works of Thorwaldsen, the Schadow brothers, Julius Schnorr von Carolsfeld, and Friedrich Overbeck. When Quandt returned to Germany he bought a large estate in Dresden and again entertained lavishly from his home, where his personal collection of works of art filled nine rooms.

Carus, who succeeded Quandt as director of the union in 1833, was by profession the royal physician and a professor at the Dresden Academy for Surgery and Medicine, but his interests were much broader. Also a close friend of Goethe, as well as of Alexander von Humboldt, he wrote several treatises on comparative physiology, zootomy, and psychology – following in the wake of Goethe's enthusiasm for biological research. He was important for Dresden culturally, for he was an accomplished sonnet writer, a talented landscape painter, and a strong supporter of Caspar David Friedrich.

This erudite cast of figures began to change in the 1830s and 1840s, as the romantic tradition of the city became revitalized by an influx of younger artists who soon seized the initiative. Among the first of this younger generation was the sculptor Ernst Wilhelm Rietschel (1804–61), who was appointed a professor at the Dresden Academy in 1832. He had studied in Dresden in the 1820s but then took his apprenticeship in Berlin under Christian Rauch, a close friend of Schinkel. After winning a three-year traveling stipend from the Prussian Academy in 1829, he set out the next year for Italy but the political unrest of the winter of 1830–31 (that which induced Semper to leave Rome for Naples) caused him to return north early. Rietschel became a popular figure in the city's vibrant social landscape, in part because of his marriage to Carus's daughter Charlotte, who was noted, among other things, for her beauty.

Rietschel's appointment was followed by that of Semper in 1834. The latter, in turn, was instrumental in luring Ernst Julius Hähnel (1811–91), a native of Dresden, back to the city in 1838. Hähnel had first studied architecture at the Academy in the mid-1820s, then went to Munich to continue his studies under Friedrich von Gärtner. From Munich he went south to Florence and Rome, where (with the help of Thorwaldsen) he shifted his interest to sculpture. He first met Semper in Rome during the latter's second stay in the city and the two remained lifelong friends.

Also joining the faculty at the Academy in the 1830s was the landscape painter and illustrator Ludwig Richter (1803–84), and the Düsseldorf painter Eduard Friedrich Bendemann (1811–99). Richter was also an alumni of the Academy; after a prolonged stay in Rome, he first found employment at a small drawing school in Meissen before returning to Dresden. Bendemann, a student of Wilhelm von Schadow, in turn convinced his friend, the painter Julius Hübner (1806–82), to join him in the city. Another painter of merit, Friedrich Pecht (1814–1903), first studied in Dresden in the mid-1830s, then returned to the city a decade later to draw once again upon the city's artistic energy.

This rejuvenation was certainly not confined to the visual arts. Parallel with the development of the Dresden Theater was the growing stature of the orchestra connected with it, first under the musical directorship of Weber and then of Karl Reissiger. The latter was joined in 1842 by the young Richard Wagner (1813–83), who (although born in Leipzig) had spent much of his childhood in Dresden. Through the connections of his real father Ludwig Geyer (a singer occasionally employed by Carl Maria von Weber), Wagner as a child had witnessed many of Wilhelmine Schröder-Devrient's early performances and thus this city had nurtured his infatuation with the theater. After his own spirited *Wanderjahre*, Wagner gave up his Paris setting to move back to Dresden, where he was offered the chance to stage a stalled performance of his opera *Rienzi*. The success of the work, first performed on 20 October 1842, at once established his artistic reputation. This performance was followed within a few years by the first performances in Dresden of two other Wagner operas: *The Flying Dutchman* and *Tannhäuser*.

Wagner's commanding presence contributed still further to enriching the life of the city, as numerous musicians were lured there for visits during his seven-year residence, among them Hector Berlioz and Franz Liszt. Clara and Robert Schumann were also attracted to the city in 1844, shortly after Robert's nervous breakdown; they remained until their departure for Düsseldorf in 1850. Another composer and pianist of high regard during this time was Ferdinand Hiller, whose salon (presided over by his beautiful "Polynesian" bride) became another important center for artistic discussions. Pecht described his evenings at the Hillers – eagerly attended by the leading politicians, connoisseurs, and artists of every trade – as the most intense gatherings of their kind that he had ever experienced.[4]

Still other younger and older artists migrated to Dresden during this period: the writer Ida Hahn-Hahn, the poet Alfred Meissner, the painter Julius Schnorr von Carolsfeld, and the actress Caroline Bauer. Dresden, particularly in the 1830s and 1840s, was a place where a score of leading artists of every persuasion met, shared ideas, and entertained each other on a regular basis.

It was into this intensely social and cultural milieu that the rebellious and somewhat nervous Semper (Pl. 23) arrived in the fall of 1834, determined to make his mark. His first impressions of the city, not surprisingly in view of his temperament, were rather negative. He found the people unfriendly and the Saxon Diet, for all its feigned democracy, a kind of cruel political hoax: "Damned the cursed rabble, damned the stupid swindle of freedom that has put the destiny of the state into the hands of peasants and wretched spice-peddlers."[5] He also bemoaned his loss of freedom and his status as a mere "civil servant" toeing an obscure administrative line. To make matters worse, bureaucratic machinations had delayed the payment of his salary until December, forcing him to fall back on his mother for financial assistance.

Semper's situation and confidence soon began to improve. By the following spring his complaints had all but disappeared and he now expressed his desire to set up a household. In reports home he boasted of the success of his lectures, of his rising artistic stature within the community, of various possible commissions, and of his extremely heavy workload. In the summer of 1835 he was approached by a city official privately, regarding the salaried position of municipal architect, but this overture proved disappointing.[6]

Contributing to his heavy workload were his lectures, and the extensive reforms he undertook for Lindenau at the department of architecture. In his first proposal for changes, dated 26 October 1834, he made various suggestions.[7] One was to bring together the different design studios into a single large studio, open from morning to evening, thereby encouraging student interaction. He proposed raising academic standards by restricting the number of students to the most talented, and he also recommended moving his lectures from the daytime to the evening in order to lessen the interruptions in the students' day. Finally, he sought to remove mathematical studies from the Academy to the nearby technical school and to have more faculty participation in students' work.

The general thrust of the report was his desire to place more emphasis on practical development, that is, on mastering the many technical aspects of the profession. He also introduced a personal studio alongside his general studio, whereby the best students could

23 Portrait sketch of Gottfried Semper, 1835. Institut für Geschichte und Theorie der Architectur, Semper Archiv, ETH-Zurich.

gain experience in working on actual commissions. The introduction of a large open studio space was an innovation deriving from his experience with Gau in Paris; in this way students could better exchange ideas and learn from one another. In addition to teaching design, Semper also delivered two cycles of lectures: the first a traditional survey of architectural history, the second a historical-comparative course on building types.

Semper's domestic life, in the spring of 1835, centered around Bertha Thimmig (1810–59), whom he married in September of that year. It was an expeditious engagement and marriage, and one toward which his mother was initially rather cool, although she contributed a sum of money for furnishings. Semper probably created this problem through his lack of tact. He first described his fiancée to his family not in terms of her intellectual or physical attributes but as the penniless daughter of a deceased Saxon major, a girl who for years had cared for her sick mother and ailing widowed sister. With the death of her mother (and the end of her widow's pension), Bertha had lost her means of support and was facing the prospect of a "dependent life."[8]

24 Portrait sketch of Bertha Semper with daughter Johanna Elisabeth, 1836. Institut für Geschichte und Theorie der Architectur, Semper Archiv, ETH-Zurich.

To allay his mother's doubts concerning Bertha's sincerity in love, Gottfried sent her several of Bertha's love letters, annotated by his own pen – a somewhat unusual if not inexcusable violation of his fiancée's privacy. Gottfried's mother responded with gratitude for this trust but said she needed some time to think about the whole surprising matter. Apparently she consented, for Gottfried and Bertha exchanged vows on the first of September and spent their honeymoon in Berlin. Between 1836 and 1848 Bertha dutifully gave birth to six children: two daughters and four sons.[9]

In a portrait of Bertha with their first daughter, probably sketched near the end of 1836 (Pl. 24), she appears as an attractive but maternal figure. Although there was genuine love between the two partners, the marriage was not an altogether happy or level affair. Bertha's first letters to Gottfried of June 1835 (those Gottfried sent to his mother) are brimming with ebullient and unaffected expressions of love. Gottfried, in turn, seems initially to have found in Bertha a certain solace or shelter from his worldly pressures. An exchange of letters of October 1836, however, reveals a quite troubled relationship. Gottfried, away in Berlin on business and staying at the same hotel in which they honeymooned one year earlier, voiced his deep-felt pain and remorse at his harsh treatment of her over the past year, a year that should have been the most beautiful of their lives – had he only moderated his "unbridled heart." Bertha's reply, in forgiving his trespasses, alluded to a quarrel in which Gottfried expressed his desire to be free of her and have his "old freedom" returned.[10]

Letters in later years, when Semper was traveling, often repeat the same format: the homesick Semper apologizes for his "bad temper" and insists that things will be better.[11] Bertha, it seems, was not a polished conversationalist and she had trouble adapting to the more sophisticated social circles in which her husband eventually moved. To some extent Semper's relationship with his mother, who was more strong willed, followed a similar pattern. At times Gottfried confided to her his most intimate feelings; at other times there was considerable tension and distance between the two. On one occasion the scorned mother congratulated her son because his "irritable mood" had succeeded in making her ill.[12] Semper's relationship with both his wife and his mother would undergo considerably more strain during and after the unsettling events of 1849.

Nevertheless, Semper's first years in Dresden were characterized chiefly by the heavy workload he began to assume through his teaching duties and by his efforts to establish an architectural practice. The profession of architecture in the nineteenth century was not so different from today, in the sense that a young architect seeking to stake out a reputation was expected to work on a variety of projects with little or no financial reward. In Semper's case – an inexperienced designer in state employment within an established and somewhat parochial environment – he had to prove his metal both personally and artistically.

One attribute that quickly became apparent was his commanding presence, even arrogance. The painter Friedrich Pecht, who first met Semper in 1836, was initially much taken aback by the forcefulness of his personality, which for him was the uncommon mark of genius: "No one who knew Semper well could doubt that he was just such an untypical nature," destined to make a significant place for himself. "When I first met him in Dresden," he continued, "I was facing a man of medium height and stocky build, with a mistrustful, measuring, and penetrating glance that at the same time seemed to listen more to inner impulses than to observe outward appearances."[13] Pecht, who later came to extol Semper as one of the artistic demigods of the century, saw him as an impassioned intellectual warrior in perpetual combat with the complacent social conventions of Dresden at that time. Semper's outgoing and assertive nature, on occasions prone to hypochondria, was not without charm, and his bonhomie was often evident at social gatherings, "particularly those in the form of cheerful bacchanal celebrations."[14]

The published correspondence between Ernst Rietschel and his former mentor in Berlin, the famed sculptor Christian Daniel Rauch, provides further insights in this regard. Rauch in the summer of 1834 had expressed surprise at Semper's appointment to the academy, to which Rietschel, who had joined the faculty two years earlier, responded with puzzlement and with some alarm that this new professor was not known in Berlin, since "Gau (archaeologist) in Paris had recommended him warmly."[15] Two years later the young Dresden sculptor seems to have forgotten his concern, as he reported to Rauch his great admiration for Semper, who "shows himself ever more a talented artist."[16]

Rietschel's opinion of Semper was high in January 1836, because of their recent success in designing the festivities celebrating King Anton's eightieth birthday. Semper had designed and supervised the construction of a series of provisional structures for various public squares and bridges in the city, including two obelisks, a Greek temple (inside of which was a bust of the King), and a triumphal arch. All were vividly appointed with polychrome decorations, and were illuminated at night. Rietschel executed in plaster the various genii and victories for these works; the engineer Andreas Schubert masterminded the complex scheme of illumination. The combined result, as Rietschel reported to Rauch, "was altogether magical" and a brilliant success; the polychrome figures and forms were nightly bathed in an amber-reddish light, silhouetted against the black sky.[17] The painted obelisks and temple were the first things Pecht saw upon his arrival in the city on Christmas Day 1835. For him the brilliance of these works against the backdrop of snow-covered streets symbolically "seemed to proclaim a new spring. And it was in fact so!"[18] Semper and Rietschel had merged their talents successfully: they were now regarded by many as the two brightest beacons of Dresden's artistic community.

The relationship between Semper and Rietschel was a complex one and was not without its rocky moments. Rietschel privately resented the fact that Semper lured the sculptor Hähnel back to the city in 1838, which resulted in fewer commissions for himself. Rietschel in the same year also complained to Rauch of the unbearable "tyranny of architects, above all Semper, who has a most irritable and choleric temperament."[19] Several months later Rietschel even went so far as to lay the blame for his own loss of confidence as an artist on Semper's neglect and ill will.[20] Aside from these difficulties, Rietschel, whose local commissions often depended on Semper's architectural designs, nevertheless revered Semper both socially and artistically. To Rauch he praised Semper's design for the pedestal to his statue of Friedrich August I, placed in the courtyard of the Zwinger, in the highest terms. He was also profoundly moved by Semper's stage designs for the 1844 production of *Antigone*.[21] On one occasion in 1843, he told Rauch how he lamented the fact that Semper's "glorious powers" – "his rare talent and refinement of ideas" – were temporarily not being put to use.[22]

If the festivities surrounding King Anton's birthday in 1836 gave Semper his first public opportunity to display his artistic bravado, it was winning the commission for the new royal theater and opera in 1837 that launched his architectural reputation on both national and international fronts (Pl. 25). Semper responded to this difficult design problem, situated adjacent to two Baroque masterworks (the Zwinger and the Hofkirche), with a production of great elegance and high drama, one that – with its rounded amphitheater form, rich sculptural effects, and lavish interior appointments – was applauded in many circles as the finest theater in Germany. His success with the Dresden Theater moved the young architect into the first rank of Dresden's cultural elite, and in 1841 the King awarded him a knighthood and a loge in the theater (number two) in perpetuity. Semper's architectural career now seemed assured.

In addition to the boost the theater gave to Semper's reputation, one should also consider its effect on the cultural life of the city. Pecht applauded its "epoch-making" design for just this reason – to him the theater represented the end of one era and the dawning of another, a sophisticated overcoming of the city's former "romantic inflation."[23] The theater also enhanced the city's reputation in more concrete ways. Its lively plastic decoration heralded the so-called Dresden school of sculpture, led mainly by Rietschel and Hähnel.

The freshness and originality of the new facility also nurtured the desire to enhance and enlarge the theatrical and operatic companies connected with the building. It may, for instance, have facilitated the special appointment of Richard Wagner as a resident conductor in 1842, and it certainly helped to lure Eduard Devrient to the city in 1844. This was not only true of the theater. Semper's other urban masterpiece for the city – the new art gallery – also played a role in Julius Schnorr von Carolsfeld's decision to leave his post

25 Gottfried Semper, exterior perspective of the Hoftheater, Dresden (1838–41). Institut für Geschichte und Theorie der Architectur, Semper Archiv, ETH-Zurich.

in Munich to become the museum's new director. Still, it was the theater, perhaps more than any other single achievement or event of this period, that came to symbolize Dresden's artistic resurgence in the 1840s.

On a more personal level, the Dresden Theater firmly established Semper's credibility among other artists. For instance, the proscenium design and renowned acoustics of the building, made it one of the best facilities in Germany for staging the operas of Richard Wagner, who later frequently shared Semper's theater loge. This friendship, which in future years would have many ups and downs, only barely survived the first fiery encounters of these two assertive personalities. In one early meeting, the composer, who was younger by eleven years, happened upon Semper in a music shop as the latter was purchasing the libretto of *Tannhäuser*. The architect, Wagner noted, wasted no time in expressing his rage over the medieval content of the lyrics: "He wanted art to have nothing to do with medieval minnesängers and Pilgrims' costumes, but made it clear to me immediately that he despised me for my choice of such material."[24] This reaction actually encouraged Wagner, for it convinced him that at least one person in Dresden was taking his art seriously. Upon further inquiry at the music shop, however, he discovered that Semper was the only person in the city to have purchased the newly printed text of his work.

This critical if not confrontational bond and friendship deepened in the mid-1840s as Semper, Wagner, Rietschel, Hähnel, Hiller, Hübner, Bendemann, Schumann, and others met weekly in a room at the Café Engel to pursue their artistic discussions in earnest. Semper was rarely on his best behavior, at least with regard to expressing his contempt for Wagner's supposed "medieval Catholicism, which he often attacked with a real fury."[25] Rietschel, it is said, was forced to intervene on more than one occasion to lessen the tension between the two men. Wagner, when he wrote his autobiography many years later, believed that he had actually succeeded in convincing Semper that his teutonic myths were less a result of medieval nostalgia and more explorations into the roots of Germanic antiquity, which somehow appealed to Semper's classical idealism: "Yet it was impossible to settle anything without heated debate, not only because of Semper's odd and contentious habit of contradicting everything flatly but also because he viewed things quite differently from the rest of the company. His paradoxical assertions, which were apparently only intended to stir up discussion, soon made me realize, beyond any doubt, that he was the only one present, in addition to myself, who was passionately in earnest about everything he said. All the others were quite content to let the matter drop when convenient."[26]

A similar story of conviction is related by the poet Alfred Meissner, who described another gathering of artists in the mid-1840s in Quandt's library – an affair that began in the afternoon and ended, after a vast consumption of Cuban cigars and wine from Bordeaux, sometime the next morning. Semper, Rietschel, Hähnel, Hübner, and Schnorr von Carolsfeld were among those in attendance and the topic of the evening was Semper's design for the new art gallery: "The debate over this building and everything related to it lasted the entire evening. I heard of nothing but half-columns and column flutes, independent and organically articulated arches, friezes, pilasters, panels and astragals, until my head began to swim." The visiting Meissner came away from the affair with the resolution that in future he would make use of the group's energy by channeling the course of conversation closer to his own interests.[27]

In various other ways the pace and intensity of the Dresden artists' social life undermined the city's former court society. The famous actress Caroline Bauer related a story of the ballerina Lola Montez, the "Spanish dancer" (later social democrat and mistress to King Ludwig of Bavaria), whose "mercury feet" took Dresden and the Saxon royal court by storm during a fortnight of performances in 1842. Each night, the number of her male admirers increased greatly – much to the chagrin, says Bauer, of the "prudish women of Dresden." The next year Montez returned to give further performances, but this time she was shunned by the court and spurned by her erstwhile worshippers, "who seemed almost embarrassed whenever her name was mentioned. Only in the society of some courageous men, among them the young architect Gottfried Semper, was the beautiful adventuress still to be seen."[28]

Pecht in his chronicles of this time was himself infatuated with "the frolicsome, seductive, and slightly mischievous" person of Wilhelmine Schröder-Devrient, whose "blond beauty was exceeded only by her genius." Often at her side at social gatherings was the mysterious countess Ida Hahn-Hahn, a writer who was no less scornful of social norms: "Both women carried the banner of indignation against societal conventions, not only within artistic-literary circles but also within the old aristocratic ones. There they played with the fire that would soon consume everything in bright flames."[29] Pecht wrote these lines with full knowledge of the political firestorm that at the end of the 1840s was to incinerate the city, extinguish its artistic life, and extract a heavy price from nearly all of its leading talents. No less a bold and gifted upstart than Gottfried Semper would also find his promising career severely charred by this conflagration.

The Crisis of Architectural Historicism in Germany

The fact that an "outsider" with as little experience and reputation as Semper could be called to the chair at the Dresden Academy in 1834 raises a number of interesting questions. By what criteria was he chosen for this relatively prestigious position? What expectations based on the city's particular architectural culture did the political and educational authorities of Dresden have for this young and untested appointee? And what unique perspective did Semper himself bring to this artistic environment?

If it is true that academic leaders in Dresden seriously entertained the possibility of attracting Schinkel out of Berlin, Georg Moller out of Darmstadt, or even the unhappy Gau out of Paris, then the appointment of Semper seems, at first view, to have fallen short of the mark. He possessed neither a significant scholarly record, nor a portfolio as a practicing architect, nor any known expertise for teaching or running a school. He had the promise of youth, but so did many other aspirants to the position. Semper's resumé boasted three main achievements: his French education under Gau; his tour of the south undertaken under difficult political circumstances; his pamphlet on polychromy with the pledge of a forthcoming and more definitive study.

The tour of Italy was itself not unusual for architectural students in the nineteenth or even in the eighteenth century. The trip was almost a prerequisite for any architect seeking admission to the higher echelons of the profession. Dozens of German students from the architectural schools in Berlin, Karlsruhe, Munich, or even Dresden could have matched this qualification. Semper's trip was exceptional only in his adventurous forays into Sicily and Greece, but even in this last regard he was not altogether unique. The Munich architectural student Eduard Metzger, as we have seen, managed to find a way to Athens in the midst of the same political turmoil, and undoubtedly there were others. From afar (that is, to those unfamiliar with the details of Semper's impromptu travel decisions), the trip therefore must have appeared as a well planned and well financed scholarly tour, and this was certainly to Semper's benefit. It also gave evidence of his ambition and courage.

The role of Semper's education in France under Gau may also be seen in a different light from that in which we may see it today. Gau himself came to view his career of these years with bitterness and a sense of frustration, but this was almost certainly not how it was regarded in Germany. He represented, rather, a native son who had migrated to the artistic capital of Europe (as many German architects were prone to do, at least in their early years for training) and found some measure of success: a governmental post and a reputation derived from his involvement with two prestigious publications on Egypt and Pompeii. Rietschel, as we have seen, referred to Gau in his letter to Rauch as an archaeologist rather than as an architect, and this attests to Gau's high standing in this field. Thus Semper's connection with Gau was viewed very positively in Dresden, as, probably, was the more general "French" character of his architectural training.

Semper's pamphlet and promise of a larger study may also have played a significant role in his appointment. It is interesting to speculate as to whether the pamphlet's preface, devoted to contemporary architectural issues, or his text, addressed to the question of polychromy, had the greater impact on its readers in Dresden. The first section displayed the fire of a young architect quite willing to take on the architectural establishment and usher in change; the second part placed him in the center of an important European controversy and held out the promise of a major recasting of archaeological history. Did the artistic adjudicators in Dresden prefer to read the words of the rebel or the archaeologist and scholar-in-training?

This question may perhaps be better considered in view of the rich architectural legacy of Dresden. If it is accurate to say that German architecture in the eighteenth and early nineteenth centuries in general followed very much in the wake of the French academic tradition, this was perhaps nowhere more evident than in Dresden, a city that also took great pride in its Baroque tradition. Indeed, the foundation of the Dresden Academy of Fine Arts in 1763 can be viewed in many respects as the overlaying of French Neoclassical reforms upon this Habsburg-inspired Rococo spirit. This is apparent, at least, in the outlook of the school's first director, Friedrich August Krubsacius (1718–89), who was also the residing court architect. He was the author of two architectural treatises dealing with classical architecture and the issue of ornament, and he is said to have greatly influenced Winckelmann's aesthetic development.[30] He was also the probable author of a 1771 German translation of Marc-Antoine Laugier's *Observations sur l'architecture* (1765), an important theoretical milepost of the Neoclassical movement.[31]

Notwithstanding his anti-Baroque teachings, Krubsacius's Neoclassicism was at best transitional. The exterior Tuscan porticos and pilaster strips of his Dresden Landhaus (1770–76; now Stadtmuseum) may in large part have been inspired, as it is frequently said, by the work of the French Neoclassical architect Jacques-Germain Soufflot, yet the grand foyer (Pl. 26) with its double staircase and cast-iron railings was almost purely German Rococo in character.

Krubsacius's Neoclassical vocabulary and teachings, however, left their mark on Dresden's architecture well into the next century, as his pupils and others in the Saxon capital continued to be impressed by French tendencies. Such influence can be seen, for instance, in the work of Krubsacius's student Christian Friedrich Schuricht (1753–1832), who late in his career (in 1812) was appointed court architect. In Schuricht's most notable commission, his addition to the huge royal complex at Pillnitz (Neues Palais; 1822–26), he had to mediate the baroque-oriental character of Pöppelmann's Rococo buildings on one side with his own Neoclassical interpretation (with some curved roof lines) on the new garden courtyard opposite. The interior of the domed festival hall, however, was executed entirely in the new style.

A contemporary of Schuricht was Gottlob Friedrich Thormeyer (1757–1842), the most active architect in Dresden in the first three decades of the nineteenth century. He presided over the demolition of the city's ramparts and in the process laid out a number of new streets and urban squares. His planning of Antonplatz in 1826 (Pl. 27) consisted of a group of alternating two- and three-story buildings on each side of a rectangular plaza with recessed shopping arcades at ground level – certainly a tribute to Percier and Fontaine's rue de Rivoli in Paris. Both Schuricht and Thormeyer also shared a sympathy for the work of Claude-Nicolas Ledoux, especially the primitive classicism of his Parisian *barrières*. This influence can be a detected in Schuricht's Third Belvedere (1814) with its recessed, Paestum-inspired, Doric vestibule (Pl. 28), and in Thormeyer's Leipziger Tor

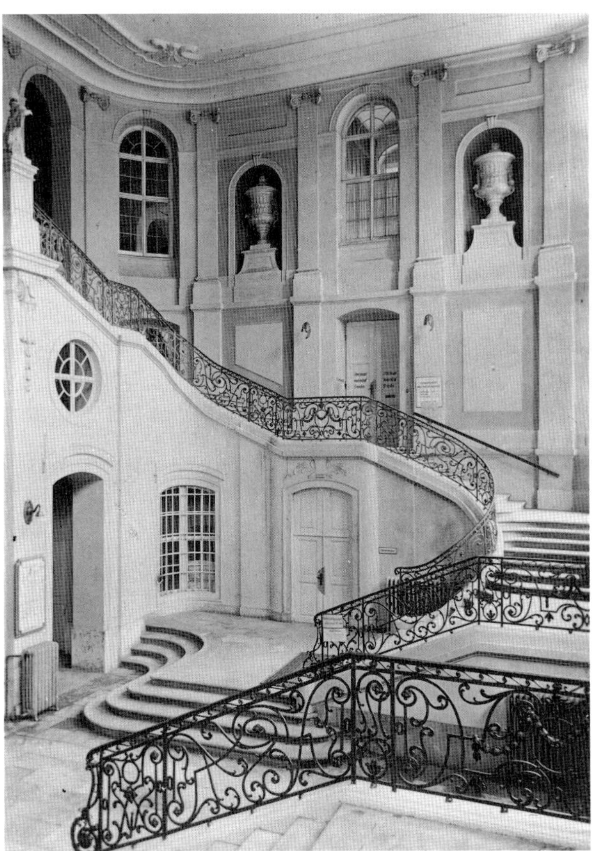

26 Friedrich August Krubsacius, Dresden Landhaus (now Stadtmuseum), 1770–76. Stadtmuseum Dresden.

27 (below left) Gottlob Friedrich Thormeyer, Antonplatz, Dresden, 1826. Stadtmuseum Dresden.

28 (below right) Christian Friedrich Schuricht, Third Belvedere on Brühlschen Terrasse, 1814. Engraving by Christian Gottlob Hammer. Stadtmuseum Dresden.

(1827–29), a pair of gatehouses with blocklike proportions and Tuscan porticos on three sides.

Another respected Neoclassical architect in Dresden was Semper's immediate predecessor, Joseph Thürmer (1789–1833), who was appointed to the Dresden Academy in 1827. As a designer, he gravitated more toward the taut, cubic simplicity of Schinkel's smaller works of the 1820s (he executed Schinkel's design for the Dresden Hauptwache in 1830–32) rather than to French models. On Thormeyer's Antonplatz he designed the large, U-shaped post office at one end of the square. His best known commission during his six years in Dresden, however, was his design of the urban villa (c. 1830) for August von Lüttichau, the general director of the Dresden Theater. This large rectangular block is marked simply by its shallow, scored rustication on the lower story, its low roof, and its rectangular windows cut into the walls without exterior moldings. Its only exterior ornamentation, aside from the pseudo-rustication, was a tall Greek fret that surmounted the top of the building as a frieze. By the mid-1830s it was, like much of the work of Schuricht and Thormeyer, quickly becoming outdated.[32]

Thürmer's quaint and conservative Neoclassicism, however, also sheds some light on Semper's selection. Thürmer was a student of the talented Munich architect Karl Fischer, but he was also a respected painter and engraver. After a long stay in Rome, he too had ventured to Greece. Like Semper, he was a relatively young outsider brought in (at the urging of Quandt) specifically to broaden the local cultural horizon, but he was seemingly admired more for his erudition (he was yet another friend of Goethe) than for his originality. Semper's appointment suggests that Dresden officials were more interested in his exposure to classical models and his potential for scholarship than in his possible skill as a designer.

.Thürmer also serves as a counter-illustration to the fundamental change taking place in the architectural profession in the 1820s and 1830s: the revolutionary perspective that Semper would bring to his new city of residence. Although architects of every era like to speak of their own period as particularly fraught with crisis, this was a time in which this claim was indeed no exaggeration. The European controversy over polychromy and the revolt against Neoclassical principles that had characterized French architectural education in the late-1820s – an insurrection that found its first major victory in France with Félix Duban's Renaissance design for the Palais des Etudes at the Ecole des Beaux-Arts in 1833 – had its equivalent in German theory and practice, even though this revolution was less coherent in its principles and more varied in its aspects. Facets of this aesthetic upheaval in Germany were also specifically Germanic in their intellectual style and this, too, complicates the picture.

Because of the political and religious fragmentation of the various German towns and states, it is difficult to speak of a uniquely German architecture prior to the nineteenth century. The progress toward a unified German culture made by Goethe, Schiller, Kant, and Fichte at the end of the eighteenth century, however, were given a great boost in the first decade of the new century by Napoleon's occupation of much of the country, which resulted in severe economic devastation. Thus one can truly speak of a national German consciousness only after 1815, though the country continued to be politically divided. This consciousness manifested itself as a collective awareness and desire to advance the country's political and cultural status, a trend that ultimately culminated (under Bismarck in 1871) with the defeat of France and the forced unification of Germany.

Architecturally, however, this consciousness had formed earlier rather than later. By the start of the 1790s, the talents of Carl Gotthard Langhans (1733–1808), Heinrich Gentz (1766–1811), and Friedrich Gilly (1772–1800) had already spawned a decidedly Prussian cast or interpretation of Greek Neoclassicism. This model was to work its way through Germany and be much emulated. The reorganization of David Gilly's private architectural school into the Berlin Bauakademie, or architectural academy, in the late 1790s was another important foundation stone of this cultural edifice.

German architecture in the first few years after 1815 thus adhered in many respects to a Neoclassical tradition, although – as in France – the style came increasingly under fire. This breakdown of values can be seen by following the principal tendencies of German design in the 1820s, a decade that was dominated by the architects Friedrich Weinbrenner (1766–1826) and Heinrich Hübsch (1795–1863) in Karlsruhe, Leo von Klenze (1784–1864) and Friedrich Gärtner (1792–1847) in Munich, and Karl Friedrich Schinkel in Berlin. During this period every German architectural student, such as Semper, had to contend – in one way or another – with one of these ideological forces.

Weinbrenner is perhaps the easiest to deal with because he was the oldest of this group, almost by a generation. A native of Karlsruhe, he did his architectural training in Vienna before migrating to Berlin in the early 1790s, where he was swayed by the new Greek Neoclassicism of the capital as well as by French "visionary" designs. After a tour of Italy he returned to his city of birth and established a busy practice as both a city planner and architect of many of Karlsruhe's principal monuments. In his architecture school, which he founded privately in 1800 (incorporated in 1825 into the polytechnic school), he taught the classical ideals of Winckelmann together with an emphasis on functional design. His urban designs can be characterized by their plain, somewhat heavy walls with small openings, accentuated here and there by columnar porches. Semper seems never to have been particularly inspired by Weinbrenner's work. His indication in a letter of 1827 that the majority of Gau's students in Paris were from the "Weinbrenner school" is phrased in such a way that it gives at least a hint of scorn.[33]

The lead of both Gärtner and Klenze in Munich, as we have seen, was also flatly rejected by Semper. Gärtner, eight years younger than his rival Klenze, also got a much later start in practice. He studied first under Karl von Fischer in Munich and then under Weinbrenner in Karlsruhe, before moving to Paris in 1812 to train under J.-N.-L. Durand as well as Percier and Fontaine. After a three-year tour of the south, which included stops in both Paestum and Sicily, Gärtner traveled to England before settling back in Munich in 1820 and accepting Fischer's former chair at the Munich Academy of Fine Arts. Gärtner's first commissions followed only at the end of the decade, beginning with the Ludwigskirche (1829–44).

Semper had enrolled at the Academy in 1825 but he seems quickly to have lost interest in both Gärtner and the school, as he left the city some months later for Regensburg. In the correspondence between Gau and Semper of the 1830s, Gärtner's architectural style was frequently raised as a point of ridicule – so much so that one wonders if Semper did not have a personal grievance against him dating from his brief stay in Munich. Gärtner's teaching and generally progressive practice were nevertheless very influential throughout Germany in the 1830s.

The eclectic style of Klenze was also a frequent object of Semper's and Gau's irreverence. He (following Schinkel) was one of the first to study at the Bauakademie in Berlin; in 1803 he went to Paris, where he worked in the office of Percier and Fontaine. Following a trip to Italy in 1803–04, he was employed by Napoleon's brother Jérôme at the court in Kassal. When Jérôme left Germany for France and Italy in 1813, Klenze searched for another patron and soon found one in Ludwig I of Bavaria, a monarch intent of transforming Munich into a major cultural capital. In 1816 Klenze won the limited competition for the Glyptothek, the sculptural gallery designed specifically to house the Aeginetan marbles then being restored by Thorwaldsen. Klenze's "Greek" design (he had

29 Leo von Klenze, Walhalla, near Regensburg. Designed in 1814, built 1830–46. From *Allgemeine Bauzeitung*. Courtesy The Getty Center for the History of Art and the Humanities.

also had a "Renaissance" and "Roman" proposal), consisted of a range of low domed galleries (one of the most accommodating sequences of rooms in Europe) surrounding an open courtyard. A central octostyle Ionic portico is the only prominent feature of the exterior; the blank walls are enlivened plastically by corner pilasters and by a series of aedicules incorporating sculpture.

Klenze, who in the 1820s and 1830s continued to extend his archaeological interests with trips to Italy and Greece, was prone to cite historical precedents in his works. He followed his sculpture gallery in Munich with an array of monumental works, nearly all of which closely imitated ancient, medieval, and Renaissance models. His Leuctenberg Palais (1816), for instance, was a Renaissance townhouse based on the Palazzo Farnese. The exterior of the Königsbau or royal residence (1826–35) was nearly a replica of the Palazzo Pitti, onto which Klenze, in the upper two stories, imposed the pilaster system of Alberti's Palazzo Rucellai. The Alte Pinokothek or painting gallery (1826–36) was also Renaissance in its forms: employing motifs from Bramante's Cancelleria and the courtyard of the Vatican Belvedere. Klenze's church of All Saints (1826–37) in Munich, his only church, emulated a twelfth-century Palentine chapel at Palermo. His grandest Neoclassical work (Pl. 29), the Walhalla (1830–46; the first competition design dated from 1814–16), was a huge Greek temple that eventually came to be situated on a hillside near Regensburg.

It is easy to see how Klenze's liberal and literal use of historical motifs in his designs made him an easy target for younger architects, such as Semper, who insisted upon greater originality in practice. Semper's sarcastic dismissal of Klenze's style in his pamphlet of 1834 – where he writes of those architects who slavishly produce "a Walhalla *à la* Parthenon, a basilica *à la* Monréale, a boudoir *à la* Pompeii, a palace *à la* Pitti, a Byzantine church, or even a bazaar in the Turkish taste!"[34] – underscores vividly the ideological crisis that had seized German architecture by this date. Semper's publication of such remarks (in which three of Klenze's buildings were mentioned in the same breath with a boudoir and Turkish bazaar) bordered on an imprudence rarely found in earlier architectural discussions, and reflected the depth of his feeling.

Actually, the first volleys of this professional debate were fired a couple of years earlier by the young Karlsruhe architect Heinrich Hübsch, who in the 1820s had taken upon his shoulders the task of liberating present-day architecture "from the chains of antiquity."[35] Hübsch had studied philosophy and mathematics at the University of Heidelberg before moving to Karlsruhe in 1815 to study architecture under Weinbrenner. In between extensive tours of Italy and Greece (1817–20, 1822–24), Hübsch published his first book, *Über griechische Architektur* (On Greek Architecture), in which he attacked with fury the Neoclassical teachings of his former teacher Weinbrenner and the Berlin art historian Alois Hirt. Hübsch refined and sharpened his arguments in a popular and controversial pamphlet of 1828, *In welchem Style sollen wir bauen?* (In What Style Should We Build?).

By means of a rational survey of the major historical styles, Hübsch attempted to underscore contemporary failings in design and in the process identify the "objective" principles on which to base a new style for his time – a style that would better accommodate modern materials, technologies, German social needs, and climate. His analysis, which was conceived only a few years before the industrial production of iron became a reality in Germany, initially limited the formal possibilities of this new style to a choice between trabeated (post-and-lintel) and arcuated masonry systems. Accepting the economic superiority of the latter, he then discussed the relative merits of the pointed-arch (Gothic) and round-arch (*Rundbogen*) systems – the last of which he much preferred. Even though Hübsch's own designs of the 1830s and 1840s would tend toward a literal Romanesque interpretation, his description of the *Rundbogen* in 1828 was much more abstract, almost ahistorical in its conception. The unornamented, exposed brick facades of his Finance Ministry (begun in 1827) and Technische Hochschule (1833–35), both in Karlsruhe, demonstrate the early application of his theory. Some of Gärtner's buildings in Munich, such as his design for the State Library (1831–42), perhaps provide a better illustration of this tendency.

Over the next two decades Hübsch's pamphlet touched off a flurry of historical and polemical essays, many of which appeared within the pages of newly founded architectural journals.[36] Klenze in Munich dismissed all such efforts as "some misguided German scribblers and dilettantes who believe . . . , that they will be able to invent a new style through pamphlets, proclamations, and articles."[37] Yet other architects and critics lined up eager to present their ideas for a more responsive stylistic paradigm. Rudolf Wiegmann, for instance, initially criticized Hübsch's materialist focus, but a few years later he too came round to the possibilities of a *Rundbogen* style.[38] The Magdeburg architect Carl Albert Rosenthal praised Hübsch's analysis but preferred the adoption of Gothic to Romanesque forms.[39] The Berlin historian Franz Kugler, while applauding the non-historical conception of Hübsch, doubted whether anything artistic could emerge from such a dry and uninspired analysis.[40]

By the 1840s this debate had caused a rift in German architecture, with camps rallying around the *Rundbogen*, the Neogothic, and the vestiges of the Neoclassical style. There was even a culmination of sorts, with the competition, organized by Maximilian II and the Munich Academy in 1850, specifically to invent a new style – a "Maximilianstil" – for an Athenaeum or cultural center. This new style was to embody the character, materials, and technologies of the time, take into account the country's political and social circumstances, employ German plant and animal forms for its ornamentation, and unite the simple and quiet character of the Greek style with the spiritually uplifting attributes of the Gothic. Not surprisingly, the result was a fiasco.

This event, however, could not have been foreseen in the late-1820s or early-1830s, as the debate was still taking shape. Semper was certainly aware of Hübsch's efforts by the time he arrived in Dresden, and some of his early designs even made use of the round-arch motif. But Semper, as we shall see, eventually came to reject this formal device in favor of Renaissance paradigms. What we have not examined thus far, however, is Semper's response to the fourth architectural tendency evolving in the 1820s and 1830s – that trend and ideology fostered by the efforts of Karl Friedrich Schinkel in Berlin.

Schinkel's influence on Semper was profound, although it is not very evident in simple stylistic comparisons of their designs. The Prussian architect had been trained at the end of the eighteenth century at the newly formed Bauakademie in Berlin (under the guidance of both David and Friedrich Gilly), before undertaking his tour of Italy, Sicily, and France between 1803 and 1805. The Prussian defeat by Napoleon's armies at Jena in 1806 greatly delayed the start of his own architectural practice. He busied himself during the grim years of Napoleonic occupation with a series of landscape and historical paintings, diorama and stage designs, and architectural fantasies. It was not until after 1815, when he was promoted to a prominent post within the Prussian state service that Schinkel was able resume his architectural career in earnest. He reverted at first to the Neoclassical vocabulary of Gentz and Friedrich Gilly for his spartan Neue Wache or royal guardhouse (1816–18). With its severe Doric portico and rich representational themes, it was actually an ennobled version of an earlier scheme that was fronted with a portico supported by plain square pillars. The sculptures in the pediment of the built work depict a raging battle with many fallen heroes; the traditional triglyphs in the frieze are replaced with goddesses of victory in applied relief.

In his design of 1817 for the Berlin Schauspielhaus or playhouse, Schinkel further simplified his use of classical language by developing a tectonic, trabeated system that he placed on top of a rusticated podium, accentuated above by the strong horizontal banding of its blank frieze. He designed the theater as a group of blocks defining the foyer and concert hall, auditorium and stagehouse, and the service wings. Each of these was embellished with its own pediment. Each block was further articulated – seemingly – by large expanses of glass recessed behind strong, square pilasters used as mullions. Schinkel admitted that in his design he avoided the use of round arches and vaults and attempted "to follow as closely as possible Greek forms and constructional methods."[41] The monument was nevertheless richly appointed, with representational works of sculpture placed in the pediment and perched on acroteria on all four sides, depicting such mythical events as the story of Niobe, and Orpheus's liberation of Euridice from Hades. A victorious Apollo in his chariot crowned the urban masterpiece.

Even before the theater was completed in 1821, however, Schinkel had begun to rethink his ideas and he began questioning the very premises of contemporary design – why should not his own period, like every great age preceding it, inaugurate a style of its own?[42] His buildings of the 1820s can also be read as a series of formal experiments: dialectical studies of historical and new constructional motifs. In some instances, such as at Glienicke (1824–32) and at Charlottenhof (1826–33), he attempted to transpose vernacular

Italianate motifs upon the Prussian landscape. For other works, such as his design for a market for Unter den Linden (1827), he produced an almost purely functional style, stripped of historical references, with factory-like blocks into which were set large rectangular openings for light and showrooms. What is most remarkable in Schinkel's search for a new visual order was the clarity with which he was able to express his intentions and – sometimes – their failings. Speaking of his experiments with non-historical designs, probably sometime around 1830, he had this to say of his efforts:

> I noticed that all architectural forms were based on three ideas: 1) forms generated by construction; 2) forms possessing traditional or historical importance; and 3) forms meaningful in themselves, taking their model from nature. I noticed further that a great treasury of architectural forms had already been created or brought into the world by different nations over many centuries of development. But I saw at the same time, however, that our use of these accumulated and often very different motifs was arbitrary – because each individual form possesses its particular charm, which through a dark presentiment of a necessary motif, be it historical or constructional, intensifies and continues to seduce us through its usage. We believe that by invoking such a motif we invest our work with a special charm. I noticed, therefore, that the most pleasing effect produced by the primitive appearance of old works was often completely contradicted by its invocation in our present works. It became especially apparent that our willfulness in this matter was the reason for the lack of character and style that seems to plague so many of our new buildings. It became my life's goal to clarify this matter. But the more I considered the problem, the more I saw the difficulties opposing my efforts. Very soon I fell into the error of pure radical abstraction, by which I conceived a specific architectural work entirely from utilitarian purpose and construction. In these cases something dry and rigid emerged, something that lacked freedom and altogether excluded two essential elements: the historic and the poetic.[43]

Schinkel's resolution of this problem centered on what he termed the cultivation of "refinement of feeling" – that is, his willingness to draw from the historical treasury of forms but at the same time to modify these motifs in an original manner, taking into account contemporary ideals and conditions. His design for the Berlin Altes Museum (1822–30) in many respects foretold his new direction.

The museum is a major urban monument (Pl. 30), situated on the Lustgarten opposite the stately royal palace and beside the newly refurbished Berlin Cathedral. It is a low but imposing building with a giant order of eighteen Ionic columns approximately 12 meters high, draped across a facade over 79 meters in length. Behind the screen of this grandiose stoa, Schinkel designed a much more elaborate facade to entertain the visiting pedestrian: not the plain marble panels that are hung on the walls today but a colossal cycle of frescoed murals, allegories depicting the evolution of the heavens, mythological deities, the human race, and – most importantly – human culture. Schinkel intended them to introduce the contents of the museum thematically, but also to stand on their own as a gesture of public civility. They functioned, in effect, as an outdoor museum.

Indeed, if we can imagine the building restored to its original grandeur, we would be hard pressed to find an artistic conception of greater magnificence in all of nineteenth-century architecture. Two large murals, one story in height and six in length, graced the upper wall at each side of the monumental staircase. The first mural depicted a lively

30 Karl Friedrich Schinkel, Altes Museum, Berlin, 1822–30. Perspective. From Schinkel's *Sammlung architektonischer Entwurfe*. Courtesy The Getty Center for the History of Art and the Humanities.

31 Karl Friedrich Schinkel, Altes Museum, Berlin, 1822–30. Perspective of stairhall. From Schinkel's *Sammlung architektonischer Entwurfe*. Courtesy The Getty Center for the History of Art and the Humanities.

procession of floating deities emerging from a gray-blue darkness into the light of day – a march beginning with Kronos and the Titans and concluding with Eros, Venus, Urania, and Phoebus on his sun chariot. The mural to the right of the staircase represented various events of early human culture with sibylline enthusiasm: a festival of nymphs, heroes, poets, and muses dancing. On the enclosing end walls, at right angles to the main facade, two other thematic studies were placed: one depicting *Uranus and the Dance of Stars;* the second, *Dream on a Tumulus,* the earth and its transfiguration. Below the large murals of this vestibule numerous smaller panels depicted other moments from the history of culture.

In the upper vestibule, behind the monumental staircase, Schinkel designed another cycle of wall paintings (Pl. 31). One panel portrayed the raw forces of nature and the human misery and death they have produced; a second depicted warring human tribes descending upon a community of peaceful earlier settlers. The colorful frescoes were executed by students of Peter Cornelius, beginning in 1841. Schinkel, however, had prepared all the designs, in great detail, in the late-1820s and 1830s. They were, as Kugler noted in 1842, widely known and admired in Berlin.[44]

The importance of the murals in this design reveals an understanding of architecture that is didactic and representational in its intentions – a conception of architecture as urban theater, as a setting for promoting cultural rituals, with the aim of refining or improving public taste. Whether for Schinkel this conception originated in his own glorious vision of classical antiquity or – as both Kurt W. Forster and Barry Bergdoll have recently suggested[45] – in his earlier fascination with stage designs and *Stimmungsbilder* (images with feeling), it was nevertheless a vision capable of sustaining the greatest architectural drama. Moreover, the colossal murals in themselves were but part of a larger urban tableau, one that extended itself to the polished granite fountain at the entrance, to the treescape of the new square, to Schinkel's newly built bridge that enters onto this square (populated with sculptures devoted to classical themes), indeed to the array of plastic works planned along Unter den Linden – as Schinkel himself seems to have envisioned it.[46] What is entirely novel in this theatrical conception of architecture, at least as it relates to similar impulses in antiquity and in the Baroque and Neoclassical eras, is its application not to a religion or to an individual ruler but rather to the newly forming, aspiring bourgeois culture of nineteenth-century Germany. Architecture, in Schinkel's view, should demand a high level of public morality and patriotism; it should provide a pause and a station for civic instruction and deliberate self-reflection. It should embrace, as Schinkel himself later suggested, the historic and poetic.

This vision had become so strong for Schinkel by the 1820s that he even adhered to it in subsequent designs of lesser monumental value, such as in his design for the Bauakademie or architectural school (1831–36). Often admired by critics in our century for its exposed brick facades and ingenious system of segmental fireproof vaults, this building perplexed many of Schinkel's contemporaries because of its lack of historical motifs, which were restricted to a few Hellenic emblems in the consoles of the cornice and at the crown of the window openings (Pl. 32). Yet the bare logic of the constructional members only underscored the richness of the iconography that Schinkel wove into the surrounds of the windows and doorways. Here he once again employed a series of narrative panels (now cast in terra-cotta and hoisted into place) to write a mythological and cultural history – this time a history of architecture and its construction and technology. Schinkel was very proud of these terra-cotta panels, for he had them exhibited at the Academy prior to their

32 Karl Friedrich Schinkel, Berlin Bauakademie, 1831–36. Elevation. From Schinkel's *Sammlung architektonischer Entwurfe*. Courtesy The Getty Center for the History of Art and the Humanities.

placement within the building, and he published their content in both his own portfolio of designs and in the first four numbers of the new Viennese architectural journal *Allgemeine Bauzeitung*.

The panels framing the two main portals represent architecture as an art and as a science, respectively. In the first case (Pl. 33), the two lower plates of the doorway depict acanthus plants, a symbol for nature from which the laws of architecture emerge. Above, the Doric order is personified on the left by Hercules with a club; opposite, Egyptian architecture is shown as one spiritual wellspring of Greek forms. In the third pair of panels the Corinthian and Ionic orders are represented by a pair of maidens. The panels above depict the mythical invention of the Corinthian order by Callimachus and on the right a genius holds a plumb-line. The top-left corner panel portrays Orpheus with a lyre, symbolizing the harmonious kinship of architecture and music. On the right, opposite, resides Amphion, who built the walls of Thebes with the musical sounds of a lyre given to him by Apollo.[47] The seven genii emerging from acanthus plants across the top of the door are said to symbolize the organic character of architecture.[48] On both bronze doors the profiles of various architects, mythical and real, are shown – from Iktinos and Vitruvius to Michelangelo and Andreas Schülter.

Schinkel advanced another narrative in the window surrounds on the second and third stories of the building. The windows were divided into three fields by herm-like mullions. Above, a terra-cotta panel filled in the space between the top of the window and the segmental brick arch; below, terra-cotta parapets portrayed different moments from the evolution of architecture. In the series of parapet designs shown here (Pl. 34), Apollo at the top is flanked by the genii of painting and sculpture. The next rows of panels, moving downward, depict a fallen Pegasus and the decline of classical architecture. This sad condition continues until medieval times, when the building trades are mastered once

33 and 34 Karl Friedrich Schinkel, Berlin Bauakademie, 1831–36. Above left: main doorway. Above right: parapet designs. From Schinkel's *Sammlung architektonischer Entwurfe*. Courtesy The Getty Center for the History of Art and the Humanities.

again and architecture subsequently revives itself. What is especially evident in this narration, however, is that Schinkel followed precisely the theatrical and didactic intention he pursued for the museum. In the early 1830s, in fact, some of these allegories were even conceived in tandem. The visual proximity of the school to the museum along the opposite bank of the canal (connected by Schinkel's bridge) only reinforced this continuity. And functionalist interpretations aside – far from losing meaning because of the absence of historical motifs, the windows and doors of the architecture school functioned rather as grand mythical tapestries stretched between the structurally innovative masonry piers. The students and shoppers utilizing the portals and shops at ground level were thus given their own processional frieze, just like their cultural ancestors in Athens.

Semper also seems to have been strongly impressed by this theatrical architectural conception. Returning north in 1833 after more than four years of travel, he postponed his (Christmas) homecoming in Altona to complete the final and most important leg of his journey: the presentation of his findings to Schinkel in Berlin. The latter at this time was in fact in the midst of finishing his allegorical schemes. Semper may even have seen the finished panels for the doorways to the school, which were exhibited at the Academy in 1834; in any case, he met with Schinkel on several occasions. After taking charge of a sister school in Dresden, Semper returned to Berlin for his honeymoon in the fall of 1835, just as work on the exterior of the architectural school was nearing its completion. The school officially opened in the following spring; in October 1836, Semper once again came to Berlin for a visit.

All of this points to the great reverence Semper held for Schinkel and certainly there were few buildings in Germany that Semper had a better chance to study than the Berlin Bauakademie and Altes Museum.

It is also important, however, in view of what has been said, not to confine Semper's early architectural approach solely to the limits of Schinkel's classical framework. Even though Semper shared Schinkel's high regard for architecture as inherently a theatrical exercise, and espoused an equally brilliant vision of antiquity, he would also come to differ from his spiritual mentor in his choice of the stylistic framework that would best articulate this drama. In fact, there were three formative pillars to Semper's architectural education. In addition to Schinkel's sense for urban theater and their shared archaeological interests in classical antiquity, there was also Semper's familiarity with and appreciation of the new stylistic developments taking place in France. All three would soon combine to lead German architecture in an entirely new direction.

The Making of an Architect

When Semper came in Dresden in 1834 he carried with him not only the educational tools and the desire to build an architectural practice specializing in large projects, but also a very specific plan on how best to achieve this goal. Little in Semper's life from this day forward would be left to circumstance; his youthful intemperance would now be overtaken by dedication, boundless energy, and a prodigious workload. Smaller commissions were viewed only as stepping stones to accomplishments on a far grander scale. His unrestrained confidence in his own abilities, his critical and forceful personality – both would now serve him to good advantage.

From his very first days in the city he reported his progress to an attentive and supportive mother. Only a few hours after he took his formal oath, he spoke to her optimistically of two possible commissions. One was for the addition of a salon to an inn, the other for the design of a new hospital.[49] The following spring, after his initial period of disappointment and adjustment to his new environment, he again wrote home proudly of several designs in progress, among them a scheme for a coffee house, proposals for the renovation of the Antiquity Rooms in the Japanese Palace, a maternity hospital, and the design of a pedestal for a large statue dedicated to King Friedrich August I. Only the first project, the coffee house, seems to have come to naught.

His renovation and layout of the Antiquity Rooms in the Japanese Palace was a suprising commission for a newcomer to the city. The Palace, one of the oldest and largest in the capital, had been extensively rebuilt on various occasions in the eighteenth century, once by Pöppelmann himself. Since 1782 the complex had housed the royal library and the royal collections of antique sculptural works – the latter under the curatorship of Carl August Böttiger, a noted classicist and historian. Sometime in the spring of 1835 Semper received the commission for rearranging the pieces on display and for providing a suitable architectural backdrop.[50] His changes to the configuration of the rooms were minimal and

35 and 36 Gottfried Semper, the Antiquity Rooms in the Japanese Palace, Dresden, 1835. Sächsische Landesbibliothek, Abteilung Deutsche Fotothek.

restricted for the most part to blocking the lower halves of existing windows to limit natural light to a higher angle.

Semper responded to the decoration of the seven rooms, however, with brilliant polychrome designs (Pls. 35, 36), recalling in their intensity his work on the Donner Pavilion. Each room was given a separate theme: several were Pompeiian in style, another Greek, another Renaissance in its ornamentation. Yet what distinguishes Semper's theme rooms from earlier models from the Neoclassical and first Empire periods was simply his vivid use of color, now made to conform to his image of classical antiquity. In one room he employed bright panels as a backdrop to the sculptural pieces, thereby limiting the additional decoration to a variegated frieze and ceiling vignettes. In another room the figurative frieze was made to compete with the works exhibited below. Greek works were placed against the background of Greek ornaments, Roman works against Pompeiian motifs. White marble pieces were silhouetted against darker tones than were the bronze pieces. Another feature of Semper's design was that the colors and motifs were variations on drawings he had made while in Italy and Greece. Hence they were authentic patterns, recomposed in a museum setting.

This visually aggressive approach to the display of classical works created at least a small sensation both within and without Dresden. Caroline von Humboldt, the daughter of the famed educational reformer and linguist Wilhelm von Humboldt, received a private tour of the rooms under renovation in October 1835 and pronounced them not to her liking, too "restless" in their effect.[51] She most likely compared the colors to those used by Schinkel for the antique sculpture gallery at her family home in Tegel, outside Berlin. Others however, particularly the younger artists of Dresden, welcomed this new use of bold color effects. The rooms were finished and opened to the public late in 1835, around the time that Semper was completing his preparations for the festivities surrounding the eightieth birthday of King Anton. Thus the controversy at the Japanese Palace combined with the popular success of his street architecture to underscore his artistic presence in the city.

Semper's design for the Maternity Hospital was less significant from an architectural viewpoint but it nonetheless reveals another dimension of his professional persona. Construction of the hospital began late in 1835. It was a simple, three-story symmetrical building, H-form in plan, mixing twenty-two birthing rooms with a chapel, administration areas, a dining hall, and a kitchen. The exterior was stuccoed with the exception of ground-floor stonework and lateral quoins; a small clock tower projected from the central pavilion. The historian Manteuffel records the spare use of sgraffito decoration on the exterior.[52] The building's slate roof was a novelty to Saxon architecture. Semper had seen such roofs in France and ordered the slate from England through family and professional contacts in Hamburg.[53]

What makes this building noteworthy, however, was less the design and more the controversies that ensued both during and after construction. Semper at various times engaged masons, carpenters, city officials, and committee members in numerous disputes. The tone was set even before work began, when Semper complained to his brother in the summer of 1835 of the "painful changes" to the design that the building committee had dictated.[54] Semper took to task city officials and his carpenters, respectively, over the truss system for the roof that he had proposed (one that was more efficient than the heavy timber systems then in use), and over changes that were made to his detailing of the window casements.[55] Another battle was waged with the building committee over their desire to add a coat of green paint to the finished stucco and stone. Semper vigorously opposed this intervention, insisting that his "principle in art, as in life, is truth!"[56]

Even more contentious was the dispute over Semper's fee. At the conclusion of construction in 1838 Semper submitted his bill: asking for a fee of two percent of construction costs. The committee countered with an offer for half of that amount. Semper responded with a lengthy letter to city officials, in which he lambasted the backward condition of Saxon architecture – in contrast to "most civilized lands" – a condition due, he felt, to the small value placed on the talent, training, and authority of architects. The letter was masterful in its tone. Semper related the history of labor relations in the building trades, the extent of his own work, the exploited and impoverished life of the eighteenth-century Dresden architect Georg Bähr and other such "martyrs of art," and the low esteem and fees afforded modern architects, resulting in continual interference with their designs.[57]

Semper's complaints certainly had some legitimacy. Architects in early nineteenth-century Germany were employed only on larger projects and even then they were seen by many as a luxury. Their authority with regard to the building trades, which still harked back to medieval guilds, had yet to be clearly established or defined. Semper's letter was at the same time a warning to municipal officials to steer clear of him in future dealings, especially on issues related to artistic conception and execution. By 1838 Semper's position and reputation in the city was sufficiently strong to issue such an edict. City officials, formerly accustomed to a quite different relationship with architects, relented and paid him the fee he demanded.

Another early project that had a major impact on Semper's career was the tall pedestal he designed for the statue to King Friedrich August I, who had ruled Saxony for fifty-eight years until his death in 1827. The sculptor Ernst Rietschel had received the commission for the bronze statue in 1831 and four years later it was ready for casting. Schinkel had also been consulted at the earlier date and had prepared a design for the pedestal. When the decision was made in 1835 to add four new smaller statues to the work (symbolizing Wisdom, Piety, Justice, and Leniency), Semper was commissioned to revise Schinkel's scheme (Pl. 37). The young architect raised the height of the whole work by inserting a leafy band of coursing below the corner statues and above the granite socle. He also made a considerable effort to procure from sources in Berlin an unusual reddish-brown granite for the pedestal, the tone of which greatly pleased Rietschel.[58]

The statue was not officially unveiled within the Zwinger courtyard until 7 June 1843, and then with great pomp and ceremony.[59] Semper headed the committee that prepared the courtyard festivities and decorations. Fifty-eight white-robed girls, the daughters of prominent local families, led a procession of people and dignitaries into the courtyard. They were followed by several battalions of the communal guard and by King Friedrich August II and the royal household. The newly installed *Kapellmeister* Richard Wagner was commissioned to compose and direct the singing of a festival song, an event followed by thirty-six canon shots.

What makes this pedestal design such an important moment in Semper's career, however, was the manner in which he seized the occasion to set in motion a much grander architectural scheme that he had been hatching since his first days in Dresden. In presenting the options for placing the statue within the Zwinger courtyard in 1835, he

37 Gottfried Semper, pedestal of the Monument to Friedrich August I. Zwinger courtyard, Dresden, 1835. From *Allgemeine Bauzeitung*. Courtesy of The Getty Center for the History of Art and the Humanities.

suggested at the same time a major addition to this celebrated Baroque complex – its extension northward toward the river by means of a new orangerie and royal theater. Over the next three years Semper orchestrated the official and public response to this proposal with the greatest care and tactical skill.

His first mention of this initiative is in a letter to his mother written in April 1835, in which he referred to his "new theater designed long ago."[60] He then warned his mother that his design should remain "between us," until it became politically wise to go public with his proposal. The phrase "new theater designed long ago" certainly seems to indicate, as Herrmann has already suggested,[61] that Semper was quite aware of Dresden's need for a new theater and actually may have started working on a scheme in the summer of 1834, when he was still at his family's home in Altona. It is also likely that shortly after his arrival in Dresden he had informal discussions with Rietschel regarding the building of such a theater and the placement of the statue. Early planning in locating the bronze sculpture probably led him to explore schemes for expanding the existing Zwinger courtyard, which had in fact been left in an unfinished state since the early eighteenth century. It was closed off along the northern end (the side parallel to the river) only by a brick and stucco wall.

There were also other factors that encouraged the political authorities to be receptive to Semper's proposal. The first was the ghetto-like condition of the so-called Italian Village, a collection of forty-odd houses that lay between the Zwinger courtyard, the adjacent palace, and the river. This grouping of small houses had come into being in the eighteenth century, when it served to accommodate emigrant craftsmen and their families from Italy, who were employed by the court in the construction of the Hofkirche and other royal projects. In the name of urban renewal, the crown had begun legal proceedings in the 1820s to expropriate this land and find a better use for it. For a decade, however, the project had been stalled by a lack of an acceptable plan and by disputes with the Saxon Diet. The second factor coming into play was, of course, the very real need of the city for a court theater and opera house.

Given the artistic vitality of Dresden, it is remarkable that a new facility had not been built earlier. The opera company formerly resided in a building designed by Andrea Zucchi, tucked into the southeast corner of the Zwinger in 1738. It was remodeled by Guiseppe Galli Bibiena in 1749–50 but then converted into a royal ballroom in 1772. The only other theater in the city was the Comedy House, a makeshift playhouse designed by Pietro Moretti in 1755; it was located at the north end of the Italian Village. Moretti's small structure was enlarged from 350 to 814 seats in 1783. Eventually it received a vestibule, but by the end of the eighteenth century it was recognized as inadequate for the increasingly complex theatrical productions.

Two proposals were made in 1803 and 1804 for reconverting the old opera building back into a theater, but Napoleon's invasion intervened. Schuricht and Thormeyer unsuccessfully prepared another set of designs in 1816 for this renovation. With the arrival of the new director Lüttichau in 1824, the matter of converting the old opera back into a theater received constant attention but made little forward progress. In 1829 Lüttichau commissioned Semper's predecessor Joseph Thürmer, and separately the Brunswick architect Carl Theodor Ottmer, to prepare proposals. The municipal architect Thormeyer reviewed both plans and then made his own proposal in the same year. Still no decision was reached. Another proposal for a theater along the Elbe was made by Woldemar Herrmann in 1831. Lüttichau revived the issue in 1834: this time asking the court architect Otto Wolframsdorf to prepare a design and cost estimate for renovating the old opera. The latter presented his scheme to Lüttichau in March 1835. In competition with his colleague, Thormeyer made yet one more proposal. Finally, the whole matter of the need for a theater was reviewed once again, this time by a state official called in from Berlin.[62]

This is where the matter stood in the summer of 1835 as Semper, shortly before his marriage to Bertha, continued to develop his proposal for locating the statue and a new theater. In August he reported to his brother that he would soon make public his scheme.[63] He did indeed present his proposal but – in a shrewd strategic ploy – not to Dresden officials. Instead, on his honeymoon in Berlin in September, he showed his months of labor to Schinkel and Karl Graf von Brühl, the latter the long-standing director of the Berlin Theater. The highly respected theater manager was evidently impressed with Semper's design for he ordered copies made, which he passed on to the Crown Prince Friedrich Wilhelm IV.[64] Heartened by this preliminary round of support, Semper returned to Dresden and in October presented the same scheme to Prince Johann, the brother of the King and the chair of the commission on royal monuments. On the same day the Prince received still another report from Lüttichau regarding the feasibility of rebuilding the old opera.[65]

Prince Johann, expecting from Semper only a site plan for the statue to his deceased father, was no doubt surprised by the elaborate set of drawings that were laid before him (Pl. 38). The young architect assumed the razing of the Italian Village and placed the new theater with its rounded auditorium wall north of the existing Zwinger complex, near the river; it was connected to Pöppelmann's complex with a narrow orangerie. The statue of Friedrich August was located in the old courtyard, along the axis of the two hemispheres and just off the intersecting north-south axis. Other sculptural monuments to Dresden's royalty were proposed for the axis perpendicular to the new orangerie. The terraces and parterres of the gardens were designed in the "Italian taste," and were meant by Semper to invoke the "market-like" character of a forum with its many fountains and its statuary.[66] In a preliminary perspective drawing of the theater (Pl. 39), it can be seen that Semper's design is already in an advanced stage. The proportions of the arcades were determined by those of the Zwinger and were carried through to the theater by the orangerie. Only the roof of the rounded auditorium was to undergo modification.

What happened next is unclear, although officials no doubt held many lively discussions, some of them probably hesitant to entrust such a prestigious commission to a relatively unknown architect. When Semper returned to Berlin in October 1836 he again brought along his plans and reported to his brother that the Crown Prince of Prussia was interested in the project and could perhaps give it a boost.[67] There was surely something more afoot here as Semper's contact with both Karl Graf von Brühl and the Crown Prince had probably been arranged by Schinkel. Even the rounded amphitheatrical form of Semper's building bears a curious similarity to a proposal that Schinkel had made in March 1835, in connection with an ideal palace complex. The auditorium of Schinkel's theater was also rounded and the main entrances had been moved to the side. Such a form for a theater, in fact, had preoccupied the Berlin master since 1813, when he first put forth proposals for renovating the Berlin National Theater. Semper's stage and auditorium reforms, as will be shown in the next chapter, also resembled the reforms proposed by Schinkel at this earlier date.[68]

The matter failed to be resolved, however, and deliberations on the project continued through 1837. Lüttichau sought out various opinions, among them that of Schinkel himself. The latter was enticed to visit Dresden and inspect the site and proposal on his return from holidays in Karlsbad. Semper anxiously awaited his arrival in mid-July.[69] After his site review, Schinkel enthusiastically supported Semper's design and even offered, if the young architect's project was accepted, to supply him with guidance and advice during construction.[70]

Schinkel's animation helped to convince Lüttichau that Semper was the right person for the job, and the theater director, in turn, put additional pressure on the King. In September 1837 Semper was asked to refine his project and provide a cost estimate, which he delivered on 23 March 1838. In a cabinet meeting in April, three years after the start of the most recent burst of activity, Semper's design received its royal approval, boosted by an interest-free loan floated by two princesses at the court. The King was evidently eager to start the project before the Saxon Diet reconvened in the fall of 1839, as both he and Lüttichau preferred not to have the parliamentary body become involved in a question that historically had been the purview of the royal court.

The official proclamation of Semper's commission did not come down until August 1838. Semper was given the artistic control, but had to operate under Lüttichau's supervision and with the technical assistance of Wolframsdorf. The Diet, which was constitutionally responsible for purchasing the land in the Italian Village, did in fact hotly debate the merits of the project throughout the following year, but construction was already too far advanced to be halted. In its final location, the theater was brought

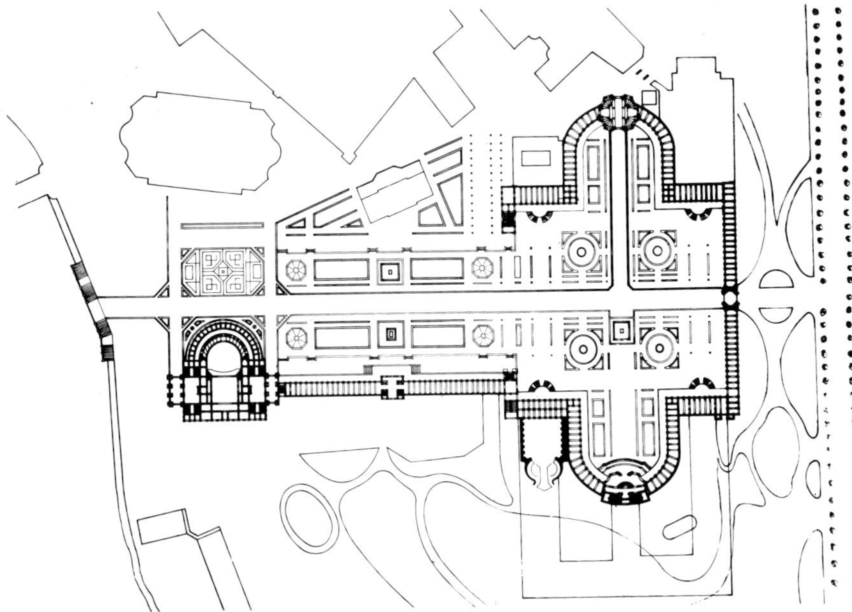

38 Gottfried Semper, preliminary plan for the Hoftheater, Dresden, with connection to Zwinger, 1835. Sächsische Landesbibliothek, Abteilung Deutsche Fotothek.

39 Gottfried Semper, preliminary perspective of the Hoftheater, Dresden, 1835. Sächsische Landesbibliothek, Abteilung Deutsche Fotothek.

somewhat closer to the Zwinger to allow the Comedy House to operate until the new edifice was built, but it was placed along the line of the west wing of the Zwinger as Semper had proposed. The money to building the connecting orangerie, however, was denied by the Diet and the vital link was not made. Thus the theater, as it turns out, forever lost an even more magnificent urban setting, much to Semper's disappointment.

As foundations were being laid in the fall of 1838, Semper and Lüttichau set out on a tour of Europe to study other theaters and to scout for decorative artists and for technical expertise for the complex enterprise. After Semper's earlier experience with hiking across the continent, his new mode of traveling by private coach and the chance to stay in fine hotels (now at the crown's expense) was a welcomed luxury. He barely tolerated the company of Lüttichau, whom he regarded as uncultivated and something of a bore. The director, however, was a prominent figure in Dresden social circles – in large part because of the great intelligence and beauty of his wife, Ida, who was said to have entranced Tieck, Carus, and a score of other worshippers.[71]

Semper and Lüttichau traveled through Weimar, Frankfurt, and Mainz, where they boarded a steamship for Cologne. After taking in the "imperfect" cathedral of that city (the construction of which was about to resume after almost three centuries of suspension), they moved on to Aachen, Antwerp, Ostende, and then crossed the Channel to London, arriving in mid-December. Semper was pleasantly overwhelmed by the size and splendor of the English capital – and put off by the already notorious high cost-of-living. He was impressed with Windsor Castle and other monuments that he saw – especially by the quality of English interiors and the refinement of their detailing. The architect and archaeologist T. L. Donaldson was one of the few colleagues that he met there.

The next stop was Paris, which allowed Semper almost a month to interview painters interested in bidding to work on the interior decorations of the Dresden theater. He and Lüttichau soon decided in favor a group of artists led by Charles Séchan, Jules Dieterle, and Edouard Desplèchin. While in the city, Semper also placed orders for the machinery and stage apparatus of the building.

Semper was unimpressed with the direction French architecture had taken during the previous decade. He found Duban's new building for the Ecole des Beaux-Arts to have many positive attributes, but more successful for him was Jean-Baptiste Lesueur's extension to the Hôtel de Ville in the French Renaissance style, which he described in a letter to Wolframsdorf as "the most beautiful building in the manner that I intend to build the theater."[72]

Toward the end of January Semper and Lüttichau traveled south to Marseille and then across to Italy, where they visited theaters in Milan, Genoa, and Naples. In the last city the two men separated and Semper returned north during February by way of Mantua, Verona, and Padua, arriving in Munich on 1 March 1839. Upon his return to Dresden he was greeted with news of the uproar that the construction of the new theater had sparked in the recently reconvened Saxon Diet, where, in Semper's words, "every blockhead reserves the right to butt in on it."[73]

During the years that Semper was involved with the theater, his architecture practice began to prosper with various other commissions. In 1837, as part of a liberalization of laws concerning religion, the Jewish community in Dresden was given the right to erect a synagogue and the next year Semper was awarded the commission (Pl. 40). Situated along the old ramparts adjacent to the river, upstream from the theater, the building was a simple cube to which was attached a narrow vestibule and twin towers defining the entrance. The stuccoed exterior walls were exceedingly plain, punctured only by groups of arched and rounded windows in the *Rundbogen* style. Inside, the polychrome effects were once again sumptuous, although most of the "Moorish-Byzantine" ornaments were painted on the plaster surfaces in imitation of more costly materials. The building was destroyed at the end of World War II.

Through these contacts with the Jewish community, Semper met and befriended Martin Wilhelm Oppenheim, the wealthy Berlin banker who was on familiar terms with the Rothschilds, Astors, and other luminaries of the burgeoning world of international finance. For the Oppenheim family in Dresden, Semper built two homes, which he and others regarded as two of his finest efforts.[74]

The Villa Rosa (1839; destroyed 1945) was situated just outside the limits of the city

40 Gottfried Semper, Dresden Synagogue, 1838. From *Allgemeine Bauzeitung*. Courtesy The Getty Center for the History of Art and the Humanities.

and served as a summer retreat on the Elbe (Pls. 41, 42). The charm of this work was due in part to its setting within spacious gardens, in part to the novelty of its decoration and the cheerful assurance of its Venetian, that is, "provincial" Renaissance motifs.[75] The almost square house was set on a rusticated (plastered) plinth with its main facade, terrace, and fountain located on the south, facing the river. This facade was the most richly articulated with its double flight of stairs, triple-arched doorways, central loggia, leafy spandrels, and caryatids. The spandrels of the side windows on the ground floor were adorned with wreaths; a more elaborate frieze panel was inserted under the balustrade. The herm-like brackets of the upper story supported a tall console table filled with ornament; the balustrade on the roof shielded a skylight. The villa was designed with gaiety and entertainment in mind and Semper provided a most successful theatrical setting for social occasions.

Inside, the plan emulated Palladio's Villa Rotunda with its nine-square division of rooms. In its middle division, a two-story octagonal salon connected a front entry vestibule with the rear (southern) garden salon. Corridors separated the central rotunda from lateral dining and entertainment rooms. The interior decoration was both luxurious and skillfully executed, especially the central rotunda illuminated by an oculus above. With its patterned marble floor, first-story wood paneling, and brilliantly lit and painted dome above, the room greatly impressed many of its early visitors. Oppenheim occupied the house with the family of his son-in-law, the painter August Grahl.

The Renaissance style of the Villa Rosa, as Kurt Milde has indicated,[76] also fell in with a more general Saxon movement of the 1830s toward Roman and Renaissance forms, as seen in Italian-inspired residences by Albert Geutebrück, Gustav Hörnig, and Woldemar

41 Gottfried Semper, Villa Rosa, Dresden, 1839. View from south. Institut für Geschichte und Theorie der Architectur, Semper Archiv, ETH-Zurich.

42 Gottfried Semper, Villa Rosa, Dresden, 1839. Section. From *Allgemeine Bauzeitung*. Courtesy The Getty Center for the History of Art and the Humanities.

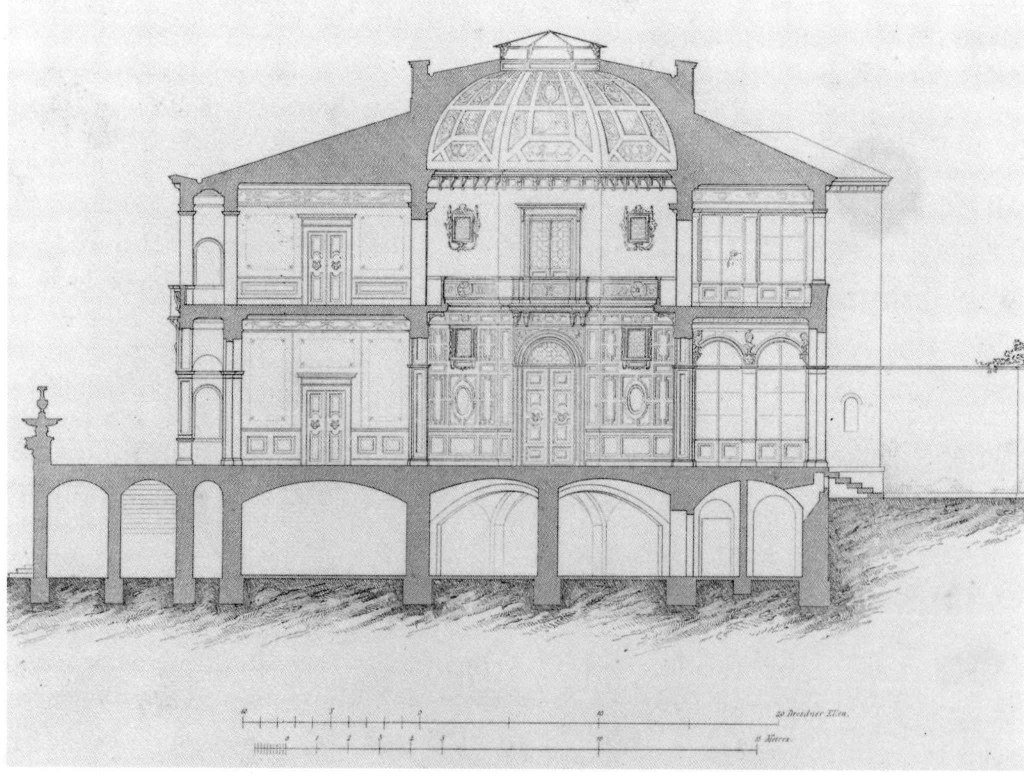

43 Georg Hermann Nicolai, Seebach residence. Dresden, 1839. Courtesy of Heidrun Laudel.

Herrmann. Georg Hermann Nicolai's Venetian design for an urban residence for the Seebach family on the Bürgerwiese (Pl. 43), a fashionable new park and residential neighborhood just outside the old town walls of Dresden, was also closely related in style and character. The talented Nicolai has thus far not received his historical due.[77] He was a Saxon native, a pupil of Joseph Thürmer, and later of Gärtner and Klenze in Munich. In 1835–36 Nicolai toured Italy and then worked for a brief period in Hittorff's studio in Paris, during which time he also met Gau. The Seebach house was designed and built in 1839, the same year as the Villa Rosa, and there is some question as to which design introduced this style into Dresden. To complicate matters further, Nicolai also seems to have worked briefly for Semper during this period but the two men had a bitter falling out – seemingly over some criticisms Nicolai made with regard to the theater.[78] Nicolai held his ground in the dispute but soon left the city to accept work in Coburg and Frankfurt. Ironically, it was Nicolai who eventually succeeded Semper in his chair at Dresden.

The second residence Semper built for the Oppenheim family in Dresden was the so-called Oppenheim Palais, a sumptuously appointed Renaissance palazzo that also faced the new Bürgerwiese (Pl. 44). Built between 1845 and 1848 (destroyed 1945) on an awkward triangular site, the more formal building took on the character of a high Renaissance palace without assuming any of the gravity sometimes associated with this style. The architectural merit of the work lies more in the exterior detailing and the decorative treatment of the interiors than in its plan, which centered around an octagonal reception hall near the center of the triangle. The layout of rooms, while workable from the inside, was also quite illogical in relation to the facade, as Manteuffel has noted.[79] Two of the imposing windows of the *piano nobile*, for instance, open onto a salon, while others are disproportionally large for the smaller bedrooms and boudoir behind.

44 Gottfried Semper, Oppenheim Palais, Dresden, 1845–48.

Notwithstanding these problems, the sandstone work chronicles Semper's growing mastery of Renaissance forms, especially the rich, plastic articulation that he would exploit so successfully in later buildings. The general physiognomy of Semper's architecture is also visible here: the stark contrast between the powerful rustication of the ground floor and the more lightly profiled detailing above. Great attention was given to the columnar windows of the main story. Wreaths adorn the lower dados of the column bases; the upper base (separated from the lower one by the sharp line of a molding) was decorated with a continuous Greek fret. The major divisions of the window pediments (borrowed, says Constantin Lipsius, from the Palazzo Pandolfini in Florence),[80] were also separated throughout by thin bead moldings, scarcely visible in surviving photographs. The upper half-story, tucked below the overhang of the cornice, was notable for its bas-reliefs, depicting stretched, flying figures. The few photographs and drawings of interior details that are preserved show once again an elegant treatment, with copious decorative fields and motifs. The building in its day was certainly heralded as a major success. Pecht notes that Oppenheim celebrated its completion with a sumptuous house-warming party, "to which half of Dresden was invited."[81]

During the 1840s Semper carried out a number of smaller designs that, while not specifically advancing his architectural stature, nevertheless fill out this busy period. Among them were a remodeling of the Elimayer shop in the New Market in Dresden (1840), the Houpe residence in the same city (1841), a military barracks in Bautzen (1842–45), a memorial fountain to victims of the cholera outbreak in Dresden (1843), a provisional triumphal arch for the return of Friedrich August II from England (1844), various vase designs for the porcelain works at Meissen, and tombs for Carl Friedrich von Rumohr (1843), Carl Maria von Weber (1844; after the return of his remains from England), and a member of the Oppenheim family (1849). Various other projects were not executed, among them Semper's design for the Leipzig railway station (1838), a Gothic design for a school in Blasewitz (1841), a remodeling proposal for the city hall at Oschatz (1842), a Freemasonry lodge in Dresden (1844), and a *Rundbogen* design for a hospital in Bucharest (1844).

Certainly one of the more intriguing of Semper's unexecuted designs was his proposal for rebuilding the Renaissance castle at Schwerin in the northern German province of Mecklenburg (Pl. 45). The Grand-Duke Friedrich Franz II invited Semper to his castle for a stay of nearly two months in the last part of 1843, during which time Semper, in competition with the Duke's own architect, Georg Adolf Demmler, prepared numerous drawings for the castle's remodeling. Semper proposed transforming the existing remnants of the castle into a large irregular pentagon with various towers in a picturesque setting. The German-Renaissance style of the original work was mixed with French and Italian elements; an extensive series of terraces and arbors was suggested along the lake. At one stage in the work Semper believed his proposal had been "essentially" accepted but the Grand-Duke quietly decided otherwise.[82] The rebuilding was carried out between 1847 and 1857 by Demmler and the Berlin architect Friedrich August Stüler (1800–65).[83]

Stüler, as it turns out, was Semper's main rival among the younger German architects for the leadership of the profession in the wake of Schinkel's death in 1841. Stüler had attended the Berlin Bauakademie and had worked for Schinkel on a number of architectural projects, beginning with the remodeling of the royal palace in 1827. At the start of the 1840s he had prepared an urban scheme for this section of Berlin (not dissimilar in scale to Semper's forum project in Dresden), in which he developed the area behind Schinkel's museum into a vast museum complex. Out of this proposal came his commission for the Neues Museum (1843–55). It was a Neoclassical work paying tribute to Schinkel (physically connected to his museum, now called the Altes or "Old" Museum,

45 Gottfried Semper, design for the castle at Schwerin, Mecklenburg, 1843. Perspective. Institut für Geschichte und Theorie der Architectur, Semper Archiv, ETH-Zurich.

with a bridge), but at the same time it was rather progressive in its construction and structural use of iron. Stüler went on to execute a number of other monumental commissions in the Prussian capital and elsewhere.

Various designs of Stüler and Semper were published during the 1840s in several of the newly founded architectural journals, which for the first time began to have an impact on the profession. Stüler and Semper were also chartered members of the first national congress of German architects and engineers, started in Leipzig in 1842. The very existence of such an organization tells of the modernization of the German building trades and the growing acceptance of architects as professionals with specific expertise in such areas as structural design, civil engineering, and mechanics. The organization was also a forum for architects to meet and exchange views on a variety of aesthetic issues. The concomitant style debate, for instance, fully erupted with a series of lectures at the second congress meeting in Bamberg in 1843.

At the first meeting in 1842, both Stüler and Semper were elected to the twelve-member executive committee. At the convention held at Bamberg in the following year both men displayed several of their new works. Stüler exhibited his Frankfurt Exchange and his proposed Berlin museum, along with several other designs. Semper displayed his proposed city hall schemes for Hamburg and Oschatz, a daguerreotype of his Cholera Fountain, and engravings of his recently completed Dresden Theater and Synagogue. At the convention held in Prague in 1844, Stüler and Semper were again voted to the executive committee, even though their heavy workloads made it increasingly difficult for them to devote much time to these events.

Semper's ascendancy within the German architectural profession in the 1840s was again highlighted by his commission for the new Art Gallery in Dresden (partially destroyed 1945; since rebuilt), a work whose "noble and self-sufficient beauty," in the words of Constantin Lipsius, "distinguishes it above all others and lets it appear as worthy of the brilliant performances of the *cinquecento*."[84] The Dresden Art Gallery is also a tribute to Semper's persistence and stamina in seeing through the realization of a monumental work in the face of innumerable bureaucratic and political obstacles.

The need for a new museum to exhibit the city's famed collection of paintings had – like the theater – been expressed for some decades. The city's collections had up to this time been housed in the Stallgebäude (now Johanneum), a building renovated for this purpose in 1745 by Johann Christoph Knöffel. Although admired at this time for its innovations, the many acquisitions of the second half of the eighteenth century had long rendered its spaces inadequate. The Stallgebäude, moreover, was situated on a busy street in the heart of the city, its contents continually exposed to street noise, vibrations, dust, and the pernicious effect of coal smoke. The lack of a heating system had further caused the building's interior to be damp, even during the few summer months when the museum was actually open to the public. A gallery commission convened in 1836 found over 900 paintings in need of cleaning and restoration, many in an advanced state of deterioration. This committee, led by Quandt and the painters Eduard Bendemann and Carl Christian Vogel von Vogelstein, recommended a new building away from the center of the city. Semper was brought in at this point to advise the committee and make design proposals.

The site initially favored, apparently at the urging of Quandt, was located on the right bank of the Elbe, opposite Brühlsche Terrasse. In April 1838, during the period when the royal theater was receiving its final approval, Semper also presented various gallery schemes to the commission. These designs, surprisingly, now drew upon Klenze's Renaissance-inspired gallery in Munich, the Alte Pinakothek (1826–36). One of Semper's schemes consisted of a large rectangular block with arcuated windows in the *piano nobile*, top-lit gallery spaces, and projecting corner pavilions containing staircases and additional gallery space.[85] His proposals differed from the Munich example, however, in the addition of a central tribunal surmounted by a drum and dome, a motif that also reappeared in later schemes.

Between May and August 1838 the commission debated Semper's proposals and became divided on the merits of both the scheme and the site. Whereas various members, led by Quandt and Vogel von Vogelstein, lauded Semper's efforts, another group, led by Rietschel, argued that the riverbank was a poor location because of its dampness, the costs of digging foundations, and its vulnerability to foreign military control. Semper continued to argue for this site but the museum commission in its consultations with members of the royal cabinet began to consider other options.

The issue became much more muddled in 1839–40, as the King and his cabinet, Semper, various committees, and the two chambers of the Saxon Diet discussed and considered the problem at length. Even though he worked in fear of "a wretched caboodle that intrigues against me,"[86] Semper continued to make proposals for different locations, now all centered around the Zwinger. In one scheme he suggested locating the gallery, U-shaped in plan, outside the Zwinger's western hemisphere – wrapping it around the two-story center pavilion and utilizing the latter as the main entrance. In another and perhaps even more imaginative scheme (Pl. 46), he proposed removing the Zwinger's

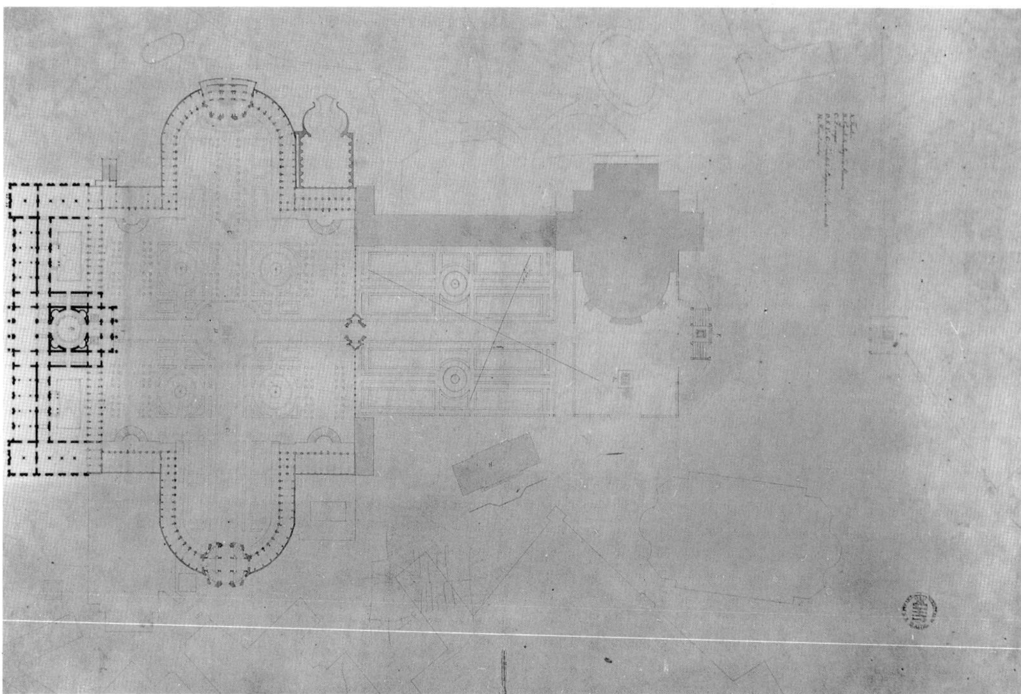

46 Gottfried Semper, early proposal for locating Dresden Art Gallery south of Zwinger courtyard, ca. 1839. Sächsische Landesbibliothek, Abteilung Deutsche Fotothek.

ornate southern gateway and situating the gallery outside this low range of galleries. The gallery's main entrance was then to be approached from the courtyard and the gateway was to be relocated at the opposite, northern side of the forum. In yet a third scheme, Semper proposed closing off this northern end of the Zwinger courtyard with the museum. This design, with its central dome and raised side pavilions (Pl. 47), was actually a modified version of his riverbank scheme. Its system of glazed arcades and sculptural niches along the Zwinger side were carefully scaled to accommodate the more fragile Baroque arcade of the Zwinger. Yet none of these proposals found acceptance, as still other sites came under consideration. By the end of 1840 Semper somewhat gloomily noted to a former student that "probably nothing" would come of his work on the museum.[87]

Nevertheless, Semper, the King, and the commission continued to pursue the matter. In the summer of 1840 the monarch sent a representative on a tour of Belgium, Holland, France, and England to examine various galleries and make a detailed report on their arrangements, illumination, and heating. Chemists conducted additional tests on the paintings and suggested optimal conditions for their preservation. The size of the gallery space needed was also more carefully studied. Semper made one proposal for rebuilding and adding to the existing Stallgebäude. In another scheme originating around this time, he proposed a centralized domed museum in the park west of the Zwinger, separated from the Baroque work altogether.

Meanwhile, other factors came into play. Near the end of 1840, the King decided to have his architect Wolframsdorf (who was also making his own gallery proposals) build a

47 Gottfried Semper, early facade study for Dresden Art Gallery, ca. 1839. Sächsische Landesbibliothek, Abteilung Deutsche Fotothek.

new orangery away from the Zwinger, thereby eliminating the architectural link by which Semper hoped to join the theater to the Zwinger complex. In response to this decision, Semper proposed to build a narrow storage building connecting the theater to the Zwinger, fronting it with an open colonnade. Reportedly at the suggestion of Lindenau, Semper then combined this proposal with still another scheme for the museum, locating the gallery as an extension of the eastern wing of the Zwinger (opposite the storage building and theater) and thereby doubling the area of the courtyard or forum (Pl. 43).

This proved to be a brilliant solution to the problem, one that Semper had previously refrained from making out of respect for Schinkel's guardhouse and arsenal, which in the early 1830s had been awkwardly set down in this location. In the new scheme, the arsenal was relocated north of the complex along the bank of the river, also centered on the forum's main axis. This scheme soon became Semper's preferred solution to the difficult problem and he set about making various refinements to it. The plan became the basis of his famous rendering of 1842 (Pl. 49), which shows the enlarged Zwinger courtyard with the theater on the right, museum on the left, and a low balustrade with two columns of Victory in the foreground, spatially defining the northern end of the complex. Recalling an aspect of Stüler's concomitant forum proposal for Berlin, a bridge connected the new gallery to the royal palace situated behind it. Also in this scheme some older buildings (among them the old opera) attached to the outside of the Zwinger's eastern hemisphere were removed and replaced by new galleries, thereby making regular an odd conglomeration of buildings. The building shown west of the Zwinger's western hemisphere was an alternative site for the gallery.

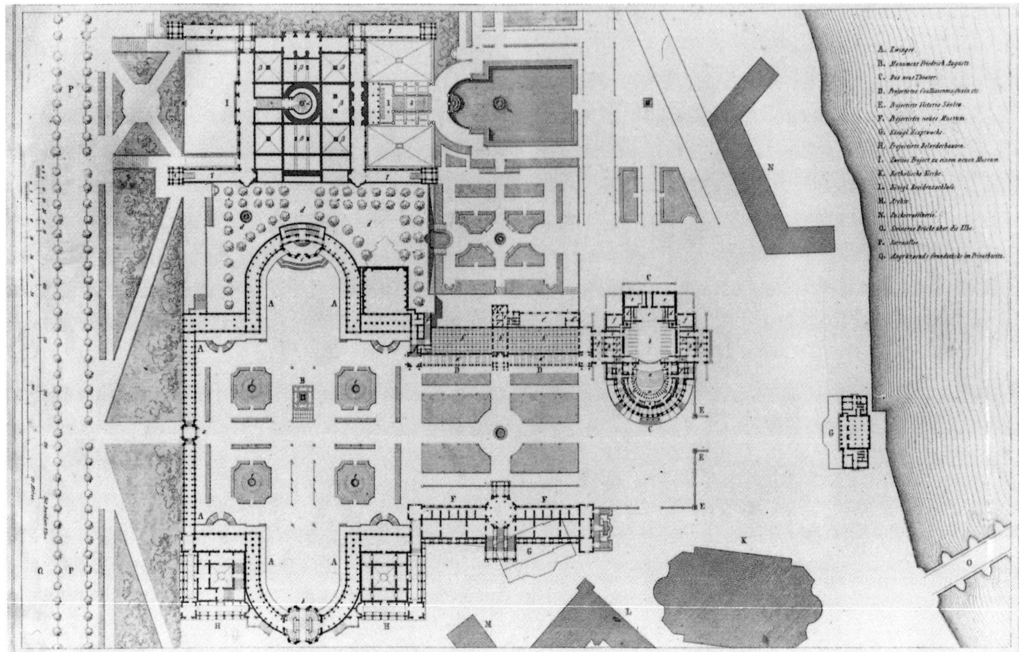

48 Gottfried Semper, plan of the Zwinger courtyard with the Art Gallery located as extension of east wing (bottom). Alternative location of the Art Gallery to west (above and separate from Zwinger). 1841. Institut für Geschichte und Theorie der Architectur, Semper Archiv, ETH-Zurich.

During this period Semper decided on another course of action that was relatively new to the practice of architecture: he set about lobbying for his scheme in the pages of architectural journals. At least this seems to be the case. When his plan for the enlarged Dresden forum appeared in the Viennese journal *Allgemeine Bauzeitung* in 1844, the unnamed author of the article, probably Ludwig Förster, touted the numerous architectural merits of Semper's design. He described the much needed link between the theater and the Zwinger, the beautiful effect of the gallery's dome on the city's skyline, the lively array of wall contours – all of which would "produce the most varied architectural-painterly effects."[88]

In another lobbying effort that suggests Semper's hand, J. Andreas Romberg, a friend of Semper and editor of the Leipzig journal *Zeitschrift für praktische Baukunst*, interrupted an article by Wolframsdorf (in which the royal architect was describing his now completed Dresden orangerie) to dispute the author's contention that it was necessary to move the orangerie away from the theater for reasons of fire safety. Romberg insisted that the last problem could easily have been solved with modern construction methods and that the city itself was the loser in the injury done to Semper's "beautiful plan."[89]

When this last remark appeared in 1846, Semper's efforts – by now after nearly a decade – had almost succeeded. He had convinced both the King and the cabinet of the artistic advantages of the extension scheme. A bill was actually sent to the Saxon Diet during the 1845–46 session to fund construction, but the Diet, now facing the additional cost of relocating the arsenal and expropriating more land in the Italian Village, balked once again. Other objections were raised: the gallery's proximity to both the palace and the theater (fire), a dusty street running between the museum and the palace, even the possibility of a "tunnel effect" produced by the prevalent direction of the wind. In the end the Diet compromised and approved funding, but only after eliminating the connecting link to the theater and forcing Semper to rotate the gallery around ninety degrees and close off the open, northern side of the Zwinger courtyard. Semper was then asked to prepare another ten variations of the design before the King made his final decision early in 1847 on a shortened variant. Work on the foundations started in March and some fifteen months later the decision was made to enlarge the work and restore the pavilions at each end.

The final location of the gallery created several architectural problems that Semper was unable to resolve in a satisfactory way. In his proposal of 1840 for locating a building on this site, he had suggested (based on smaller spatial requirements) a lower and narrower building mass, articulated with lateral wings and a central dome. In this scheme he also created a three-arched passageway through the central pavilion and into the Zwinger courtyard; a staircase was located on each side of the courtyard passage. In Semper's first variation on this scheme in 1846, the passageways into the Zwinger courtyard were retained (connected underneath by a low dome), but the twin staircases were moved to the pavilions at the north and south ends of the building. This proposal was pondered by the authorities for some time but then rejected, and Semper was asked to limit the vertical circulation to one staircase, which he located along the south wall of the gallery to one side of the archway.

This decision had a disastrous effect on the floor plan of the building (Pl. 50). Not only

49 Gottfried Semper, perspective of the Zwinger courtyard with the Art Gallery left foreground, 1842. Institut für Geschichte und Theorie der Architectur, Semper Archiv, ETH-Zurich.

was the ground floor now bifurcated by the center passageway, but the main stair also arrived at the second level in a central entrance hall at the south, which allowed access only to the east side of the museum. To make matters worse, the construction of the lower vaulted passage raised the floor level of the central tribunal almost a half-story above the adjacent wings, thereby separating the tribunal from the stair landing (with a wall) and the tribunal from the gallery spaces (with stairs). This, in turn, required a somewhat messy structural solution on the ground floor. Moreover, the central domed rotunda, which was originally conceived by Semper as the "sanctum for art" for the placement of Raphael's *Sistine Madonna*, now lost its monumental purpose; the large painting was moved by Schnorr von Carolsfeld to another location.

Increasing the spatial program of the museum also made it difficult to mediate the work compositionally with the smaller proportions of the Zwinger (Pl. 51). In response to this problem, Semper stepped down the Zwinger facade a half level to ease the transition, but the sensitivity to the Zwinger's height and scale that characterized his earlier scheme was all but lost in the executed version. The massive gallery simply overwhelms the more fragile Baroque elements of the Zwinger. On the theater side, however, the enhanced mass better defines the square of the theater and the church; here a concealed third story was placed behind the raised brow, lit only by skylights.

Notwithstanding these problems, the Art Gallery with its colorful and tasteful selection of materials was greatly admired, even exalted as one of the finest architectural creations of the day. Overall, the long rectangular block is dominated by the central dome and two-story, triumphal archway. The last Roman motif, of course, celebrates the spiritual triumph of art and provides a grand public entrance to both the Gallery and Pöppelmann's "Roman Theater." From the river side, the visage of the whole work is actually controlled by the horizontal layering of the two stories, set apart not only by their respective degrees of rustication and detailing but also by the use of two different shades of sandstone – one yellow and one white. The horizontal rhythm of the whole is greatly enhanced by the exquisitely detailed, monumental aedicules (similar to those of the Oppenheim Palais and Palazzo Pandolfini), which are applied to alternating windows along the main story. Full columns are used only at the center and at the end pavilions.

The strength of Semper's work, however, is always in part derived from his gift for detailing (Pl. 52), and here the Gallery forms a worthy companion to the nearby theater. Foremost is Semper's mastery of rustication: the linear design and control of the width and depth of joints, which in this and in later buildings became a trademark of his distinctive personal style. "No modern architect," said the nineteenth-century critic Josef Bayer, "has thought out the actual idea of stone with similar thoroughness, none has applied this artistic motif with an equally exceptional understanding, from which arises such a powerful intensification of the building upward: from elementary coarseness into variety and splendor."[90]

Semper's preference for a strong lithic rustication was closely related to his developing theory of architecture; in his later text on style he devoted several chapters specifically to exalting the process of "taming this coarse natural motif." Rustication, he argued, was principally an aesthetic idea, an expression of the network of lithic forces and of the building's more general relation to the ground. The two elements to be considered are the framing "edge" and the force-laden "face." This last effect can be enhanced, for instance, by increasing the projection of the face from the regular frame of it edge and by

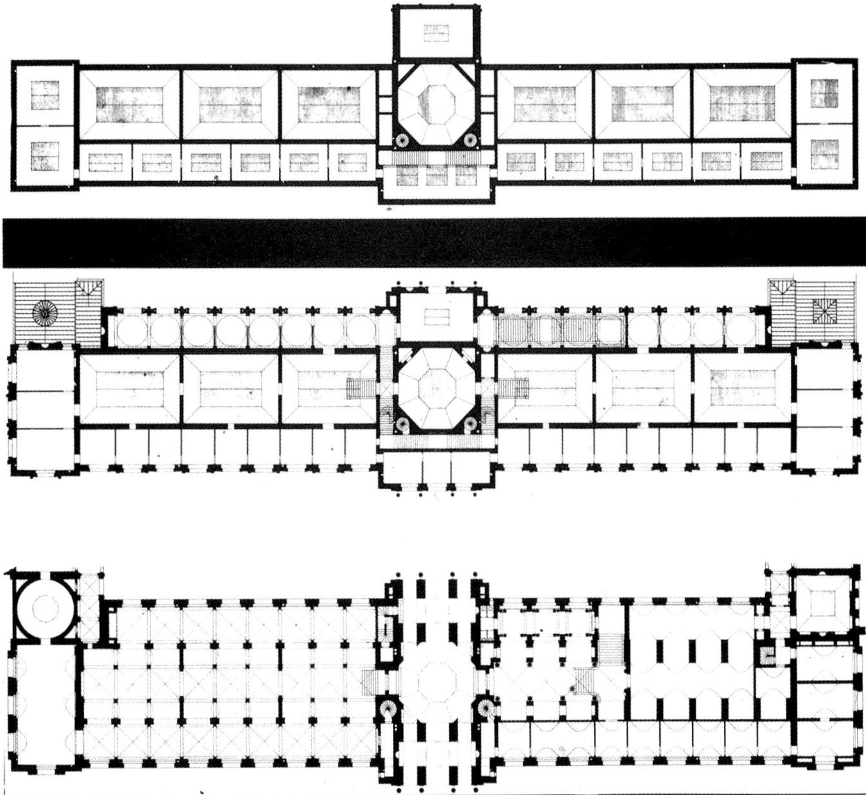

50 Gottfried Semper, Dresden Art Gallery, 1839–55. Plans. Institut für Geschichte und Theorie der Architectur, Semper Archiv, ETH-Zurich.

51 Gottfried Semper, Dresden Art Gallery, 1839–55. Aerial view with the Zwinger in background. Institut für Geschichte und Theorie der Architectur, Semper Archiv, ETH-Zurich.

52 Gottfried Semper, Dresden Art Gallery, 1839–55. Facade toward Theaterplatz. Photo by author.

controlling the direction of chisel work – the bossage he developed for the Dresden Gallery derived from early Renaissance examples.

Exploiting the contrast of face and edge also lends it a symbolic value, in that "the bands of the joints between the bulges acquire a regular 'beat,' one that has a decorative effect because of its rhythm and different surface treatment. The same effect is also achieved by the careful beveling of the joint surfaces. Thus the rustic coarseness can be clad in a certain manly elegance and gain an expression similar to the symbolism of the Doric order."[91] This eurythmic and crystalline strength below, for Semper, also contrasts with the smoothness and delicacy of the detailing above, that point at which the stone now becomes fully tamed by art.

The rustication on the Zwinger side of the Gallery is less forceful than its counterpart, as here Semper had to contend with the more delicate proportions of the Baroque work. The arcade rhythm of the windows along the main story is somewhat lightened and the windows allude in their detailing to the facade of Andrea Sansovino's library in Venice. The triumphal arch (Pl. 53), however, becomes more prominent and richer in its decorative treatment, as Semper here had to respond to Pöppelmann's extraordinarily

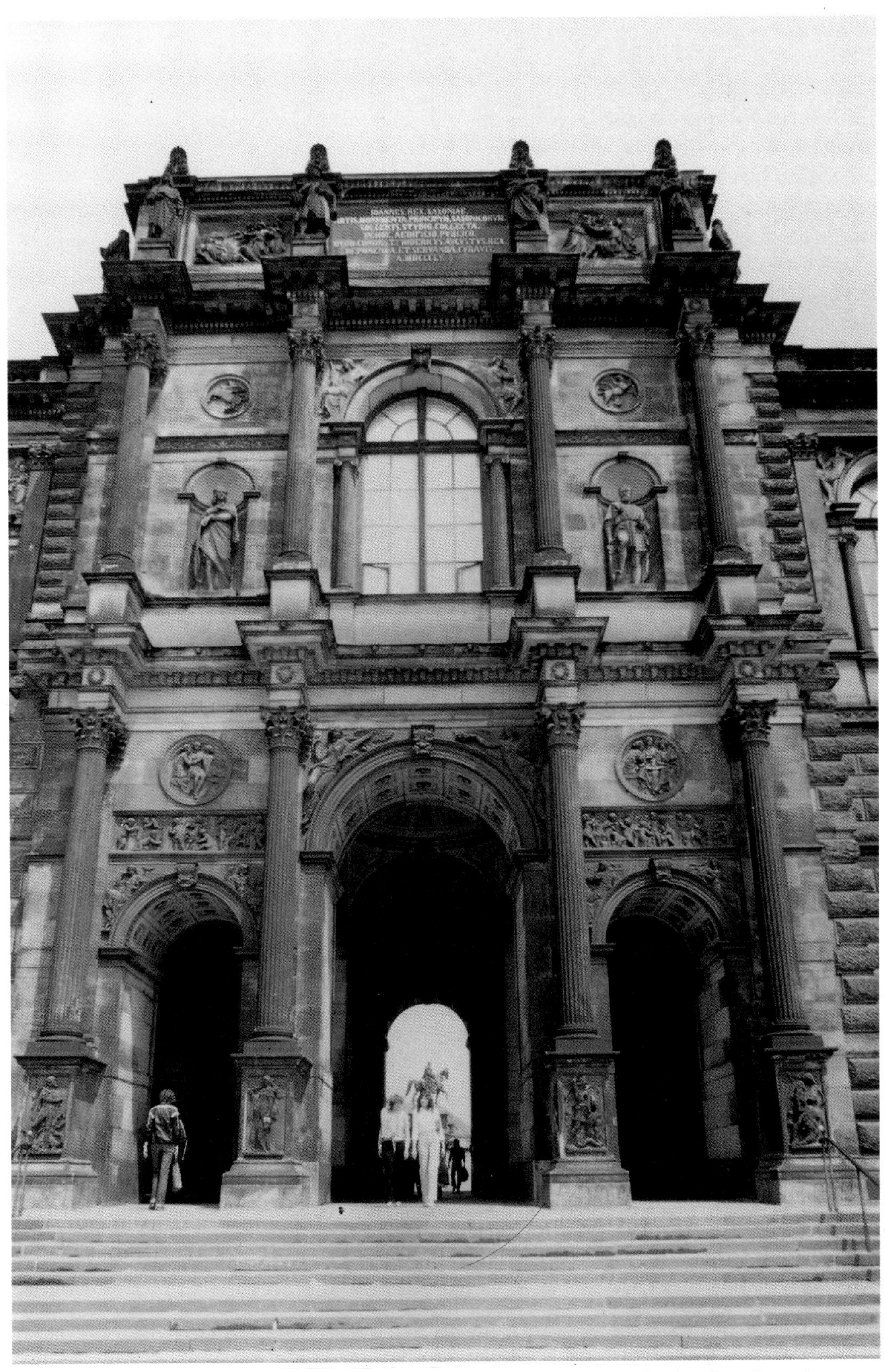

53 Gottfried Semper, Dresden Art Gallery, 1839–55. Archway on Zwinger facade. Photo by author.

ornate south gateway. The balustrade of the lower roof line was originally intended by Semper to be populated with an array of statues, which would have dissipated the visual forces still further.

There was still another facet of the building that greatly pleased its early admirers: its iconographic program. In an 1855 review of the recently opened museum, the art historian Wilhelm Lübke listed what he perceived to be several of the building's shortcomings (principally the plan), but he felt all had been compensated for by the building's artistic merits, chief of which was the intricate allegorical program woven into its fabric – a stupendous narrative that, as in Schinkel's earlier museum in Berlin, depicts important moments from the mythical and historical development of art.

As Lübke analyzed it, the program unfolds on both sides of the museum at the triumphal archway. On the facade facing the theater, all sculptural reliefs are taken from Greek mythology and classical antiquity, and thematically they revolve around the spandrel figures of the upper archway: Hesiod (relating to gods) and Homer (relating to heroes). The progenitors of human culture appear on the face of the lower column plinths: Theseus slaying the Minotaur, Jason and the golden fleece, Perseus with the head of Medusa, and Hercules with the hydra of Lerna. In the spandrels of the two side arches the four elements are represented; in the frieze panels above are shown the athletic contests of the Greeks. Prometheus and Pygmalion are represented in the two medallions: the former as a master-craftsman fashioning a man, the latter with a statue of a woman about to be given life by Aphrodite. In the spandrels of the central arch is an allegory to the power of art to tame nature and inert matter. On one side Amphion builds the wall of Thebes; on the other Orpheus is shown with his lyre. The four statues at the top of the triumphal arch, representing the two golden periods of Greek art, portray Pericles and Phidias on one side, Lysippus and Alexander the Great on the other. The spandrels of the windows along one wing of the facade represent Greek deities. Those along the opposite flank show heroic figures. Across the top of the building between aedicules are ten medallions, portraying Apollo and the nine muses.

The themes on the Zwinger side of the museum are devoted to the Christian era. The narration revolves around the two sculptural figures of Raphael and Michelangelo, set in the niches of the archway: the former, as Lübke explains it, representing intuitive creativity in peaceful harmony with the world, the latter a more complex and contemplative creativity often in conflict with life. At the plinths of the lower columns are four heroes displaying these tendencies: St. George and Siegfried on the side of Raphael, Samson and Judith on the side of Michelangelo. The spandrels of the side arches portray four sibyls. The frieze above depicts painting on one side, sculpture and architecture on the other. In the medallions of the first story are represented the three graces (Raphael's side) and the three arts (Michelangelo's side). In the medallions of the second story are victories holding a palm branch on one side, a laurel on the other. The frieze in the attic story on the left shows Pegasus on a winged horse; the other, on Michelangelo's side, shows a sphinx. In the spandrels to the central window are allegories depicting events in the life of Jacob. The six statues crowning the triumphal arch portray Holbein, Giotto, Dante on the side of Raphael; Dürer, Cornelius, and Goethe on the side of Michelangelo. The spandrels of the facade left and right of the central archway represent themes from the Old and New Testament.

Motifs on the side facades of the museum mediate between the classical and Christian periods. At the northwest end are medallions of old and new Rome. Among the motifs portrayed are Hellas and Rome, Italia and Germania, Faust and Helen, and Armor and Psyche.

What is most interesting in Lübke's very detailed litany of the plastic works is the conclusion he reaches at the end of it. Not only does he laud this journey through time, "under the intellectual guidance of such a skillful master," but he also goes on to compare this "tree of human culture" specifically to the two museums in Berlin by Schinkel and Stüler.[92] Whereas Stüler's recently completed work, Lübke felt, lacked a sense of monumental "repose and clarity," particularly in its interior, Semper's museum "clearly and firmly held in view the meaning and purpose of a museum – such as Schinkel had shown so well in his older Berlin museum – namely, to express the ideal purpose of the building on the exterior through its monumental treatment, and to let the interior be as simple as possible so as to have as its sole and most precious adornment the display of artistic treasures."[93]

It was certainly easier to make this connection in 1855 than it is today – prone as we are to dwell exclusively on the formal or stylistic aspects of architecture. But this link forged between Schinkel and Semper, discussed in Dresden 150 years ago, today serves to underscore just how discernible Semper's theatrical intentions were. If Semper in Dresden constructed his own urban stage for art, it was a stage that in many respects was dedicated to Schinkel, that is to say, to his artistic conception and lead. The ennobling force of Semper's monumental forms and the communal procession of apotheosized emblems were intended – like Schinkel's colossal murals in Berlin – to dramatize cathechistically the capacity of art to shape a culture, as well as to bring some joy or delight to the Sunday afternoon stroller. In this sense, the artistic dressings of the Dresden Art Gallery expanded Semper's theoretical basis while at the same time building on its founding impulses. His literary promulgation of these ideas was but a few years away.[94]

What is different, of course, is Semper's transposition of Schinkel's vision of a Greek stoa into a sanctified Renaissance palace. This most important stylistic transformation – like the Hoftheater, largely deriving from the Gallery's proximity to the arcuated forms of the Zwinger – at the same time combines with other aspects of Semper's artistic make-up: his sense of scale, his preference for ornate, highly plastic forms, above all, his compositional skill. It is in this last respect, in particular, that Semper elaborates upon Schinkel's earlier vision of theatricality. The Art Gallery is also but a stepping stone, a transitional work, to still greater achievements.

The Dresden Hoftheater

We can better explore this aspect of Semper's artistic personality by returning to and considering more fully the design of the Hoftheater: the court theater and opera that first established his high artistic reputation and to which his name has since been invariably linked.

By every contemporary account the theater was considered a grand success. It opened on 12 April 1841 with a performance of Goethe's *Torquato Tasso*, the tragic drama of the Renaissance poet and genius who succumbed to mental illness. Newspaper correspondents from all over Germany flocked to the city to observe the much anticipated event. One columnist from Hannover recorded the audience's initial reaction to the new building: "Everyone was overwhelmed by its splendor and brilliance. No one expected something so richly decorated and royally adorned, yet not overladen. Everyone marveled. And as the King entered they showered applause on him with indescribable rejoicing. He was besieged with a thousand cheers and thanks because he had provided Dresden with such a magnificent theater, one with few rivals in all of Germany."[95]

The new theater (Pl. 54) in many respects broke with established prototypes and is today seen as an important development in the nineteenth-century evolution of this building type. In contrast to earlier theaters, which generally wrapped their complex functional program within rectangular forms, Semper chose to articulate the different components of the building individually. In its formal composition, it was an especially successful ensemble of various architectural parts: the rounded wall of the auditorium and corridors facing the main public square, giving way at the sides to rectangular circulation blocks and carriage entrances, surmounted with pediments. Even the rear of the theater was given an impressive elevation, with the stagehouse terminating in a squared, three-story facade, arcuated and crowned with a tall bacchanalian frieze. Semper justified the motif of the rounded facade on the public square on functional grounds – with the argument that the outer forms of a theater ought to represent interior uses.[96] There was also the planned link or arcuated connection with the Zwinger, which would have brought the theater in greater formal harmony with the Baroque complex.

The formal unity of the work was considerably enhanced by Semper's decision in 1835 to align the elevation of the stagehouse with the rounded block of the interior auditorium wall, combining both under one large roof. The gabled circulation wings on each side, whose ridge was also raised in height to this cornice line, recall those of Schinkel's Berlin playhouse, with their blocklike articulation and enrichment of the urban setting. Semper's rounded form was also a conceptual play on the expansion of the Zwinger forum into a much larger urban square: the positive mass of the theater reflecting the negative spatial mass of the two existing hemispheres of this Baroque gallery.

If this rounded theater front was the most noticeable innovation, it was also a design motif that – as various historians have pointed out – was a culmination of several decades of attempts to reform the stage, deliberations going back to the eighteenth century. The idea of such a motif, it seems, was first raised as early as the 1770s by the Italian architect Francesco Milizia.[97] The period around 1800, when interest in the Greek arena stage as an alternative to Baroque prototypes was great, was the time of several proposals for circular theater forms, among them separate designs by the Berlin architects Friedrich Gilly and Ludwig Catel, as well as a proposal by the French theorist Jean-Nicolas-Louis Durand.[98] The same tendency continued after the Napoleonic years, with Pietro di Sangiorgio making a proposal for the Via del Corso in Rome in 1821 in the form of an amphitheater. A few years later the architect Clemens Wenzeslaus Coudray, in collaboration with Goethe, proposed a rounded theater design to Grand-Duke Karl August of Saxe-Weimar; both men cited antique precedents.[99]

In 1829 construction was even started on two theaters with rounded fronts, although neither was similar to Semper's scheme. Pierre Bruno Bourla's design for the city of Antwerp was much smaller in scale and very different in its appearance and layout. Georg Moller's City Theater in Mainz was larger but much heavier in its classical Roman proportions. Finally, Schinkel was at work in 1835 on a theater with a rounded end, as

54 Gottfried Semper, Dresden Hoftheater, 1835–41. Institut für Geschichte und Theorie der Architectur, Semper Archiv, ETH-Zurich.

part of his larger design for an "ideal palace."[100] It is possible Semper may have seen this proposal or even discussed it with Schinkel. What distinguished Semper's design from all of these other efforts, however, was the great assurance and sensitivity with which he handled this particular theme.

Another innovative and influential aspect of the Dresden Hoftheater was Semper's use of Renaissance forms. The most obvious reason for selecting this particular stylistic dressing, one clearly apparent in sketches for the work, was the need to link the theater with the arcuated galleries of the Baroque Zwinger. In his sketches for the connecting orangery and – later – the connecting storage building, Semper simply continued the Zwinger's line of arches with the same proportions. When this link reached the theater, he placed a second story of arches on top of the first to accommodate the new spatial necessity.

But this decision was a startling departure from recent precedents as well as being an attempt by Semper to formalize his notion of organic architecture. Not only was every theater built in Germany in the first half of the nineteenth century (save Moller's theater in Mainz) Neoclassical in character, but Renaissance-inspired motifs had not even made their way into the contemporary stylistic discussion in Germany. It was not that the

Renaissance and its forms had been overlooked as a historical style, but rather that this period was regarded as a false style: a corruption of an already suspect Roman style, a corruption that had led to the greater debacle of the Baroque. This was true for Renaissance painting and sculpture as well. When Franz Kugler in 1842 published one of the first major histories of art, he devoted all of eight pages to Italian art in the fifteenth century.[101]

In Germany, Renaissance forms were also seldom applied to other building types. The Munich architect Karl Fischer employed various Renaissance motifs in his very original practice in the first decades of the century, but his reputation as a designer was soon eclipsed by the heralded entry of Klenze into that city. Klenze himself, who had worked for Percier and Fontaine in Paris, designed various works in a literal Renaissance style, but until the end of his life he adhered to the belief that only the Greeks had achieved artistic perfection. Schinkel, who in his early years had argued that "the best style of architecture had finished with Bramante,"[102] generally avoided the subject of the Renaissance in his musings, but occasionally in his practice, as with his renovation of the urban residence of Count Redern, he flirted with Renaissance elements – although few seem to have noticed.

This quite arbitrary and selective "effacement of four hundred years of art history," as Semper later referred to it,[103] is somewhat surprising in light of the increasing popularity of this style in France during the 1830s, and here of course was Semper's inspiration. French fascination with the Renaissance style, in fact, can be traced back to the late eighteenth-century publications of Percier and Fontaine, in which these two former *grand-prix* winners at the French Academy in Rome praised the beautiful order, happy disposition, simplicity of means, and picturesque effects of Renaissance style.[104] In the 1820s this was the style around which the *pensionnaires* at the French Academy rallied in their search for an alternative to Neoclassical forms. Félix Duban's new building for the Ecole des Beaux-Arts (1832–39) was Renaissance in its motifs, as was the earlier design for this building by François Debret (1819). And in 1838, the same year the Dresden Theater began construction, Henri Labrouste in Paris was preparing his design for the Bibliothèque Ste-Geneviève, which drew its principal formal inspiration from Alberti's San Francesco in Rimini. It must be stressed, however, that neither Semper nor the French designers ever employed this style in the literal and eclectic way that Klenze had done in Munich. Renaissance forms, as Semper later argued, were simply elements of a language capable of further evolution, a language that provided a more plastic and more functional alternative to nascent Neogothic and *Rundbogen* tendencies.

Thus the Renaissance style was seen by Semper as a progressive and logical way out of the contemporary style debate, but this was not the only reason for his attraction to it. Like his French contemporaries, he regarded the style with its vast treasury of formal motifs as possessing great expressive possibilities. Most especially he was attracted to its capacity for plastic articulation and allegorical narration. In his later monograph on the theater, written in the mid 1840s, Semper defended his selection of Renaissance forms – notwithstanding their "solemn rigor" – just because of this style's capacity to allow a "play with forms." Recognizing the exuberance that is also inherent in a theater design, he noted that he had sought to evoke that "chameleonic color that sometimes laughs, sometimes cries, but is always playful, and that seems all the more justified in that (characteristic of the direction of our dramatic art) it recalls the century in which the principles of antique architecture found a rather free and whimsical interpretation, in which Shakespeare endowed drama with new life, a life that has blossomed again in a second youth through that great poet and artistic magistrate of recent times."[105]

This "second youth" – a spirited homage to Goethe's poetry and dramas – is enormously revealing of Semper's attitude toward his art and might well serve as an abstract for his theory. His grasp of the theatrical impulse underlying monumental architecture, however, was yet not as fully developed as it would be in many of his later works. Unlike Semper's Art Gallery of a few years later, the principal exterior motifs of the Dresden Theater were still isolated in their narrative themes. He filled in eight arcades of the rounded wall with niches, in which he placed the statues (exemplary works of Hähnel and Rietschel) of Goethe, Schiller, Gluck, Mozart, Molière, Shakespeare, Sophocles, and Euripides. And Karl Rolle, under Semper's direction, applied black-and-gray sgraffito decorations (a Renaissance technique re-introduced by Semper) to parts of the arches and third story. (Sgraffito is the process by which the ornamental design is scratched into a layer of plaster, revealing a plaster of a different color beneath.)

One area, however, where he allowed his natural inclination to reveal itself was in the thematic selections he made for the two pediments and rear frieze. The side pediments, like Schinkel's theater in Berlin, expounded the dual themes of "tragedy" and "music." Yet whereas Schinkel, on the advice of Tieck, had chosen for the tragic theme the lamentable story of Niobe mourning her slain children, Semper preferred the more forceful events of Orestes avenging the murder of his father Agamemnon, as told by Homer and later playwrights – featuring the death of Aegisthus and Clytemnestra, the pursuit of Orestes by the Erinyes, and his acquittal by the Athenian Areopagus, represented plastically by Sophocles, Aeschylus, and Euripides.

The "comic" motif was portrayed by the bacchanal celebration in the large frieze across the rear (Pl. 55), in which an ecstatic Dionysus joyfully led a train of satyric followers in revelry. This last theme, as Semper's later artistic efforts would show, was an idea particularly dear to him, and it demonstrates that his use of Renaissance forms was a means to reach back to the more primitive artistic emotions of the classical and preclassical past, just as Greek forms were to Goethe and Schinkel. In this respect, Semper's proclivity for the Renaissance was a psychological bridge to more profound artistic sensitivities, since mollified perhaps by the advent of civilization. The nineteenth-century critic Edouard Conte, in eulogizing the French architect Charles Garnier and his desire to tap the classical nerve through his own use of Renaissance forms, once said that "he loved the epoch when the flesh announced through the monument, as through books, paintings and sculpture, its joy in the rebirth of pagan pleasure without being poisoned by the idea of sin."[106] The Dionysian verve and high sensuous content implied in this statement seems better suited to the carnalist Semper (with his fleshy tectonic forms) than to his more intellectually detached French contemporary. Semper's materiality is already evident in the exterior of this work.

The Hofheater was also famed for a number of interior innovations, both technical and theatrical, and many of these again go back to Schinkel (Pl. 56). Semper, in fact, envisioned more of them than he was able to realize. In his monograph on the building, he complained of the many hindrances and changes that were forced upon his earlier stage schemes. Working together with Ludwig Tieck, with whom he had also collaborated in the mid-1830s on the reconstruction of a Shakespearean stage, Semper initially proposed

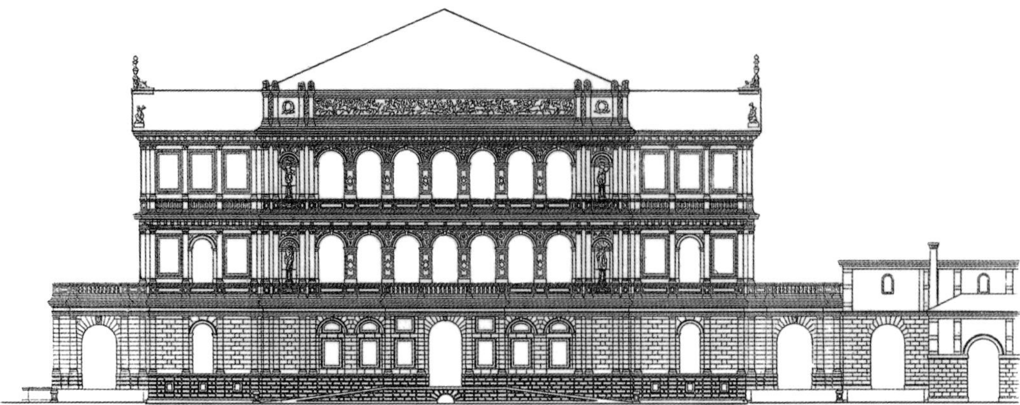

55 Gottfried Semper, Dresden Hoftheater, 1835–41. Elevation from Semper's *Das königliche Hoftheater zu Dresden* (1849).

a plan containing a wide and shallow backstage area, fronted with a relatively narrow proscenium opening, with antique-like scenery and stage entrances to each side of the opening.[107] The vast machinery and range of coulisses that moved up and down on the Baroque stage were eliminated. A podium area in front of the proscenium, accessible from the side entrances, was to be the main performance area, similar to the classical precedents of arena stages. The orchestra pit was made nearly invisible – later entirely so. The intention was to bring the actors as close as possible to the audience and to make the scenery less literal and illusional and more theatrical in effect.

Schinkel's efforts in Berlin had grown out of an architectural competition of 1800, in which Carl Gotthard Langhans's more traditional design for the Berlin National Theater had been chosen over the amphitheatrical design of Friedrich Gilly. The latter had been inspired by the theater reforms of Goethe and Tieck, who suggested simplifying the backstage area by bending the stage forward into the auditorium, thereby placing the actors on line with the proscenium opening. Schinkel sought the same end in 1813 with his proposed modifications to Langhans's building. He not only bowed the stage forward but collapsed the space immediately behind by proposing four Corinthian columns on each side behind the proscenium. The aim was to simplify the costly and unwieldy Baroque stage sets by reducing each scene to a single backdrop.[108]

When Langhans's playhouse burned to the ground in 1817, Schinkel was soon appointed the architect for the new theater. Working directly with Tieck and Goethe this time, Schinkel again proposed a platform stage, lit from the sides as well as above, and the reduction of the backstage area, which could now be enhanced by a unified pictorial backdrop. His design was not accepted in all of its details, but he did succeed in bringing the action forward and creating a greater sense of intimacy between the actors and audience. Thus Semper's proposals in 1835, again made in consultation with Tieck, were nothing more than a reiteration of these efforts in Berlin, and even the final results were similar. As built, the Dresden proscenium was widened over Semper's first proposal and the side entrances were lost.

A reconsideration of the auditorium itself, which seated 1750 people, was also a major concern for Semper, as it was for Schinkel. Semper cited antique precedents for the curved form of the auditorium, claiming that it was "prescribed to a certain extent by nature herself" – that is, the psychological tendency of people in public venues to encircle an event.[109] And just as Schinkel in Berlin had attempted to do away with the traditional loges or theater boxes (set aside for royalty and aristocracy) in favor of open seating, so did Semper. In addition to their sightline problems and aristocratic connotations, the loges also had the disadvantage of creating a beehive effect through their many tiers, thereby deadening the room's acoustics. Schinkel in Berlin had succeeded in reducing them to a single row at each tier, in front of which he placed open seating. Semper was less successful in his efforts, although he did recess the partitions separating the loges, thereby giving the tiers the appearance of continuous seating. On the fourth level he was able to create an open gallery. The recessed partitions of the loges also had the advantage of improving the sightlines from the more forward boxes. The openness of the boxes, moreover, defeated private conversations, thereby turning the focus of their occupants to the stage itself.

Combined with these novelties in the interior design were other technical accomplishments that greatly enhanced the final product. Semper rationalized the elimination of interior columns and the related improvement in sightlines on the grounds that theaters, even court theaters, should be expected to examine their gate receipts and maximize their proceeds. The machinery of the stage apparatus, in part based on Semper's research in London and Paris, was carried out by the Mannheim mechanical designer Mühldorfer. The interior of the Dresden Theater was lit throughout by gas lamps, another recent invention.[110]

In his design, Semper also paid much attention to the acoustics of the large auditorium and in this respect his theater was unsurpassed. Because the theater was to be used for both drama and opera, his task was especially complex. In his monograph he argued that an

56 Gottfried Semper, Dresden Hoftheater, 1835–41. Floor plans from Semper's *Das königliche Hoftheater zu Dresden* (1849).

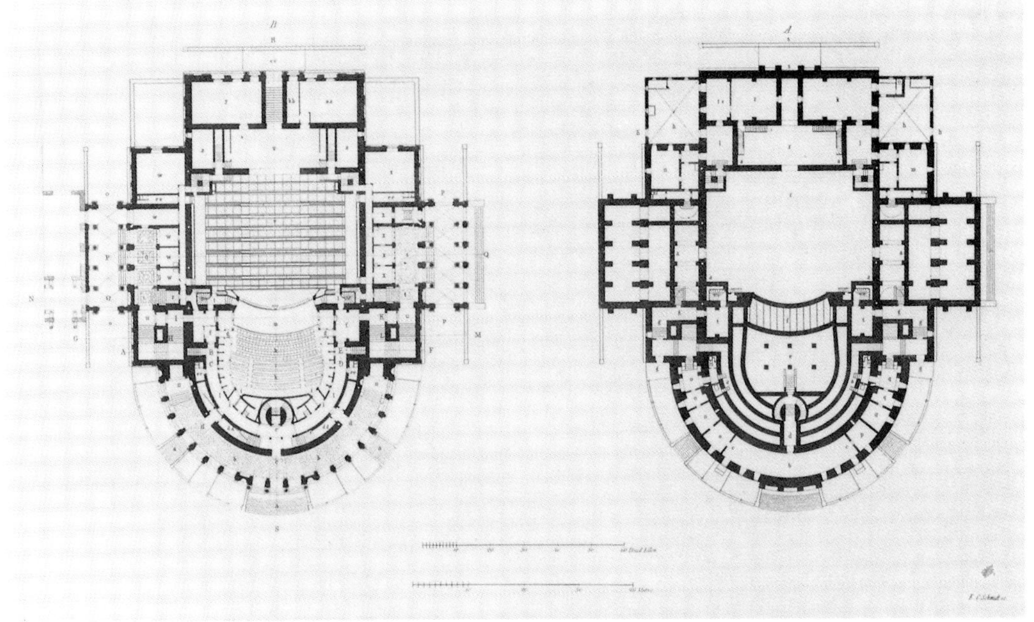

elliptical form had a superior acoustical effect to that of a rounded form for auditorium seating, since it matched the natural projection of sound better. He also specifically opposed the prevailing trend in acoustic design toward smooth walls and balcony parapets; he correctly asserted the necessity to disperse or diffuse sound waves at varying angles by means of extensive surface projections. The height of the auditorium was, of course, another important variable, and the large circular disk of the ceiling platform was designed, in effect, as a flexible soundboard to deflect and disperse sound. The faces of the proscenium and balcony parapets were angled and amply filled out with relief. The conch or clam-shell form of the baldachins above the loges was a motif used by Semper once again to deflect and diffuse sound. He structurally isolated the floor of the orchestra pit and supported it on a post-and-beam system that was designed to be, in his words, "the crater of a large drum." Recognizing also the inherent acoustical advantages of wood, he used this material extensively throughout the auditorium to enhance reverberation. The hall in its totality was consciously regarded, in itself, "as a musical instrument."[111]

If all of this is not sufficiently impressive, several hundred pages of mathematical calculations have survived from the project, demonstrating that Semper personally did all of the structural engineering for the building.

Yet it was the theater's visual charm or stately appearance that most impressed its visitors. Inside, the basic tones of the auditorium were white and gray, with decorations highlighted in gold. The panels inserted into the parapet fascias were blue. The rear wall of the loges and the drapery of the proscenium were a deep crimson. The large circular disk of the ceiling was painted *en grisaille* by the French painters Edouard Desplèchin and Jules Dieterle; a drawing by Semper, however, shows that he himself worked out the design. The four oval fields were allegorical representations of music, tragedy, comedy, and fine art. The four circular portraits closer to the center were of Goethe, Schiller, Weber, and Mozart. Desplèchin and Dieterle, both of whom became lifelong friends of Semper, designed the draperies of the proscenium, although the figurative scene on the main curtain was carried out by the Dresden painter Julius Hübner. In the center of this design were scenes from Tieck's prologue *Kaiser Octavianus*; below was a procession of figures from works of Shakespeare, Molière, Calderon, Lessing, Goethe, and Schiller. The royal box, lobbies, corridors, and staircases were likewise richly decorated with various allegories and the names of renowned poets, composers, operatic singers, and actors.

The painter Friedrich Pecht was deeply moved by the theater's overall "elegance of decorative taste," as well as by the "organic nature of the decoration growing out of the construction and the glorious perfection of form." Above all, however, he was impressed by the "very special, deeply saturated distinction of color," which he believed far outstripped any similar artistic effort of his day.[112] Constantin Lipsius, writing about the first court theater in 1880, noted that though there have been theaters built since that have invoked a more imposing and grander impression than the first Dresden Theater, the latter with its "engaging, harmonious, finely sensitive, charming, and noble effects had not been equaled up to now, let alone surpassed."[113]

Semper's artistic talent, as demonstrated by this building, which obviously had a profound effect on many of his contemporaries, has in recent times rarely been acknowledged or appreciated. The destruction of so many of his buildings in Dresden (including this theater, which was destroyed by fire in 1869) has certainly had much to do with this historical shortcoming. The great emphasis that has been placed on his written legacy, as we noted earlier, has also contributed to this problem. But it is unfortunately evident that we have to some extent lost our ability to discern the very formidable artistic intentions of this period.

Lipsius, in attempting to summarize the artistic appeal of the Dresden Hoftheater in 1880, could think of no higher compliment than to invoke the word "character," by which he meant to underscore the originality and command of an artistic personality. But the theater at the same time also influenced Semper's artistic outlook, that is, as his first major commission it helped to give concrete form to his very conception of monumental architecture – thereby shedding some light on the subsequent development of his theory.

If Semper, as his letter seems to suggest, began designing the theater while still in Altona or shortly after his arrival in Dresden, it places the theater's genesis not only close in time to his first Berlin exposure but also to the writing of *Preliminary Remarks on Polychrome Architecture*. Hence, it is easier to connect this work with his image of the Greek temple: that sanctified edifice brilliantly painted and decked out with metal ornaments, gilding, draperies, baldachins, curtains, and moveable implements, but above all made magical by the ceremonial processions of priests and people (substitute actors and audience). This vision certainly compares well with Semper's desire to paint the theater with a "chameleonic color," that is, to invest the work with the capacity to laugh and to weep, and playfully exploit its sensuous physiognomy. Aspects of Friedrich Schiller's aesthetics can certainly be found here, especially Schiller's insistence that the plastic and graphic arts must become music and move us through their immediate sensuous presence.[114] This same attitude can also be found in Semper's later writings, not the least of which is the passage in which he, in pondering the origin of monumental architecture, refers to the "haze of carnival candles" as the true atmosphere of art.[115] The last image is so overtly theatrical in its invocation that it deserves elaboration. In dwelling upon this "carnival spirit," which as he said is so very essential to the artistic thinking of sculptors, painters, architects, poets, musicians, and dramatists, Semper noted:

> For similar reasons the drama could also be meaningful only in the beginning and at the height of the progressive education of a people. The oldest vase paintings give us an idea of the early material masques of the Hellenes – in a spiritual way, like those stone dramas of Phidias, the ancient masque is taken up again by Aeschylus, Sophocles, Euripides, as well as Aristophanes and the other comic dramatists. The proscenium is used for framing a noble piece of human history that does not occur at some time somewhere but that happens everywhere as long as human hearts beat. "What's Hecuba to him?" The spirit of masks breathes in Shakespeare's dramas; we meet the humor of masks and the haze of candles, the carnival sentiment (which truly is not always joyous) in Mozart's *Don Juan*. For even music needs a means to shatter reality.[116]

We can also find concomitant expressions of this thinking in contemporary French architecture, in what David Van Zanten has termed "*tableaux* of building masses," or the design of works by impressionistic effects. In a lecture given to the Académie des Beaux-Arts in 1832, the architect A.-L.-T. Vaudoyer, in commenting on the Renaissance fantasy *Hypnerotomachie Polphili*, summed up the process:

> [The architect's] spirit takes fire and is transported into a domain of elevated and vivid illusions. His heated imagination yields a kind of delirium, or better, an ecstasy; he

> penetrates new and unknown places, he passes through magnificent palaces, enchanted gardens, cool and mysterious grottoes; and a dream, like a second hypnerotomachia Poliphili, a vision, causes him to experience successively diverse sensations; here a rich and imposing architecture brings him to recognize a temple to the deity; further on a majestic but simpler building, severe in character, open and easy of access, discloses the seat of justice.[117]

This impressionistic vision of architecture is also reflected in the new approaches to architectural drawing making their appearance at this time. The architects Charles Percier (1764–1838) and Pierre Fontaine (1762–1853), who were first responsible around 1800 for reappraising the merits of Renaissance architecture, tried to magnify the latter's "picturesque effect" with their linear interior perspectives: often by placing the spectator under the curved framing line of a vaulted enclosure. In perspectives such as those for the Farnese and Massimi palaces in Rome, it is nearly impossible to distinguish what is enclosed and what is open to the sky.[118] This scenographic device was advanced in the nineteenth century by the studies of Pierre Gauthier (1789–1855) and Paul-Marie Letarouilly (1795–1855) (Pl. 57). In his folio of 1818 on the palaces of Genoa, Gauthier not only defended the use of the perspective in design presentations but also extolled the theatrical effects that could be captured by them. Letarouilly's *Edifices de Rome moderne* greatly expanded the studies of Percier and Fontaine into three volumes, bringing into play other building types under the same scenographic layout.[119]

Semper certainly studied the spatial and representational devices of both authors. On his trip to Paris in the winter of 1838–39, he purchased Gauthier's *Les plus beaux édifices de la Ville de Gênes* and the first volume of Letarouilly's *Edifices de Rome moderne.*[120] He recommended both works in lectures to his students in the 1840s – no doubt also for their Renaissance models. And when, in the mid-1840s, he laid out his interior perspective of the Dresden Theater (Pl. 58), he framed it not from behind the stage, as Schinkel framed his theater in his published designs, but from the curved rear of the auditorium, from underneath the first tier of loges, thereby endowing the image of the stage with considerable visual tension.

Yet Semper's sense of theatricality in architecture should not be interpreted simply as a sensitivity toward visual and spatial imagery. His feeling for spatial drama during his Dresden years was, in fact, still at an early stage of development. His architecture during this period is characterized, rather, by a certain fleshiness or corporeality that takes delight in exquisite material execution and detailing – a tendency that later will be better described by his notion of "dressing." To this sensuousness must be added the intellectual or didactic content of both his early and later monumental works: his heavy reliance on iconography, allegory, pictorial and plastic elaboration, as is perhaps made more explicit in the Dresden Art Gallery. Once again, we see in Semper's designs of the 1840s the conception of architecture as a grand unity of effects gleaned from all the fine arts: his powerful use of painting, sculpture, and architectonic form to animate and enliven surfaces.

The German language, of course, has a word for this artistic conception – *Gesamtkunstwerk* – the "synthesis of the arts." It is a theatrical conception already articulated by Semper in *Preliminary Remarks on Polychrome Architecture* but it is also an idea that – notwithstanding its wide diffusion at this time – is today almost universally attributed to Richard Wagner.

57 Paul-Marie Letarouilly, Villa di Papa Giulio. From *Edifices de Rome moderne.*

58 Gottfried Semper, Dresden Hoftheater, 1835–41. Interior perspective from Semper's *Das königliche Hoftheater zu Dresden* (1849).

Although affinities between the artistic visions of Semper and Wagner have on occasion been noted, no one has really emphasized the extent to which the intellectual and artistic ideas of these two individuals not only converged but also found support in one another.

Various passages from their writings, in fact, are so close in subject and outlook that they could have been penned by the same person. The profoundly religious and civic expression of the Greek temple and theater, the necessity of a people or nation to institute a spiritual alliance and partake of its communal utterance, the decline of the individual arts after the dissolution of this beautiful synthesis in classical times – all are themes that Semper and Wagner expounded in unison. Given these similarities, it is small wonder that their conversations in Dresden during the 1840s were often intense.[121]

Wagner's views regarding architecture, as articulated in *The Future Work of Art* (1850), provide further insights. For him, the demi-urge for a self-conscious architecture grew out of no mundane impulse or craven need, but emanated in unison with the other arts in a moment of high dramatic necessity. In alluding to the ancient sanctuary first mentioned by Homer in the *Iliad*, he gave full range to his wildly Romantic vision:

> Before the *divine oak* at Dodona, the *original Hellene* bowed in anticipation of the natural oracle. Beneath the shady thatch of leaves and surrounded by the verdant tree-columns of the *god's sacred grove*, the *priest* raised his voice. Under the beautiful structured gabled roof and among the ingeniously arranged marble columns of the divine temple, the happy and artistic *lyric poet* choreographed his dance to the sounds of the metric hymn. And in the *theater* that was raised around the altar to the gods (as its centerpoint), with its oracular stage and broad spaces reserved for the audience seeking understanding, the *tragic actor* performed the most vital work of the most perfect art.[122]

It was thus in a primitive natural commune that mankind first came to fashion artistic impulses, that architecture as an art was called into being through the collective epiphany (to use a Wagnerian term) of the temple and theater. Only in the "sweet repose and noble charm" of these two building forms, Wagner argued, arose the true spiritual meaning of architecture. When Greek drama began to decline, so did architecture; in Rome this art gave vent to its individual excesses by displaying the false values of luxury and egoism. Conversely: "Only with the redemption of the egoistically isolated and purely human arts into the collective future work of art, with the redemption of the *utilitarian man* into the future *artistic man*, will architecture also find redemption from the bonds of serfdom and its curse of impotency and become the freest, most inexhaustibly creative artistic activity."[123] Thus the most compelling artistic task of the present, for Wagner, was to revive first and foremost the drama (the highest and most perfect union of the arts) and – with it – the theater, the highest calling of architecture: "Only that edifice [the theater] is formed according to necessity when it best serves human needs: the highest human purpose is artistic purpose, the highest artistic purpose is the drama."[124]

And it was this Dresden Hoftheater, of course, that cemented the sometimes intimate, sometimes strained friendship of Semper and Wagner. The latter's artistic fame and maturity, following directly upon Semper's, was achieved mainly in the 1840s. His early works, *Rienzi*, *Der Fliegende Holländer*, and *Tannhäuser*, made their debut on Semper's newly finished stage. And in Wagner's architectural vision of the future theater, we find what seems to be a reiteration of the sentiments rehearsed by Semper in his monograph on the theater. The ideal theater, in Wagner's view, is one in which art alone gives each detail, however insignificant, its law and measure, in which sightlines must be carefully resolved and acoustics absolutely perfected – all in service, of course, to the clarifying oracle of dramatic action. "Everything that breathes and moves upon the stage," says the impassioned Wagner, "breathes and moves through the emphatic desire to commune, to be seen and heard in a space that, although limited in its dimensions, the actor imagines from his scenic standpoint to embrace the whole of mankind."[125] In this edifying burst of activity of almost mystical transfiguration, all reality is suspended and the space of the stage becomes transformed into an impersonal, that is, world-space. The theatrical intention of the architect and dramatist entirely merge into one another: "Such wonders blossom from the building of the architect; he is able to give a real basis and footing to such magic when he takes the intention of this highest human work of art as his own, when he summons forth from his own artistic resources the terms of drama's enlivening."[126]

Even the one specific criticism of contemporary theaters that Wagner made in his essay of 1850 – the undemocratic nature of the loges, by which the public is parceled out into "the most distinct classes and civil stations" – is in complete accord with Semper's assertions in his monograph, his plea for open seating. Wagner wrote his essay *The Future Work of Art* in the second half of 1849, soon after his departure from Dresden. He certainly knew Semper's earlier pamphlet on polychromy, but the monograph on the theater had yet to appear. It is quite possible, however, that Wagner read the text in August 1849 when he visited Semper in Paris, just as the architect was completing the final drawings for the work. In any case, Wagner paid a second visit to Semper in the French capital in February 1850, during which time Wagner asked Semper to read his essay and comment on it.

Thus it seems fair to say that two theatrical composers made their debut in the 1840s upon this Dresden stage. Both took pause at each other's presence. Both took delight in the nuances of their dialogue, and neither flinched before the unreal harshness of the stage lights. And both, after many troubling years had intervened, would later join their talents in a theatrical encore of truly astounding, monumental proportions.

Setbacks in Hamburg

In contrast to the fame and professional accolades that Semper enjoyed during his fifteen years in Dresden, there was during these same years a series of less successful and more painful encounters with his native city of Hamburg. Indeed, this parallel scenario composes a fascinating, if not a distended story of its own – one filled with more than its share of personal duplicity, petty jealousies, political and civic mismanagement.

Semper's first contact with his native city after his departure for Saxony grew out of the architectural competition for a new trading exchange building, which was announced in Hamburg on 31 January 1837. As a seaport town and "free city" whose economy was based in part upon international trade, the Hamburg Exchange had always been an important symbol for the city. The first open markets for the sale of commodities were set up as early as the sixteenth century. Between 1791 and 1830 numerous attempts were made to build a new and more modern exchange, but a series of calamities – economic setbacks, wars, plagues, Napoleonic occupation, political infighting, and, in general, the unwillingness of the city fathers to spend the money – had repeatedly conspired to defeat its realization. The architect Axel Bundsen had proposed more than a dozen schemes for a new exchange in the 1820s, and it was the defeat of his last design in 1829, in fact, that had inspired the student Semper, then residing in Paris, to make his first design for the exchange in 1830.

In 1834, the year Semper moved to Dresden, the project was again revived and over the next couple of years the issue slowly moved its way through the political bureaucracy. The first hurdle, an exploratory committee, was formed in 1835; the following year the city Senate gave preliminary approval for the building. In 1836 an architectural commission was appointed to write a program, set down the guidelines of an architectural competition, and see the building through construction. It was headed by the attorney Johann Christian Kauffmann, but largely controlled by Senator Christian Matthias Schröder. One of its members, as it turns out, was Friedrich Heeren, Semper's former roommate at Göttingen and travel companion to France.[127]

But the final building program, written by the consulting architects Carl Ludwig Wimmel (1786–1845) and Franz Forsmann (1795–1878), was not specific in many of its details, and the amount of money budgeted for the building was deemed by many potential competitors to be grossly inadequate. Thus the competition, once it was announced at the start of 1837, got off to a somewhat rocky start when nine local architectural firms boycotted the event.

Semper was informed of the competition and its ensuing controversy by his friend Franz Georg Stammann, the architect who had just completed his Donner Pavilion and who was still awaiting payment from either Donner or Semper for his services. Stammann wrote Semper twice in early February, discussing the "disgrace" of the program, the poor site, the lack of an adequate budget, and the selection of an artistically unsophisticated jury – composed, as it was, of two senators and eight businessmen. Stammann urged his colleague to write a critical article about the event in a Dresden newspaper and send copies to him in Hamburg, so that it could be used by the disgruntled local architects as fodder in their campaign to scuttle the project.[128] Semper's response is not preserved, although he probably declined Stammann's request.

The local architects, in any case, were unsuccessful in their tactics and various designs were submitted to the jury on the first of May. Two weeks later Stammann reported to Semper that the committee had received around thirty projects (actually twenty-six) from architects as far away as London, Munich, and Berlin; he remained convinced, however, that only "stupidity and arrogance" would prevail in the choice of the best project.[129] The competition submissions that have survived (Pls. 59, 60) vary considerably in their quality. One of the most talented local architects, Alexis de Châteauneuf, a student of Gärtner, submitted a Schinkelesque pseudo-medieval scheme. Another project of interest was the accomplished Greek design of J. Andreas Romberg, an architect who would in a few years become better known for his editorship of the architectural journal *Zeitschrift für praktische Baukunst*.

What Stammann did not know in May was that Semper was already secretly involved with the competition, although not in the way that his friend had initially hoped. Shortly after Semper had received his first letter from Stammann in early February, he had also been appraised of the Hamburg proceedings by his old gymnasium friend Eduard Sthamer, who had since been elected a senator.[130] Sometime during the winter or early spring, Sthamer, who was put off by the behavior of the boycotting architects, convinced Semper

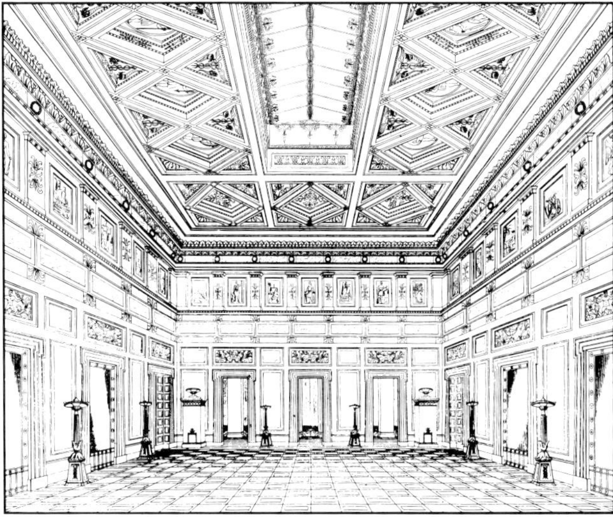

60 J. Andreas Romberg, competition design for the Hamburg Exchange, 1837. Staatarchiv Hamburg.

59 (left) Alexis de Châteauneuf, competition design for the Hamburg Exchange, 1837. Staatarchiv Hamburg.

that it would be in his interest to submit an unofficial design for the Exchange privately to the committee, as an alternative or fall-back proposal to the official schemes. This ethical lapse on Sthamer's and Semper's part seems not to have been the only impropriety here. Wimmel and Forsmann, who had written the architectural program and were employed as professional consultants to the committee, had also entered the anonymous competition with their separate schemes.

What happened next was a series of miscalculations and political intrigues. When Semper sent his scheme to Sthamer, he refused to send the prescribed budget for the design, arguing that the amount allotted by the program was inadequate. He also laid down a set of conditions for the acceptance of his project, among them that his "ideas" would not be used by other architects and that if his scheme were approved, he would have complete control of its execution.[131] The committee, it seems, had quite naively left open the possibility of combining parts of various schemes and appointing their own contractor if no single winner emerged. Semper's scheme (Pls. 61, 62), which has only recently resurfaced, resembled a Renaissance palace, and consisted of a rectangular building block with a central trading hall. Tucked behind the arcade of one facade, situated along a canal, were two monumental staircases, reminiscent of but running in the opposite direction to Schinkel's solution for his Berlin museum. Semper's design was competent but by no means superior to most of the other schemes.

In early May Sthamer presented Semper's proposal privately to his colleague Senator Schröder, who appears to have welcomed the secret entry but was perplexed by the architect's conditions. This is not surprising in view of the more utilitarian issues upon which much of the work of the committee was focused. For instance, the principal issue of debate engaging the committee during this time was the question of whether the exchange would have a central heating plant.

Throughout the month of June, Sthamer continued to inform Semper (almost on a daily basis) of the jury's private deliberations, in particular the jury's fascination with a scheme by an undisclosed Berlin architect.[132] At the start of July, Semper was still wrangling with Sthamer over his conditions and even threatened to withdraw his unofficial project if his demands were not met. He also continued to balk at submitting a budget proposal, but sent two revised drawings – an elevation and a perspective (both now apparently lost), in which he added a campanile to this scheme as a civic gesture.[133]

By the middle of July the jury deliberations had stalled and Sthamer saw his opening. He sidestepped gingerly Semper's demands (the jury had been adamant in adhering to the conditions of the program) and presented Semper's scheme formally to the jury with a letter explaining that this native son had been deterred from officially entering the competition because of the boycott by local architects, and that, out of civic pride, he would give his scheme to the committee free of charge, providing that he exercise sole artistic authority throughout construction.[134] Sthamer also advised Semper at this time to go public with his design and provide the jury with an honorable way out of the controversy by denigrating not the jury itself but the program that they had been forced to follow. In this way the jury could award the two prizes to official participants but give the actual commission to his non-official scheme. The jury seems to have had no qualms at this suggestion, but what Sthamer did not know was that the committee members were also being lobbied on behalf of Wimmel and Forsmann for a similar resolution of the competition in their favor. In a secret vote taken near the end of July, in fact, the jury awarded the commission to Wimmel and Forsmann.[135]

Both Sthamer and Semper, as well as the public, were unaware of this decision. The controversy surrounding the competition continued through August as the drawings (minus Semper's scheme) were first put on public display. Romberg published a stinging critique of many of the projects during that time. Sthamer, who was still optimistic of Semper's success in the first part of August, advised Semper to make his design known to Stammann, in the hope that the local architects who had excluded themselves from the competition might rally around his design.[136] This was highly improbable as the local firms, now believing that no consensus had been reached, wanted to be considered again for the project. Finally, in the middle of the month the jury announced its decision and awarded two prizes, but it also recommended that neither be built. Only in September did the jury finally admit that Wimmel and Forsmann had been hired to collaborate on a new scheme. Semper, whose covert design may have prompted this resolution, was thus handed a rather stinging defeat. Wimmel and Forsmann's new building – an admirable architectural work – opened in the spring of 1841, a few weeks after Semper celebrated the first performance at his court theater.

It is unclear whether Semper, who was still without the official commission for the Dresden Theater, would have moved back to Hamburg in 1837 had he been awarded the commission for the Hamburg Exchange, but his desire to return to his native city becomes

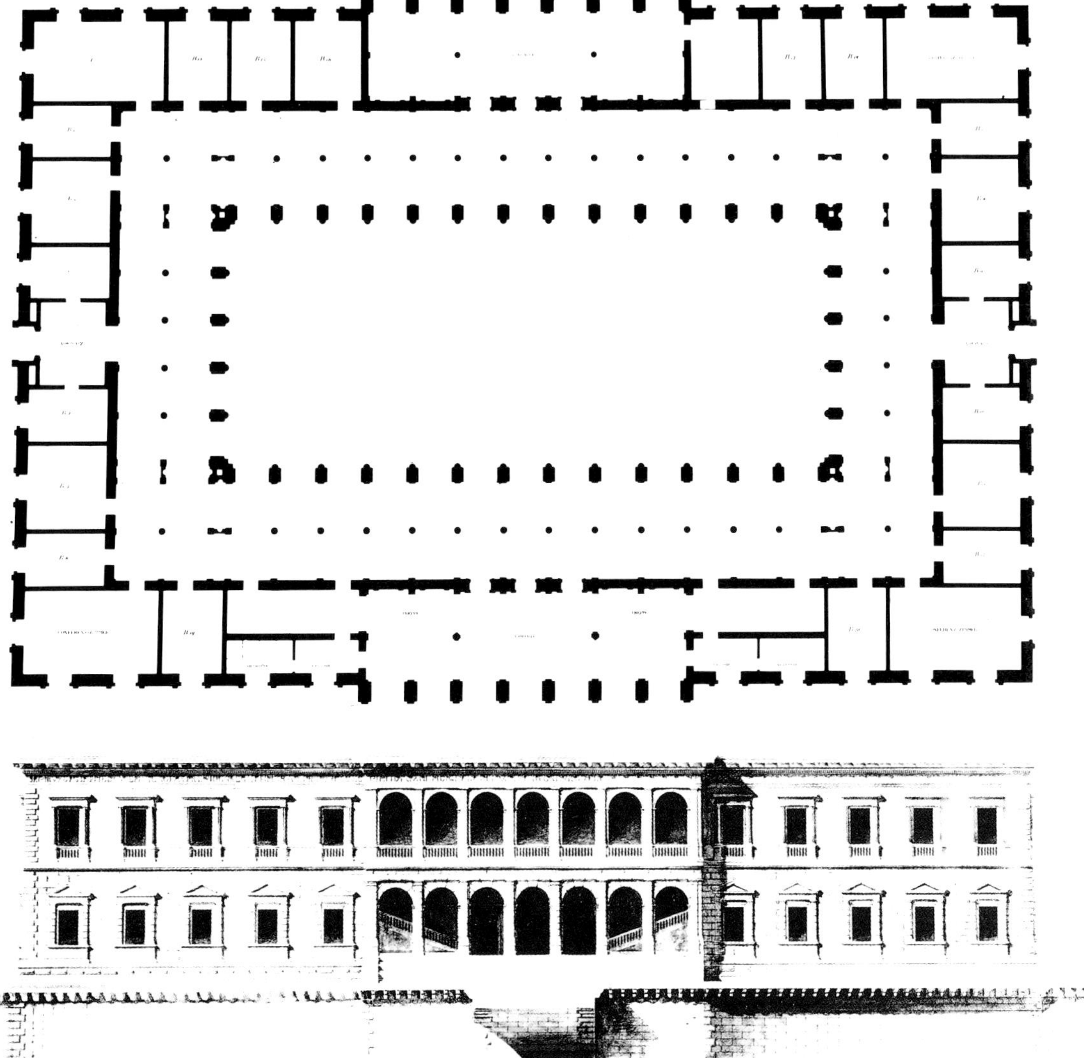

61 and 62 Gottfried Semper, competition design for the Hamburg Exchange, 1837. Top: plan. Bottom: elevation. Institut für Denkmalpflege, Dresden.

clear from two other contacts he had there, the first of which took place in the spring of 1842.

The immediate cause for this involvement was the great fire that devastated the heart of the old city in early May. Over a three-day period, between 5 and 8 May, more than 60,000 people, almost one-third of the population, had been forced to flee their dwellings; 20,000 people had been left homeless by the blaze. Nearly every major building in the center of the city had sustained severe damage (Pl. 63). Architecturally, the greatest loss was the city's cathedral, the Nikolaikirche or church of St. Nicholas. One of the few buildings left standing after the conflagration, oddly enough, was the new Exchange, which had been saved by a heroic effort. Semper was first informed of the blaze in a letter from his mother dated 7 May. Three days later his brother Carl sent him a plan of the burned-out area, along with the news that their brother Wilhelm's newly purchased pharmacy, together with his home and belongings, had been lost. Semper immediately left Dresden on a hurried trip north.

The city authorities moved rapidly in the wake of the devastation.[137] On 9 May the English engineer William Lindley (1808–1900), who for several years had lived in Hamburg as the engineer in charge of constructing the new rail line to Berlin, began working on a plan for rebuilding the city. He completed his first proposal on 12 May and submitted it to the Senate. One week later, a technical commission consisting of several architects and engineers was officially called into being to plan the massive task of reconstruction. Lindley was elected its chairman.

On 19 or 20 May, at his mother's home in Altona, Semper received an unexpected visit from his friend Sthamer, who had advised him on the earlier competition. Sthamer, now speaking on behalf of the Senate, urged Semper to participate in the meetings of the technical commission as a special advisor. Semper hesitated at first but soon felt that the exceptional nature of the situation warranted an affirmative response to this urgent request. Over the next seven days he attended all of the commission's lengthy meetings in Hamburg as an outside observer and made various and important contributions.

Semper's work for the commission initiated a series of events that consumed much of his energy over the next three years – energy spent almost entirely in vain. These problems grew out of the make-up of the initial commission, which was ill-chosen for the particular task at hand. Lindley, although a highly competent engineer, had no particular talent or interest in the artistic aspects of city planning. In his plan for rebuilding the city, he was guided solely by such technical concerns as the optimal placement of the sewer lines. And other architects on the commission, among them Wimmel, were not particularly happy to have their erstwhile rival from Dresden suddenly brought into the deliberations. Moreover, Semper as an outsider observer had no real authority or power, even though in the end he dominated the commission's work.

The result was almost predictable and generated almost as much heat as the fire itself. At the very first session, Semper read to the commission a lengthy memorandum that encouraged the creation of urban squares and the demolition and relocation of the extensively damaged Nikolaikirche.[138] He rejected Lindley's first plan, which had imposed a rigid street grid on the city's old historic center. Over the next few days Semper – taking Venice as his model – began sketching an alternative plan that sought to connect a series of religious and civic monuments with one another and with the city's waterways. At the heart of his plan was the preserved Trading Exchange, which he placed within a large urban forum, adjacent to a new city hall. The axis formed by the new City Hall and Exchange connected in a northeastern direction with a series of streets and squares parallel to the Alster Basin. To the south of the City Hall, across another canal, Semper created another large urban square, in which he placed the rebuilt markets and new Nikolaikirche, shifted slightly from its original site.

Semper's proposal, sketched on 26 May, seems to have met with little understanding. One engineer on the commission, Heinrich Hübbe, reported that Semper's scheme had certainly broadened and enlivened the discussion, although he was uncertain as to just what end.[139] Apparently many of the other commission members felt the same way, for two days later, on 28 May, Lindley's plan was approved unanimously by the committee with a few small changes. The published version of the plan contained an addendum in

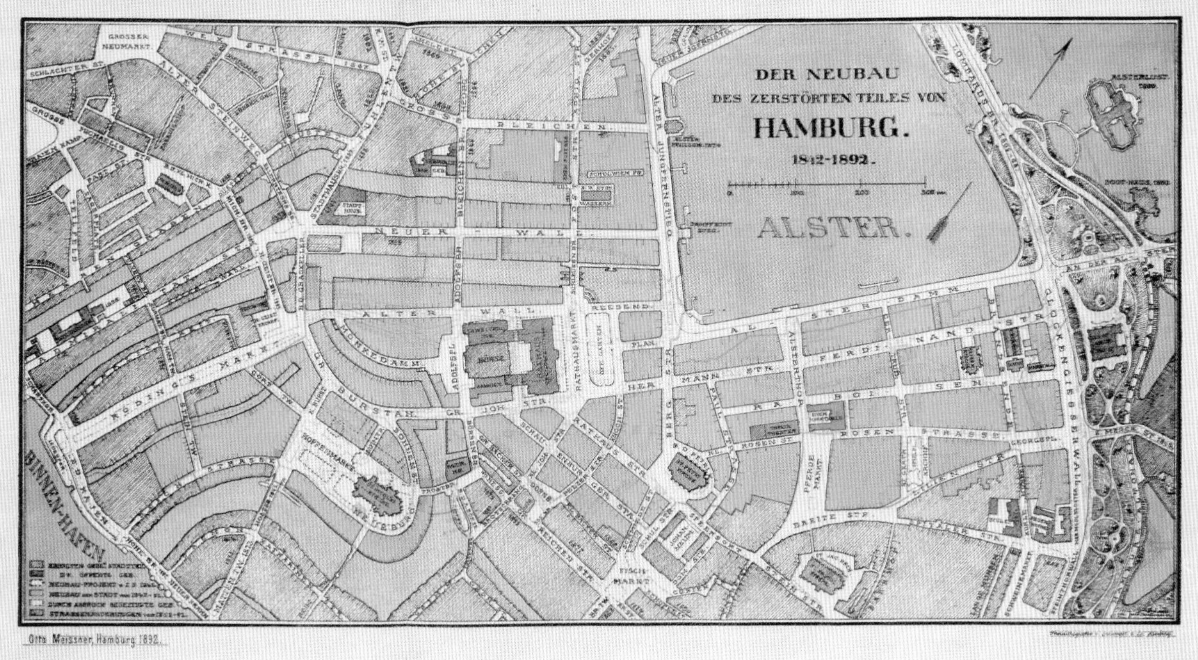

63 (top) Hamburg, parts of the city destroyed by the fire of 5–8 May 1842. From Julius Faulwasser, *Der grosse Brand und der Wiederaufbau von Hamburg*.

64 Hamburg, rebuilding plan of August 1842. From Julius Faulwasser, *Der grosse Brand und der Wiederaufbau von Hamburg*.

which Semper once again decried the emphasis that had been placed on utilitarian issues at the expense of an artistic restructuring and revitalization of the urban center, all of which he felt could be implemented with little or no additional cost.[140] The next day he returned to Dresden, no doubt feeling that he had accomplished little despite his efforts.

But the matter was not yet finished as Lindley's plan soon came in for its share of criticism, both directly and indirectly through a number of alternative proposals. On 5 June, the architect Friedrich Stammann, the brother of Franz Georg, published his plan for the city. During the same month the architect Carl Friedrich Riechardt published a brochure that severely criticized Lindley's plan for its lack of artistic sensitivity. Other alternative proposals were soon put forth by the architects W. D. Holmes and Wimmel. The most significant development, however, was the restructuring of the technical commission and the replacement of Lindley with Alexis de Châteauneuf, an architect of some ability.

Châteauneuf was sympathetic to Semper's artistic ideals, but at the same time he was warding off political pressure to come up quickly with a revised final plan. On 16 June a second commission, known as Advisory and Citizens' Council, was formed to review the first commission's plan, raise money, and revise the expropriation laws and building codes for its rapid execution. Throughout the month of July, Châteauneuf orchestrated a sensitive revision of the Lindley plan (Pl. 64), which gave greater attention to the urban spaces surrounding the City Hall (now relocated east of the Exchange) and to the area around the burned-out church of St. Nicholas. The new scheme further developed the suggestions made by Semper for creating urban foci and relating the canals to the new urban spaces. The modified plan was approved by the first commission at the start of August and by the advisory council a few weeks later.

Semper, meanwhile, was no passive observer of these developments. As early as June he wrote to Sthamer and another friend Voight, discussing with both men his possible relocation to Hamburg. Not only had the fire created a glut of architectural work but Semper was also interested in an official position, either with the city or with one of the rebuilding committees. Both men strongly discouraged his efforts and urged him to keep his permanent position in Dresden. Sthamer argued that Hamburg with its mercantile spirit was an exceptionally bad place for anyone with artistic talent, and in any case Semper had already made quite a name for himself in Germany – a reputation that would be little respected in his native city. Voight answered in a similar vein, pointing out that the bureaucratic offices were already filled and that a talented architect would not survive six months in such a contentious atmosphere anyway.

Semper continued to receive reports from Sthamer and family members on the work of the committees. Toward the end of August, as the revised plan of the first technical commission was receiving its final approval, Châteauneuf, through a mutual acquaintance, sent Semper two copies of the plan with an expression of gratitude for his efforts. He even solicited from Semper his critique of the final plan.[141] Semper, of course, was not one to let such an opening pass. He soon prepared a revision of the areas around the church of St. Nicholas and the proposed City Hall. He made a perspective design for the new City Hall, which – from its Venice-like vantage point on a canal – depicted a crenellated parapet and a tall picturesque tower. This was the drawing he exhibited at the architects' congress in the following year.

Semper decided to take up his fight in the Senate as well. He sent another sketch of his

City Hall to Sthamer, who dutifully distributed it to his senate colleagues. Semper should have known that he was waging a hopeless battle. With the plan for rebuilding now approved by the two commissions there was little possibility for any further revisions. Châteauneuf, if anything, seemed puzzled by the revised sketches, since he felt the final plan had already been quite sympathetic to Semper's original design.

The only concrete thing to emerge from this phase of his involvement with the city was his design for his brother's pharmacy (Pl. 65), whose construction began in 1843. Given a free hand artistically, Semper chose an early Renaissance facade for this urban townhouse, which contained the apothecary on the ground floor, his brother's residence on the main floor, and rental apartments above. The rusticated masonry of the lower story was cut and finished in Dresden and shipped down the Elbe by barge. For the upper stories Semper decided on an elaborate sgraffito ornamentation, carried out by the Dresden artist who had worked on the Hoftheater.

The design in all of its attributes related to the meaning of a pharmacy. The sculptural figure in the center of the main story is St. George, the patron saint of health and pharmaceutical endeavors. On the parapets of the two balconies are depicted a griffin and a sphinx, the protectors of nature's secrets. The four figures between the windows of the second floor represent the Oriental, Chinese, Negro, and European races and regions, from which the raw materials (portrayed by the baskets with fruits and plants) for a pharmacy are imported. In the frieze above boys are depicted playing with retorts, a still, mortars, bellows, and other laboratory equipment. Interspersed are the interactions of the four elements. The same four elements are repeated above as four seated women. Once again, Semper put much effort into his narrative depicting the building's use. The architectural journal *Allgemeine Bauzeitung*, in publishing the plates of the building in 1848, felt it was one of the few genuinely artistic solutions to the middle-class house to appear in Hamburg since the great fire.[142]

With the plan for Hamburg now approved and the city starting to rebuild, Semper next turned his attention to the problem of the church of St. Nicholas, the oldest part of which dated from 1195. This historic building posed a most delicate architectural question: the problem of whether to raze it and build anew or reuse whatever parts of the older church could be salvaged. Opinion was sharply divided in December 1842, as many parties vied for attention. Semper had earlier concurred with the technical commission in opting for the demolition of the old church, but more recent structural investigations had raised the possibility that the foundations, parts of some walls, and perhaps the tower could be saved.

By the end of December Semper had changed his mind, and he came down firmly on the side of rebuilding the existing work. He announced this shift in a letter to Sthamer at the end of December 1842, in which he also sent along a sketch of his design.[143] His argument for preserving what remained of the church was twofold: the economic advantages of salvaging the old work as well as its historic importance as a landmark to the city. Sthamer distributed the letter to his colleagues. On the day after Semper mailed his letter to Sthamer, he received from Hamburg three letters from friends there – the painters Martin Gensler and Otto Speckter, and the architect Theodor Bülau – all urging him to join their efforts in saving the tower. Bülau, who had been a close friend of Semper since their earlier time together in Regensburg, thought the tower could serve as a memorial to the fire by becoming a hose tower for the fire department.

In reversing his position regarding the church, Semper may have sensed the changing

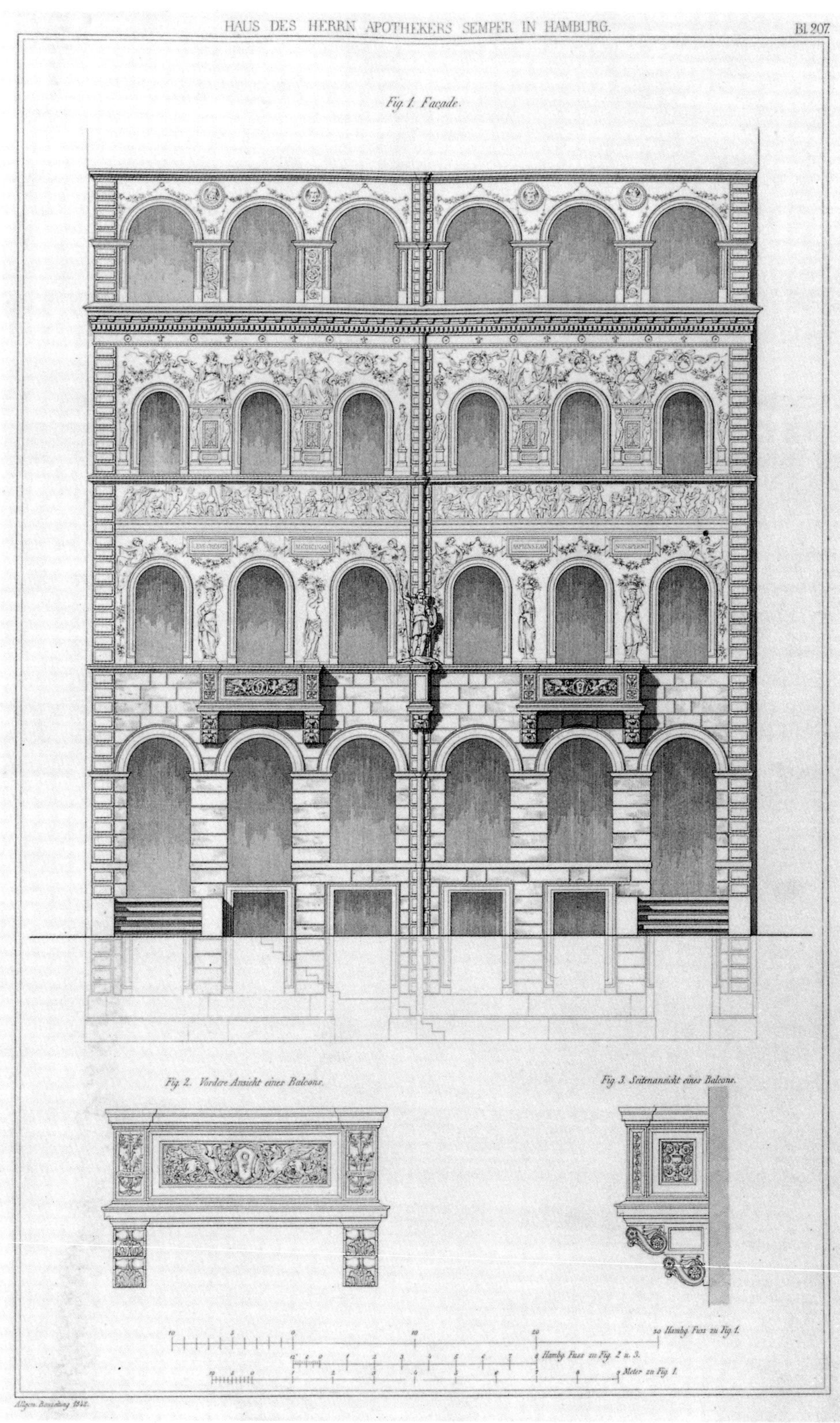

65 Gottfried Semper, apothecary for Wilhelm Semper, 1843. From *Allgemeine Bauzeitung*. Courtesy The Getty Center for the History of Art and the Humanities.

course of public opinion in Hamburg. He was also moved to re-examine his earlier ideas as he was simultaneously preparing a report on the preservation and rebuilding of the cathedral at Meissen, published in January 1843. In the report, Semper referred to the changing attitudes toward medieval architecture, the greater appreciation and respect for the masterpieces of the twelfth, thirteenth, and fourteenth centuries, the artistic lessons that can be gleaned from the study of these works. "From out of the labyrinth of the conflicting tendencies of modern artistic efforts," he noted, "it even seems as if Ariadne's thread could most surely be found if we were to return to those truly national principles and apply them to our time. False originality would thereby be held in check and many new elements would lie open to the true artist for specific development."[144] As Wolfgang Herrmann has shown, Semper had been quite receptive to the beauty of both Romanesque and Gothic architecture up to this stage in his career, demonstrating a flexibility that – from someone who built in a quite different manner – was relatively rare within the sharpening style debate of the 1840s.[145]

His efforts in Hamburg now conformed, for a while at least, with these nationalist tendencies, as the political factions in the city coalesced. Hübbe was the most prominent member of the technical commission lobbying for the church's preservation; he was opposed by the commissioner Wimmel, who was also the city architect in charge of the Nikolaikirche and therefore in line to receive the commission for a new building. Many reports were produced over the next few months, advocating both sides of the issue.

As the controversy was entering its final stage, in mid-January, Semper received a supportive letter from Châteauneuf, who suggested that the time of reckoning was at hand and that Semper's interests would best be served by coming to Hamburg. Châteauneuf also expressed the hope that Semper might thereby gain the architectural commission for rebuilding the church.[146] Two other plans for rebuilding the old church surfaced at this time, both of which have been attributed to Semper.[147] One depicts a Gothic church modeled on the cathedral at Regensburg; the other is a centralized design, most likely Romanesque in style. Bülau, who in the 1820s and 1830s had prepared the large monograph on the Regensburg work, may also have played a role in overlaying the Regensburg design on the old Nikolaikirche foundations. Sthamer was also encouraging Semper to come to Hamburg, and in the middle of February he once again traveled north.

The ostensible reason for this trip was to set in motion the construction of Wilhelm's pharmacy and residence, for which Semper engaged the supervisory services of the local architect Heinrich Wilhelm Burmester. During his stay, however, Semper quietly teamed up with Burmester in preparing a report on the old church, complete with floor plans, sections, and elevations. The report was finished by 4 March. In it, Semper and Burmester proposed rebuilding the church in a late-Gothic style, employing the old foundations and incorporating the damaged tower. The latter was to be structurally reinforced on each side by a pair of tall flying buttresses.[148]

This work, however, once again came to naught. Even though Semper's report was soon backed up by two additional structural studies by Hübbe and Burmester, the technical commission once again proved itself incapable of reaching a decision. Wimmel, who wanted the old church and tower torn down, prepared a negative report for the commission in April; other objections were raised concerning the high cost of preserving the old fabric, although it almost certainly would have cost less than starting a new church from scratch. During the spring and summer the issue bounced back and forth between the governing church council, the technical commission, the advisory and citizen's council, and the Senate. Finally, the faction led by Wimmel proved victorious and the latter's plan for the church's demolition was approved by the commission in late July 1843. The Senate gave its consent in September.

The demolition of the historic monument prepared the way for a new church, which was now to serve as the single great symbol of the city's rebuilding efforts. The design of the church was not given to Wimmel, but instead a major architectural competition was announced. The governing church council was dissolved by the Senate in favor of a new competition committee. With all of the difficulties that the city had recently had with its numerous other committees and commissions, one might have hoped that a more judicious choice of committee members would have been made. But the political leaders had learned nothing from their earlier mistakes and the expertise of the jurors for the new architectural competititon could not have more incomprehensible: one senator, one attorney, eight businessmen, and a painter. As Bernd Franck has noted, it had no one with architectural knowledge or experience and no one representing the parish of the church.[149] These omissions would prove disastrous to nearly everyone involved.

In the winter of 1844 the committee slowly tackled the difficult task of writing the program for the competition. Such a program is difficult to write because if its lacks the necessary detail, if the most basic design decisions are not defined in specific ways, the competitors face the prospect of having many weeks, if not months, of hard work quickly eliminated by some unknown bias on the part of the jury. The committee prescribed a church with a seating capacity of 1200–1400 people, and a total standing capacity of 3000 people. The program gave no indication of the form or style to be employed in the design, although a tower was mandated. The program was published at the end of May 1844; the competition schemes were required in Hamburg by the end of November.[150]

Semper, of course, was very intent on participating and felt confident he could win the competition. He asked both Burmester and his brother Wilhelm to send him the program as soon as it was printed. During the summer months he labored intensively over his competition design, and in the end he produced a stunning solution of great originality (Pls. 66, 67).

The design in its stylistic features contained both Romanesque and Renaissance elements. At the heart of the scheme was a large hall, square in plan, crowned with a tall drum and elongated dome, reminiscent of Brunelleschi's dome for Santa Maria del Fiori in Florence. Around the hall was grouped a lively ensemble of lower towers, apses, choir, nave, and narthex, all lending structural support to the superstructure. Since the church, like its predecessor, was to be constructed out of brick, this solution, which was so happy in both its interior use and exterior forms, was logical and economical. The full force of the work within its urban context was captured in a large sepia perspective drawing that Semper prepared (Pl. 68), the earlier version of which appears as if drawn for a stage set. Its artistic spirit and imagination, in fact, had few parallels in all of nineteenth-century church building, although it calls to mind H. H. Richardson's similarly polychrome Romanesque design of the 1870s for Trinity Church in Boston.

By autumn, however, Semper began to have doubts about how well his scheme would be received or interpreted. He first feared that his tall dome might not be considered a "tower," and he set to work on a variation of his design in which the dome was replaced by a more conventional tower. He then wrote to Wilhelm in November, asking him to

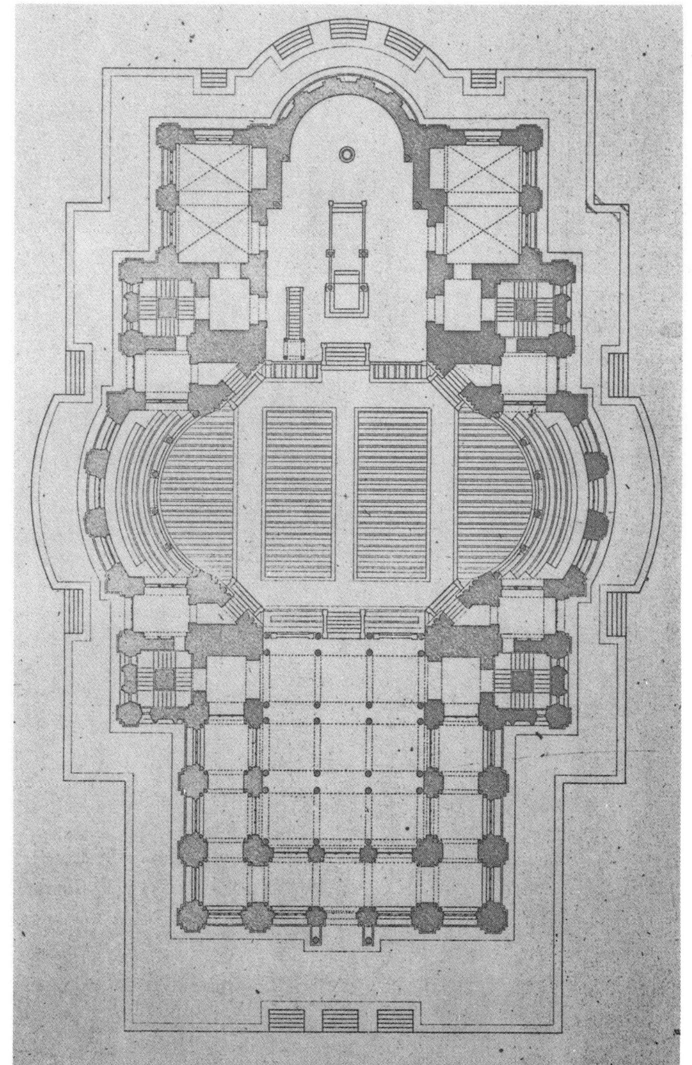

66 and 67 Gottfried Semper, competition for the church of St. Nicholas. 1844. Above left: plan. Above right: section. Institut für Geschichte und Theorie der Architectur, Semper Archiv, ETH-Zurich.

approach someone from the competition committee and ask if the committee had any objections to a domed church in the "Byzantine" style.[151]

Wilhelm spoke with two committee members separately and neither had any objections in theory to such a scheme. Semper, however, was already at work on an alternative Gothic scheme (Pl. 69), although by now he had no hope of finishing it on time. He did manage to complete it in late December and sent it to the committee in January. Most of the competition entries arrived on time and were publicly displayed from the middle of December through to the middle of January. A late scheme by the English architect George Gilbert Scott (1811–78), which had been held up in Cuxhaven by an early frost, was allowed into the competition. Altogether, there were forty-four schemes sent in by thirty-nine architects.

Semper's logic in coming up with the particular scheme that he did was indicative of both his strengths and weaknesses as an architect and tactician. In an age when architects

68 Gottfried Semper, competition for the church of St. Nicholas. Perspective, 1844. Institut für Geschichte und Theorie de Architectur, Semper Archiv, ETH-Zurich.

increasingly prided themselves on their historical learnedness, when designs were sometimes pasted together from sketches collected in notebooks on travels across the continent, Semper remained to some extent the exception. Not only did he consider design to be a creative or artistic process but also a dialectical one, that is to say, one indicative of a certain amount of soul-searching for the proper means of expression. Given the state of crisis that architecture was perceived to be in, he felt it imperative to examine the premises of each building type and to make departures whenever necessary from accepted norms and practices.

69 Gottfried Semper, competition for the church of St. Nicholas. Gothic variant. 1844. Institut für Geschichte und Theorie der Architectur, Semper Archiv, ETH-Zurich.

But the Hamburg competition for the Nikolaikirche must also be seen against the backdrop of the great excitement and expectations raised by the resumption of construction of Cologne Cathedral. The recent decision to complete this Gothic work, on which construction had been suspended in the sixteenth century, resonated with political overtones. Napoleon had partially incorporated the Rhineland into France in 1801 and after 1815 the control of this region went to Prussia. The people of Catholic Rhineland, however, harbored a deep distrust of Lutheran Prussia and their minority status within the Prussian government. As a concession to Rhenish Catholics, Friedrich Wilhelm IV, upon his ascension to the throne in 1840, pledged 50,000 thalers a year toward the completion of the work. After another two years of deliberations, the Rhineland finally agreed to match his expenditure. The young architect Ernst Zwirner (1802–61), who as early as 1833 had prepared plans for the completion of the Cathedral in consultation with Schinkel, was placed in charge of the work. The Prussians saw the Cathedral, for the most part, as a symbol of German nationhood; the Rhenish people, however, saw it rather as a monument to Catholic Rhineland. In any case, the new cornerstone was laid on 4 September 1842, that is, as the future of the Nikolaikirche was about to be decided.

Impelling this work forward were various religious reform movements in Germany, led by such disparate personalities as Sulpiz Boisserée (1783–1854) and August Reichensperger (1808–95). The older Boisserée, who was perhaps best known for his remarkable collection of early German paintings, had long-standing ties to German Romanticism and was a friend of Goethe, Friedrich Schlegel, and Ludwig Tieck. Even though his view of Gothic architecture was shaped by Romanticism, he had established himself as a leading authority of this historical period. The younger Reichensperger, by contrast, was representative of a younger generation whose connection to Gothic architecture was more religious than Romantic in origin.[152] He was a zealous follower of Augustus Welby Pugin and a vocal protagonist in the style debate of the 1840s. He viewed the reimposition of Gothic architecture and Catholic practice, the former in its most authentic form possible, largely in terms of a religious crusade that would, in his view, subsequently revive society as a whole. The Gothic Revival and its allied reform movements, of course, were not limited to Germany, although they sometimes took on different characteristics in other countries. Like Pugin in England, French architects were active in the 1840s, led by Eugène-Emmanuel Viollet-le-Duc and Jean-Baptiste-Antoine Lassus, who were working on the restoration of Notre Dame in Paris (1846–50).

In his lectures of this time, Semper generally spoke favorably of the constructional logic, interior perspectives, and spatial grandeur of Gothic works, even though among medieval works he preferred the compositional possibilities of the Romanesque.[153] His criticisms of Gothic works really related to his sense of form and for the most part centered on Gothic architecture's lack of exterior wall surface, which to him presented "the impression of being unfinished or as if it still needs to be clad."[154] On another occasion this criticism transformed itself into the view that Gothic works reveal too much "openwork," as if they "were in the process of being built, surrounded by scaffolding."[155]

In preparing his scheme for the church of St. Nicholas, however, Semper rationalized his design in a different way. In both his written explanation to his competition drawings and in the later defense of his scheme, he stressed the appropriateness of the more centralized floor plan for Lutheran church services, and conversely the inappropriateness of the long nave of the traditional Gothic cathedral. Liturgically, the long Gothic nave and basilica division of the church had evolved from Catholic processional rites and the daily celebration of the mass, often taking place simultaneously at various altars. The Gothic style, he believed, further embodied the hierarchy of the Roman Catholic Church, whose service centered around the priest bringing forth the act of transubstantiation. The Lutheran service, he insisted, was more community-oriented and egalitarian in its features, and thus emphasis should be given to the communal prayers, readings, and songs. These activities demanded the closeness or proximity of its participants. To these liturgical distinctions there were also added some stylistic questions:

> A theater must surely remind us of a Roman theater if it is to have character. A Gothic theater is incomprehensible. Churches in the old-Doric or even in the Renaissance style of the 16th century have no spiritual meaning for us. With this viewpoint we agree. Even if this were not so, it would still be impossible to invent a brand-new style; only the gradual passage of time, following many changes, imperceptibly brings forth altogether dissimilar results.[156]

Thus, although initially wavering between a Romanesque or a Gothic-inspired solution,

Semper argued that the earlier style provided much the better alternative model for modern design, from what he termed a "world-historical" viewpoint. With this decision behind him, Semper next embarked on a search for the "primordial type" (*Urtypus*) of Western churches, which he did by studying the more centralized solutions of churches found in Constantinople, Antioch, Ravenna, Milan, and Venice. The vaulted, round-arch solution, for one, permitted a widening of the nave and therefore greater proximity of participants within its confines, but more importantly it also allowed the feature of galleries. These had largely disappeared in the Catholic rites with the Gothic style but they had an obvious advantage for Protestant services. Moreover, the development of the Romanesque style on German soil at Bamberg, Naumberg, Worms, and Cologne, among other places, had stamped this style with an authentically Germanic character. And unlike the Gothic style, which had more or less perfected its forms, the Romanesque style – Semper argued – had been prematurely superseded by Gothic forms and was thus capable of further formal development and refinement.[157] These reflections on the various aspects of the problem led him to his unique "Byzantine" solution: fully flying in the face of the current interest in the Gothic style.

Semper's reasoning was quite difficult to convey to the competition jury, unschooled in architectural matters and with little basis upon which to reach a decision, other than personal biases and the visual appeal of the presentation drawings. The committee did, of course, have the assistance of the local press, which quickly reduced the pile of drawings to four or five leading entries, and let their authors (supposedly anonymous by the mandate of the competition) be known.

Early in the deliberations, interest settled on the Gothic scheme of G. G. Scott, whose London office (which employed the gifted draftsmen Henry Edward Coe and George Edmund Street) had produced several highly seductive, colored perspectives. Scott, who excelled in harvesting examples from the past, was in the process of establishing one of the largest and busiest offices of the Victorian age: a modern paradigm for the division of labor. He believed his historically "correct" Gothic design was representative of the period 1270–1300. It was distinguished by its soaring tower and filigree spire, which dwarfed the relatively modest church behind it. Since it was based on a Catholic model, it contained no galleries. In his written explanation sent along with the design, Scott skillfully played to the nationalist feelings of the German public, who still regarded the Gothic style as the *Alt-Deutsch* or Old-German style, even though historical research had by this time proved that Gothic forms actually had their origin in France. Scott, as his *Personal and Professional Recollections* later show, relished using this particular stratagem; in the previous year he had toured Europe and had met many members of the Gothic Revival movement on the continent – including both Boisserée and Zwirner.

Interest also focused on the competition design of the Berlin architect Johann Heinrich Strack (1805–80); this also contained an openwork Gothic spire. Strack was a pupil of Schinkel and a skillful architect whose practice was just coming into its own. His design was less derivative than Scott's scheme but not as polished; the tripartite Gothic nave was kept at the same height and featured galleries running along each side.

By the start of 1845, Semper, who was regularly appraised of the public discussions by his friend Bülau, began to worry about the course of events and wrote to Hans Porth, the lone artist on the competition committee. Semper's letter was evidently about the late delivery of his Gothic alternative scheme, but Porth's reply described the enthusiasm generated locally by Scott's design and he suggested that Semper might prepare a perspective to strengthen his proposal.[158] In another letter of early February, Porth asked Semper to prepare a response to the criticisms with which his scheme had met in the local press. This time Porth was even more laudatory of Scott's design – "so beautiful, so pure in the German style" – and all but conceded it the first prize.[159] He was only awaiting the decision of a sub-committee of specialists that had been set up by the competition committee to evaluate the architectural merits of the various schemes.

Porth's second letter certainly gave Semper little comfort. The only positive sign was that the competition jury had finally come to realize its basic incompetence in reaching a judgment on this matter, and had become aware of the politically difficult situation in which it now found itself. Scott's scheme was strongly supported by the active groups of evangelical reformers but there was also a backlash forming, strengthened by local architects, because Scott was a "foreigner." Semper's scheme – that of the famous native son – would have provided an easy alternative, were it not vehemently opposed by the same religious reformers because it was Romanesque in character. No other clear alternative had emerged and the competition jury was now forced to conclude, at least in a perfunctory way, that perhaps it might be proper to examine the architectural merits of the different schemes. Thus a sub-committee composed of seven local architects was formed to appraise the larger committee of the programmatic, technical, and artistic advantages or shortcomings of the leading designs. Bülau was selected for the committee, although he compromised his position on the same day by publishing a review laudatory of Semper's scheme. Yet other members of the sub-committee, such as Wimmel and Forsmann, were certainly expected to be cool toward Semper's entry.

Porth's letter to Semper also made another allusion that would soon become a matter of deep concern to the Dresden architect. Apparently forgetting to whom he was writing, Porth described the appointment of this technical sub-committee as something of a ruse: as merely a pacifying gesture to local architects before the committee turned, if necessary, to "outside" specialists. Although Porth did not mention specifically who these outside specialists might be, the competitor Scott had already done so in three confidential letters addressed to the committee.

Already in December Scott had begun lobbying committee members to seek the advice "of some eminent antiquarian," and suggested the expertise of Georg Moller in Darmstadt, Boisserée in Munich, and Johann Claudius Lassaulx in Coblenz – all Gothicists.[160] The same names appear in a later letter from Porth, where they are grouped with Zwirner, the architect of Cologne Cathedral. Scott, who insisted to his German judges that he was himself a member of the reform movement led by Boisserée, no doubt felt that he was defending his interests as a foreigner in a German competition. But since the competition program had never demanded a design in the Gothic style, it was hypocritical of the competition committee to seek the advice only of specialists known to prefer Gothic schemes. But of course any pretense of a disinterested jury had now been dropped by Porth altogether.

Semper's position would, over the next several weeks, become almost untenable, as a coordinated campaign to purge the competition of all non-Gothic solutions was undertaken by the more determined members of the evangelical reform movement. Porth in his second letter had sent Semper an anonymous article from a layman that fiercely attacked various aspects of his design: among them its structural integrity, illumination, and acoustics. This article was but one of a series of articles and brochures, nearly all anonymous, that appeared between February and May – all exalting Scott's "German" solution against its "heathenish" rivals. Various of these authors have since been identified, among them Ferdinand Stöter, Burmester (the former collaborator with Semper), and Georg Palm.[161] That their efforts were coordinated is shown by a letter of Boisserée to Stöter written at the end of April, in which Boisserée thanked Stöter for sending him several articles and then encouraged the efforts of his group in their fight against the "sophistry" of Semper.[162]

Semper, in fact, was now forced to give nearly all of his time to defending his scheme. He first answered, point by point, the article Porth had sent him in early February.[163] In reaction to Porth's mention of Boisserée, Moller, and Zwirner, Semper wrote a frantic letter to a friend in Hamburg, asking him to meet with Porth personally and point out that all of these men were Gothicists and that it was important for the committee to maintain its impartiality.[164] Against another hostile article, Semper published a retort in a Hamburg newspaper on 12 March.[165] His most comprehensive defense was a lengthy brochure, *Über den Bau evangelischer Kirchen* (On the Building of Protestant Churches), which he wrote in late-March and published in Dresden at his own expense. He sent copies to his brother Wilhelm in early April for local distribution.[166] In it he gave a detailed summary of the problems that should be considered in the design of a Lutheran church and how they had been solved historically and by himself. The most interesting footnote to the work was his response to a charge made by Stöter – that he was unfamiliar with Bunsen's treatise on early Christian churches. Semper, who had known Bunsen personally from his time at the Archaeological Institute in Rome, not only countered Stöter's hyperbole but did so by citing Bunsen, chapter and verse. Yet the one charge that Semper could not refute, however much reason he used to appease the religious opposition, was that his design was somehow "un-German." The Gothicists were simply unrelenting in their virulence.

Early in March, however, came the most surprising development within the whole competition: the verdict of the technical committee. As Bülau later informed Semper,[167] the sub-committee that convened in February was at first rather hostile toward Semper's design but then began considering its merits with regard to the other works, on such programmatic criteria as its cost, sightlines, and seating capacity (Scott's design, which fell far short of the required number of seats, was nearly discarded for this reason). Much discussion ensued over the dome and whether it complied with the requirement of a tower. After consulting various dictionaries and encyclopedias, the committee of architects determined that it did in fact conform with the technical definition of a tower. Its monumental appearance was further compared with other major churches in London, Paris, Florence, and Constantinople. Near the end of the two-week proceedings, the committee-member Wimmel, who was also the city architect in charge of the old Nikolaikirche, suddenly died. His death left an important municipal vacancy – a lifetime appointment – that the winner of the competition might be in line to inherit. Once again, this pointed to Semper's scheme and his interest in moving to Hamburg. The committee of specialists came to its decision by a secret vote at the end of February. The decision was soon leaked to a newspaper and then published at the beginning of March all over Germany. Scott's entry was placed third. Strack's design gained second place. And Semper, with all of the publicity that this entailed, was declared the winner!

This was the stage, however, at which things took a more treacherous turn, as the competition jury, now embarrassed by the verdict of its committee of specialists, was prepared to take any steps necessary to nullify the decision. In a letter to Semper at the beginning of March, Bülau noted that he had heard that this committee was thinking of soliciting the outside advice of Boisserée and Zwirner, but he believed this rumor was simply a "villainy" perpetuated by Lindley and his followers.[168] Semper was aware from Porth's letter that the rumor was in fact true. The competition committee waited until April to write to Boisserée and Zwirmer and ask them to come to Hamburg and review the decision. Boisserée declined the trip on his doctor's advice, but he sent to the committee his monograph on Cologne Cathedral with his advice that Hamburg's new church should also be Gothic in style. Zwirner, who as a practicing architect was crossing an ethical line by questioning a decision already made by a formal committee of architects, arrived in Hamburg at the end of the month. During the first ten days of May he went through the dodge of reviewing the sub-committee's decision on the schemes. He now become, in effect, the sole judge of the competition.

In yet another piece of chicanery, Scott left London early in May for Germany, where – quite by accident he said – he ran into Zwirner and other jury members in Lübeck. Although Scott later admitted the "chance" encounter (which was immediately known in Hamburg), Zwirner, in his competition report of 11 May, denied ever meeting the Englishman: a blatant lie. The German historian Franck, who has recently reviewed the matter, has suggested that Scott must in fact have been in Hamburg – incognito – since 4 May.[169] Scott's presence, however much it infuriated the local community, did nothing to change what was already a foregone conclusion. Zwirner's report gave Scott's scheme the first prize; Strack was again the runner-up. The third prize went to a Gothic design by the Munich architect Ludwig Lange. Semper, who had now devoted a full year of his life to the design and defense of his work, was not even granted an honorable mention.

The competition jury's final decision, given on 19 May, was greeted with controversy and bitterness. The spurning of the committee of specialists drove a spike into the heart of the local architectural community. A letter sent by Bülau to Semper in the second week of May reveals the intensity of the emotion generated by this act. After noting the conspiratorial meeting of Scott and Zwirner in Lübeck, Bülau went on to describe Zwirner's constant companions during his stay in Hamburg – Burmester ("this abortion of mud and slime"), Porth ("this old woman, this nervously sweating miscarriage, this caricature of a regular Christian, this eccentric fool"), and Châteauneuf ("this ignorant windbag"). Even more virulent was Bülau's reaction to the pending decision:

> It is not however the educated architects, not the knowledgeable craftsmen who oppose you [Semper], but miserable cowards of architecture, pious vermin living on tea, chaps who become intoxicated when they see an empty wine glass, and who lower their eyes when a beautiful woman passes across the way. Our city's castrated *chevaliers de l'industrie*, led around by the nose, conspire with the traitors of the state to squander the financial resources of our native city and, for a small sum of money, play into the hands of the English, that contemptuous pack of enemies. Their scheme will not be successful, for it slips too deeply into the slime of infamy. The devil take them one and all.[170]

Opinion was also divided in other factions within the city. Although members of the evangelical reform movement rejoiced at their victory, it was in the end a somewhat hollow one in view of the many delays and cost overruns that plagued the construction of the church – difficulties to some extent predictable in an effort to build a Gothic cathedral out of brick. The behavior of city officials was also roundly condemned outside Hamburg. The Viennese journal *Allgemeine Bauzeitung*, in reviewing the architectural competition in 1848, criticized the selection of Scott's scheme with its basis in Catholic liturgical rites and then went on to describe the competition itself as a fiasco, the repetition of which would make it impossible in the future for any "honorable artist" to participate in a competition in that city.[171]

The most embittered victim to emerge from the competition was of course Semper himself – who incidentally never expressed and did not share the anti-English bias of Bülau's letter (his rage became directed, instead, at the "tendentious" Gothic party). After being declared the winner of the competition, he had been humiliated by the jury; in full public view he had had his professional competence questioned. Through his friend and attorney Sthamer he briefly threatened litigation – on the basis of the Lübeck meeting of Scott with members of the jury, of the seating capacity of Scott's scheme, and of Zwirner's competence as the jury's lone and final arbiter – but faced with a counter-suit for libel he backed down.[172]

Later in the summer of 1845 he sought (for the sake of history, he noted) to publish his design with a defense, and he repeatedly requested from the competition jury a copy of that part of Zwirmer's report dealing with his design. He was not, however, afforded the courtesy of a reply. The anger he felt toward the city did not soon subside. For more than six months he could not bring himself to write to his mother, and then he explained in the saddest terms the "rebukes, misgivings, admonitions, criticisms, and mistrust" that had haunted every effort to write. "I have crossed Hamburg, that unworthy Sodom, off from my geography," he noted, "I avoid everything that reminds me of its existence. Unfortunately, Altona lies so close to it that it automatically reminds me of Hamburg and everything that goes with it."[173]

In the end, a few Hamburg politicians felt compelled to do something to ease the city's collective bad conscience. Later that year, on 13 December 1845, the sheepish Senate awarded Semper six Portugals for his "willing, enthusiastic, and patriotic participation" in the plans for the rebuilding of the city, following the great fire.[174] These six gold coins were his compensation for over three years of the most laborious efforts and bitter disappointments.

Assyrian Alabaster

In view of the extent of Semper's architectural activity during his years in Dresden, it is easy to forget that he was also a professor and head of the architecture department at the Academy of Fine Arts. In fact, the bulk of his time during this period, especially during his first few years in the city, was given to his duties at the Academy: on the one hand to its reorganization (a process that continued into the early 1840s), on the other hand to his lectures (some cycles of which lasted three years). Moreover, the historical, archaeological, and aesthetic foundations for his later theories on architecture and art were built in these relatively subdued but nevertheless important years of European intellectual development.

Semper did not come to the consideration of architectural theory from a background of well cultivated intellectual interests and a fixed ideological framework. But he did possess a natural curiosity and intellectual stamina that lent themselves to the consideration of philosophical matters within the broad scope of his artistic perspective. Over time, the pace of his learning even accelerated, so much so that by middle age, when most individuals delimit their intellectual experiences and fall back into familiar patterns of thought, Semper continued to expand the range and depth of his concerns. We can see evidence of his early lack of refinement and of his critical demeanor in his inaugural address to the Dresden Academy, given in 1834. It was a lecture that, with its derivative and pseudo-philosophical affectations, is quite unsophisticated when compared with the more engaging direction of his later thought. Still, it also shows the focused intensity that is characteristic of his artistic efforts.

Work on the address was probably started in Altona in the summer of 1834 and seems to have been inspired by two books. The first was the *Handbuch der Archäologie der Kunst* (Handbook for the Archaeology of Art; 1830) by Carl Ottfried Müller (1797–1840); the second was a three-volume text in art history, *Italienische Forschungen* (Italian Investigations; 1827–31), by Karl Friedrich Rumohr (1785–1843).

Semper had personal contacts with both authors. Müller was on the faculty at Göttingen during the years Semper attended the university and it is possible that he sat in on some lectures by this young and celebrated archaeologist (six years older than Semper), who received his chair at the tender age of twenty-three. Müller also wrote a relatively positive review of Semper's *Preliminary Remarks on Polychrome Architecture* for the *Göttingische gelehrte Anzeigen* in 1834. Semper had met Rumohr while in Italy in 1833, although the details of their contact are not known. But throughout his life Semper held a very high opinion of Rumohr. He designed his grave stone in Dresden in 1843 and cited him as late as 1869.

Semper's inaugural address was intended to introduce and explain the conceptual foundation of his lectures on architectural history, which commenced with Egyptian architecture. In reacting against the abstract terminology and antiquarian predilection of so many German writers on art (Winckelmann and Lessing chief among them), Semper proposed a more straight-forward historical and practical approach to the study of architecture, one that sought to cultivate the architect's feeling and critical powers of observation.

Semper referred to Müller's text only in passing; on one occasion he praised the archaeologist for his "philosophical acuity and erudition" as well as for his "correct sensitivity to art and personal artistic ability."[175] Müller was perhaps the foremost Hellenic scholar of his day. His *Handbuch der Archäologie der Kunst* proposed "to reduce the body of archaeological literature to a scientific order," although Müller for the most part restricted himself to Greek antiquity.[176] Of all the branches of the Indo-European race, Müller believed that only the Greeks (chiefly the Dorians) combined artistic sensitivity with spiritual equipoise; only this civilization forged an independent culture with perfect artistic forms. Müller, working of course from a limited body of archaeological material, viewed the Etruscans as merely an "episode" of Greek art; he summarized the entire artistic cultures of the Egyptians, Phoenicians, Babylonians, and Persians in only a few pages in the appendix of his book.

Perhaps more interesting from Semper's perspective were the theoretical prolegomena Müller attached to his text: his effort to ground his new science within the proven framework of – mostly Kantian – aesthetic formulae. Thus the reader learns that art is a "representation" (*Darstellung*), an activity by which something internal or spiritual is revealed to the senses. Further, art is a kind of "play" without exterior or practical purpose and this makes it different from "mere handicraft." Art is again a making, a creating of sensuous form, manifesting an "artistic idea." The latter is not a concept but an intuited "mood and activity of the mind from which proceeds the conception of the particular form." Artistic ideas are also particular and possess meaning only within the context of the specific work; they express feelings of the soul, like a simple melody.[177]

From this epistemological basis, Müller embarked on defining the most general laws of art, the conditions under which the soul can be excited to agreeable emotions. He first divided artistic forms into those manifesting mathematical relations and those representing the organic forms of nature. The former was an artistic category introduced by German Romantic philosophers and others around the turn of the century in order to endow architecture and music with some measure of respectability as fine arts.[178] Instead of imitating natural models, architecture was then said to embody nature's invisible laws – principles such as regularity, symmetry, and proportion. The problem with Müller's acceptance of such a category was that he had earlier sought to exclude concepts from artistic activity, even going so far as to deny art the use of allegory. Given this basic inconsistency, it was only fitting that Müller in the end fell back on Winckelmann's Neoplatonic conception of beauty, defining beautiful forms as those that "induce in the soul a feeling that is appropriate, salutary, and entirely conformable to its nature, producing vibrations, so to speak, that correspond to its innermost structure."[179] Beauty is now made mysterious. It dwells neither in the forms of representation nor in the artistic idea, "hence the profound remark of Winckelmann, that perfect beauty, like the purest water, must have no particularity."[180]

It is difficult to understand what Semper may have gained from his reading of Müller's somewhat forced aesthetic reasoning – other than a rudimentary and for the most part irregular understanding of Kantian aesthetics. In fact, as Semper's inaugural address unfolds, it soon becomes apparent that he was himself very much opposed to just such an overly conceptual approach to art. German idealist aesthetics, in fact, beginning with Winckelmann and Lessing but continuing with Schelling and Hegel, had very little to offer Semper in the 1830s and in later years. Semper's first efforts at theory were made in opposition to these tendencies, and Rumohr's critique of such trends was the vehicle Semper initially seized to promote his contrary vision.

Rumohr, who has nearly been forgotten in recent times, was a well-respected historian in his day. Semper was evidently impressed with the force of his personality, describing him in his lecture as someone admired by everyone for "his investigative and organizing spirit," and as "a sensitive architect who knows his material, and as such, appears always highly disciplined and tactful in his social intercourse with men."[181] Wilhelm Waetzoldt later characterized Rumohr the art historian as "the first in the line of art-historical specialists of the nineteenth century," and "the last of the great scholarly dilettantes of the eighteenth century," therefore as a transitional figure between the traditions of Winckelmann and Jakob Burckhardt.[182] This is not an unfitting portrayal of the man who first honed his artistic instincts in the Humboldt circle in Rome in the first years of the century, and who then drew upon his extensive archival research to fashion a double-edged assault against both Romantic and Neoclassical theories of art. Rumohr's approach to art history has been described as "philological," "stylistic," and "oriented toward positive objectivity," but such appellations merely cloud the range of his concerns. The aim of *Italienische Forschungen* was to build "a documentary foundation for the new art history," to bring scholarly precision to a field of research formerly plagued with aesthetic preconceptions.[183] Wilhelm Dilthey once praised Rumohr for correcting the idealistic bent of Hegelian aesthetics, for promoting "a well-balanced approach to art which also encompasses the sensuous and technical aspects."[184]

Only in volume three of *Italienische Forschungen* did Rumohr deal with the subject of architecture, in the essay entitled "Über den gemeinschaftlichen Ursprung der Bauschulen des Mittelalters" (On the Common Origin of the Architectural Schools of the Middle Ages). Its leading thesis was that the early Christian and Byzantine schools in the Eastern Roman empire carried on the Graeco-Roman tradition of architecture uninterrupted until Gothic times. With his emphasis on historical continuity, Rumohr argued – in the way that Alois Riegl would seventy-five years later – that the formal changes appearing within this tradition were not signs of a declining taste, but rather modifications brought about by local, climatic, and historical needs. Applying this reasoning to an earlier period, Rumohr suggested that the external factors that transformed the Greek trabeated system into the Roman arcuated system were the colder climate of Rome (requiring the roofing of public spaces), the new Imperial and public building types necessitating longer spans, and the greater urban density, which promoted vertical expansion into multi-story structures. Thus the column, the essence of Greek architecture, became a decorative appendage to the pier, the new support for the vaulted interior spaces. Although most German historians in the 1820s regarded Roman architecture as degraded by this change, Rumohr insisted that such criticism ignored the historical process of design. Roman architecture, although built upon Greek architecture, responded to a set of variables different from those of its predecessor and could only be evaluated within this context. Implied here was a relative notion of beauty: "Thus we learn to see more and more that with regard to beauty no lines, no form, no proportion can be completely the same within a new combination."[185]

The two main branches of architectural development of the classical Roman tradition were the Byzantine and northern Italian schools of the Justinian era. Rumohr traced both schools back to Roman themes and building methods. In the Hagia Sophia, for example, "in the prudent selection of the materials out of which the dome was constructed we recognize the Roman school, which in the preparation of bricks was unrivaled."[186] Similarly, the building tradition of northern Italy, Rumohr argued, continued Rome's technical advances, even during the time of the so-called barbarian invasions:

> What could the Italians of the sixth to eighth centuries have to borrow from the architecture of the Eastern kingdoms? Technical skill? Not at all, because, as I have shown, both architectural schools based their techniques on Roman traditions. We have no reason to assume that Roman building methods were totally eradicated in Italy during Gothic and Lombardian times – an assumption for which Ghiberti and Vasari, but not our contemporaries, could be forgiven. Not even the example that they assert for it – the church of San Vitale at Ravenna! As if it has not long been known that this was a work of the late-Visigothic period, which Justinian only decorated with mosaics and to which he added a vestibule."[187]

In his critical attitude Rumohr's new "scientific" approach to art history can clearly be seen, as can his healthy skepticism toward the once unquestioned sources and explanations of events. Even where Rumohr's historical detachment begins to break down, as in his preference for employing the terms "*germanisch*" (Germanic) and "*deutsch*" (German) for Gothic architecture, his aim was still to draw out its "organic" character as a novel response to a new set of demands, and not to promote its forms as adaptable to nineteenth-century needs. Rumohr, in fact, cited the concomitant preoccupation with historical styles as one of the leading causes of historical distortion: "By showing its historical and, so to speak, organic development, I have tried to suppress the views that ascribe to an imbecilic urge for imitation what in fact was solely based on necessity, intention, and purpose."[188] Whereas Rumohr's aesthetics is not entirely materialistic, there is little sympathy in this concept of history for Winckelmann's ideal or for any form of a spiritual *Zeitgeist*. Semper in his lecture, and also later, adopted very similar reasoning.

The aesthetic basis of Rumohr's art historical conception was spelled out in his lengthy critical introduction, which he entitled "Household of Art." His main tenets, many of which were carried over verbatim by Semper in his address, are in large part a critique of the ideas contained in Schelling's lectures on art, which dealt with many of the idealist paradigms of Winckelmann. The outlines of this struggle were presented by Schelling in his Munich lecture of 1807, which began with a discussion of the conflict between Winckelmann and Lessing on the respective aims of sculpture and poetry, as they related to the Laocoön statuary group. Winckelmann had praised the sculpture's expressive restraint, in contrast to the piercing description of the event depicted by Virgil. Lessing responded that the two arts have very different goals – beauty without distracting emotion being the aim of sculpture. In essence, Schelling agreed with Lessing that sculpture had a very different aim, but he insisted that passions in sculpture should not be moderated for the sake of beauty; rather, the passions should be fully expressed and tempered, as it were, by beauty. Schelling then went on to describe the plastic arts in general as an intense artistic struggle, a parallel world to that of nature, in which the artist wrestles with nature – "in strong and courageous battle"[189] – imbibing the vital force, creative energy, and universal laws of nature so that he can achieve a mystical union with it, thereby ascending to the realm of pure ideas. Whereas Winckelmann had raised the artistic ideal above nature, in effect substituting the imitation of antiquity for the imitation of nature, Schelling countered with a more vigorous and refined naturalism, one in which (although beginning with a severe style) the artist must search out the finest form or fullest bloom in order to transcend particularity and portray the species. Hence he ended with the somewhat paradoxical Romantic formula – modified by Semper some years later – that "only through the perfection of form can form be annihilated, and this, the characteristic idea, is indeed the final aim of art."[190]

Rumohr, while accepting most of the tenets Schelling laid down, sought to carry this new naturalism a stage further – not only by denying the mimetic premise of Neoclassical idealism but also by moderating the contrary response of Romantic theory. Thus in delineating the different goals of the literary and plastic arts, Rumohr specifically excluded from the plastic arts both moral and religious sentiments, as well as any discussion of art and its ascension from the profound depths of "being." Rumohr still allowed art to operate in the realm of the mind or spirit, but his interest lay more in unveiling those general and objective laws that lay behind the physical making of art, that is, he sought to establish a framework for investigating the work of art itself rather than the subjective process of its creation. It was this concern with the execution of the work of art that earned him the reputation of a realist, and it was no doubt this quality that the practically inclined Semper found so appealing.

Following Schelling, Rumohr accepted intuition (*Anschauung*) rather than concepts (*Begriffen*) as the means by which the plastic arts convey their meaning. The specific work of art consists of the conception (*Auffassung*) and the representation (*Darstellung*). The former is the spiritual content to be intuited; the latter its material realization. But whereas the conception should be correct, moving, and charming, the representation "is the only guarantee for the strength or weakness of the conception."[191] Only it affords the critic the possibility of meaningful discussion. With this, Rumohr embarked on his course of naturalism by reiterating Schelling's view that organic forms could hardly be "improved" upon. He traced the contrary false view to poorly defined terms used by artists – to Raphael's statement, for instance, that he painted from a "*certa idea*" in his mind (this, says Rumohr facetiously, "after twenty years devoting himself to the most loving and personal study of nature") and to Vasari's emphasis on invention in his definition of mannerism.[192] The errors of modern idealism, Rumohr felt, could be found in such pretensions, which stood in stark contrast to ancient times, in which artists, unburdened by such aesthetic distractions, enjoyed a proud and profound relationship with nature and their medium. Naturalism for Rumohr was not a mechanical reproduction of nature, something that portrayed the ugly as well as the beautiful, but was – like Schelling said – a tool by means of which the artist transcends the seemingly endless display of organic variation "by bringing the types of nature in their original and particular sense into use."[193]

Later in Rumohr's analysis, he turned to the notion of style, a concept that Winckelmann had popularized in German theory with his chronological division of Greek art into four styles. Rumohr, however, discarded this understanding of the term and underscored its etymological sense – the *stylus* of Roman time that was used as a tool for writing on wax tablets, which later came to signify a general literary excellence. Against the temporal appropriation of this word, Rumohr now redefined style qualitatively "as the successful accommodation of the artist to the inner demands of the material, by which the sculptor actually creates his forms, the painter makes visible his images."[194] Style thus signifies neither a school of artists nor some temporal phase, but the general and particular demands of the raw material to be treated. In the case of architecture, which responds to spatial needs, the most general principle of style is the "harmony of spatial relationships," which requires a cultivated artistic instinct. This harmony, for Rumohr, was akin to the compositional laws of music.

Hegel, whose artistic theory preferred to dwell on the spiritual content of a work, took issue with Rumohr's materialism in this regard.[195] But it is also interesting that Semper (who was certainly unaware of these objections, and probably of Schelling's writings directly) did so too.[196] In fact, in Semper's address of 1834 the question of style was the only aspect of Rumohr's thought about which he offered any elaboration. Semper accepted all of Rumohr's other major points: the central importance of intuition (feeling), the failed terminology of Winckelmann's idealist paradigm (not to mention his "incompetence" with regard to architecture),[197] the duality of conception and representation, and the general outlines of his naturalism.

He also followed Rumohr's lead in his definition of style, which Semper defined as "a general advantage in the handling of the artistic material, as well as a subordination of the representation to a certain lawfulness."[198] This legality, however, was both general and specific to each art, that is, it dealt with principles of form and color, harmony, and proportion, but also (and here is where he expanded on Rumohr's scheme) "the positive laws of convention and the specific cultural stage of a people and a period."[199] In essence, Semper brought his definition of style closer to Rumohr's analysis of late-Roman and medieval architecture, but he did so for reasons other than logical consistency: he was troubled by how to incorporate architectural polychromy into this stylistic discussion.

Rumohr, as has already been noted, expressed the view privately to Müller that he had no use for theories of ancient polychromy, since (as we now see) the arts of sculpture and architecture, which deal primarily with mass and space, can be defined without this attribute. Yet Semper, who was unfamiliar with Rumohr's views on color, was clearly perplexed at how classical polychromy could be viewed within these delimiting material conditions. In his lecture he thus argued, on the one hand, how there were historical periods in which religious beliefs had tyrannized art with excessive conventions, thereby impeding art's formal development. He noted, on the other hand, how in the flowering of Greek art, style laws were less rigidly adhered to than is now imagined. Following Rumohr, he insisted that "the arts only evolve to their most beautiful maturity when the free spirit appropriates the generally understandable language of natural expression, which elevates mysticism to symbolism and allows taste and convention to set limits to excessive degeneration."[200]

The problem that Semper faced, however, was how to make a convincing case for this symbolism and convention, given his materialist premises. In attempting to explain in his lecture why the Greeks, for instance, had employed bronze reins and color on the frieze of the Parthenon, he could only speculate that the arts were surely more closely allied in classical antiquity and that marble may initially have presented material difficulties that have since been overcome. If his explanation comes up rather short, it is because in 1834, in working within a borrowed conceptual framework, Semper as of yet had no resolution to these issues. He was in fact only just becoming aware how complex and multifarious the style problem really was – a problem that eventually became a central focus of his thought. In later years he returned on two occasions to Rumohr's notion of style, but within an entirely different aesthetic framework.

After Semper's inaugural address, he settled into a cycle of historical lectures for the remainder of the 1830s, lectures that systematically surveyed ancient and recent architecture. Only parts of them have survived – fragments dealing with Egyptian, Persian, Greek, and Scandinavian building.[201] They depict a somewhat scholarly survey of a limited range of published material. His main sources seem to have been texts by Gau, Müller, and A. H. L. Heeren.[202]

In 1840 Semper restructured the content of his lectures, arranging his material by nine building types, with a tenth rubric devoted to city planning. The new course, which he referred to as a "*Lehre der Gebäude*" (Theory of Buildings), represented a significant change of viewpoint, both in terms of how he now analyzed architecture (by climate, function, traditional and religious influences, materials) and in the considerably widened range of his sources. In a few pages of one lecture dealing with dwellings, Wolfgang Herrmann has recorded cited texts by Percier and Fontaine, Letarouilly, Gutensohn and Knapp, Gradjean de Montigny, Cicognara, Hittorff and Zanth, Gauthier, Thiersch, Quatremère de Quincy, and Vasari.[203] In another section of a lecture discussing educational buildings, Semper devoted almost five pages to a description of the various botanical, mineralogical, and anatomical collections at the Jardin des Plantes in Paris.[204] Not only were his interests expanding, with an encyclopedic range, but a much more critical attitude now permeated his analyses. He was beginning the search for "original forms" that were exemplified in his coeval design for the church of St. Nicholas, only with respect to all building types.

This search may not have gone anywhere, however, were it not for a letter Semper received in July 1843 from the Braunschweig publisher Eduard Vieweg. On a recent trip to Dresden Vieweg had renewed his acquaintance with Semper, who had promised to send him an outline of his new course of lectures. Semper apparently expressed interest in publishing his lectures with illustrations. Vieweg countered this proposition with the suggestion of incorporating the lectures, if suitable, into a new edition of David Gilly's *Handbuch der Land-Bau-Kunst* (Handbook of Rural Architecture; 1797–1811).[205] Semper did not respond at once but gave careful consideration to the matter. When he did reply near the end of September he gracefully declined Vieweg's request but again expressed an interest in a new and more encompassing work based on his lectures. Vieweg warmed to the second proposal and a book contract was drawn up in August 1844. Over the next six years, Semper struggled unsuccessfully with the very ambitious task he had set for himself.

What makes Semper's letter of 1843 so important is that he took the occasion to articulate in a succinct and elegant manner a theme that would become a preoccupation for the remainder of his life. The problem he had with the Gilly textbook was that it was too technically oriented: it tended – a criticism harking back to Rumohr – "to elevate the material over the idea," whereas in nature "the material always serves the idea." The contrary approach of making theory "from above" – the aesthetic ordination of a set of rules or precepts – was equally to be disdained, Semper felt, because architecture in effect was much too complex. He proposed instead a theoretical approach that seeks to explicate the "original models" (*ursprüngliche Gebilde*) of architectural production: "We call architectural forms organic when they arise from a true idea, when in their formation they display the lawfulness and inner spiritual necessity by which nature herself creates – that is, creates only the good and the beautiful, and even uses the ugly as a necessary element to harmonize the whole."[206]

The goal of the "thoughtful architect," Semper continued, should be to clarify these original models or forms, compare them with one another, and ultimately to derive the simplest and most original laws governing architectural creation. In his most vivid formulation of his new approach he indicated his intentions in this way:

> We therefore come to the view that nature in her variety is ever simple and sparse in her basic ideas, renewing continually the same basic forms by modifying their graduated development a thousandfold according to their conditions of existence, developing parts in different ways, that is, shortening some parts and lengthening others. So, I say, that architecture is also based on certain normal forms conditioned by an original idea, which always reappear and yet allow infinite variations conditioned by more specific circumstances.[207]

By identifying and applying these "normal forms," Semper argued further, the architect could overcome monotony and willfulness in design by modifying these models according to the variables of place, time, custom, climate, materials of execution, and artistic imagination. Drawing two examples from natural science, Semper spoke of the limbs of a seal that have evolved into fins, while the rear legs of a rabbit have responded to an entirely different terrain. In both cases the original idea of the limb remains apparent. Architecture, too, can create truly beautiful forms by taking into account its normal or original forms.

Although Semper's biological analogy may well be appropriate for this stage of his thought, we should be somewhat cautious in ascribing too much importance to it. Ten years later, in a lecture given in London, he repeated virtually this same passage but coupled it with a reference to the quasi-evolutionary researches of Georges Cuvier and Alexander von Humboldt – a reference that has led many historians to far-reaching conclusions regarding Semper's later methodology.[208] The matter of defining these "normal forms" in 1843, however, especially as they related to contemporary, pre-Darwinian conceptual models within the natural sciences, was an exceedingly complex one. The mere coupling of Cuvier and Humboldt in the same sentence was in itself problematic. The biologist Cuvier adamantly opposed the idea of transmutation across species and was a pious defender of the Biblical story of creation, according to which the earth underwent a series of "catastrophes" or floods that successively inundated its surface and eliminated animal life. The human species was a divine creation following the last catastrophe. Humboldt, by contrast, was an agnostic in religious sentiment and a Heraclitean in his cosmology; he regarded change, and species mutability, as being as natural as changing wind patterns or ocean currents.

Still, the respective methodologies of Cuvier and Humboldt, the two most famous scientists of this period, do offer a glimpse of the intellectual ferment at this time.

Cuvier was firstly a comparative anatomist, and he was best known for the osteological and paleontological collections that he put on display at the Jardin des Plantes in Paris – "those rooms," as Semper later noted in English, "where the fossil remains of the animal tribes of the primeval world stand in long series ranged together with the skeletons and shells of the present creation."[209] At the center of his methodology was his "law of correlation," which stated that every part of an organism stands in a mutual relationship, functionally defined by every other. Cuvier applied this principle at times with some dramatic results, such as with his first reconstructions of dinosaurs. His method worked across functions. Given a tooth, for instance, he might reconstruct the jaw, which suggested a digestive system, in turn a native habitat, and finally a full skeletal description. He boasted of his ability to reconstruct any animal from a single part, and this was amply demonstrated by his extensive collections, which were open to an enthusiastic public. Semper visited them when in Paris as a student and perhaps on his return trip of 1838–39. Even though Cuvier described animal systems by function (circulation, respiration, nervous system, etc.), the descriptions were essentially morphological, since form was a strict result of function. He viewed his work as a *physique particulière*, which was different from physics proper. Whereas the physicist was allowed a speculative latitude in search of universal laws, the comparative anatomist should be concerned only with observation and description and refrain from all speculation. Cuvier thus saw his work very much in the tradition of Aristotle and Linnaeus, as a "System of Nature, or a great catalogue."[210]

Cuvier's views on the unchangeability of species, however, were not upheld by scientists everywhere. There was also a school of evolutionism in France, going back to the environmental theses of Jean Baptiste Lamarck at the turn of the century. Here the question of species mutability grew ever more prominent in the first decades of the century; it came to a head on 22 February 1830, when the naturalist Geoffroy Saint-Hilaire debated the issue with Cuvier before the French Academy of Sciences – an event sensationalized by the press. Semper was living in Paris at the time.

A keen observer of the proceedings was Johann Wolfgang von Goethe, who by this date had amassed his own impressive body of botanical and morphological studies. Goethe, in reporting the event to German readers, noted that the "tireless" systematizer Cuvier could never hope to succeed in science by utilizing a method that constructed the whole from out of the individual parts. He was much more sympathetic to the evolutionary thrust of Saint-Hilaire's reasoning, because it "preserved the inner sense of the whole and proceeds with the conviction that the individual part later evolves from out of the whole."[211]

Goethe's own evolutionary beliefs centered around the notion of "type," the idea of prototypical plant and animal forms. At late as his trip to Italy in 1787–88, he still believed he might locate his *Urpflanze*, the oldest, archetypal plant species from which all other plants evolved. By the 1790s his search had became more an intellectual attempt to define conceptually the laws by which plant forms operate. The distinguishing plant parts – leaves, stems, roots, blossoms – generated their forms, he argued, in response to external conditions, and these differences were then perpetuated by hereditary factors. In a similar way, his discovery of the atrophied, human intermaxillary bone allowed him to postulate a primeval type for vertebrates, thereby linking the human being to other animal types in skeletal structure. Goethe's scientific and poetic writings after 1790 are filled with allusions to *Urformen* (original forms), *Urbilden* (original shapes), and *Urphänomene* (original phenomena). In his theory changes in biological form followed the doctrine of metamorphosis: "Form is a flexible element, a becoming, a passing away. A theory of form is transformational theory; the theory of metamorphosis is the key to all the manifestations of nature."[212]

In such a view the boundary between the organism and the environment dissolves, merging both systems into a single biological process. Form evolves according to one cardinal principle: "Function and form are essentially bound. Function can be conceived as the being in activity."[213]

Goethe's theories had an enormous influence on German thought. When Alexander von Humboldt later attended Cuvier's lectures on the history of science in Paris, he was known "not to scruple to controvert during the lectures in whispered comments to his neighbors" Cuvier's own impassioned attacks on Goethe's theory of structural unity in vertebrate animals.[214] Humboldt later admitted that the idea of his major work, *Cosmos: Sketch of the Physical Description of the Universe* (1845–58), originated in Jena in 1796, when he, his brother Wilhelm, and Friedrich Schiller, all came in regular contact with Goethe and his morphological theories.[215] *Cosmos* was one of the most ambitious attempts, in the first half of the nineteenth century, "to apprehend Nature as a whole, animated and moved by inward forces."[216] From his extensive travels to the Americas and Asia, Humboldt was able to add considerable breadth to Goethe's ideas on morphology:

> The series of organic types presented to our view gradually gains enlargement and completeness, as previously unknown regions are penetrated and surveyed... Amid this immense variety of animal and vegetable forms and their transformations, we see, as it

> were, incessantly renewed the primordial mystery of all organic and vital development, the problem of metamorphosis, so happily treated by Goethe – a solution corresponding to our intuitive desire to arrange all the varied forms of life under a small number of fundamental types.[217]

Since these words were printed a little over a year after Semper's letter to Vieweg, it should be noted that in Dresden Semper also had contact with another of the leading physiologists and comparative anatomists of his day, Carl Gustav Carus, who was also the head of the artists' association. Between 1836 and 1838 – until the early death of his daughter Charlotte – he was the father-in-law of the sculptor Ernst Rietschel, perhaps Semper's closest friend in the city. But Carus was foremost a physician, physiologist, professor at the Dresden School of Surgery and – beginning in 1827 – the personal physician of the King.

Early in the 1820s Carus had become enamored with Goethe's theories and soon began producing an impressive array of scientific textbooks devoted to morphology and comparative anatomy, comparative physiology, comparative zootomy, and psychology – all of which he dutifully sent to the sage of Weimar for his blessing. By the 1840s the term "comparative" was bandied about in every field of scientific research. It signified above all a new respect for empiricism, but it could also be associated with more traditional speculative models. In his researches Carus sought to combine the primeval types and metamorphic principles of Goethe with the metaphysical "world-soul" of Schelling and Lorenz Oken. In his evolutionary model or "genetic" theory, organisms were inwardly and ceaselessly propelled toward ever greater species differentiation and feature articulation, everywhere moving from simpler to more complex organisms.

But if we return to Semper's lectures, we see that it was not only progress in the field of natural science that was causing him to reconsider the accepted models of architectural development. In the 1830s and 1840s, in fact, there was a flurry of activity in the fields of anthropology and archaeology, which once again called into question many earlier assumptions. Most of scientific and artistic theory up to this time had been predicated on the Biblical dating of human creation, which generally assigned the human race a 6000-year history. This meant that the eighteenth-century European explorers of Asia Minor, Persia, Egypt, and China were thus discovering architecture, in theory, dating from mankind's presumed beginnings in time. On this basis Quatremère de Quincy in 1785 postulated three distinct and essential "types" underlying architectural creation: the cave, the tent, and the hut. He related these autonomous types both to the three modes of living of hunters, shepherds, and farmers and to the respective architectural cultures of Egypt, China, and Greece.[218] As has recently been demonstrated, Quatremère de Quincy based his theory on contemporary ethnographic research, Cornelius de Pauw's *Recherches philosophiques sur les Chinois et les Egyptiens* (1773).[219] As late as 1836, Raoul Rochette could point out that one of the more egregious, that is, "unscientific" errors of Semper's *Preliminary Remarks on Polychrome Architecture* was his mention of Egypt in connection with Greek architecture, since the respective architectural types of the two nations (the cave and the hut) were fundamentally different.[220]

Such a view, however, was fast becoming outmoded. Various discoveries in the 1820s, of human bones mixed with those of antediluvian animals such as the mammoth, challenged Cuvier's "catastrophe" theory. The fate of this theory was more or less sealed by Charles Lyell's epoch-making study of 1830–33, *The Principles of Geology*, which interpreted the stratification of the earth not as evidence of catastrophic floods but as the long-term results of the agents of water, ice, volcanoes, and geological convulsions – thereby reckoning the age of the earth in spans of millions, not thousands, of years. Lyell may not have wanted to accept the implications of his geological theories with respect to the human species, but Darwin, who on his voyage around the world between 1831 and 1836 was collecting the evidence for his theory of natural selection, was of a very different view.

On another front, Franz Bopp's *Comparative Grammar of the Sanskrit, Zend, Greek, Latin, Lithuanian, Gothic, German, and Slavonic Languages* (1833–52) consolidated decades of linguistic research and proved unequivocally that differences in the various Indo-European languages – far from being attributable to Noah's sons, Shem, Ham, and Japheth – were a result of a complex and lengthy linguistic evolution. The question of the derivation and uniqueness of Hellenic civilization itself became an issue of debate. Speaking of Sanskrit's grammatical affinity with the Greek language, Bopp noted, "Who could have dreamed a century ago that a language would be brought to us from the Far East, which should accompany, *pari passu*, sometimes surpass, the Greek in all those perfections of form which have been hitherto considered the exclusive property of the latter, and be adapted throughout to adjust the perennial strife between the Greek dialects, by enabling us to determine where each of them has preserved the purest and the oldest forms?"[221]

Anthropological models were frequently adjusted to reflect these new facts, as can be seen in the three editions of James Prichard's *Researches into the Physical History of Man*, which appeared between 1813 and 1847. In the first edition, working from the assumption of species fixity and the paradigm of monogenesis, Prichard argued that the original family had black skin and was an inhabitant of the Middle East. Migrations took place prior to advanced linguistic formation, hence later physical and intellectual distinctions (such as increasing lightness of skin) was a result of the civilizing process. In the second edition of 1826 Prichard doubled the size of the work and dropped the single trunk line. Climate, rather than civilization, was now the main cause of species variation. In the five-volume, third edition of this work, which started appearing in 1836, Prichard distinguished seven "classes of nations" but still sought to interpret these within the Biblical story of creation. Only by the fifth volume of his work, appearing in 1847, did he finally admit that the idea of the seven-day creation was no longer tenable.

Prichard's solution to the problem can be found in *The Natural History of Man* (1843). Against Cuvier's explanation that after the flood the seats of human existence came to rest on Mount Caucasus, Mount Altai (Mongolia), and Mount Atlas (Ethiopia), Prichard brought the cradles of civilizations into the fertile plains and river valleys of three nations: 1) the Semitic or Syro-Arabian nation; 2) the Japetic or Indo-European stock; and 3) the land of Ham or Egypt. Prichard believed that other races and nations arose as variations or degenerations of these three types, with differences becoming more extreme the more physically remote from the original source. To each stage of cultural life – aligned with head and skull form, brain size, and the practice of hunting, pastoral, or agricultural ways of life – Prichard assigned both physical and moral attributes. Thus the Semitic race (comprising Syrians, Hebrews, Arabs, and southern Arabians) occupied the geographic center and always maintained moderate physiques and human features, even though their mode of living resulted in "the splendour and luxury of Nineveh and Babylon."[222] From the Japetic stock of Persia, however, came a "remarkably fine and handsome race," not "strictly Grecian," but noble and dignified, intellectual and "indicative of reflection."[223] This Aryan race was, of course, the precursor to the Greek and European civilizations.

Anthropological evidence of a slightly different sort was compiled by the German ethnologist Gustav Klemm in his major undertaking, *Allgemeine Cultur-Geschichte der Menschheit* (General Cultural History of Mankind), which appeared in ten huge volumes between 1843 and 1852. Klemm and his famed collection of artifacts resided in Dresden. He moved to the city in 1831, first to work at the royal library. By 1834 he had gained the post of librarian, as well as overseer to the porcelain collection at the Zwinger. Klemm's interest, however, lay entirely with the ethnological material he was assembling. By 1843, when he began publicly lobbying for a museum of ethnology (Semper, who was engaged in the planning of the art museum, no doubt took notice), his collection of artifacts numbered 5000 pieces; by 1852, his description of his private museum, by section title alone, filled out eleven pages.[224]

Klemm defined the task of this new science of "cultural history" as dealing with the gradual development of mankind, from the rudest beginnings in time, "into organic, social bodies," the last manifesting itself in customs, knowledge and skills, domestic and public life, religion, art, and science. "We must search for the succession of cultural conditions with the various peoples of the old and new world, of old and recent times," he noted, "to set them beside one another and try to recognize from them the process of human development."[225] Klemm discerned three stages in cultural evolution: savagery, tameness, and freedom. The phenomenon of culture itself, coinciding with the development of the fixed abode, the use of fire, and property ownership, appeared first in such locations as Malaysia, Mexico, Egypt, the Middle East, and China. The third stage, of freedom, he identified largely as a Western event, taking place once the yoke of autocratic or religiously-dominated political systems was shattered, first by the Persians and Arabs, later by the Greeks, Romans, and Germans (Europeans).

Klemm's taxonomy of human activities was exhaustive, as he methodically reviewed human societies of each region of the world for their physical and mental characteristics, family and social life, eating and burial habits, dwellings, dress and personal decoration, tools, weapons and utensils, religion, and language – each category expanding with cultural progression. His work in effect became an anthropological compendium, as he combined the discoveries of more recent travelers such as Humboldt with the exotic descriptions of such eighteenth-century travelers as James Cook, Etienne Marchard, and Jean-François de La Pérose.[226] Ornate nautical implements from the South Seas (Pls. 70, 71) could – for the first time – be appraised and compared with decorated Egyptian headpieces.

Still, the most compelling anthropological event of the 1840s, at least with regard to the development of Semper's architectural thinking, was the unearthing of the Assyrian civilization by the competing archaeological expeditions of Paul Botta and Henry Layard. The existence of the Assyrian civilization (ca. 1350–612 BC), in what is today central Iraq, had been known earlier through the exuberant descriptions of Herodotus, Didorus Siculus, and the Old Testament, but little modern archaeological study had been carried out, beyond the few sketches of the region done by Robert Ker Porter in the 1820s.[227] Thus the first discoveries of the 1840s met with considerable interest and confusion in Europe. Paul Emile Botta, the French consul at Mosul, began diggings across the river

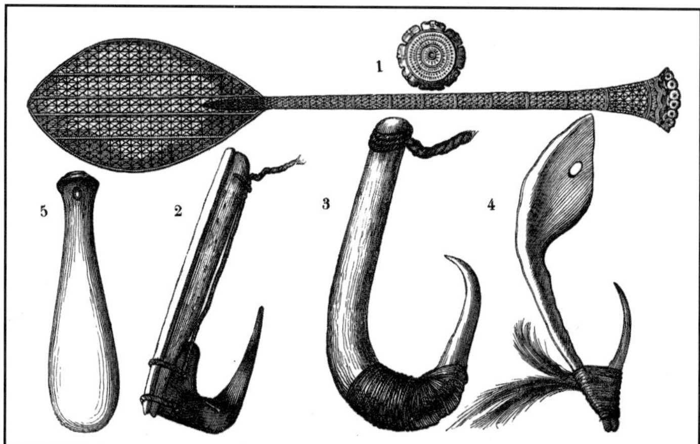

71 Oar and implements from the South Seas. From Gustav Klemm, *Allgemeine Cultur-Geschichte der Menschheit*, vol. IV, 1845.

70 (left) Egyptian head-pieces. From Gustav Klemm, *Allgemeine Cultur-Geschichte der Menschheit*, vol. V, 1847.

from Mosul in 1842, but, having little success, soon moved to a site fourteen miles north, where he uncovered the huge palace of Sargon II (721–705 BC). Botta actually found Khorsabad, although he believed it to be Nineveh; he quickly published his five-volume *Monument de Ninive* in 1849–50. The Englishman Layard, meanwhile, in fierce competition with Botta, had at the same time been excavating the remains of several Assyrian palaces at Kuyunjikl, Ashur, and Nimrud – the last of which he believed to be Nineveh.[228] Only on a second trip to the Middle East in 1849–51 did Layard eventually find the actual city of Nineveh, at Botta's original site across the river from Mosul.

It is difficult today to imagine the excitement generated by these findings, as the first colossal winged-bulls and alabaster wall panels began arriving back in London and Paris in the late 1840s (Pl. 72). Here was evidence of that opulent empire of almost mythical proportions – the sinful place so vividly portrayed in the Old Testament. The Assyrian cities were at this time not culturally distinguished from the older Sumerian and Chaldean cities to the south, and thus they were believed to be the important third seat of civilization that made up the preclassical past. At Khorsabad, Botta excavated a palace, city walls, portals, and the remains of a ziggurat – discovering sufficient detail to allow fabulous reconstructions of giant buildings arranged around regular streets and courtyards. The Frenchman interpreted his bas-reliefs as an artistic mean between the sculpture of Egypt and Greece. Whereas Egyptian art (with its figures generally portrayed in profile, without regard for anatomical accuracy) reflected the rigid theocratic system of its place of origin, Greek art and its political system had broken the fetters of theocracy; its art was free in the sense that its forms were based on the ideal of beauty. Assyrian art mediated these two stages: in its execution and naturalism it surpassed Egyptian art, even though it remained wedded to traditional forms. Thus it was interpreted as being at an early stage in an artistic process that found its perfection in Greece.[229]

Cuvier, Carus, Prichard, Klemm, Herodotus, Diodorus Siculus, Ker Porter, and Botta – all found their way into Semper's lectures in the second half of the 1840s, as his descriptions of early architecture swelled with ethnological detail and his attention became focused on the beginnings of architectural form-making and its implications for theory. In one fragment of a manuscript for a lecture, probably prepared in 1848 (although alluding to concerns voiced in 1843), Semper spoke of *Urformen* or the original forms underlying architectural creation. He mentioned only two. The first was the "vertical encosure" (*Umfriedigung*), which provided a spatial boundary and protection against enemies; it was a wall motif particularly developed in the courtyard style of architecture in the south. The second was the "gabled roof," which was widely used in the huts of the northern climate. It was a motif suited to individual dwellings, such as villages laid out along a river, rather than to the large communal cities of the south.[230]

In another lecture from this same period Semper defined the enclosure (*Gehege*) as the "first element of ancient architecture" among the southern races, the "original seed" (*Urkeim*) of the dwelling, later of towns and cities. The wall acquired this essential value by virtue of its "inner spatiality," its metaphysical creation of a small isolated world. Within the enclosure was the "hearth" that served as its domestic centerpoint, later

72 Assyrian courtyard. Reconstruction of Khorsabad, drawn by Eugene Flandin, from Paul Emile Botta, *Monument de Ninive*, 1849.

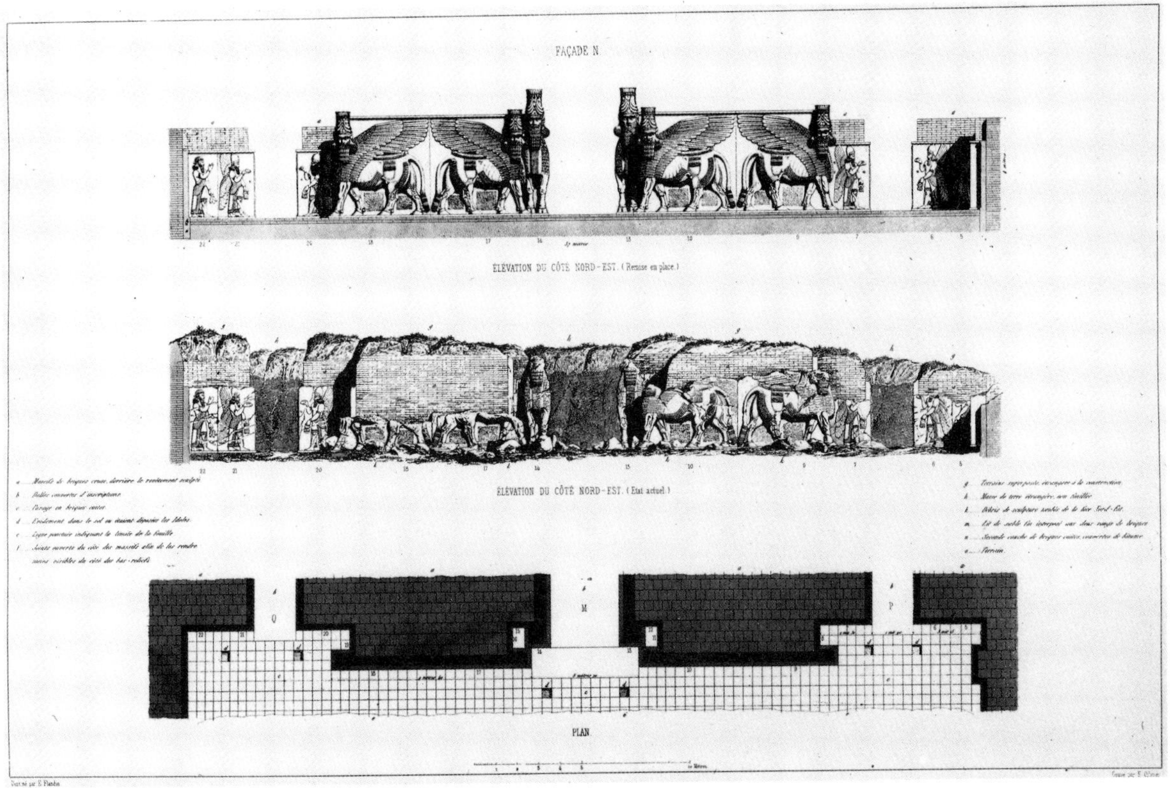

acquiring its particular religious significance in the temple: "Likewise, market towns and cities evolved according to this model...a godhead safeguarded the city as a protective patron. To him was dedicated a special hearth in the market with a cella behind serving as his dwelling. If the religion allowed several deities, then there was consecrated to each a separate district, in which stood his altar and temple."[231]

Semper struggled with these ideas. In responding to pressure from his publisher Vieweg in 1845, he attributed his delay in complying with the schedule of his book contract, as well as with completing the text for his monograph on the theater, to a "thousand hindrances," and promised from now on to arise at 5:30 in the morning and move both projects ahead.[232] Two years later, in January 1848, Semper excused his delay as now due to a broken rib suffered in a fall.[233] By the following December he had completed the text on the theater and indicated to Vieweg that he was in correspondence with Gau in Paris and Donaldson in London and would soon make serious progress on his book.[234] Another fourteen months later Semper consoled the ever patient publisher with the fact that it was a good thing that he had not finished his work earlier, since the recent archaeological discoveries by Botta and Layard would have already rendered his work obsolete.

The one constant in all of his efforts to write this book was his desire to lay bare the original conditions of architecture and therefore the formative elements and stylistic principles of its later development. "Do not believe that my concern for development at the beginning of art is superfluous," he cautioned Vieweg, "on it is based the idea that I propose to carry through the entire work, the red thread that binds it together."[235] These last words were penned after a dramatic event had once again forcefully shaken the very core of Semper's existence. He was now writing to his publisher not as an architect and professor in Dresden, but as a German refugee in political exile.

3

Refugee in Paris and London 1849–1855

"Today in the *Deutschen Allgemeinen* I read my name among those for whom a warrant of arrest has been issued. Thus the bridge between my future and my past has been broken! So be it!"
(Letter from Gottfried to Bertha, 22 May 1849)

The "Semper Barricade"

For Semper, as for most educated Europeans, the political convulsions of 1848–49 did not come as much of a surprise. Certainly the underlying social, political, and economic problems of central and western Europe had been simmering for several decades – in Germany since 1815, when the thirty-odd separate sovereignties comprising the German-Austrian landscape, with all of their rival and vested interests, made the first unsuccessful overture toward a national government.

By 1848 little progress on unification had been made and social conditions were scarcely improved. Dominated militarily by Prussia in the north and Austria in the south, the German states were economically more backward than France or England, and political liberties were curtailed to a greater extent. If the situation in France was slightly better than in Germany, this country too was hurtling into turmoil. The promised political reforms of 1830, especially electoral reforms, had never really come to fruition, and the liberals of 1830, among them the aging King Louis Philippe and his chief minister Guizot, had now became the conservative defenders of the status quo with its vastly unequal distribution of wealth. Social factors were bringing additional pressures to bear upon this situation. The advancing forces of industrialization were creating an impoverished and therefore increasingly militant working class, and socialists such as Louis Blanc and Auguste Blanqui were attempting to marshal this new political energy. Even.more ominously for royal interests, in 1848 Karl Marx and Friedrich Engels were in exile in London writing *The Communist Manifesto.*

Still, it was an accidental discharge of a soldier's musket in France that set in motion the catastrophic events of 1848–49. Crowds of demonstrators had become commonplace on the streets of Paris since the beginning of the year. On the evening of 23 February a particularly large group of workers had gathered in front of the Ministry of Foreign Affairs. They would almost certainly have been placated by the unreported news that Guizot had just been ousted from the cabinet – were it not for the accidental shot that was fired as a soldier was affixing his bayonet. The troops guarding the Ministry, misreading the direction of the shot, fired several volleys into the crowd, killing fifty-two demonstrators. That night the bodies of the fallen heroes were piled onto a cart and led through the streets of Paris, accompanied by the ringing of church bells. It is claimed that 10,000 people at once took up arms and by the next morning over 1500 barricades were in various stages of construction. Within the next few hours the "bourgeois king," Louis Philippe, was planning his abdication and flight to safety in England.

The events in Paris sparked numerous upheavals across Europe, from Ireland to the Balkans. One of the largest of the first cycle of protests took place in Berlin during the first days of March, as protesters surrounded the palace. At first the demonstrators met with some success. King Friedrich Wilhelm IV was forced to withdraw his troops from the capital and he gave his promise of a Prussian constitution and other reforms. The widely reported events in Berlin sparked similar incidents in other German cities and also encouraged the demand for national unity. This time events pushed forward quickly. By the end of March, fifty-one self-appointed democrats had gathered in Heidelberg and made the necessary preparations for the first national elections. In May, following the elections, a republican parliament of 574 members convened in Frankfurt and began writing a constitution of national unity.

The political power of this parliament, however, proved largely illusional. One of the first items of business for this solemn assembly was the emotional issue of the Danish duchies of Schleswig and Holstein, whose German-speaking populations had revolted in March against Danish rule. The parliament asked Prussia to send in troops to support the insurgents, which Prussia did during the summer of 1848. But England and Russia preferred to keep the Baltic seacoast under the control of the less threatening Danes and during the summer months a major military conflict loomed. Semper, whose family home and textile factory was in the Holsteinian town of Altona, avidly followed the events. Early in the standoff he wrote his brother Carl, who was an officer in the local militia, and suggested various military strategies for defending Altona against the possible onslaught of Danish, Russian, or English troops.[1] He also promised to return to Altona and defend his homeland at a moment's notice – this the sister city to the one that he had only a few years earlier referred to as an "unworthy Sodom." The war, however, never materialized, as Prussia in the fall signed an armistice with Denmark and quietly retreated.

Work in Frankfurt on the constitution and national unity proceeded through the autumn with sporadic uprisings throughout Germany endowing it at least with popular authority. Yet the parliamentary members, dominated by lawyers, magistrates, and college professors, proceeded exceedingly cautiously. Prussia's retreat from Danish territory was the first of several affronts to its governing mandate. A few weeks later one of its more prominent members, Robert Blum, was summarily executed by Austrian troops after being captured at a barricade in Vienna. The Parliament demanded that Austria punish the officer responsible for the execution but no action was forthcoming. The Parliament, however, continued its work and in March 1849 completed a draft of the constitution, which was based in part on the English model. Parliamentary representatives soon ventured to Berlin to offer the Prussian monarch Friedrich Wilhelm IV the titular national crown. The King, who in the intervening year had ample time to reconsider the convention's actual power and his earlier promises for reform, haughtily refused it and insisted that the other German monarchs follow his lead. The German public, which had previously supported the work of the Parliament, this time did not rise to the occasion.

Only in two states – Baden and Saxony – did active sympathy for the Parliament's democratic work lead to political action.

Baden, which in southwestern Germany shares a border with France and Switzerland, had for several years been a stronghold of republican sympathies, but this was less the case with Saxony. The Saxon civil unrest of 1830, it is true, had ushered in a liberal government that was untypical for Germany, but it advocated only a moderate liberalism, in service to the King, without the slightest revolutionary pretensions. Leipzig with its flourishing book industry was perhaps the leading town for political progressivism in Saxony. Yet Dresden, where the Saxon Diet and Court resided, was the more logical focus of political activity.

King Friedrich Augustus II, the Saxon monarch, evidently felt little threatened as events unfolded in March and April 1849. He still allowed noted revolutionaries such as Arnold Ruge and August Röckel to roam freely in Saxony, although they were watched more closely as tensions heightened. The political coalition that formed around the issue of a constitution and national unity consisted for the most part of middle-class or moderate liberals; there was also some support from the working class and from peasants. The political leadership that stepped to the forefront in April and May, however, contained few serious radicals.

The Dresden uprising, in fact, may never have happened were it not for the indecision of Friedrich Augustus II and – once again – the overreaction of the military. Throughout the month of April, after the Prussian monarch had rejected the crown, the Saxon king vacillated on whether to support the national constitution and it was only in response to pressure from Berlin that he decided near the end of the month to dissolve the Saxon Diet, which had become the legal vessel for progressive demands. The Diet did disband on 30 April with a proclamation in support of the constitution, forcing at least one of its more vocal members, August Röckel, to flee the state because his grant of immunity from arrest had ended with the session. A parade scheduled by the local militia or communal guard for the first of May was canceled, and in response crowds began to mull around in the streets. On the morning of 3 May the Saxon king rejected a petition from the democrats for face-to-face discussions. That same afternoon the Vaterlandsverein, an association founded in March 1848 to campaign for national unity (Semper was a member), had an urgent meeting and there was some talk of "armed" resistance. It is unlikely, however, that they would have taken any action. But before this meeting broke up, another crowd of demonstrators marched on the city's arsenal and began pelting the defending Saxon troops with stones. The guards returned the assault with gunfire, leaving by one account as many as twenty dead. This incident, like the one in Paris, sparked the uprising; over 100 barricades soon appeared around the city.

The activities at this point could still have been halted with some judicious action on the part of the King. Instead, he panicked and petitioned the Prussian monarch for military assistance, further inciting the populace. In the predawn hours of 4 May Friedrich Augustus and his cabinet ministers fled the royal palace by foot and boarded a boat on the Elbe, bound for the fortress in Königstein. This effectively ended all hopes of mediation, as now there was no one with whom to negotiate. Leaders of the demonstrators, for the most part members of the Saxon Diet, had no alternative but to form a provisional government in support of national unity, expecting the blessing of the Frankfurt Parliament. But even these acts were carried out with some ambivalence, as the majority of

73 (above) Julius Scholtz, *Barrikadenkampf im Mai 1849*. Stadtmuseum Dresden.

74 Unknown artist, *Wilhelmine Schröder-Devrient calls to Battle*. Stadtmuseum Dresden.

democrats still hoped for a reconciliation with the crown. Militarily, the new government had the control of the local militia (with few guns and munitions), but the leaders also believed they had the sympathy of the Saxon army (which they did not). They also hoped that Prussia would be diverted from immediate intervention by the threat of scattered uprisings throughout Germany. Some even viewed their actions – quite naively as it turns out – as a signal for the whole of Germany to unite around the national cause without bloodshed. These hopes were soon shattered.

A ceasefire on 4 May allowed the Saxon military to gather its forces in the "new city" (the part of the city north of the Elbe) and plan an offensive. The next day the fighting began in earnest, as the Saxon troops crossed the river and encircled the palace and arsenal. That evening the first of two Prussian battalions arrived. On Sunday, 6 May, a three-pronged attack was launched on the barricaded "old city" and the Zwinger was retaken. Altogether, about 5000 well-equipped troops (2800 Saxon, 2200 Prussian) continued to encircle and make probes into the city. The poorly armed insurgents, supported in small part by groups of people from the countryside, numbered at most 3000 (Pls. 73, 74). Fighting became ferocious as the armies pressed into the city center, and within a few days the situation for the rebels became hopeless. In the early hours of 9 May the leaders of the provisional government started to flee as the royal armies began the final assault. Prisoners captured by the military were brutally treated; some were summarily bayoneted and tossed off the Augustus Bridge. All in all, over 250 rebels were killed in the fighting; another 250 were wounded. The Prussians lost eight soldiers; the Saxon army twenty-two.

Even though Semper's activities during these frenzied days are easily chronicled, it is more difficult to establish the depth of his commitment to the revolutionary cause. Certainly since his political experiences in France and Greece in the early 1830s, he had been an ardent republican with all of the anti-royalist sentiments that this position implied. His joining of the Vaterlandsverein in 1848 confirms his belief in the cause of national unity and political reform. He was, however, by no means one of the political leaders of this uprising. Like so many of the participants in this rebellion, he seems more to have been swept away by the electric fervor of the moment than by some deep-felt need for revolutionary action.

He was encouraged in this radicalism by Richard Wagner, who during the same months (in large part due to his growing personal debts and conflicts with the royal theater company) had become ever more extremist in his views. But among both men, there was also a certain ambivalence. Both were civil servants with relatively comfortable lifetime positions; their salaries were paid by the Court. Thus any opposition to the government, even mild criticism, put their professional appointments in danger. At the same time both were respected leaders within the community, which had now been forced into a defensive position by the impulsive actions of the King. This dilemma can be best seen in a story related by Richard Wagner of a chance encounter with Rietschel and Semper shortly after the barricades went up. Rietschel was troubled and complained to Wagner that he did not know how to reconcile his democratic sentiments and duty as a "citizen" with his professorship at the Academy of Fine Arts. Wagner was amused at his squeamishness and, glancing toward Semper, slowly repeated the word "citizen." Semper responded with "a peculiar smile" and looked away, apparently in disgust.[2]

His own personal misgivings aside, Semper belonged to the militia's "academic legion" and was also a member of its sharpshooter company. Thus he was also in a certain sense duty-bound to be involved in the fighting, as the militia was now under the authority of the provisional government and Diet. But later, even privately to people who had some sympathy for his position, he remained somewhat defensive of his actions. In apologizing to Bertha, for instance, he attributed his excitement during the siege to a glass of schnapps, laced with opium, he had shared with a companion at the riding caserne.[3]

At other times Semper's euphoria was very real. Wagner mentioned seeing him early in the affair in full military uniform, wearing a hat bedecked in German national colors. Semper first served as a sentry at the City Hall, the site of the provisional government, and it was probably at this post that he pointed out to Wagner the faulty construction of a barricade on Wilsdruffergasse, one of the main entrances into the city. Wagner, so he said, referred Semper to the military commissioner for defense and Semper was soon given the order to improve it. The Prussian commander in charge of retaking the city singled out the "Semper barricade" – as it soon came to be known – as an exceptionally imaginative work, a "small fortress" built to a height of one story.[4] Wagner, too, was very impressed; in his autobiography he related that Semper led the reconstruction of the barricade "with all the conscientiousness of a Michel Angelo or Leonardo da Vinci."[5] To further protect this barricade against attack, the provisional government ordered the nearby old opera house (attached to the west corner of the Zwinger) to be set afire. This was the building in which Wagner, only a few weeks earlier, had publicly fanned the revolutionary flames with his spirited performance of Beethoven's ninth symphony.

On the fourth day of the conflict Semper returned home exhausted, after defending his barricade for three nights. He was awakened shortly after going to sleep with the order to build and take charge of another barricade on his own street. This barricade soon came under attack by Saxon troops, led by a commander known to him, and Semper again defended the work in battle. In later explaining his actions to his brother he made some telling remarks about his own character: "Everyone must know what his sense of duty demands of him and act accordingly. Half-heartedness is, in any case, too often found among the educated classes, who, even though taking up a cause, will not sacrifice anything for that cause. In short, I feel myself free of blame."[6]

Semper exposed his revolutionary complicity in other ways. He had requisitioned some materials from the riding caserne to build make-shift shelters for the barricade and left a written receipt. He engaged in both verbal and written negotiations with the English ambassador (who lived on his street) on behalf of the provisional government. He attended various meetings, exhorted the young men of the technical legion to battle, and also spoke at a public gathering for the cause of German unity and freedom. When the situation worsened he sent his wife and six children to safety in the nearby town of Pirna, but he himself remained behind until the very end. He was one of the last of the revolutionaries to flee the city on the morning of 9 May, as Prussian and Saxon troops were storming into town.

Semper fled the city with the son of Sophie Schröder-Devrient, to the latter's nearby estate. The two then continued on what Semper described as a harrowing journey to Zwickau, eluding the military and civil authorities who were seeking to round up the fleeing revolutionaries. To arrive in Zwickau, Semper and the younger Devrient had to pass through Chemnitz, the city into which – as Wagner's autobiography famously relates – several members of the provisional government were lured and captured. Once in Zwickau, Semper first sought refuge from Bertha's sister, but her husband threatened to have him arrested. Semper then boldly walked into the local police station and with the help of his Holsteinian passport obtained the necessary traveling papers to leave Saxony. He crossed into Bavaria and arrived in Wurzburg on 15 May, where under an assumed name (Victor Leu) he wrote the first of several letters to his brother Carl asking for assistance. In addition to requesting money for himself, he begged his brother to travel to Dresden to see that his wife and family were safe. He was also uncertain if he was specifically being sought by police and thus did not know what precautions he should take. The same evening he traveled to Frankfurt where he stayed with the architect Nicolai, who, as fate would have it, would later be awarded the professorship vacated by Semper. A few days later he pressed on to Heidelberg, arriving there on 22 May.

In Heidelberg Semper first read the newspaper report that a warrant had been issued for his arrest. He also now began to understand the gravity of his situation. He had been charged with treason and thus, if captured, possibly faced death by firing squad, almost certainly many years in prison. For the moment Semper was safe in this university town located in the state of Baden, as their provisional government was still holding out against Prussian threats. He waited for funds from Carl and pondered where to go next. He considered trying to make it to Altona but felt it too difficult to travel around Germany and through Holland. At the end of May Semper was in Karlsruhe, the capital of Baden, where he was offered a commission in the Baden revolutionary army, which was preparing for battle against the invading Prussian troops. Semper declined the request with some hesitation – "If I were rich and twenty years younger, without wife and children, then they would have heard more from me."[7] At the beginning of June he crossed the French border into Alsace. In Strasbourg he purchased a ticket for the two-and-one-half-day coach ride to Paris. He was forced to ride on top of the coach, exposed to the weather, as he traveled with "eight or ten" uniformed men who had been sent to Strasbourg as military substitutes. The contrasting daytime heat and evening chill caused him to be quite ill when he arrived at the Paris home of Desplèchin. This decorative painter, whom Semper had employed on the Dresden Theater, provided the new exile with a temporary home and refuge.

In Paris, with few possessions other than time on his hands, Semper now came to grips with the fact that his life had now been irrevocably altered. He had, in his frightening escape, abandoned (temporarily he hoped) a wife and his six children. He had not only lost his home (which the Saxon state soon threatened to confiscate) but also the bulk of his personal possessions, his friends, his lifetime appointment to the Dresden Academy, and – not least – a highly successful and prestigious architectural practice. His existence was now reduced to the desperation of an unemployed refugee: in his words, an "outlaw" who was perhaps forever banned from returning to his homeland.

In the first days after his flight from Dresden, his mood had been positively defiant, almost buoyant, as he confessed to Bertha the feeling of being awakened by a fresh life, by a new sense of freedom, which he much preferred to his "vegetated" existence in Dresden, particularly now under the "victorious aristocratic party." He comforted Bertha: "Let the sails be set for America! . . . perhaps the day of retribution is closer than we think."[8] From Heidelberg he even asked Carl to caution Bertha against seeking a personal amnesty or clemency on his behalf: "I am not repentant and would gladly speak and answer for my deeds and words." He added emphatically, "Let the penalty then be paid!"[9]

Once in Paris, however, his resolve began to weaken and collapse, as his marriage and living situation entered a most difficult phase. He was greeted upon his arrival with a bitter and reproachful letter from Bertha, who rebuked him for destroying with indifference their means of livelihood and social situation, and for abandoning her to the recriminations of the townspeople and authorities. Semper was devastated by Bertha's letter and, in reaffirming his devotion to her, asked her to inform the judge that he would return and stand at the court's disposal: "I almost repent having fled . . . the world is only a large prison for me. I almost long for the solitude of a prison cell."[10]

The courts were indeed harsh on those who had participated in the activities. Many of the captured leaders were sentenced to death, although later these sentences were commuted to lengthy prison sentences. In the wake of the violence and destruction to the city, public opinion had veered sharply away from the democratic demands of the provisional government and any general amnesty or leniency was now politically out of the question. The government, in fact, became vehemently reactionary and repressive in its measures. It is said that over 10,000 people in the city were subsequently investigated by the police for their political views and possible sympathy with the events.[11] Semper experienced this intimidation firsthand, as he found out how many former associates and friends now no longer wished to correspond with him or with any known participant in the uprising.

In answering a letter from Gau on Semper's behalf, the self-righteous Quandt insisted that Semper had dishonored himself by breaking with the state and leaving his family behind, and that it would be an injustice to all if the state showed any mercy in his case.[12] The director of the Dresden Academy, H. W. Schulz, who was one of the few people genuinely interested in seeing Semper return, felt that the architect would be considered neither as one of the leaders of the rebellion nor as one of the thoughtless participants, but as one of its more prominent fighters. Thus he could be assured of a prison sentence of several years.[13]

Nevertheless, Bertha continued her efforts on her husband's behalf and began to petition officials within the government for amnesty. Semper also now began to have second thoughts of his own, as he became aware that his academic post and his supervision of the building of the Art Gallery would be filled by someone else, thereby precluding any hope of his return. Work on the gallery had only proceeded up to the walls of the first story when Semper left the city. "I find it terrible," he noted in a letter in late June, "that my work, the museum, will now be finished without me. I may not even think of it."[14]

Semper was unaware that his former traveling companion Lüttichau, in two confidential memoranda to the King, had already taken legal steps to have him and Wagner dismissed from their positions because of their absences from the city. Meanwhile, Schulz promised Semper to delay the new appointments as long as possible, although he admitted he was without power in this regard. He suggested to Bertha that Semper should petition the King for clemency directly.

Semper hesitated, then in July wrote the letter asking for clemency to Friedrich Augustus, only to regret this futile gesture a few days later. In his letter he spoke of the enthusiasm that the German people had fostered since the spring of 1848 for a strong fatherland, and how this idea "found also in my heart the liveliest accord." His disappointment at the turn of events led him to his inadvertent participation in the Dresden uprising, but he concluded with his "most humble plea" that final action on his academic and architectural positions be delayed until the resolution of his legal status.[15] The wording of his letter, containing really no apology, was sure to have little effect in persuading the cabinet to reverse its decision. The Englishman Henry Cole, who visited Dresden in December 1851, heard the story still told locally that the King had sworn "to hang him in his own theater" if he ever got his hands on Semper.[16]

With his plea unanswered, Semper gave up any hope of returning. His first preoccupation upon fleeing Dresden was to obtain his Academy lectures so that he might begin working again on his promised book for Vieweg. His second concern was his desire to emigrate to the United States and begin a new life, as many of the German refugees were disposed to do. German immigration was, in fact, very much on the rise in the 1840s, as an average of 100,000 annually made their way to the shores of North America in this decade. The number more than doubled in the first years after the events of 1849. Even while still living in Dresden, it seems, Semper had discussed with Bertha his fascination with emigrating to America, but now the issue was taken up in earnest.[17]

In Semper's first letter from Paris, addressed to the Dresden architect Bernhard Krüger, he discussed his plan to leave for the United States at once.[18] In a letter to his brother written the next day, he reiterated his intentions and was optimistic of his prospects. In June Semper also wrote to his publisher Vieweg and asked him for a letter of recommendation for North America. Vieweg, who had promised to mediate his case in Dresden, urged him not to make such a hasty decision until he had exhausted every hope in Germany and Europe.[19] The major stumbling block to Semper's plan, however, was Bertha, who firmly opposed such a move. She may well have been, as Semper complained to his brother, "rooted in Dresden," but she also feared undertaking the long journey with several young children, the last of whom was born in 1848.

Even though he temporarily gave in to her wishes, Semper continued to solicit information about working prospects in America. One former student who had fled Dresden with him, Wilhelm Heine, wrote back to him in September with a glowing report of the architectural opportunities in New York city. He had discussed Semper's situation with "the young Astor" (apparently John Jacob, 1822–1890) and the latter seemed pleased and interested in helping Semper relocate. Heine also stressed the material wealth and busy pace of architectural activity in the city. If all else failed, he would offer Semper a partnership in his own office.[20]

Semper's prospects in Europe, as it turned out, were quite limited. Immediately upon fleeing Germany, he sought to renew his book contract with Vieweg, which he hoped to complete "with some diligence" in three months – a hope that was far too optimistic in view of the actual complexity of the matter before him. He had to wait well over a month to get his lecture notes sent out of Dresden, before he could even begin to reconsider the work. He also made a proposal to Vieweg, perhaps as an intervening book, to write the memoirs of his flight from Dresden, a proposal carrying the intriguing title "Letters of an Outlaw." These letters, to be addressed to a fictitious party, were to deal not only with the underlying social conditions and politics of the revolution but also with the topics of art and nature. This project never advanced beyond the proposal, however. Semper also tried his hand at a translation of François Mazois's *Le Palais de Scaurus* but soon gave it up. He had thoughts about returning to Hamburg or Holstein and made some futile overtures to friends there. For the short term, at least, he was left with only the prospect of remaining in Paris and trying to scratch a meager existence.

His earlier association with various French artists at the Dresden Theater now provided him with some solace. The painter Despléchin initially took him into his Paris apartment but within a few days Semper moved out to Sèvres to the home of the artist Jules Dieterle. The latter, together with his wife, not only gave Semper some psychological comfort but also employed him from time to time to do some drawings. In December Semper moved in with the third French artist active in Dresden, Charles Séchan. While living in Sèvres, Semper traveled into Paris on occasion and conversed with other artists and refugees. Gau, as already mentioned, tried to intercede on Semper's behalf but was unsuccessful. Gau's architectural practice, like his health, was in sharp decline and he could provide only little assistance.

Richard Wagner, after his own narrow escape from the authorities in Chemnitz and a stay with Franz Listz in Weimar, showed up in Paris a few weeks after Semper arrived, and the two artists greeted each other warmly. Wagner soon left for Switzerland but returned again to Paris the following February to give a series of concerts. On both occasions the two discussed Wagner's book.

But whereas Wagner now found himself to be a celebrity of some international stature, Semper's career prospects in Paris gradually turned from bad to worse. Repeatedly he hatched far-fetched schemes that he felt would somehow extricate him from his impoverished existence and spiritual alienation, but each attempt only met with frustration. His first scheme, harking back to his early years, was to appeal to the Greek government for work. At the same time he wrote to General Jochmus, whom he had met in Greece in 1831–32, and asked for letters of recommendation for someplace in the orient, "perhaps Constantinople, Athens, or Alexandria."[21] His whimsicalness became even more fanciful the following spring, as he wrote to Bernhard August Lindenau, the former Saxon cabinet minister. Alluding to a conversation that he had had many years earlier with him, Semper informed him that he would now be willing to undertake a scientific-artistic expedition to the orient (Egypt, the Middle East, Turkey). In this way he hoped first to atone for his criminal misbehavings; second to remove himself from the political confusion of Europe; and third to "serve my fatherland that I know and love."[22] Lindenau was understandably taken back by the request and pointed out that he had given up his governmental post in 1844. Still, he promised (obviously with no hope of an affirmative response) to forward the architect's strange request to governmental officials in Prussia and Austria.[23]

Closer to Paris, Semper also pursued more sensible avenues. In September 1849 he met with Charles Blanc, the noted theorist and teacher who Semper described to Bertha as the "director of all art institutions in France." He left feeling optimistic that a teaching position might come out of the meeting; it did not. Around the same time a professorship was advertised at the University of Bern but Semper's efforts to have himself seriously considered were in vain, in part because of his uncertain legal status. Toward the end of September 1849 he was informed by a friend of a teaching position at the drawing academy in Ghent. In October he collected what meager resources he had and ventured to Belgium, where he was rudely greeted by an official who had no interest in his application. To compound this rejection, he had trouble with the police over his passport and became seriously ill and was forced to spend ten days in bed. A sad and pitiful letter to Dresden recapped the events: "Oh Bertha, if you knew how much all of this hurts, how sick at heart I am – yet courage!"[24]

His spirits lifted slightly in December as Dieterle and Séchan received a major decorative commission for the Paris opera and offered him a stage design to work on, a perspective of an Egyptian town. Semper was sufficiently buoyed by this gesture to speak to his mother of a possible partnership with these painters, but this hope too proved to be unfounded. In the winter of 1850 another prospect of a teaching position in Geneva proved ephemeral. And Wagner, now back in Zurich, had several discussions with the politician Jakob Sulzer about a position for Semper in the town, but these talks ended when the new conservative government was elected.

Financial support for Semper and the seven members of his family in Dresden during his first year of exile came mainly from his mother and brother, from the charity of a few people in Dresden (among them Oppenheim and Krause), and from his literary activity. He renewed his book contract with Vieweg and – out of the latter's kindness – received relatively substantial advances, especially for a book whose progress was often frustrated by his futile gestures to find other work. In the autumn of 1849 he approached J. Andreas Romberg, the editor of the architectural journal *Zeitschrift für praktische Baukunst*, and offered his services as a foreign correspondent; he called attention to the fact that he knew nearly all of the architects of Paris and was quite familiar with the city's many exhibitions and collections. Romberg accepted the request and several articles by Semper appeared in the last issues of 1849 and the first issue of 1850. There was a description of the cathedral at Amiens, various travel sketches from Belgium, a report on colored asphalt, and an extensive analysis of the gardens and buildings at the Jardin d'Hiver in Paris.[25] Semper and Romberg, however, soon had an argument over the content of the articles and the association ended.

Other architectural prospects also failed to materialize. A "more or less" promised commission by Count Larochfoucault-Liancourt to design an extension to his chateau was never officially proffered. When Semper first arrived in Paris he received from the banker Oppenheim a letter of introduction to the Baron de Rothschild. Semper met with him twice and was referred to a local congregation that was considering a renovation of its synagogue. The building committee initially decided against this option but in the winter of 1850 came up with the proposal for a new synagogue on a different site. Semper designed the new scheme but his hopes for a major work once again ended in disappointment, as the committee postponed its decision to build soon after.

With his frustrations mounting, in fact becoming intolerable, it was inevitable that Semper once again turned his attention to emigration – to England and to America. At the start of 1850 Dieterle recommended Semper's drawing skills to a Mr. Graham in London, who owned an interior decoration firm. Semper, who at this point was willing to accept such a "dependent" position, prepared some sample drawings and ordered some other of his designs to be sent from Dresden. Several months went by without a response.

Meanwhile, Semper's supporter in Dresden, Dr. Krause, had written to his friend William Lindley in England and inquired about prospects there. Lindley was the author of the Hamburg rebuilding plan of 1842 – the plan that Semper had so vehemently opposed. The Englishman, however, promised to let bygones be bygones and help his former antagonist with letters of recommendation. But in Lindley's letter to Semper in the spring of 1850, he presented the now desperate architect with a very candid assessment of the difficult working conditions Semper could expect to encounter, in view of the fact that he was unknown and would be competing against more established colleagues and against anti-foreigner sentiments. He suggested that Semper would not find such obstacles in North America.[26]

By the spring of 1850, Semper had already concluded that the United States was his last remaining option. In March, after hearing that his academic position in Dresden had been filled by the architect Nicolai, he discussed with his sister and Bertha his plans to travel to New York and work as both an architect and teacher, the last at a private architectural school that he would open. He asked Bertha to solicit letters of introduction. He wrote to his sister as an intermediary to plead for a substantial loan from his mother or Carl, part of which would purchase the necessary books to found his school, the rest for travel and setting up a home so that Bertha and the children could join him. All plans to leave, he insisted, now hinged on the outcome of the Paris synagogue project, which was shortly to be decided. He used a similar ploy in his April letter to Lindenau, in which he asked for a positive response to his oriental proposal within fourteen days or his fate in American exile would be sealed.

He again wrote to Heine in New York, but he had to wait several more months for a response from his sister on the loan. In the meantime Heine responded in May with a long letter, in which he discussed further the working conditions in New York city and the possibility of a partnership for Semper with the architect Charles Gildemeister. In 1852 the latter eventually teamed up with the architect Georg Cartensen, to win the competition for the New York Crystal Palace, a polychrome variation on the London building of the previous year. Gildemeister wrote Semper in early July and responded to various proposals he had made, among which was a suggestion to open a candle factory in addition to an office and a school.

All seemed settled in early August when Semper's mother and brother consented to the loan and Semper began purchasing the texts for his school.[27] He first booked a passage on a steamship sailing from Liverpool on 19 August but changed his plans and decided on another one departing from Le Havre on 19 September. He sent his baggage ahead to New York and, in a somewhat anxious state, boarded the vessel on the eve of its departure. Once on board he received a completely unexpected letter from Dr. Emil Braun, the secretary of the Archaeological Institute in Rome. Braun, who was unknown to Semper, praised his past artistic efforts and urged the architect to reconsider his departure: "I believe I can offer you, or at least suggest, a field for your artistic activity, a field that promises to be no less brilliant than the one you have left behind."[28]

Semper was dumbfounded, and drafted two responses, an affirmative and negative one. After several more hours agonizing over his plight, he finally decided to leave the ship and travel back to Paris to hear more details of Braun's offer. Twelve days later he wrote to his brother from his new location: "You will surely be astonished to receive from me a letter from London. In fact, the whole thing is rather like a Shakespearean play . . . something akin to the last act of Hamlet."[29]

Thus Semper surrendered his American dream for one last attempt to reconstruct his life in Europe: this time in England. It is fascinating to speculate on what might have happened had he stayed the course for the new world. Work was indeed plentiful in New York as there was a scarcity of trained architects. He would perhaps, with his energy and speculative instincts, have made a small fortune. Had he succeeded in establishing a school of architecture, it would have the first of its kind in the new country. But it is also very likely that he would have become far too busy with his practice and other pursuits –

candle factories or whatever – to give much time to his growing interest in theory. For this, his proximity to the major libraries and museums of Europe was essential to his further development.

The Four Elements of Architecture

It was through his interest in architectural theory, in fact, that Semper was able to retain some measure of intellectual dignity during the most difficult and painful period of his life. After securing his lecture notes from Dresden, he threw himself into work on his long-promised book, although he faced many obstacles. He was most worried about the status of his publishing contract and shortly after arriving in Paris he wrote a beseeching letter to the publisher Vieweg, imploring him to honor his earlier obligation. Semper's concerns were twofold. The long-delayed monograph on the theater was important because it would help to keep his name and work in public view. And his proposed book on building theory would help to establish his prominence as one of the leading architects in Europe.

Vieweg responded quite magnanimously to Semper's letter. He expressed joy that Semper's lecture notes for his "more serious work" – the book on theory – were not destroyed and he even offered to mediate Semper's sad predicament with various Dresden officials.[30] Semper promptly finished the monograph on the Dresden Theater. By the end of August the woodcuts for the drawings were being printed. The text may also have been in Vieweg's hands at this time, although the portfolio did not appear until March 1850 – much to Semper's chagrin.

Work on the text on architectural theory proceeded more slowly and was frequently interrupted by its author's "accursed bread-work" and efforts to find permanent employment. He seems to have started writing in earnest near the end of July but then he suspended his efforts in the fall when he traveled to Belgium and became ill. Through most of December he worked exclusively on the stage design for the Paris opera, but he resumed his writing at the start of 1850. In February he sent Vieweg an insightful letter in which he noted the intellectual anxiety inhibiting his progress.[31] Chief among his problems was the recent proliferation of studies devoted to the origins of art in early historical times. Semper cited the two recent studies on Assyrian art by the Englishman Layard and the Frenchman Botta, Coste and Flandin's *Voyage en Perse,* and Christian Lassen's study of Indian Architecture. These works had led him to reconsider the relevant parts of the text that he had previously composed, in particular the preface, which he had already now revised twice. Yet he felt that progress was being made and that he had, in fact, won for architecture "a fundamentally new perspective." The special access he obtained to areas of the Louvre that were closed to the public also caused him to adjust his earlier views. His privileged access meant he was able to examine closely the Assyrian sculptures and wall panels that were arriving from Khorsabad.

This rare positive note soon gave way to another fit of depression, but this gloom was also brought on in part by the nature of the task that Semper had posed for himself (Pl. 75). His "Comparative Building Theory," as the projected work now came to be called, was conceived as a comprehensive review of eleven building types, each category being considered historically from its inception until modern times. For several years he had

75 Ernst Kietz, *Gottfried Semper*, 1850. Institut für Geschichte und Theorie der Architectur, Semper Archiv, ETH-Zurich.

been struggling with the text but he was still in the first category of the "dwelling" and then had advanced his study only to the start of classical times. The proposed framework for the scheme was simply beyond reasonable expectation and this in turn aggravated the tensions of his already strained existence. Only a few weeks after his positive remarks to Vieweg, he noted to Bertha that he would be happy if the publisher would not respond to his last letter, for then he would be free of his contract and would no longer be chained to Europe.[32] Nevertheless, he stayed with the work through the spring and in May 1850 he sent to Vieweg a 380-page manuscript consisting of a preface and twenty chapters. These sections reviewed the domestic architecture of eastern Asia, India, Mesopotamia, Assyria, Persia, and Egypt in ancient times. All in all, they represented only a small fraction (less than half of the first category of eleven divisions) of his projected treatise.

Yet this manuscript in many ways represented the wellspring of Semper's theoretical activity, for the rudiments of nearly all aspects of his later theory were proffered here for the first time. In the preface devoted to topical themes, Semper attributed the current malaise in architectural thought to the absence of any integrating "world idea:" there was no comprehensive vision such as Newton, Laplace, Cuvier, and Humboldt had brought to the sciences. Architecture, he felt, was following the early course of the physical sciences with their fragmentation and specialization; in architecture this resulted in a plethora of texts devoted to aesthetics, construction, materials, or certain building types. Durand with his typological framework, he argued, had come closest to such a comprehensive vision but only superficially so, in that – influenced by the Neoclassical proclivities of the time – he soon lost himself in inaccuracies and fell into a "lifeless schematism." Rondelet's treatise on building construction, by contrast, had approached architecture purely from its practical aspect but this was also its limitation: with its technical bias a true theory of architecture lay beyond the projected field of inquiry. The Germans, in general, had produced excellent works on aesthetics and art history, but the architects of this country currently lacked the innovative technical experience common to French, English, and American efforts. This absence of an integrating theoretical perspective was, in Semper's view, the main reason why so much contemporary architecture was devoid of originality.

Semper proceeded to divide contemporary developments into three main schools. The first, the historicist or "historical-eclectic" school, came about through the ease by which the monuments of other cultures and times could now be studied and reproduced. The principal failing of these architects was their lazy imitation of such models – an approach, Semper felt, that implicitly rejected the more daunting task of creating an autonomous work of art from the specific requirements of the task at hand.

The architectural school of "aestheticians," by contrast, was attempting to reduce the practice of architecture to rigid precepts and formulas, without any coherent architectural theory giving substance to this abstract conceptualization. One offshoot of this school, interestingly enough, were the disciples of Schinkel in Berlin – architects so dominated by the master's genius that they had succumbed to aesthetic schematization. Notwithstanding this school's shortcomings, Semper argued that their works revealed an underlying faith and conviction that was absent from both the romantic (Gothic) and classical tendencies.

The third architectural trend of his day, the "materialists," Semper felt were enraptured with the new materials and technologies and therefore fettered the "idea" too much to these restraints: "Regarding construction as the essence of architecture, the materialists stray as far from the goal as those who think of architecture as a kind of sculptured or painted decoration to be applied to houses."[33] The choice and application of any material, Semper argued further, should always be subservient to the idea, since this is how nature forms her creations. Moreover, architecture has over centuries accumulated its conventional store of forms, upon which the architect should draw in shaping his designs. This language of forms remains legible and understandable to everyone and should not be arbitrarily cast aside: "The architect who spurns these conventional forms is like an author who constrains his own language by adopting an antiquated, foreign, or self-invented order of words and manner of expression. He will be understood only with difficulty and, at least as an author, will not find success, whereas he would have lost nothing in originality had he used simplified but intelligible terms."[34] This was a viewpoint that Semper would reconsider over the coming months but to which he would eventually return.

Semper concluded his preface by weaving in passages from his letter of 1843 to Vieweg, in which he drew on the analogy of nature and its infinite variation, based on a very few "normal forms." He again expressed his belief that the architect creates "original formations" [*ursprüngliche Gebilde*], not based on natural models but springing forth from a correctly conceived basic idea. These architectural formations are organic if they make manifest the rule of law and internal necessity also found in nature. Therefore, "the task of an intelligent architect should be to seek and pursue the rise and development of basic ideas and to reduce to its simplest expression the law that lies hidden within the artistic covering."[35]

In the first few chapters of his text, Semper introduced another important theme that would become a preoccupation of his later writings – the four elements or formative motives underlying architectural development. These motives long preceded its conception as a fine art. The first motive, the hearth, is given as the symbolic element giving rise to civilization. Around the open fire the first groups of hunters gathered after the chase; the hearth was therefore the germ, the embryo of all social institutions. Later the hearth became sanctified through religious customs; still later, in modern times, the fireplace remained the spiritual focal point of every household. It was thus the hearth that bonded human beings into families, tribes, and nations. The other three elements – the mound, roof, and vertical enclosure – arose to safeguard the sacred flame. The mound raised it off the damp earth and protected it from inundation; in its later manifestation in masonry, the mound became transformed into the foundation and stylobate for the temple. The gabled roof shielded the flame overhead from bad weather. The enclosing walls sheltered it from the wind and at the same time defined a spatial interior, a habitable private world distinct from the outside world.

A second theme to emerge from these chapters was his division of these four motives into two fundamental dwelling types: the isolated gable-roof huts of the northern Europeans and the wall-dominated courtyard-style of housing common to the southern races. Only these four motives and their distinct cultural evolution were important to the rise of monumental architecture, Semper insisted.

In his tenth chapter devoted to Assyrian-Chaldean architecture (also in his later chapter on Egyptian architecture) Semper again broke new ground by developing for the first time his notion of the "dressing" (*Bekleidung*) and its central importance to ancient architecture. His firsthand viewing of the Assyrian alabaster wall panels at the Louvre led him to this concept, although it was also latent, as we have seen, in his own fleshy treatment of monumental architecture. His reasoning was quite original in this regard.

In primitive dwellings, as cultural anthropologists had already shown, the vertical enclosure was often formed of crude mats with interlaced grasses and branches. Over time these mat-dividers gave way to textile fabrics manufactured from synthetic cords and threads. The Assyrians were renowned for their tapestries, which were sometimes hung vertically as wall hangings over more durable backdrops. For Semper this was simply the symbolic transformation of the earlier spatial motif once the more durable core walls had been constructed: "Hanging carpets remained the true walls; they were the visible boundaries of a room. The often solid walls behind them were necessary for reasons that had nothing to do with the creation of space; they were needed for protection, for supporting a load, for their permanence, etc."[36]

Later, as these textile hangings in turn gave way to gypsum and metal paneling, stucco and glazed tile (even mosaics), the artistic character of the new wall dressings for a long

76 Assyrian winged figure. From Austen Henry Layard, *The Monuments of Nineveh* (1849). Courtesy The Getty Center for the History of Art and the Humanities.

time emulated the textile style of their predecessors (Pl. 76). From this Semper drew a far-reaching conclusion connecting his ethnological studies with his earlier polychrome interests:

> The artists who created the painted or sculptured decoration on wood, stucco, stone, or metal, following a tradition of which they were hardly conscious, imitated the colorful embroideries of the age-old carpet-walls. The whole system of oriental polychromy and consequently also the art of painting and of bas-reliefs arose from the looms and [dyeing] vats of the industrious Assyrians or from the discoveries of prehistoric people who preceded them.[37]

This same dressing motif eventually culminated, Semper was convinced, in the brilliantly painted walls of classical Greece.

As his despondency increased, Semper again suspended work on his book after sending the first installment to Vieweg. During the summer of 1850, as has already been described, he turned his attention exclusively to his emigration to the United States. Early in the fall, after he had changed his mind and crossed the Channel to England, he resumed his literary activity, but now his focus reverted to polychromy. He began an essay in defense of his earlier views on polychromy and wrote several chapters. Sometime around November he decided to join these chapters with the leading ideas of his manuscript on building theory.

Nine weeks later, in January 1851, he sent this new book to Vieweg. He noted that it had actually been written for an English market and was in the midst of being translated into English. He asked Vieweg for its immediate German publication as he feared a "literary theft" of his ideas. After considering such titles as "The White Market of the Siphnians" and "On Polychromy and its Origin," Semper proposed for his new study the title *Die Vier Elemente der Baukunst* (The Four Elements of Architecture).[38] The unhappy Vieweg, disappointed at not receiving another installment of the promised work on building types, initially balked at publishing the manuscript but eventually he accepted it. Some months later, after Vieweg had brought the galleys to London, Semper attached the instructive subtitle, "A Contribution to a Comparative Study of Architecture."

Even though *The Four Elements of Architecture* was in its conception a two-part work, for Semper the dual themes of polychromy and the cultural origins of architecture were closely related. The first four chapters devoted to the question of polychromy were indeed written with London in mind. Here there was considerable current interest in the question of color, on classical Greek monuments and elsewhere. Earlier, England had made a belated entry into the European debate over polychromy when, in 1836, the British Museum convened a panel of experts. The architects C. R. Cockerell and Thomas Donaldson, together with the chemist Michael Faraday (among others), were brought together to ascertain whether color remnants might be found on the Elgin Marbles. Although the committee was disappointed at not finding traces of paint on the frieze panels themselves (which earlier had twice been washed and scrubbed by the museum staff with soap lees, an acid), other evidence was introduced. A letter from Mr. Bracebridge in Athens reported on the decorative patterns and traces of color then seen on the fascias and columns of the Erechtheum; he also gave the results of an excavation undertaken in 1835–36 at the southeast corner of the Parthenon, in which fragments of colored triglyphs, columns, and statues were uncovered.

A letter by Hittorff was also sent to the committee as evidence. The architect Donaldson, who had visited Greece prior to the outbreak of civil war, submitted various remnants of paint he had scraped off Athenian monuments and these samples were chemically analyzed by Faraday. The committee's report, written by Donaldson and published in 1842, concluded that there "appears no reason to doubt" that color had been applied to broad surfaces of Athenian monuments. Faraday's analysis of the paint samples "proves that the surface of the marble of the shafts of the columns of the Theseum, and other parts of the edifices from which these specimens were taken, were covered with a colored coating."[39]

In the 1840s British interest in polychromy widened into other areas. In the middle of the decade the architect Matthew Digby Wyatt studied the polychrome mosaic schemes of a number of medieval works in Germany, France, Italy, and Sicily. In 1848 he published his findings under the title *Specimens of Geometric Mosaics of the Middle Ages*. He also presented various papers on his theories, among them a lecture to the Royal Institute of British Architects (RIBA) in December 1850, entitled "Polychromatic Decoration in Italy."[40]

The Welshman Owen Jones was another partisan of antique and modern polychromy. In 1833 he had teamed up with Semper's friend and Greek traveling companion, Jules Goury, on a tour of the Middle East and Egypt. The two returned to Europe by way of Spain, where they recorded the color schemes of the Alhambra near Granada (Goury there died of cholera in 1834). Jones visited the Alhambra again in 1837 for further studies, and five years later he published his impressive folio on this monument, *Plans, Elevations, Sections, and Details of the Alhambra.*

In the fall of 1850 Jones was engaged in another controversy over color: his proposed scheme to paint the interior of Joseph Paxton's iron and glass structure for Hyde Park. The building, which was to house the international exhibition of the following year, was just beginning construction. On 16 December Jones publicly defended his proportional color scheme of blues, reds, and yellows before the Royal Institute of British Architects. He attempted to counter what he termed "Puritan prejudices on colour" by explaining the chromatic theories of George Field and Michel Chevreul.[41]

Even the Paris architect J. I. Hittorff decided to re-open the European debate around this time. Since the 1830s he had been preparing a major folio study of his Sicilian findings, a book that appeared in 1851 under the title *Restitution du temple d'Empédocle à Sélionte; ou l'architecture polychrome chez les Grecs*. Semper viewed the chromolithographic plates in the architect's studio when he first met Hittorff during his Paris exile. In the fall of 1850 Donaldson invited Hittorff to London to present his ideas to the Royal Institute of British Architects. Semper, too, received an invitation to participate in the discussion, shortly after he arrived in London in October. Altogether, three sessions were devoted to polychromy in January and February of 1851. Semper was present at all three.

As Hittorff's views were presented by Donaldson at the first session, several of Semper's polychrome drawings of 1833 were exhibited in the room, among them his partial restoration of the Parthenon, a study of a building at Pompeii, an Etruscan tomb at Corneto, and his colored rendering of the Theseum. Owen Jones also exhibited his own "more ideal" study of the Parthenon facade, in which the entire work was painted in tones of red, yellow, and blue.

Semper too addressed the assembly, at the second session on 26 January, probably in French. According to the transactions of the proceedings, he explained his colored drawings and discussed his interpretation of a passage of Herodotus. On his views concerning the use of polychromy on ancient monuments, the minutes conclude: "It was his opinion that a transparent layer of coloured enamel or varnish was laid over the surfaces generally, the colour being of an opaque nature only on the ornamental bands and mouldings."[42]

The first four chapters of *The Four Elements of Architecture* deal exclusively with the issue of polychromy. The first chapter opens with a brief review of the earlier controversy, beginning with Quatremère de Quincy's *Le Jupiter olympien* – "one of the most important events in the literature of art and a triumph of our century."[43] Quatremère de Quincy had presented a "more correct" way of seeing Greek art by raising questions not previously considered by the majority of scholars and artists. Hittorff's first studies and the ensuing debate on polychromy (even its negative moments) consolidated this beginning by calling attention to the many allusions to color made by classical authors, passages that were still being disputed by critics. Semper's own contribution to the debate, his brochure of 1834, was little more than, in his words, "an unexpected diversion," by which he had intended only to introduce his larger work. This project, he rather misleadingly noted, had been "completely prepared for publication," but had been held back for various reasons, among them the poor conceptual design of the work and the fact that the issue of polychromy on the Continent had fallen out of favor by the mid-1830s. Kugler's harsh attack on his ideas was also cited as a contributing factor in his decision to let the work languish.

Over the next three chapters Semper makes a point-by-point rebuttal of Kugler's earlier charges. Considering the difficult personal circumstances that Semper had been enduring over the past eighteen months, it is easy to read in these pages a certain emotional catharsis, as he bitterly ridicules each of Kugler's objections, sometimes very personally. After discussing passages of Pausanias, Pliny, and Seneca, Semper turns to the important passage in the third book of Herodotus (sections 57–58), which Kugler felt to be an incontrovertible piece of evidence against the practice of polychromy. The passage speaks of an oracle related to the defeat of the Siphnians, inhabitants of one of the wealthiest of the Aegean islands. The oracle urged the town fathers to "beware of the day when white is thy high prytaneum, white-browed thy mart likewise," for that day their city was to be assailed.[44]

Since Herodotus also mentioned that the forum of Siphnos was at that time built of Parian marble, Kugler had concluded that all Ionian monuments built of marble were therefore principally white. Semper, however, gave a very different interpretation to the passage, insisting that poetic invention mandated that the "white" condition of the forum was actually an anomaly: in this case, the market had just been built of Parian marble and had yet to be painted. He supported this interpretation by referring to the second part of the oracle, in which mention is made to a "red herald," when in fact the color of dress worn by Greek heralds was white.

After presenting this philological evidence, in the next chapter Semper tackled the issue of "chemical proof" raised by Kugler. In addition to reiterating his own observations of Greek works, he quoted extensively from Donaldson's report to the British Museum, which had cited Bracebridge's letter and Faraday's chemical report. Semper even tried to contest C. O. Muller's interpretation of the Greek word for "polish," with which the latter had opposed Semper's conclusion in his Göttingen review of Semper's brochure of 1834. At the conclusion of these chapters, Semper felt, all that was left for Kugler to do was "to hoist the white flag."[45]

What emerges in a more general way in these chapters is the legendary value Semper now attached to Greek art. If art in pre-Greek times was isolated and fragmented, it had by the time of the classical age of Greece evolved into a harmonious whole – a great democracy of the various arts. In relating how difficult it is for the nineteenth-century mind to comprehend this vision of unity, Semper returned to the theater as the fitting metaphor for art's resurrection: "Can he [the nineteenth-century mind] once again summon the chorus from Orcus, the chorus that had given birth to drama, in which all the arts and the Greek earth and sea and sky and even the whole nation worked together for their common glorification? For everything will only remain an eerie phantasmagoria until our national life develops into a harmonious work of art, analogous but richer than Greek art in its short golden age. When this happens, every riddle will be solved!"[46] In these pages Semper seems to be paying homage to Richard Wagner's passage on Dodona, published the previous year.

In the fifth chapter of his book, which carries the book's title "The Four Elements," Semper presented for the first time in print his theory of the hearth, roof, enclosure, and mound. Although much of this chapter is an adumbration of his manuscript on comparative building theory, some new and insightful remarks are added that allow it to read as a lucid exposition of his theme.

One aim of this chapter is to recover the original intentions underlying the Greek temple and, more generally, of Greek art. It was, for Semper, a civilization not autonomous in its artistic traditions, as was generally assumed around 1850, but "a culture that could only have arisen on the humus of many past traditions long since dead and decayed and from alien motives brought over from without."[47] The aim is thus to explore the development or evolution of classical forms.

Semper's choice of the term "elements" (the word he also used in his earlier manuscript) to designate this process is somewhat misleading, in that he actually speaks of these elements more as "motives" or "ideas" that came to shape formal development. Certain technical skills are also associated with these motives. The hearth of prehistoric times gave rise to ceramic and metal arts. The roof spawned carpentry or the concept of a fixed structural framework. The notion of mounding first became developed through the building of dams and canals, but it also evolved into terracing, construction of masonry walls, and vaulting.

The last element, the vertical enclosure, is once again described in a digression, as Semper traces examples of this spatial and dressing motive from its primitive inception as a mat-like divider to the painted and paneled dressings of Assyrian, Egyptian, Chinese, Indian, and Phoenician architecture.

At issue here is really the conceptual underpinning of all of nineteenth-century architectural theory. In the popular formulations of Quatremère de Quincy, architecture took its basic forms and ontological basis from the three primitive dwelling types of the cave, the tent, and the hut, each one of which was associated with the modes of living of hunters, shepherds, and farmers. Placed within the advancing ethnological framework of the early nineteenth century, this model allowed various architectural historians, such as Thomas Hope, to view the sloping ridges of Chinese roofs, for instance, as the formal imitation of the catenary curve of the nomadic tent.[48] Semper ridiculed such simplistic formal associations and proffered instead his "new perspective": a model of types for architecture based specifically on formal motives rather than on the forms themselves. It was an attempt to de-mystify the origins of architecture and provide it with a sounder foundation.

Again, it is important to interpret Semper's "elements" not as specific entities, such as a wall or mound, but rather as thematic processes generating formal development. If the motive of mounding, for instance, led to the idea of stacking rocks on top of one another for a foundation (stylobate) and eventually to the idea of a masonry wall, the masonry wall was essentially different from the spatial dressing, the symbolic sheathing that was applied to this masonry core. The dressing had evolved from the motive of the textile enclosure, and thus only the dressing symbolized the original spatial idea contained in the enclosure.

The masonry core was only a prop to support this dressing; only the latter alluded to a private human world distinct from the world "outside."

Semper's model also differed from earlier paradigms in that he based it on recent anthropological research. The gable-roof hut, for example, was associated with the start of patriarchal life and came to function symbolically, in the Mediterranean area, during the first phases of tribal federation. In the north and in more rugged mountainous regions, however, huts of greater durability and warmth were necessary. Often they were simple timber roofs placed over excavations in the soil. These primitive, single-roof houses, which Semper connected to certain Saxon settlements of northern Germany and Scandinavia, sheltered all of the family's possessions, including its livestock. Expansion of this architectural motive was possible either by the addition of independently roofed rooms or by another story.

The appearance further south of the wall or "courtyard" style of dwelling, on the other hand, was more closely aligned with the beginning of monumental architecture, an event taking place in the cultural phase that Klemm had designated as "tameness." In his earlier manuscript, Semper alluded to the Amphictyonic League at Delphi, the Twelve Tribes of Israel, and the Twelve Kingdoms of Egypt as the surviving remnants of tribal federations, which either became hierarchic oligarchies or were overturned by dynastic absolutism. Such a development was important not only because it led to the emergence of civilization but also because each culture exploited in its own special way one or more of the four architectural motives. The common theme of both modes of government was centralization, which in the Mesopotamian valley and in Egypt was necessary to carry out the building of huge dams, embankments, and monumental edifices. By the time of recorded history, however, none of the building motives had survived in their pristine form but rather had evolved, combined, and become more complex. Semper illustrated this with his review of the "four noteworthy" building directions of the Chinese, Phoenician (Semitic), Egyptian, and Assyrian peoples.

For instance, the isolated units of Chinese cities (devoid of a focusing hearth or altar), emanated according to his theory from the Tartar military camp, which had integrated the gable motive into a regular and convenient planning scheme. By contrast, the Phoenician or Semitic tribes, with their religion based upon the mosaic (hut-like) tabernacle, developed the walled or courtyard style of architecture that focused attention spatially on the tabernacle. Egyptian civilization proceeded in a slightly different way. The cast system of oligarchic priests typified a hierarchic government. The combination of Egypt's warm climate and the fact that its geographical isolation left the country free, for the most part, from foreign conquest allowed a wall or courtyard style of building to develop that was different from that of the Semitic peoples. Yet the core of the temple complex, for religious reasons, was the hidden *sekos* or tabernacle from which evolved a series of processional yards (Pl. 77), formerly open or covered with canvas, later with a roof. At the culmination of this process were the "pilgrim chapels" found at Karnac and Luxor. Semper interpreted the pointed, roof-like forms of the pylons and the pyramids as the residue of the primordial tribal tabernacle.

Quite different architectural forms evolved in Assyria, which shared the dynastic or despotic principle found in all Asian states, co-opting the socialistic-militaristic values of "coordination and subordination." The absolutist political system was necessary to undertake the national enterprises and to protect the emerging cultures from foreign invasion or

77 Egyptian Temple of Edfou. From J. Gardner Wilkinson, *The Manners and Customs of the Ancient Egyptians*, 1837.

migrations. The original inhabitants of Mesopotamia were a nomadic, Semitic people, whose early cultural progress and wealth drew the envy of neighboring tribes. Their subsequent conquest by these neighbors, Semper believed, transformed the nomadic tents into solid settlements. As a consequence, a mixture of elementary motives characterized Assyrian architecture. The canal and embankment terrace was the motive of the original inhabitants, who developed it in order to secure a dry spot for their hearths and tents. Their conquerors were the sons of hut-dwelling mountain people, from whose military escapades had emerged the "fortified camp," that is, a field of tents arranged around an elevated core. In the center was the satrap's dwelling surrounded by the tents of the courtiers, then those of the armies. Expansion was possible only through the addition of new units or by the repetition of the same. This plan of encampment also carried over into the layout of Assyrian cities, where the ring of courtyards also became modified vertically by terraces. The town planners separated the aulic precinct from each successive or secularized layer by a system of walls or periboli. The space between the two outer rings was set aside for the tents of the nomadic traders, harking back to the past. Yet as the walls and terraces came to dominate this scheme, the roof (that element introduced by the mountain invaders) atrophied; it only survived symbolically on the temple atop the ziggurat.

Whatever may be said about Semper's reasoning today, it represented one of the first attempts in modern times to interpret architecture and its evolution in cultural terms, rather than on the basis of quasi-mythical values.

With respect to Assyrian art and architecture, Semper followed Botta's analysis, but he expanded on the latter's ideas and made clear his ethnological perspective. Whereas Botta had viewed the alabaster bas-reliefs found in his excavations as an artistic mean between the sculpture of theocratic Egypt and democratic Greece, Semper – although concurring fully – turned to his four-element theory to explain Assyrian traditionalism. The fact that the Assyrians used bas-reliefs of the size and in the locations they did suggested to Semper that the organic interplay of the wall and roof (a feature first evident in Greek architecture) had not yet taken place, and that this style, in fact, more faithfully adhered to the original textile motive. Of all the ancient nations the Assyrians had best preserved the wall's original motive: the mat or wickerwork spatial divider. This anachronism was at the same time due to the very high artistic level of their famed tapestries.

The Greeks inherited from them or their neighbors this "dressing" principle, but this complex civilization joined it with various other motives that had been tribally transmitted, among which was the peristylar courtyard of the Semites and Phoenicians and the hypaethral temple form of aboriginal Caucasian tribes. But Greek architecture, with all of its grand unity of artistic effects, was still affected internally by conflicting tendencies. Only when Dorism combined with the Hellenic (Asian) instincts in Attica, did the more phonetic arts of painting and sculpture ultimately follow an Ionic tonality. At other times and places, Doric impulses took precedence, such as in the colonial works of Sicily. The same duality was reflected in Greek polychrome schemes: "It is surely more than mere conjecture that Dorism – as in music, so also in the practice of the two named arts, and especially in their application to the temple – differed fundamentally from Ionism, and that there was a Doric color key, just as there was a Doric musical key."[49]

In his sixth and final chapter Semper presented a few practical rules for applying polychromy to modern designs. Here for the first time he acknowledged that antique polychromy had lost is historical footing once the masonry wall and roof (vault) began to be treated tectonically by the Romans. Thus only in secondary instances, such as when the material of the wall needs to be preserved or its material is not aesthetically pleasing in itself, is some interior or exterior dressing mandated. Semper even provided several suggestions for applying the wall dressing properly, such as taking into account the climate, the purpose of the building, and the structural nature of certain parts. Most importantly: "The wall should never be permitted to lose its original meaning as a spatial enclosure by what is represented on it; it is always advisable when painting walls to remain mindful of the carpet as the earliest spatial enclosure. Exceptions can be made only in such cases where the spatial enclosure exists materially but not in the idea. Then painting enters the realm of theater decoration, which it often may be able to do with good results."[50]

Semper also suggests in this chapter – perhaps in response to his exposure to the English theories of John Ruskin and the polychrome effects of William Butterfield – the exploitation of different colored materials. His most curious remark of all, however, is the footnote that appears on the next to last page of his text, in which he apologizes for his own historicist inclinations: "How unfair it is to reproach our architects for a lack of invention, when there is nowhere a new concept of universal historical importance being pursued with force and vigor. First provide some new ideas; then we architects shall find architectural expressions for them. Until then, we have to be content with the old."[51]

This apology reappears in one of his later writings, but it is important to note that Semper was already wrestling with the issue during his forced retirement from his architectural practice. Even when he returned to it later the issue would not go away. It is not unfair to suggest that Semper, from this time forward, defended his formal historicist language with something of a bad conscience, although I think it is wrong to construe this statement as an indication of bad faith. The lack of "a new concept of universal historical importance" (of which others of his generation also spoke) must also be placed within the context of a rapidly changing profession that in another sense was satiated with too many new ideas, at least in the realm of construction. Time was necessary for these tectonic possibilities to be sorted out and assimilated into architecture – a so-called art, moreover, that had always been controlled by higher political and social interests. Yet Semper's admission is certainly curious in light of his own artistic conviction.

Notwithstanding the great significance that *The Four Elements of Architecture* possesses today as a "fundamentally new perspective" for architectural theory and history, Semper's book had very little impact initially. In the pages of *Deutsches Kunstblatt* in 1852, the antiquarian Alexander Ferdinand von Quast defended himself and his friend Eduard Schaubert against the charge of plagiarizing some of Semper's drawings of Athenian monuments – a charge that Semper had made in his book in passing.[52] A few issues later Semper's old adversary Franz Kugler, now the editor of this same journal, took up the cudgels once again to assail Semper's vision of polychromy. Kugler had not altered his viewpoint at all in the intervening seventeen years and he criticized Semper, especially his interpretation of Herodotus, vociferously. In his rage, however, he almost overlooked entirely the chapter on the four elements, which he conceded as having only a "very peculiar, cultural-historical and poetic interest." He dismissed Semper's line of thought in a terse and sarcastic way:

> The author goes back to the primitive conditions of the most ancient people and develops from them and from their different historical position the basic elements of architecture and the direction that the latter must take. . . . It is a pleasant experience to descend into those dark regions of world history guided by an artist full of imagination, and since the interpretation of hazy images from the past requires a good deal of personal fantasy, our own thinking receives a most valuable stimulus.[53]

In England, the appearance of Semper's text proved equally uneventful. The English translation that friends of Semper had begun was never completed, but a shortened, revised version of the polychrome section did appear in Edward Falkener's *The Museum of Classical Antiquities*.[54] Few seem to have taken note.

Because of its accessibility, *The Four Elements of Architecture* has in recent times always figured prominently in discussions of Semper's thought, but the importance of the book should not be overestimated. Its promised new perspective was only in a stage of incubation as far as his later theory is concerned, and within this context the book represents at best a transitional stage toward more coherent and more incisive deliberations. Its main ideas, in fact, within a decade were almost entirely superseded by Semper's much larger study of the problem of style.

The "Great University of 1851"

After Semper made the difficult decision to leave the American-bound steamer at Le Havre, he returned to Paris expecting to meet with Emil Braun, who had set up a tentatsive date. In the French capital Semper found not Braun but a second letter from him from Scotland, where the archaeologist had been called to attend to the death of his father-in-law. This letter urged Semper to proceed at once to London, where Braun would meet him and help him establish a foothold. Braun was still sanguine about Semper's prospects in England, but he had few details to add to his first letter. He indicated that the architect William Falkener had agreed to give Semper some space in his office. He also made a passing mention of a cemetery project and noted that when things in the office were slow he would commission from Semper "several designs for furniture."[55]

Semper now realized that Braun had little concrete to offer. In a draft of his response, he wrote that after discussing "your kind invitation" with Hittorff, Gau, and other friends, he had decided to proceed with his emigration to New York and that he had re-booked a passage on 29 September.[56] He changed his mind again, however, and sent Braun a different version. For with no speaking knowledge of English, he departed Paris for London, arriving at the Hotel d'Allemagne et du Commerce on the evening of 28 September. The next day he met his optimistic German benefactor for the first time, and with him another gentleman: the prominent social reformer Sir Edwin Chadwick (1800–1890).

The well-intentioned Braun, in diverting Semper from his departure for New York, had, in fact, nothing firm to offer him in London – only prospects. The most promising of these, the reason for the hotel meeting of the 29th, related to a government bill that Chadwick was pressing before the British Parliament to create a number of public cemeteries in the wake of the cholera epidemic then afflicting the country. The problem of internment had become especially acute in London, as hundreds of people were dying each day and cemeteries were quickly reaching capacity. Chadwick had proposed the government sponsorship of several new cemeteries: the first ten miles downstream at Woolwich. The bodies would first be transported by barge to receiving morgues and from there to a 240-hectare cemetery. It was suggested that a series of thirty-five connecting chapels should be built, a sufficient number to accommodate 100 funeral services a day.

Chadwick's bill, as Herrmann's touching and detailed history of this period of Semper's life makes clear, ran up against innumerable obstacles in making its way through the two Houses, and in the end the parliamentary wrangling managed to survive the epidemic.[57] Semper, who was completely oblivious to the political situation, began sketching variations on both rectangular and hemispherical schemes on the day of the meeting (Pl. 78). He did not become fully aware of the tenuous nature of this project until well into 1851, after he had put much labor into his design. Late in June of that year his plans were rejected outright by the Board of Health for reasons of style (they were not Gothic), cost, and practicality. Here was yet another major setback.

Much had happened in the intervening nine months, nearly all of which was similarly painful. Chadwick in particular took it upon himself to assist Semper by introducing him to several potential patrons and employers. At a dinner at his house in November, Chadwick asked Semper to bring along his portfolio so that he could show it to Joseph Paxton, the newly appointed designer of the "Crystal Palace." Paxton was a man of varied and considerable talents. Through his well publicized scheme for a huge glass-and-iron structure in Hyde Park, he had become much sought-after and he was just then attempting to build a major architectural practice – eventually he had offices in London and Sydenham. In 1850 he had been given the commission to build Mentmore, the seat of Baron Mayer Rothschild, in Buckinghamshire. Within three years he also gained the commission for Baron James de Rothschild's estate at Ferrières, near Paris. The day after the dinner, Semper asked Chadwick to approach Paxton about the position of interior

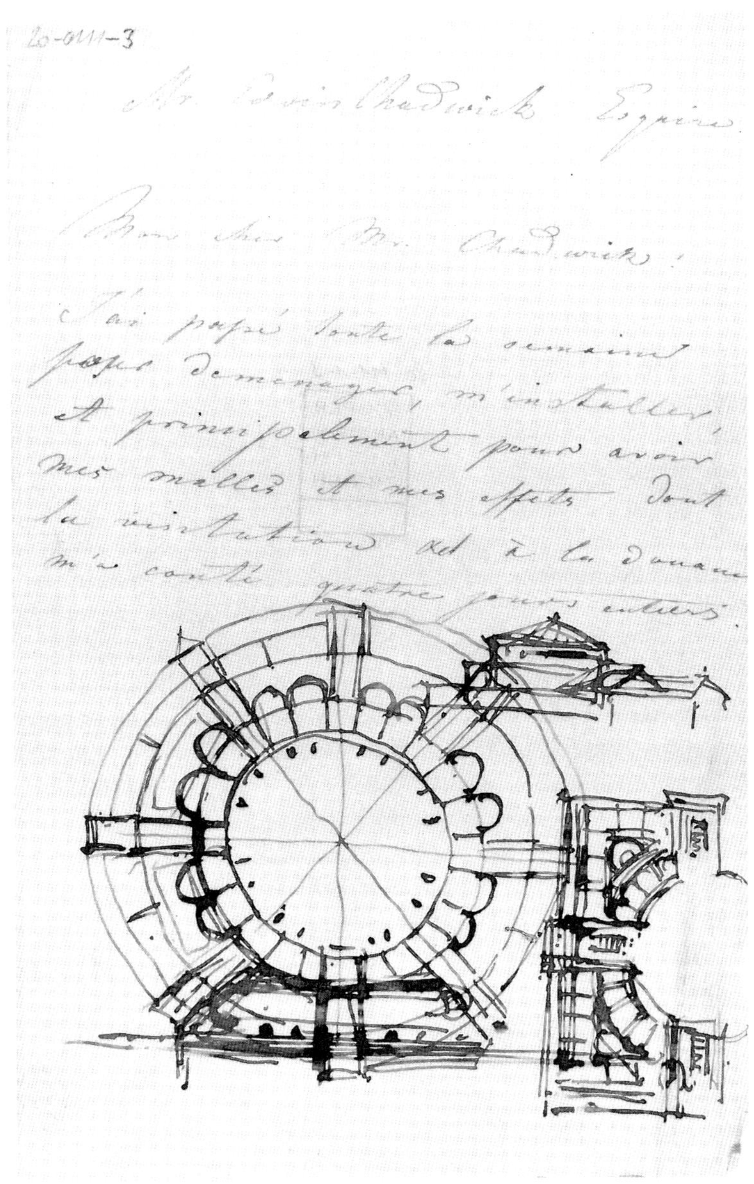

78 Gottfried Semper, sketch of a plan for a national cemetery, London, 1850. Institut für Geschichte und Theorie der Architectur, Semper Archiv, ETH-Zurich.

designer for the exhibition building, thus revealing his naiveté in English matters. Owen Jones had already been appointed to this post by the Royal Commission and was shortly to give a public lecture on his color scheme.

The Four Elements of Architecture consumed much of Semper's energy through the remainder of 1850, but at the start of 1851 he found himself still unemployed and was again thinking about leaving for the United States. This decision was once more put aside as, against the advice of all his friends, he devised a scheme to open an architectural school and boarding house in London, aimed at attracting German and French students. In February announcements were placed in several European newspapers, including one in Zurich in which Richard Wagner made several laudatory remarks about Semper.[58] The advertisements, however, seem to have garnered no response. Semper's optimism even led him, in early March, to turn down a position in Paxton's architectural office – a decision he soon regretted.

Braun, after luring Semper to London, had since returned to Rome; in trying to counter the idea of a boarding school he wrote to Semper with the prospect of a partnership in a "galvano-plastic" factory, but this offer also had little substance. By the start of summer 1851, with the collapse of the cemetery project, Semper fell into a terrible fit of depression and in his letters he began speaking of "intrigues" and of the "invisible powerful hands reaching out from over there . . . to destroy us."[59]

This fear and dread expressed the other dimension of Semper's exile, in addition to his economic distress. He had not moderated his political views during his first two years of exile, but this could hardly be expected in view of the humiliation he was continuing to endure. Bertha and the children were still in Dresden, and Semper in his isolation and frustration grew increasingly more lonely and despondent. In his first letter to Carl from London, he sharply criticized some negative comments that his brother had made regarding democrats and he went on to condemn Carl for snuggling up to "our open enemies," the aristocrats: "they do what they do to save themselves . . . they are no less your enemies than ours and all your efforts to gain their favor will be in vain. In the end gunpowder and bullets will again decide the issue."[60]

While in London, Semper participated in an association formed by German political refugees, the "United Democrats." It was organized for the most part by Arnold Ruge, the former co-editor (with Karl Marx) of the *Deutsch-Französische Jahrbücher*. Another member of the group, and a close friend of Semper, was the Prussian Lothar Bucher, an erstwhile National Assemblyman and later the personal secretary and confidant of Otto Eduard Leopold von Bismarck. Bucher was earning his living in London as a correspondent for the *National Zeitung* and in the spring of 1851 he wrote about Prussian agents spying on German refugees in the city. Soon thereafter, there was also talk of political assassinations by undercover agents. There was a legitimate basis for this concern on the part of the refugees. Records from the Dresden state archives, recently brought to light, reveal that Saxon police informants were monitoring the activities of the Saxon exiles closely. Semper, it was reported, frequented the Blue Star tavern on Maddox Street, where he reportedly met "with many red brothers."[61] This secret surveillance continued throughout his stay in London and even during the first years of his tenure in Zurich.

In addition to being subjected to the hostile scrutiny of German spies, exiles such as Semper and Bucher were scorned by more serious political revolutionaries for their moderation. In the summer of 1851, for instance, a charge of embezzlement led to a purging of the leadership of the United Democrats, and in their place Semper and Bucher were elected to the executive committee. This vote infuriated Karl Marx, who sarcastically noted in a letter to Friedrich Engels: "A new provisional committee has been selected, consisting of Herr Kinkel, Graf Reichenbach, Bucher, and the Saxon Semper. You see from this that a new phase has begun. They [the refugee community] have thrown themselves into the arms of respectable *hommes d'état*, ever since the former 'leader' was compromised as a bourgeois rag."[62]

During all of Semper's first year in London, in fact, there was but a single bright spot: his limited association with the Great Exhibition of the Industry of All Nations of 1851. This event was one of the more important episodes in British history, if only for the international boost it gave to industrial development and to the dawning of the "modern" age. Behind the Great Exhibition stood an individual who over the next few years had an equally dramatic effect on Semper's life – the short, portly, but determined and energetic figure of Henry Cole (1808–82).

For most of the 1830s, Cole had been an obscure civil servant, a record keeper for the Exchequer of Pleas and for the Public Records Office. Yet he had the respect of a number of people who later attained prominent positions within and without the government, among them Edwin Chadwick and John Stuart Mill. Cole was gifted with a sometimes ruthless tactical skill to go along with his abundant energy. After creating a public scandal to facilitate reform at the Records Office in the early 1830s, he turned his attention to a host of other issues: uniform penny postage (1838–41), railways and docks (1845–49), and the curriculum of British schools of industrial art and trade (1841–49). His interests were always far ranging. Later in life, in addition to his continuing efforts at reforming artistic education, he devoted time to such disparate matters as drill for boys in public elementary schools, sewage disposal, and musical church services. Cole has been described by some historians as the perfect Victorian: hard working, religious, family oriented, and always ready to serve as a spokesman for a matter that he deemed to be in the public interest. Others, however, were less polite in their evaluation. One of his contemporaries, the Prime Minister, Lord Derby, once called him "the most generally unpopular man I know."[63]

In the early 1840s Cole began to develop an interest in art, as he sketched in his spare time at such places as Westminister Abbey and Hampton Court. A few years later he started a series of children's books called the "Summerly Home Treasury" series. Under the pseudonym of Felix Summerly, Cole wrote the texts but hired a number of respected artists such as John Horsley and Richard Redgrave to produce the illustrations. The next stage of this enterprise was the creation of Summerly Art Manufactures, an alliance of artists, led by Cole, which was formed to sell designs to manufacturing firms. This venture coincided with Cole's work in the mid-1840s for the Society of the Arts, which, under the aegis of Prince Albert, was studying the problem of Britain's lagging competitive position with respect to the export of manufactured goods. Merging these two interests, Cole managed a series of ever larger exhibitions between 1846 and 1849, conceived to put the fruits of English industry on public display. Cole aligned himself with Herbert Minton, a friend since 1842 and director of the pottery works at Wedgwood. At the first exhibition in 1846, a tea-set designed by Cole and produced by Minton won a silver medal. Cole arrived at his prize-winning design by visiting the British Museum and looking at specimens of Greek earthenware.

As a result of the success of these exhibitions, Cole was invited to give a lecture in 1848 at the School of Design in London. Here was yet another opening that he would most skillfully exploit. The School of Design – actually one of seventeen such schools that had to been set up within the previous decade in many of the manufacturing centers of England, Scotland, and northern Ireland – was the first effort at state-supported, applied arts education in Britain. The mission for the schools, as conceived by an act of Parliament in 1837, was to further exports by upgrading British design skills and thereby to counter the economic menace of French designed products. They were thus placed under the jurisdiction of the Board of Trade. The schools may even have succeeded, had they been shielded from continual political interference. Unfortunately their history, as Quentin Bell has noted, presents a fascinating yet sordid story of "scandal, confusion, and disaster; they were distracted by feuds, encumbered by debts and convulsed by mutinies."[64]

The first director of the London school, John Papworth, soon became its first victim. His curriculum of drawing, modeling, and industrial design, combined with "the study of the history of taste and theoretical knowledge of style," was replaced in 1838 by another conception, that of William Dyce, the second director, who was a talented painter then under the influence of the German Nazarenes.[65] Dyce seemed to side with some of the reforms carried out in Berlin by Gustav Waagen, who envisioned such a school as being an artistic fellowship, emphasizing craftsmanship. In 1843 Dyce was replaced by Charles Wilson. This new director met with a student rebellion in 1845, in part supported outside the School by Augustus Welby Pugin.[66] Wilson survived, temporarily, but in 1846 Richard Redgrave led a faculty revolt against his reign, indicating in a letter to Lord John Russell that the School was successful neither in the "inculcation of a pure taste," nor in conveying to the students a "knowledge of manufacturing processes."[67] A special committee of investigation was set up by the Board of Trade and out of it a triumvirate emerged to run the School, consisting of H. J. Townsend (Master of Form), J. C. Horsley (Master of Color), William Dyce (Master of Ornament). The next year new quarrels erupted and Horsley and Dyce resigned in favor of J. R. Herbert (Ornament) and Redgrave (Color).

It was at this juncture, in the autumn of 1848, that Cole was asked to lecture, but he declined for the reason that the schools in general were in disarray. He was then asked by the Board of Trade to write a report and Cole wrote three. In the first report he indicated the need for a state industry to give a creative and financial outlet for the schools; in the third he pointed out that the schools were in need of thorough administrative and educational reform. And lest it was not clear to everyone who was the man most capable of carrying out this difficult task, Cole embarked on yet another venture, the *Journal of Design and Manufactures*.

This new journal, both funded and run by Cole, proposed to be a "pattern book for all decorative manufactures," which offered to the industrial designer "treatises developing sound principles of ornamental art, and to keep him thoroughly informed of all that is likely to be useful and instructive to him in his profession."[68] But Cole also made no attempt to conceal the fact that the journal was there to criticize (as a "friend") the various schools of design with all of their obvious failings. Not only should these schools "be reformed and made business-like realities," but the civil servant Cole did not shy away from the most drastic measures: "We profess that our aim is to foster ornamental art in all ways, and to do those things for its advance, in all its branches, which it would be the appropriate business of a Board of Design to do, if such a useful department of Government actually existed."[69]

Despite its inflammatory rhetoric and persistent lobbying, the *Journal of Design* was an articulate and discerning voice during its three-year history. This was due in large part to the literary contributions of Richard Redgrave, Matthew Digby Wyatt, and Owen Jones – all of whom formed a very effective ideological circle supporting Cole's political power.

Richard Redgrave (1804–88), like his equally famous brother Samuel, was trained as a painter at the Royal Academy, but divided his interests between painting, teaching, and administrative duties. In 1843 he was selected by Prince Albert and the Commissioners of

Fine Art as one of six artists to form a committee to further decorative painting in England. By this date Redgrave had acquired a reputation as a painter, first for his historical themes and landscapes, then in the 1840s for the sentimental and sermonizing attributes of his female-dominated subjects. He was elected an associate member of the Royal Academy in 1840 and became a full member in 1851. Redgrave's tenure at the School of Design in London in the second half of the 1840s brought him into contact with Cole, and from 1849 onward their political and artistic interests were inseparable.

Matthew Digby Wyatt (1820–77) was descended from a long line of famous architects, beginning with the Neoclassicist James Wyatt. After studying the polychromy of mosaics and stained glass on his European tour in the 1840s, he returned to England to make a name for himself as a lecturer at the Royal Society of Arts. Better known as a "committee man" than as a designer, he was a shrewd critic of contemporary events and this no doubt was the attribute that Cole found so attractive – notwithstanding Cole's generally negative attitude toward architects. It was almost certainly Wyatt who penned the journal's review of John Ruskin's *The Seven Lamps of Architecture* in 1849, which bravely attempted to oppose Ruskin's "lopsided view of railway architecture." The anonymous reviewer went on to characterize the already influential Ruskin as one who "either puts his back against their further development, or would attempt to bring back the world of art to what its course of action was four centuries ago!"[70] This was one of several occasions when the aesthetic sensibilities of the Cole circle and Ruskin crossed.

The final member of the group was Owen Jones (1807–74), a Welshman who also had a keen critical eye but only a modicum of architectural talent. After his tour of the Middle East and Spain in 1834 with Jules Goury, from whom he certainly learned of Semper's efforts with Goury, Jones returned to London to establish a small architectural practice in the 1840s, designing a few villas and shop interiors in a "Saracenic" or "Moorish" style. His chromolithographic study on the Alhambra, *Plans, Elevations, Sections and Details of the Alhambra* (1836–45), was well received, but proved to be merely a prelude to his equally brilliant and more famous decorative study, *The Grammar of Ornament* (1856). This last work, with its normative propositions and visual patterns, can also be read as an exposition of the educational and decorative reforms that Cole was attempting to institute in the 1840s and 1850s.

It was Cole, however, who orchestrated all these talents and provided them with a political mantle. As he was mounting his multifaceted campaign against the design schools in 1849, the investigative committee of the Board of Trade was in the midst of concluding its deliberations. Yet the final report insisting on reform, tediously written and taken through the committee by Cole, did not achieve its intended purpose. This was due in part to the fact that Cole, in one of his rare political lapses, published private evidence in the *Journal of Design* before the official report was presented. The suggested reforms thus entered the public political arena and a bitter fight ensued; the matter of reforming the schools ended in a draw in the summer of 1849.

By this time, however, Cole was back at work organizing exhibitions for the manufacturing arts. In the course of planning a national exhibition for England in 1851, Prince Albert asked Cole and Wyatt to visit France in order to report on a national exposition there. Cole went, and upon his return made the spirited suggestion of an international exhibition to be held in London. Prince Albert embraced the idea and soon the planning

79 Transept of the Crystal Palace. From *The Illustrated Exhibitor: A Tribute to the World's Industrial Jubilee*, 1851.

process began. Cole was given a leading position on the commission; his friend Wyatt was appointed the commission's secretary (he later became the architect in charge of erecting Paxton's building; Fox Henderson and Co. were the builders). Cole also saw that others of his circle were drawn into the proceedings. Jones was hired to design the Saracenic cresting for the roof as well as to devise the internal color scheme for the iron-and-glass structure. Redgrave was appointed to the head jury in charge of design and he later prepared the official exhibition report.

It is nearly impossible today to imagine the excitement and drama generated by the first international exhibition for industry and art (Pl. 79), which opened in Hyde Park on 1 May 1851: a half million people in Hyde Park awaiting the arrival of the Queen and Prince Consort; 30,000 people inside the glass structure; the royal salute fired from a model frigate moored on the Serpentine (with the worry that the sound would shatter the glass roof of the exhibition building); the flourish of trumpets; the prayers; the benedictions; the innumerable speakers. Next there was the building itself. It was designed by the soon-to-be-knighted Paxton and was by far the largest in the world. It enclosed eight hectares or 935,000 cubic meters. Its distant colorful parts appeared "to be enveloped in a blue haze, as if it were open to the air, the warm tint of the canvas and roof contrasts with the light blue colour of the girders into which it is insensibly lost, and harmonising with the blue sky above the transept, produces an appearance so pleasing, and at the same time so natural, that it is difficult to distinguish where art begins and nature finishes."[71]

Finally, there was the exhibition itself: wares from around the world disposed over

93,000 square meters; 14,000 exhibitors; 100,000 articles (including industrial machinery, agricultural implements, wagons, carriages, and locomotives); goods from both the industrialized and "primitive" nations, arranged by Cole and Wyatt into divisions of minerals and raw materials, machinery, manufacturers, and fine arts. *The Times* reported that "the edifice, the treasures of art collected therein, the assemblage and the solemnity of the occasion, all conspired to suggest something even more than sense could scan, or imagination could attain."[72] One critic, William Whewell, referred to the Crystal Palace as the "magical glass" cabinet that brought together in time and space goods from different nations in different stages of artistic progress, revealing that mankind "is, by nature and universally, an artificer, an artisan, an artist."[73] Cole viewed the event as something that might help "to keep nations from going to blows as hastily and foolishly as they have been accustomed to do," in that it would increase awareness of other countries and travel. It was also, he was convinced, a signal of London's coming-of-age as a cosmopolitan center, a demonstration "that England, even in the question of art, was not behind other European nations."[74] Even though Semper's role in this grand affair was very small, its effect on his artistic education was enormous.

Semper first met Cole at the latter's home on Kensington High Street in December 1850. The meeting had been arranged by Chadwick, who had hoped Cole might be able to facilitate the publication of Semper's paper on polychromy. At the end of the meeting Cole kept Semper's portfolio, yet several weeks passed with no further communication. Finally Semper, who was then intent on furthering his scheme for an architectural boarding school, decided to seek Cole's favor by contacting him at the construction site of the Crystal Palace. He was denied entry, so he wrote a letter to Cole explaining his new plan for a school. Cole, who spent most of January trying the solve the problem of the building's leaking glass roof, responded with a short note in early February 1851, promising to promote Semper's plan. Later that month Cole returned Semper's portfolio with another short note offering his best wishes. At that time he must have placed Semper's name on the list of local interior decorators who were available to assist participating countries with their layouts. Early in the spring Semper received four requests (in most cases couched as diplomatic orders) to appear before various embassy officials and take charge of their country's layouts. He coordinated the displays of Turkey, Canada, Sweden, and Denmark, and also seems to have talked to officials of the Greek and American delegations.[75]

The jobs were relatively simple and consumed only a few weeks of time. But they allowed Semper not only the chance to examine the wares of these countries carefully but also to have access to the exhibition hall, at the time that the goods were being brought in and arranged. The exhibit for Turkey was the most important of the schemes for Semper, for it occupied a location at the corner of the main transept. The exhibit for Canada, for which several of Semper's sketches have survived (Pl. 80), was also interesting in that he could examine original North American Indian artifacts for the first time: polychrome implements, sandals, and clothing sewn from natural threads, feathers, animal and vegetable skins.

Over the course of the summer the still unemployed Semper visited the exhibition almost daily. He was much impressed both with the machinery of industrialization (far in advance of what he had known in Germany) and with such anthropological items as the "Caraib hut," a full-scale reproduction of a dwelling from the Caribbean island of

80 Gottfried Semper, sketch for the Canadian exhibit, Crystal Palace, London, 1851. Institut für Geschichte und Theorie der Architectur, Semper Archiv, ETH-Zurich.

Trinidad (Pl. 81). This simple habitat exemplified for him perfectly his "four elements" of architecture in their prototypical form. The clay hearth was set on a platform, a roof of reeds supported on a tectonic framework protected it from the weather, and mat-walls were hung vertically between the roof supports: "Every element of the construction is speaking for itself alone and has no connection with the others."[76]

Also of interest were the hedge-like lattice works of aboriginal tribes from the South Seas, which provided Semper with indisputable documentation of the authenticity and originality of the textile motif. Their binding together of branches or sticks with twine was raised to the symbolic level of a fetish, in that similar knot-like decorations were also found on household utensils, weapons, and canoes. Similarly, some grass skirts on display from Africa demonstrated for Semper so-called primitive man's intuitive grasp of color principles, in this case simple but effective compositions of yellow, black, and red strands: "It is generally recognized that the products of the most naive methods of material fabrication, as well as models for pattern and color, far surpassed the refined works of the civilized nations in what one calls style."[77]

The juxtaposition of these artifacts with the latest implements of technology made a very vivid impression. Machine products such as steam hammers, bessemer pumps, and boilers were placed alongside such raw and processed materials as the finest silks, satins, cottons, velvets, lace brocade, flax, and hemp. Rare woods and suits of armor competed for review against perfumes, tobaccos, exotic foods, and magnificent oriental carpets.

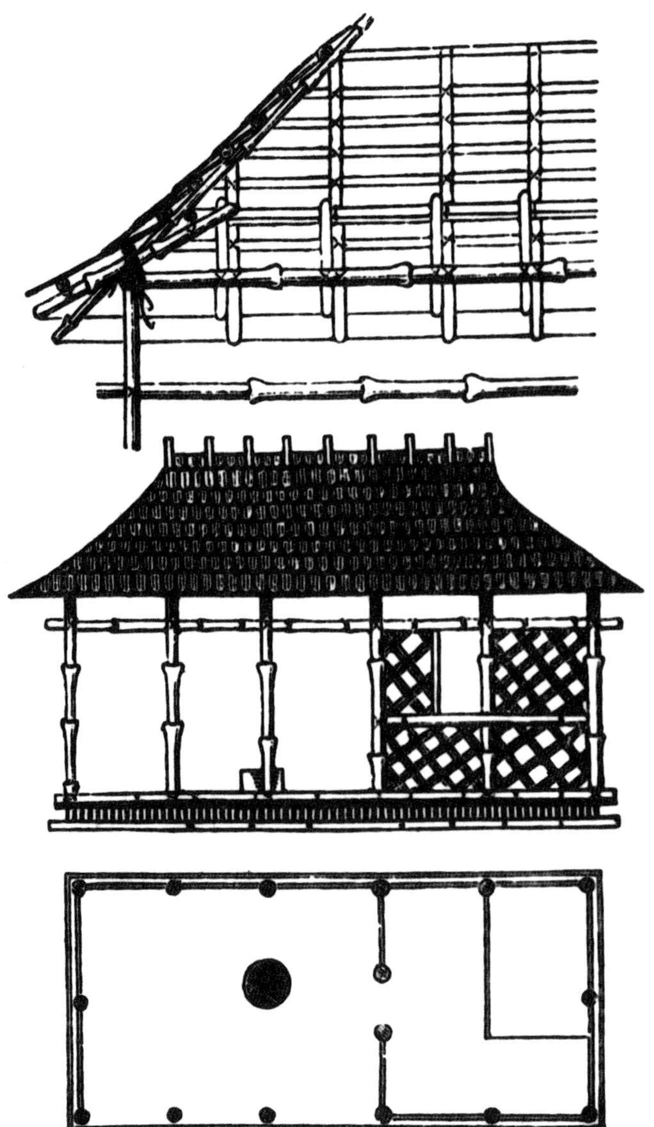

81 Caribbean hut from Trinidad on display at the Great Exhibition of 1851. From G. Semper, *Der Stil*, vol. II, 1863.

Interspersed throughout the gargantuan glass building were abundant specimens of contemporary art: jewelry, porcelain, carved furniture, and marble statuary. It was for this reason the Great Exhibition was often contemporaneously referred to as the "great university" of 1851. The cultures and the products of the West and the East appeared side by side for the first time.

Semper took in everything, while developing his ideas further. But the hot summer, his very real poverty, and the isolation of his personal life were also continuing to take their toll on him – psychologically, physically, and politically. By the end of August he had fallen into an altogether desperate condition and felt he could no longer continue. He wrote Bertha a tearful letter, in which he insisted on seeing her immediately; they arranged to meet in Belgium. After fretting over receiving his traveling papers in early September, Semper was able to spend two happy weeks with his wife in Bruges: their first face-to-face encounter in nearly two and a half years. Bertha, who was also enduring the separation with great distress and poverty, brought with her the two oldest boys, Manfred and Conrad. The three helped to give Semper a new fortitude.

On 3 October he was back in London, somewhat strengthened but also saddened by the vivid reminder of how brutally his once happy existence had been destroyed. The exhibition itself was just closing and Semper took the occasion, along with many others, to write a report on its meaning; a few weeks later he sent Vieweg a manuscript of three short chapters. The publisher, who had seen Semper in August during his visit to the exhibition, agreed to publish it only if its author promised to include in it a formal announcement of his long-delayed book on building theory.

Semper began to rework his manuscript and – on the advice of someone in London who was aware of the pending changes at the School of Design (almost certainly Chadwick) – he added four new chapters that surveyed some of the wares on display at the exhibition and outlined his views for improving artistic education. Thus early in 1852 Semper's second book written in political exile appeared in Germany, under the title *Wissenschaft, Industrie und Kunst: Vorschläge zur Anregung nationalen Kunstgefühles bei dem Schlusse der Londoner Industrie-Austellung* (Science, Industry, and Art: Proposals for the Development of a National Taste in Art at the Closing of the London Industrial Exhibition). With it, he took another significant step in his intellectual development.

The Future of Art in the Industrial Age

Few events in the history of English arts have given rise to as much literature, both contemporary and retrospective, as the London Exhibition of the Works of Industry of all Nations of 1851. And whereas the vast majority of writers, in particular those of the twentieth century, have tended to deprecate the art displayed – and, more specifically, the period's love of ornament – this view has not always been so generally shared, or at least earlier was given a different interpretation.

Writing in 1891, that is, forty years after the event, the architect Robert Kerr, for instance, derided those who cast "scorn and derision" on the exhibition and its artistic productions. The Victorian era symbolically commenced in the year 1851, he argued, and it was this particular event, this great "popularising of Art," that started a course of steady artistic improvement, not only for England but for Europe as well. It was at the exhibition, Kerr believed, that the exhausted academic tradition and its formulae finally spent themselves, that the constrained and pedantic "Fine Art of Architecture" stepped down from its pedestal to join hands with the "Minor Arts" and became the new "Industrial Art of Architecture." The arts and crafts, once deemed ornamental and inferior, were embraced by architecture in 1851, "no longer of unequal dignity with herself, but of altogether equal and similar comeliness of grace."[78]

Kerr's view on the importance of this event in reversing contemporary artistic tendencies found much support in the various commentaries that appeared around the time of the exhibition, writings that for the most part exemplify a very high level of analysis. Criticisms, in general, were quite similar in their direction and conclusions, and at heart they were not so different from Semper's slightly broader cultural analysis. It is against this body of criticism that Semper's own review should be measured.

One thing that is clearly evident in turning to this literature is that the crisis of art and its root causes at a time of advancing industrialization were apparent to nearly everyone. Thus Ralph Wornum's prize-winning review of the exhibition for the *Art Journal* inscribed the crisis of art within the broader stylistic debate, and he found much of contemporary art to be wanting. Of the objects on display, Wornum noted that there was nothing new in the sense that all works conformed to styles of the past. On the whole, the best understood style, particularly with regard to execution, was what he termed the mixed Cinquecento or early Renaissance style. The antithesis to the excellence of this mode was the inauthentic style of Louis Quinze, a taste strapped with all the overladen infelicities of the Rococo. This last style disregarded detailing, was superficial in its choice of motifs, degraded ornament in its search of display, "and where such a style prevails the paramount impression conveyed to the critical mind must be a general want of education in taste, just such an impression as the Great Exhibition gives at the moment."[79] This Rococo proclivity toward the "overloaded" was therefore the chief fault of Victorian art but at the same time a problem, he suggested, that could be easily corrected.

As for the British products on display, Wornum found them – with the possible exception of carpets, porcelain, and glass – very inferior to French designs. He attributed this limitation, however, to England's industrial advantage, that is, to the focusing of her efforts toward the "million" rather than toward the few. This was an important distinction, for whereas French items may possess great individual beauty, they "are not the fruits which will bring about the great results which should accrue from this unexampled event, though they may aid them negatively by rather warning us that beautiful objects may arise from infinitely less outlay of either time or substance."[80]

Aspects of Wornum's analysis also reveal just how deeply the principles of Augustus Welby Pugin had already penetrated English theory. A carpet should express flatness: no water lilies, no shaded recesses, no rococo scrolls. With pottery, porcelain, and glass, the shape of the vessel is the first consideration to be taken into account. Only with Wornum's acceptance of contemporary eclecticism, with his choice of conventional over naturalistic treatments within any given style, was he at odds with some of his peers. "A proper distinction between a picture or model and an ornament," he wrote, "is of the utmost importance to the designer, for the mere power of imitation of natural objects, and even their exact imitation, is perfectly compatible with the total ignorance of Ornamental Art."[81]

Wornum, like many at this time, opposed any naturalistic ornamental treatment, the "horticultural school," because it did not give proper attention to the object being decorated, and because of its inherently antifunctional result. The designer, he believed, should return to the proven and conventionalized themes of the past and continue to apply them in a pure or uncorrupted form, even if this would mean a continuation of eclecticism. In fact, there was no other option for him: "The time has perhaps now gone by, at least in Europe, for the development of any particular or national style, and for this reason it is necessary to distinguish the various tastes that have prevailed throughout past ages, and preserve them as distinct expressions; or otherwise, by using indiscriminately all materials, we should lose all expression, and the very essence of ornament, the conveying of a distinct aesthetic expression, be utterly destroyed."[82]

It was on this issue of whether the present style should remain bound to historical examples that Wornum's analysis differed from that of Richard Redgrave, whose official jury report for the exhibition presented one of the most comprehensive and incisive analyses of contemporary artistic developments of this time. Redgrave began his study, entitled "Supplementary Report on Design," by first distinguishing between ornament and design. He wrote that the latter includes ornament but refers more specifically to the construction of a work; ornament is limited and secondary, that is, it is the decoration of the thing constructed. This was an important distinction for Redgrave, as it was earlier for Pugin, and it formed not only the basis of his criticism but also led to what he deemed the foremost error observed at the exhibition – that of constructing ornament rather than ornamenting construction. The result was an excessive use of ornament, which in a negative sense led the visitor to develop an admiration for "those objects of absolute utility (the machines and utensils of various kinds), where use is so paramount that ornament is repudiated, and, fitness of purpose being the end sought, a noble simplicity is the result."[83]

This quasi-functionalism of Redgrave permeated his entire stylistic review. The true styles of the past, he argued, reflected a tradition neither good nor bad in themselves but always sustaining a local use and symbolic life. Moreover, ornamental details were conceived in certain materials at a certain scale, and for a particular situation, none of which could be duplicated today. Thus the task of modern "ornamentists" was to search out the principles of the past, but not imitate historical models in themselves. Redgrave further argued that the two classes of modern ornamental designers – the traditionalists and the modernists – both failed in this requirement. The traditionalists were the eclectics, "men of limited ideas and small progress," for whom art bears no responsibility to be original; the moderns were those who advocate the present course of naturalism, where "or-molu stems and leaves bear porcelain flowers painted to imitate nature, and candles are made to rise out of tulips and China asters, while gas jets gush forth from opal Arums."[84]

This last tendency, he concluded, has its roots in industrialism and here the second and more serious dimension of the problem emerges. Whereas the ornament of the past was founded and practiced as a handicraft, now it was the product of the machine. Whereas the artist was once the ornamental designer and executing craftsman, now the stamp, mold, press, and die have removed the product to the factory where it is produced in the thousands. Whereas each product was before rendered unique by the individual efforts of the artist, now the same are stamped out commercially in a "sickening monotony." Finally, whereas the artist of old worked out of love of labor, piety, or fame, now the designer in the factory is paid barely better than the workman and both are ill-trained for their tasks. As a result, "Whenever ornament is wholly effected by machinery, it is certainly the most degraded in style and execution; and the best workmanship and the best taste are to be found in those manufactures and fabrics wherein handicraft is entirely or partially the means of producing the ornament as in china and glass, in works in the precious metals, carving, etc."[85]

This same qualitative disparity between machine-made and hand-crafted items, Redgrave believed, also carried over into architecture:

> In other ages of the world, nations have been fortunate in so adapting design to prevailing wants, and in sympathy with existing feelings, as to produce a national style. But in the present day men no longer attend to such considerations; they are wholly without such guiding principles, and consequently are totally without a characteristic

> style. They are satisfied with the indiscriminate reproduction of the architecture of Egypt, Greece and Rome, or of Christendom in any, or all, its marked periods. Originality they have none.[86]

There were, of course, other factors leading architecture into this condition. Differences in climate were not being taken into consideration by modern imitators, nor were the conditions of contemporary society, its fiscal limitations, and modern habits. In the end, the dual crises found in architecture and in the industrial arts were inseparable: "It is this merely imitative character of architecture which has so largely contributed to decorative *shams,* to the age of putty, papier maché, and gutta percha. These react upon architecture; and, from the cheapness with which such ornament can be applied and its apparent excellence, the florid and the gaudy take the place of the simple and the true."[87]

In this way the uplifting of architecture's degraded condition was bound to the problem of industrial reform, which of course pivoted on the reformation of the design schools. Redgrave's whole report, in fact, echoed in each and every detail the editorial position of the *Journal of Design.*

A few years later, Matthew Wyatt would refer to Redgrave's exhibition report as an endorsement and amplification of the principles that Owen Jones had laid down in his "Gleanings from the Great Exhibition of 1851," a series of articles published in the summer of 1851 in the *Journal of Design.*[88] Jones and Wyatt may indeed have been the guiding intellectual forces within the Cole circle, for in many respects their ideas and analyses were in advance of both Cole and Redgrave.

Jones, in his capacity as the exhibition correspondent for the *Journal of Design,* argued that the Eastern countries – India, Tunis, Egypt, and Turkey – offered the most instructive lessons in ornament at the exhibition, in particular with regard to textiles. The decorative repose and the harmony of color and line of these textiles were due to the fact that their ornamental designs were considered first as a unit, second materially, and third for their use of conventional forms. Moreover, the designs were always abstract surface decorations – "no carpets with flowers whereupon the foot would fear to tread" – fully conforming to the perceptual laws of color. "The patterns of their shawls and carpets," noted Jones, "are harmonious and effective from the proper distribution of form and colour, and do not require to be heightened in effect by strong and positive oppositions; the great aim appears to be that coloured objects, viewed at a distance, should present a neutralized bloom – each step nearer exhibits fresh beauties, a close inspection reveals the means whereby such effects are produced."[89]

The "bloom" for Jones, which derived from the theories of Michel Chevreul, was the perfect proportional balance of contrasting hues so as to produce from afar a neutral, even white, radiance of warmth. Jones concluded his "Gleanings" with six principles that should govern ornamental design, at the head of which was the now familiar tenet that construction should be decorated, decoration never constructed. In two lectures given in 1852 Jones expanded his principles first to twenty-two, then to thirty-three propositions.[90] In their final form, in the *Grammar of Ornament,* the same list was enlarged to thirty-seven propositions.

Wyatt reviewed the exhibition from the commercial and industrial, as well as the ornamental viewpoint. To Jones's six summary principles he added a few other "dicta" dealing with the adjustment of an ornament's scale and pattern to fit the fabric, with material considerations, with color, and with the making of the initial decision to select a "pictorial" or "mosaic" type of decoration (with or without a background). In his formal exhibition lecture presented in 1852, he attempted to define the principles of design in a slightly more metaphysical way, as when he came to speak (echoing Semper) of the wondrous variety of nature operating from a few select laws. The education of the artist should begin with learning to see and feel nature, then with enjoying, selecting, and storing in his memory the characteristics of natural forms.[91]

More important were various remarks that Wyatt made on the commercial and industrial ramifications of the exhibition. In his preface to *The Industrial Arts of the Nineteenth Century: A Series of Illustrations of the Choicest Specimens Produced by Every Nation at the Great Exhibition of Works of Industry* (1851), Wyatt saw the event as the culmination of a thirty-six year industrial process (commencing with the end of the Napoleonic wars), reflecting the "universality of development attained by combining the division of labour in manufacturing with the aggregation of results in commerce."[92] The exhibition, he felt, had become the beacon to the industrial age, just as the Olympic games were to Greece or as fairs were to the Middle Ages.

In another article published in the *Journal of Design*, entitled "The Exhibition under its Commercial Aspects," Wyatt described the pace of industrial change as "double speed," and sought to allay the fear that the exhibition would work to the profit of foreign competitors. Not only did he deem these fears unfounded, but he hoped that the exhibition was softening the nationalist prejudice that prompted such feelings in the first place: "The kindly spirit and style in which the truly distinguished foreigners who are now visiting this country have been received gives us hopes that much most unworthy prejudice has been done away with."[93]

Both Jones and Wyatt saw important ramifications for architecture arising out of the Great Exhibition. Jones's denunciation of historicism recalls that of Redgrave, yet he traced the problem to the proliferation of publications chronicling each and every style, from Stuart and Revett's folio on Greece to Pugin's more recent efforts exalting Gothic architecture. "I mourn over the loss which this age has suffered, and still continues to suffer," he admitted, "by so many fine minds devoting all their talents to the reproduction of a galvanised corpse."[94]

This aping of the past had recently gone from bad to worse with the casting of classical or Gothic details, and most recently Elizabethan details, in iron. "We have no more business to clothe ourselves in medieval garments, than to shut ourselves in cloisters and talk Latin," he said – a refrain that became popular later in the century.[95] Yet the blame for the various revivals should not be shouldered solely by architects, for it was the public too that demanded that steamhouses appear as "mosque tombs of the caliphs of Cairo" with chimney shafts decorated as minarets. Jones hoped that the Great Exhibition would have the salutary effect of opening the eyes of the British public to this want of taste.

Jones admonished architects to press their talents forward rather than backward, but he was somewhat vague as to how this "new style" could be accomplished. He viewed architecture, in effect, as an evolving decorative language of conventional forms. The Moors, for instance, inherited the egg-and-tongue molding from the Roman arch, a motif that they doubled and tripled to form their stalactite pendentives. The Greeks had done the same with certain Egyptian and Assyrian forms, such as the honeysuckle ornament.

Jones in the end thus advocated a potpourri of selected principles from the past: the symbolic attributes of Egyptian architecture, the purity and grace of Greek forms, and the polychrome system of the Arabs and Indians. In this last regard, he was an even more unabashed exponent of polychromy than Semper. He defended his color scheme for the exhibition building by insisting that color would enhance the grandeur of Paxton's structure by increasing the height, length, and breadth of the building, giving solidity and distinctness to the structural lines, and "bring the building and its contents into one perfect harmony."[96] He also sought the "bloom" effect: a neutral merging of hues of blue, red, and yellow in the proportions of 8:5:3, separated by lines of white. By all accounts, his scheme enjoyed great success.

It took the critical acumen of Wyatt, the architect supervising the construction of Crystal Palace, to relate Paxton's iron-and-glass design to the new suspension bridges and to industrialization in general. He concluded a highly negative assessment of contemporary iron design in one article in late-1850 with a somewhat guarded yet nevertheless enthusiastic appraisal of the exhibition building in Hyde Park, then under construction: "Whatever the result may be, it is impossible to disregard the fact that the building for the Exhibition of 1851 is likely to accelerate the 'Consummation so devoutly to be wished,' and that the novelty of its forms and details will be likely to exercise a powerful influence upon national taste."[97]

It was thus in an effusive, and sophisticated, artistic climate that Semper penned his own remarks on the Great Exhibition in his pamphlet *Science, Industry, and Art.*

The metaphor Semper first selected to characterize the exhibition and its effect on the arts was that of "a kind of Babel," the confusion of which pointed to "certain anomalies within existing social conditions."[98] These anomalies were the result for the most part of the fast pace of change, induced by scientific breakthroughs and rampant industrialization. Whereas in the past the invention of a new material or a product evolved slowly from a recognizable problem, now the process had been reversed: industry had flooded the marketplace with new methods, materials, machines, and implements, which in themselves were inducing change. Quite simply, "Practice wearies itself in vain in trying to master its material, especially intellectually. It receives it from science ready to process as it chooses, but before its style evolved through many centuries of popular usage."[99] As a result the artist has had little time to reflect upon the proper applications of these abundant means. The hardest granites could now be cut like chalk, ivory and rubber could be molded to imitate other materials. Metal was being processed in ever more efficient ways, and machines in general "sew, knit, embroider, paint, carve, and encroach deeply into the field of human art, putting to shame every human skill."[100] This devaluation of labor has led, in turn, to a devaluation of meaning, such that art produced in a traditional way, by hand, now comes to be seen as eccentric.

This superabundance of means was only one aspect of the problem, however, in that the direction of art was also being fundamentally altered by the speculative forces of capitalism. The marketplace was not merely responding, as it did in the past, to existing needs, but it was actually creating new needs and concomitant desires. Capitalism was in a certain sense insinuating itself into the marketplace along with the arbitrary forces of public taste, creating fad, fashion, and an economic system predicated on consumption; this amalgamation became the new arbiter of taste and commercial success. In working for the forces of capitalism, the industrial artist had now become doubly dependent:

"a slave to his employer and to the latest fashion that provides the employer with a market for his wares. Man sacrifices his individuality, his 'birthright,' for a pottage of lentils."[101]

Artistic forms, once the realm of the few and knowledgeable, were now directed to the many, and the quality of the goods produced necessarily became degraded when everything was "calculated and tailored for the marketplace."[102] And because items intended for mass consumption lacked a specific place or occasion for their use, they needed to be made for the broadest possible use and be capable of becoming neutral with every possible surrounding. With certain items, such as with carriages, weapons, and musical instruments, Semper argued, this denuding of forms of their traditional ornamental vocabulary worked to the advantage of all. But in other respects, in particular with regard to high art, a very interesting and even more profound transformation was also taking place: "While our art industries carry on aimlessly they unconsciously fulfill one noble task: the *disintegration of traditional types* by their ornamental treatment."[103]

It is on this issue that Semper's critique departs markedly from those of his British colleagues. Whereas critics such as Wornum and Redgrave – with all of their progressive tendencies – still saw the solution to the contemporary artistic crisis largely in terms of a choice between conventional or naturalistic ornaments applied to more rational construction, Semper in his analysis now rejected both avenues of development. Rather, he began to see that these "certain anomalies" within artistic production, phenomena induced by the forces of industrialization and capitalism, were in essence destroying the historical basis of art altogether, the traditional art of Europe's past. Moreover, this was a process that could not be halted; nor was it an aberration peculiar to the "backwoods Anglo-Saxons" as opposed to the Continental defenders of Europe's old art: "Let us not delude ourselves! Those conditions most certainly are going to have a general validity for us [Germans and French], because they correspond to circumstances that prevail in all countries; and second, we are becoming aware only too painfully that high art especially is being fatally hit."[104]

If this remark seems like an extraordinary insight for 1851, it is doubly so in view of the startling conclusion Semper drew from it. Rather than decry this loss of art's traditional values – the replication of historical motifs that he described as "borrowed or stolen" – Semper applauded this process of "disintegration" and insisted that for the future of art it could not happen fast enough: "*This process of disintegrating existing art types must be completed by industry, by speculation, and by applied science before something good and new can result.*"[105] These are the words of the same author who only one year earlier had apologized for his appropriation of historical forms, because his age lacked "a new concept of universal historical importance"!

Semper's analysis of the situation also differed from that of his British colleagues in another crucial respect. Even though his criticism in passages paralleled the remarks of Jones and others in its exaltation of "those simple melodies of form and color" found in the artistic productions of non-European cultures, Semper never viewed these non-industrialized paradigms as something that could be grafted onto a conventionalized European system. The contemporary artistic crisis was on the contrary a style problem – but not in the historical sense that Wornum cast it. Rather, style was the process of defining the proper normative values for artistic production, which had to rise within the European cultural system.

82 Augustus Welby Pugin, "Mediæval Court." From *The Illustrated Exhibitor: A Tribute to the World's Industrial Jubilee*, 1851.

Semper's text, in fact, revolves around his style theory, which defines this concept in this way:

> Style means giving emphasis and artistic significance to the basic idea and to all intrinsic and extrinsic coefficients that modify the embodiment of the theme in a work of art. According to this definition, absence of style signifies the shortcomings of a work caused by the artist's disregard of the underlying theme, and his ineptitude in exploiting aesthetically the means available for perfecting the work.[106]

This is nearly the same definition that he developed in his earlier lectures and again it unfolds in three distinct parts. First there is the basic idea or motive of the work of art, the intention and theme that should embody and convey its meaning. Second there are the internal factors affecting artistic production, such as the material and the technical means employed in a work's fabrication. Third there are the external variables influencing style: the local, temporal, national, and personal forces. It must be emphasized that none of these so-called coefficients in themselves determine a work's form, but merely bring certain pressures to bear on the underlying motive or idea. This theme, "like a musical theme," remains the ideological and idealistic heart of Semper's style conception. Such a tripartite definition also became the organizational basis of all his future deliberations on style.

It was only in the second half of *Science, Industry, and Art*, in those chapters added in the last months of 1851, that Semper actually reviewed some of the art works and products on display at the exhibition. Yet even here – sandwiched between his condemnations of modern sculpture, Lyon fabrics, Gobelin tapestries, and the endless English ornamental permutations on *Victoria regia* – Semper reverted back constantly to the underlying style problem and extolled the educational measures needed to correct it. Curiously, one area of English design that he praised, in addition to the ceramics of Herbert Minton, were "some truly good things" assembled in Pugin's "Mediæval Court" (Pl. 82). Cole and his *Journal of Design* had been championing Pugin's design principles for several years, very recently against the political backdrop of antagonism toward his Roman Catholic beliefs and liturgical designs on display in Hyde Park.[107] It is an interesting question if Semper – whose own antogonism toward Gothicism and Catholicism had remained unchanged since the campaign waged against him in Hamburg – was aware of Cole's support for Pugin in this regard.

Other chapters of *Science, Industry, and Art* seem to have been written precisely with Cole in mind. One chapter is entirely given over to discussing the inappropriate division of the industrial and fine arts: in essence a tirade against the European academic and industrial-art system of education in general. Another chapter is devoted to Semper's proposals to reform public taste, which, as he noted in his letter to Vieweg, were conceived and written for an English public. These proposals stressed the need for collections (arranged thematically according to Semper's four elementary motives), lectures, workshops, and prizes – all of which he proposed should be housed in the "glass-covered vacuum" of the Crystal Palace. Some scholars, among them Leopold Ettlinger, have placed much emphasis on the progressive nature of these proposals, regarding them as a prophetic blueprint for the future South Kensington complex.[108] Although there may indeed be some basis for such a reading, the proposals probably had a much more pragmatic basis in the need to find employment in England.

Nevertheless, *Science, Industry, and Art* is unique within Semper's literary works just for its revolutionary views regarding art and industrialization. Semper's ebullience in discussing the destruction of Europe's traditional art was clearly related to the vast spectacle before him, to the overwhelming juxtaposition of this half-Victorian, half-industrial, half-modern panorama of cultural artifacts. Indeed, the lure of the exhibition for many was owing to the contradictory answers that it presented with regard to the future. Near the end of his essay, Semper reflected on three American daguerreotypes – fixed *tableaux vivants* – in which "Past, Present, and Future" were represented by three young women. But one women was darker and more serious than the other two: was she the past or the future?, he asked with great concern.

The same question could be posed with regard to Semper's transitory enthusiasm for the destruction of traditional art, for in a few years he reverted to a defense of these same artistic values against the social and industrial pressures to do away with them. But this seeming contradiction can be explained more by the circumstances under which this text was written than to any failing of his theory. It underscores this most difficult period of the author's life, when the pain and pressures of fitting into a foreign society were most acute.

Professor at the Department of Practical Art

The Great Exhibition was in every respect a resounding success. Throngs of curious visitors streamed into London from across the British Isles, the Continent, and the Atlantic during the summer of 1851. Less than two months into the event, it became evident that it was going to produce unexpected profits of a magnitude sufficient to require some major public gesture. Toward the middle of August various royal commissioners were already discussing to what end the vast surplus of proceeds might be directed.[109]

Dr. Lyon Playfair, the respected chemist and a special advisor to the committee, made various suggestions for educational institutions, among them a Museum for Economic Geology. Cole soon convinced him of the need for a College of Art and Manufacturers, one that would also assimilate the School of Design. Prince Albert was also in favor of this plan for cultural institutions, and suggested purchasing a large tract of land in South Kensington on which to build the complex, leaving open the question of the number and types of facilities.

Around the same time another decision was made, no doubt prompted by Cole, to spend a portion of the profits on selected wares from the exhibition itself, so that a design museum might be established for the School of Design. Early in October an acquisition committee consisting of Cole, Redgrave, and Jones – joined as well by Pugin – scoured the exhibition hall for suitable items. Pugin was not at all happy with some of the selections and a few weeks later he became ill with what eventually turned out to be his final nervous breakdown. These purchases formed the basis of the collection today housed in the Victoria and Albert Museum.

Cole's political star, with the exhibition behind him, was very much on the rise. At the end of October, three weeks after the close of the exhibition, he was privately offered the prize he had long coveted: the administrative directorship of the School of Design and its affiliates. The official announcement was made in January and Cole wasted no time in correlating his plans for his school with those of Prince Albert for South Kensington.[110] The Prince Consort formally proposed the purchase of land in South Kensington in early January 1852, and he offered Cole the use of Marlborough House for his institution on an interim basis – that is, until new buildings could be erected. The School had formerly operated out of Somerset House, but its quarters were too confining. Around the same time Richard Redgrave was appointed by the Board of Trade to be the Superintendent of Art for the School of Design, in charge of revamping the artistic curriculum for the entire network of schools.

Also in January, the various schools of design and the design museum for the London school were reorganized by the Board of Trade into the Department of Practical Art. Its new mission, as suggested by Cole, was to give special instruction in the knowledge and in the practice of ornamental art, the "practical application of such knowledge to the improvement of Manufactures."[111] The *Journal of Design* ran its last issue as Cole poured all his energy into building his new bureaucratic empire. By 1864, from his offices at the Department of Science and Art (so named in 1856) in South Kensington, he was managing over ninety art schools, the museum, and 16,000 students with the same administrative efficiency he had earlier applied to the postal system and public records office.

Semper's eventual connection with the Department of Practical Art emerged only after frustration and difficulty. In the middle of November 1851, as Cole was preparing for a short tour of Germany and Austria, he discussed with Chadwick his prospective new appointment – although by this time it surely could not have been much of a surprise to anyone.[112] Shortly thereafter, Chadwick probably informed Semper of the pending reorganization of industrial-art education. At least this seems plausible, for it was around this time that Semper decided to write the last four chapters to *Science, Industry, and Art* and outline his views on reforming national taste.

When Cole returned to London at the end of January, Semper sent him a formal letter of application for a faculty position at the School of Design, pointing out his qualifications as a teacher. These included his experience with decorative works, furniture design, silversmithing, china production, and bronze casting.[113] Cole had in fact visited Dresden on his tour through Germany, to view Semper's architectural work firsthand, and he recorded some positive remarks about the Dresden Theater.[114]

Despite this, Semper was still far down on Cole's list of priorities, as the new director was much more concerned with securing the resignation of some existing faculty members and appointing more loyal replacements. He was, at least, sympathetic to Semper's agonizing financial plight and in a charitable letter of acknowledgment he sent Semper a check for £5, "until you get rich enough to repay it to me." He also offered to assist Semper in securing "the commission for [drawing] some simple outlines of objects."[115]

In February, Cole acquired the services of J. Simpson to teach a class on "Painting on China." During the same month the former director of the School of Design, William Dyce, lobbied for a position as a lecturer in Applied Ornament, but his efforts were unsuccessful. Cole was also engaged in some delicate negotiations with Ralph Wornum, who had been the highest paid lecturer at the school during the previous year. The new director was unable to ease him out as he wished, but he did manage to restructure and expand Wornum's duties to include that of librarian; he also commissioned him to write a catalogue on the museum's acquisitions.

Cole was unsuccessful in some of his other efforts, too. It is probable that he would have preferred to have Pugin become connected with the School, but the prominent architect and ornamentalist showed no signs of recovering from his mental collapse. Cole also lost the assistance of Owen Jones and Digby Wyatt, both of whom – for a handsome fee – had received in May the commission to relocate the Crystal Palace in Sydenham. After failing to come to a suitable arrangement with Cole over his fees, Jones did give a series of lectures at the School in June 1852, but he never became officially connected with the Department of Practical Art.[116]

It was in March that Cole apparently first considered Semper for teaching a class on ceramics. In the middle of the month he asked Semper to visit Minton at the pottery works in Stoke-on-Trent, in order to prepare for a lecture and write a report on some nearby schools of design. He was trying, in fact, to ascertain the extent of Semper's expertise in this field. Minton himself was confused by Semper's unannounced visit (which was to last several weeks) and felt the architect had "much to learn," although he did not doubt his good taste.[117] Semper in his report upon leaving Stoke-on-Trent commented very positively on Minton's designs for decorative tiles and majolica wares, although he found the glazed roof tiles to be less than perfect.[118]

Minton's first letter seems to have dissuaded Cole from considering Semper for a class on ceramics, but by the end of April he had come up with an alternative. He commissioned the architect, for the very large fee of £180, to prepare what Semper referred to as a *catalogue raisonné* of decorative metal works: a comprehensive historical description of this field. He also hinted that if Semper were able to complete this task successfully, there would be a teaching position for him at the Department of Practical Art.

Semper was naturally excited about the project and he plunged into the task with great enthusiasm. In seeking examples and information he wrote to a host of longtime and more recent friends on the Continent: Braun in Rome, Vieweg in Braunschweig, Séchan in Paris, Julia von Zerzog in Regensburg, Bülau in Hamburg, even his successor Nicolai in Dresden. He put in long days at the British Museum: making sketches of various collections and exhausting the museum's rich library. He confided in Bertha that he was working seven days a week, every evening till seven or eight, taking only a piece of bread and cup of tea during the day. Semper even hired a draftsman at one stage to accelerate progress. The scope of the project within such a limited time frame, however, was once again beyond reasonable human expectation, but the manuscript Semper delivered to Cole in early August – entitled "Practical Art in Metal and Hard Materials (ware): Its Technology, History and Styles" – was notable in that he brought together many of the theoretical issues that he had been developing previous to and since his experience with the Great Exhibition.

The text begins as a discourse on museology, in which Semper extols the importance of collections as "a sort of index to the history of culture."[119] He likened them in their intellectual spirit to the values Immanuel Kant espoused in his essay, "Idea for a Universal History from a Cosmopolitan Point of View." Also contained in this introduction was his "Plan for an Ideal Museum," a conceptual framework within which to organize and consider all artistic productions. His earlier "four elements" are more clearly identified as motives here, placed in the four production categories of 1) twisting, weaving, spinning, or the fabrication of thin, pliable materials (such as textiles); 2) ceramics or the kneading of soft, plastic materials; 3) the carpenter's art or the framing of sticklike components into constructional systems; and 4) masonry, the idea of cutting up hard materials into given forms and combining these small hard pieces into larger objects. In this scheme, the particular materials used in each of these processes is irrelevant; what counts is the motive itself. For example, a metal tripod represents the carpentry or tectonic motive, while a zigzag motif on a ceramic vase alludes to its textile origin in basket weaving. The so-called ideal museum was to arrange its artifacts according to the four categories, with a fifth division to be reserved for the combination of the four motives in such higher arts as architecture. This proposed scheme of Semper's later proved very influential when the first applied-arts museums began to take shape, including the one in South Kensington.

The same conceptual framework was then applied to the topic of metal artifacts. The first section deals with metal leaves, plates, and threads; the second with objects cast in metal; the third with trellis works and metal assemblages; the fourth entails the "cutting out of massive pieces of hard and costly materials." A fifth section treats "monuments in metal, high art." With this framework defined and laid out, Semper next offers a wealth of examples illustrating each category.

A seventeen-page bibliography at the end of the manuscript attests to the wide variety of sources he consulted in his research. This was without question the most important aspect of his study, as he was now gathering material for his later book on style. Passages in fact appear in the catalogue on metal objects that reappear in the later text. For the first time, for instance, Semper attempted to draw his famous comparison between the Greek *hydria* and Egyptian *situla*: interpreting the ethnographic cultures of the two nations through the forms of their respective vessels for carrying water. Thus this commission proved of great importance to Semper. Through his preparation of the manuscript, although it was hurriedly written and never published, he was able to carry out research in a field with which he was unfamiliar and to refine his ideas on style one stage further.

Semper presented the final parts of his manuscript to Cole in the first half of August 1852, amid another fit of depression. In a tearful letter to Bertha he complained bitterly of his contempt for his own impoverished existence and how much he yearned to flee to America and start his life anew. This suffering, however, could have been avoided, because Cole had been lobbying the Board of Trade for permission to hire the political refugee since early July. Cole had to demonstrate that he was not hiring a revolutionary.

On 19 August Semper received from Cole the happy news of his new professorship. In the official letter from the Board of Trade, which followed almost one month later, he was appraised of his duties "to afford instruction in the principles and practice of Ornamental Art applied to Metal Manufactures."[120] His salary was paltry (£150 annually), but there was the promise of additional income from outside commissions and public lectures. "I am resolved to pass this test like a true philosopher," he now wrote to Bertha, asking her to bring herself and the children to London "without having to ask Mother again for money."[121] After more than three years in desperate isolation, under living conditions that would have broken many lesser spirits, Semper was finally able to reclaim some measure of dignity.

His appointment, in fact, completely transformed his life and brought him into contact with groups of people who, long after this association had ended, continued to influence his intellectual outlook. Cole and Redgrave were chief among them. Both within and without the department, Cole fought all the political and financial battles to keep the schools running and expanding. Redgrave was charged with setting out the educational theory and syllabus for the schools, although Cole had considerable authority in this area as well. He preferred to make the schools as financially independent of government subsidies as possible, and to this end he sought paid commissions from manufacturers, and charged special fees for lectures (except for those students on scholarship), made inventories, took attendance, mandated desk sizes, and prepared extensive annual reports that underscored his administrative efficiency.

Redgrave's pedagogy, in general, stressed the teaching of geometrical perspective and copying from prescribed examples in lieu of the former emphasis on figure drawing. Theory was almost totally excluded from the program. General instruction – excluding those special classes on metals and other topics – was given under the four headings of drawing, painting, modeling, and composition, and comprised twenty-two stages. The student passed from geometry and the sketching of flat patterns to three-dimensional ornaments and figures, before concluding the process with a final course on elementary design.

Redgrave, like Cole, was also an avid catechist in his teaching of art. Semper's very first task, as we learn from a note of Redgrave to Cole, was to produce a set of axioms, "something in the shape of Owen Jones's propositions," to be displayed in his classroom.[122] Incidentally, the Marlborough House, a spacious, red-brick mansion located at the west end of Pall Mall, adjacent to Buckingham Palace, provided very respectable temporary accommodation for the School.

It was Cole's belief that the heart of the Department of Practical Art should be the museum, whose collections were greatly enhanced by the items selected from the Great Exhibition, mostly from the Middle Eastern and Asian sections. The museum expanded rapidly in the 1850s as first Wornum – and beginning in 1853, John Charles Robinson – made extensive purchases on travels to the Continent. Other faculty members occasionally argued for certain acquisitions. Redgrave confined most of his attention to paintings and in 1856 he was successful in obtaining the Sheepshanks Collection of English works for the museum. At this stage, there was even political skirmishing between the Department of Practical Art and the National Gallery over which institution would house the best British paintings.

Shortly after joining the faculty, Semper advised Redgrave and Cole to purchase some castings of antique gems and medals from Berlin, and in the following year he wrote a report on the new acquisitions in the metalworks division.[123] One of the more infamous episodes connected with the museum (satirized by Charles Dickens in a short story) was its "chamber of horrors," a special room set aside for contemporary objects designed according to "False Principles." A brief political firestorm ensued when the manufacturers of some of these horrors complained to the Board of Trade and the room was quickly turned over to more worthy items.

Semper maintained a respectful and professional relationship with the other faculty members, although he developed no special friendships beyond a certain cordiality with the museum curator, J. C. Robinson. Semper's new position and the arrival of Bertha and the children required that he take a larger flat near Hyde Park – from which he could walk to from work, occasionally with Cole. Robinson, was both knowledgeable about and sympathetic toward art of the Renaissance period, and hence shared some of Semper's tastes in design. Semper's polychrome and archaeological interests should have been appealing to Owen Jones and Digby Wyatt, yet there was little contact and even less warmth between these men. Jones, for some reason, was particularly cold, even hostile toward Semper. At no time during the latter's unemployment did Jones seek to assist him in any way. Later the Welshman privately opposed all of Semper's minor commissions in connection with the Sydenham Crystal Palace in 1854, and with the British section at the Paris Exposition of 1855.[124] Jealousy is perhaps the best explanation for this behavior.

The only architects of stature that Semper did converse with regularly in London were Thomas L. Donaldson and C. R. Cockerell, both of whom had initially made their reputations as archaeologists in connection with Greece. Semper had first met Donaldson on his London visit in 1839, and in the mid-1840s he wrote to him from Dresden regarding his planned book on comparative building theory. Donaldson returned the favor in London by inviting Semper to the meetings of the Royal Institute of British Architects at which the issue of polychromy was discussed. In March 1853, Semper advised Cockerell on the acoustics of the concert hall for St. George's Hall in Liverpool. The work had been started by Harvey Lonsdale Elmes in the 1840s, and was being completed by Cockerell after Elmes's premature death. Semper had his son translate his monograph on the Dresden Theater, which discussed his ideas on acoustics extensively. He passed this to Cockerell along with a copy of the original German text. Cockerell in return sent Semper a "trifling gratuity" for his advice and counsel.[125]

Semper's closest friends in London, in fact, were two Germans: Lothar Bucher and Karl Wilhelm Siemens. He had met Bucher through the association of German refugees and the latter later played a very important role in the unification of Germany through his work for Bismarck. Karl Wilhelm Siemens (later Sir William) was the younger brother to the founder of the electrical conglomerate, Ernst Werner Siemens. Karl, after his education in Germany, had come to England to promote several of their inventions, and he eventually installed a subsidiary of his firm there to take advantage of the progressive patent laws. His principal invention of the 1840s was the differential governor for steam engines, and profits from this helped start the British branch of his family's business. He became Semper's closest confidant in London, as their range of intellectual interests often overlapped and mutually benefited each other.

At the Department of Practical Art Semper easily settled into a routine of teaching and undertaking small commissions. When he first joined the faculty in September 1852 he had only two paying students, with eight others on scholarships. Beginning in the summer of 1853 he incorporated his metals class into a larger division on "Practical Construction, Architecture, and Plastic Decorations." He gained eight architectural students and taught a second class on geometrical perspective to seventeen students. These two classes grew to a combined thirty-five students in 1854.[126] In addition, in his annual report Semper listed fifty students in his "masters in training" studio, in which he focused on the general principles of style. By this date he had become an important and respected member of the School's faculty. Among his London architectural students was his oldest son Manfred (born 1838), who was just embarking on his own career.

Semper's educational beliefs had not changed since his teaching days in Dresden and they were to some extent at odds with those of Henry Cole. He outlined his ideas in his first departmental report, prepared in December 1852, and entitled "Scheme of Instruction for the Metal, Furniture and Pottery Division." In it he cited the importance of workshops or atelier instruction instead of classroom exercises. He thought students should not be segregated by age or level of advancement, and that they should also be given experience by being allowed to assist the professor with his own commissions. Semper broke his instruction down into three parts. The first consisted of geometric principles of design (including perspective); the second, the principles of style. The third part of his course was intended to teach students "how to invent objects of ornamental art," that is, to foster imagination and creativity, so that the students need not "pass the whole of their time copying and making studies after nature, without trying their forces on their own creations."[127]

This third part of his program opposed Redgrave's approach of teaching by imitation, and it is not surprising that Cole deleted it from the final published report. Cole also did not care much for Semper's suggestion of bi-weekly and bi-annual competitions for his students. The first competition was to take place every other Monday and be a one-day exercise; the latter, on a somewhat reduced scale, imitated the awards traditionally presented to the best students at academies. In later reports, Semper noted the problems and progress of his students. In his 1853 report he requested that the Department purchase a textbook for his class on architectural design, Paul-Marie Letarouilly's *Edifices de Rome moderne* – "the best collection of fine specimens of modern architecture for use in schools of architecture."[128]

The commissions that were passed down to faculty members from various manufacturers, and the evening cycle of lectures, were both intended by Cole as revenue-making enterprises for the Department of Practical Art, although they were not always successful in this. The most famous of the commissions, granted a few days after Semper joined the staff in October 1852, came about through the death of the Duke of Wellington. The Crown, after rejecting earlier designs, charged the Department of Practical Art with the task of designing and building the funeral wagon to transport the Duke's coffin from Whitehall to St. Paul's Cathedral. The much heralded military commander and politician, the hero of Waterloo, was to be afforded an impressive state funeral – postponed two months in fact by the preparations. The hearse itself was a gilded, six-wheeled wagon, richly appointed with a fabric canopy, satin casket covering, and decorative trophies. The day of the funeral was declared a bank holiday and over a million people watched the solemn procession of soldiers and mourners' carriages.

Both Redgrave and Semper made several designs for the hearse. The Prince Consort selected Redgrave's design (adding to it some features from Semper's drawings) and Semper was placed in charge of constructing the vehicle and attending to the ornamental details. The exceptionally ornate carriage was a great success.

Semper's commissions over the next few years were otherwise quite spare and this was without doubt his biggest disappointment in London. In his annual report for 1853, he listed as outside work only an ebony sideboard commissioned by Sir James Emerson Tennant of Ceylon, and a furniture exhibition he produced for the Gore House. Various drawings for other projects exist: a kiosk for telegraph messages, a departmental certificate, a silver punchbowl, and separate architectural designs for a pottery school, a hostel, and a bath-and-laundry establishment. None, save the certificate and punchbowl (executed by Alexander Schönauer of Hamburg), was actually carried out. Semper also made plans for adding a building to the complex at the Royal Arsenal at Woolwich, but the officer-in-charge saw fit to rework the scheme by altering the elevation and roof parapet so that its silhouette would conform to the contour of a cannon. Semper's efforts, in view of his former architectural glory, could hardly have been more degrading.

The most important of his London designs was his "Mixed Fabric Court," a commercial shop placed inside the revamped and enlarged Crystal Palace at Sydenham. This last building, relocated in a wooded, eighty-hectare park on the outskirts of London, was to be transformed into one of the first theme parks, as much money was poured into its enlargement and its horticultural setting. Paxton, Jones, and Wyatt combined to create a vast winter park and garden, which brought together exotic plant life and special works of art. Altogether, there were seven commercial courts including Semper's court inside the building, all small profit-making ventures. They were secondary in stature, however, to the several fine-arts courts – the Egyptian Court, Renaissance Court, Medieval Court, Pompeian Court, Roman Court, and Alhambra Court – nearly all of which were executed by Wyatt and Jones. It was Paxton who offered Semper the design of the Mixed Fabric Court in February 1854, three months before Crystal Palace was scheduled to open its doors to the public.

Little is known of the design other than the fact that its execution nearly proved a fiasco. Semper was slow in coming up with the design and this delay angered one of the corporate administrators.[129] One month later another administrator noted that the construction of the court was far behind schedule and needed the architect's personal attendance.[130] In May Semper requested from Paxton an additional £500 to complete the court but his request was denied.[131] The court was not completed by the beginning of summer, when the enlarged building was opened to the public. Finally, Paxton authorized an additional £800 to complete the work and Semper imported the talents of Séchan and Dieterle from Paris to execute the design. It was not finished until the end of the year, and then not before work was again scaled back due to cost overruns.

In letters to his French associates, Semper viewed his commercial court as a stepping-stone to the larger commission that he hoped to procure: the design of an ancient Roman amphitheater that was to be placed inside Crystal Palace, modeled on the theater at

83 Gottfried Semper, colored design for Roman amphitheater, Sydenham Crystal Palace, 1854. Institut für Geschichte und Theorie der Architectur, Semper Archiv, ETH-Zurich.

Pompeii (Pl. 83). One large polychrome drawing by the hand of Semper exists, together with a colored copy of the design by another hand. Paxton must have raised the possibility of this commission, but apparently no money was ever found for its execution. The drawing in itself would have little value, were it not for the fact that within a few years Semper replicated the scheme in connection with an even more grandiose proposal inside an iron-and-glass structure in Munich.

Semper's evening cycle of lectures at the Department of Practical Art went a little more smoothly, and was perhaps the most successful aspect of his time in London. Altogether, parts of twelve English lectures have survived. On 20 May 1853, Semper presented his inaugural lecture to the Department, which Cole described in his diary as "thoughtful and suggestive."[132] He followed it in November and December of the same year with a cycle of five lectures. This cycle was modified and given in the fall of 1854 over seven evenings. The lectures were relatively well attended. In the cycle of 1854, Semper averaged 44 listeners, of which 14 were paying guests. During the same school year lectures by Wornum were read to an average audience of 140 members, by Redgrave to 95, by J. C. Robinson to 20, and by Octavius Hudson to 45.

The London lectures, many of which were posthumously assembled and translated by Hans Semper for publication in *Kleine Schriften* (1884), were largely based upon Gottfried's earlier Dresden lectures. Their overall importance within the development of his architectual theory is therefore less than has generally been assumed, although they display some very instructive passages in light of his later thought. For instance, in the first of three lectures on ceramics in 1853 (Ms. 133), Semper devoted several pages to outlining and critiquing the ideas contained in Alexandre Brongniart's *Traité des arts céramiques* (1844) and Jules Ziegler's *Etudes céramiques* (1850), both of which became important sources for his later work on style. In another lecture, which Hans Semper titled "On Architectural Symbols," the architect signaled a new phase in the development of his ideas by giving greater attention to the symbolism of decorative forms.

Since these essays were, for many years, the most accessible of all of Semper's published writings, they have always been seen as the best introduction to his theory. Only recently however, as the original English manuscripts have again become available, has it been noticed that Semper's son altered the content of some of these lectures in his German translation. These posthumous changes, as it turns out, eventually worked much to the detriment of his father.

As Wolfgang Herrmann first chronicled them,[133] these corruptions ranged from the careless omission or editing of certain words and phrases to the unacknowledged amplification – and misreading – of certain crucial passages. Semper's inaugural London lecture of 20 May 1853, for instance, was drafted as a critical response to the tenet: "The decorative arts arise from and should be attendant upon architecture." In the German translation this axiom is placed into the text as if it were being presented by Semper himself; it comes, however, from the lecture given one year earlier by Owen Jones and was one of those axioms placed on a wall at Marlborough House for the students to follow. The point of Semper's lecture was rather to show that just the opposite was true: that the practical and industrial arts had arrived at a high degree of development centuries before the invention of monumental architecture, and that architectural forms and principles could only be understood by first considering these prototypical works. In his various drafts for the lecture, it is even possible to trace how Semper toned down his objections to the tenet, so as not to make his challenge to Jones, Redgrave, and Cole too explicit.

Far more problematic was Hans Semper's reworking of his father's principal lecture on his theory of style, entitled by Hans, "Outline for a System of a Comparative Theory of Style." The translation was based on two manuscripts, as Gottfried Semper clearly had to struggle to render his ideas into English. In particular the problem centered around the definition of style, which Semper had earlier defined in his native German as the satisfaction of an artistic idea, mediated by internal and external influences.

In the final draft of this London lecture, he altered this definition of style slightly: "The term is used for the notification of certain achievements in works of art, arising: 1) *from using artistically the means*, and 2) *from observing the limits*, which are contained in and defined by the task and problem in question, as well as by the accessories which modify the solution of it in every case."[134] Not only does he now separate out "the means" from the other influences "contained in and defined by the task and problem in question" but also his former high regard for the artistic "idea" or theme is now veiled under the ambiguous locution "certain achievements." I suspect this change resulted from the difficulties he found in composing a lecture in English, or perhaps it was an adjustment he felt necessary to accommodate an audience of industrial-art students. In any case, the change became problematic when he invoked a mathematical analogy to clarify his definition of style:

$$U = C\ x, y, z, t, v, w$$

where "U," the work of art embodying style, is defined as a mathematical "function of an indefinite number of quantities or powers which are the variable coefficients." The designation "C" refers to this functional operation; "x, y, z, t, v, w" refer to the variables affecting style. In this manuscript Semper divided his variables into two classes: the first "comprises the exigencies of the work itself" (including the "elementary idea" as well as such internal influences as the material and means of fabrication); the second comprises those "outward influences," the local, temporal and personal factors.

Hans Semper no doubt found his father's explanation of the formula vague or puzzling, for after presenting the mathematical analogy in his translation he rejected the text of this manuscript (Ms. 122) and turned to an explanation for the formula given in an earlier draft of the lecture (Ms. 124). The problem was that the two drafts were incompatible.

In manuscript 124 Semper also wrote of the "exigencies of the work of industry and art in itself" (the artistic idea) but, unlike in manuscript 122, he subsumed this idea under the designation "C." He also separated this idea from those internal and external coefficients represented by "x, y, z, t, v, w, etc.," which he now divided into three groups. These coefficients, "which act upon . . . and modify the appearances of the elementary ideas," are: 1) the materials and modes of execution; 2) the local and ethnological influences, climate, political institutions, and national tendencies; and 3) personal influences.

This only compounded the problem for Semper's son, who altered the text and gave his own explanation of this formula without acknowledging his changes. Thus, in returning to the text of manuscript 122, he assumed that "C" (represented by "F" in his translation) comprises not a mathematical operation but a "class of variables," chief of which he identified as the function or "purpose" of the artistic work. This textual corruption in itself has led to ruinous consequences, as Semper's theory again and again has been interpreted as blatantly "purposeful." Because of this interpretation he has either been praised as an early modernist or denigrated as a utilitarian functionalist – the latter being nearly the antithesis of his whole theoretical stance.

What makes this hermeneutic imposture all the more embarrassing and inexcusable from a historical perspective is that Semper, in manuscript 124, after presenting his formula, went to some lengths to point out that an artistic problem could by no means be reduced to the level of a mathematical problem, and that those variables influencing the style of any work could in no way supersede the artist's talent and good taste. He resorted to this analogy, he explained in apology, simply "as a crutch" to delineate the framework of his theory.

Semper returned to the same mathematical analogy in another manuscript prepared a few years later in Zurich, but this time – composing his ideas in German – he was much more precise and concrete. He divided the "variablen coefficienten" into two classes: style's internal and external influences. The first class included the use, material, and means of execution; the second class comprised style's local, temporal, and personal influences. In his definition of style he also returned to the paradigm presented in *Science, Industry, and Art,* which stressed the underlying artistic theme or idea: "Style is therefore the emergence of the basic theme raised to artistic meaning, and all the inner and outer coefficients that cause its embodiment to be modified in a work of art."[135]

It is a pity that this Zurich manuscript has surfaced only recently. For nearly a century historians have attempted to characterize Semper's ideas – sometimes exclusively on the misreading and mistranslation of this single London lecture.

Greek Tectonics and Ancient Missiles

On the whole, Semper's years in London were a time of reflection and research, and in this regard two little-discussed events would have a large impact on the redirection of his earlier ideas. The first was his reading of another major work of architectural theory by Karl Bötticher (1806–99), which led Semper to reevaluate in a more sophisticated manner the conceptual foundations and limitations of his earlier ideas. The second event was the composition of a small, unheralded text by Semper himself. Largely mathematical in nature, it has thus far escaped any critical review and has almost been forgotten.

Bötticher's *Die Tektonik der Hellenen* (The Tectonics of the Hellenes; 1844–52) represents in many respects one of the great intellectual achievements of the nineteenth century. Together with Semper's better known writings, it dominated German thinking on architecture in the second half of the century; it not only established several key architectural concepts but also provided the ideological framework for much subsequent discussion. As late as 1896 a doctoral dissertation was devoted to analyzing its many nuances – a discursive study that considered both its many merits and its contemporary limitations.[136]

Bötticher was a professor of architecture at the Bauakademie in Berlin. He began his studies at the school in 1827, focusing his attention at first on ornamentation and textiles. After teaching at several Prussian technical schools in the 1830s, he was brought back into the academy as an instructor in 1839, promoted to professor in 1844. Urged on by Schinkel, and – like Semper – inspired by the analyses of K. O. Müller, Bötticher turned his attention to Greek architecture in the early 1840s. His study on Greek tectonics was an attempt to unravel the symbolic scheme of the various parts and decorative attributes of Doric and Ionic temples; it sought to explore the aesthetic hierarchy of classical forms by considering the artistic meaning of their underlying structural principles. Even though the first volume of his work did not appear until 1844, an earlier and shorter version was put on display at the first congress of German architects at Leipzig in 1842. Semper, who was present, apparently took no notice and it was another eight years before his first encounter with it in the reading room of the British Museum.[137] He must surely have been taken back by the relevance of many of Bötticher's ideas to his own; important aspects of his thought, such as his notion of dressing, had been anticipated if not preempted.

As has often been noted, Bötticher's literary style was excessively opaque, even by nineteenth-century German standards. The author himself was aware of this problem, as he made various attempts to reformulate his ideas in later editions of the text. His analyses of the Greek temple were predicated upon three principal terms: the "core-form" (*Kernform*), "art-form" (*Kunstform*), and "juncture" (*Junktur*). He defined the core-form as the "mechanically necessary and statically functional scheme," the working structure of each architectural member of the temple – for instance, the capacity of a column to carry a load.[138] Related to it in a way that progressively sought to define its meaning, was the column's art-form, that is, the idealized manner in which this core-form was characterized in an artistic sense. The art-form was, in this way, the representational explanation of the core-form. Bötticher also referred to the art-form as a veiling (*Hülle*) or decorative attribution of the core-form, but he was at the same time explicit in stating that this symbolic "dressing" (*Bekleidung*) was conceived simultaneously with its mechanical function and thus was no willful or arbitrary appendage.[139] Still, the core-form, when concep-

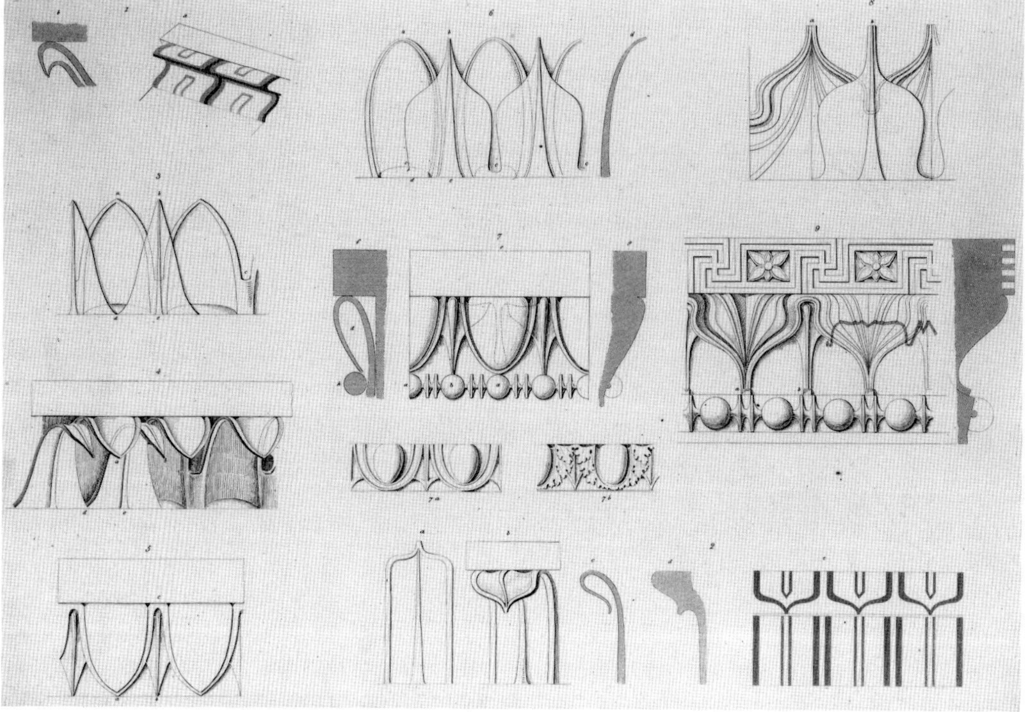

84 Bending of leaves under burden, forming the egg-and-dart motif. From Carl Bötticher, *Die Tektonik der Hellenen*, 1844–52.

tually considered, was all that was necessary to carry out the architectonic function; the member's art-form, especially as interpreted later in the century, came to be seen as the artistic dressing applied to the core-form, symbolizing in effect its mechanical or structural function. Bötticher defined the juncture as the relational deference each member maintains toward others – the working together of the parts in the indissoluble unity of the structural organism.

Bötticher then examined various members of the Greek temple within this framework: delineating how the symbolic representation of the mechanical function was carried out. For instance, Bötticher interpreted the Doric cyma, a double-curvature molding that is applied at transitional points in the paradigm of a temple, as a symbol for load and support, a seam within the structure signifying the notions of upright-standing and free-finishing. The curvature of the molding varied, depending on the intensity of the load that was thus symbolically expressed. When placed high in the entablature, for example, the molding might incline in a more vertical profile; at a lower point of greater stress, for instance, in the case of the Doric echinus, the curvature might become more severe and horizontal in its form. This theme of conflict was represented by the Greeks artistically as a folding or bending of leaves (Pls. 84, 85). The folding of certain types of leaves eventually created certain standard motifs, such as the egg-and-dart ornament.

The point of this exercise for Bötticher – as well as for Semper – was that this symbolic representation (art-form) of each part was essential to an understanding of Greek tectonics. The motif of egg-and-dart leaves, for instance, always appeared with a particular molding, either plastically formed or painted. This type of analysis thus explained certain aspects

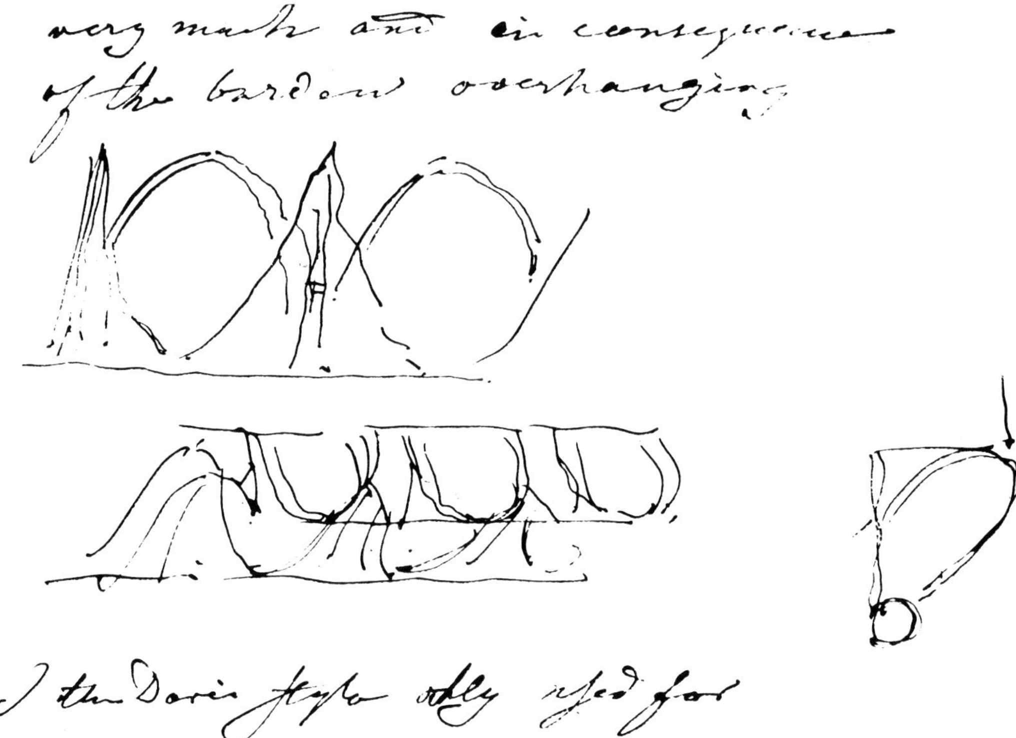

85 Gottfried Semper's sketch of Bötticher's plate. Institut für Geschichte und Theorie der Architectur, Semper Archiv, ETH-Zurich.

of Greek polychromy and at the same time it allowed the symbolic dressings to be seen as having important semantic values of their own, inherited from earlier times. In short, Bötticher's exhaustive investigation gave scholarly validation to some of the vague ideas on Greek formal development contained in Semper's *Preliminary Remarks on Polychrome Architecture*.

Several sets of notes preserved in the Semper Archive in Zurich reveal that the recently employed professor, after his initial exposure to Bötticher's book on 13 December 1852, returned to the same study on several occasions over the next weeks and months to delve further into its contents. In one manuscript he even translated some of Bötticher's remarks on the cyma into English, which he then utilized to a significant extent in his London lecture, "On Architectural Symbols."[140]

Semper was also shaken by the extent to which Bötticher's analyses presaged many of his own recent ideas and he responded in a very mean way to his colleague. In a draft to an archaeological article he was preparing in December 1852, he railed against this "vicious little mystagogue from Berlin, the founder of a new era in architecture, the Pythagoras of the nineteenth century revealing the secrets of tectonics, and the rediscoverer of the 'Analoga,' before whom and his trismegistos Schinkel the world had groped in the dark and had no idea of Greek architecture or of architecture in general."[141] He continued his campaign in other later writings; on one occasion (after pointedly rejecting his distinction between a core-form and art-form) he sarcastically referred to Bötticher's "learning, taste, and acumen."[142]

103

Setzt man $y_{,} = z^2$ ist

$$2\sqrt{2}\,m\int\sqrt{\frac{V^2}{k}+z^2}\,dz = (X-x)$$

also

$$(2)\quad (X-x)=\sqrt{y_{,}}\,\sqrt{(2V^2+2my_{,})}+\sqrt{\frac{2}{m}}\,V^2\,log\,nat\left(\frac{\sqrt{y_{,}}+\sqrt{y_{,}+\frac{V^2}{m}}}{\sqrt{\frac{V^2}{m}}}\right).$$

Ist k positiv, also $= m$, so wird:

$$(3)\quad (X-x)=\left\{\begin{array}{l}\sqrt{y_{,}\,(2V^2-2my_{,})}\\ +2\sqrt{\frac{2}{m}}\,V^2\left(Arc\left[tang=\sqrt{\frac{\sqrt{\frac{V^2}{m}}+\sqrt{y_{,}}}{\sqrt{\frac{V^2}{m}}-\sqrt{y_{,}}}}\right]-\frac{\pi}{4}\right).\end{array}\right.$$

II. Abfallende Bahn.

Dem positiven k der aufsteigenden Bahn (mit Einschluss von $k = 0$) entspricht das positive $k_{,}$ der abfallenden Bahn. Für diese Fälle wird also (Seite 99)

$$(4)\quad (x)=\left\{\begin{array}{l}\sqrt{y\,(2V^2-2k_{,}y)}\\ +2\sqrt{\frac{2}{k_{,}}}\,V^2\left(Arc\left[tang=\sqrt{\frac{\sqrt{\frac{V^2}{k_{,}}}+\sqrt{y}}{\sqrt{\frac{V^2}{k_{,}}}-\sqrt{y}}}\right]-\frac{\pi}{4}\right).\end{array}\right.$$

Hat $k_{,}$ negativen Werth und ist es $= - m_{,}$ so wird

$$(5)\quad x=\sqrt{y}\,\sqrt{2V^2+2m_{,}y}+\sqrt{\frac{2}{m_{,}}}\,V^2\,log\,nat.\left(\frac{\sqrt{y}+\sqrt{y+\frac{V^2}{m_{,}}}}{\sqrt{\frac{V^2}{m_{,}}}}\right).$$

Es sei $A = 45^0$ $a\,C''_{s=0} = 1.$ so wird

$$-2k=(1-2\,a\,C''_{s=0}\,sin\,A)\,cotang\,A^2=-(\sqrt{2}-1).$$

86 Gottfried Semper, page from *Ueber die bleiernen Schleudergeschosse der Alten*, 1859.

There were, however, a number of legitimate differences in the architectural theory of the two men. Semper, for example, rejected Bötticher's claim for Greek cultural and artistic autonomy, for the creation of these tectonic symbols in stone temples rather than in other prototypical forms, and also the pervasive esoteric tenor of some of Bötticher's investigations. But these differences should not obscure the very great debt that Semper's thought came to owe to Bötticher's analyses. It is not unfair to characterize Semper's reading of Bötticher's multi-volume text in December of 1852 as a pivotal point in his intellectual development – the point at which he made his all important shift from a quasi-materialistic to a symbolic reading of artistic forms.

This point can be underscored by Semper's other important intellectual project of this period: his mathematical study on the shape of Greek slingshot projectiles. The immediate impetus to this investigation, curiously, was a meeting of the Royal Institute of British

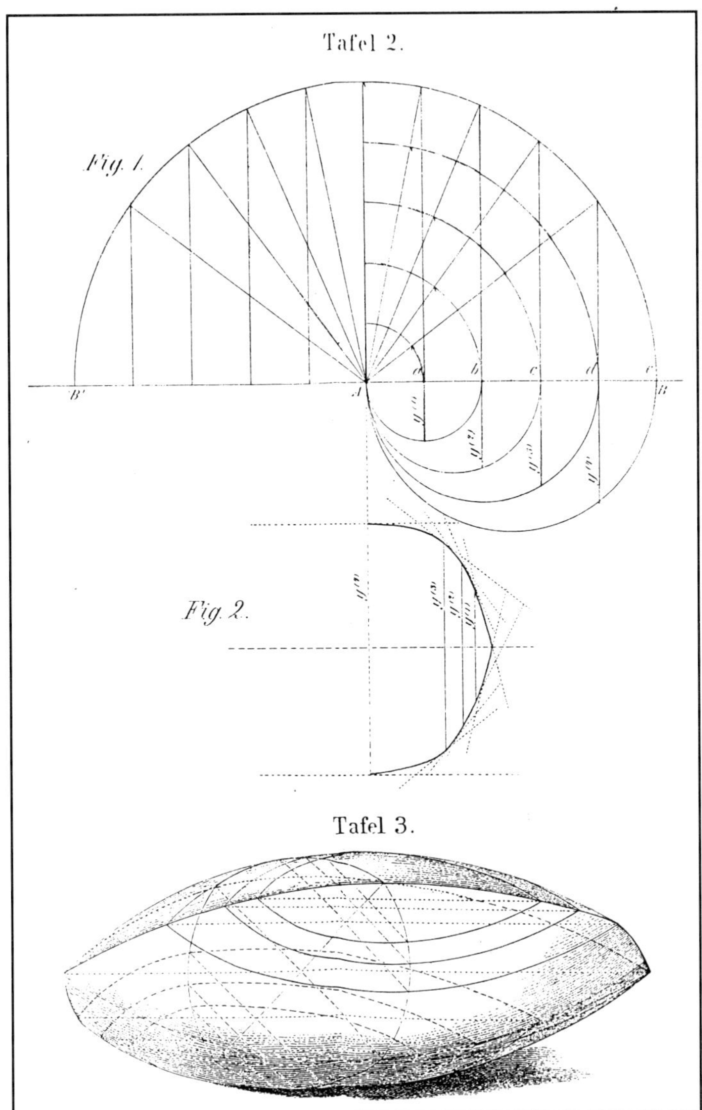

87 Gottfried Semper, page from *Ueber die bleiernen Schleudergeschosse der Alten*, 1859.

Architects held sometime in late 1852 or early 1853, when there was a discussion as to whether the Greeks possessed universally valid laws of proportion and formal beauty. Semper, who by instinct and practice had always resisted the idea of absolute systems of proportion in general, was moved to consider the problem from a slightly different perspective; he began to examine mathematically some artifacts of ancient Greek and Arabian slingshot projectiles on display at the British Museum.

Initially he hoped to resolve the riddle of their mathematical properties within a few days, but the more he became involved with the physics of projectiles (taxing his considerable mathematical talents) the more complex the matter became. Finally, in January 1854, he sent to a friend in Dresden a paper consisting of a series of several hundred – mainly – trigonometric and derivative functions (Pls. 86, 87), the fruit of more than a year of intense labor.[143] His Dresden friend examined it, then passed it on to a better qualified mathematician for review. After some minor corrections, Semper reworked it over the remainder of 1854 and throughout much of 1855, before sending it to his publisher Vieweg. An intervening legal dispute with this former friend delayed the work again and it was not until 1859 that this remarkable little study, *Ueber die bleiernen Schleudergeschosse der Alten und über zweckmässige Gestaltung der Wurfkörper in Allgemeinen* (On the Leaden Slingshot Missiles of the Ancients and the Functional Shape of Projectiles in General), appeared in Zurich.

The pamphlet's sub-subtitle – "An Attempt to Demonstrate the Dynamic Origin of Certain Forms in Nature and Art" – sheds further light on Semper's proposed problem, which in many ways was a bold departure from his earlier assumptions. And in his thoughtful and highly lucid Preface, stylistically perhaps the most elegant of all of his writings, he wasted no time in announcing his intention to challenge the view of Greek forms as "mere scaffolds or so-called 'structural schemas' that are decorated by means of attached symbols from the animal and vegetable world, as Professor Karl Bötticher in Berlin wants to represent them."[144]

Semper's Preface, in fact, touches upon art only in an indirect way. Underlying his discussion is the tenet that every true artistic form must express an inner necessity of form, as in nature, where no parts are superfluous and all are essentially conditioned by the environment and by the part's function. Absolute schemes of beauty fail because a form's beauty can only be judged within its own context, that is to say, within its compliance with these norms. Yet even if we discount the hope of absolute numerical schemes, Semper argued that there are still eternally valid and simple laws of beauty governing art, similar to the mysterious "vital forms" ruling nature. High art exhibits greater artistic perfection the more successfully it allows the organic conflict between elementary and vital forces to be shown and resolved.

Semper illustrated this point with the example of Greek caryatids and atlantes, or the use of human forms to support parts of the temple. By accepted nineteenth-century standards of taste, this practice of the ancients was generally frowned upon as an error. But for Semper, the practice depicted rather the artistic courage and élan of the Greeks (for him unique among the ancient nations), that is, their desire to enliven their architectural creations specifically with such powerful human analogies. Whereas many other major styles were equally successful in delineating the principles of their structural systems, only the Greeks dared to do so with such vivid images drawn from the repertoire of natural forms. For this reason alone, Semper felt, this style will survive into perpetuity: "For the mysterious organic law that is also valid in art must – when it will become clearly conceived as a principle in periods of high artistic development – time and again lead to forms and analogies that closely resemble those once produced from this spiritual seed in such a splendid golden age."[145]

Semper next took his reader through an impressive series of propositions, diagrams, and mathematical equations. Using them, he discussed the dynamics of moving bodies in voids, liquid and gaseous mediums; aerodynamic forms; acceleration; pneumatic pressure; the directional axes of birds and fish; and rotating bodies. His aim was to prove mathematically that there is an optimal, almond-like form for moving or thrown objects, and that the Greeks investigated these principles in order to configure their projectiles optimally.

In the last paragraph he closed with some aesthetic observations that make evident the artistic point of these exercises. The elastic curvatures found in Greek projectiles, he pointed out, resemble those seen in Greek art – that is, the contours of their tectonic and architectonic forms (strictly distinguishable from those found in other artistic cultures) can be characterized by a similar tendency toward the straight line with pronounced bending taking place along relatively short axes. This similarity was not coincidental, Semper believed. He argued that the Doric echinus, for instance, borrowed its name from the Greek word for sea mussel. Such forms are thus mussel-like in their profiles, in contrast to those of other nations, which often appear tumescent or swollen. From this it "should not be maintained that the Greeks designed their forms according to mathematical formulas (which in art would be absurd) but that the law of nature followed by the Greeks in the limits of their form-making, everywhere letting the tension dominate, was not vaguely intimated but clearly recognized."[146]

This is Semper's first, but not last, response to Bötticher's relatively abstract scheme of Greek tectonics. Moreover, these analogies between art and natural forms, which in many ways portend his stylistic analyses of the second half of the decade, also provide the best indication of what Semper generally meant by the "organic" nature of Greek art.

Semper's intellectual maturation was thus largely complete by the time of his departure from London in the middle of the decade. Early in August 1854, as he was revising his work on Greek projectiles as well as frantically trying to bring to completion his Mixed Fabrics Court in Sydenham, Semper received a letter from Richard Wagner. The latter, who early in their exile had pleaded Semper's case to Swiss authorities, had remained a good friend.[147] (The friendship was strengthened further in the first half of 1855, when Wagner served as a guest conductor with the London Philharmonic.)

Wagner's lobbying on Semper's behalf now came to fruition in the summer of 1854, when the Swiss government finalized its plans for a new technical college in Zurich (now the Eidgenössische Technische Hochschule, Swiss Federal Institute of Technology). Semper's name was proposed for the directorship of the department of architecture, a suggestion that was passed on by government officials to three local architects for recommendation. These three – Albert Wegmann, Ferdinand Stadler, Johann Caspar Wolff – all gave firm support. Semper, whose revolutionary activities and exile had made his name something of a household word throughout the German-speaking world, was also receiving considerable architectural praise at this time for his Dresden Gallery, which was finally nearing completion. State officials then approached Wagner and asked him to inquire whether his friend would be interested in the post. In his letter to Semper, Wagner described the position in somewhat inflated terms as "the highest architectural authority for all of Switzerland."[148]

Semper answered Wagner's letter in a positive way, and in the middle of September he set out for Zurich to be interviewed. The meetings went well and he hired an attorney to negotiate the contract. Early in October 1854, he received the offer of the directorship of the school and the first professorship, with two faculty members under his direction. Semper did not respond right away, in fact he began to have second thoughts about accepting the position. He tentatively accepted the offer in December, but by the end of the month he once again began to have doubts. He did not formally notify the president of the school of his acceptance until January 1855; and then his position was not ratified by the Swiss parliament until February. Once this process was completed, he began to delay his move to Zurich because of his misgivings.

Semper's reluctance to accept the post stemmed from a variety of factors. He had over the last year continued to gain stature in Cole's Department of Practical Art and he hesitated to give up the intellectual and cultural resources of the English capital, which in 1855 were far superior to those of Zurich. Secondly, some members of his family resisted the idea of moving once again. His eldest son Manfred, in particular, had adjusted well to London and was contemplating a career in architecture there; at first he insisted on remaining behind. This resistance was apparently very strong with other family members as well, as in one letter to Bertha, written from Paris in March 1855, Semper voiced concern at the "personal animosity" of his children, perhaps a natural aftermath of his earlier, forced abandonment of them.[149]

Thirdly there was the issue, or rather the possibility, of returning to architectural practice. Germanic Zurich, with its long-established tradition of political sanctuary, offered him this possibility, just as London had afforded him so little opportunity. But signs that the situation in England might be changing began to appear early in 1855, shortly after Semper had formally accepted the Zurich offer. Henry Cole had arranged for the Department of Science and Art (formerly the Department of Practical Art) to carry out much of the British design work associated with the Paris World Exposition of 1855 (a follow-up to the London exhibition of 1851). Semper hoped for important commissions, as he was first asked to design a monumental trophy for the British Navy, which he conceived as a large column. When he arrived in Paris in March, however, he found his design scaled back and all of the more prestigious projects already snatched up by British architects. Once again he complained in a letter to Bertha of the ill-will of the British architects toward him.[150]

Another possible commission that led him to reconsider the position in Zurich was the design of what would become the future Victoria and Albert complex in South Kensington. In 1855 Prince Albert and Cole were advancing their plans to move the school to South Kensington and join it with sundry other cultural activities on the land purchased after the Great Exhibition. In a meeting with Prince Albert in February 1855, Cole was asked to have Semper begin preparing plans for the new complex and the Prince offered to pay him personally. Semper was elated at the prospect – unaware that the Prince had done this before and that Cole had a personal aversion to hiring architects to design buildings.

Semper threw himself into the project during his ten-week stay in Paris, beginning in mid-March. He designed not only a new school and a museum but also the concert hall (later Royal Albert Hall) that the Prince had requested. In June he presented his plans and a painted cardboard model to the Prince and Cole, both of whom seemed pleased with the design. At the end of the same month, however, the Board of Trade once again insinuated itself and voted down Semper's project as being too costly.

The absence of an approved plan, together with the need for Cole's department to vacate Marlborough House (the official residence for the Prince of Wales, now coming of age), led Prince Albert in the spring of 1855 to propose a temporary "iron museum" on the Brompton Park Estate in South Kensington. This iron building with corrugated-iron infilling, erected by the firm of Charles Young and Company, soon became known as the "Brompton Boilers" – and was subsequently painted with green and white stripes to tone down the crudeness of its design. Cole housed his school temporarily in four nearby houses. The first permanent buildings of the South Kensington complex were eventually designed by Captain Francis Fowke, who was not an architect but a royal engineer by training. Fowke had a distinguished career, and eventually designed many of the buildings in South Kensington, as well as galleries in Scotland and Ireland.

All of this activity or promise of activity, however, came too late for Semper. The disappointing rejection of his plan by the Board of Trade in June forced him to sever his ties with England. A few days afterwards he and his family left London for Zurich – there to open a new and in some respects more challenging chapter to his life.

88 Gottfried Semper, ca. 1855. Institut für Geschichte und Theorie der Architectur, Semper Archiv, ETH-Zurich.

4

The Zurich Years 1855–1869

"Liszt extends his hand. The architect of sound salutes the musician of stone!" (Princess Carolyne Sayn-Wittgenstein to Gottfried Semper, 8 December 1857)

A New Start in Switzerland

Notwithstanding his reluctance to leave London for Zurich, Semper approached his new position at the Zurich Polytechnikum with much energy and great optimism (Pl. 88). The new technical college had been created by the Swiss federal government in 1854 to provide higher studies and training in the building arts and sciences: from architecture and engineering to chemistry and astronomy. Semper's task was to lecture, write the curriculum for the school, and hire faculty members as the department expanded.

The work initially was tedious, as this type of technical training in architecture, which was intended to be different from the artistic emphasis of the older fine-art academies, was a relatively new educational concept. France had formed its Ecole Polytechnique in 1794, but this was a school originally set up to train military engineers. Germany took the concept of technical schools in a slightly different direction by viewing such institutions more broadly, as colleges of higher education that were technical alternatives to the liberal-arts-based universities. Relatively few German technical colleges – such as those at Karlsruhe (1825), Dresden (1838), and Stuttgart (1840) – preceded Switzerland's federal example. By the close of the nineteenth century, however, this type of institution (later renamed technical universities) became prevalent, and were the most prestigious centers for architectural education in the German-speaking countries. In essence, they came to supersede academic training.

In the early years students at Zurich were few. Semper had less than a half-dozen students for the fall term of 1855, and by the fall of 1860 his first-year students numbered only nine. This might be compared with the fifty-five students enrolled in preliminary courses in mathematics in the same semester. By 1869 first-year student enrollment in the architectural school had grown to eighteen and total enrollment in the school was forty-one. Enrollment in the engineering department in the same year, however, was almost triple that of architecture. After 1860, the architecture program had become sufficiently known and respected to attract students from other countries, such as Germany, Poland, Hungary, Russia, and Italy. Even after Semper left the school at the beginning in 1871, many foreign students – such as the Dutch architect Hendrik Berlage – were lured to Zurich specifically by Semper's program and the high reputation of the school.

The three-year curriculum Semper inaugurated consisted of preliminary courses in calculus (differentiation and integration), geometry, archaeology and history, construction, ornamental design, and drawing. In the second year the student followed Semper's own courses in comparative architectural theory and composition, together with courses in structural engineering, petrography, shadow delineation, road and hydraulic design, drawing, and ornamentation. In the third year there were courses in architectural theory, composition, drawing, and ornamentation, in addition to those in geology and civil law. Notwithstanding Semper's own theoretical bent, the technical training was demanding and reflected Semper's own mastery of architectural materials and technology.

The curriculum changed little during Semper's tenure at the school. The most notable faculty member in the department, other than Semper, was the historian Wilhelm Lübke (1823–92), who joined the staff in 1860 and taught archaeology and ancient art for a few years, before accepting a chair at the Stuttgart technical school. Lübke, who had praised Semper's Dresden Art Gallery highly in his review in *Kunstblatt* in 1855, was a specialist in the German Renaissance, but he soon gained a much broader audience with his *Grundriss der Kunstgeschichte* (Outline for a History of Art; 1860). At the center of the program at Zurich, however, were Semper's own courses in composition and comparative architectural theory. Semper always taught the last course alone but increasingly came to rely on his capable assistants, Julius Stadler and Georg Lasius, for the exercises in composition or design.

The Polytechnikum in other ways offered intellectual and personal companionship for Semper. The creation of this new institution of higher learning (soon to be housed in the same building as the University of Zurich) attracted a number of outstanding scientists and scholars to the faculty – among them Jakob Moleschott (1822–93), Friedrich Theodor Vischer (1807–87), and Jakob Burckhardt (1818–97).

The physiologist and philosopher Moleschott was born in Holland but he spent the first part of his academic career at Heidelberg. He was, like Semper, outspoken and contemptuous of contemporary mores, and was known in particular for his condemnation of the hold that conservative Hegelian ethics exerted in German academic, political, and social life. The so-called materialist bent of his teachings – that is, his repeated challenges to the interference of university and local religious authorities in matters of scientific inquiry – soon made his position untenable in Germany and he welcomed the move to the somewhat more liberal climate of Zurich. Little is known of his friendship with Semper except that the two men met regularly at a tavern for evening drinks. Moleschott later moved to the University of Rome, where in 1879 (as described earlier in this book) he delivered the contested eulogy over Semper's grave.

Another colleague of Semper and Moleschott was the philosopher and writer Friedrich Theodor Vischer, who also sometimes joined them in the evenings. The tempestuous Vischer had been appointed to the chair of aesthetics and German literature at Tübingen in 1844, but he immediately earned a two-year suspension for his fiery inaugural address, in which he vehemently denounced – among other things – certain demagogic adversaries, police surveillance, the display of art in museums, and the "sanctified order" of the state. His forced sabbatical allowed him time to begin work on his celebrated *Aesthetik oder Wissenschaft des Schönen* (Aesthetics or the Science of the Beautiful), which appeared in six lengthy volumes between 1846 and 1857. This prodigious work, although superficially Hegelian in its structure, embodied a complexity of ideas matched by few intellectual endeavors of this period. In 1848 he was elected to the German parliament at Frankfurt and lamented the unsuccessful labor of this body. In Zurich Vischer concentrated his efforts mainly on German literature, although he also began to rethink his earlier philosophical positions and aesthetic ideas. With his wide range of cultural interests he was certainly an intellectual match for Semper and the later re-evaluation of his aesthetic ideas may very well have benefited much from Semper's radical opposition to his earlier approach.[1]

Burckhardt received his call to the Polytechnikum as professor of art in the spring of 1855 and he arrived in the city in October. He had by this date completed his book on Constantine the Great and he was then finishing work on his travel guide *Der Cicerone*, after spending the previous two years living in Italy. His first project after settling in Zurich was his masterpiece *The Civilization of the Renaissance in Italy*, which appeared in 1860, after he had accepted a chair at the University of Basel. Burckhardt's high regard for the art of the Italian Renaissance certainly appealed to Semper, and his work as a Renaissance historian at the same time validated and popularized Semper's architectural approach. But he was politically conservative, uncomfortable with socializing with German political refugees, and seems to have had few contacts with Semper. Only several years later, in a letter to Semper after he had moved to Basel, did Burckhardt speak warmly of the days "when he had the honor of being called Semper's colleague."[2]

Much more is known of Semper's intimate friendship in Zurich with the novelist Gottfried Keller, who had lived several years in Germany and was well-known in intellectual circles. He returned to his native city of Zurich in 1855 almost penniless, shortly after completing his lengthy, semi-biographical masterpiece, *Der grüne Heinrich* (Green Henry). He knew of Semper's artistic achievements through his friend Hermann Hettner, an art historian and curator of antiquities in Dresden and a great admirer of Semper's talent. In his letters to Hettner after his arrival in Zurich, Keller often spoke of his great fascination and respect for Semper's "profound and multi-faceted genius," or his "pure artistic nature" – attributes that were often shamefully being neglected, he noted, because of Semper's lack of substantial architectural commissions.[3] Keller remained a close friend. On Christmas Eve, 1879, seven months after Semper's death, he admitted that he was still unable to come to terms with the passing of his dear friend. In May of the following year, he was haunted by a dream in which Semper returned from the dead to warn him of the "bad lodgings" there.[4]

Keller was also part of the social circle around Richard Wagner in Zurich – at least until the composer abruptly quit the city in August 1858, after his affair with the wife of one of his principal financial backers became publicly known. Two other members of the circle were Johann Jakob Sulzer (1821–97) and Georg Herwegh (1817–75). Sulzer, a young philologist from a respected Swiss family, had given up a promising academic career to pursue politics and he eventually became very successful in this field. He had idolized Wagner, since meeting him in 1850, and as his friend he sought to help other German refugees resettle in Switzerland. Sulzer was the person most instrumental in bringing Semper to Switzerland and helped him secure his most important architectural commission there.

The exiled, revolutionary poet Herwegh, by contrast, was a caustic political writer and is perhaps best known today for mobilizing an army of German students in Paris in

1848–49 to return to their homeland in the cause of its liberation. He actually led the army across the border into Germany and it engaged Prussian forces, but a series of quick defeats caused him to flee to Switzerland.

Wagner, of course, stood above all others. He had achieved international fame as an operatic composer by 1855, but he had been unable to stage any of his works since his departure from Dresden. As a consequence he was plagued during his Zurich years (not to mention some years beyond) by constant financial worries that were greatly magnified by his extravagant style of living. He was delighted to have lured Semper to Zurich as the architect had a good knack for animating social gatherings. The two men once again got along famously, despite their many artistic disputes.

The pianist and composer Franz Liszt was also close to Wagner during these years. He and Princess Carolyne Sayn-Wittgenstein graced Zurich with their presence during a six-week visit in 1856. The brilliant but brooding Sayn-Wittgenstein quickly stole the show. She was a vivacious, cigar-smoking sophisticate, who had forsaken her Russian husband to live with Liszt out of wedlock, and by every account she enchanted the city with her own incessant quest for entertainment – "as if Zurich had suddenly become a metropolis."[5] To Wagner's annoyance, she sought the companionship and intellectual stimulation of many of Zurich's professors: "If I looked in for a moment from my regular midday walk, the lady would be dining alone, now with Semper, now with Professor Köchly, then with Moleschott, and so on. Even my very peculiar friend Sulzer was drawn in, and, as he could not deny, in a manner intoxicated."[6]

Her temperament, however, was very much an extension of Wagner's own personality. Evenings for him and his circle of acquaintances were typically filled with musical and dramatic recitals, always followed by lively conversation. At one birthday gathering in March 1858, the Wesendonck family presented Wagner with an ivory conductor's baton, designed by Semper.[7] On another evening, when Wagner first read his score for *Tristan and Isolde*, Semper harshly criticized the seriousness of the content, a charge that reflected Semper's artistic outlook. The architect argued, as Keller recorded, "that the charm in the artistic construction of such material consisted in the fact that the tragic element was broken up in such a way that one could extract enjoyment even from its most affecting parts. That was just what pleased him in Mozart's *Don Juan:* one met the tragic types there, as if at a masquerade, where even the domino was preferable to the plain character."[8] Semper's and Wagner's spirited interchanges in the years between 1855 and 1858 recalled those they had enjoyed in Dresden, and they were the last happy exchanges that the two men shared until the mid 1870s.

Many of these festive gatherings almost did not take place for Semper, who soon after moving to Zurich, fell into another fit of depression and sought to return to England. His letters list his complaints: his small salary, the superficiality of his students, the heavy workload that prevented him from pursuing serious literary and architectural activities. But he also genuinely missed the cultural resources of London; his years spent there now seemed "brilliant."[9] In the spring of 1856 he decided to take action and wrote to Siemens in London, asking him to ask Cole whether he might return to the School of Design. Siemens was unable to meet with Cole until August, but the latter indicated his interest in having Semper back on the faculty, although he would need at least three to six months to make arrangements.

It was not until July 1857 that Cole got back to Semper; he did so, however, with a plea for his return and he asked him, if he was still interested, to state his conditions.[10] Semper responded with a long letter, in which he indicated his desire for a change. He also noted that he longed for architectural employment and the library resources of London, and felt dissatisfied with the physical smallness of Zurich as well as with the "theoretical" inclination (as opposed to Cole's more practical emphasis) of the Polytechnikum. Semper was also involved with a competition design for an administrative center in Whitehall during this period. For this he proposed realigning the area of London defined by the triangle of Westminister Palace, Buckingham Palace, and Nelson's Column. He apparently never officially submitted his drawings, however.

Later that July, Cole noted in his diary that he was busy with the "re-engagement of Semper." On the first of August he made a rather generous offer: an annual salary of £200, a spacious teaching hall and private office space, and another £100 in fees for work commissioned by the Department. More importantly, he indicated a willingness to let Semper pursue architectural commissions.[11] Apparently this had not been allowed in the conditions of Semper's earlier employment.

Once again Semper was faced with a difficult decision and once again he wavered. He responded by asking for a £300 annual salary and indicated his willingness to negotiate. He also suggested that he should come to London and negotiate directly. As it turns out, Semper met Cole in Paris in September and the two friends had a long conversation. Cole talked about the extensive building activity to take place the next year in South Kensington and the need for Semper to have an official position with the Department in order to participate in it. Semper, in a letter to Bertha, stressed their son Manfred's attachment to the English capital, and its educational and professional possibilities. Cole gave Semper until the end of December 1857 to come to his decision.

Semper's anxiety only intensified. He wrote to his brother Wilhelm that he would probably be returning to London to resume his former professorship. He referred to the position as a means to an end, that is, as a way to resurrect his architectural career with all of the expected new building activity. He also spoke, somewhat incomprehensibly, of a "certain Catholic party" in Zurich conspiring against him, as they had done in Hamburg. Another reason he cited for returning to London were his financial problems: the recent money crisis had lowered the value of his stocks and he had lost much money in some recently failed railway securities.[12]

None of these reasons, save the first, sound very convincing, but another letter from this period sheds additional light on his emotional condition. After the visit of Princess Sayn-Wittgenstein to Zurich in 1856, she had become something of a confidante to Semper and the two exchanged several letters in the following years. Upon returning to Germany in 1857 she visited Dresden and sent Semper a glowing description of his newly completed gallery (opened in 1855), together with a photograph – the first opportunity for the architect to examine his creation (and the changes of others), a design of well over a decade earlier.[13] Semper responded in December 1857 with a long letter in which he defended himself against criticism of his design, pointing out the changes that had been made to it (the lowered dome as well as Lübke's minor criticisms of the floor plan), but near the end of the letter he also raised his dilemma about returning to London. He began with a somewhat startling political pronouncement:

> My situation here has turned out to be very unpleasant. I am coming to the conviction – to be no republican. Or rather, the basic principle of my republic is different than the Swiss or any other existing type. My polity is a community of trust, which grants to him who measures up to its mark full authority in matters of work, giving him free reign in that which he best understands and surrendering to him the full responsibility of his position. Here it is the republic of majority rule, which provides the small fellow with desired security, so that he – despite his worthlessness – counts just as much and works just as much as another.[14]

In another remark made to a colleague around this time Semper also noted quite bitterly: "Republicans have no money for art, the most despotic prince and the most fanatical pope do more for art and the artist than the free state."[15]

Semper's emotional turmoil at this time had very little to do with his changing political views. His reunion with Richard Wagner had reminded him not only how abruptly his very promising architectural career had been terminated but also how much more difficult it is to practice architecture. Whereas poets and musicians are able to continue their work even under the most difficult fiscal circumstances, he complained, architects are completely dependent on the good will and money of patrons. Semper was now at the height of his artistic powers and the past decade of architectural inactivity, as he was now becoming painfully aware, was irretrievably lost. To compound this problem there was the administrative formality and tedium of his new position, in his words, the "committee work, meetings, special committees, joint committees, yearly reports, and time-consuming schemes to improve the effectiveness of teachers and the progress of instruction" – all of which, he felt, reduced him to the level of a "junior teacher at a technical school."

Always near the surface in his dealings with people was his deep-seated, desperate yearning to return to architectural practice. When Princess Sayn-Wittgenstein in her letter recounted his glorious achievements, it only made Semper maudlin and more painfully aware that his past could not be recovered in his present circumstances. After the passage quoted above, he discussed an architectural competition in Zurich for the new Polytechnikum building, but he noted: "I am expected to enter although it is readily conceded that the whole thing is only *pro forma* and that the commission for the building is already decided. The nature of my past experiences do not entice me to go after this lime-twig."[16] And even though Semper was also aware that London afforded him "no great prospect" and that the promise of South Kensington would for him probably "be limited, as before, to furniture odds and ends," he was seriously considering at this time – as he also acknowledged in the letter – abandoning his wife once again to pursue the phantom of an architectural practice.

This state of mind was also exacerbated, if not in part induced, by the death of his mother (who died in April 1857), and by the deteriorating health of his wife Bertha, who was now becoming bedridden for extended periods of time. The combination of multiple childbirths and her difficult personal circumstances in the first years after 1849 had conspired to destroy her physical well-being, and the move back to Zurich only worsened her condition. She died in Zurich on 13 February 1859. Semper now assumed full responsibility for the children.

In the end, however, Semper decided not to return to London and he worked his way through his difficult predicament in Zurich, that is, until he gradually resumed his

89 Gottfried Semper, competititon design for Zurich City Hall, 1858. Institut für Geschichte und Theorie der Architectur, Semper Archiv, ETH-Zurich.

architectural practice. One of his few projects during his first three years in Zurich was a modest proposal in 1857 for a lodging and small department store near the Tiefenhof in Zurich. This was undertaken for a speculative client, and it consisted of a large palazzo-like urban dwelling set on a triangular site, attached to which was a shopping bazaar, featuring two stories of shop windows framed by paired columns.

In the following year, in 1858, Semper became involved with a competition for the Zurich City Hall and the reorganization of the surrounding Kranz quarter (Pl. 89). As with his earlier efforts in Dresden, Hamburg, and Whitehall, he was attracted here to the realignment of the streets of an entire district, to the search for new urban axes and focal points. The difficulty in this instance was how to relate the new buildings both to the Limmat River and to Lake Zurich. He was of two minds, and actually prepared two schemes, in which the respective city halls were aligned at right angles to each other. In the project in which the city hall was oriented to the lake, he opened up a large swathe of park area down to the shoreline. The Rathaus and its adjoining tower were in German Renaissance style and the immediate square was defined by shops and large apartment buildings. But the project never came to fruition.

The competition for the new Zurich Polytechnikum resulted in a project that was realized, although so modified that Semper expressed the wish that it had followed the suit of his other unexecuted designs.[17]

The blame for its architectural shortcomings falls on many shoulders. Late in 1857 Semper was asked to prepare the competition program for the large building, which was to house both the Polytechnikum and the University of Zurich.[18] Semper kept his promise to Sayn-Wittgenstein and did not submit an entry, but he did have a seat on the design jury. What happened during the jury's deliberations of the following spring is unknown, although it is quite likely that Semper used his vote (not necessarily with self-serving intent) to fight the selection of any of the proffered entries. In April 1858 the jury recommended that none of the submitted proposals be accepted and the issue of the new building was thrown back to the federal and cantonal governments for a resolution. Private discussions ensued and in June Semper and the state architect Johann Caspar Wolff were named co-architects for the new complex. The site was an eastern bluff of the Limmat overlooking the city of Zurich, its river, and its lake – promising to make the new building an important new addition to the cityscape.

The forced union of two architects of very different abilities and perspectives proved disastrous to the realization of the work. Wolff, who more or less conceded control of the design to Semper, assumed the administrative and supervisory duties of construction. Yet in defending what he perceived to be the state's economic interests, he seems to have fought every artistic endeavour of his colleague, leading to ever increasing friction and to considerable bitterness on Semper's part. In cutting back on material in the building's foundations, Wolff even seriously undermined the structural integrity of the fabric, causing (some decades later) the building's near collapse and a major rebuilding effort.

Semper, for his part, failed to assess realistically the fiscal limitations of the federal and cantonal governments, although his project was by no means extravagant relative to his past efforts. He was no longer in a court city where he was answerable only to the high ambition of an artistically inspired monarch, but was in a city and a country with few monumental buildings in its history and a widespread intolerance for the pretension and cost of such. The sheer scale of his work, answering the needs of an extensive program, inevitably led to cost overruns and therefore cost-cutting in other areas. The finished work thus turned out to be a pale replica of its much grander, original conception.

In plan the building was a large three-story, rectangular block, oriented west, with an interior court bisected by a one-story wing running east and west, connecting the midpoints of the longer sides. The north and south lateral wings were given over to the activities of the Polytechnikum and University of Zurich respectively, with the middle areas on the longer sides reserved for collections, administration, and library support. The one-story wing running east-west within the courtyard was an antiquity hall (since torn down), in which were displayed plaster casts of ancient works. It was reminiscent in its intention (although not in form) of Duban's antiquities court for the Palais des Etudes in Paris. A separate chemistry building (also now demolished) was located parallel to, and east of, the main building. Extensive renovations and additions have since expanded the size and character of the original work; the plain, cold facade that now peers out over the city owes its appearance more to subsequent rebuilding than to the original design. Only the crisp, heavily scored, lithic detailing of the lower story shows Semper's artistic hand.

It is easier to gauge his intentions for the work in a perspective drawing he prepared at the time of its design (Pl. 90), in which the building, located within its natural landscape on the outskirts of the city, was placed on a large socle and plaza. Viewed from the southwest (the view from the city and of the perspective), the main facade is dominated by the triumphal arch at the center of the west wing. At plaza level this pavilion serves as the ceremonial entrance for the school. The entrance to the University of Zurich is defined by the smaller pavilion along the south side; the Polytechnikum entrance is on the opposite side. Above the main entry is a mezzanine story, which houses the administrative offices of the school president and rector. Above this story, signified by the large arcuated

90 Gottfried Semper, Zurich Polytechnikum (now ETH-Zurich), 1858–63. Institut für Geschichte und Theorie der Architectur, Semper Archiv, ETH-Zurich.

windows, is the thematic heart of the complex, so to speak – the aula, a ceremonial room set aside for the special academic events of the two institutions.

Like the triumphal arch of the Dresden Gallery, only now even more forcefully defined, this three-story arched pavilion in this instance symbolizes the victory of knowledge. As the drawing indicates, Semper envisioned abundant sculptural works for this pavilion to fill out, as it were, its iconographic framework; almost all of the sculptures, however, were later omitted. In another perspective study preserved in the Semper Archive, he also placed another row of statuary atop the crowning parapet of the west facade. Again, he added decorative pilasters in the upper two stories around the building, and he filled in the square fields between the second and third-story windows with decorative panels. Budget restrictions forced all of these attributes to be eliminated.

The only exterior decoration realized was the sgraffito work on the upper two stories of the north (Polytechnikum) side of the complex (Pl. 91), which depicts through allegories the aim of the school to forge a union of the arts and sciences. A row of sgraffito medallions across the lower frieze presents an honor roll of famed artists and scientists, from Homer to Michelangelo, Newton to Laplace. The placement of this ancient technical process only on the north side of the building suggests it was little more than an experiment with this procedure, but it is more likely – the lack of sketches notwithstanding – that Semper would have preferred to have continued it on the complementary university entrance on the south side of the building, if not on other parts as well.

Semper also prepared sundry drawings for the decoration of many interior areas of the school. The main entrance hall, for instance, was to be elaborately outfitted with pictorial and plastic works, only a few of which were put in place. The most extensive decorative work, however, was reserved for the aula, the ceremonial room above, for which the ceiling panels were actually executed. Semper was much involved with his iconographic

91 Gottfried Semper, Zurick Polytechnikum (now ETH-Zurich), 1858–63. North elevation. Photo by author.

scheme and he prepared a detailed handwritten description of the overall layout.[19] The aula itself is a large rectangular room, highly polychrome, with a colonnaded tribune at each end (Pl. 92). Semper's decorative plan consisted of four huge wall paintings (not executed) glorifying human progress through: 1) the school of pure knowledge (philosophy); 2) the school of exact knowledge (natural science, mechanics, etc.); 3) the school of rhetoric, poetry, and music; and 4) the school of fine arts. Two of these paintings were to be inserted into the perspective arch of each tribune, which would then serve as a theatrical backdrop to the person speaking to the audience. Around the top of the room and reminiscent of Schinkel's work on the front of the Altes Museum, Semper designed a continuous frieze depicting the quintessential aspects of cultural history.

It is unfortunate but understandable that so many of these designs were not executed, with the exception of the ceiling panels (Pl. 93), which revolve around mythological themes: the birth of Pallas Athene from the head of Zeus, with Eos (the goddess of dawn) and Clymene (the goddess of evening) at her side. Hephaestus, Eileithyia, Eros, and Hermes stand at the base of Zeus's throne; in the lunettes above and below are the river gods Ciphissus and Ilipus, situating the scene in Athens. On adjoining thrones sit four emanations of Athene, depicting her as the war goddess, the health goddess, the goddess of the fine arts and tectonic arts, and the goddess of music, rhetoric, and poetry.

The two large panels in the next row portray the goddess at war against darkness and the raw forces of nature, and the creative, artistic loving goddess marrying Hercules. The four oval panels above and below these represent the genii of victory, music, artistic skill, and wealth. The central panels above each side tribune depict knowledge (represented by three female figures) and art (symbolized by three graces). Whereas this scheme was not different in spirit from that of many other architectural works of the period, the unforced

92 Gottfried Semper, Zurich Polytechnikum (now ETH-Zurich), 1858–63. Design for a tribune in the aula. Institut für Geschichte und Theorie der Architectur, Semper Archiv, ETH-Zurich.

93 Gottfried Semper, Zurich Polytechnikum (now ETH-Zurich), 1858–63. Ceiling design. Institut für Geschichte und Theorie der Architectur, Semper Archiv, ETH-Zurich.

theatricality of this overall composition, with its abundance and thematic deatail, recalls Semper's similar programs for Dresden. Thus this room, in its conception at least, reaffirms the continuity of his architectural approach after the ten-year lapse of his practice, and serves as a harbinger of the even more ambitious efforts he later made in Dresden and Vienna. His buildings on their various levels had to speak to their occupants: he believed they had to communicate cultural values and serve educational purposes.

The construction of the Polytechnikum was undertaken between 1859–64. In the interim Semper became involved in a number of other projects, almost all of which were unrealized. In addition to his futile efforts on the Zurich Rathaus, he prepared a design in 1862 for the town hall in Glarus. The city had lost nearly 600 buildings in the great fire of 1861 and was in the midst of major rebuilding. Semper was brought into the project secretly to appraise the scheme of another architect, Bernhard Simon, but he was also encouraged to submit his own proposal. Semper's stark, rather inappropriate and expensive Neoclassical block proved even more unacceptable to the city leaders and the commission was rightfully carried out by Simon.

In the early 1860s Semper also made several designs for hotels and resorts. In 1860–61 he prepared for the Swiss town of Bad Ragas a grand proposal for a hotel – replete with large basin, hippodrome, and gardens – but this project proved too costly. In 1862 he made plans for a remodeling of the Hotel Schweizerhof in Lucerne, but these designs too were abandoned. Perhaps Semper's most inspired resort scheme was his design of 1866 for a health resort for the Swiss town of Baden (Pl. 94), a massive complex reminiscent in its forms of a Roman bath. It was to house a casino, theater, gallery, library, restaurant, and

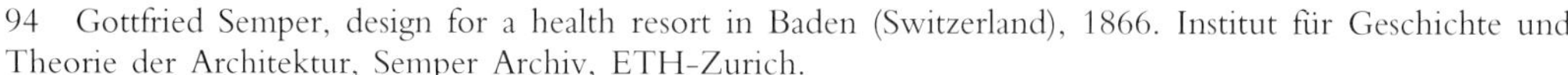

94 Gottfried Semper, design for a health resort in Baden (Switzerland), 1866. Institut für Geschichte und Theorie der Architektur, Semper Archiv, ETH-Zurich.

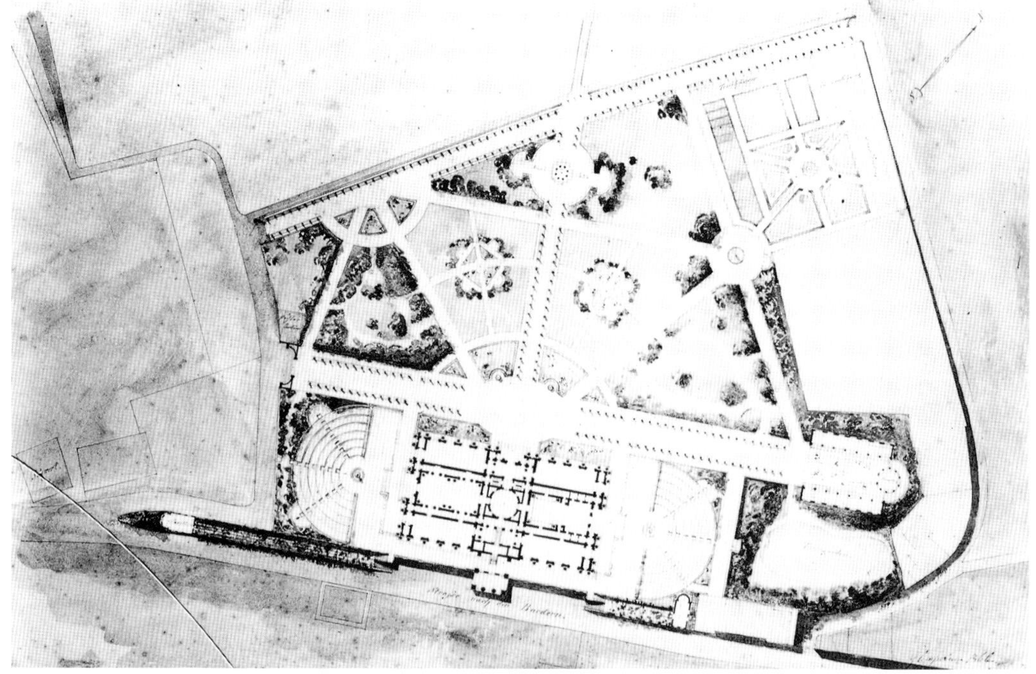

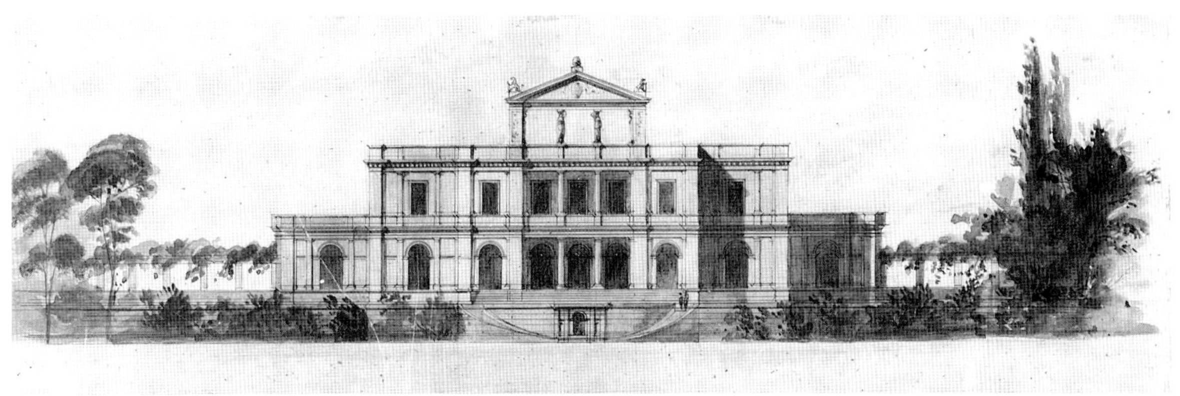

95 (above) Gottfried Semper, design for Villa Rieter-Rothpletz, Zurich, 1864. Institut für Geschichte und Theorie der Architektur, Semper Archiv, ETH-Zurich.

96 Gottfried Semper, design for Schloss Zichy, Hörisök (Hungary), 1869–71. Institut für Geschichte und Theorie der Architektur, Semper Archiv, ETH-Zurich.

cafés. Outside, two amphitheaters at each end gave way to lavish gardens in the rear, approached by wide, pedestrian allées. This proposal was certainly not one of Semper's more modest schemes.

In the same period he also prepared a number of housing designs. In 1862 he made a proposal for remodeling the exterior of a villa in Brunnen – a design that, with its tall roof and wrought-iron window railing, emulated a French chateau style. In the southern Swiss town of Castasegna, Semper built the Villa Garbald, a small home for the family of one of Manfred's schoolmates. This modest project, whose tall gabled wing is complemented by a strong horizontal arbor, is not untypical for the area and served as something of a training project for Manfred.

Unexecuted designs for the Palais von Segesser in Lucerne, the Villa Rieter-Rothpletz in Zurich (Pl. 95), and the Schloss Zichy in Nagyhörcsök, Hungary (Pl. 96) also date from this time. The first project, modeled vaguely on Bramante's House of Raphael, offers little of interest. Semper's various designs for the Villa Rieter-Rothpletz (1864), which was conceived five years earlier, are also rather traditional villa schemes. Their layout was symmetrical and in two variations of the elevation the mass steps up vertically to central motifs. In one case, it ends in an open roof-temple, supported on columns and caryatids; in the other, it concludes with a domed rotunda.

But Semper's design for the rebuilding of the Schloss Zichy in Hungary (1870–71) is unique within his oeuvre. A Gothic castle had been built in 1852–55, but in the late 1860s

Princess Zichy, the maid of honor to Queen Elisabeth in Vienna, decided to have it thoroughly reconstructed. Through the auspices of Mathilde Wesendonck she approached Semper, who responded to the problem by removing the tower, making the floor plan more regular, and organizing the front facade in a symmetrical fashion. But what was most original in the design, more so even than the remodeling of the villa in Brunnen, was the French Mannerist playfulness of the detailing, that is, the steeply angled roof, textured brickwork, banded columns, and broken pediments – all punctuated with plastic decoration.[20]

Potentially, one of Semper's most important projects during his Zurich years was his design for the Zurich Hauptbahnhof (Pls. 97, 98), the city's main railway station. Semper, along with three other architects, was invited to participate in a limited competition in 1861. The first wave of these large European railway stations, most built with iron roofs over their sheds, took place in England and France during the late 1840s and 1850s, among them such notable examples as the Lime Street Station in Liverpool (1848–49), King's Cross in London (1851–52), and the Gare de l'Est in Paris (1847–52). Thus Semper's project of 1861 can almost be viewed as a second-generation development of this building type, falling in a category together with such grand engineering feats as St. Pancras Station in London (1868–69), with its iron trusses spanning 73 meters.

The Zurich station, however, was never intended to be so large, and Semper's design should be compared with Hittorff's almost contemporary work on the Gare du Nord in Paris (1861–65). Both works were influenced by François Dusquesney's Roman bath motif of a large lunette for the Gare de l'Est in Paris. Yet whereas Hittorff carried this motif to the main street facade at the Gare du Nord, Semper terminated the narrow end of the train hall (facing the river) not with a large lunette but with a colossal, two-story triumphal arch stretched across the facade, with the same projected columns at the center that he employed on his museum in Dresden. The clerestory lunettes appear only on the

97 Gottfried Semper, design for Zurich Hauptbahnhof, 1861. Limmat facade. Institut für Geschichte und Theorie der Architektur, Semper Archiv, ETH-Zurich.

98 Gottfried Semper, design for the Zurich Hauptbahnhof, 1861. Interior perspective. Institut für Geschichte und Theorie der Architectur, Semper Archiv, ETH-Zurich.

longer elevations of the building parallel to the railway tracks, and then are well recessed on the town-facade behind the lower roofs of the ticket and waiting areas. What he seems to have tried to do was to relate the exterior triumphal arch (although this is mitigated by lower carriage porches in one version of the scheme) to the two-story system of interior arches that are employed on all three sides of the enclosed terminal. With the lunettes above providing the natural light, the interior for him, in its formal conception, thus truly became an Imperial bath.

In his competition report, Semper argued for the suitability of these lunettes, against a charge of unoriginality, on functional grounds – an argument curiously picked up by Nikolaus Pevsner over a century later.[21] But Semper is hardly functional in his architectural reasoning. The most remarkable aspect of the design are his saddle-like trusses spanning the main hall (whose structure would have been concealed in their final form), which also define these clerestories; they do not spring from low on the ground, like the iron trusses in so many English and French examples, but rather from the top of the second story of arches – and then from colossal atlantes! This decision can only be explained by Semper's comments in his book on Greek slingshot projectiles: his praise for the organic analogy (and artistic audacity) of using such human forms. In the textual description accompanying his competition project, Semper made no mention of the many contemporary English or French structural innovations; rather, he took as his model the composite roof systems that Karl Theodor Ottmer (1800–43) employed on Braunschweig

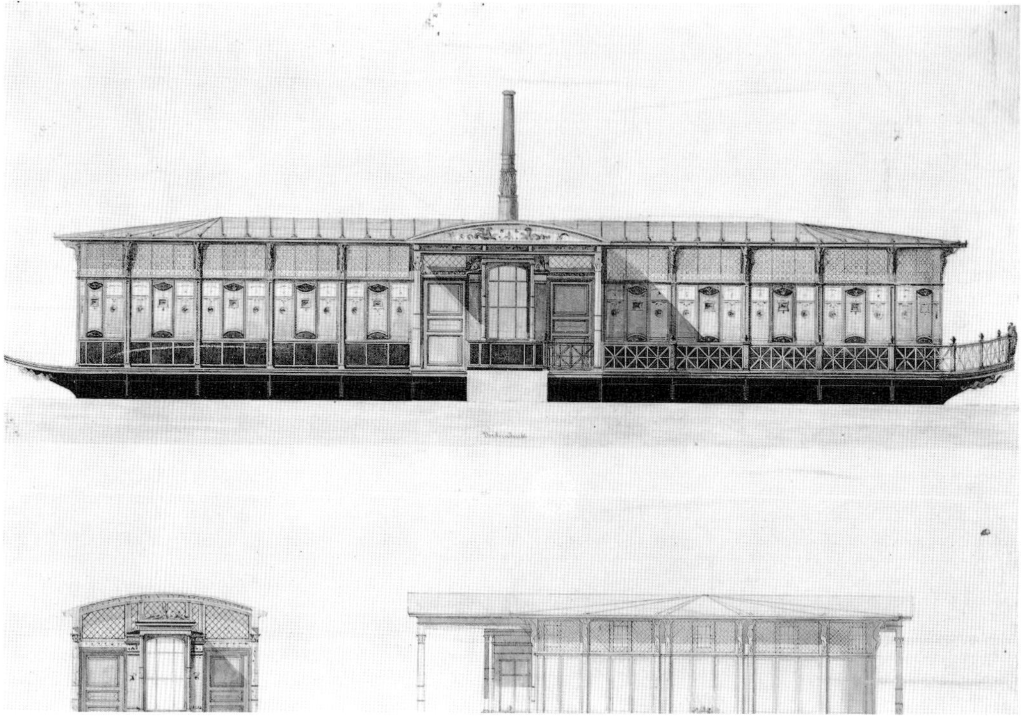

99 Gottfried Semper, floating laundry, Zurich, 1861–62. Institut für Geschichte und Theorie der Architectur, Semper Archiv, ETH-Zurich.

Castle (1831–38) and Railway Station (1843–45), which Semper considered to be antique in their inspiration. The classical form of his roof was to be formed, said Semper, out of wood panels on the interior and cast-iron tiles outside. Braunschweig Railway Station seems to have served as a model for Semper in another respect. One of the few Renaissance-inspired works in Ottmer's abbreviated repertoire, its main entrance was also invested with an imposing triumphal arch.

The final outcome of this competition was no doubt another major disappointment for Semper. The railway agency paid each of the competitors a nominal fee, then had its own railway architect, Jakob Friedrich Wanner, prepare a new design, drawing at will from the ideas of the various schemes. The blame for this perhaps really lay with the inability of Semper and the other architects to work out the many technical problems of this relatively new building type in their designs.

Another Semper project from these years, which has been widely published, was his floating laundry (Pl. 99), a barge design that was prepared in 1861 or 1862. The design of the Pompeii-inspired metal panels that concealed twenty laundry tubs, was surely something of a diversion. The city grudgingly gave a permit for this venture (which was originally moored on the waterfront) with the stipulation that the barge present a good appearance and display no hanging laundry. The colorful, intricately painted, wall panels that composed the design seem not, however, to have pleased city officials. The barge was anchored at Zurich only from 1864 to 1872, and was then moved out to Wollishofen. The idea of using mural designs from Pompeii (now rendered in aquamarine, ochre, and red) for such a purpose is difficult to justify in artistic terms. Instead of the traditional modillions or brackets supporting the overhang of the roof, Semper once again employed human forms (this time female) with Ionic scrolls atop their heads. Among other smaller projects carried out during these years, in addition to various tombs, was the rebuilding of the top of a church tower for the town of Affoltern am Albis.

Semper's design for the Polytechnikum Observatory (Pl. 100), built between 1862 and 1864, was more important architecturally. This project was related to but separate from the nearby Polytechnikum and its chemistry building and in this instance Semper had full control of the design and construction. The Observatory operated almost as a separate institute with its small instrument museum, lecture hall, and a meridian room with library (off the terrace) on the ground floor. Upper floors contained offices for other scientific activities as well as private living quarters for the director. The eighteen-meter tall tower was outfitted with a rotating telescope and copper roof.

The asymmetrical layout of the building, which was dictated by its scientific function, allowed the work to appear as one of the more relaxed of Semper's designs and there is a playfulness to the work in other respects. Decoration was kept to a minimum and consisted only of a rusticated ground story, pilaster strips above (a fixture of his later architecture), and green sgraffito work on the drum of the dome (not apparent in the later photograph). Once again, he had planned a more extensive use of sgraffito decoration on the walls of the upper story. The building, originally situated within a natural setting and vineyards, was further enhanced by a terrace, garden, and rubble coursing of the terrace walls, leading Georg Lasius in 1880 to characterize the work overall as "reminiscent of Bramante" and as one of Semper's most "truly poetic" solutions.[22] Another important architectural feature missing from the built work was the arbor planned for the terraces.

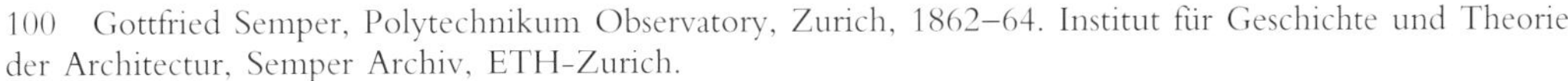

100 Gottfried Semper, Polytechnikum Observatory, Zurich, 1862–64. Institut für Geschichte und Theorie der Architectur, Semper Archiv, ETH-Zurich.

Nearby to both the Observatory and Polytechnikum buildings, Semper built an office complex and warehouse for the Fierz textile concern in the late-1860s. The owner of the building was a prominent politician and Semper designed for him a large Renaissance palazzo along the steeply sloping street. Its main entrance, however, was accessible only from a passageway leading up a level and into a private courtyard. An arbor figures prominently in the design; its lightly projecting timber work contrasts vividly with the strongly rusticated ground story along the street. The rustication here, more so than in any other Semper project, is intensified by the rough facial treatment of the ashlar, squared with the geometric network of the deeply recessed joints. Surely the textile origin of the "dressing" theme is here given full plastic articulation.

Semper's Zurich works of the 1850s and 1860s, however, are generally disappointing compared with his more monumental Dresden offerings, and the architect appears to have been struggling for a sense of direction while accommodating his artistic instincts to Switzerland's frugal building tradition. His strength as a designer, as well as his interest, still lay with design on a monumental scale, and his small projects sometimes seem to suffer from a lack of attention, which may also have been due, at least in the first half of his Swiss tenure, to the arduous pace of his literary activity. A single work that elevates this period above a certain mediocrity, however, was the design he was able to execute successfully in the town of Winterthur – the city's new Town Hall.[23]

Semper's connections with Winterthur, an industrial town 30 kilometers north of Zurich with roots in Roman antiquity, grew out of his friendship with Sulzer, who was a local son and an influential public figure in the city. By the late 1850s or early 1860s Semper had already prepared several designs for an apartment building in Winterthur, but this project never came to fruition. In 1862, no doubt at Sulzer's urging, Semper was also invited by the mayor of the city to participate in a limited competition for the new Catholic church. Yet the Renaissance style of his design, not to mention his vehemently anti-Catholic sentiments, were poorly suited to this particular problem. His proposal for a nine-square, centralized scheme with a dome, attached to which was a single tower, was expensive in its conception and the church's congregation eventually decided on a competitor's Gothic scheme.

He was not disappointed, however, with the result of the competition for the Winterthur Town Hall, which was without question the most important of his executed works during his years in Switzerland. Local discussion concerning a need for a new community hall had started in the late 1850s, and at one stage Semper's co-architect on the Polytechnikum, Johann Caspar Wolff, was appointed by the city to propose solutions on two different sites with two different programs. Yet the project languished until the summer of 1863, when a site was purchased and a building program prepared. First the local architect Wilhelm Bareiss was asked to submit a design. In December of the same year, at Sulzer's urging, Semper and another Zurich architect, Ferdinand Stadler, were also asked to prepare schemes for what amounted to a limited competition in which all three architects were to be paid. The timing was perfect, as Semper had just completed the publication of his work on style, and for the first time since his move to Zurich he could now devote much of his time to his practice.

Bareiss proposed a large rectangular block in what might be called an official Swiss cantonal style. Stadler proposed another tall rectangular block with arched windows and rooftop crenelation borrowed from early Italian urban palaces. Semper's "Roman" design

101 Gottfried Semper, Winterthur Town Hall, 1864–70. Institut für Geschichte und Theorie der Architectur, Semper Archiv, ETH-Zurich.

with its Palladian allusions was judged in the spring of 1865 – in a memo prepared by the town clerk Heller – to be "a monumental work of art in the fullest sense of the word," whose "artistic value and unaffected beauty would be matched by no other building in Switzerland."[24] And even though the work was estimated to cost twenty-five percent more than the other two entries, Semper's exquisitely rendered sepia of his design (Pl. 101) received a ringing endorsement from the community in a city-wide referendum. Work on the building's foundations began in the summer of 1865.

Simply to call Semper's Town Hall design a "Roman" work somewhat depreciates his artistic efforts. If the theme of its templar form had its origin in the Roman roots of the town of Winterthur (Vitudurum), early design sketches depict a design that is more Palladian in character (Pls. 102, 103). One is an almost conventional domed capitol with a four-column porch and a nine-square plan. The second is a richer version without the dome but with a central portico and projecting side pavilions. The rustication of the base is strongly horizontal and the main story is treated in a very plastic way with Renaissance aedicules and niches filled with statues.

In its final form, however, the building assumes a life of its own with an especially lucid delineation of building masses. The temple-like central pavilion with porch, under whose gabled roof the two-story community hall resides on the second level, extends from front to rear and lends a distinct vertical emphasis to the complex. It is seemingly intersected by two lower lateral wings that house the municipal offices; the intersection is accentuated by the row of windows placed under the main portico, wrapping around the sides. A grand exterior staircase affords a strong and luxurious entry to the civic functions. Beneath its first landing, along the main axis of the building, is a secondary and crypt-like entrance to the town archives. Compositionally, it is an exceptionally happy and theatrical ensemble of forms.

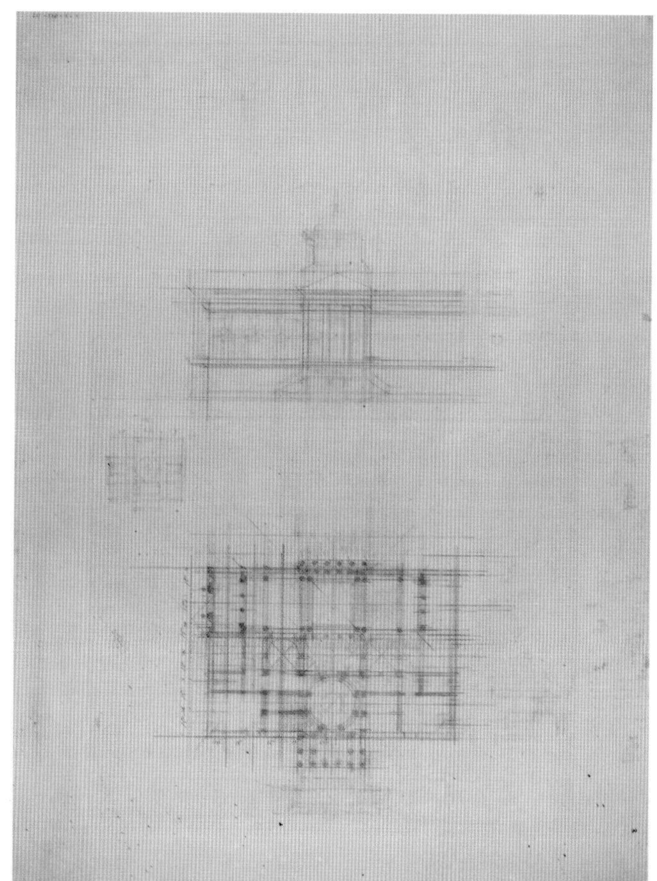

102 Gottfried Semper, Winterthur Town Hall, 1864–70. Early plan and facade study. Institut für Geschichte und Theorie der Architectur, Semper Archiv, ETH-Zurich.

103 (below) Gottfried Semper, Winterthur Town Hall, 1864–70. Early facade study. Institut für Geschichte und Theorie der Architectur, Semper Archiv, ETH-Zurich.

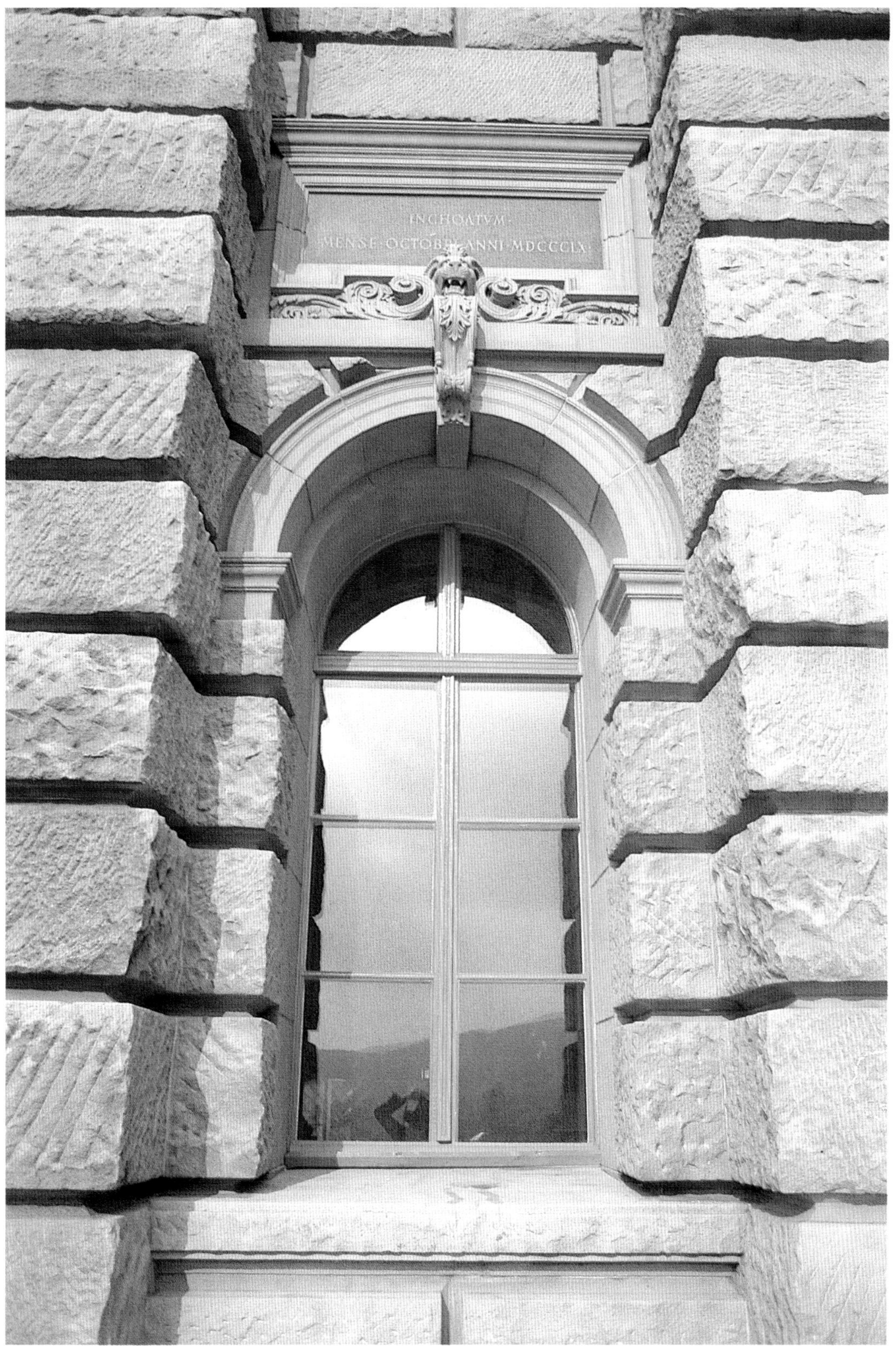

104 Gottfried Semper, Winterthur Town Hall, 1864–70. Detail of rustication around window. Photo by author.

What makes the building one of Semper's best works, however, is the care lavished on the detailing, which greatly advances the expressive lithic qualities of the stonework found in the Dresden Gallery and Zurich Polytechnikum (Pl. 104). And since the Town Hall was the first major design after he wrote his section on stereotomy in his book on style, we have specific explanations for much of this thinking. The entire first story is forcefully rusticated in a crisply conceived and skillfully executed pattern, whose shadowy lineaments and overall form compose, as it were, a sacral-like socle to the civic temple. The various chisel patterns on the face of the stone at the same time present a mosaic of different textural techniques. The joints are made especially powerful by the depth of their projection, but also by their treatment. As Semper explained it: "Ashlar expresses rusticity and the roughness of a fortification when the roughly chiseled surface – in its natural state or after being cut with a hand punch – is surrounded with rectangular, deeply sunken grooves or edging. A similar effect can be achieved by so-called diagonal beveling of the edges of the stone, which creates triangular joints. Here the bossage blends with the joint to form a unit."[25]

Semper chose the second option in this instance, which makes the mortar in the joints almost disappear. Always of interest in his detailing, is the contrast between the roughness of the rusticated stonework and the smoothness of such finished parts as window and door frames – in this instance the smooth arches. The plastic decoration is again sparse in these areas, and is limited on the ground floor to the plaques and lion-head keystones over the windows. The latter, as Peter Wegmann has interpreted them, have various meanings. He reads this motif in Semper's vocabulary as a structural symbol for strength: with its powerful body, as it were, assimilated into the stonework itself. The lion was also a heraldic animal for the city of Winterthur.[26] Semper always paid the greatest attention to his supervision of the masonry during this phase of construction.

Other features of the exterior are also significant. The window aedicules of the main story are relatively plain and semi-recessed, which has the result of accentuating their visual effectiveness. In Semper's competition design, the smooth parapets of the lateral wings wrap under the windows of the central porch and become a ceremonial frieze, no doubt intended to depict historic moments in the city's foundation. The dentils with their exaggerated cantilever visually enhance the even more strongly cantilevered roof. Atop the building are six plastic figures: three in front and three in rear. In front of the exterior staircase are two other reclining figures.

The interior as well can be studied on various levels. Perhaps the most interesting feature is the community hall, the shape and forms of which Semper modeled on the ancient basilica of Fano, as described by the Roman architect Vitruvius. They were colorfully animated with textile hangings placed within the side seating areas. The whole Town Hall, in fact, can be viewed as a pre-Imperial temple or theater to Swiss democracy.

Once again, Semper's many artistic decorations and finishes failed to be executed, even though in this case the city of Winterthur proved to be one of his more sensitive clients. Cost overruns combined with the town's financial distress during construction (the national railway, on which Winterthur's economy was based, went bankrupt during these years) forced the city to cut back on artistic finishes. Inside, the many planned murals and plastic reliefs were omitted. The ceremonial frieze on the exterior remained unexecuted, as were the lower plastic works. The figures on the roof were reduced to two human figures (the city's mythical Nemesis and Pallas Athene) and four seated griffins, and even these had to be commissioned by private funds. This gap between Semper's grandiose conception for this small monument and its somewhat emaciated reality was made even more enormous by the crude expansion and renovation of the building in 1929–34. All statuary was removed and the denuded parliamentary hall was virtually transformed into a Neoclassical work. Even in its chastened form, however, the urbane monumentality of its presence – with its spatially impressive interior staircase and simply appointed assembly hall – is still enormously popular with local people. It is highly esteemed today, as the architectural jewel of the city, and can be counted as perhaps Semper's lone artistic triumph during all of his years in Switzerland.

Richard Wagner and the Munich "Episode"

When Semper fled his home in Dresden in 1849 he had acquired his artistic reputation on the basis of a single architectural masterpiece, the Dresden Hoftheater. Over the many years of his inactivity he continued to view himself preeminently as an architect of theaters. Indeed, he knew the history of this building type well, including its technical requirements. He also viewed the challenge of designing a theater as the most difficult artistic problem for the architect, indeed as his highest calling.

England, of course, afforded him little creative outlet in this regard. His only sketch for a theater in England was for the antique amphitheater that he proposed for the interior of the Crystal Palace in Sydenham. But this project never went forward. And early in 1855, he briefly joined forces with his longtime friend Séchan, who was in London assisting him on the Mixed Fabrics Court, on a competition design for a new theater in Brussels (Pl. 105). The design was completed but the commission went elsewhere.[27]

A few years after arriving in Switzerland, in 1858, Semper entered a competition for an operatic theater in Brazil.[28] Within a few years this design proved to be very important

105 Gottfried Semper and Charles Séchan, design for a theater in Brussels, 1855. Institut für Geschichte und Theorie der Architectur, Semper Archiv, ETH-Zurich.

106 Gottfried Semper, design for a theater in Rio de Janeiro, 1858. Institut für Geschichte und Theorie der Architectur, Semper Archiv, ETH-Zurich.

in terms of his development of this building type, but the immediate results of the competition were again negative. A certain Ferrero, the Brazilian Consul in Leipzig representing the Emperor Dom Pedro II, had approached Wagner shortly before with the invitation for Wagner to come to Rio de Janeiro and produce *Tristan and Isolde*. Wagner, who was desperately seeking the production of one of his works, was intrigued with the possibility but the Brazilian emperor never followed up the invitation. A competition for a new theater was apparently related to this proposed visit and Semper, also beguiled by the prospect of a monumental commission, prepared a lavish design (Pl. 106), complete with a ceremonial emperor's box within an exedra (facing the city) and a double tier of open porticos, behind which were the rounded walls of the auditorium proper. The events that transpired during the competition are unknown.

It must certainly have been a happy surprise when in mid-December 1864 Semper received a letter of extraordinary promise from Richard Wagner. The letter began with the heralding, even ecstatic words: "The King of Bavaria wishes to commission you to build a large theater in Munich in the noblest style for the special purpose that I will indicate. My young patron deeply believes in the truth of my ideal regarding a dramatic work of art, which is essentially and fundamentally different from a modern play or opera." Wagner went on in his letter to say that the idea for the theater grew out of his proposed *Ring of the Nibelung* cycle and the theater was to service the unique problems of this new operatic production. To assist in solving the difficult technical problems, the King proposed the erection of a provisional theater as well, so that Semper and Wagner could first study the technical problems of this new theater type before carrying it forward in monumental forms. The commission was so great in importance, Wagner stressed, that it could be offered only to "a true architectural genius."[29]

Semper, who had just passed his sixty-first birthday, responded as one might expect:

> If I have let two days pass before answering your letter that has been in my possession since the day before yesterday, it is due to the emotions by which I have felt myself staggered. In truth, all of my senses and my whole being have since been fulfilled by its content and utterly claimed. What can be more welcome to an ambitious artist than the occasion to dedicate his service to the noble plans of a young monarch enthused for truth and beauty, and to bring about their execution through his frail efforts?[30]

By the end of the month Semper had traveled to Munich to meet with the young monarch, Ludwig II of Bavaria. Thus began the most Melpomene scene of Semper's artistic career – a script with sufficient mental frailty, personal duplicity and betrayal, and simple political chicanery to tax the imaginative powers of a playwright of Sophoclean stature.

The problems, for the most part, had their basis in the sometimes impulsive, sometimes mopish personality of Richard Wagner. Since fleeing Zurich in 1858 following an adulterous affair, the gifted composer had lived an exceedingly unsettled existence. He sent his ailing first wife Minna to the care of a physician in Dresden and took up residence in Venice for a period of seventeen months, during which time he completed the second act of *Tristan*. He moved to Paris in January 1860 to conduct several concerts there and to prepare the ground – he hoped – for the stage production of his new opera. His efforts were unsuccessful, especially after three failed performances of *Tannhäuser* placed him in great financial distress. After his ban from visiting Germany was partially lifted in the summer of 1860, he was on the road for nearly all of 1861 and 1862 seeking stage productions of his works in various German cities. When these efforts did not achieve their end, he roamed Europe in 1863 as a visiting conductor, giving concerts in Vienna, Prague, St. Petersburg, Moscow, and Pest. During all of these years his penchant for extravagant living far outstripped his modest income and he survived by borrowing large sums of money from various benefactors eager to ransom his future works.

By 1864 he was in a desperate financial plight, fearing his imminent arrest for debts and thus traveling incognito to elude the creditors pursuing him. In this panic-stricken condition on a trip to Germany, on 28 April 1864, he received a calling card from the personal secretary of King Ludwig. Thinking it was a trick from a creditor in disguise, Wagner nearly left town, but he decided to stay one more day for the meeting. What he heard that day would forever change his life. The young King, who idolized Wagner as the greatest artist of his day, commanded him to come to Munich and offered to provide him with luxurious summer and winter villas, a sumptuous salary, and large sums of money to pay off his debts. More importantly, he wanted to produce all of his artistic works in a new theater specifically designed for Wagner's operas. The euphoric composer immediately sent for his favorite Viennese milliner to prepare a new wardrobe and furnishings in the most exotic silks, satins, and velvets – in brilliant shades of brown, red, blue, yellow, and fiery pink.

This generosity on the part of the King would prove to have its limits, not least because of Ludwig's tenuous grasp of reality. When he ascended the throne in 1864, on the sudden death of his father Maximilian II, he did so with no particular education or experience in the affairs of state, and with absolutely no knack for coping with brutal bureaucratic and political infighting. He was a shy, withdrawn child of eighteen years with a tendency to fantasize, and his fantasies – since first viewing *Lohengrin* in 1861 – had tended to revolve exclusively around Wagnerian themes and images. They tended toward the mythological content of the librettos rather than the increasingly eccentric views of the anti-Semitic writer. Driven emotionally by his homosexuality, Ludwig was never able to come to terms with his sexual proclivities within the context and expectations of his royal position. His fragile self-image and feeble political skills were further weakened by the events of the mid-1860s, and in the years after he resorted to ever more exotic flights of imagination in both his costume and domestic surroundings.

In 1886 he was officially declared insane. One day after being incarcerated in one of his childhood homes he was found drowned, the sad victim of either an accident, suicide, or murder.

Other sordid facts regarding the Munich festival theater have been well established by earlier studies.[31] Semper traveled to Munich on 27 December 1864 to meet with Wagner, then two days later had the first of two audiences with the King. He was offered the commission for both a monumental and provisional theater and asked to start work at once. A preliminary site for the permanent festival theater was selected on Munich's Gasteig bluff along the east bank of the Isar River, just south of the Maximilianeum. The provisional theater, by contrast, was to be housed in Munich's "Glass Palace," an iron and glass replica of London's Crystal Palace, erected by the architect August von Voigt in 1853–54. Ludwig, in his enthusiasm for the project, somewhat naively asked that the monumental building be finished and in operation by the summer of 1867: the projected date of the completion of Wagner's *Ring of the Nibelung* cycle.

Semper returned to Zurich and began work with great enthusiasm. The design of the provisional theater took precedence, since it was here that he wanted to work out the technical difficulties of this new type of theater. While in Munich he and Wagner discussed doing away with the traditional loges in favor of an arena (classical) seating arrangement. They also decided to sink the orchestra pit lower than usual so as to make it invisible and thus mute, but not injure the sound. They both agreed that the proscenium should be designed in such a way that it would enhance the necessary separation of the real world of the viewer from the ideal world of the production. The model used for the provisional theater was Semper's proposal for a Roman amphitheater within the transplanted Crystal Palace in Sydenham, the drawings for which had been in Wagner's possession for several years. In this respect, the drawing for the London proposal almost certainly gave rise to the notion of a provisional work in Munich.

Even as Semper began his work at the start of 1865, there were already signs that the

107 Gottfried Semper, design for a provisional theater for the Glass Palace, Munich, 1865. Plan. Museum für Kunst und Gewerbe, Hamburg.

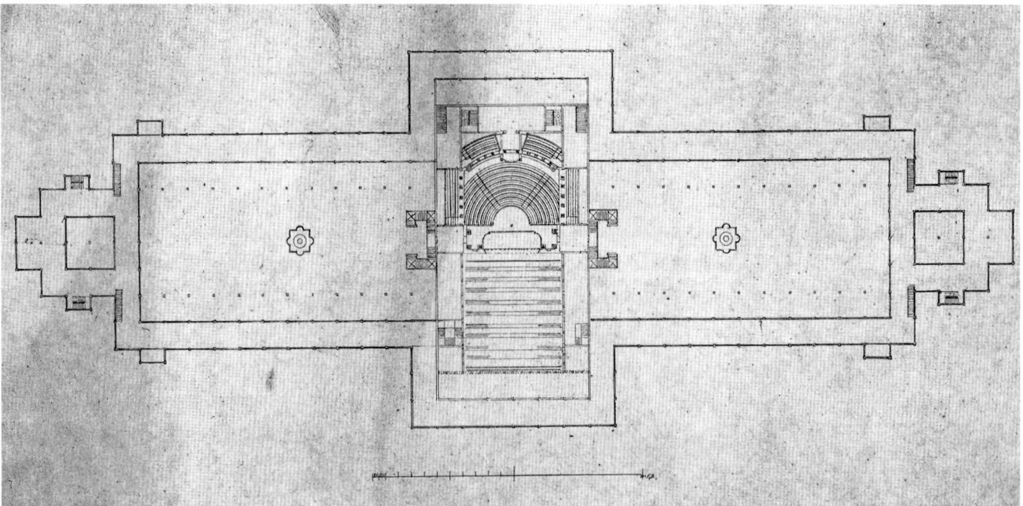

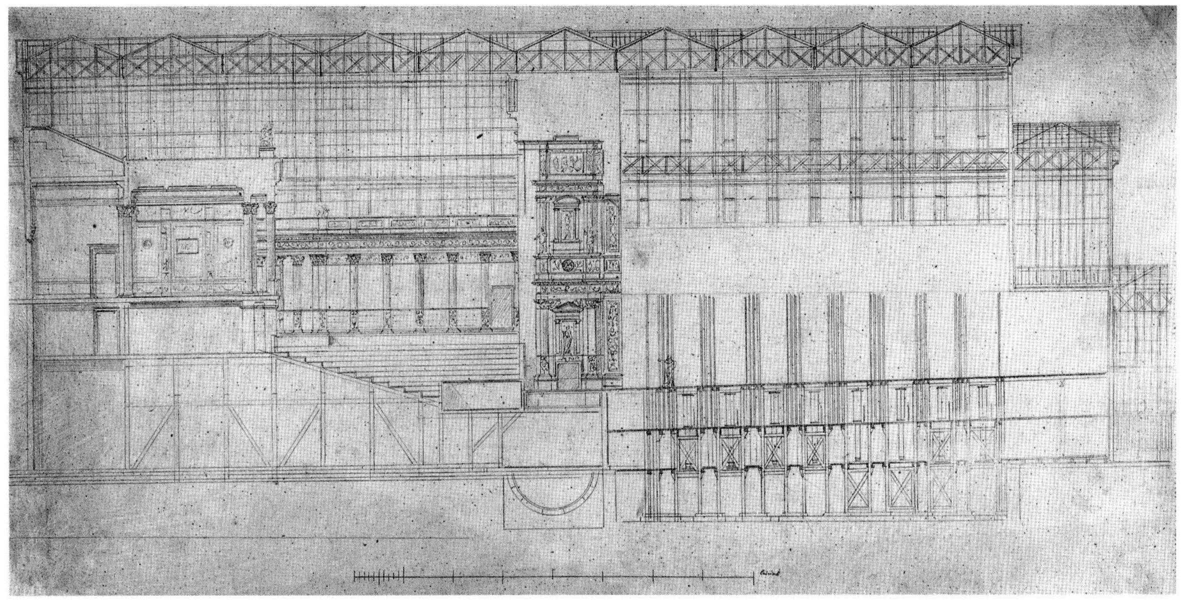

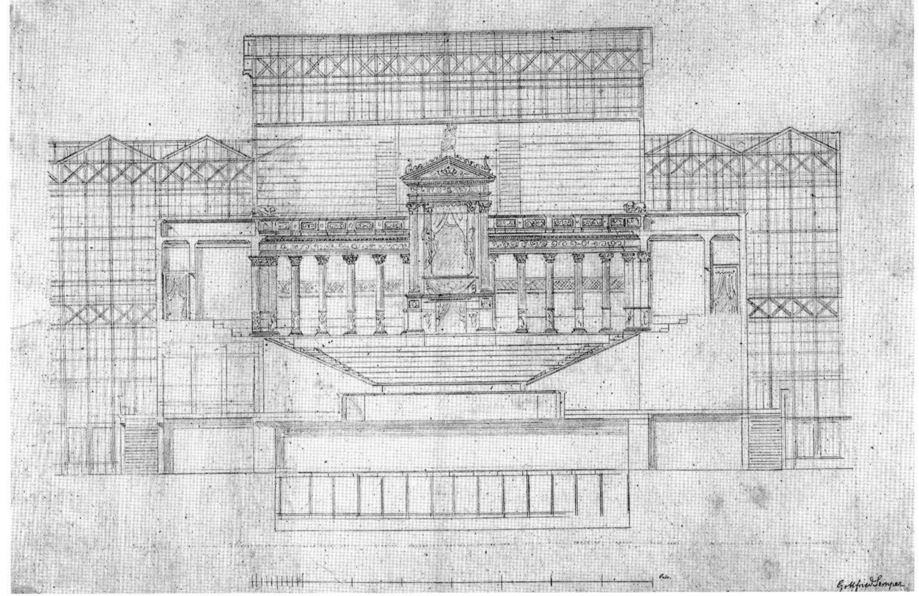

108 (above) Gottfried Semper, design for a provisional theater for the Glass Palace, Munich, 1865. Longitudinal section. Museum für Kunst und Gewerbe, Hamburg.

109 Gottfried Semper, design for a provisional theater for the Glass Palace, Munich, 1865. Transverse section. Museum für Kunst und Gewerbe, Hamburg.

King was running into difficulties. The architect had expected written confirmation of his commission but none was forthcoming. Wagner insisted that to press for a written contract after Semper had received the King's "word" would put the composer in a difficult position and be unseemly.[32] Moreover, Semper's design work – despite Wagner's and the King's demand for prompt delivery – was seriously delayed by the failure of cabinet officials to provide him with either a topographic map of the proposed site for the permanent theater or the plans of the Glass Palace.

Semper eventually contacted two old friends, the painter Friedrich Pecht and the architect Gottfried Neureuther, to ask for their assistance on his behalf. Pecht in several letters informed Semper of the local opposition brewing in Munich against Wagner and the operatic theater (never officially announced), as well as the hampering efforts of various government officials.[33] Wagner confirmed that there were problems, but he announced in March 1865 that Semper would soon receive another royal invitation to come to Munich over the Easter holidays. No invitation arrived but in April the King's secretary Pfistermeister, who was secretly leading the opposition against both theaters, sent Semper two letters: the first confirming the commission for the provisional and monumental theaters and asking for detailed plans of the former; the second asking for only "a kind of sketch" of the latter.[34] No mention of payment was made.

On 10 May, 1865, a few days before Wagner's production of *Tristan* in Munich, Semper sent to Wagner two alternative schemes for the provisional theater, seeking his review and comments. The first scheme (Pls. 107, 108, 109), seating 1000 people in moveable seats, followed closely the Roman layout of his Sydenham proposal, with a rotunda of columns surrounding the amphitheater and the King's loge (defined by an aedicule with a gable) in the center at the rear. Behind the royal loge was a private salon. The amphitheater seating was raised significantly in order to allow for the sunken orchestra pit. The squared proscenium was deep for technical reasons and in order to provide, in Semper's words, "the necessary separation of the real world from that of the stage."[35]

The second scheme, which seated 1500, was worked out in less detail and was formed like a semi-circular Greek amphitheater. An important aspect of both alternatives was Semper's overall vision for the Glass Palace. He suggested that the entire area to one side of the central theater become a grand foyer and conversation area during intermissions; he recommended that the area on the opposite side become a large banquet hall for suppers after the performance. Both areas were to have exotic greenery and multiple works of fine art; in essence, they served as leisure and cultural parks.

Wagner did not respond to Semper's package, in fact, he passed the two schemes straight to the King without studying them. Only several months later – a sign of his abating interest in the project – did he ask to have the plans returned to him for his perusal. Royal officials did not respond to Semper's two schemes either, and at the beginning of July, after almost two months of waiting, Semper wrote to Pfistermeister to ask for an explanation. The latter noted only that the King had reviewed the plans with great interest and as yet had made no decision. Pfistermeister also suggested that Semper might consider making another trip to Munich in September in order to examine possible sites for the permanent theater and make a recommendation in that regard. What Semper did not know was that from the very beginning of the process Ludwig had little interest in the provisional theater and was looking forward only to the monumental design.

During the summer Ludwig pressed Semper again for the design for the permanent theater as well as a cost proposal.[36] Semper, who was still awaiting feedback from Wagner on the provisional work, as well as topographic information, had held back on the monumental design, but he decided to travel to Munich in September and present his earlier Brazilian scheme, from which a cost estimate could be made. His trip proved awkward: the King had gone away unexpectedly to his mountain retreat because of illness and Wagner, for reasons that only later became apparent, was in no mood to see him. With Wagner's assistance, however, Semper did decide on two alternative sites north of the Maximilianeum, one of which involved the building of a new street and a bridge to connect it with the royal residence. And shortly after his return to Zurich, after ten months of delay caused by the lack of cooperation of cabinet officials, Neureuther was at last able to send him a topographic map of the general area. The King, utterly oblivious to the cause of the delay, pleaded not only for Semper's design drawings of the permanent theater but also for a gypsum model.

What had been transpiring in Munich in 1865 between Wagner, the press, and the King was beginning to have an effect. Wagner had arrived in Bavaria in the summer of 1864 seemingly with his earthly (financial) problems forever behind him, but his extreme conceit and extraordinary greed soon began to jeopardize his good fortune. Soon after joining the King at the summer villa on Lake Starnberg, Wagner sought to secure the appointment of Hans von Bülow as the conductor of the Munich orchestra. This allowed him to resume his affair with Hans's wife Cosima, also the daughter of Franz Liszt. This intrigue was soon known to everyone – everyone, that is, except Ludwig. When the composer followed the King back to Munich in the fall, he was given a palace on the Briennerstrasse for his use. He immediately installed himself in great luxury, flaunting a satrapic splendor that was an affront to the citizenry of Munich.

To the press, his outrageous behavior brought to mind the scandal of Ludwig I and Lola Montez (Semper's former acquaintance in Dresden) in 1848, which resulted in Ludwig's abdication. Ominously, newspapers in Munich even began referring to Wagner as "Lolotte." Despite the implications of this epithet, Wagner refused to tone down his act. There was a furor in February 1865 when he presented Ludwig with a gift of a portrait of himself – together with the gift of the painter's invoice to the state treasury. Opposition to him became intense as he sought to fill key musical posts within the city with his cronies. There was even talk of his meddling in the political affairs of the state. Rumors of the huge theater to be erected in his honor and funded by the taxpayers certainly did not in any way mitigate this growing resentment toward his presence in the city. Ludwig, however, ignored the rancor and remained loyal to his resident genius. He was completely unaware that his ministers, intent on saving a government hurtling toward collapse, were privately working to remove Wagner from Munich.

A successful performance of *Tristan* in June temporarily staved off the inevitable. This performance almost did not come about as police officials, acting on behalf of creditors, entered Wagner's mansion shortly before the opening; they were seeking his arrest or the immediate settlement of a debt. Only a quick trip by Cosima to the Bavarian treasury to snatch 2400 florins in cash prevented his being taken into custody. It then became apparent that much of the money that Ludwig had given him earlier to settle past accounts had gone instead to his interior decorator.

In July the sudden death of the tenor Ludwig Schnorr von Carolsfeld, who had shortly before played Tristan, sent Wagner into a fit of depression that exceeded even the usual bounds of his neurosis. He was still in this condition in September when Semper arrived for a consultation. Wagner now found the visit of his friend "odious" and he seemed to have lost interest in the new theaters that were to bear his name. As he noted in his diary: "I am not able, and do not care, to see any human being, not even the dearest and most intelligent [Semper] when Cosima is not there: anything that happens when she is not there is torment to me. How I hate this projected theatre, indeed, how childish the King seems for insisting on this project so passionately: now here I am with Semper and supposed to deal with him, talk about the senseless project! I known of no greater torment than this which now faces me. – You see – that is how I am!"[37]

This was indeed how he was. His near dementia, however, did not prevent him from planning another run on the state coffers. In August, he insisted that his salary be amended; he demanded another 200,000 gulden, of which 40,000 was to be granted outright. The King, who had no defense against Wagner's threat of departing the city, soon relented. This last ploy did, however, lead to the composer's eventual downfall. When the conditions of his emotional blackmail leaked out in late November, the King, fearing for Wagner's physical safety as well as the immediate fall of the government, had no alternative but to send his dear and only friend out of the city – temporarily he prayed. Thus on the morning of 10 December Wagner boarded a train for Switzerland, where he and Cosima, with the King's continued financial support, took up residence. The theater projects were at this point doomed, although their demise was clear only to Wagner.

Wagner's departure from Munich indeed merely strengthened, rather than lessened, Ludwig's resolve to erect this grand monument to his friend. Throughout the fall of 1865 Semper remained at work refining the design of the provisional theater – sheets that he completed in late November and sent to Wagner in Munich. These arrived, unfortunately, just as the scandal broke and were put aside by Wagner unopened, then lost during his packing and departure. They were not found until the following February, by which time numerous objections (technical, aesthetic, and financial) had been raised against building a theater inside the Glass Palace. Cabinet ministers were also intent on preventing any project that might bring Wagner back to the capital. The King, on the contrary, had the view that the theater was precisely what would lure his now sulking friend back.

Semper next turned to the design of the monumental theater, which Ludwig was again pressing him to complete. Early in November 1865, Semper sent to Ludwig a copy of his new book on style, which was well received. The King expressed a burning desire to view the model of Semper's ingenious design and thanked the heavens for his good fortune in uniting the talents of the century's "greatest of architects" with the century's "greatests of poets and musicians" – in "a work that will last until the end of time."[38] Strong words!

In the middle of December, shortly after Wagner's departure from the capital, Pfistermeister wrote to Semper to assure him that the two theaters would still be built.[39] Semper, who had now been at work on the two projects for over a year, stepped up his efforts and in March 1866 he informed Neureuther that the final design of the permanent work was well advanced, although the task was "great and difficult."[40] Around the same time, the King's decision to start work on the provisional theater met with fierce opposition from the finance minister. Wagner's intervention at this point could probably have saved the provisional theater, but he preferred to continue to brood. The project soon lost momentum.

By the middle of May, 1866, Semper had completed work on his design for his monumental theater and he sought from Frau Wesendonck the address of Wagner who, although living less than fifty kilometers away, had not written him since his latest exile.[41] Wagner was lodged at Tribschen, near Lucerne, and had visited Zurich on several occasions without calling on his friend.

Semper took the plans to Wagner's estate, then in June he sent them to the King. Once again the timing could not have been worse, as Bavaria had just entered the

Austrian-Prussian war on the wrong side. The routing of Bavarian and Austrian troops by the Prussian army mercifully brought the conflict to a quick resolution by summer's end. Semper continued working on the huge model of the theater, a project that was not finished until the end of the year. A now ebullient Wagner, with Cosima and Hans von Bülow in tow, made the trip from Tribschen to Zurich on New Year's Eve to view the finished model. He was deeply impressed with the physical representation of his "conception" and he described it in a letter to the King as "the noblest work of architecture in centuries."[42] Ludwig made special arrangements to have the model shipped to Munich without its container's being opened by customs as it crossed the border. He too was overwhelmed by its noble form and on 9 January, 1867, Semper received an urgent telegram, summoning him to the royal residence. He prepared himself for what he assumed would be his triumphal entry into the Bavarian capital.

He was indeed received royally. He had his first two-hour audience with Ludwig on 11 January and returned to the palace the next day for another. The King was ecstatic with the beauty of the design and made the decision on the spot – with his "royal word and handshake" – to build the work and to offer Semper the highest architectural post in Bavarian state service. Ludwig also ordered his ministers to make final arrangements for the purchase of the land. The King's new secretary, Lorenz von Düfflipp, promised Semper as he was leaving the city that royal decrees formalizing these decisions would be mailed to Zurich within a few days. Semper departed Munich feeling elated, his lifetime ambition as an artist had found its consummation. He could not have imagined how much treachery was to follow.

Despite many grim details, the subsequent events can be summed up in a few lines. The King's will, even though he found support within influential circles in Munich, once more collapsed in the face of cabinet opposition to his plan; meanwhile, speculative interests made the purchase of the land for both the theater and its new street a difficult venture. Had the King had some signal from Wagner of his willingness to return to Munich, he would have probably proceeded in the face of these obstacles, but Wagner (although describing Semper in a letter of 11 January as "the greatest architectural genius of our time")[43] again failed to rally around the design. His response to Ludwig was that he would, in fact, never return to Munich.

Wagner, at least, had an excuse for his duplicity toward Semper. He felt he could not live without Cosima at his side and that their illicit relationship would forever prevent his returning to Munich. Typically, he salved his bad conscience with baseless accusations of disloyalty on the part of Semper.[44]

Perhaps even more ignoble, however, was the deception practiced on Semper by the King's new secretary Düfflipp. While privately directing all of his efforts in Munich to scuttling the project, he actually had Semper at the start of 1867 begin the costly process of producing working drawings for construction. He did not, however, send Semper the promised contract, claiming it awaited the final purchase of the land; rather, he maintained his silence until the following September – that is, nine months later – and only then, after Semper had written to him, did Düfflipp request a meeting at Zurich railway station.[45] Disappointed at not receiving the long-awaited letter of commission, Semper demanded a truthful account of the situation but Düfflipp did not respond candidly. Three months later, Semper, who had finally caught on to the game taking place in Munich, sent his son Manfred to the city to negotiate on his behalf, as well as to present

110 Gottfried Semper, design for the Munich Festspielhaus, 1864–67. Elevation. Architektursammlung der TU München.

the requested cost estimate and building description. The same assurances of a written building contract and a state appointment were given to Manfred, and once again he was promised the letter of commission would be mailed out within a few days. Once again Düfflipp simply lied.

In a letter sent to Semper in the middle of January, 1868, Düfflipp finally admitted that the building, as budgeted, simply could not be financed on existing state revenues. But this acknowledgment came too late in the process. As a contingency to Manfred's negotiations in December, Semper had asked his son to lay out the history of the case to a local Munich attorney, Friedrich Schauss. When Düfflipp later insisted that he had mailed out Semper's contract after his meeting with Manfred, Semper gave Schaus, early in 1868, the authority to pursue the matter legally, beginning with an invoice for his three years of labor. Cabinet officials again fought a delaying tactic and it was only with the very real threat of a lawsuit against the Crown that they consented in January 1869 – another twelve months later – to pay Semper something for his massive efforts and expenses.[46] The scandal of the lawsuit eventually came to be seen as a dark stain on the reputation of the royal house, but King Ludwig, who had been misled by everyone, seems never to have understood what had happened.

In the midst of this skullduggery, what cannot be overlooked is the sublime architectural creation of Semper. If it had been built, it would have been not only his greatest architectural accomplishment but without question the grandest theater of the nineteenth century (Pls. 110, 111, 112). The heart of this – his most theatrical – conception was the treatment of the orchestra and proscenium. In his first solution for the provisional theater

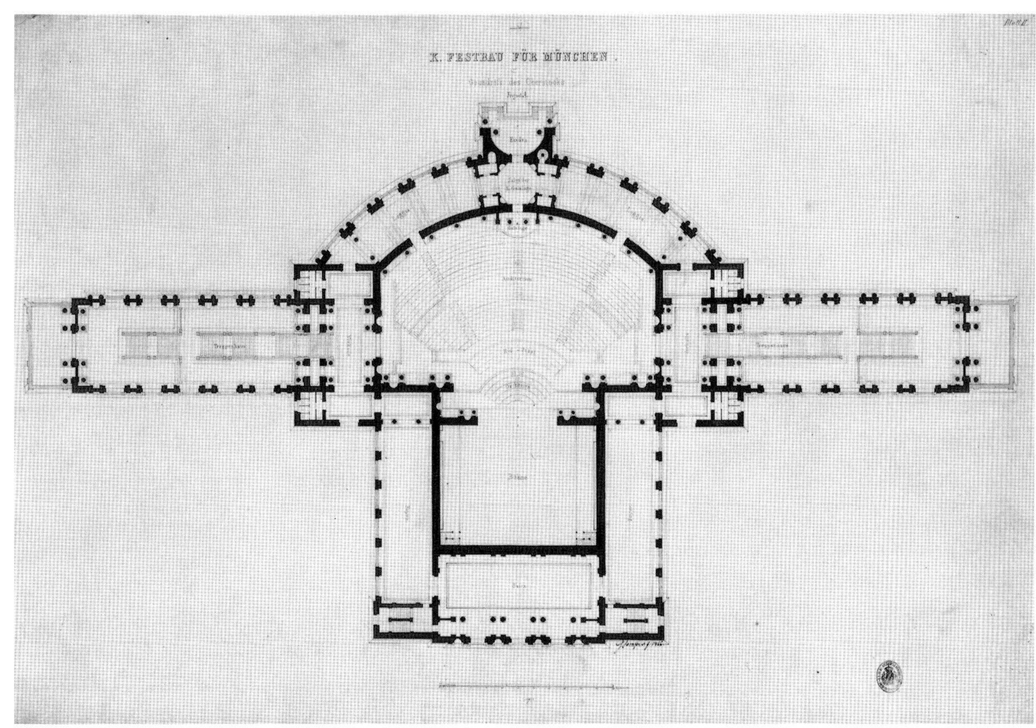

111 and 112 Gottfried Semper, design for the Munich Festspielhaus, 1864–67. Above: plan. Below: section. Architektursammlung der TU München.

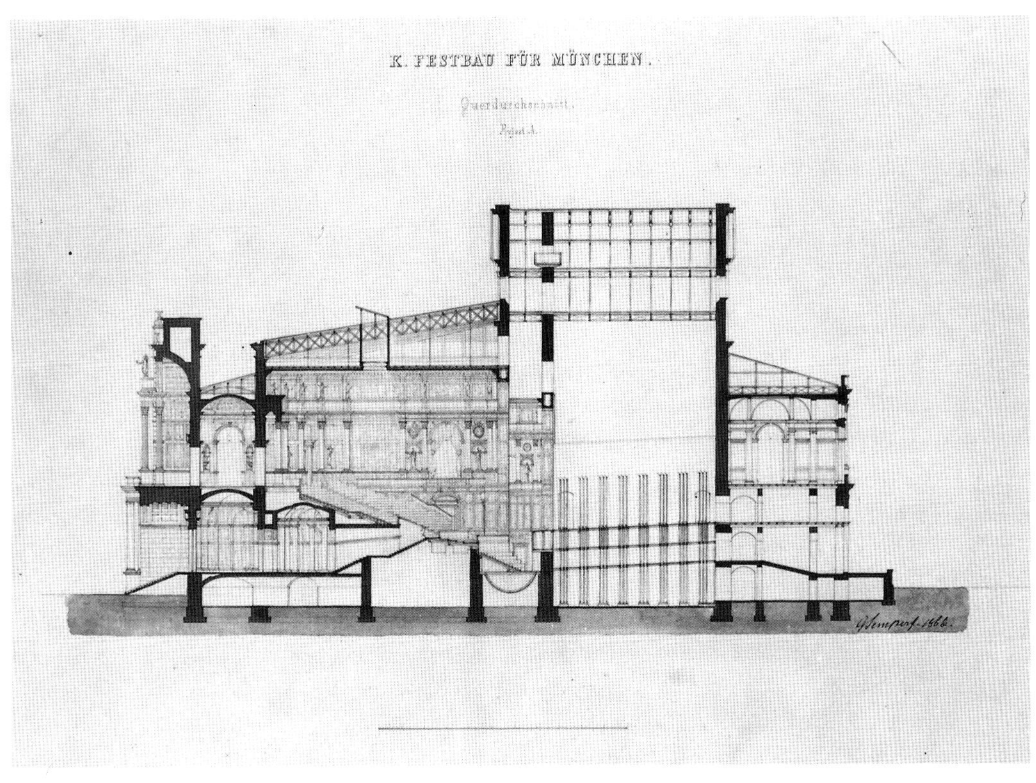

of May 1865, which grew out of conversations with Wagner, Semper had already spoken of the need to remove the orchestra from the audience's view and enhance the distinction between the action on the stage and the audience. His deep proscenium, he suggested, solved the second problem, although he rationalized its depth at that time as necessary also to bring the stage lighting forward as far as possible.

In Semper's revised scheme for the provisional theater, carried out in the fall of the same year, he hit upon an ingenious solution that solved the problems of both the orchestra and proscenium at the same time. Instead of regarding the orchestra as a single, flat pit partially submerged into the floor, he now designed it as a continuation of the stepped auditorium cavea (although stepped deeper), separated from it by an aisle and solid banister. Behind the screen the conductor looked down over the musicians. This smaller arena was made spatially distinct by virtue of its own proscenium. Several meters behind it was placed another proscenium that defined the stage proper. This solution was doubly bold for now, by manipulating the proportioning of the two prosceniums in a receding or a false perspective, the appearance of the actors on the stage could be visually enlarged, thus also enhancing their "other-worldliness" or unreality.

Semper incorporated this solution in the design of his monumental theater and discussed the reasoning in the written explanation accompanying his design drawings. The double proscenium, he said, defined an "in-between space," which permitted a new system of lighting to be shielded from view and also, more importantly, allowed the activity on the stage to seem visually enlarged:

> The decoration of this anterior proscenium is – in its motifs, orders, and proportions – the same as the posterior stage proscenium although its actual dimensions are different. Thus there comes about a perspective distortion since the eye is unable to distinguish the true dimensional differences within the perspective. It is an illusion that, according to every condition and circumstance, can be enhanced and modified by every conceivable trick of illumination.[47]

Wagner devotees have been quick to take this visually modified proscenium (which Wagner's architects later incorporated into the theater at Bayreuth) as yet another indication of their master's fertile genius, but it is more accurate to view it as a Semperian device. It came about in this instance, it is true, through the conversations of Semper and Wagner, but this line of reasoning and sensitivity to the unreality of the stage hark back to Semper's earliest reflections on the Dresden Theater and to his treatment of the proscenium there. This idea was a major preoccupation of Semper in the late 1850s, when he greatly refined his artistic theories in his main work of theory. Here he spoke specifically of the need for art to mask or camouflage its material (physical and thematic) in order to enhance its magic and seduction. In fact the passages cited in an earlier chapter regarding the "masking of reality" and "the haze of carnival candles" were penned by Semper in 1858 or 1859. It was thus inevitable that the matter of re-defining the shape and role of the proscenium should arise in the conversations of Semper and Wagner in 1864–65. The difficult part of every architectural conception, in any case, is how to realize the desired end in a convincing way, and Wagner was of absolutely no assistance in solving this aspect of the problem. The rather crude continuation of this motif along the side and rear walls of the auditorium at Bayreuth only rendered banal a device of great subtlety as originally conceived.

113 Gottfried Semper, design for the Munich Festspielhaus, 1864–67. Site plan. Institut für Geschichte und Theorie der Architectur, Semper Archiv, ETH-Zurich.

Semper's creativity in choosing the grand situation of the theater on the high bluff on the east bank of the Isar (Pl. 113) is also not always recognized. When he first traveled to Munich late in 1864, it was quickly agreed by all parties that the monumental theater was to be located on other land owned by the Crown along the river, south of the existing Maximilianeum. The latter work, ironically, had been the building on which Maximilian II had pinned his hopes for inventing the future "new style" in 1850. In 1864, shortly before his death and after the construction was well underway, he had the architect Friedrich Bürcklein change its exterior features from Gothic to Renaissance.

Semper's first site plans of 1865 locate the theater near this building, but in August of the same year he received from Pfistermeister a letter requesting him to come to Munich and search for another possible site. On this trip to Munich in September – the visit that the now uninterested Wagner found "odious" – Semper and Wagner discussed site alternatives, and out of these discussions came the astute idea of extending what is now Galeriestrasse from the rear of the royal gardens through the Anna district to a site on the opposite river bluff, and creating in the process a new bridge over the river as the ceremonial entrance to the majestic edifice. Wagner also suggested widening the profile of the building (making it similar in width to the Maximilianeum) to enhance its monumental appearance. Semper accomplished this by extending the main staircases in a line out from the sides of the auditorium at right angles.

This notion of a major restructuring of city streets to enhance a monumental work was also central to various of Semper's other urban schemes. There were plenty of precedents in Munich, as both men knew, for the inauguration of new streets: both Ludwig I and Maximilian II had had major arteries laid out in their honor. A more compelling example in this instance, however, was the new street being created in Paris in the early 1860s for a new opera building, a project that both Semper and Wagner also knew firsthand. This conception, then, was in keeping with the very similar attitudes of these two men. The result in Munich would have been an edifice that would have graced the city on the scale of its other monuments, and – with its grandiose formal composition and elevated situation – would have dominated the cityscape down to the present day. The expense and audacity of the conception, however, combined with the feebleness of the King, unfortunately prevented it from being carried out.

It was thus within the context of a highly theatrical setting that the massive scale of the work was conceived (Pl. 114). The sheer size of the composition also played into Semper's strengths as a designer. The building's width would have measured 183 meters; the ridge line of the stagehouse gable (with a colossal pedimental relief that would have been visible only far in the distance) towered above its already elevated terrain 52 meters in the air. The new masonry bridge with its sculptural works, supported on piers and segmental arches, was modeled on the Maximiliansbrücke several hundred meters to the south. At the bridge's east end carriages were directed to the two side wings, while pedestrians ascended to the theater sanctum by climbing a series of monumental staircases. A modified triumphal arch formed the central motif of the theater itself; the large cornice surmounting the upper story was broken in the center by a large exedral apse that became, in essence, the imperial canopy enclosing the symbolic seat of the monarch. In Greek times, an exedra was that part of the gymnasium furnished with a circular seat and was often a place where philosophers and their disciples world converse. The gloriously articulated exedra itself was crowned with a victorious quadriga – perhaps, as later in Dresden, Dionysus conducting his bride Ariadne up to Mount Olympus. The exedra became the motif most associated with Semper's name, in many ways the symbol of his architectural theatricality.

The exterior plastic detailing was also especially ornate. The heavily rusticated arcade and pilasters of the ground story, similar in their plasticity to those of the Winterthur Town Hall, became in effect a giant plinth for the entire complex. On the main story the arcade was fitted at each abutment with a pair of three-quarter columns. One sketch shows statuary slipped in between the paired columns and a string of garlands above each

114 Gottfried Semper, design for the Munich Festspielhaus, 1864–67. Photo of model rendered into drawing. Institut für Geschichte und Theorie der Architektur, Semper Archiv, ETH-Zurich.

window. Plastic relief was also inserted into the spandrels and concentrated heavily in the central archway. Various sketches of both the exterior and interior, show how early in the process Semper wove his allegories and vignettes into his design (Pl. 115), even if little can be discerned of the iconography other than an indication of a pantheon of composers to be placed on the exterior. This was a *Gesamtkunstwerk* on a scale never before attempted. Had it been built it would certainly have rivaled in ostentation and grandeur the new Opera in Paris and vastly exceeded it in size; the auditorium in Munich would have been over twice the width of the Paris Opera and nearly twice as deep. The city would have become the operatic center of Germany.

The relation of the proposed Munich festival theater to the one built the following decade at Bayreuth is interesting. Even as Semper labored on the Munich project, Wagner and Ludwig were privately contemplating moving the location to Nuremberg, where opposition was presumed to be less intense than in Munich.[48] After the fiasco of the project's collapse and Semper's threatened lawsuit against the Crown, the friendship of Semper and Wagner (as that of Wagner and Ludwig) cooled considerably, thus making any further collaboration between the architect and composer unlikely. Early in 1869 Semper insisted to his attorney Schauss that he did not want Wagner injured by the legal proceedings in any way, but he raged privately about the shoddy treatment he had received and refused to have anything to do with his once close friend. In Wagner's case, the problem was simply one of a bad conscience, and while still living on the handsome salary of the King, he wrote a rambling letter to Semper in the spring of 1869, recounting in a somewhat fantastic way the events that had led to the theater project's collapse. He also feigned an apology while at the same time admonishing Semper for his lack of trust in him. Semper, who knew Wagner's personality only too well, simply wrote across the bottom: "This letter, out of which I

115 Gottfried Semper, design for the Munich Festspielhaus, 1864–67. Interior details. Architektursammlung der TU München.

cannot make head or tail, I have left unanswered."[49] This ended their personal contact for several years.

Wagner, however, continued to scheme for a festival theater and was not above preparing new deceptions against Ludwig. Although under contract to deliver the Ring operas to the monarch, Wagner began to have second thoughts as he was nearing the completion of *Siegfried* – the score of which he refused to surrender to the King. With the unification of Germany becoming a reality in 1870–71, Wagner was well aware that political power now resided in the north, in Berlin, and he did not hesitate to play the Bismarck card. In a meeting with the new Chancellor in 1871, he sought political and financial backing for his project by presenting it in a nationalistic light. A short time earlier he had visited the town of Bayreuth to examine an old theater as a possible site for his works, and he found the town amenable to the idea of hosting a new festival theater.

When federal money for the Bayreuth project proved elusive, Wagner decided to finance it through subscriptions. These, however, did not raise enough revenue to complete the construction – even though Ludwig pledged 25,000 thalers to the cause. In the end it was the Bavarian treasury that picked up the bill, although Wagner at the same time was refusing the delivery of *Siegfried*. What is even more incredible, Ludwig, at Wagner's request, also sent to the composer Semper's plans for the Munich theater and the composer instructed his architects at Bayreuth, Carl Brandt and Otto Brückwald, to execute its principal ideas in timber and brick. Neither designer possessed much in the way of talent, but work slowly progressed and the undistinguished theater opened with the Ring Festival in August 1876.

But the story of what Manfred Semper once referred to as the Munich "episode" does not stop here. In the early spring of 1875 Wagner met Semper in Vienna at a soirée at Hans Markart's atelier; he sought him out again in visits to the city in May and November of the same year as he wanted to renew the friendship. Semper, by now in his seventies, had aged noticeably and was having both personal and health problems in his new city of residence. He was at the beginning of an illness that would soon force him to retire from the city and practice, and was "very tired and old," but he could become quite animated when the discussion turned to such subjects as Michelangelo.[50] In November the two friends celebrated Semper's seventy-second birthday by reminiscing about their Dresden days. The next year Semper accepted an invitation from Wagner to attend the first Bayreuth Festival as a special guest of honor. It was only some months later that Wagner admitted to what Semper certainly knew, that "the theater, even if crude and artistically lacking, was executed after your design."[51]

Semper was certainly not consoled by this admission. Although the idea of a government's spending enormous sums of money on an artistic venture of this magnitude may be criticized in social terms, the sad result of this joint venture of two of the most artistically fertile minds of the century was simply the erection of the much inferior theater in Bayreuth. It was an unworthy monument to an era in which people could still dream of art on the scale envisioned for Munich, a theatrical vision of unparalleled grandeur. Some historians have viewed the Munich episode in terms of its destruction of Semper's career and health, but this is surely overstating the facts.[52] The tragedy of Munich – in both its countenance and historical character – was much more Wagnerian than Semperian.

Prolegomena to a Theory of Style

Throughout the five years that Semper lived in London, he never gave up the idea of completing his long expected textbook on comparative building theory. The history of the technology of metals that he had prepared for Cole prior to his tenure at the Department of Practical Art, his yearly cycle of lectures at the school, his mathematical study of Greek projectiles – all furthered his endeavor intellectually, even if work on the actual manuscript was slow. In fact, he apparently did no further writing for the project after the summer of 1851, that is, after his publisher Vieweg had visited London for the Great Exhibition and asked Semper to revise and shorten the work.

Yet immediately upon his arrival in Zurich in July 1855, Semper wrote to Vieweg to renew his commitment once again: "My yearning for that exterior calm and leisure, which alone will make it possible to complete the long cherished plan of publishing my comparative building theory, was the main reason for the acceptance of a professorship and directorship of the architectural department of the Federal Polytechnikum here."[53] Although Semper may have sought to appease his publisher with this somewhat embellished reason for his moving to Zurich, he at least now was serious about making progress on the work. In the same letter he also intimated that the project was now broader in its scope than earlier anticipated; it would not just be a textbook on comparative building types but a work that would embrace "the entire world of form." The next eight years were to be, in fact, the most intellectually productive of his lifetime.

At Vieweg's request, Semper met with him in August at the Swiss resort town of Ragaz, to discuss these changes to the work as well as the terms of the contract that had been written several years earlier. Vieweg's publishing house, founded in 1786 by his father, was among the most respected in Germany. Eduard Vieweg was an honorable and well educated man with a genuine interest in advancing knowledge. Semper seemed satisfied with the new conditions. Nine months later, in June 1856, he sent to Braunschweig the first installment of his new work, now entitled "Theory of Artistic Forms" (*Kunstformenlehre*); it consisted of approximately 100 woodcuts, a preface, an introduction, and two of the six sections he had promised for the first volume. The first section, consisting of approximately sixty handwritten pages, was entitled "Simplest Combinations," and dealt mainly with the principles of ornamentation. The second section of 350 pages was devoted to ceramics.

It was at this point, as Wolfgang Herrmann's exhaustive scholarship has shown, that problems surfaced with the publisher.[54] Semper, through his acquaintances in Zurich, had learned of the more lucrative book contracts of other faculty members (among them his friend Moleschott), and he made known to the publisher his dissatisfaction with his fees. Vieweg, too, seemed puzzled at the new direction of Semper's work, and he suggested another meeting in Zurich in September 1856 to review both issues once again. Vieweg also promised to bring along with him Semper's old manuscript for the architect's revision and inclusion in the new study.

The two men met in the middle of September and worked through their respective concerns amicably. Vieweg raised Semper's fee once more and the architect presented him with his manuscript on ancient Greek missiles for publication. The publisher departed Zurich but within days Semper began to have second thoughts as to his literary value once again. A few weeks later he made an undignified decision, that eventually seriously delayed and harmed the results of his labor. In a telegram to another publisher in Frankfurt he offered his proposed book for a higher fee. Thus began several years of conflict and near litigation that did his reputation no honor.

Semper's decision cannot be excused simply by his unhappy living situation in Zurich. Only after signing his revised contract with Vieweg in September did he sit down and actually recalculate his new fee; he found it still below what Moleschott, in particular, had been paid for his most recent book on physiology. Contacting Friedrich Suchsland of the Bruckmann publishing house in Frankfurt was apparently at first simply a ploy to justify yet another demand for an increase in fees, but the strategy soon backfired.

In his letter to Vieweg, who was still on holiday, Semper complained of his financial worries and spoke of offers from other publishers; then he laid out his new demands.[55] The publisher – who for years had been patient with Semper's many delays, who had awarded him ample advances and had given financial assistance to his wife and children in the first months of his exile, who had even offered in 1849 to be his mediator with the King of Saxony over his legal problems – was deeply offended by this crude expression of greed. He left Switzerland without responding to the letter, taking with him Semper's manuscript on ancient projectiles and the new work on artistic forms.

Only then did Semper realize that he had betrayed a longtime friend – in addition to making a grave tactical blunder. Moreover, Suchsland, the publisher in Frankfurt, had also accepted the conditions of his telegram as the "first step" toward a legal contract and Semper was forced to admit, sheepishly in a letter written the day after his telegram was sent, that he was already under "some obligation" to Vieweg.[56]

In several letters to Vieweg, Semper first begged for the return of the two manuscripts, then coupled his pleas with threats of legal action.[57] Both men hired attorneys and prepared to battle in court. It was only several months later that Suchsland realized that the conflict was not simply a business disagreement but had now escalated into a bitter personal feud. For legal reasons, Vieweg eventually returned the manuscript on Greek projectiles but he held onto the first sections of "Theory of Artistic Forms" and insisted on the legality of his contract with Semper. The latter, worried at his predicament, waited until the start of 1858 to sign another contract with Suchsland's firm in Frankfurt. It was not until 1860 that the first volume of his now expanded and partially rewritten work appeared, under the title *Der Stil in den technischen und tektonischen Künsten oder praktische Ästhetik: Ein Handbuch für Techniker, Künstler und Kunstfreunde* (Style in the Technical and Tectonic Arts or Practical Aesthetics: A Handbook for Technicians, Artists, and Patrons of Art).

Given the sustained controversy surrounding the publishing rights to Semper's major theoretical text, it is remarkable that he was able to write it at all. It was a work that had undergone considerable evolution since its conception in 1843. Before coming to Zurich, Semper saw the text as a kind of architectural typology in which various building types would be compared and analyzed formally with respect to their founding motives. In Semper's version of the plan laid out for Vieweg in 1855 and 1856, he described it as a two-part work surveying formal combinations, ceramics, textiles, masonry, carpentry, and metal works in one volume, with a comparative history of architecture in the second volume. This version, as it turned out, was close to the final structure of the book, although his intervening legal difficulties forced Semper to work through several other conceptual alternatives.

After his break with Vieweg, he first considered writing an architectural dictionary, patterned on Eugène-Emmanuel Viollet-le-Duc's *Dictionnaire raisonné de l'architecture française* (10 vols, 1854–68). He abandoned this plan, however, when he heard that a new edition of Christian Ludwig Stieglitz's architectural dictionary was about to be reissued. Semper then proposed to Suchsland, in October 1856, a text entitled "Cultural-Historical and Artistic-Technical Studies on Architecture," also consisting of two parts. The first volume would deal with the origin of architecture's basic forms and symbols, their evolution in the course of cultural history (in effect a comparative cultural history of architecture); the second volume would treat the material with regard to style.[58]

Two days later he offered Suchsland an altogether revised plan, entitled "Theory and History of Style in Architecture, and the Other Technical and Fine Arts in their Relation to Architecture." Again a two-part book, it was to consider first such themes as the notion of style, the genesis of art, the practical principles of aesthetics, the origin of the most basic forms and symbols in architecture, and their development through national cultures from the first beginnings to modern times. The second part would contain a theory of composition, consider the most important tasks of the present in a cultural and historical regard, and conclude with a section on the architecture of different nationalities and a critique of the main building trends of the present.

This plan, Semper stressed, was different from the study proposed for Vieweg, in that the various technical arts (ceramics, textiles, masonry, carpentry, and metalworks) would be considered together and not given individual sections, as before. Semper also noted that the practical principles of aesthetics would be a replay of the principles he indicated at the conclusion of his small brochure on ornament, just published in Zurich.[59]

This published lecture on ornament was in fact another important stepping stone in the evolution of *Der Stil*. In effect his inaugural address at the Polytechnikum, it was presented on 24 January 1856 and was part of a weekly cycle of lectures given, for the most part, by the new intellectual luminaries imported into the city. Jacob Burckhardt, for instance, presented a talk on 27 December 1855 on the character of Queen Agnes; in February 1856 Friedrich Theodor Vischer gave a lecture on Shakespeare's *Macbeth*.

Gottfried Keller described the lecture series as "a very respectable and harmless *rendez-vous-system*" for "the prim and bigoted women of Zurich," enabling several hundred people every Thursday evening to assemble for "academic lectures *à la* Singakademie in Berlin."[60] Semper's talk, entitled "On the Formal Lawfulness of Ornament and its Meaning as an Artistic Symbol," went well. Keller, in fact, found the discussion both "charming and profound."[61] In it Semper introduced several new themes indicating the new direction of his thinking.

The lecture was built around the double meaning of the Greek word *kosmos* (cosmos, also cosmetic), signifying both the "order" of the heavens and "ornament." This ambiguity suggested to Semper that the early Greeks viewed adornment as a process of applying a decorative order (*Gesetzlichkeit*) to form: "When one decorates, one more or less consciously imposes a natural order on the object that is adorned."[62] It was this instinct, he felt, that held the key to Greek tectonics, particularly in its earliest stages. It was an attitude also manifested quite vividly in the ornaments used in everyday life: "The aesthetics of the Hellenes, insofar as it relates to the order of formal beauty, is based on the simple principles that arise in their most original clarity and intelligibility in the adornment of the body."[63]

To demonstrate this point Semper considered the development of the decorative instinct in its early stages: first as the impulse to terrify a foe through bodily accessories that modify one's physical appearance. Here he once again drew upon recent ethnological evidence, such as the war dances of the North American Indians in which alligator and bison heads were worn. Similar animal masks and talismans, he noted, could be seen among the aborigines of the South Pacific. Masks and amulets were also prominent in ancient times, as Assyrian and Egyptian wall paintings demonstrate. And a Gorgon mask adorned the aegis of both Zeus and Athena: "The mask was a meaningful symbol long before its use in the plastic arts, before drama took hold of it."[64]

The painting and tattooing of the body was another early manifestation of this tendency, as seen not only among the people of the South Seas, but also throughout antiquity, among the Oriental races and the Celts. "It would not be too paradoxical," he concluded, "to seek the origin of certain traditional surface ornaments in the art of tattooing."[65]

Semper argued that it was this instinct that the Greeks were the first to acknowledge consciously and to exploit artistically. He divided their decorative elements into three classes or types: 1) hanging ornaments, such as earrings, the tassels of certain head dresses, hair styles, and even the folds of Greek and Roman chitons; 2) ring ornaments, such as necklaces, bracelets, wreaths, and belts; and 3) directional ornaments, such as found on diadems, miters, and warrior helmets. The value of this division became evident when Semper applied it to the various decorations of the Doric temple. Expanding upon his earlier reading of Bötticher – the corona, as its name implied, was now viewed as a crowning diadem; a torus, tania, and astragal were ring elements, often painted with a binding motif or maanders; the guttae and mutules were hanging elements; the directional frieze panels formed a necklace eurythmically tied together with sculptural gems, and the palmettes of the acroteria, as well as the ridge tiles, were viewed as the plume ornaments of its head dress.

A large part of Semper's lecture was given over to his criticisms of the recently published ideas of Adolf Zeising. This writer first came into prominence with his book of 1854, *Neue Lehre von den Proportionen des menschlichen Körpers* (A New Theory of the Proportions of the Human Body), in which he sought to analyze both the cosmic world (planetary) and microcosmic world (minerals, plants, and animals) in terms of the golden section. Whereas this approach owed something to the aesthetic formalism of Johann Friedrich Herbart and Robert Zimmermann that was gaining popularity in the 1850s, Zeising's new study of 1855, entitled *Aesthetische Forschungen* (Aesthetic Investigations), attempted to merge this formalism with Hegelian idealism.

Semper utilized Zeising's terminology and systematization to a certain extent. For example, he grouped architecture with dance and music as "cosmic arts;" he also utilized the designations "macrocosmic unity" (a synonym for symmetry) and "microcosmic unity" (a synonym for proportion).[66] At the same time, however, he was highly critical of Zeising's new Hegelian framework. The aesthetician had admitted in his Preface that the goals of the artist and aesthetician were essentially different, in that the artist strives to introduce ideal beauty into the phenomenal world, while the philosopher traces phenomenal appearance back to the Idea. Semper saw the role of aesthetics in the much more practical sense of providing theoretical guidelines for the artist. He was also vehemently opposed to a particular paragraph of Zeising's abstract analysis, which stressed that since aesthetics only concerns itself initially with phenomenal appearance, it therefore only involves itself with planimetric appearance.[67] Semper's thesis, articulated through his analysis of Greek ornaments, was fundamentally at odds with this approach in that the genius of Greek aesthetic principles (still representing for him the highest of human artistic endeavor) was for him always three-dimensionally presented.

The architect's line of reasoning at this time was also drawing upon other sources. From Arthur Schopenhauer (whom he as well as Richard Wagner was reading in the mid-1850s) he adopted the notion of the visible world as something that can be read through its volitional statics and dynamics. Form is thus no mathematical abstraction but a vibrant balance of forces, in which gravity is opposed by will (leading to modifications of form) and movement and growth are governed by the resistance of a moving body to its medium.

In bringing together these ideas Semper sought to do several things. First to consider architectural form through the spatial properties of symmetry, proportion, and direction, each of which he aligned with a spatial axis. Thus these were not abstract features of form but dynamic principles of growth and development. From such a paradigm, secondly, he could review architectural forms first as base elements (structural-mechanical parts of a building: quiet masses, simple detailing, dark colors) and second as dominant elements (expressive features: richness of articulation, glowing and bright colors, extensive decoration).

In the next section of his talk, he turned to the question of how and why certain works typically emphasize certain formal features. Whereas symmetry for Semper was predominant in such monumental forms as tumuli and pyramids; proportion, which evolved vertically, was found especially in domed works and towers. The directional movement into depth was especially notable in the design of such forms as ships, but also in such built works as the basilica church with its extended nave. The greatest architectural marriage of these principles for him was – once again – found in the Greek temple, where symmetry, proportion, and direction were combined in a perfect static and dynamic balance.

The final part of Semper's Zurich talk was given to his theory of style. After delineating such internal variables as the work's purpose, material, and means of fabrication, and such exterior variables as its many local and personal influences, Semper returned to his definition of style formulated a few years earlier, as "the emergence of the basic theme raised to artistic significance, and all internal and external coefficients that modify the embodiment of the same in an artistic work."[68] With this, Semper strove to bring his new thoughts on formal aesthetics and ornamentation in line with his earlier style theory.

Very much related to Semper's Zurich address of January 1856 are a number of fragmentary manuscripts, some quite lengthy, whose lineage cannot be established with certainty. All were written some time between 1855 and 1860 and they can therefore be viewed as theoretical precursors to his work *Der Stil.*

One manuscript of this group (Ms. 186), which can be dated, carries the title "Theory and History of Style in Architecture, and the Other Technical and Fine Arts in their Relation to Architecture." It is the outline of Semper's reformulated work (done after his dispute with Vieweg), which he described to Suchsland in late October 1856.[69] His new work was to be no architectural primer, no historical study, no treatise on pure aesthetics, no abstract theory of beauty – but rather an artistic and practical solution to the question of beauty for architects. In his outline Semper promised a review of ancient and modern aesthetics (Winckelmann, Rumohr, Goethe, and Schiller), as well as the definitions of harmony, symmetry, and eurythmy. Style theory, in his view, had to deal with the matter practically; it was no simple sum of factors but rather a product or result that emerged in the acknowledgment of certain principles. It shared with physics and physiology the attribute that its laws arise not from ideal speculation but from experience and observation. It was also related to linguistics in its concern with the formal development of language.

This outline was most interesting for its promise to review the definitions of style of Hegel, Rumohr, Vischer, and Schopenhauer. This is the first indication that Semper had read Hegel's lectures on art, in particular Hegel's comments on style in which he criticized Rumohr's earlier definition for its materialism.[70] The mention of the philosopher Friedrich Theodor Vischer is also important as it is the only such mention of him in Semper's writings. In the light of Vischer's earlier multi-volume study *Aesthetik oder Wissenschaft des Schönen* (Aesthetics or the Science of the Beautiful), Semper could have been expected to be critical of the idealistic and abstract nature of the philosopher's scheme. But perhaps Semper's friendship with him precluded him from being too harsh. As Herrmann has already suggested,[71] Vischer may have had a minor influence on the organization of Semper's concepts during this period, but as Vischer was at the same time contemplating a critical revision of his earlier aesthetic scheme, it is more likely that he would have been influenced by Semper's critique of Zeising and other speculative thinkers.

The various Semper manuscripts that have been inventoried under the title "Attributes of Formal Beauty" (Mss. 168–181) are somewhat more difficult to place.[72] Herrmann has considered these texts as comprising a relatively autonomous intermediary work, first written in London or shortly after Semper's arrival in Zurich, with revisions being done as late as 1859. The content of many of these texts is so close to the published form of the Prolegomena to *Der Stil*, however, that they can also be viewed as preparatory drafts for it.[73] They are perhaps best considered by turning to the final published version of the Prolegomena of 1860, which serves as a forty-three page introduction to the two volumes of *Der Stil*.

The Prolegomena, it has often been said, is a somewhat disjointed work with regard to the main body of the text, and this disembodiment has much to do with the legal confusion induced by Semper's signing of two contracts with two publishers. Moreover, the Prolegomena itself is divided into two thematic parts: the first half is a wide-ranging review of the crisis of contemporary art; the second is given over to the formal and mathematical concerns raised by Semper's reading of Zeising. The axioms of the second part are never really integrated successfully into the main body of the text, and the analysis of the first part – the crisis of contemporary art and architecture – is made fragmentary by the fact that the sections Semper planned to devote to architecture in a later volume of the text were never written.

Art's contemporary crisis, the subject with which Semper began the Prolegomena, he said was rooted in many factors. The empyrean image he chose to depict art's sorry condition was not that of an existing celestial system dispersing or breaking up as it approached extinction (a hypothesis he felt was hopeless and unproductive), but rather an image of scattered cosmic dust forming around the nucleus of a new stellar system. Thus out of the present chaos a new order and condition of regeneration was emerging, and the existing social conditions giving rise to the problems of contemporary art were but temporary abnormalities within this larger cosmic process. The task of his study, in effect, was to examine the orbital patterns of this artistic re-formation: "To explore the inherent order that becomes apparent in the phenomena of art during the process of becoming, and to deduce universal principles from what is found, the essentials of an empirical theory of art."[74]

Semper's "empirical theory," as noted in his earlier manuscript, was an important distinction for him, but it needs some further explanation. The phrase "practical aesthetics" that is buried in the work's main title was proposed by him at one point as the only title for the book, underscoring his firm belief that aesthetics should serve art and not become an isolated intellectual exercise riddled with conceptual abstractions. But Semper's "empiricism" did not have the same meaning for him as it does for us today. It is almost better defined, in fact, by what it is not. *Der Stil* is not a handbook for the practice of art, that is, it does not show the making of form but rather its becoming, or the various factors conditioning form. It is no history of the arts, in that it does not seek to apprehend facts or explain art according to the conventions of historical periods or localities; rather, it strives to reveal the inner necessity of style, the principles that govern artistic form in the way that these same principles govern organic form. Again, Semper proposed – taking aim at Hegel and Schelling in particular, and the whole body of German speculative aesthetics in general – not an abstract theory of beauty but a theory of style. The latter "seeks the constituent parts of form that are not form itself but the Idea, the force, the task, and the means, in other words, the preconditions of form."[75] In this way Semper's viewpoint was not really empirical at all but remained to some extent lodged within the bounds of German idealism – even if the focus was entirely different and novel.

Another methodology invoked by Semper for his study is seen in his adoption of Rumohr's term "Household of the Arts."[76] For Rumohr the term indicated that the various arts were similar in that they could be grasped intuitively rather than conceptually. Semper, however, equated this term with the notion of a *Gesamtkunstwerk*, that is, with the grand unity of the arts in their founding principles, with architecture occupying only one suite. The proper entrance to this household and its principles is through the so-called lower arts: through the study of adornment, weapons, weavings, pottery, and domestic implements. This is so because at this level aesthetic necessity is the main criterion, because the codex of practical aesthetics was formulated and applied to these simple works prior to the invention of monumental art, and because precisely these arts are being most harmed by present conditions, especially by the failings of the educational system as applied to the arts.

Next in the Prolegomena, after repeating some of the arguments of *Science, Industry, and Art* concerning the detrimental effects of capitalism and mass production on art, Semper discussed the direction of mid-nineteenth-century architecture in three major categories – all of which he criticized. First there are the architectural "materialists," those who were swept away by the new constructional possibilities and who elevated material and technical tools over the artistic Idea, whereas the material should be "subservient to the Idea, and is by no means the only decisive factor for embodying the Idea in the phenomenal world."[77] He also placed in this category, almost as an afterthought, those who call for a naturalistic style of ornament instead of the conventional and structural principles of adornment. This argument against artistic materialism is repeated in several other places in the text of *Der Stil*.

The second school of architects against whom Semper argued were the "historicists," that is, those "eager to take as models certain works of art from times long past or of other cultures and imitate them with the greatest possible critical and stylistic accuracy," rather than let the solution "evolve freely from the premises that the present offers."[78] Although Semper's criticism was directed at eclectic tendencies across the board, his main attack was against Neogothicism, which he saw as the predominant eclectic trend. This tendency, in his view, took root in Germany with the Romanticism of Goethe, Schlegel, and others, and later the banner was taken up by the restoration movement – in Germany with the resumption of building of Cologne Cathedral. In its present form, this movement had come under the control of a "very active political-religious party": religious zealots who treated "the northwest and northern Europe as a pagan country to be conquered anew for Christianity." In an earlier manuscript Semper had also accused this group of trading "in Catholic and crypto-Catholic propaganda."[79] In the Prolegomena, however, this passage is restricted to a passing shot at the Catholic activism of August Reichensperger. It is clear that the wounds inflicted on Semper in the competition for the Nikolaikirche in Hamburg had yet to heal, but Semper nevertheless clearly viewed this mixing of the ideals of art with religion as quite destructive to art. "Tendentious art" is in fact a codeword used throughout the text to allude to this tendency, always with the greatest vehemence or disdain.

His treatment of the historical classicists, by contrast, was almost benign. Although not to be followed, the "little renaissance of Louis XVI and the latest Hellenistic movement (whose coryphaeus is Schinkel)" at least had the saving grace of being "creative from the start." Even the Neorenaissance school posed certain dangers in its eclecticism, although its damage was somewhat mitigated by the fact that – in contrast to Neogothic designs – it could be practiced only by a "true artistic hand." Architecture, in general, will have emerged from the historical morass when it had left archaeology behind and arrived at the viewpoint of "comparison and synthesis."[80]

The third trend of contemporary architecture is perhaps the most interesting from a historical perspective today. This is the school of "purists, schematists, and futurists," led by the abstract formulas of contemporary aesthetics. Semper's remarks about this begin as a critique of the division created by contemporary trends in aesthetics, that is by German idealists in particular who want to reduce art to "an intellectual exercise, philosophical delight, consisting in tracing the beauty of the phenomenal world back to the Idea and dissecting it into its conceptual kernels."[81] But a closer reading of these few paragraphs reveal that his aim was really to censure much of art theory since classical Greek antiquity. Thus philosophy itself, after its Attic golden age, grew old and conceived "dead categories;" thus Gothic architecture became the "lapidarian transformation of the scholastic philosophy" of the Middle Ages.

From recent times, Semper singled out for criticism "the aesthetic Puritanism" found in a certain school of architecture in southern Germany, by which he meant Weinbrenner's work in Karlsruhe. Its failing, he felt, was especially apparent in monumental works, where its paucity of means deprived art of its expressive possibilities. Moreover, this proto-functional design denied – and here Semper's historicism assumes its essentially conservative posture – "some of the oldest traditions of architecture that are fully consistent with the logic of building and with artistic creation in general and that have symbolic values that are older than history and cannot possibly be represented by something new."[82]

Under this same category Semper also condemns the "iconographic art" of the trendists and futurists, that is, the hunt for new ideas and the boastful display of meaning. "Art in its highest exaltation," Semper wrote, "hates exegesis; it therefore intentionally shuns the emphasis on meaning."[83] Viewed within the context of his own practice, these passages are somewhat difficult to understand, although they can be interpreted as a warning against the architect seeking excessive or oblique meanings.

With these views set out, Semper opened part two of the Prolegomena with a few pages of general remarks on the origin of art, which are among the most powerful, in a literary sense, of all of his writings. His discussion of architecture in earlier manuscripts as a primitive "cosmic art" – cosmic in the sense of the double etymological meaning of "order and ornament" – is here partially subdued; or rather, it is prefaced with an impassioned and pessimistic discussion of the primeval human condition of pain and alienation, induced by mankind's early and terrible struggle for survival, and of the physical and mental sufferings that ultimately led to the ennoblement of the human intellect.

Surrounded by a world full of wonder and of sublime forces that could be divined but never completely understood, the first humans etched out a few fragmentary harmonies and thereby conjured up a missing perfection in their instinct for play. They reconstructed a tiny world for themselves and formed fanciful images that displayed, expanded, and deepened their many moods. They took delight in mimicking spatial and temporal sequences – through the interlacings of a wreath, the curl of a scroll, the circular dance, or the beat of an oar. "These are the beginnings out of which music and architecture grew," Semper noted, "both are the highest purely cosmic (nonimitative) arts, whose legislative support no other art can forego."[84]

There are, of course, aspects of Schiller's Romanticism and his "play instinct" behind these lines, but also the aesthetics of Schopenhauer and – quite possibly encountered for the first time by Semper during his period in London – the ethics of Thomas Malthus, captured in one frightening ethical principle: "the individual is created only to serve the whole as nourishment."[85]

Darwin, of course, was wrestling with similar concerns in his contemporaneous writing of *The Origin of Species* (1859). But for Semper, as for Schopenhauer, "the nonsensical and the absurd" that we confront at every step along the path of life, together with our own internal "chorus of passions at war with themselves," find their natural outlet – if only momentarily – in art. Basically, then, it is this pain that gives birth to the "lyrical-subjective and the dramatic manifestations of art."[86] Thus the metaphor for the origin of art and architecture is once again the theater; art remained for Semper preeminently a dramatic exercise.

Some important categorical groupings that Semper made in an earlier manuscript with respect to the various arts are missing from these introductory remarks. He wrote that as a cosmic art, architecture formed a triad with dance and music, in that each have similar laws of form, structure, and ornamentation (harmony, symmetry, analogy, eurythmy, and rhythm). Parallel to these three arts are the "microcosmic" arts of sculpture, song, and melopolastic (movements of the human body); in a third division there are the three "historical" arts of painting, poetry, and drama.[87]

The Prolegomena ends, however, not on this profound note but rather with Semper's presentation of his aesthetic principles – which in their schematic presentation approach the abstract aestheticism that has just been criticized. Following Zeising once again, Semper posited three principles of configuration that govern the creation of all organic and artistic form: symmetry, proportion, and direction. These principles are manifested in an aesthetic sense as three formal "authorities" – the eurythmic-symmetrical, proportional, and directional authorities – which are aligned with the three spatial directions of width, height, and depth.

Semper borrowed the term "authority" from Vitruvius and it signified for him "the emphasis given to certain formal components of a phenomenon that stand out from the rest and thereby become within their respective sphere the leaders of the chorus, as it were, and the visible representatives of a unifying principle."[88] These three authorities are, in effect, the principles that describe formal development in both the organic and artistic worlds. In art, as in life, there is also a fourth authority that provides a "higher order" for these three principles. He terms it "unity of purpose" or the "content authority." This principle is manifested in such formal properties as regularity, type, character, and it is the principle most responsible for artistic expression.

As we noted earlier, this aesthetic schematism found little outlet or application in the main body of the text, aside from an occasional reference to the concept of eurythmy. Whereas in its overall logic it is the most confusing and least considered aspect of all of his theory, its appearance in the Prolegomena is due, probably, to Semper's desire to salvage some important ideas from his earlier manuscripts that he had never had time to develop satisfactorily, while at the same time – for obvious legal reasons – not basing his text too closely on the text in Vieweg's possession. With this concern and in his haste, he thus omitted some of the crucial passages and concepts of his earlier manuscripts, not the least of which was his definition of "style" – the main word in the title of his book![89] The fact that such an important book should suffer from such conceptual lapses only underscores what a high price Semper paid for his earlier behavior toward Vieweg. Yet notwithstanding its shortcomings, the Prolegomena in the end in no way detracts from the extraordinary insights and novel line of reasoning that Semper laid down in the following 1100 pages.

Theory of Artistic Forms

Although *Der Stil* was seen by many architects and non-architects in the nineteenth century as one of the greatest intellectual productions of the period, its fate in later times has not always been so happy. Certainly one reason for its lack of attention in more recent times has to do with its very inaccessibility: the fact that this untranslated and out-of-print work is also a difficult, if not an altogether abstruse text to penetrate.

Its recondite character is due to many factors, not the least of which were Semper's literary shortcomings. It is a diffuse work, filled with inexplicable tangents, repetitions, and sometimes excessive technical detail, some of which could easily have been omitted. The book also lacks a single articulated goal: on many occasions there is no sense of direction and no coordination of its many arguments. It reads, as one critic has recently noted, "like a voyage of discovery through the history of architecture and applied art, with unexpected findings all the time, but with no clear prospect as to where the trip will end – if it will end at all."[90]

Another reason for the difficulty of this two-volume study is the manner in which the book was conceived and put together. These problem can be attributed to Semper's heavy work load, to his general aversion to refining earlier drafts, and, once again, to the already mentioned contractual problems with two publishers. In his early drafts he generally preferred a two-part study – the first part dealing with the technical arts of ceramics, textiles, tectonic frameworks, and masonry. This volume would compose the ideological basis of his study and be followed by a second part devoted to architecture proper.

When the critical introduction and the first section on ceramics was taken in pawn by Vieweg in 1856, Semper continued working on the other sections in the hope that his opening chapters would eventually be returned. This was even the case when Semper signed the contract with his new publisher in 1858. It was only after he realized that Vieweg was indeed not going to return the section on ceramics that he made the important decision later in 1858 to begin the first volume with the section on textiles. This was perhaps a good decision as far as the treatment of his many themes was concerned. But it created the problem that in the course of writing this section, its projected size continued to expand. And when the author, some time late in 1858, decided to add to this section a 316-page excursus on the principle of "dressing," his earlier scheme now became untenable, as this first section on textiles alone filled out the entire first volume. For a few months he vaguely held out the hope of combining the other three technical arts along with architecture in the second volume. The next year, however, he admitted to his publisher that this was impossible.

Thus in October of 1859 a supplemental contract was signed, which expanded the proposed work from two to three volumes. The first volume would treat textiles and Semper's theory of dressing; the second volume would survey ceramics, tectonics (carpentry), stereotomy (masonry), and metals. The third volume was to review "as the most powerful factors of style in architecture, the social structure of society and the conditions of the times, which to express artistically and in a monumental way has always been the most eminent task of architecture."[91] This culminating volume, however, never appeared. As a consequence, the two volumes that did appear in 1860 and 1863 outlined Semper's theory only with respect to the technical arts, and here almost exclusively with regard to their material and technical factors. Thus style's so-called extrinsic coefficients – the factors of climate, culture, personal proclivities of the artist – never came under his critical purview.

Similar complications also affected the title of the work. In Semper's initial proposal to Vieweg he had suggested the title "Theory of Artistic Forms." After the two men fell out he scurried to find an alternative title and a new conceptual framework for the study, that is, one that would draw upon the same content but would not result in a lawsuit. Semper first preferred the simple title "Practical Aesthetics" but his new publisher rejected it as too bland. After numerous variations, another title – "Style in the Technical and Tectonic Arts: A Handbook of Practical Aesthetics" – found its way into galley. The still unhappy publisher then proposed his alternative: "The Theory of Artistic Forms, or Style and its Practical Application in the Technical and Tectonic Arts." This variation was once again rejected by Semper because of his legal concerns. The amended and final title of the book, "Style in the Technical and Tectonic Arts or Practical Aesthetics: A Handbook for Technicians, Artists, and Patrons of Art," thus only superficially depicts the content of the finished work. With all of these changes, "Theory of Artistic Forms" remained the title closest to the book's content and leading theme.

Notwithstanding these difficulties, the book was enormously popular later in the nineteenth century. As a work sandwiched between Charles Darwin's *The Origin of Species* (1859) and the first volume of Karl Marx's *Das Kapital* (1867), *Der Stil* shares with these efforts not only a great novelty of method but also a driving ambition to promote a radically different attitude toward its particular field. And if the book was conceived to some extent to countervail against the same materialist tendencies of the period, it can also be grouped with these works in its attempt to strip away the metaphysical (as well as ethical and religious) underpinnings of its subject. The principal aim of *Der Stil* was nothing less than to delineate and explain the origin and transformation of the formal motives of the technical and tectonic arts over the course of their historical development. If Semper failed in this task, it was not for a lack of effort on his part. Indeed much of the initial appeal of the book was due to its extraordinary erudition, which even today is astonishing in light of the other demands on Semper's time. The whole of the final result, perhaps because of the many new pathways of research that it suggested, somehow became greater than its many parts.

Perhaps the best guide to the conceptual inspiration for the book remains the section on ceramics, which – although rewritten – was probably based in part on the manuscript held in pawn by Vieweg (since lost). This was the first section that Semper wrote in 1856, when he regarded ceramics as the most important of the four technical motives. And two texts earlier referred to by Semper played a prominent role in its conception: Alexandre Brongniart's *Traité des arts céramiques ou poteries, considérée dans leur histoire, leur pratique et leur théorie* (1844), and Jules Ziegler's *Etudes céramiques, recherche des principes du beau dans l'architecture, l'art céramique et la forme en général* (1850).

Alexandre Brongniart (1770–1847) was the son of the famed Parisian architect Theodore Brongniart and a member of a family noted for its intellectual and artistic accomplishments. Trained in medicine, geology, chemistry, and natural history, the younger Brongniart was an early and close friend of Georges Cuvier; in fact, he collaborated with Cuvier on a book on the mineralogy of soils in the geological basin of Paris. He also contributed several articles to Cuvier's grand *Dictionnaire des sciences naturelles* (18 vols., 1802–9).[92] Beginning in 1800, Brongniart took over the directorship of the national porcelain manufactory at Sèvres, and it was his work there – over the next forty-seven years – for which he is best known today. He completely reorganized the royal enterprise, greatly expanded its museum, and carried out extensive research on the chemical composition of ceramic and porcelain and the techniques of their production, all of which gave the products manufactured there a high reputation.

Brongniart viewed his new museum at Sèvres, in particular, as an important pedagogical tool – not so much for the casual visitor as for the artist and ceramic manufacturer. These collections, like their anatomical counterparts at the Jardin des Plantes, were arranged with the same logical rigor that Cuvier employed on his fossilized artifacts. They were organized not by relationships of form, composition, or design but rather by their material and technical origin, and only then were they divided into historical periods and geographic regions. Similarly, the *Traité des arts céramiques* was principally concerned with the historical ordering of ceramics by materials and production techniques, and thus aimed to provide the archaeologist, for instance, with important lessons by which to date newly discovered artifacts. In the plates to his *Description méthodique du Musée céramique* (1845), Brongniart provided the visual documentation of his taxonomic scheme (Pls. 116, 117). Some plates arranged ceramic forms by techniques across cultures and periods; others became, in effect, a typology of formal production within a single culture. That a field so formally complex as pottery could be treated as or reduced to a few general forms could not have escaped the attention of the architect Semper. As early as 1843 he had proposed doing precisely the same thing with architecture.

Semper was intimately familiar with Brongniart's work. In fleeing Germany in 1849 he lived for several months at the home of Jules Dieterle in Sèvres. He visited the museum often and developed a personal relationship with the museum's new curator M. Riocreux, who had worked closely with the recently deceased Brongniart in the development of his classificatory system. In *Der Stil* Semper described the *Traité des arts céramiques* as a work that, "notwithstanding some gaps and omissions that it contains, remains always the first

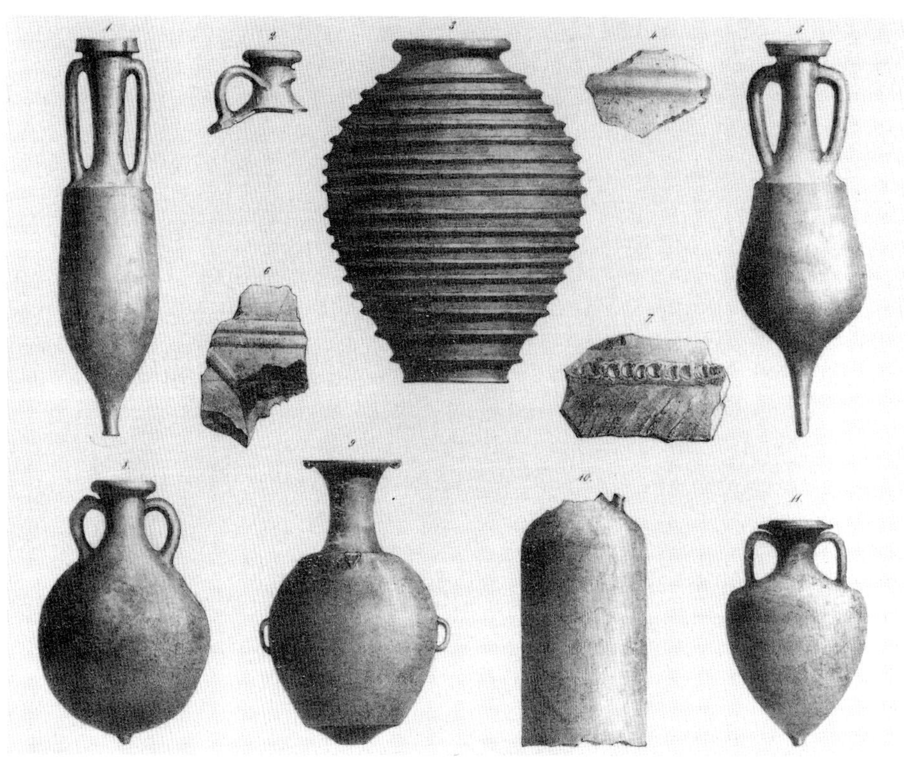

116 and 117 Alexandre Brongniart, plates from *Description méthodique du Musée céramique*, 1845.

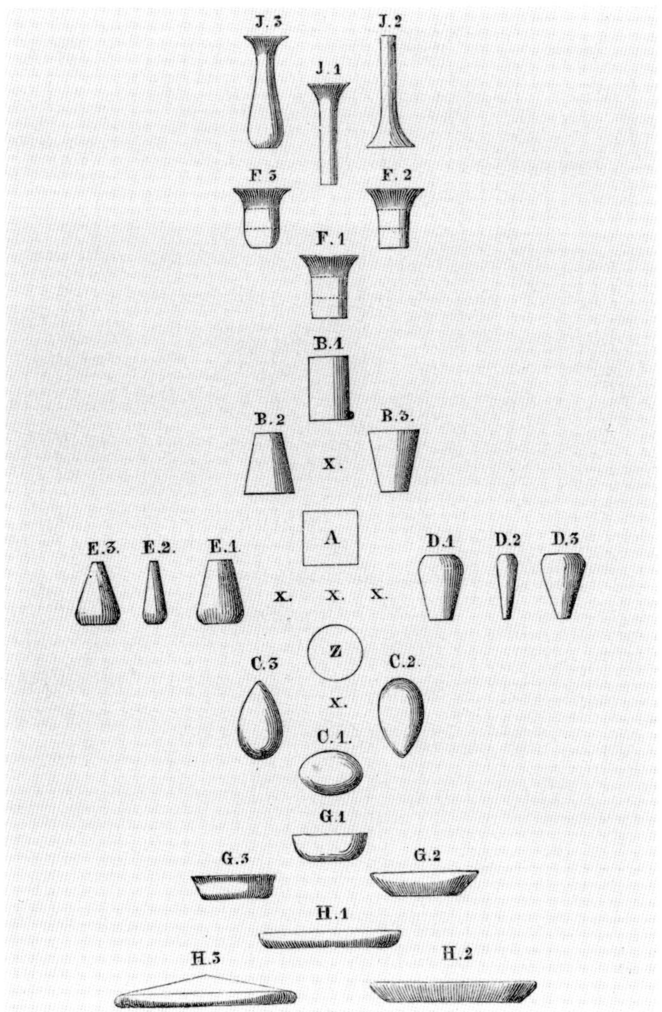

118 Plate from Jules Ziegler's *Etudes céramiques*, in G. Semper, *Der Stil*, vol. II, 1863. Courtesy The Getty Center for the History of Art and the Humanities.

authority" in its field – high praise from someone not prone to giving accolades.[93] Semper's section on ceramics, and the structure of the analyses of each of his primeval motives, owe much in their formulation to Brongniart's taxonomic efforts, as well as to his high regard for materials and technical processes.

The *Etudes céramiques* of Jules Ziegler (1804–56), although less grandly conceived in its scope, similarly and profoundly colored Semper's conceptual outlook. A painter by avocation, in fact trained by Jean-Auguste-Dominique Ingres, Ziegler brought a critical artistic perspective to the subject of ceramics. He made his first debut as a painter in the Salon of 1831 and worked for several years on murals for the church of the Madeleine. In the late-1830s he opened a pottery studio at his country residence near Beauvais, and between 1838 and 1842 he even worked at Sèvres itself, where he also brought his formal schemes of classification to Brongniart's attention.[94] Ziegler continued to view the problem strictly from his artistic perspective, however, and his book, published in 1850, was conceived as twenty-four Cartesian meditations on the beauty of certain ceramic forms. With his illustrative plate classifying ceramic forms (Pl. 118), which made its way into

Semper's book with acknowledgment, he attempted to demonstrate how compound ceramic forms can be generated from the primitive mathematical forms of the circle and cube. Even more complex forms could be fashioned, Ziegler explained, by combining these primary forms in another set of variations; thereby producing the neck, belly, and base of a vase, for example.

But Ziegler for the most part displayed his ceramic models not for their morphological values but for the artistic lessons that could be gleaned from their study. He reflected on the original artistic impulses giving rise to these first ceramic essays, taking place alongside the other primitive artistic expressions of music, dance, and poetry. By defining ceramics as one of the first arts, that is, one that produced what he called "inventional forms," Ziegler attempted to demonstrate the influence of the ceramic shapes on the formal development of architecture. He argued that the ceramic quarter of Periclean Athens acted, as it were, as a training center for artists of every persuasion, thus becoming a school for formal experimentation and invention – with formal "discoveries . . . brought to light by a potter a hundred times a day," in which "one is able to find the rudiments, the foundations of a national and new architecture."[95]

In a similar way, the laws of proportion, symmetry, eurythmy, and ornamentation, said Ziegler, were developed first in ceramics, then later passed to other arts. Ceramics also became the first art to study and appreciate the abstract purity of contours, which too preceded the advent of monumental architecture. Ziegler's analogies in this regard, such as his connection of the three parts of a column with a tripartite vase, are sometimes forced, but at other times they are quite instructive. His lengthy discussion of the principle of eurythmy would certainly have been of interest to Semper, as would his comparison of the profile of certain architectural moldings with prototypical ceramic forms. In short, Ziegler stressed the limited store of successful formal variations within the seemingly boundless number of formal possibilities.[96]

Semper acknowledged Ziegler's contributions to *Der Stil*, although in a footnote he also disassociated himself from the Frenchman's "many strange remarks."[97] But he was generally in agreement with the tenor of Ziegler's reflections on the primacy of ceramics and its formal influence on architectural development. For Semper the circle of ceramic forms, even though evolving from technical and utilitarian conditions, helped to compose a formal language that in Greece became adopted by all the arts. This circle of forms supplied architecture not only its "general basic principles of formal articulation and the contrasts between the parts that constitute this articulation," but also "a large part of the traditional signs and [linguistic] terms of its formal language."[98] And whereas other primary technical arts, such as textiles, exerted a similar influence on the building art, ceramics and architecture – even up to the present time – enjoy an especial relationship because of the similar range of their formal languages.

But Brongniart's and Ziegler's analyses really only provided Semper with a starting point for his investigation, as the architect's desired mark far exceeded the framework of these earlier schemes. An illustration of Semper's broader concern is also given in the opening pages of his section on ceramics, in which he makes his famous analogy between an Egyptian *situla* and a Greek *hydria* (Pl. 119). This example was first presented by him in a London lecture of 1853, which demonstrates how long this aspect of his stylistic conception had been in his wind.[99] The Egyptian *situla*, or pail, was formed for the purpose of drawing water from the Nile; its raindrop-form, it was presumed, evolved from

119 Gottfried Semper, comparison of an Egyptian *situla* with a Greek *hydria*. From *Der Stil*, vol. II, 1863. Courtesy The Getty Center for the History of Art and the Humanities.

earlier leather prototypes. It was carried on a yoke, one pail in front and one behind the bearer. The Greek *hydria*, by contrast, was borne on the human head: vertically when filled, horizontally when empty. Its form evolved not with the purpose of scooping water from a river but from collecting it from a spring or fountain. These double conditions required a high center of gravity to allow maximum stability and balance, giving the *hydria* its unique shape.

The instructive aspect of this comparison, however – that which later enchanted Heinrich Wölfflin and so many other art historians of his generation – was Semper's attempt to interpret the Egyptian *situla* and Greek *hydria* as "religious and national emblems," emblems conveying in effect the spiritual demeanor of these two cultures.[100] These formal distinctions were not specifically racial or physiognomic, as so many other authors were then speculating, but rather purely spiritual. In "spring worshipping" Greece, for instance, design proclivities were represented theatrically in the early Pan-Athenian celebrations by processions of maidens carrying a *hydria*. Thus Semper attempted to read "the basic features of all Egyptian architecture" in the low center of gravity of the

Egyptian pail; likewise, "no less striking is the relationship of the form of the hydria with certain types found in Doric architecture!"[101] Both cultures, in effect, echoed these prehistoric reminiscences in their monumental forms.

With this in mind it is easier to grasp Semper's methodology and overall intentions, as he articulated them in the introductory chapters of *Der Stil*. Art, he explained, has its own special language built upon primeval types and symbols, which has undergone extensive change over the course of cultural history. In the past, speculation about these types and symbols has often been rather naive. Theorists such as Quatremère de Quincy have, for example, settled on such motifs as the rustic cabins of the forest dwellers, the caves of troglodyte cultures, and the tents of nomadic tribes in trying to explain prototypical architectural forms. Semper dismissed such speculative efforts out of hand and likened his own research to that of comparative linguistics. Here investigations into the interrelationships of certain idioms and the transformation of words has shown human linguistic development to be a far more complex phenomenon than previously believed: with regressions taking place as well as displacements and advances. One example of this complexity is the Finnish language, which, despite the present (1860) impoverishment of the nation, possesses a rich poetic lore and great linguistic sophistication, all harking back (in Semper's view) to a time of higher social development.

Semper then posited two theses to govern his analyses: 1) there exist certain basic types or motives for art, sometimes clearly and distinctly seen, which are older than the existing social organizations in which they have been formally interpreted; and 2) these types or motives are borrowed from the four primeval technical arts, from the very earliest times. Over time, they also acquired symbolic values and thereby became agents for the subsequent transformations of architectural forms.

Although these types or motives are often constructional and technical in their origin, Semper insisted that his approach was unrelated to the coarsely materialist view that tries to reduce architecture to such factors as materials and construction. This was a very important distinction for him and he made the point on several occasions. These types or motives are, as it were, functional themes that continually reappear in architecture and influence the development of its basic forms.

Another very important concept for Semper, which sometimes governs the formal development of these motives, was signified by the term *Stoffwechsel*, which has the literal meaning of "material transformation." It was a relatively new term in Germany at the time, signifying the biological "metabolism" or "metabolic process." The term was first employed, in fact, by the chemist Justus von Liebig in the 1830s and 1840s, but gained greater currency in the chemical and materialist theories of Semper's friend and colleague at the Polytechnikum, Jakob Moleschott. The latter even brought the term into the title of his 1851 study *Physiologie des Stoffwechsels in Pflanzen und Thieren* (The Physiology of Metabolism in Plants and Animals), which dealt with the circular biological process by which the organic compounds of plants were eaten by animals, chemically broken down in the digestive and circulatory processes, then expelled from the organism, subsequently enriching a new cycle of plant life.

Semper used the term in a very different sense. For him it signified the process by which artistic forms undergo changes of material but carry forward vestiges or residues of their earlier material styles in later forms, symbolically alluding as it were to the materials used in the past. One obvious illustration of this process for Semper was how textile

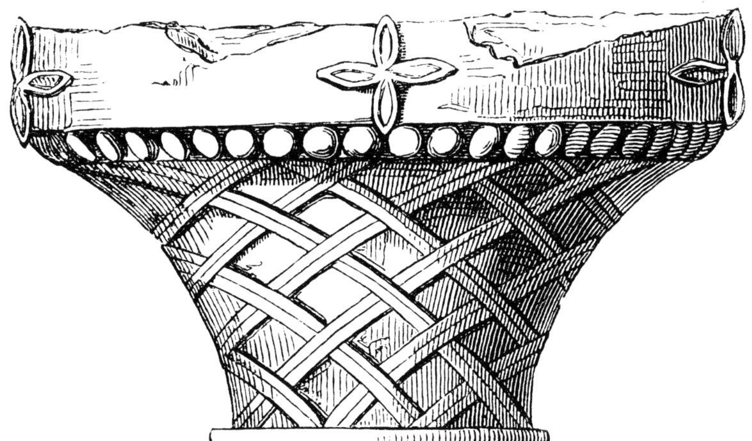

120 Gottfried Semper, basket pattern applied to a column capital. From *Der Stil*, vol. II, 1863. Courtesy The Getty Center for the History of Art and the Humanities.

patterns that had developed in wall hangings were retained or applied to Assyrian bas-reliefs executed in stone. Another was how the geometric patterns originating in baskets might be transposed into conventional geometric designs on ceramic vases or even applied to column capitals (Pl. 120). This last suggestion later proved to be very useful to archaeological theory.

The question has never been asked, however, as to why Semper borrowed this particular biological term for his artistic theory – given the ideological baggage that the term had acquired in the 1850s. In Moleschott's theory it was certainly no innocent term, as the scientist was then engaged in a bitter dispute with the German academic community (and with Liebig in particular) over the supposed "materialist" nature of his research. The controversy grew out of a paper Moleschott presented in 1850, in which he speculated on the importance of the chemical phosphorus to human thinking. His research provoked a terse response from Liebig for its "dilettantish" premises.[102] Moleschott responded in 1852 with his best-known work, entitled *Kreislauf des Lebens* (Cycle of Life), in which he both developed and expanded his biological thesis into an attack on idealism in general and religious interference with science in particular. The biological conflict, as Moleschott now framed it, was between the progressive spirit of scientific investigation and those staunch defenders of Christian theology (also aligned with Hegel's political conservatism) who still impeded scientific research by holding to some divine explanation for organic events. Moleschott went so far as to argue that human vital energy and thought processes were not only inseparable from the physiological processes of the organism but essentially conditioned by them.

Surely the iconoclast Semper was aware of the implications surrounding his choice of this biological term; he was, it should also be noted, quite sympathetic to Moleschott's social and political beliefs. At the same time he was careful to distinguish his own artistic investigation of formal types and their transformations from the concomitant materialist explanations then prevalent in art. In architectural theory, these tended to reduce the development of new forms to new materials or technological factors. It seems that by choosing the term *Stoffwechsel* Semper wanted to align himself with what he saw as the progressive forces of the scientific community, while at the same time countering the main thrust of recent German theories in art.

After postulating the notion of symbolic types undergoing formal development, Semper next in his introductory chapters divided his subject matter into four material-functional categories: 1) the material qualities of being pliable, tough, and tensile, those qualities found in textiles; 2) soft, malleable, plastic materials capable of being hardened by drying in the sun or over the flame, such as are found in ceramics; 3) stick-like elements that possess strength along their length, as found in tectonics or carpentry, and 4) dense, aggregate materials resistant to compression, the basis of stereotomy or masonry.

These categories replaced his earlier "four elements" and once again it is important that they be interpreted as functional categories rather than as actual materials. The category of ceramics, for instance, deals not only with clay but its stylistic motives and principles might also be applied to glass, stoneware, metalware, even wooden pails and some baskets. Conversely, some terra-cotta panels might be better treated under the textile category of the dressing because this is the decorative motive they are following. And metal, which in its many treatments shares different properties of style, at times displays attributes of all four functional classes, and it is even afforded its own – the fifth – section in Semper's study.

With this division made, the daunting task thus confronting Semper was to follow these technical motives from their origin to their appropriation into architecture, thereby clarifying the stylistic limitations of certain architectural forms. If Semper's proclivity to expound upon the nuances of technical processes often reduces his discussion to the level of a technical manual or handbook, his approach to the origin and transformation of artistic form is so radically different from any previous study – his guiding principles and insights so suggestive – that he cannot avoid, as it were, bringing to light a host of major connections that forever recast the framework of discussion on both style and architecture. Moreover, he produced not only what is at heart the first modern textbook devoted to style or design but he also did so within the artistic ideology of nineteenth-century historicism. Indeed his book served as his principal apology for it. This dialectic of classical and modernist concerns is, at least with regard to architecture, never fully resolved, but it is at the same time gravid with results.

Nowhere is Semper's anxiety better seen in this regard (and with very different consequences) than in the architectural arguments that evolve from his reflections on the tectonic and masonry motives.

The focus of the "tectonic" (carpentry) analysis begins with the Greek pedimental roof and its supports – a pegma or structural framework in Semper's terminology – which he regarded as one of the oldest symbols for divinity since prehistoric times. But the formal language of its ornamental detailing, he argued, was fixed long before the tectonic or carpentry motive was used in monumental building. In short, the elements of the prototypical wooden and stone temple did not evolve out of their own premises, nor did they borrow their principles and ornamental language from each other, but rather both were based on earlier essays in the technical arts. In Semper's ever-present linguistic analogy, their word-formation was derived from the even older artistic syntax used in textiles and the ceramic arts.

This so-called genetic approach (a term sometimes applied to Semper's methodology on later occasions) allowed the architect, first of all, to dispense with various hypothetical explanations still current in architectural thinking. One was the explanation that the stone

121 Gottfried Semper, household and religious implements. From *Der Stil*, vol. II, 1863. Courtesy The Getty Center for the History of Art and the Humanities.

temple materialized as a transposition of the Vitruvian wooden hut; another was Bötticher's contention that the stone temple arose – "like Pallas Athene, fully armed and ready"[103] – out of its own symbolic premises. Semper even goes out of his way to deny some of Viollet-le-Duc's more positivistic assertions, such as his argument that the rounded form of the Doric stone column appeared because it facilitated the rolling of the heavy stone drum to the site.[104] In rejecting these approaches as purely speculative, Semper dwelt on the contrasting aesthetic and formal conditions of the structural or tectonic framework (that is, its frame, filling, supports, and joints). This he did at times by reiterating various general aesthetic principles formulated in earlier sections, such as those concerning bands, covers, knots, seams, and borders.

Typical of his method is his tendency not to analyze the products of carpentry proper, or even their later evolution in the forms of the Greek temple, but rather such precursors as household and religious implements – candelabra, tripods, steles (Pl. 121). It is in these artifacts, he insisted, that the formal and ornamental motifs for the pegma were earlier developed before their assimilation into monumental art. And in this regard the Greeks, as might be expected, were particularly adept at distinguishing between structurally active and inactive fields; they restricted higher art (representational art) for the most part to the latter areas but at the same time they also endowed the active framework with extra-structural values, such as might be done with the column capital or by adjusting the particular angle of the pedimental roof line.

It was in fact when Semper turned to the second part of his tectonic analysis, that is, to a consideration of modern wooden and iron frameworks, that problems emerged. His analysis, in effect, is tinged with long-standing prejudices toward the display of iron in monumental architecture – first enunciated in a report of 1842 on a proposed parish church by Eduard Heuchler and reiterated in his article of 1850 on the iron structure of the Jardin d'Hiver in Paris.[105] His criticism of iron on both occasions was that the structural thinness of this material fundamentally precluded its use as a monumental material, since the slight dimensions of iron called into question its own structural stability. In the later article of 1850, he even alluded to the aesthetic failing of Labrouste's Bibliothèque Ste-Geneviève in Paris: the lack of warmth and coziness of its reading room, which was caused by a ceiling supported on these thin iron lattices.[106]

In *Der Stil* – with the experience of the Crystal Palace behind him – Semper continued to frame his argument in a similar way. The structural properties of iron allow its tectonic members to be thinner in dimension than those of wood, he reasoned, so thin in fact that when they are used most logically they tend toward invisibility. This attenuation therefore put it into an essential conflict with the aims of monumental art, which was proportionally and symbolically defined by mass. With this attenuation of form, the traditional ornamental treatment of its filling also suffers, thereby reducing iron construction in principle to a "poor soil for art!" He continued: "It is not possible to speak of a monumental style for rod and cast metal, its very ideal is invisible architecture! For the thinner the metal is spun, the more perfect is its manner."[107]

Semper and many others of his time were already quite aware that this attenuation of form had already taken place, for the invisibility of the ceiling members was one of the more frequently heard criticisms of the "glass-covered vacuum" of Paxton's Crystal Palace. But whereas other critics praised this technological innovation and saw it as a precursor of future architecture, Semper could scarcely bear the thought of it. His conception of monumental architecture required the visual attribute of mass in order to allow for the possibility of symbolic play and the explication of stylistic motives. The only concession to iron he made in *Der Stil* – a single sentence added to the text at galleys stage – was that if this material were treated in a tubular fashion, so that its form or dimension could be visually enhanced, "it might be possible to attach some hope for the future of art to this development."[108] Evidently the image Semper had in mind were some tubular trusses then used in bridge building.

The limitations of Semper's theoretical position nevertheless soon became obvious to many of the next generation of architects. Still, for the next forty years in fact, the German debate regarding the architectural use of iron became largely construed in Semperian terms, that is, the issue became one of how to define monumentality with iron in the face of its logical tendency toward invisibility. After 1871, this debate in the new economic and military superpower of Germany was particularly sophisticated in all of its aspects. It was, if anything, more widespread than similar debates taking place in France, England, or the United States. And it was this German debate that set the stage for the German Modern Movement of the turn of the century – despite the efforts of Sigfried Giedion and others to bury this important chapter of modern architecture.[109]

A very different result came, however, from Semper's treatment of the masonry motive. In this section, the fourth of his elementary motives, he first reviewed the thematic development of aggregates, mounding materials, and stone from their early use in foundations, beehive tombs, and stylobates to the refinement of the masonry motif in polygonal blocks or ashlar – citing such examples as Mycenae and Epidaurus. He next treated the same development in a technical sense even more exhaustively, as he followed the development of the masonry or stereotomic motive – first as a sheathing or dressing applied to other surfaces, and secondly as a formative element in itself, that is, cut stone in the creation of walls and vaults. Implied in both developments is the underlying "spatial idea," an idea that he felt developed quite slowly in architectural history.

Among the first examples of this motive are the clay brick and tile facings applied to the earth ramparts of the Chaldeans and early Assyrians. They provide, Semper argued, some of the oldest monumental embodiments of spatial ideas, as these sheathings, later replaced by mosaic, stucco, and alabaster panels, re-enacted the primordial spatial values of their original textile predecessors. A further stage of masonry and spatial development can be discerned in Persian and Egyptian monuments. In Persian architecture it is still possible to find the surface of the stone being treated as a sheathing, even though the stone itself is no longer cut into thin panels; rather, the walls are formed of enormous blocks of stone precisely cut and dimensioned. In Egyptian architecture there is a third stage of development, for this notion of a surface sheathing or dressing idea is done away with altogether and the stone structure is conceived fully in terms of carefully cut, solid ashlar blocks. The Greeks, as might be expected in Semper's scheme, perfected the isodomen or ashlar wall in a technical sense, while at the same time (as the next chapter will show) divesting the stone's monumental form of its material vestiges with a dressing of paint.

Developing alongside the regular patterns of the ashlar wall, however, was the cut stonework applied to the arch and the vault – a lithic-spatial motif that, in effect, stood in a fundamental opposition to the symbolic post-and-lintel forms employed in earlier monumental works. The Greeks were conscious of the arch's inherent contradiction to their trabeated systems and for this reason, argued Semper, they banished the arch and vault (whose structural possibilities they were quite familiar with) to foundation substructures. This same arcuated technology, however, was revived and brought above ground by the Romans, who were in all other respects conservative guardians of Graeco-Italian customs. Although they greatly advanced the technology of arcuated construction they were by no means the inventors of this new vaulted "spatial art" in stone, "which would have related to Greek architecture like a symphonic concert does to a hymn accompanied by a lyre, were it perfected to the same extent as the latter."[110] They did, however, forcefully pursue the spatial superiority of the vault over the tectonic framework; in their culture it came to symbolize, says Semper, their adoption of Alexander the Great's idea of world domination. In effect, the "dressing" motive that dominated classical architecture became superseded by the more direct "spatial" motive of stone – an understanding long implied thematically. A new avenue for architecture now lay open for artistic exploitation.

Such an understanding for Semper carried important implications for nineteenth-century practice, which in more ways than one was seeking a new creative resource to overcome the long-recognized problems of historical imitation. These implications did not become apparent to Semper himself until a few years later, when – in a lecture given in 1869 – he reiterated just this passage from *Der Stil* and concluded with the stirring sentence: "Herein [in the mighty art of space creation] lies its future and the future of architecture in general."[111] If other theorists – such as Bötticher[112] – had to some extent preempted Semper in suggesting the importance of spatial design for architecture, it was Semper who brought the idea to its logical conclusion. Like his comments on iron, this short passage of *Der Stil* set in motion a theoretical debate that culminated with the notion of space becoming a central issue of modern theory. As early as 1878, in fact, the art critic and aesthetician Conrad Fiedler prepared a lengthy commentary on these passages of *Der Stil*, in which he projected the vault's "spatial art" as precisely the means by which architecture could escape from its imitative course and set out on a new path of artistic development.[113] And Fiedler was not alone in developing the implications of this passage.

Both the Berlin architect Richard Lucae (in 1872) and the Swiss architect Hans Auer (in 1885) were sufficiently moved by Semper's suggestion to posit their own view of architecture as the creation of space.[114]

The most extensive development of this theme, however, was made by the German art historian August Schmarsow. In his inaugural address, entitled "The Essence of Architectural Creation," before the Leipzig faculty and student body of 1893, he proposed that architecture could now be historically reviewed exclusively as the "creatress of space." Dismissing Semper's thesis of dressing so as to enhance his own position, Schmarsow in his zeal somehow forgot that it was Semper who had provided him with both the methodology and intellectual basis (in more ways than one) for his own "genetic" and spatial outlook.[115] It was nevertheless not until a few years later that European architects, such as Hendrik Berlage, once again picked up this Semperian theme and began to define modern architecture almost solely as the art of spatial creation. Over a half century later, modern architectural historians such as Bruno Zevi – seemingly unaware of these many earlier discussions – could still claim to have found a novel historical approach with this spatial theme.

The Masking of Reality in the Arts

None of the three main sections of *Der Stil* so far considered – ceramics, tectonics, and masonry – begins to offer the wealth of new material presented by Semper in the first of his main divisions concerning textiles. This is due to a number of reasons, not the least of which was the near Faustian fervor that seized control of his investigation in the course of preparing his lengthy excursus on the theme of the "dressing." These last several hundred pages of his treatment of textiles (in many respects a culmination of his long-standing interest in polychromy) not only brought to light a host of new factors influencing stylistic development but also, in Semper's characteristic and singular way, best exposed the precise nature of his theatrical conception of monumental architecture.

Interestingly, it was also the theme of textiles that initially frustrated him in finding the appropriate direction for his research. Notwithstanding his long interest in tracing the influence of textiles on the development of architecture, he had, prior to the mid-1850s at least, not done much research into the field of textiles proper. Consequently, in first reflecting on this proposed division of his book after his arrival in Zurich, he wrote to his friend Lothar Bucher (then living in Paris) in search of suggestions for reference material.[116] A few months later, in September 1855, he also wrote to John Robinson in London and asked the museum curator at the Department of Science and Art to approach Cole or Redgrave. Semper wanted to know if they could obtain a grant from the Board of Trade so that Octavio Hudson, the head of the textiles program at the Department of Science and Art, could co-author this section with him. Robinson responded that the Department would not be able to cooperate financially and in any case both Cole and Redgrave felt that the "thoroughly impractical" personality of Hudson would make him an undependable collaborator.[117]

Semper proceeded to work on the introduction and ceramic section through the fall and winter of 1855-56. After sending these sections to Vieweg in the spring, he began to pursue information on the history of textiles in earnest. By this time he had overcome

Alle diese Sorten sind unter sich charakteristisch verschieden, gemeinsam leicht von Klöppelwerk dadurch zu unterscheiden, das alle aus Variationen der beiden Stiche bestehen, die auf den unterstehe Figuren 1 und 2 dargestellt sind.

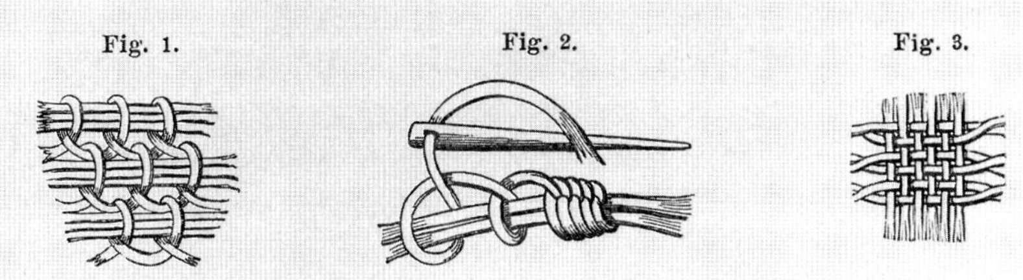

2) Bobinet, Kissen- oder Klöppelarbeit ist eine Erfin der neuern Zeit. Man nennt Barbara Uttmann aus Sachsen als die finderin und gibt das Jahr 1560 als das Jahr der Erfindung an.

122 Gottfried Semper, stitching patterns in lace. From *Der Stil*, vol. 1, 1860.

some of the obstacles to finding reference material, even though in the text he repeatedly complained about the lack of research material in Zurich. The first volume moved forward rapidly, although he continued to add to it until its publication in 1860.

London provided many sources of information to help with Semper's conception and treatment of the theme. Several times in the text he either referred to or quoted extensively from Redgrave's "Supplementary Report on Design," the report that the painter had prepared at the conclusion of the Great Exhibition. These citations for the most part refer to the principles of textile design taught at the Department of Practical Art, which Semper adopted more or less as a whole. And the entire section on lace (Pl. 122) was also taken over, nearly verbatim (with the accompanying illustrations), from the report "Observations on Lace," written by Hudson for Cole.[118]

None of this, however, detracts from Semper's originality. In introducing his textile theme he explained that this field should now take precedence in his study (over ceramics) because it is the most original of all the technical arts, that is to say, it is the art from which all other arts, including ceramics, have borrowed artistic types and symbols. Semper next divided the field of textiles into two primary stylistic motives: first linear forms used as bindings or connected in a series; and secondly flat covers used to protect and enclose.

With this, he began a relatively exhaustive stylistic review of the many materials, techniques, and ornamental themes found in textiles – in both Western and Eastern cultures, in modern and ancient times. The wreath is presented as "perhaps the earliest series" with its primordial interlacing of branches or flowers in a eurythmic order (Pl. 123). It had long been a symbol of coronation or upward limitation, he noted; a principle manifested in floral patterns around the neck of a vase as well as in an architectural frieze at the top of a building. The characteristic of bands is their linear strength and suppleness. Fluttering decorations such as flags and pennants were presented as symbols of unrestraint. The textile category of the cover was defined by its spatial and planimetric surface, as opposed to the linear attribute of bindings. Illustrations of both motifs are copious and most imaginative. Perhaps one of Semper's more far-flung analogies is his interpretation of

123 Gottfried Semper, wreath as primordial artistic symbol. From *Der Stil*, vol. I, 1860. Courtesy The Getty Center for the History of Art and the Humanities.

the Doric triglyph; he dismissed the accepted explanation that it represents the face of a beam in the prototypical wooden temple, prefering to trace it, in his motivational theory, to the unhemmed edges of textiles.[119]

Not all of his analogies are so imaginative. In his section on textiles special attention is given to the ornamental treatment of a seam (*Naht*) and a border (*Saum*). Here in fact is where Semper's investigative method proves itself most fruitful. His analysis turns on a couple of etymological connections. The German word for "seam" or stitching motif, *Naht*, is related to the German word for "necessity," *Noht*, from which Semper deduces the stylistic principle that the purpose of the seam is "make a virtue out of necessity," that is, the seam should represent itself functionally as an expedient that joins or stitches together pieces in an undisguised fashion. This meaning is reinforced by the similarity of the word for seam with the word for "rivet" (*Niethe*), which also serves as a self-evident symbol when found in textiles as a button. Exemplary models for seams vary from the stitching of Iroquois leather moccasins to a stone engraving of an Assyrian carpet pattern, which Semper recorded in a sketch from the British Museum (Pl. 124).

Similarly, the German word for a hem or "border," *Saum*, bears a linguistic affinity with the German word for "hedge," *Zaun*. Both terms also have the additional architectural meanings of – respectively – "fillet" and "fence." The textile border shares symbolic attributes of both the band and seam, in that it both ties together the edge and frames the garment or dress. The range of Semper's sources in explaining these motifs over the next several hundred pages almost defies description, as he draws upon such disparate and surprising sources (to quote only a few of his many ancient ones) as a Pliny discourse on sheep breeding (in discussing wool manufacture), Plutarch's description of the animal headpieces worn by Cimbrian warriors (in discussing furriery and tanning), and a report by Salmasius on Egyptian embroidery. Among the modern etymological sources that are cited are the studies of Jakob and Wilhelm Grimm, Karl Gustav Albert Höfer, and L. Diefenbach, although the work of Wilhelm von Humboldt and Franz Bopp are also of importance.

Chapters of especial interest include those on the ornamental tattooing of human skin

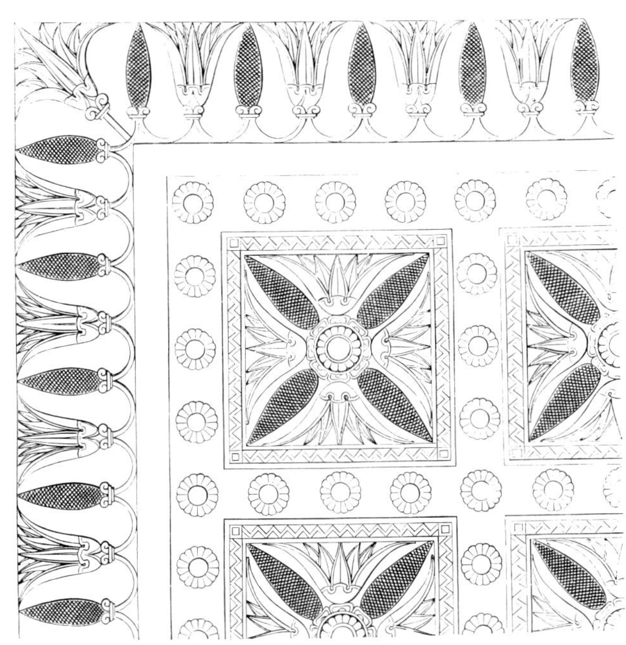

124 Gottfried Semper, Assyrian carpet pattern engraved in stone (in the British Museum). From *Der Stil*, vol. I, 1860. Courtesy The Getty Center for the History of Art and the Humanities.

(one of the earliest of the decorative arts) and the "knot," which Semper identified as "perhaps the oldest technical symbol." His method in pursuing this last motif was most ingenious. After identifying the knot as an expression of some the earlier cosmogonic ideas among various nations, Semper followed its development in ancient cuirasses and Egyptian decorative nets, before proceeding to discourses on plaiting, braiding, canework, matting, and embroidery. In the fields of ceramics and architecture, the network made of knots is often applied as an adornment on projecting or bulging parts, such as on the paunch of a vase.

These chapters end with a lengthy excursus on the theme of the "dressing," by which means Semper returned the discussion to architectural theory. Once again etymology became a powerful tool with which to make points that otherwise would not be evident. The German word for "dressing," *Bekleidung*, derives from the German verb *kleiden*, meaning "to clothe, to dress." In a technical sense, however, *Bekleidung* can also refer to the "covering, paneling, wainscoting, and sheathing" of a building, although most of these meanings emerged in later centuries. Semper's initial point was that there is a close correlation between clothing and fine arts, or rather – nearly all symbols, as well as the members used in architecture, are actually motives borrowed from the realm of costume and finery. He demonstrated this by citing a number of German terms with textile and architectural meanings. In addition to *Saum* and *Naht*, he pointed to the words *Wand* (wall, partition, screen) and its derivative *Gewand* (dress, garments, clothing), and to *Decke*, which has the meaning of both "cover" and "ceiling." His second and less obvious point, however, is much more far-reaching. This is the seemingly innocent proposition "*that the beginning of building coincides with the beginning of textiles*" (his italics).[120] The exposition of this theme, with all of the rich and profound implications that it holds for architectural theory, is what fills out the remainder of this excursus.

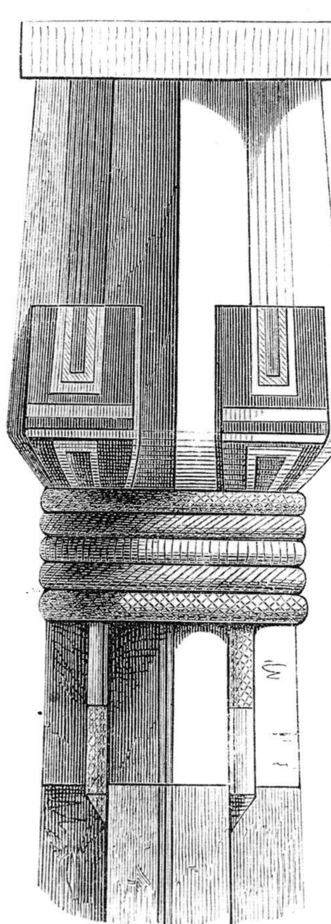

126 (above) Gottfried Semper, Egyptian hair ornaments. From *Der Stil*, vol. I, 1860. Courtesy The Getty Center for the History of Art and the Humanities.

125 Gottfried Semper, lotus blossoms inserted into Egyptian capital. From *Der Stil*, vol. I, 1860. Courtesy The Getty Center for the History of Art and the Humanities.

It is important in discussing this section to see how this argument unfolds, as the line of reasoning concerning the dressing is developed in a way that is neither linear nor altogether transparent at first reading.

Logically, Semper's account begins with his earlier description of the origin of the wall motif: the primitive screen or woven mat-wall, bound together from sticks and branches, hung vertically as a spatial divider. The transition from the plaiting of branches to the plaiting of bast was an easy and natural one for early men and women. From the use of threads spun from vegetable or animal matter came the invention of weaving, followed by the pattern when two differently colored threads were used. Then came the dyeing and knitting of colorful carpets that were hung vertically as wall dressings. This phase of textile production was an important one, for these polychrome tapestries remained the symbolic spatial membrane even after solid and more permanent walls were built behind them. When textiles eventually gave way to other, more durable wall dressings, such as brick, wooden or stone paneling, the principle of their decoration, following this material transformation, often remained the same.

This coincidence of the material origin of the wall dressing with that of textile weaving is a direct and concrete connection, but the cultural analogy of textiles and architecture was manifested for Semper in other ethnological ways, especially in costume and jewelry (Pls. 125, 126, 127). One of his more imaginative examples, certainly, was the parallel he drew between the insertion of lotus blossoms into Egyptian capitals and the same flowers similarly inserted into hair ornaments worn by Egyptian women.

127 Gottfried Semper, helmet ornaments and Greek acroteria. From *Der Stil*, vol. 1, 1860. Courtesy The Getty Center for the History of Art and the Humanities.

The thematic relationship of clothing to architecture was indeed almost a fixation with Semper. The development of free drapery, he believed, was an area in which the Greeks excelled over all barbarian nations. The Attic chiton with its free fall of folds and balance of masses – "the robe as an ornament that can regularly bring about and accentuate all three moments of beauty"[121] – was for Semper perhaps the most sublime creation in the history of clothing. It was (according to a passage of Athenaeus) an invention of Aeschylus for the stage; only later was it worn by priests and torch-bearers, and eventually by the population at large. The significance of the chiton's theatrical roots does not become evident until several pages later in Semper's text. Initially, he was content simply to imply that these same Greeks at this advanced stage of artistic development would naturally evolve an equally perfect textile dressing for their architecture.

In the opening paragraph of his excursus on the dressing, Semper cited another obscure fragment of a passage from Democritus, said to be from a work describing the Temple of Artemis at Ephesus. The fragment itself, however, describes not the temple but rather the various types of Ephesian dress, including the violet-blue, purple, and saffron undergarments, the apple-green, purple, and white *sarapeis*, and the purple (sometimes hyacinth color) *kalasirei*. Semper's point in reciting these few lines was to show that if only a slightly longer passage of this text had been preserved, we would today (and for the past several centuries) have had a very different image of Ionian architecture – no doubt equally colorful.

This analogy between architecture and costume even extends into the domain of household furnishings. Some of the more impassioned pages of the section on the dressing are given to discussing the invention of the Ionian marble capital, which Semper traced back not to scrolls or other such formal emblems but rather to Assyrian empaestic techniques employed in domestic furnishings. The key to his argument is, in effect, the absence of any material evidence of Assyrian columns to be found in diggings at Nimrud and Chorsabad, although the profiles of ionic-volute, column capitals are represented pictorially. Just as the textile-inspired, alabaster bas reliefs unearthed in these cities faithfully preserve the motive of their woven predecessors, Semper reasoned, so the empaestic or embossed works of Assyrian chairs, stools, candelabra, steles, and chariot wheels hold important clues of the technical procedures used in the production of Assyrian column capitals.

Ancient embossed works are of two types: first flat boards with sheet metal nailed or riveted to their surface; and secondly pieces of wood arranged in a non-planar manner, so that the sheet-metal dressing must now be folded or bent around the frame and seamed with raised and sunken areas, as seen for instance in ancient cast-bronze doors. With the development of this second technique, Semper argued, the metal acquired sufficient strength and rigidity to dispense with the hidden wooden core, leaving a hollow body or tubular type of construction to convey both the structural and symbolic (religious) meaning. This was the stage reached by Assyrian art. The survival of several such tubular column capitals from the later Persian empire (with their volutes stylistically misapplied) lent further credence to this thesis (Pl. 128). Semper did not mean by this to deny the rather complex historical development of this tubular system prior to its Greek assimilation into the stone style.

Another element of Assyrian design that was a factor in the formation of the classical

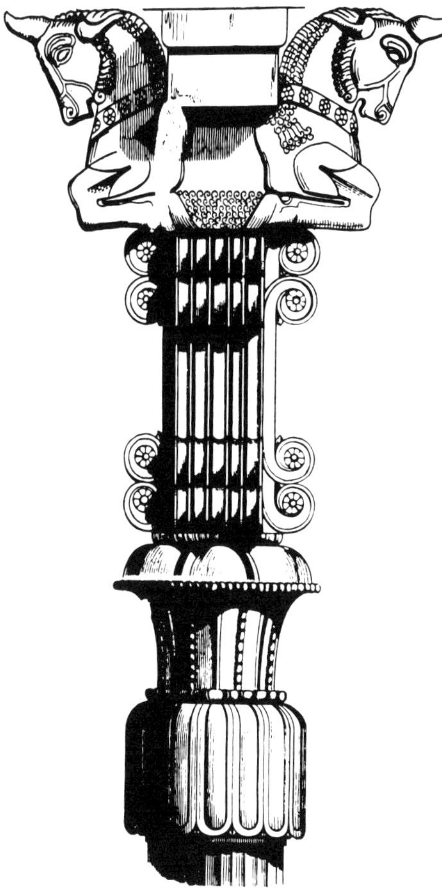

128 Gottfried Semper, Persian tubular column capital. From *Der Stil*, vol. I, 1860. Courtesy The Getty Center for the History of Art and the Humanities.

Ionic capital was the tendentious or religious nature of Assyrian artistic forms – the fact that they combined a technical or utilitarian meaning with a religious symbolism, allowing these furnishings and other implements to function on two symbolic levels, as it were. Semper was convinced that the ionic-volute columns of Assyria had their basis in religious symbolism – the volute chalices of the Sacred Tree[122] – and that the Greeks, in later appropriating these customs and forms, downplayed but did not entirely suppress these earlier cult meanings. This was very different from the artistic tendencies of Egyptian architecture, for instance, in which the artistic covering always remained separate from the structural core, as with the lotus blossoms being inserted into the columns as separate or unintegrated blocks. Here Semper's reasoning was intended to dispute Bötticher's earlier contention of a distinction between the "core-form" and "art-form," at least as far as Greek architecture was concerned.

The Greek Ionic style executed in stone, in fact, significantly advanced this ancient Asiatic empaestic technique artistically, by elevating its forms precisely in a higher "structural-symbolic" sense: that is, both by liberating figurative art to a neutral or non-structural field and by a more refined treatment of the dressing itself. Ornaments, for Semper, were "structural-symbolic" when the art-form, in essence, enhanced the structural values of the core-form; this is opposed to free ornaments that may be present in neutral fields or non-structural areas.[123] In Semper's words: "It was merely a matter of transforming the mechanically necessary forms of Asiatic dressing-construction into dynamic organic forms, of animating them, of rejecting or remitting to neutral ground everything that has no morphological purpose, that is foreign or even opposes the purely formal idea."[124]

Even the fluting of the column, which was originally a decorative device to enhance the rigidity of hollow columns, later became a means, an art-form perhaps, to mask the column's structural role. The new empaestic-inspired stone-style of the Ionian Greeks thus avoided all unnecessary references to weight and support. In portraying its structural function in this way, it thereby emancipated form from any suggestion of material presence and from the more mundane need of bearing a load.

With its refinement also came the development of a new dressing for the column – the coat of paint. "Following this tendency," Semper concluded, "the Hellenic building principle had to vindicate and nurture *color* as the subtlest, most bodiless dressing. It is the most perfect way to do away with reality, for while it dresses the material it is itself immaterial. It also corresponds to the freer tendencies of Hellenic art. Polychromy replaces the barbaric dressing of noble metals, incrustations, inlaid gems, paneling, and the other accessories with which Asiatic works are so extravagantly outfitted."[125]

The decisive step that Semper had already taken in his argument, already suggested in his earlier writings, was to tie the concept of the dressing to his notion of antique polychromy, which he did by recounting in this text the main issues of the debate over color during the 1820s and 1830s. He here insisted that the earlier discussion on polychromy could not have been satisfactorily resolved because the main archaeological evidence explicating the diffusion of "this principle of dressing or incrustation" – evidence eventually unearthed in Assyria, Persia, Asia Minor, Egypt, Italy, and Cyrenica, he said – were discovered only several years later. Thus Quatremère de Quincy in his lengthy text on colossal chryselephantine statuary came close to solving the riddle but he failed to connect this ancient practice of color incrustation with other arts such as architecture. François Mazois and Gau published their informed study of the wall paintings of Pompeii, but they still viewed them as a manifestation of a specifically Roman technique from a capricious period, undetached from earlier practices in Greece and Egypt. Similarly, Raoul-Rochette and Latronne debated extensively the issue of whether the Greeks painted murals on walls directly or on panels inserted into the wall, but neither saw the connection that these paintings had with the history of wall decorations in general.

The crucial discoveries for Semper, once again, were the textile-inspired, Assyrian alabaster panels found by Botta and Layard in the 1840s. These were important not just because they were signs of the more general cultural and historical practice of polychrome dressings but also because they – and here Semper was entirely correct – upended the outmoded historical prejudice of viewing Greek art as an indigenous growth of Greek soil. For Semper, the creative genius of the Greeks had a nobler task than simply inventing new artistic types and symbols. They – in seizing this principle of dressing or incrustation from the East – apprehended "*in a higher sense* these materially already fixed types and motives in their nearest tellurian expression and idea, grasped them as a symbolism of form, in which the opposites and principles that excluded and fought one another in barbarism were united in the freest collaboration and in the most beautiful, richest harmony."[126]

Thus the motive of the dressing, that had become manifest in its latest development on the alabaster panels and brick facings of Assyrian and Babylonian walls, was elevated by the Greeks in a "highly spiritualized" manner and was made to serve beauty in a more "structural-symbolic" than "structural-technical" sense.

What Semper was discussing here, although it is not immediately apparent through his juggling of so many themes, is the actual beginning of monumental architecture, which now pivots in a conceptual and symbolic sense on this "highly spiritualized" layer of paint that the Greeks applied as their new dressing. All building up to this point, even when on the colossal scale found in Babylonia and Egypt, was pre-architectural for Semper; or perhaps it is better to say that these buildings were pre-theatrical, which means that they preceded the conceptual development of the monument proper. It was left to the Greek people to take the momentous step of actually creating monumental architecture; they took this step concomitantly with the invention of the chiton and the fixed stage for Greek drama. The monumentalization of architecture for Semper was simply the making permanent of this primitive theatrical instinct and event – in a strict architectural sense, giving permanence to the temporary and mobile theater stage:

> The festival apparatus, the improvised scaffolding with all the special splendor and frills that indicate more precisely the occasion for the festivity and enhance the glorification of the day – covered with decorations, draped with carpets, dressed with boughs and flowers, adorned with festoons and garlands, fluttering banners and trophies – this is the *motive* of the *permanent* monument, which is intended to recount for coming generations the festive act and the event celebrated.[127]

Never mind that Semper's immediate ethnological evidence (Lycian tombs preserved in the British Museum) for marrying the birth of monumental architecture with the making permanent of the theatrical scaffold is slim. This grand vision, which points in his view to the essence of architectural creation, can be justified only on Semper's own artistic terms. Moreover, he was not the only theorist attempting to make such connections at this time. In a near contemporary philological study of arborolatry, or the tree cults of the ancient Greeks, Semper's longtime antagonist Karl Bötticher was considering the evolution of ancient rites centered on specific trees and sacred groves – how these natural and solemn features (the forerunners to the religious temple) became outfitted (*bekleidet*) with primitive images, garlands, votive offerings, clothing, ornaments, musical instruments, altars, sacrificial victims, weapons, and implements.[128] All were later affixed to the scaffold of the temple.

Semper's account fundamentally differs from Bötticher's, however, in that he believed that these textile-adorned scaffolds (although certainly sacral in origin) reflected in their spiritualized aspect less the image of their religious nursemaid and more the underlying theatrical impulses simultaneously giving rise to Greek drama. Saying this another way – Semper pointed out that the more primitive religious instincts were in essence *theatrical*, and that these instincts were artistically exploited not only in the monumental temple but also on the "richly decorated and dressed performance stage" that made its Dionysian entry in Attic times.

This connection, for Semper, carried with it yet one other quite extraordinary implication, which reached into the very heart of his vision of monumental architecture:

> My main interest in introducing these examples is to draw attention to the principle of *exterior decoration* and the necessary *dressing* of the structural scaffold of the improvised festival stage, which always and everywhere conveys the nature of the thing. From this I deduce that the same principle of veiling the structural parts – associated with the monumental use of canopies and carpets stretched between the structural members of the prototypical scaffold – must also appear natural when seen on early monuments of architecture. [Semper's italics.][129]

Thus through his description of this practice of "veiling" structural parts – what Mark Wigley has recently referred to as the "dissimulating fabric" inextricably woven to "the fabrication of architecture"[130] – Semper attempted to overturn, as it were, the tectonic basis of nearly two thousand years of architectural theory. Monumental architecture, as he viewed it, is no longer the construction of an edifice, but rather the masking or veiling of constructional parts in a dramatic conundrum or artistic play. That crude spatial mat first plaited with branches (contemporaneously represented for Semper in pens built by the Maoris in New Zealand), later achieving artistic perfection on "the looms and vats of the industrious Assyrians," underwent another significant metamorphosis with the Greek coat of paint – the paint becoming less a "dressing" and more an artistic "masking" of the material and structural reality. In short, monumental architecture was born out of this same theatrical instinct; both arts embraced the same goal to mask the reality of their respective subject matter: in the case of drama the masking of life's tragic and comic underpinnings; in the case of architecture the symbolic masking of life's ennobling cultural forms. It is through this primordial masking, as Semper saw it, that one comes to grips with the existential human condition of alienation. This also explains the meaning of Semper's famous footnote to this last citation, which makes his approach to architectural practice fully explicit:

> I think that the *dressing* and the *mask* are as old as human civilization, and the joy in both is identical with the joy in those things that drove men to be sculptors, painters, architects, poets, musicians, dramatists, in short, artists. Every artistic creation, every artistic pleasure presupposes a certain carnival spirit, or to express myself in a modern way – the haze of carnival candles is the true atmosphere of art. The denial of reality, of the material, is necessary if form is to emerge as a meaningful symbol, as an autonomous human creation. [Semper's italics.][131]

The German phrase that Semper used for this "denial of reality" is *Vernichtung der Realität*, which can be rendered more literally as "annihilation of reality."[132] In this context, however, it seems to refer less to reality's destruction than to its theatrical suspension, such as when a theater-goer puts aside everyday worries during his or her absorption in the unreal world of the stage. But it is important to see that this masking or suspension of reality operated on many levels for Semper. The architectural dressing camouflages the material in a physical sense, as Greek polychromy concealed the material nature of the marble beneath, thereby rendering it as pure form. The artistic dressing, however, also has the noble purpose of concealing the work's thematic content:

> Let us forget the means that must be used to achieve the desired artistic effect and not proclaim them loudly, thus missing our part miserably. This untainted feeling led primitive man to the denial of reality in all early artistic endeavors. The truly great

> masters of art in every field returned to it – only these men in times of high artistic development also *masked the material of the mask.* This instinct led Phidias to his conception of the two tympana on the Parthenon. Evidently he considered his task, the representation of the double myth and its actors (the deities), as *the subject matter to be treated* (as was the stone in which he formed them), which he veiled as much as possible – thus freeing them of any material and outwardly demonstrative expression of their nonpictorial and religious-symbolic nature. Therefore, his gods confront us, inspire us, individually and collectively, first and above all as expressions of true human beauty and grandeur. "What's Hecuba to him?" [Semper's italics.][133]

These remarks support Richard Wagner's account of his first reading of the score of *Tristan and Isolde* to Semper and others in 1858 (perhaps during the very same days that Semper was working on this footnote), at which time the architect fiercely reacted to the overtly tragic content of the libretto, unmediated in his view by the theatrical mask. Semper felt that Wagner had proclaimed the tragic content of his work too loudly and – unlike Mozart's *Don Juan* – had put too little emphasis on disguising the material and the means. "Even the domino," if we remember Semper's response, "was preferable to the plain character."[134] The confluence of Semper's and Wagner's artistic perspective becomes apparent in other ways as the footnote continues:

> For similar reasons the drama could also be meaningful only in the beginning and at the height of the progressive education of a people. The oldest vase paintings give us an idea of the early material masques of the Hellenes; in a spiritual way, like those stone dramas of Phidias, the ancient masque is again taken up by Aeschylus, Sophocles, Euripides, also by Aristophanes and the other comic dramatists. The proscenium is used for framing a noble piece of history that does not occur at some time somewhere but that happens everywhere as long as the hearts of men beat. "What's Hecuba to him?" The spirit of masks breathes in Shakespeare's dramas; we meet the humor of masks and the haze of candles, the carnival sentiment (which truly is not always joyous) in Mozart's *Don Juan*. For even music needs a means to deny reality. Hecuba also means nothing to the musician – or should mean nothing.[135]

And of course what is true for the stage, for Shakespeare (the refrain of Hecuba is taken from *Hamlet*),[136] for Phidias, and for Mozart, is also true for architecture:

> How Greek architecture also justifies what has just been discussed, how it is ruled by the principle that I have tried to intimate, according to which the viewing of a work of art makes one forget the means and the material with which and by which it exists, how it has an effect and as form becomes self-sufficient – to show this is the most difficult task of style theory.[137]

But one must be careful, Semper warned, when that which is behind the mask (both materially and thematically) is false or the mask in itself in its details is no good. For if the theatrical masking of reality is to be successful, it is essential that this material – the indispensable – be completely mastered:

> Only by complete technical perfection, by judicious and proper treatment of the material according to its properties, and by taking these properties into consideration while creating form can the material be forgotten, can the artistic creation be com-

pletely freed from it, and can even a simple landscape painting be raised to a high work of art.[138]

With this formulation of this dissimulating mask Semper completed at least a part of his artistic odyssey. It was an odyssey that had begun thirty years earlier in Greece and one that had wound its way through the intellectual alleys of Rome, Berlin, Dresden, Paris, London, and Zurich. This journey did not end with the publication of *Der Stil*; it had for the moment merely found a resting point. There remained within Semper's heart, still, the most burning desire to enact this vision in his own architectural practice.

The Third Volume of Der Stil

Even so, Semper's work on the theoretical front was not done. The projected third volume of *Der Stil*, which was to apply these principles and findings to nineteenth-century architecture, was never written. But this failure to complete this volume, which would have made his ideas far more accessible to both the professional and lay public, also tells us something more of the strength and fraility of the character who sought to glean from Greece the artistic solution to the problem of contemporary design.

The birthdate of Semper's projected third volume was 7 October 1859.[139] Up to this time, Semper had planned to write a two-volume study of style, but the swelling of the first volume on textiles to 525 printed pages had made this plan untenable. When his new publisher Bruckmann agreed to re-write the contract to include a third volume on architecture, he asked Semper to prepare a new prospectus for the book as a whole.[140]

Semper addressed for him both the thematic framework of the third volume and its content. In addition to reviewing "all functional, material, and constructional factors" related to the problem of architectural style, he proposed tackling the social or cultural conditions giving rise to certain forms. As he described it:

> A vast field of inventiveness will be revealed to us once we try to make artistic use of *our* social needs as factors in the style of *our* architecture in the same way as has been done in the past; whereas it would hardly ever be possible only through new materials and their use in new methods of construction to bring about a decisive and lasting change in architecture, and even less so through the simple power of a genius who has dreamed up his so-called new style (Semper's italics).[141]

This two-part division of his style theory conformed once again to Semper's definition of style as presented as early as 1852, which "means giving emphasis and artistic significance to the basic idea and to all intrinsic and extrinsic coefficients that modify the embodiment of the theme in a work of art."[142] Functional, material, and constructional factors comprised style's internal or "intrinsic coefficients," social or cultural issues its "extrinsic coefficients." The artistic theme remained the basic idea underlying the work of art.

The content of Semper's so-called comparative method as postulated for the third volume was somewhat more traditional in its structure. He proposed to achieve his end by surveying architecture from its earliest known appearance in antiquity through its historical development, down to modern conditions. This would certainly have made the projected volume topical, as the debate on the contemporary crisis of architecture in Germany was still raging during this decade.

Two questions were to be posed at the end of his analysis. The first was whether the current "medieval trend" had a future in architecture – a question that it can be assumed would have been answered with a thundering no. The second question or set of questions are more difficult to answer in retrospect: "Has Renaissance art solved what it set out to achieve? Has a new era already started for us, or are we only at the beginning of the Renaissance? How do we recognize and make use of the social motives and innovations that the present offers with true stylistic and historical understanding? What are the most important tasks in this regard at the present time? How have they been solved up to now?"[143]

For well over a century architects and historians have pondered the answers to this series of questions, often with the assumption that the manuscript recording Semper's answers had been lost or even destroyed by Semper himself. Only in recent times, through Wolfgang Herrmann's cataloguing of Semper's literary estate in the 1970s, has it become clear that the third volume was definitely never written – save for an introductory, forty-two page manuscript composed in 1869.[144]

The confusion about the existence of the third volume arose because Semper (in response to the constant prodding of his new publisher, and the threats of legal action that took place without interruption between the years 1863 and 1877) repeatedly insisted that the third volume was written and needed only minor revisions. This insistence was taken at face value by Semper's early biographers, who were further misled by his frequent references to a third volume in the first two published volumes, in which he often promises to give in his future volume his answer to the most challenging architectural questions. But it is now known that this volume was seriously pondered only for a few months in 1869 and then given up. It is interesting to ask why this was the case, in the light of Semper's great mastery of the issues in the earlier volumes.

The forty-two page manuscript of 1869, and the lecture of the same year upon which it was based, are both informative in this respect. The lecture, entitled "On Architectural Styles," was presented to a crowded auditorium at the Zurich Town Hall on 4 March 1869 and was well received.[145] The manuscript is obviously based on the text of the lecture, although it restructures the content in certain sections. However, it only works its way through two-thirds of the printed, thirty-two page lecture, although in doing so it also brings a little more depth to the discussion. Because the content of the two texts is nearly identical, they can be considered together.

The most notable difference between the two works is their opening remarks. Semper began his lecture by alluding to his long-standing conflict with the now deceased Franz Kugler over the issue of polychromy. He assailed Kugler for his negative review of *The Four Elements of Architecture*, and once again blamed him for his (Semper's) own failure to complete his projected book on polychromy in the 1830s – he claimed that Kugler's criticism deprived him of trust in his own convictions.

These remarks, however, merely cloud his proposal to investigate the origin of architectural styles. Because the arts under the hegemony of architecture have always symbolized prevailing social, political, and religious systems, he noted, styles could also be examined precisely under such cultural criteria. And if his effort at devising a kind of "art topic" or theory of invention based on his study of the origin, transformation, and meaning of traditional types was too high a mark at which to aim, at least he hoped to set up some boundary posts to help the next generation understand the vivid profusion of architectural development in history, as well as to provide some useful parameters for accurately assessing the present. For the present was a time of invention, he concluded in his opening remarks, and architects did not want to disgrace themselves by a lack of invention.

With this said, Semper started his lecture proper with a critique of contemporary architecture – now updated a decade from his remarks at the start of *Der Stil*. He referred sarcastically to those architects who would conjure up a new style on the spot, a class into which he put the "charivari" of the French Néo-Grec architects (exemplified for him in Garnier's new Opera building and Joseph-Louis Duc's Palais de Justice), as well as the failed "Maximilian style" of the Bavarian king. He took to task the eclecticism of the "tourist architects," including those who from moral and nationalistic instincts (in addition to a lack of imagination) sought to re-impose a modern Gothic style.

In the text written to introduce the third volume, Semper avoided making general remarks, and started with a discussion of the four building motives – the mound, wall, and roof, centered around the social hearth – from which all architectural development arose. In what was essentially a critique of his earlier presentation of these motives in *The Four Elements*, Semper insisted that architectural form can neither be satisfactorily explained by these motives alone, nor by such other factors as geography and climate, but only by the broader considerations of a more encompassing style theory. It is with the outline of this style theory that both the lecture and manuscript for the third volume of *Der Stil* converge.

It starts with a definition of style, the notion that was absent from the Prolegomena to the first volume of Semper's study, published in 1860. And it is interesting in view of the intervening decade to note the subtle changes to his earlier definition of this term. "Style," said Semper in his lecture, "is the accord of an art object with its genesis, and with all the preconditions and circumstances of its becoming."[146] In the later manuscript he defined it similarly, and even more succinctly as the "harmony of form with its inner-lying idea."[147] In both texts (drawing once again upon Rumohr) he discussed the etymology of the word "style," the Roman *stylus* used for both writing and drawing. But in his manuscript to the third volume he added a few sentences on how the shapeless matter of art should be fashioned into form. In what is certainly an allusion to his lengthy footnote in *Der Stil* on the masking of reality in the arts, Semper pointed out that the physical material (*Stoff als physische Materie*) should be completely mastered as physical matter but also "spiritualized," so that "it can be forgotten in the pleasure of pure artistic form." And then, by way of rejecting a style theory occupied simply with such material considerations, he noted further:

> But under material [*Stoff*], in addition to the material [*Material*] of the art-form, we also understand something higher, namely the *task*, the given *problem* or *theme* for artistic exploitation. *This content-factor of artistic form is in any case* the most important of all other previously named factors, because it makes form into the absolute expression of its content. [Semper's italics.][148]

Thus he explained how the denial or annihilation of form by the artist is the negation of form in both a material and thematic sense.

Another important expansion on his style theory is his reference in the Zurich lecture to Darwin's *Origin of Species* and to those historians (Hermann Grimm is noted in the published text; Wilhelm Lübke's name is cited in a draft to the lecture but later deleted)[149] who view architectural history as some deterministic biological model, governed by laws of natural selection, heredity, and adaptation. This is a fascinating reference for 1869 and it demonstrates that already by this date the social application of Darwin's theory to history and art was becoming quite fashionable.

Semper's argument, in opposing the axiom that "nature makes no leaps," is that art does indeed make leaps, often through the creative genius of a single individual. This is another forceful rejection by Semper of any mechanistic or materialist historical conception of art: "We can quite rightly describe the old monuments as the fossilized receptacles of extinct social organizations, but these did not grow on the backs of society like shells on the backs of snails, nor did they spring forth from blind natural processes, like coral reefs. They are free human creations, upon which we employed our understanding, observation of nature, genius, will, knowledge, and power."[150]

Therefore, Semper argued, the "creative human spirit" is the first and most important factor in the genesis of a style, even though it would certainly be reigned in by "certain higher laws" of tradition, demand, and functional necessity. The irony inherent in these lines was that Semper was falsely categorized, and condemned by many as just one of those Darwinian determinists in the first few decades of the twentieth century.[151]

Thus, in both his lecture and in the third volume of *Der Stil*, Semper proposed to examine the issue of style thematically, that is, through social, political, religious, and personal motives. He attempted to do so by considering humanity under the following three rubrics:

1) the individual;
2) collective mankind, the state;
3) the human ideal as the highest task of art.

These three distinctions conform roughly to three successive but not mutually exclusive stages of human development. In the first stage of existence mankind sought to express human individuality principally through acts of self-adornment and the decoration of implements. Art in the service of religion or state later became most apparent in the centralized and autocratic civilizations of Egypt and the Mesopotamian valley, among other places. Mankind as a human or liberal ideal arose for the first time in Greece, when the people "no longer held the divinity captive in hidden cages" but personalized him or her, thereby turning gods into symbols of human perfection.

The text of Semper's lecture races through these three categories and, like his very first publication on polychromy, can be criticized for its sweeping historical generalizations, which demonstrate his weakness as a historian. The manuscript for *Der Stil* goes into slightly more detail but adds little of substance, and its does not reach the third division before it breaks off. The one surprising aspect of the lecture, from what we know of his earlier writings, is Semper's quite positive discussion of the architecture of Imperial Rome, rating it over and above that of the Renaissance. He described Roman architecture as containing "the cosmopolitan future of architecture" because "it represents the synthesis of two seemingly contradictory cultural forces: namely, striving toward individuality and merging into the collective."[152]

Semper was lauding not only the spatial motive inherent in arcuated design, but also the great innovations of Roman architecture in both the design of the floor plan and in composition – where each element is necessary for the whole but does not yield its individuality, or reveal the need for material support. Only Michelangelo's brilliant dome for St. Peter's added to these spatial and compositional innovations at the time of the Renaissance, but this divine creation of Semper's favorite artist was subsequently bungled by the papacy, which placed a Baroque basilica in front of it. Semper's anti-Catholicism continued to influence his thinking as strongly as ever.

It was this delicate issue of architecture's present and future course that Semper was unable to resolve, as his abandoned manuscript makes clear. The first several hundred pages of the third volume would have been relatively easy for him to write, for he had already brought his opening remarks to the point at which he could have drawn heavily upon his earlier lectures and manuscript for "Comparative Building Theory." It was, however, what lay behind or at the end of these several hundred pages – the conclusions he would have to draw – that troubled him.

Wolfgang Herrmann, who has done extensive research on the publication history of *Der Stil*, concluded that Semper was hampered in his efforts to write the third volume by two concerns: first by the recent advances in historical knowledge, a proliferating body of material that he was now hesitant to tackle or lacked the confidence to master; and secondly by his fateful decision to append his lengthy discourse on the "dressing" to the first volume. Herrmann argued that by adding this section, Semper essentially robbed himself of the legitimate content of the third volume, because this principle could also be applied to all of architecture's technical motives.[153]

Semper's concerns are certainly evident. In 1861 he discussed with his publisher his worry that a critical assessment of modern conditions would be difficult, first because he was not a disinterested observer of contemporary developments, and secondly because he was still unable to travel to Germany or keep up with the recent architectural developments there, due to his political banishment.[154] In another very revealing letter to Bruckmann of 1873, Semper frankly accepted the blame for the third volume's long delay, and admitted the fact that the general and specialized researches of Hirt, Stieglitz, Schnaase, Kugler, Bötticher, Lübke, and many others since, had advanced historical understanding to the point that it was now difficult to forge a new path. This erudition of his rivals, combined with his own old age, had robbed him of his "former spontaneity," thereby forcing him "to put down my pen whenever I took it up again to complete finally the partly finished opus I had conceived more than twenty years ago."[155]

There were perhaps two further reasons why Semper was unable to write the final volume of his most important work of theory. The first was time, or rather, the extraordinary demands made on his time in the mid-1860s with the design of the Winterthur Town Hall and the Munich Festspielhaus. By contrast, when he arrived in Zurich in 1855 he was for the first time in many years free of financial worries and could direct some of his time to writing. Between 1855 and 1858, when most of volume one of *Der Stil* was written, he had in fact no major architectural commissions to distract his attention. Even when the second volume was written, between 1860 and 1863, his practice was still modest. But things changed quite suddenly in 1864, when he should have been starting the third volume. He first became involved with the competition for the Winterthur Town Hall and then, in December of that year, with the Munich Festspielhaus. The latter, in particular, was particularly draining of his time and energies. It was a large work in both scale and complexity and it was of great importance for his professional identity. Moreover, it was a design that only he could fashion, both conceptually and in its various details. In addition, its design over several years had to be carried out during Semper's semester breaks – time previously devoted to his literary work. Thus it seems reasonable to suggest that his failure to write the final section of *Der Stil* was yet another byproduct of the Munich tragedy.

The other reason he failed to complete the third volume, it can be argued, was what can be called the crisis of his intellectual and artistic spirit – his inability to cope with the implications of his theory on his own architectural practice.

When Semper began his architectural practice in the 1830s and 1840s he had utilized Renaissance forms in a very innovative and progressive fashion: first to re-think the problems of the cultural theater and museum, and second to consolidate his own theatrical approach to design. He was almost alone in Germany at this time in his use and development of such forms. But by the mid- to late-1860s, the architectural conditions in Germany were quite different. In part through the influence of his own works, in part through a new recognition of the artistic accomplishments of the Renaissance period, the so-called Neorenaissance style had become quite popular in the Germanic countries, especially among the younger generation of architects. The popularity of the Neorenaissance did not peak, in fact, until the late-1870s, at which time it passed into a phase called the Neobaroque. Thus what had been innovative in the 1830s became more the norm in the 1860s, and Semper was not inclined to fall in easily with the movements of the pack.

The same was to some extent true with regard to his theory. In the 1830s and 1840s he began a line of theoretical development that provided architectural theory first with a more solid ethnological footing (as opposed to the myths of classical theory), and second with a means of mining the rich seam of historical artistic values. Against the *Rundbogen* theories of Heinrich Hübsch, for instance – which preached the superiority of the *Rundbogen* or rounded-arch style because it better satisfied contemporary needs and was structurally more efficient – Semper held out for an artistic solution to the style crisis, the key of which lay in the polychromy of classical antiquity. This line of thought culminated with his masterpiece on style at the start of the 1860s, in which the "haze of carnival candles" now emerged as the "true atmosphere" for monumental art.

Although this image would prove to be highly seductive for the next generation of architects coming to the fore, it – like Hübsch's theory – was also a theory predicated on the architecture of stone or mass. But the Germany of the 1860s was changing rapidly. It was a collection of cultures and states on the verge of achieving political unity and by the start of the next decade this new country had become the leading military power of Europe. Industrialization was speeding ahead and even beginning to outstrip that of England and France. The implications of what this trend held for architecture were becoming evident to everyone. The question of whether iron would become an important architectural material was no longer seriously debated in the 1860s; rather, the issue became how best does one treat it artistically.

In this light Semper's dilemma becomes clear. On the one hand he had been one of the first architects in Europe, following his review of the Great Exhibition of 1851, to recognize the revolutionary changes that industrialization and mass production would bring about in art and architecture. On the other hand he had built an architectural practice and constructed an elaborate theoretical model predicated solely on the use of stone, whereby mass or the monumentalization of the theatrical impulse conveyed architecture's essential meaning. He must surely have worried about how his critical review of contemporary developments would be received by the younger generation of architects, and how his theory could be justified in the light of the changing conditions of architecture. Would the whole underpinning of his theory be seen as something of little value or would it simply be regarded as anachronistic? In short, Semper with his diminished spontaneity would have been unable to draw the conclusions already evident in aspects of his theory – that if these refined nuances of architectural design were to survive in the coming years, they would have to do so in other than historical forms.

Thus at the age of sixty-five – rather than come to this logical conclusion – Semper retreated. The ending to his lecture of 1869 candidly revealed his decision. Borrowing words from his text of 1851, he lamented once again his architectural predicament and simply apologized for it: "People reproach us architects for a lack of inventiveness – too harshly, since nowhere has a new idea of universal historical importance, pursued with force and consciousness, become evident. We are convinced that wherever such an idea would really take the lead, one or the other of our younger colleagues will prove himself capable of endowing it with a suitable architectural dress. Until that time comes, however, we must reconcile ourselves to make do as best we can with the old."[156] Here the onus of innovation is placed on "one or the other of our younger colleagues."

But this complacency in the face of such momentous change – now clearly visible only a few years away on the architectural horizon – should not be interpreted as a concession to his artistic integrity. If Semper was the one architect and theorist who brought German theory and architecture to the brink of what we today term Modernism, he should not be faulted for lacking the fire, the "spontaneity," to complete the process. For this decision would also have denied him his own strengths as a designer.

And indeed one other factor should be taken into account: namely, that when he spoke these words in 1869, at the age of sixty-five, he believed that his architectural practice was more or less coming to an end. He could not have imagined that the next decade of his life would be (in terms of the number of monumental commissions) by far the most prolific decade of his lifetime. He could scarcely have believed that he would have another chance to give form to his artistic ideals in one last and brilliant monumental design. What could Hecuba mean to him?

5

The Monumental Builder 1869–1879

"It is an exhausting trade – architecture – and I would rather be a swineherd."
(Gottfried in a letter to his son Manfred, 19 May 1871)

Overtures from Vienna

Despite his disappointment with the theater in Munich, Semper's professional stature and artistic reputation continued to grow during the 1860s in several ways. His high standing as an architect was still largely based on his Dresden works, his Hoftheater and Art Gallery in particular. And his move back to Zurich (now as a quite well-known political refugee), together with his designs for the Polytechnikum and Winterthur Town Hall, re-established his presence on the Continent. The publication of the two volumes of *Der Stil* in the first years of the decade also came to add another dimension to his reputation. Its erudition initially seems to have overwhelmed its readers, but as the decade progressed more and more architects, art historians, aestheticians, and archaeologists came to appreciate both its research and many artistic insights. By the start of the 1870s it would be regarded in Germany, at least, as "a canon for modern aesthetics."[1]

Even the bitter experience in Munich did not in the end prove injurious to his stature. If anything, it enhanced his image as a heroic monumental builder and fighter who, with his expansive and valiant artistic vision, was willing to take to task the frailties of kings and lesser political spirits. Contemporary observers of German architecture were also fully aware of the ambition and grandeur behind his theater proposal, even though the design was never officially made public. One of the leading art historians of the day, Wilhelm Lübke, expressed privately to Semper his high regard for the design and he added the comment – somewhat injudiciously it turns out – that if Wagner's music and his following proved to be short-lived, Semper's new theater, at least, would survive to the next century.[2]

Respect for Semper's abilities also manifested itself in growing professional recognition. The Amsterdam Society for the Advancement of Architecture (Maatschappy tot Bevordering der Bouwkunst) made Semper an honorary member in 1863, the first of a string of similar acknowledgments.[3] The Royal Bavarian Academy of Sciences followed suit three years later, as did the Vienna Academy of Fine Arts in 1868.[4] The Royal Institute of British Architects was not yet prepared to go so far (they did in 1877), but in the spring of 1863 its acting president, Charles Nelson, wrote to Semper (in French) to ask for a nomination for its gold medal, awarded every three years to an architect from abroad.[5]

The University of Zurich awarded Semper an honorary doctorate in 1864, allowing him to affix this respected appellation before his name. These accolades continued throughout the 1870s; even the American Institute of Architects bestowed its honorary membership in 1872.

In the summer of 1867 the architect received a letter from Rudolf von Eitelberger, demonstrating Semper's influence on another front. The director of the newly founded Österreichisches Museum für Kunst und Industrie, asked Semper for a copy of the "Metals Catalogue," the unpublished report that Semper had written for Henry Cole just prior to his being hired at the Department of Practical Art.[6] The request signaled the very strong impact that Semper's four-motive theory was beginning to have on the planning and layout of industrial-art museums. A museum dedicated to the applied arts was in itself a relatively new phenomenon within the German-speaking countries, first making its appearance with the Germanisches Museum in Nuremberg (1852) and the Bavarian Nationalmuseum in Munich (1854). The model for the more recent wave of these institutions was, however, Henry Cole's museum at the Department of Science and Art in London.

Eitelberger, who received his directorship of the yet to be built Vienna museum in March 1864, advanced the notion of such a museum in a significant way. Trained first in law, philology, and philosophy, he shifted his interest to the arts in the 1840s and became the University of Vienna's first professor of art history in 1852. His interest in the arts, however, was more practically based and, after traveling to London for the World Exhibition of 1862, he became impressed with the goals of the South Kensington museum and school and urged the founding of such an institution in Austria. It was in London that Eitelberger probably first became aware of Semper's earlier manuscript for the Department of Science and Art. He was also quite familiar with the architect's other writings and even arranged his first collections at the new building in Vienna (completed in 1871) in part according to Semper's four-motive theory. Like Cole, he saw the aim of this new museum to be the display of design models for the instruction and inspiration of the craftsman and designer, and to this end he also incorporated a library and industrial-art school into his institution.

Semper's ideas on the organization of such institutions at this time came to be recognized in other cities as well – in particular at the newly founded industrial-art museums in Berlin (1867) and Hamburg (1874).[7] In the case of Vienna, Semper sent his manuscript to Eitelberger, who had a copy made of it. Semper became aware at this point of the high regard in which he was held in Viennese artistic circles.[8]

Another indication of Semper's growing reputation in the 1860s was his appointment to the juries of various international competitions – events not totally unrelated to the lifting of his warrant of arrest in Germany and the rapidly changing political situation. The 1860s were dominated politically by the aggressive diplomatic stratagems of Otto von Bismarck and by the expanding military might of Prussia. Bismarck was named Minister President of Prussia by King Wilhelm in 1862 and soon began to implement his plans for a confrontation with Austria, so as to settle once and for all the question of who would unify and dominate the still independent German states. By sending Prussian troops into the former Danish duchy of Holstein, he induced the Emperor Franz Josef into war in the summer of 1865. The Prussian forces quickly routed the Austrian and Bavarian armies at Sadowa, clearing the way for their conquest and assimilation of the other German states.

Prussia's eventual defeat of France in 1870–71, and its imposition of unity to this new entity of Germany at the same time, consolidated this country's position as the leading European economic and military power, a position it maintained until World War I.

The suspension of Semper's warrant of arrest for his political activities of 1849, which allowed him greater freedom of travel, was affected by these events only in the reverse sense that it was prompted by a liberal backlash to Bismarck in Saxony. August Röckel, Wagner's former assistant in Dresden who had been captured in 1849, was released from prison in 1862 under the new policy of leniency by Saxon officials, and in the same year Wagner himself petitioned the Saxon king and was allowed to return to Germany to attend to his ailing wife Minna. Semper at this time was engaged with Saxon authorities in a legal dispute over the status of his two sons, Manfred and Conrad. Saxon officials insisted that since the boys had been born in Saxony they were required to perform military service or pay a substantial fine. Semper ended the matter shrewdly by having his whole family naturalized in Switzerland. This resolution of the legal dispute allowed him to petition the Saxon crown for the right to travel to other German states, a request that Friedrich Augustus personally granted in the spring of 1863.[9]

The reason for Semper's request was a letter he received in March 1863 from the chair of a building committee for the Kunsthalle in Hamburg, Dr. Abendroth, requesting his presence on the design jury.[10] A competition for this fine arts museum had been announced late in 1862 and Semper initially intended to participate. Various sketches for the design by his hand exist and they depict a variation on his Dresden Gallery, a rectangular building with a central pediment and low dome above. Semper apparently put the design aside when he traveled to Hamburg in July 1863 to join the competition jury, which included the Berliners Dr. Gustav Waagen and August Stüler, in addition to his old Dresden friend Julius Hähnel. The jury selected the team of Hermann von der Hude and Georg Theodor Schirrmacher as the architects. Their very handsome sandstone and terracotta building, a near square in plan with its open loggia courts at the centers of all four sides, was built between 1863 and 1866.

Semper's return to his city of birth may have led to a small commission he received from the city of Altona in 1864 to add a new front and waiting hall to that city's railway station. The source for the commission was probably Semper's brother Carl, who was also a director with the railway society. When Semper received the details of the commission in February 1864, however, he seems to have lost interest. The city wanted to modify the existing station by shifting its main entrance to another side, yet it had very little money with which to execute the work. Plans by another architect were sent to Zurich and Semper apparently was asked only to deal with the architectural facade. He saw the work, however, as an opportunity to further Manfred's architectural skills and he called his son north from Italy to carry out the project. Correspondence between the father and son indicate that Manfred handled most of the design work on site with regular comments from his father. One suggestion of the latter, intended to reduce the cost and more aptly deal with the bad taste of the "philistines," called for eliminating the pilaster projections in the waiting room and treating its walls in a "tapestry style."[11]

The railway station in Altona was not the only commission outside Switzerland for which Semper was considered. In January 1866, just as he was finalizing his designs for the permanent Munich Festspielhaus, there was some discussion about inviting him back to

London to design the Royal Albert Hall. Semper, of course, had made a rough design for a concert hall in South Kensington just prior to his departure from London in 1855, but this project was soon forgotten. In the interim Captain Francis Fowke, a Royal Engineer, was named Inspector for the Department of Science and Art, and was therefore in charge of building the South Kensington complex. Fowke, who was also a brilliant inventor, soon built the first permanent museum building, the structure housing the International Exhibition of 1862, and the Great Conservatory for the Royal Horticultural Society Gardens. With the death of Prince Albert in 1861, Cole and others revived the idea of a concert hall in the Prince's honor – a project for which Cole began to raise money in 1863. In the fall of that year Cole and Fowke traveled to the south of France to study the Roman amphitheaters at Nimes and Arles, from which arose their joint scheme for an elliptical building. Fowke died in December 1865, while revising the design.

The next month talk focused on his successor. General Charles Grey, the Queen's secretary, was apparently the first to recall Semper's earlier design. In letters to the Prince of Wales and Lord Derby (soon to become Prime Minister) Grey spoke of the Prince's high regard for Semper, this "most scientific man."[12] Cole was consulted and preferred "to do without any fresh architect – by means of Fowkes' draftsmen – if not: then Semper certainly."[13] Cole also felt that should Semper be employed, it should be only "for his designs;" for reasons of economy, the actual execution of the building should be placed in the hands of Major-General Henry Scott, another Royal Engineer.[14]

Cole was practicing a charade here, as he had already approached Scott in December and promised him the entire job. Yet it seems to have been the particular opposition of Lord Derby that sealed Semper's fate. In strongly worded letters to both Grey and the Prince of Wales, he referred to the suggestion of hiring Semper as "a slur on the whole body of British architects."[15] The irony of this was that Cole wanted nothing to do with any architect, and the Royal Institute of British Architects had been contesting for years Cole's use of engineers for his many architectural projects. While all of this discussion was taking place in London, no one seemed to be aware that Semper was then designing what would have been the grandest opera house of the nineteenth century. Semper also seems to have had no inkling of this discussion in London concerning his services.

In the last years of the decade Semper sat on the jury of three highly visible, international competitions. The first, taking place in 1867, dealt with the design of the facade for Florence Cathedral, the conclusion to the famous church and dome of Filippo Brunelleschi. Earlier jury deliberations had tendered first place to the Florentine architect Emilio de Fabris, who was then asked to make some modifications and re-submit his design to a second jury. Thus the jury that was seated in the spring of 1867 had the task of finalizing the conditional result of the first jury against a few token competitors. Two members of the earlier jury – Viollet-le-Duc and the French sculptor Dupré – declined to participate in this second round. Semper was joined on the new jury by his Swiss colleague Jakob Burckhardt and by the Italian Count della Porta. From the start, Semper opposed the modified scheme of de Fabris and preferred instead the basilica scheme of another entry by Cipolla. He lost his argument, however, and in the end the scheme of de Fabris was accepted and built.[16]

In the following year Semper received an invitation to head a jury in Palermo, which was deciding a competition design for the Teatro Massimo. Semper looked upon Sicily with a certain nostalgia, and various travel sketches by his hand testify to his enthusiasm for revisiting the destinations of his youth. The jury awarded first prize to the theater design of Giovanni Battista Filippo Basile, a proposal that – after much delay – was ultimately completed by his son Ernesto in 1897.

The third competition jury that Semper sat on in this decade considered the new cathedral proposed for Berlin in 1867–69. It was, in view of Prussian ascendancy in Europe, one of the more widely watched architectural events of the day. Berlin was shortly to become the new capital of a unified Germany and this project, situated on the Lustgarten alongside Schinkel's Altes Museum and opposite the Royal Palace, was viewed by many Prussians as both a religious and national symbol – in its proposed scale a Protestant challenge to the Vatican's church in Rome. The relatively small church then located on this site dated from 1747 and needed replacement. Schinkel had remodeled the cathedral in the early 1820s by adding three domes and an Ionic portico. The architects Wilhelm Stier and August Stüler made designs for a new building in the 1840s; the latter's proposal was accepted and construction was started on a new church in the mid-1840s but this work was halted due to the political events of 1848–49.

Little more was done until the time of the upswing of the Prussian economy in the 1860s. After protracted consideration, a new architectural competition was announced in August 1867, yet – as in so many other cases – it was plagued with a badly defined program. Altogether, forty competitors submitted fifty-two entries, but the jury report (only published in 1869) disappointed everyone. No entry was accepted for execution, although ten entries were cited for the excellence of their design. The architect Friedrich Adler was awarded honorary first place. But the jury's report at least had the merit of arguing that it was the program, and not the work of the architects, that was responsible for the failed quest for a solution.

Semper regarded both the program and majority of the designs with a great deal of skepticism, if not hostility. In his Zurich lecture given in March 1869 he castigated the proposed size of the project in general, and one of the Gothic designs in particular (perhaps that of E. Klingenberg) as an "Asian-Roman triple-crown miter" transformed into "a colossal medieval spiked helmet."[17] He then went on, with typical sarcasm, to question the political motivations behind the work: "If Count Bismarck takes an interest in the building department, we believe he would sooner find inspiration for *his* ideal of a national monument by taking as a model the previously discussed great building undertakings of the imperial depressor of princes, Ch'in Shih Huang Ti, or the labyrinthian government palace of the Egyptian dodecarchy, than by making inquiries from St. Peter."[18]

There are several reasons to account for this sharpness of the tongue, somewhat characteristic of Semper at this stage of his life. Even though sitting on juries implied a certain honor and prestige, it also implied a senior status within the profession, and in Semper's case his semi-retirement from practice. In 1869, for instance, he was approaching his sixty-sixth birthday and was a scant four years short of his mandatory retirement from the Polytechnikum chair in Zurich. And even though the 1860s had been kind to Semper in some ways, this was not especially the case architecturally. The building of the Winterthur Town Hall was his only significant work of the decade to be erected and the bitterness about Munich was still very much with him. His long-standing problem with asthma was worsening and he was becoming aware, as his letters increasingly suggest, not only of his loss of youthful spontaneity but also of his vigor – that is, his mortality. These problems were not reconcilable with the lofty ambition of younger days.

He was perhaps gripped with such inquietude when toward the end of the decade he received a letter that was to shape forcefully the last ten years of his life. It was a note from the Viennese architect Carl Hasenauer, dated 7 August 1868. Hasenauer apologized to his elder of thirty years for taking the liberty of writing to him unannounced, and then spoke of his involvement in an architectural competition in Vienna for the design of two museums, of the long delay by two design juries in arriving at a verdict, and of the death of the jury's first leader, Eduard van der Nüll. He asked Semper if he could suggest his name as a possible replacement for the deceased architect.[19]

Hasenauer was writing about one of the largest and most prestigious architectural commissions of the day. Since the late 1850s Vienna had been one of the busiest hubs of building activity in Europe. The stimulus to this work was the decision made in 1857 by the young Franz Josef to take down the ramparts and broad glacis defending the historic city and replace them with a grand boulevard – the Ringstrasse – thereby providing a location for much needed housing on one hand and a score of cultural amenities on the other. Plans for a number of monumental works were soon put into effect, beginning with Heinrich von Ferstel's Votivkirche (1856–79) and Siccardsburgh and van der Nüll's Opera (1861–69). Even the crushing loss to Prussian forces in 1865 did not slow down this activity; it seems only to have fortified Franz Josef's resolve to compete with, if not overwhelm, Berlin culturally. Over the next decade construction on a string of other monumental works was started, among them Heinrich von Ferstel's Museum of Art and Industry (1868–71) and University of Vienna (1873–84), Friedrich von Schmidt's City Hall (1872–83), and Theophil von Hansen's Greek Parliament (1873–83). The proposed Art Museum and Natural History Museum were potentially the most prestigious of these additions, as they enjoyed a privileged site just above the historic Burgtor (royal gate), peering down over the busy complex of the Hofburg Palace. The palace in itself also needed expansion and remodeling and there had already been talk of a new royal playhouse or theater.

Discussion concerning the need for the museums had started as early as the 1830s but it did not become serious until the end of the 1850s; a formal program for the works was not drafted until 1865. A limited competition was announced in that year and four local architects were asked to prepare proposals: Theophil von Hansen, Heinrich von Ferstel, Moritz Löhr, and Carl von Hasenauer. Hansen and Ferstel were obvious candidates for the prestigious commission as they were at the top of the architectural profession in Austria at this time. The selection of Löhr, who was a civil servant, was accepted by many within the profession with less excitement, even though in his governmental capacity he had prepared a number of studies for the museums and their locations. Hasenauer's admittance to the limited competition was somewhat surprising, as he was by far the youngest and least experienced of the three men. After completing his studies under van der Nüll in Vienna, Hasenauer had traveled widely before returning to the city at the end of the 1850s to begin his architectural practice. His built works were still few: some villas and an impressive designs for the Paris World Exposition of 1867. He participated in the competition for the facade of Florence Cathedral in 1867 and won an honorable mention. A few years earlier he had received third place in the competition for the Vienna Opera. With his election to the Vienna Academy of Fine Arts in 1866, however, he solidified his position as one of Vienna's most talented and promising architects.

But the architectural competition for these two large museums, like virtually every other government-sponsored competition of this era, had completely misfired.[20] The failing was spectacular even for this city, so long noted for its covert political alliances and courtly intrigues. The large jury that was seated in July 1867 quickly eliminated the submissions of both Hansen and Ferstel on the grounds that neither had complied with the program requirement of designing two separate buildings. Both men had objected to this restriction and joined the two buildings into a monumental complex. Hansen did so by joining his two buildings with a colonnaded sculpture gallery on one side; whereas Ferstel added wings to both sides, thereby creating a semi-enclosed garden and courtyard. Of the two remaining entries, Löhr's design was judged more functional than Hasenauer's (Pl. 129), but its artistic grandeur was derided. In the end, none of the four projects was recommended for execution.

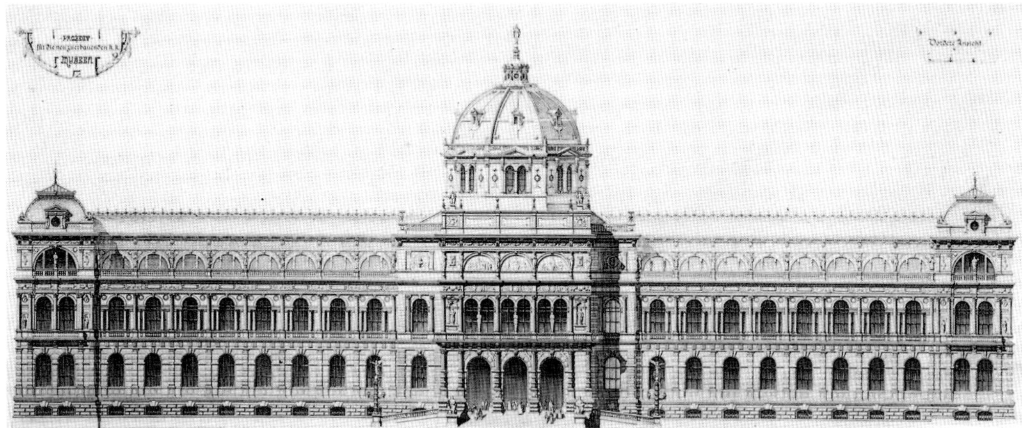

129 Carl von Hasenauer, first competition design for the Vienna museums, 1867. Institut für Geschichte und Theorie der Architectur, Semper Archiv, ETH-Zurich.

In August of that year Franz Josef decided to initiate a second stage of the competition and restrict it to the revised projects of Löhr and Hasenauer. This decision provoked nothing but criticism from the professional community and the local press, members of whom insisted that artistic values were being short-changed by a faulty program. Thus there was much lobbying for Hansen's and Ferstel's reconsideration and in December 1867 the Emperor was forced to relent and allow their projects to be judged again. By this date criticism had started to focus around the program itself, which was deemed too narrowly conceived and rigid in its design parameters. Eitelberger, who wrote to Semper during these months on behalf of the layout scheme for his own industrial-art museum (now under construction), led the charge in Vienna by writing a pamphlet that appeared in December. It proposed a thoroughly revised program. Eitelberger was also the first individual at this juncture to raise publicly the question of defining the relationship of the two museums with the planned extension of the nearby Hofburg.

The second stage of the competition took place in the summer and fall of 1868 and was no less happy in its result (Pl. 130). Hansen and Ferstel refused to revise their proposals and the former even questioned the competence of the local jury by insisting that other jurors be brought in from outside Austria and that their judgment be accepted by the Crown

130 Carl von Hasenauer, second competition design for the Vienna museums, 1868. Institut für Geschichte und Theorie der Architectur, Semper Archiv, ETH-Zurich.

without delay. Once again the submissions of both Hansen and Ferstel were eliminated on technical grounds, even though several members on the jury preferred Hansen's original scheme. The majority decided in favor of Löhr and his project was recommended, without particular enthusiasm, for execution.

This last project, however, was the solution least admired by the professional community, because of its severity and lack of artistic character. Hasenauer wrote to Semper after presenting his submission to the second jury and prior to the jury's decision in favor of Löhr. Hasenauer's suggestion that Semper might take van der Nüll's spot was a misrepresentation of the facts, as the deceased architect had for some months already been replaced on the jury by Johann Rösner. Hasenauer seems to have picked up on Hansen's demand for an international juror or outside judgment, and was seeking the good will of this prominent architect, whose work he personally admired.

Semper at first made no response to Hasenauer's letter, even though he was undoubtedly monitoring the events in Vienna closely. Because of his trip to Palermo, he did not respond until November, that is, until a few days after the second verdict was made public. The jury's selection of Löhr's project was quickly assailed by the professional community and in the press. This popular commentary on the judgment was shortly thereafter supported by another commission reviewing the competition process, which found that the jury's work had been biased in Löhr's favor. Professional groups also objected to the dismissal of the projects of Hansen and Ferstel on technical grounds. The Emperor's cabinet took preliminary steps to commission Löhr officially, but soon shied away from taking final action in the face of the intensifying uproar. The demands for an outside arbiter were by now growing more widespread.

Pleased at finally getting a response, Hasenauer wrote Semper a second letter toward the end of November, saying that he had proposed his name for this task.[21] On almost the same day, the architect and jury member Karl Tietz, who had earlier been a supporter of Hansen's design, also wrote to Semper with the same request – this time suggesting that he be joined by Wilhelm Lübke and Friedrich Theodor Vischer in evaluating the results of the second jury.[22] Tietz may have been encouraged in part by Hasenauer, but he was also representing the Congress of Austrian Engineers and Architects, which was quite eager to make its voice heard in this important artistic decision. Semper thus had the major professional organization in Vienna pressing for his advice.

In December 1868 Hansen also added his support when he suggested Semper's mediation during an audience with the Emperor.[23] This request now gained the favor of the Crown, which was desperately seeking some way to resolve this highly contentious affair. During the same month Hasenauer again wrote to Semper, who had not yet responded to the second letter and had not yet expressed interest in judging the matter. Hasenauer explained that the ministry had already decided on seeking Semper's advice, and he sent Semper his published designs for the two stages of the competition – thereby overtly attempting to compromise the fairness of any possible decision.[24]

A few days into the new year Semper received a second letter from Tietz, also confirming that he would soon be contacted by someone from within the cabinet. The official letter was dated 15 January 1869 and was sent from the Austrian Embassy in Bern.[25] Semper was asked to evaluate the projects of Löhr and Hasenauer and render his judgment to the Crown. The competition drawings were then packed up and sent to Zurich, arriving at the end of the month. By acceding to the Crown's request, Semper now became, in effect, the Emperor's personal and – presumably – final arbiter of the matter.

Thus at the start of the year the situation was complex. Ferstel had for the most part dropped out of consideration, although he still had some support from within professional circles. Hansen's project was clearly the favorite of many locally, but it had been eliminated on a technicality and was not even in Semper's hands for review. Löhr, who had officially won the drawn-out competition, was opposing any outside intervention, as he was feeling – quite rightfully – that he was being cheated out of his hard-won victory. And Hasenauer, without Semper's encouragement, was not only privately feeding him his own version of events in Vienna but he was also shamelessly promoting his own interests. It is thus to a certain extent surprising that Semper decided to take up the matter at all.

Nevertheless, he studied the proposals conscientiously during February. In March, just before he left to sit on his design jury in Berlin, he sent his decision to Vienna in the form of a report: he recommended that neither of the projects be executed but not for the obvious reasons.

Semper's view on this matter truly turned on his talent as a monumental builder and it drew upon a line of reasoning that first took shape in his early days in Dresden. The failure of the Vienna competition was, in his analysis, a failing of the program, that is, a conceptual failing on the part of government planners to connect the site of these two large museums with the extension of the nearby Hofburg. In short, Semper suggested that given the ideals of recent Viennese expansion along the Ringstrasse it was only proper to bring together these vast enterprises into a single urban whole – into the symbolic heart of the ruling and cultural elite, the physical heart of the city.

As Semper characterized it, there should be "a far more comprehensive building idea, focusing itself around the new palace, to which both museums have to be subordinated."[26] This lack of a "clear idea" stigmatized both schemes, as neither proposal possessed an urban "inner connection." In addition, Löhr's scheme suffered from its monotony and arid schematism; the proposal of Hasenauer, by contrast, was too busy in its massing and lacked any sense of harmony. Semper thus suggested a thorough revision of both proposals, based on this new urban premise.

How correct Semper's analysis was can be gauged by the immediacy by which Franz Josef was willing to rethink the entire project. Semper left for Berlin in the middle of

March, probably feeling his work for Vienna had ended. Next he traveled to his family home in Altona, where he hoped to relax for the Easter holidays. He was certainly surprised to find a letter from the Emperor's secretary there, requesting him to come to Vienna as soon as possible and speak personally with Franz Josef. Semper now became aware that something much larger than advice was possibly in the offing.

He halted his holidays and hurried south to Vienna, via Berlin, Dresden, and Prague, arriving in the city on 6 April. Franz Josef was spending the holidays at his palace in Ofen and Semper next traveled there. Although he was received with the greatest cordiality – lodging near and dining with the Emperor – he was initially disappointed with their conversations. He reported to Manfred that Franz Josef was still vacillating between Hansen and Hasenauer and that he was nothing more than a "middle person" giving advice. On the topic of his possible involvement with the project Semper lamented: "I see myself in my retirement back in Zurich. Everything is only a problematic honor!"[27]

His fortune changed one week later, after the Emperor and his coterie, together with Semper, returned to Vienna. He was asked by the young monarch, tentatively it seems, to prepare a design for the two museums and Hofburg extension, for which he was to choose a local partner, preferably one of the architects in the competition.

This request amounted to the architectural commission and it did not take long for the artistic community of Vienna to become aware of Semper's presence and intervention. Semper, however, remained aloof and met with only some of the competitors for the project. Hansen, because of a serious illness, asked to be excused from consideration of a partnership. It is unclear if Semper met with Löhr, but the latter in any case remained quite hostile to his presence. Semper really had no choice but to select Hasenauer as his associate in this new venture, although the latter's youthful energy, talent, and decorative skill no doubt contributed greatly to this decision. Semper returned to Zurich to ponder the design.

He devoted the summer of 1869 to working out the plans for the new complex. Hasenauer dutifully supplied him with the necessary programmatic requirements and other information regarding the site; his regular recounting of the bickering still taking place in Vienna (in large part because a "foreigner" was taking control of this important Habsburg monument) no doubt unsettled Semper as well. The sour recollections of Munich were still haunting him. Löhr seems to have been heading the opposition; he did not hesitate to put his own municipal office to work on designing an alternative scheme for the museums and Hofburg – effectively in competition with Semper.

Hasenauer, at first elated with the joint appointment, was soon harboring resentment at Semper's command and control of the revised design. During the first half of May he was even unclear as to what exactly Semper was doing over his drafting table in Zurich. The older architect later became aware of this anger and invited Hasenauer to come to Zurich in June to participate in the design.

The first birdseye perspective of the new buildings (Pls. 131, 132) indicates the massive overhaul the project underwent at the hand of Semper. He had created, in effect, a gigantic "Roman" forum, defined by the two museums (in the foreground) and – crossing the Ringstrasse – by three buildings housing the Emperor and the government. The old Burgtor was kept intact along the central axis. The domed Imperial offices and banquet halls culminated the sightline at the far end of the colossal urban square. The residence of Franz Josef (right) and Imperial guest apartments (left), both with exedrae, continued up

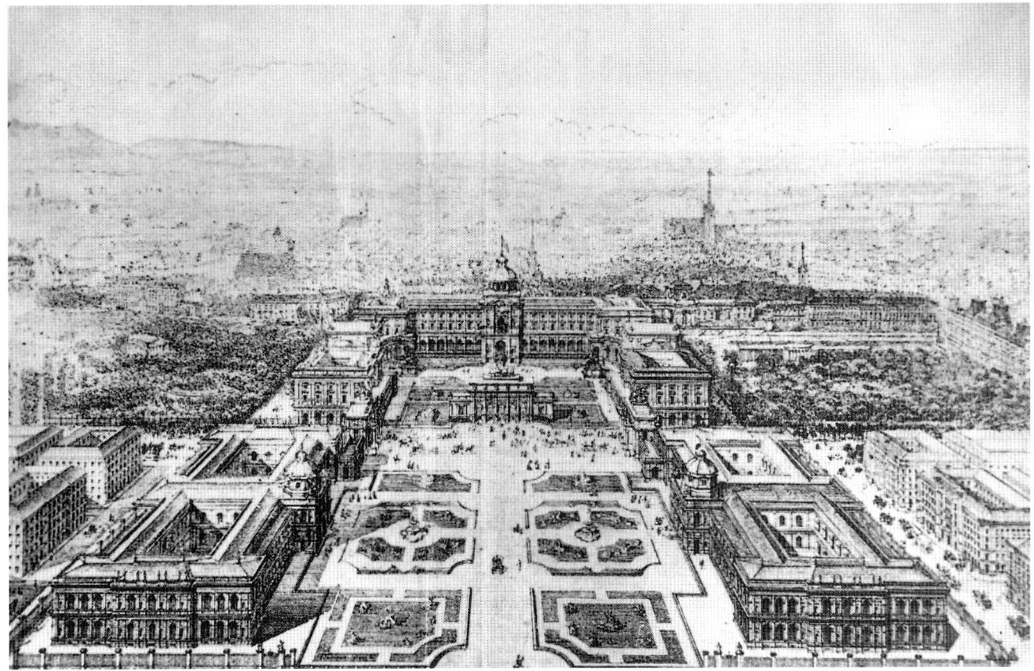

131 Gottfried Semper and Karl von Hasenauer, birdseye perspective of the Imperial forum with two museums in foreground and imperial offices at far end, 1869. Institut für Geschichte und Theorie der Architectur, Semper Archiv, ETH-Zurich.

132 Gottfried Semper and Karl von Hasenauer, plan of the Imperial forum, 1869. Vienna Akademie der Bildenden Künste.

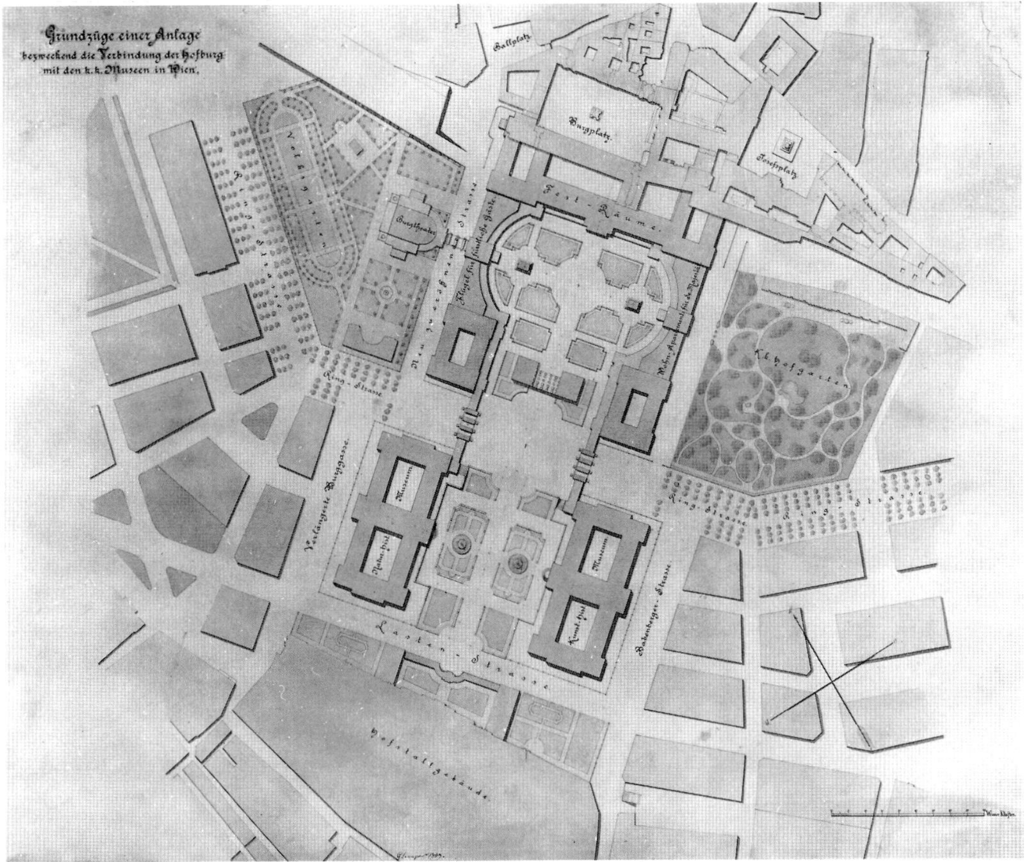

toward the grand boulevard and aligned with the two museums. The overall design and cornice line of the latter were also simplified and made less fussy. The plan, apparently composed at the same time, also shows a theater or playhouse to the northwest. This building may have been a late addition to the ensemble.

Hasenauer returned to Vienna with the plans and on 2 July he presented the drawings to the Emperor, who was suitably impressed with the grandeur of the new proposal. Following several high-level meetings and another audience with Franz Josef, the young architect greeted Semper on 21 July 1869 with the joyful decision in favor of their efforts: "Victoria! Victoria! The victory is ours."[28]

Semper, however, was not so sure. He had received no written confirmation from the court of his commission and, quite naturally from his past experiences, he trusted no one. Hasenauer, however, carried the presentation drawings back to Zurich and together they began to refine the design. They also worked together in drafting a letter on Semper's behalf to Prince Hohenlohe, the secretary to the Emperor. In it Semper expressed gratitude at having heard from Hasenauer the happy news of the acceptance of their design scheme. He then pointed out that such a large design would necessitate his relocation to Vienna and thus the resignation of his chair in Zurich. He asked for a salary commensurate with his present one and the security of a pension matching that available to him in Zurich.[29] It seems remarkable in retrospect that none of these matters had been discussed during his earlier visit to Vienna, but it seemed to be a difficult request to discuss in official circles. The Emperor's absence from the city for the summer holidays had, in any case, brought the governmental bureaucracy to a halt, at least until the end of September. This allowed Semper and Hasenauer plenty of time to follow with concern the continuing opposition being voiced in Vienna (and even within the Emperor's cabinet, it seems) over Semper's "foreign" intrusion into the project.

This was, at least, where matters stood on 21 September 1869, when a tragedy of an altogether different kind quickly unfolded. In Zurich Gottfried Keller entered a tavern at his usual late-afternoon hour and was handed the newspaper that he customarily read at the table. He was entertained at a distance by a local violinist known as "Paganini," who often played to customers for tips. Suddenly Keller, after glancing at the headlines, pounded his fists on the table and muttered some incomprehensible words. At this instant, a witness reported, Semper entered the tavern and took his usual seat opposite Keller, breaking the silence with his habitual inquiry into the state of the world. With a lazy hand he took the paper grievously extended to him by Keller; he suddenly jumped up and stared at the headline before him. Running both hands through his unruly white hair, he sank back into the chair, devastated. Keller tried to console him.

Just then Paganini appeared at the table and, unaware of the drama being played out, began a melancholic tune by Mendelsohn. Semper slowly raised his head and stared at the violinist as if in a dream, before he gave way to wild sobbing and fell back with his head in his hands. After a few minutes he sprang up and rushed out of the door. Keller paid his bill, tipped the violinist, and also left. The astonished onlooker, who had witnessed the scene from an adjoining table, walked over and glanced at the harrowing headline.[30] In a telegram format no doubt lifted straight off the wire service it relayed the tragic news just out of Saxony:

The Hoftheater in Dresden, Gottfried Semper's masterpiece, stands in flames!

The Ringstrasse Monuments

In Dresden, shortly before noon that day, a fire had broken out in a storage room above the main chandelier of the theater, as some workers were repairing the fixture's wiring. Within minutes the entire interior and roof of the building was engulfed in flames; by evening only the pitted and charred arches of the theater's exterior ashlar remained standing. The population of the city mourned the great loss: "No building in the city had become so dear to the hearts of Dresdeners, none had delighted the public with such veneration or was the object of such pride as the glorious Hoftheater, which the great talent of Gottfried Semper had bestowed upon Dresden."[31]

These words of Cornelius Gurlitt, reflecting back on the first theater, were written not in 1869 but in 1878, as Semper's second Hoftheater was preparing to open its doors and artistic splendor to the world. The design and construction of this building did not interrupt Semper's building activities in Vienna; his work on the monuments in both cities had run in tandem. And as in Vienna, the Dresden commission was not secured without some early difficulties.

One of the first acts of the King after the fire was to provide funds for the building of a provisional theater, so that the large theater company and its staff would not be forced into idleness. In the meantime, a building committee was formed to study the problem of the ruined fabric, consisting (among others) of the sculptor Ernst Julius Hähnel, Hermann Nicolai, and the longtime gallery director Julius Schnorr von Carolsfeld. The committee released its report in early December 1869. In view of the extensive destruction of the old building, it recommended not the rebuilding of the original work on its old foundations but the commissioning of an entirely new design.

The report also suggested moving the new building away from the Art Gallery and the Zwinger complex because of the danger of fire spreading among all three buildings, and because of the earlier theater's intrusiveness with regard to the museum's splendid front facade. Semper had originally situated the theater close to the Zwinger with the intention of making a physical connection to the latter – a possibility that was denied him by the Saxon Diet in 1845.

Other functional reasons were also cited by the commission for not restoring the theater to its original design. Among these were the limited wardrobe and changing rooms, the absence of coat rooms for the audience, and the lack of depth of the backstage area. The commission concluded its report with the vague proposal for a limited competition, with Semper competing against "some other architects of great prominence."[32]

Within days Semper published a response, which reacted angrily to the commission's criticisms of his earlier building, but most especially to the suggestion of yet another competition: "The maneuver to draw me into a limited competition is very cunningly devised to appease public opinion and to get rid of me in the best way; for everyone knows very well that I will never participate in any competition."[33]

Semper was certainly correct in his mistrust of the committee and the politics of competitions, but he was at the same time somewhat buoyed by the popular support that had been gathering over these few months for his artistic sovereignty over the theater. This interest in having him design the new work first became apparent at the end of November, when the leading arts society in Dresden presented a petition to the King, which insisted upon his artistic reinstatement. In December the *Deutsche Bauzeitung*, which since its inception in 1867 had become Germany's leading architectural journal, also took up the cause. While not denying the importance of architectural competitions when a new idea was being sought, the paper defended Semper's artistic claim to the design of this "national monument" and it pleaded strongly for "piety toward art and toward the artist."[34] The same feeling was echoed by 1200 Dresden residents who attended a special meeting of the Saxon Diet on the last day of December 1869, all of whom insisted not only upon Semper's command of the project but also on the rebuilding of the work on or near the old site.[35] Talk of Semper being lured to Vienna by Emperor Franz Josef must surely also have galvanized support for him on his former homefront.

Collectively, these events forced both the Saxon Diet and King Johann to overturn the recommendation of the building committee and directly seek out the services of Semper. A package of material was mailed to Zurich in early February 1870; it consisted of a few photographs of the ruins, an invitation for Semper to come to Dresden, and the request for his architectural advice – if he were not, in fact, too preoccupied with work in Vienna.[36] Semper then made his first visit to Dresden in almost twenty-one years, at the end of February, and within a few days he had signed a contract. He asked that his son Manfred be placed in charge of the construction in Dresden; cabinet officials also appointed the state architect Karl Moritz Haenel to superintend the work and its finances. The ruins and rubble of the old theater were soon removed.

Semper sent his first designs back to Dresden at the beginning of May from his office in Zurich; they consisted of two variants in plan and elevation. The first design, more or less modeled on the original theater, retained the rounded auditorium front with the relatively tight restriction on the staircases at the side. The second design proposal, however, expanded these staircases and servant spaces, with the result that the rounded auditorium form in plan became truncated into a segmented arc, similar to Semper's proposals for theaters in Rio de Janeiro and Munich.

The second scheme was favored by officials in Dresden and Semper refined it over the summer. By September he had produced the main features of the final design, which was shown to the city's residents in December 1870. Having received a warm reception, the project moved forward, even though not all of the building's funding had been arranged. The cornerstone for the new theater was laid in the middle of February 1871. The budget for the new edifice was never satisfactorily worked out and the inflationary spiral of the 1870s further drove up the cost of labor and materials, thus plaguing the project fiscally and politically over the next seven years. But many of these problems were quickly forgotten by the residents of the city on the evening of 2 February 1878, when the new and even more glorious Dresden Theater opened with a production of Goethe's *Iphigenia in Tauris*.

Much had happened in the interim, however, as Semper had both moved his place of residence to Vienna and then quit the city. After his letter to Prince Hohenlohe in August 1869, negotiations with the Crown regarding his role in the Vienna museum project had moved ahead very slowly. Semper traveled to Vienna at the end of September and remained there for several weeks, refining the design of the museums in Hasenauer's office. At the Emperor's urging he returned to Vienna around Christmas, but even after speaking directly with high governmental officials no legal contract was forthcoming. By the following spring, when Semper was at work designing the Dresden Theater, talks had more or less come to a standstill.

The reasons for this bureaucratic delay was simply the political and military malaise gripping the ruling powers in Vienna. Since the Prussian defeat of the Austrian army in June 1866, the once mighty Habsburg Empire had been unraveling at the seams. Bismarck seized the Prussian victory as his opportunity to begin the process of assimilating the states of the German confederation in the north, thereby excluding Austria from its traditional political and economic interests there. Austria's price for French neutrality before the war was to cede Venetia to French control (Lombardy had been ceded to France in 1859). But the most serious blow to former Habsburg glory after the war were the concessions that Austria was now forced to make with the Magyars in the east. The Austrian Empire now became supplanted by the Austro-Hungarian Empire, a dual monarchy with autonomy afforded to the eastern half of the coalition in all areas except the army and foreign affairs. But this German-Magyar spit of the government in no way addressed the nationalist aspirations of the Slavs, Bohemians, Poles, Slovenians, Croatians, and the many other ethnic groups under Habsburg control. These problems continued to consume Franz Josef's time and efforts for many decades.

During the years 1870–71 the situation in Germany reached its conclusion. Prussia marched its armies into France to conquer its main competitor for continental supremacy. Semper was following events with keen interest, and even with a certain measure of nationalist pride. When the painter Friedrich Pecht visited him in his Zurich studio in August 1870, the architect was in a jubilant mood over the early reports of German victories around Metz.[37] Among Semper's archival papers are also military maps that were contemporaneously published and sold in bookshops, which showed the changing positions of the German and French lines. Semper's youthful fascination with the military strategies of such heroes as Napoleon I apparently remained a lifetime passion.

It was in this political climate that Semper negotiated with Vienna in 1870. In January of that year he had written to Hohenlohe to confirm in writing the substance of their meeting in December.[38] He gave his assurance that he would place his creative powers at the disposal of Franz Josef, but he also noted that he was having doubts about moving to Vienna. He pointed out that his vacillation, expressed in his December meeting in Vienna, was due in part to his loyalty to a country (Switzerland) that had harbored him for fourteen years, and in part to the grave responsibility for undertaking such a major commission at his advanced age. Nevertheless, an artist, he noted, should courageously strive to accept a call to arms, as it were, and he would not hesitate to carry out his task if he were formally summoned. Cabinet changes within the government and the strong opposition of interior minister Karl Giskra to Semper, however, delayed any official response for months, but this pause had the benefit, at least, of allowing Semper the time to prepare his design for the Dresden Theater.

It was not until July 1870 that Franz Josef decided to move ahead with earlier plans, and then his decision turned out to be less certain than it initially seemed. Hasenauer first informed Semper on 22 July that he had heard from private sources that the project had surmounted "all the chicanery, intrigues, and vicissitudes" of opposing factions and received "the sanction of His Highness."[39] A few days later Semper received the official letter of Hohenlohe, which commissioned both men for the designs of the two museums, the Hofburg Palace extension, and the attached Hofburg or court theater.[40] The last project for a playhouse had been discussed on earlier occasions but until this time only as a possibility. This decision, however, was only tentative, for soon thereafter the theater disappeared from serious consideration – only to resurface in the following year. What unfortunately was not spelled out in the letter of July was any mention of professional fees, the exact professional relationship of Semper and Hasenauer, and whether Semper would move to Vienna. All of these details, which were so vital to the successful and timely progress of this colossal architectural project, were left for a yet-to-be-nominated building committee to decide at some unspecified later date.

Nevertheless, the letter renewed the architects' interest in the design, and Semper traveled to Vienna during October to begin the next stage of design development. Even after he returned to Zurich he continued to work on both the playhouse and the facades for the two museums. Correspondence between Semper and Hasenauer at this time indicates that Semper was still directing the design. This collaboration continued through the fall and into the first four months of 1871.

It was only in May, fully ten months after the commission had been presumably awarded, that the cabinet met and named a building committee. Hohenlohe was given charge of the committee and the architects together were given but one vote – a precarious situation as far as the artistic control of the project went. In the same month Semper also received the letter, with the three seals of the Emperor, which commissioned him officially once again and named the building committee members. The matter of compensation, however, was not raised.[41] To his son, Semper expressed disappointment with the lack of influence he would have over the committee. He also expressed for the first time his reservations at working with Hasenauer, whose attitude toward him, he noted, was changing.[42] Yet he voiced none of these reservations to Hohenlohe in accepting the commission – although he did make known his demands concerning salary, pension, and the need to relocate to Vienna.[43]

Hohenlohe quickly conceded all points and Semper, within weeks, seemed perched to make his move to the Austrian capital (Pl. 133). Privately, however, he again expressed his "grave concerns" about Hasenauer, "for whom the Prince and also the others (as it seems) hold no particular respect, yet who, as I feared, perceives nothing of this but rather considers me as only a symbol, as an annoying concession to public opinion, a drag on his profits, and treats me accordingly whenever possible."[44]

Perhaps it was the sense of this impending conflict with his younger partner that led Semper to write to Hohenlohe that he could not come to Vienna until after Easter 1872, because of his contractual commitment to the Zurich Polytechnikum. The Prince would not hear of it however, and – after years of delay– the Austrian court quickly intervened to stay the opposition of Swiss authorities and to secure Semper's release from his contract. It was with some trepidation, then, that Semper set out for Vienna, his new home, at the end of September 1871: he was now to place his artistic talent in the service of Habsburg glory.

The scope of the work in Vienna was exceedingly demanding: the design of two large museums, a court theater, a governmental administration building, and a new Imperial residence. If executed according to plan, it would have become one of the most costly and elaborate architectural projects of the century. And to add further to Semper's work load, Hasenauer had recently been engaged by state officials as the chief architect for the Austrian World Exhibition of 1873. In short order Hasenauer dumped the entire project into the lap of Semper, who was approaching his sixty-eighth birthday. Their relationship continued to deteriorate over the next several years, as Hasenauer became more and more

133 W. Ungers, *Gottfried Semper*, 1871. From *Zeitschrift für bildende Kunst*, 1879.

preoccupied with his own interests and came into their joint office less and less. When he did appear he often afforded his partner little respect and imperiously made changes to the design without consultation. A major conflict thus became inevitable.

Work on the foundations for the new museums began in the fall of 1871 and construction slowly gathered momentum. By 1874 over 1200 workers (a tenth of them masons) were occupied with construction. The size of the two museums remained huge: each block 168 meters long, 74 meters deep, and 64 meters high, each with two courtyards.

Even though some of the basic features of Hasenauer's original proposals remained intact, the executed design underwent significant changes under the hand of Semper. His criticism of Hasenauer's earlier scheme – for having too many pavilions, projections, and setbacks – resulted in simpler, more compact overall forms, crowned by tall domes with their four satellite lanterns (Pl. 134). Only the central entrance and corner pavilions step forward, but they do so quite forcefully. They have the effect of accentuating and terminating the strong line of the frieze and roof balustrade.

134 Gottfried Semper and Carl von Hasenauer, view of the Art History Museum, Vienna, 1869–91. From *Zeitschrift für Bildende Kunst*, 1892. Courtesy The Getty Center for the History of Art and the Humanities.

The somewhat delicate, second-empire influence apparent in several of Hasenauer's schemes is also strengthened by Semper with a more authentic Renaissance vocabulary. To be properly appreciated, the heavily encrusted facades must be imagined within the context of Semper's idea for a grandiose forum, as captured in the beautifully rendered perspective drawing for the World Exhibition of 1873 by Girard and Rehlender (Pl. 135). Here the connection between the museums and governmental buildings is made spectacular by two equally colossal triumphal arches that straddle the Ringstrasse. The feeling of urban vacuity that surrounds the two museums today is thus quite alien to the teeming, piazza-like character that Semper had originally intended for the forum. Its grandeur, Semper believed, should match that of the forums of Imperial Rome – the leitmotif of the design.

The main features and details of the two museums also underwent much refinement. The large, recessed, third-story clerestories (later lunettes) were eliminated, or rather, changed into skylights that were screened from below. In their place is also a row of small rectangular clerestory windows tucked under the architrave. The rhythm of these windows with the arched openings on the main story is mirrored by their counterparts in the rusticated socle below, where the squared windows provide light for the basement areas. Although the upper or main story follows for the most part the formal lead of the Dresden Gallery, its much larger surface area is even more compacted with large-scale decorative reliefs and celebrational attributes.

The masonry rustication of the lower stories, by contrast, is treated with less edging and projection of the individual blocks than some of Semper's earlier works. The narrow, recessed bands surrounding each block is shallower than those of the Dresden Gallery, for instance, and it gives way at the mortar line to a seemingly razor-thin joint. The chiseling of the face of each block is more regular and non-directional in its hammering; from a distance its fine grain or texture appears almost carpet-like in its density. The pilasters that Semper adds to the lower stories accentuate the great height of the facade. This sense of verticality is strengthened by the end pavilions, which are especially successful with their

135 Gottfried Semper and Carl von Hasenauer, Imperial forum. Colored rendering by Girard and Rehlender for the World Exhibition of 1873. The Natural History Museum (with dome) in immediate foreground. Institute für Denkmalpflege, Dresden.

triumphal-arch motifs above. The finishing glory of both museums is, however, the theatrical prop of each entrance pavilion. The tripartite openings, framed on both sides by the deep projecting porches of double columns, festooned upper frieze, and triumphal wreath-bearing angels compose one of the most luxurious moments in all of Semper's architectural oeuvre (Pl. 136). And this takes no account of the abundance of other figurative pieces in the spandrels, the ornate lanterns, and the colorful dome surmounted (on the art museum) by Pallas Athene.

This sense of elation is by no means diminished by the spatial drama of entering the two buildings. The Art History Museum, with its ornate and polychrome splendor, is particularly luxurious in its ascension. Visitors arrive in the first vestibule under a low circular canopy, at the apex of which is an oculus sufficiently large to open a vista to the expanse of domed space high above. The staircase leading to the main level, situated along the central axis of the building, is one of the most monumental creations of the nineteenth

136 Gottfried Semper and Carl von Hasenauer, Art History Museum, Vienna, 1896–91. Entrance pavilion. Courtesy Institut für Geschichte und Theorie der Architektur, Semper Archiv, ETH-Zurich.

137 Gottfried Semper and Carl von Hasenauer, Art History Museum, Vienna, 1869–91. Stairhall. From *Zeitschrift für Bildende Kunst*, 1892. Courtesy The Getty Center for the History of Art and the Humanities.

century (Pl. 137). A half level up the central flight is a glorious stairhall (with a Canova sculpture of Theseus on the axis of the landing, black marble columns above), returning at both sides to the second level. Klaus Eggert attributes the stair motif to Luigi Vanvitelli's design for the Royal Palace at Caserta (1751–74).[45] The upper vestibule or polygonal reception room satisfactorily completes the spatial progression; it is a two-story room with a stupendous lantern and dome above. The abundance of variegated marbles on every surface (selected by Hasenauer) informs the spectator that this is no mere temple to art but rather a Habsburg cathedral erected in honor of its own memory.

As with so many of his monumental projects, however, it is Semper's iconography that becomes the red thread holding together his artistic conception. On no other buildings did he have as much control over this aspect of the design, but the result, if anything, suffers from its very complexity. He finished the selection of the figurative themes in the spring of 1874 and passed his written proposal on to the building committee, where it eventually received Franz Josef's personal approval. The publication of this program by his son in 1892 allows us a very important insight into the theatricality of his architectural thinking: in this case the connection of his practice to his theory.[46]

He first of all conceived this building's figurative works as the visual representation of his style theory. The definition of style that he had so recently promulgated in his Zurich lecture of 1869 is repeated in the preface to the written program: style is "the correspondence of a work of art with the history of its becoming."[47] And just as his tripartite style theory deals with the material (internal), social-cultural (external) and ideal (the artistic interpretation of the idea) factors of style, so the iconographic conception of the museum is now divided into its "material" (ground story), "cultural-historical" (main story), and "personal" (roof statuary) realms. In short the pictorial and sculptural themes form one evolutionary chronology in a vertical direction – arising out of the materialist and formative influences of certain technical arts and achieving their cultural and historical unfolding on the main story, then subsequently glorified at the apex by art's transformation under the guise of individual artistic genius.

Thus the motifs proposed for the ground story are objects drawn from the various technical arts: vases, ornaments, weapons, tools, and instruments. As Semper noted, it should contain the treasury of old and new artistic techniques, it should inform the viewer of the role played by technology in influencing the course of art. By contrast, the spaces of the main story, behind which are housed the museum's main collections, are to be reserved for high art. Its themes, the program says, should be arranged to demonstrate not only the social, political, and religious conditions under which the art of each epoch and culture took form but also the essential civilizing power of art. The third realm of the roof should be populated by those individuals who opened significant new paths for art – not only artists but also the poets and scientists who shaped artistic development. Here, as in the lower two realms, Semper proposed that the program unfold through a series of dualities. He did this not by juxtaposing the classical and post-classical periods of art; rather, he sought to articulate what he deemed to be the classical and romantic tendencies within each era. These might be represented by such formal dualities as Doric versus Ionic art, or through such diverse artistic personalities as a Raphael or a Michelangelo (as in Dresden), a Mozart or a Beethoven.

To complement this vertical unfolding of his style theory, Semper's program also called for a horizontal division of the thematic content into historical epochs, arranged by facades. Thus the rear facade of the museum on Babenbergerstrasse is given over to antique art; the south-west side facade on Lastenstrasse to Byzantine, Romanesque, and Gothic art. The main or entrance facade on Maria Teresa Platz features Renaissance art, whereas the side of the museum facing the Hofburg and the newly created Ringstrasse is reserved for modern art. It would take too long to chronicle the dozens of works proposed for each side, but an indication of Semper's thinking process can be seen by examining a few of the pieces proposed for the classical side.

The principal works of the lower story are the three geniuses representing the forces and the materials found in nature; figurative themes in the lower frieze of this story depicts the inventors of the six technical arts: Dibutades (pottery wheel), Rhoecus (casting), Clarchus (hollow metal and embossing), Glaucus (forging and welding), Daedalus (wood construction and carpentry), and Melos (marble sculpture). Sub-themes are also portrayed on the keystones to the openings (Pl. 138). The two sitting figures between the double columns in the central pavilion represent architecture (Pl. 139) and industrial art. Above, on the main story, are paired the figures of Minyas and Polycrates (pavilion toward the Ringstrasse), Pisistratus and Pericles (central pavilion), Alexander and Augustus (south pavilion). These figures were described by Semper as representatives of the social, political, and individual influences on art. A series of medallions in the spandrels of the main story also portrays the victory of art and science over savageness and barbarity. These include such

138 and 139 Gottfried Semper and Carl von Hasenauer, Art History Museum, Vienna, 1869–91. Keystone detail and figure of Architecture.

incidents as Perseus slaying Medusa, Hercules killing Hydra, and Theseus destroying the minotaur. The highest realm of the roof is inhabited by the standing dualities of Theodorus and Bularchus, Canachus and Polynotus, Phidias and Polycritus, and Pythagoras and Aristotle.

The crowning element of the whole museum is the dome, upon which stands the proud figure of Pallas Athene peering out over the city. She also ennobles the city with her stately presence. In the four adjacent tabernacles surrounding the drum of the dome are seated figures depicting the four attributes essential to artistic mastery: talent, strength of will, passion, and self-restraint. Below the front two tabernacles stand the four wreath-bearing angels that later (in 1902) became such important artistic emblems for Otto Wagner in his design for the Post Office Savings Bank.

Nearly all of Semper's suggestions were accepted and implemented. The Vienna Art Museum is one of the few institutions in the world where one literally needs a program to read the contents of the building's exterior. If this type of schematism appears today perhaps as somewhat "bookish" to modern sensitivities, it at least underscores the critical gulf that divides our two eras and their respective artistic conceptions. An architect of Semper's stature could expend so much effort on what would be regarded today as the decorative accessories of a building only because this means of articulation and eloquence was so central to his overall approach. Whatever its relative success or failing, Semper's Vienna museums should be seen as a continuation, indeed as the culmination, of the cultural and historical scheme that Schinkel had imposed on the front facade of his Berlin museum nearly a half-century earlier. It may very well have been the last offspring of this glorious lineage.

Various of the interior motifs of the museum were also given some attention, although Semper himself was forced to resign from the project before working out his scheme. Works here are better known for their artists than for their iconographic structure. The most highly regarded among the works of the entrance are the Canova sculpture of Theseus on the main stair landing, the stairhall ceiling lunettes by Hans Markart, and the spandrel frescoes on the back wall by the young Klimt brothers – all of which gathered rave reviews when the museum finally opened on 17 October 1891.

The Natural History Museum, opposite the temple to art, follows suit in its iconographic complexity. The leitmotif here for Semper was Alexander Humboldt's comment that the proper methodology for the natural sciences lay in the quest to gain a concept of unity from the vast multiplicity of worldly appearances.[48] The sculptor Hähnel, Semper's friend in Dresden, prepared the first program for the building, but Semper made some changes to downplay the mythological content. Atop the dome stands Helios, the sun god; surrounding him in the four tabernacles are Gaea (earth), Hephaestus (fire), Urania (air), and Poseidon (water). The elevation again unfolds in a tripartite division, representing ways of making scientific discoveries. These realms are emblems related to the independent striving for knowledge of natural laws or contemplative reflection, world events that suddenly extend the horizon of observation, and the invention of technological media that allow one to examine phenomena both up-close and afar. The four sides of the building also portray different scientific epochs. The two prominent figures of modern science are, as might be expected, Georg Cuvier and Alexander von Humboldt.

The two museums were intended to be part of the much larger ensemble of the Hofburg Forum, yet they were the only two components actually started in Semper's lifetime. Only in 1879, the year of his death, did Franz Josef give the go-ahead for construction of his palace on the south-east wing of the forum, continuing the line of the art museum. This delay eventually proved extremely costly in more ways than one. Hasenauer's plans were approved in 1881 but work on the excavations did not start until 1885. A severe white stone was chosen for the exterior walls, but this was only the first of a series of catastrophic mishaps that plagued the building for many years. Cost overruns and slow construction hampered progress for nearly a decade. When Hasenauer died suddenly in 1894, the exterior walls (minus the roof) were in place but little work had been done on the interior. A series of governmental architects succeeded in bringing the project to a standstill by the mid-1890s, and more talented architects, such as Friedrich Ohmann and Ludwig Baumann, were unable to bring the project to a successful conclusion in the following decades. Work on the interiors continued through World War I and until some years after the Habsburg monarchy itself, which ended in 1917 with the death of Franz Josef. It seems that Semper's divine conceit of a grand Imperial forum had in some manner aroused the fury of the gods. On the more mundane level, the project all but bankrupted the Empire itself.

The two museums were not, however, the only projects with which Semper was involved during his Vienna years, and from the very beginning of his association with the city various possibilities presented themselves. Late in 1869 – that is, before matters regarding the museums were settled and while the second Dresden Theater was being discussed – Semper participated in a limited competition in Vienna for a new stock exchange, or Börse, against the Viennese architects Theophil Hansen, Carl Tietz, and Anton Baumgartner. The Palladian design for the exterior (in plan vaguely recalling Semper's proposal for Hamburg of many years earlier) was rejected and faulted by the jury for its ventilation, structure, and bad proportions.[49] Around the time work on the museums was starting up, Semper teamed up with Hasenauer on two other projects: an apartment complex on Löwelstrasse and a warehouse for the Hofburg theater's scenery, both designed in 1872. The former, with its great terrace and arcade below, was not built, but the theater depot was erected after several years of delay. This makeshift Florentine palazzo, however, does not stand high among Semper's completed works.

One non-Viennese project of importance during this period, was the design for a new theater in Darmstadt, on which Semper worked briefly in 1872–73. The old theater of Georg Moller had been destroyed by fire on 24 October 1871, and after some discussion of re-creating the old design the King of Hesse-Darmstadt asked Semper to prepare a new one, taking into account the existing foundations. The project, with its squared front facade, was worked out for the most part by Manfred, and notwithstanding its rectangular appearance it borrowed much from the first Dresden Hoftheater. The design did not please Darmstadt officials, however, and a new theater was rebuilt in 1875–79 by the architect Horst, on a plan closer to the original design by Moller.

The Hofburg Theater in Vienna is the other major work with which Semper's name is still associated. Essentially a playhouse presented to the city by the crown, the Hofburg Theater is perhaps the happiest architectural production of the Ringstrasse era from the point of view of its scale, animation, and situation. It first appeared on the forum plan in the spring of 1869 as an appendage to the guest wing of the Crown. Its original outline resembled that of the first Dresden Theater, but in another plan of the forum, presented by Hasenauer and Semper later that year, the theater took more definitive shape as a scaled–down version of the Munich Festspielhaus. For the next year or so the matter of a playhouse was put on hold, as the ministry apparently was considering locating it in the old opera house.

Early in 1871 the question of the new theater and its location again came under consideration. Since the guest wing of the Hofburg Palace, to which it was earlier attached, was projected only in the distant future, it was decided to give the theater an independent form and a site was considered at the west end of the Volksgarten, also along the Ringstrasse. When Semper moved to Vienna in the fall of 1871, he and Hasenauer first focused their attention almost exclusively on the design of the theater. In one proposal it was situated parallel to the Ringstrasse, with one of its long sides fronting the boulevard (Pl. 140). The overall form was rectangular – quite dissimilar to any of Semper's other theater designs. One month later a revised design was presented, consisting of an H-shaped plan (Pl. 141). The axis of the auditorium had been shifted perpendicular to the street and carriage drop-off ramps were placed at the two sides, one for the Emperor and one for the public.

Finally, in December 1871, a third scheme was presented, which drew quite specifically upon Semper's theater designs for Munich and Dresden. The main foyer followed the segmented form of the auditorium and contained the familiar exedra at the center (Pl. 142). As in Munich, the staircases were extended out from the auditorium at right angles, thereby enhancing their interior grandeur and exterior monumental form. The theater was still conceived at a much reduced scale, however.

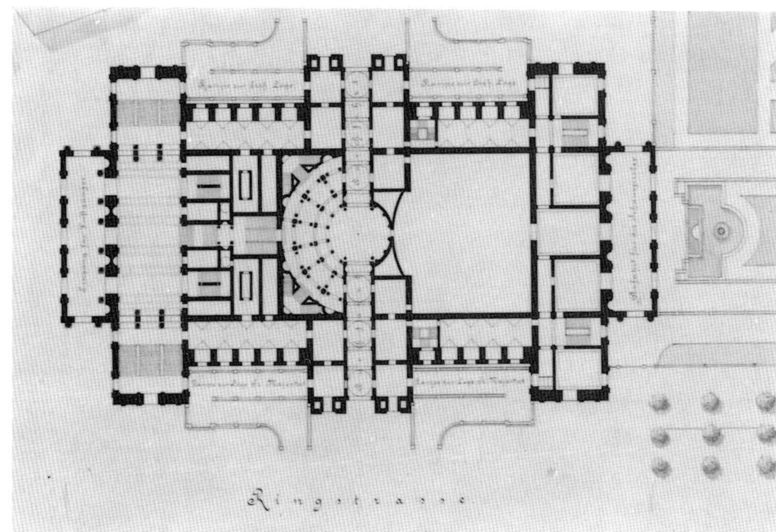

140 Gottfried Semper and Carl von Hasenauer, Hofburg Theater, Vienna, 1871–88. Preliminary design. Vienna Akademie der Bildenden Künste.

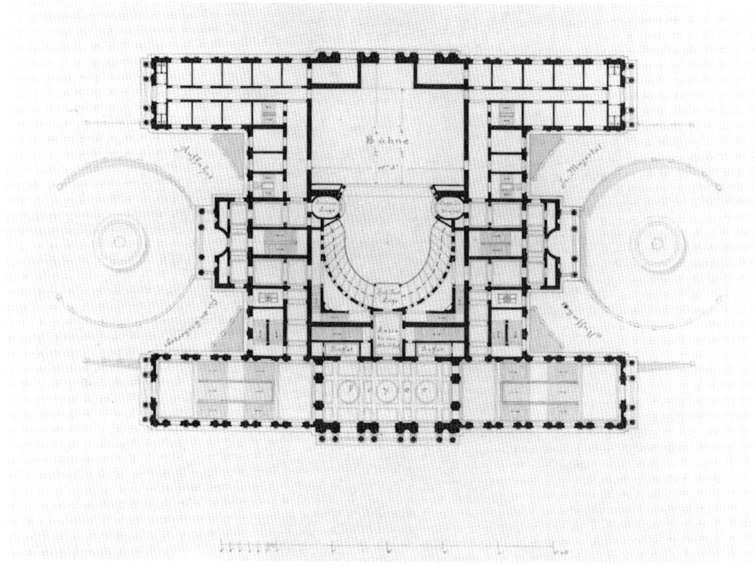

141 Gottfried Semper and Carl von Hasenauer, Hofburg Theater, Vienna, 1871–88. Preliminary design. Vienna Akademie der Bildenden Künste.

Franz Josef and his cabinet considered the schemes in the winter and spring of 1872. Differences between Semper and Hasenauer began to appear. Hasenauer preferred the first scheme presented to the building committee in the previous year, the one whose axis was parallel with the street; Semper's preference was for the third scheme. Both the cabinet officials and Franz Josef eventually decided in favor of Semper's choice and the program was finalized. The need for working drawings for the two museums apparently pushed the theater project aside for many months and it was not until the summer of 1873 that further refinements to the design could be seen. The central exedra (at Hasenauer's instigation) was replaced by a flattened projection of three bays, above which was placed a giant frieze (Pl. 143). All other elements of the theater conformed essentially to Semper's design. The presentation drawings even showed that many of the decorative details, such as the design of the auditorium ceiling, had already been worked out.

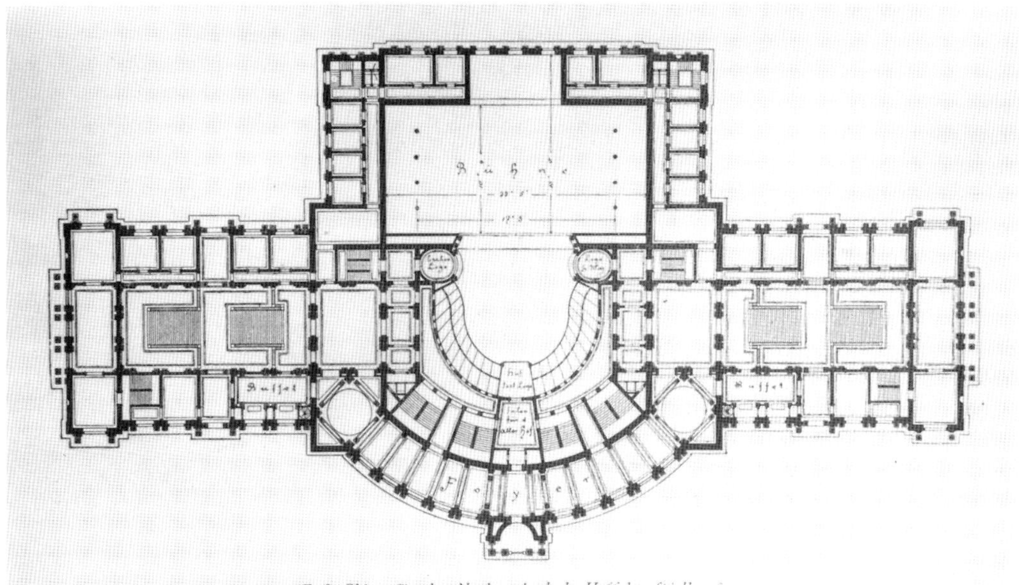

142 Gottfried Semper and Carl von Hasenauer, Hofburg Theater, Vienna, 1871–88. Final plan. Institut für Geschichte und Theorie der Architectur, Semper Archiv, ETH-Zurich.

143 Gottfried Semper and Carl von Hasenauer, Hofburg Theater, Vienna, 1871–88. Institut für Geschichte und Theorie der Architectur, Semper Archiv, ETH-Zurich.

The major change on the exterior with respect to Semper's other theaters was the use of a giant Corinthian pilaster order on the segmental front facade of the theater, behind which was recessed the two-story vestibule and foyer. This decision imposed a grand unity on the middle portion of the facade, even though it gave way at the side to the two-story stairhalls. The tripartite composition of the foyer, auditorium, and stagehouse was also reduced to two parts in this design. The rounded copper roof of the auditorium (reminiscent of the Paris Opera) was a later change made by Hasenauer, but it nevertheless fits in well with the composition. Even the flattened giant frieze at the center of the front facade (crowned, at Hasenauer's instigation, by a seated Apollo and two muses) is a very dignified solution. The story of Dionysus and Ariadne assumes a subservient role within the frieze.

The theater, particularly when aglow with foyer lighting for the evening performances, virtually comes alive to the passing pedestrian – both along the grand boulevard and in the park across the way. It is exceedingly well scaled to its location, even though it is much harmed in its broader context by its formal juxtaposition to Hansen's Greek parliament building and to Friedrich Schmidt's Venetian Gothic Rathaus. The stylistic, almost comic disjunction of these three buildings, in fact, seriously undermines the effectiveness of all of them and for many years they have collectively epitomized the architectural futility of the so-called Ringstrasse era. If it had been within a more sympathetic architectural context, I suspect the theater would have had a better reception by historians.

Construction of the Hofburg Theater began late in 1874 – at the point at which the working relationship of Semper and Hasenauer was on the brink of collapse. Up until this time Semper's life in Vienna had been relatively happy. The one tragic event of his three years in the city was the death of his daughter Johanna Elisabeth (born 1836), who passed away from an illness in June 1872. His other children, however, were becoming quite successful. Manfred (born 1838) was working under his father's direction as the architect in charge of building the new Hoftheater in Dresden. Conrad (born 1841) was a businessman who later emigrated to Philadelphia. Anna Catharina (born 1843) was also close to her father. She married the history professor Theodor Sickel and lived in Vienna. Hans Semper (born 1845) also soon joined the academic community as a professor of art history in Innsbruck. Gottfried's youngest son Emmanuel (born 1848) had been trained as a sculptor and was working on various pieces for the Dresden Hoftheater. He, too, later emigrated to the United States.

In November 1873 Semper, now having persistent health problems brought on by his worsening asthma, celebrated his seventieth birthday. Congratulatory letters, telegrams (twenty-six have survived), and notes streamed into the city from princes, artistic luminaries, and professional organizations across Europe. It was a fitting testimony to his belated but still growing fame. With German unity now a reality his life – including many years of professional achievement sacrificed by his political exile – now took on a heroic light: that of a fearless fighter for democracy who had taken on the old regime and who had still somehow managed to survive. His new monuments under construction were of course adding to this aura. After his seventieth birthday, laudatory articles on his life's work began to appear across the German-speaking countries: one featured his bust placed on a pedestal with his head crowned by an angel holding a laurel leaf.[50]

The chilly relationship with his Viennese colleague, however, soon took a turn for the worse, as the world exhibition closed and Hasenauer, after being occupied for almost three years on the event, reclaimed the architectural partnership. He returned to the office with a very different and much harsher attitude toward the aging master; earlier lack of respect now gave way to outright abuse. The fact that Semper and Hasenauer in the spring of 1874 favored two entirely different schemes for the theater underscores their inability to work together any longer, but the building committee took no action to alleviate this problem.

By the beginning of 1875 face-to-face dialogue between the two men ceased altogether. This breakdown is first seen in a letter from Semper to Hasenauer, in which the older architect indicated the difficulty of dispersing funds on the projects for which they were both legally responsible, and he then suggested that all further communication be in writing. The tone was tense and terse: "Yet should you, contrary to my expectations, not concur with my understanding and formulation of your demands, understand these demands differently, or even wish to place on me even more extensive demands, I ask you, in order to avoid any further unpleasant oral discussions, to communicate likewise in writing and state the reasons for your demands in this regard."[51]

The situation, however, only worsened. Manfred blamed the subsequent decline in his father's health on the stress and increased workload placed on him during this conflict. In May 1875, Semper asked both Manfred and his son-in-law Dr. Sickel to mediate the dispute. But their meeting with Hasenauer proved fruitless and in fact only exacerbated the problem. The situation came to a head in the fall of 1875 when Hasenauer, in speaking to these intermediaries, demanded Semper's resignation from the partnership and – according to Manfred – even made threats of violence against the father, son, and Dr. Sickel. To the building commission, Hasenauer used a different ploy – threatening his own resignation if Semper were not removed as his partner.

The commission still seemed unable or unwilling to understand the seriousness of the breach, and Semper had no choice but to seek legal counsel. A letter to Hasenauer from Semper's attorney Dr. Haerdtl, dated 23 December 1875, related a sad account of outrageous behavior on Hasenauer's part, and went on to insist that all communication cease except in writing, and this time through Semper's attorney. Against Hasenauer's threat of physical violence, Semper countered with the threat of a lawsuit.

The attorney now also represented Semper's interests in the meetings with the building commission, but given Semper's age there was only one viable resolution. In the spring of 1876 the commission met and, at Semper's urging, released the seventy-two year old architect from his contract for the work, although it still insisted on retaining him as a building commission member and artistic advisor. Semper now lost control of the detailing of the Hofburg Theater, and thus had little to do with the interior decoration. And Hasenauer wasted no time in making some near fatal changes to the design. He altered the configuration of the auditorium and the loges, which had disastrous consequences on the room's acoustics. A major reconstruction of the auditorium was thus made necessary some years later to correct these problems.

It was in the summer of 1875 that Semper and Wagner also had their reconciliation in Vienna. The great deterioration in Semper's physical appearance that Cosima noted was due much more to his personal difficulties and declining health than (as she attributed them) to the earlier Munich situation.[52] Her report of Semper's poverty (his inability to afford a carriage to take him to the theater) was again somewhat exaggerated. Semper, unlike Wagner, had never been richly rewarded for his endeavors, but he had managed to put together sufficient funds for a dignified retirement. His son in Dresden was investing money for him and Semper was able to augment his salary with the accrued interest. He had always been rather frugal in his outward appearances and this moderation no doubt appeared to Richard and Cosima as poverty. Semper and Wagner met at Hans Markart's atelier in the spring of 1875 and on two other occasions that year. In 1876, at Wagner's invitation, Semper made the trek to Bayreuth to witness the opening of festivities there.

The Semper-Hasenauer conflict has an interesting conclusion that adds nothing positive to Hasenauer's historical reputation. After the Viennese architect had ousted his older partner and taken over the office in the spring of 1876, his name – quite naturally – came to be associated more and more with the three buildings under construction, so much so that by the start of the 1880s he was often referred to in Viennese circles as their sole author. One commentator taking issue with this claim asked somewhat sarcastically in 1880: "Does anyone still remember Gottfried Semper"?[53] His question was seemingly raised in vain.

In 1884, on the occasion of Hasenauer's appointment to the chair at the Vienna Academy of Fine Arts, the *Neue Freie Presse* published a laudatory biography in which the author (Em. Ranzoni) insisted that Semper had very little to do with the design of the two museums and theater and that he was credited with the design earlier only because of his famous name. He further insisted that it had been Hasenauer who had first come up with the idea of the Hofburg Forum.[54] This article precipitated a series of responses in various German periodicals, nearly all of which refuted these claims. Even the Berlin journal *Deutsche Bauzeitung* published a retort, written by Semper's former students Arnold Cattani, Albert Müller, and Hans Pestalozzi, which pointed out the significant fact that nearly all of the design work for the museums was carried out in Zurich.[55] But these accounts did little to change the perception of Hasenauer in Austria, as the latter began to insist more and more on his authorship of the original designs. It took, in fact, a serious miscalculation on his part to straighten out the historical record and reveal the shortcomings of his character.

In December 1889, shortly after the opening of the Natural History Museum, Hasenauer sent a letter to a close friend that outlined his version of the earlier events. The letter did not surface until just after Hasenauer's death in 1894, when parts of it were published in the Vienna journal *Fremden-Blatt*.[56] The letter went to extreme lengths in its attempted distortion of the facts. After complaining that many people still considered him no more than a tool in Semper's design of the museums and theater, Hasenauer argued that he had now endured the insults in silence long enough. He only attempted to have Semper made a juror in 1868, he imagined, because of the "agitation" against his competition scheme. During his first trip to Vienna, he wrote, Semper had asked him in private if he could be made a partner. Semper indicated at this time that he was too old and could not help with the design, and in addition was having problems with Zurich colleagues. But at least he could give advice. Out of blind trust and a sense of pity, Hasenauer said, he accepted the request from the old master. He soon found out that Semper only wanted to come to Vienna because he was nearing retirement and had no pension. Once in Vienna, Semper was of no help in the design process because he was consistently in bad health. Due to his concern for Semper's medical condition, Hasenauer asked him – out of the depth of his infinite kindness – to seek out a warmer climate, such as Italy, in order to prolong his life. Hasenauer promised, in effect, to cover for him in Vienna. He concluded: "He [Semper] was therefore nominally my partner for four years and two months, while I have since 1866, for twenty-four years, been ceaselessly engaged with these works."[57]

This fanciful and self-serving letter soon prompted a devastating rebuttal. In 1894 Manfred Semper scrupulously pieced together the historical details of their relationship – mainly through the publication of Hasenauer's own letters to Semper. The pamphlet quickly put an end to the discussion of Hasenauer's supposed authorship, even among his most steadfast supporters in Austria. His artistic reputation, surely of considerable merit, has yet to overcome the darker side of his character.

Semper and the Birth of Tragedy

Although it is easy to be swept away by the excitement and praise found in contemporary accounts of Semper's second Dresden Hoftheater, the work is still seen today as one of his greatest achievements, the second great masterpiece of his career (Pl. 144). It is, like its earlier example on nearly the same site, a complex work in its design and formal intentions, but it also drew upon a lifetime of involvement with the theater and of other theoretical interests, and on Semper's experience of forming a new type of theater in Munich. When it opened in 1878, two years after the inauguration of the Festival Theater in Bayreuth, it eclipsed with ease its spiritual counterpart to the southwest. In Europe, it was rivaled in its grandeur only by the much more costly Paris Opera, which first opened its doors in 1875.

Few German architectural works of this era, in fact, received more widespread approbation. The usually temperate *Deutsche Bauzeitung*, poured forth pages of laudatory comments in its first review, characterizing the building as an "artistic confession of faith" by Semper, one that successfully crowned his "glorious career" and placed him behind only Schinkel in terms of his profound and enduring influence. The author of the article, the journal's editor K. E. O. Fritsch, was especially impressed with the Dresden Theater's "truth of the building organism," that is, by the functionality and compositional unity of its hierarchical grouping of masses.[58]

Semper's biographer Constantin Lipsius, who himself rose within a few years to become Dresden's leading architect, was also overwhelmed by its "characteristic expression," as well as by the grandeur of its setting. Lipsius felt that this theater towered over Semper's other works because of its functional logic, its "nobility and boldness," and the way in which Semper "truthfully expressed the innermost nature of the whole edifice on its exterior and invested it with a physiognomy of articulate clarity and triumphant beauty."[59]

The most considerate analysis of the new work, however, was Cornelius Gurlitt's forty-four page pamphlet, published on the occasion of the theater's opening. Gurlitt, who became one of Germany's best known critics and exponents of "modern art" in the last years of the century, tried to bring a critical detachment to his analysis, but his disinterestedness on occasion simply collapses under his emotional reaction to this stately "temple of art." Semper, he reasoned, had traversed the sixteenth century with his first theater: with this new work, he advanced from the modest flowering of the early Renaissance style to the more powerful energies of the high Renaissance. Everything in his new design had now become "more conscious, prouder, and more expressive," in both its overall mass and detailing.[60]

Gurlitt also praised the compositional logic and unity of the new work: the graduated ensemble of auditorium, stagehouse, staircases, dressing rooms, practice halls, and carriage porches. He was moved by the "overpowering strength" of its curved front and crowning exedra, "which with a loud voice announces that here is a house that gladly opens itself to friendly communion."[61] The rusticated pilasters of the lower stories, together with the rich detailing of the paired Corinthian half-columns and arched windows of the upper story, combine to produce the "rare grandeur" and "majestic effect" of its exterior appearance. At the same time, the work distinguishes itself from the almost contemporary opera houses in Paris and Vienna: "One clearly recognizes as a basic idea an expansion [of effects] executed with logic and wise moderation – from noble simplicity to a luxurious unfolding of all decorative means," says Gurlitt, "but there also lies in the final intensification of splendor a certain seriousness of emotion that very well suits our conception of a theater."[62]

The interior staircases, foyers, and auditorium also displayed, Gurlitt felt, that rare "festive beauty" and "intensified emotion" that elevates architecture over music as the art that speaks most directly to the human heart. In this respect, Semper's new masterpiece formed a worthy companion to the nearby efforts of Pöppelmann, Chiaveri, and Schinkel: "Only such a gifted nature could have so happily fallen in line with their creations, only an artist such as Semper, with such a broad knowledge of style, could blend in with such diverse works and form such a happy and harmonious accord . . . He knew how to apply the achievements of modern art theory practically."[63]

What seems to have affected Gurlitt and so many others of his generation was the very theatricality of this artistic ensemble. The setting of the new work is indeed spectacular. Pushed back from its earlier site, the theater opens up the full facade and decorative splendor of the gallery, against whose height and length it easily holds its own. At the same time the theater's plasticity and enlarged masses form a more worthy counterpoint to the tall Baroque church of Chiaveri opposite, and to the tower of the German-Renaissance royal palace. The small Neoclassical guardhouse of Schinkel protrudes into the square as a minor note, atonal by virtue of its angular axis. Through the triumphal arch of the museum one still gains access to the grand courtyard of the Zwinger. At the other end of this vast architectural field (although screened in 1878 by a row of smaller houses) is the river Elbe.

Yet what truly sets off the building as a distinguished architectural monument – its wonderful situation notwithstanding – is the very skillful handling of the masses. The tall gabled stagehouse, crowned with Hellenic lyres and griffins, was criticized by some initially for the plainness of its walls, but this severity is what anchors the theater compositionally and at the same time complements its graduated richness. In front, the stagehouse descends into the tall third story of the auditorium, which in turn descends into the double stories of the vestibules and foyer; the rear of the stagehouse is buttressed by a three story backstage and practice wing. To the sides the theater steps down again to the one-story carriage porches (originally conceived as two stories), which form the lowest plastic masses. From the center of the theater square, however, the stagehouse is shielded by the lower masses and the composition as a whole is dominated by the colossal exedra with its crowning quadriga. This motif, first used on the theater designs for Rio de Janeiro and Munich as a royal emblem, may – as Gurlitt suggested – have had its origin in Bramante's Vatican Belvedere, but it is treated here with a polychrome splendor (mosaics,

144 Gottfried Semper, second Hoftheater, Dresden, 1870–78. Institut für Geschichte und Theorie der Architectur, Semper Archiv, ETH-Zurich.

marbles in giallo antico, rosso antico) rarely seen in Renaissance exteriors. It is for Semper more Roman than Renaissance in its inspiration.

The detailing of the stonework, especially the rustication, also follows the very lithic and plastic qualities of his later works. The rounded wall of the front is punctured at the ground floor by the series of archways and doors, which allows pedestrian access into the building (Pl. 145). The rustication is especially bold, even violent in its chisel work, and the blocks are projected out far from the smooth face of their edging. On the double pilasters the texture presents the appearance of a dressing – or rather, of a taut dress that is too small and therefore exposes the bare, smooth stone at the neck and ankles. Leftover parts of this coarse fabric even appear to be inserted into otherwise empty areas, such as in the recessions between the keystones and pilasters. It is accentuated at the keystones of the archways by the equally exaggerated theatrical masks, carved by Semper's son Emmanuel. The second story of the foyer succeeds to a more delicate realm, but even here the blocks are scored by their joints. The main motif, aside from the window arcade and double Corinthian order, is the frieze filled with oversized festoons (vivid from below), masks, sacrificial implements, and other festive symbols. The theater is also liberally endowed with individual plastic works, some of which were salvaged from the earlier building.

In its coherent and concise plan, the theater also brings together aspects of the designs for Rio de Janeiro and Munich with the historic features of the first Hoftheater (Pl. 146). Both the configuration and dimensions of the new auditorium are nearly the same as the

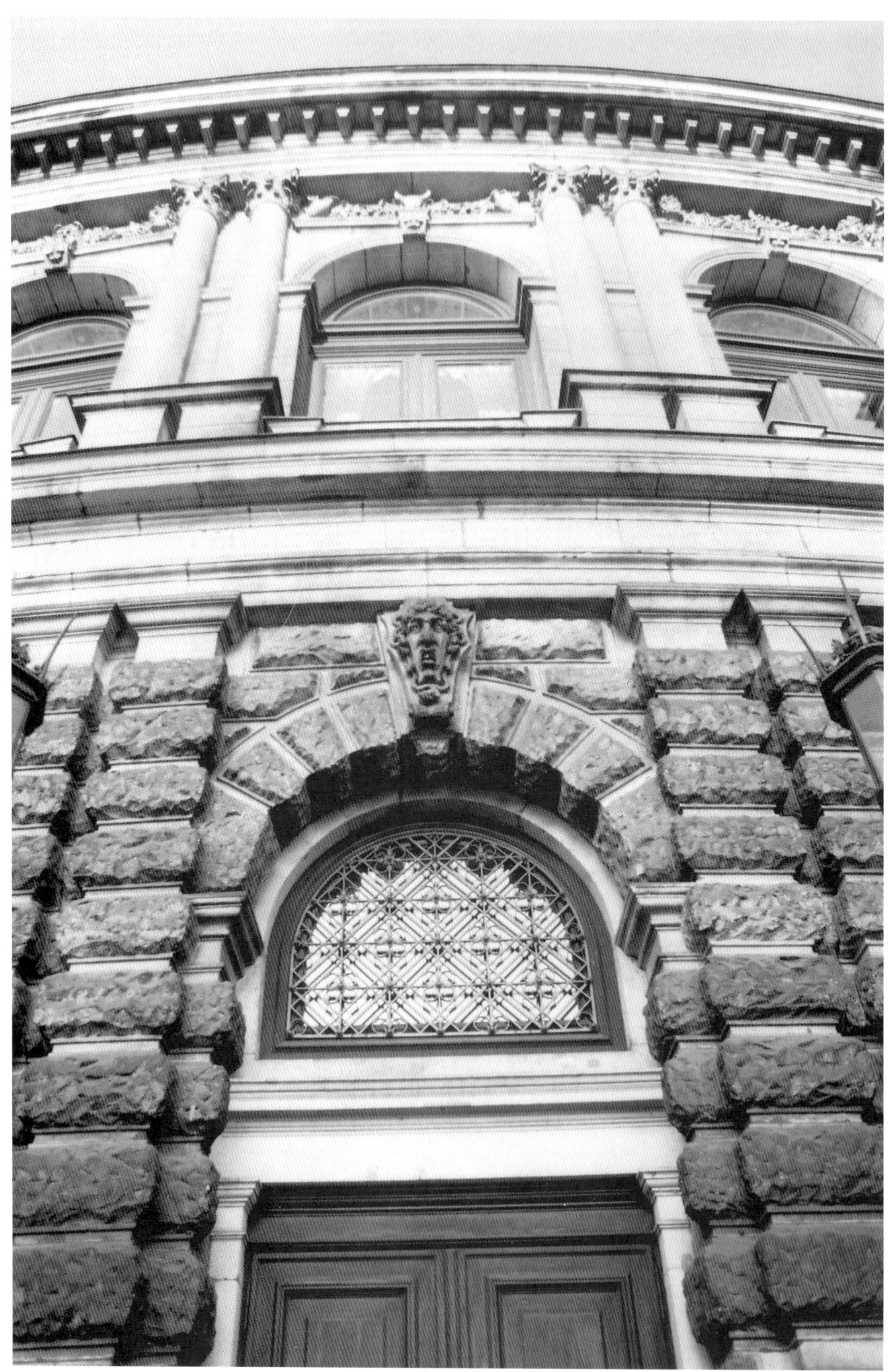

145 Gottfried Semper, second Hoftheater, Dresden, 1870–78. View of bay. Photo by author.

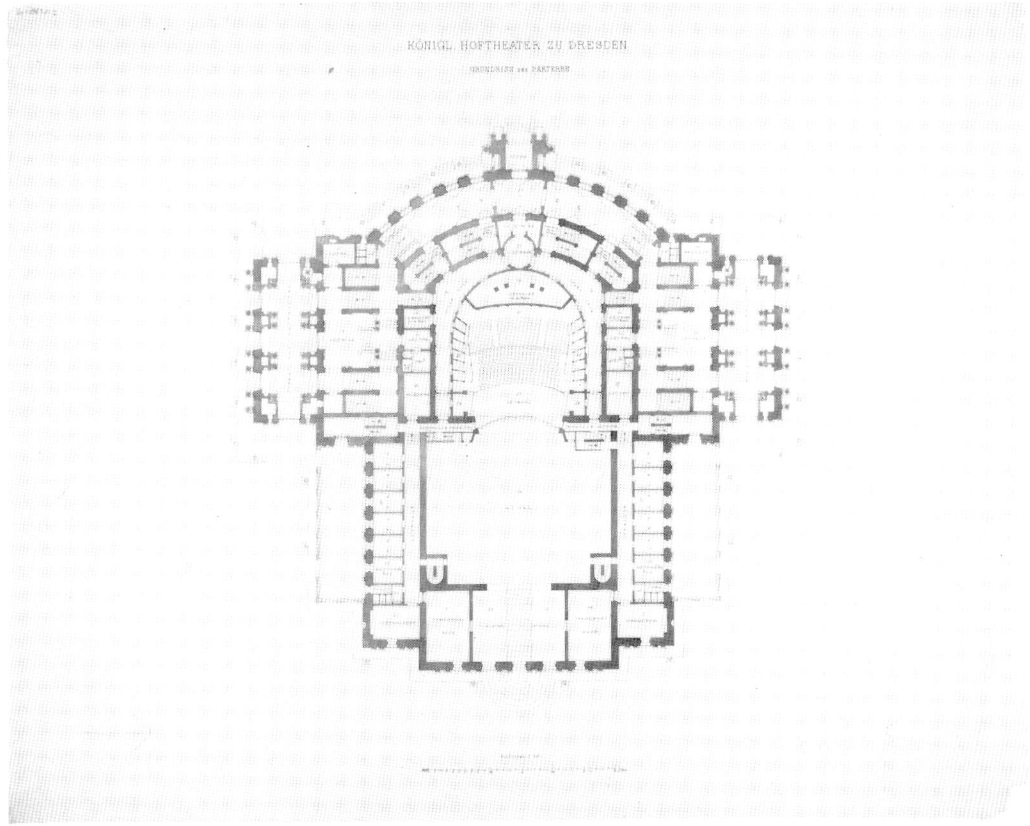

146 Gottfried Semper, second Hoftheater, Dresden, 1870–78. Plan. Institut für Geschichte und Theorie der Architectur, Semper Archiv, ETH-Zurich.

earlier one, although the height of the ceiling is raised considerably with the addition of a fifth gallery. The wedge-shaped seating layout at Munich is here only slightly intimated, as Semper follows rather the gentle curve of his earlier seating arrangement. The stage likewise bows out in the same arena-like manner; the acoustic qualities of the sunken orchestra pit again dictate the form of an independent wooden drum suspended within the structure. Only in the loges are changes introduced. On the upper levels, the half-private loges of the earlier scheme have their partitions recessed even more, and the seating becomes a true arena on the fourth and fifth levels. Semper's intention with the interior seems to have been to follow the original design as closely as possible. The acoustics, like in his earlier work, are exceptional.

The two largest differences in plan between the earlier and later designs are the treatment of the staircases and the sharp separation of the auditorium from the stagehouse. The linear, highly theatrical staircases, thrown out at right angles to the main axis of the auditorium in the Munich and Vienna schemes, are here inappropriate because of the restrictions of the site. But Semper corrected the flaw of his earlier Dresden scheme by giving the circulation areas greater dimension and luxury. This is done by widening these areas, but also by shifting the staircases forward to meet the segmented line of the auditorium. If they in their spatial drama fall far short of the theatricality of Garnier's main staircase for the Paris Opera, these somewhat crowded areas are at least compensated for

147 Gottfried Semper, second Hoftheater, Dresden, 1870–78. Interior view. Sächsische Landesbibliothek, Abteilung Deutsche Fotothek.

148 Gottfried Semper, second Hoftheater, Dresden, 1870–78. Interior view. Sächsische Landesbibliothek, Abteilung Deutsche Fotothek.

by the rounded upper vestibule, highlighted by its abundant and tasteful decoration (Pls. 147, 148). Many of these decisions were, of course, governed by greater budgetary constraints.

The constructional separation of the auditorium from the stagehouse was made partly because of considerations of fire, but it is also an integral part of the composition itself. The proscenium becomes a more forceful divider between the auditorium and the stage, recalling the accentuated but controlled separation proposed for the theater in Munich. The height and depth of the backstage areas, against Semper's proposed reforms made in the 1830s, are considerably enlarged over his earlier solution. These now speak to the ever more complex demands of a new generation of theaters.

As with all of Semper's monumental works, however, it was through the iconography that he orchestrates the decorative effects to a high pitch of theatricality (Pl. 149). The leitmotif here is the bronze quadriga atop the exedra, in which Dionysus leads his bride Ariadne to her apotheosis in a chariot propelled by four panthers. As the cumulative decorative effects make clear, Semper viewed the theater in emotional terms as the frenzied realm of a Dionysian dithyramb – or as Schiller has described it, the chorus as "a living wall which tragedy had drawn around herself to guard her from contact with the world of reality, and maintain her own ideal soil, her poetical freedom."[64] Nietzsche, of course, exenterated the implications of this passage more cogently: "The idyllic shepherd of modern man is merely a counterfeit of the sum of cultural illusions that are allegedly nature; the Dionysian Greek wants truth and nature in their most forceful form – and sees himself changed, as by magic, into a satyr."[65]

Apollo, who more typically epitomized the higher developments of civilization such as the arts, is in Semper's ornamental scheme consigned to a relatively minor position (to a panel beneath the vault of the exedra) and then to a secondary role within this placement – joined with the flute-playing satyr Marsyas (whom Apollo flayed alive) in framing the three Graces.

Below Dionysus and Ariadne, atop columns at the corners of the exedra, stand the four muses: Terpsichore (dance), Thalia (comedy), Melpomene (tragedy), and Polyhymnia (mimic art).[66] Semper in his program preferred placing these figures in the interior of the auditorium, and seconded a suggestion of the sculptor Johannes Schilling that these spots be reserved for the more active (and unclad) figurative dualities of Hercules and Hebe, Eros and Psyche. He was overruled, however, by the program committee that had been set up by the Saxon court.

Semper did, however, have his way with many of the plastic figures on both sides of the theater, above the carriage porches. As with the nearby museum, he divided his thematic content into classical and post-classical periods, but this time conceived his figures as a series of conflicts drawn from theatrical themes. Thus on the side of antiquity (the river side) were placed the statues of Zeus and Prometheus, Antigone and Creon, Medea and Jason, and a bacchante and a satyr; on the Zwinger side were the dramatic figures of Macbeth and Hecate, Faust and Mephistopheles, Don Juan and the Commendatore, and Oberon and Titania.

In two memoranda presented to the program committee in 1874, Semper also explained his reasoning.[67] In contrast to such brutal natural laws as the survival of the fittest and the rights of the stronger, he pointed out that he was appealing in his theater to the higher law of humanity, that is to say, to the causal connection of history, best understood in mythical

149 Gottfried Semper, second Hoftheater, Dresden, 1870–78. Exedra at entrance. Photo by author.

terms and when directed to the national consciousness of a people. In the second memorandum he also indicated that the figurative dualities were motivated by his division of the arts in macrocosmic (architecture, instrumental music, and orchestra), microcosmic (sculpture, song, mime), and historical (painting, drama, and pantomime) categories. Thus Prometheus and Zeus, drawn from the "old tragedy" of Aeschylus, represented the macrocosmic category on the classical side, while on the Zwinger side he recommended Siegfried and Brunhild or Kriemhild and Hagen. The microcosmic division was portrayed by tragedy with pathetic content, such as found in the drama of Sophocles and Euripides. To represent this he recommended Antigone and Creon, Agamemnon and Clytemnestra, Medea and Jason, and Faust and Mephistopheles. He suggested Midas and Silenus, Oberon and Titania as figures portraying the historical arts of painting and drama. The satyr and bacchante, in his view, combined macrocosmic and microcosmic impulses.[68]

The program for the theater interior was no less complex, but fewer of these decisions were made by Semper himself – particularly from 1875 onwards as his health began to decline. Altogether, there were over 120 separate pictorial and plastic pieces commissioned for the theater's interior, allowing a panoply of mythical and historical themes to be summoned. Semper lost more battles than he won here, as his proposals were repeatedly rejected by the program committee and finance minister. Some of his earliest drawings of the interior, beginning around 1873, were made for the circular auditorium ceiling panel, which drew both its geometrical organization and iconography from the first theater. The main oval images again depicted the four geniuses of tragedy, comedy, music, and fine art; the medallion portraits were of Goethe, Schiller, Weber, and Mozart. For the curtain he proposed the allegory "The Birth of the Arts from Darkness," reminiscent in itself of a theme from Schinkel's Altes Museum. This suggestion was rejected, and by means of a competition (with unspecified theme) arose the winning design of Ferdinand Keller, under the title *Providentiae memor.* Semper was also unsuccessful in selecting the subject of the large ceiling frieze above the proscenium, for which he proposed a scene from the life of Dionysus painted *en grisaille.* The executed allegory on "Poetic Justice" was, by contrast, decidedly un-Semperian in its content.

The theme of Dionysus, however, was approved by the program committee for the ceiling panels of the main foyer. Not only does the large central panel – between the royal loge and the royal balcony of the exedra – pay homage to the "Return of Dionysus," but this theme is reinforced in several of the other ceiling panels of the foyer: among them Persephone and Thanatos (the Orphics in particular associated Dionysus with the Nether World), the defeat of Dionysus by the Titans, Dionysus punishing the pirates, the nourishing of Dionysus by the Maenads, and the discovery of Ariadne. Once again Apollo, the tamer of the orgia and benefactor of both Dionysus and the arts, is relegated to a secondary role; he is allotted but one panel, shared with a swan and a lyre.

This very explicit Semperian "priority of the Dionysian over the Apollonian" – as Heinrich Magirius has already aptly described it[69] – does indeed share something more than a historical coincidence with Nietzsche's almost contemporary book, *The Birth of Tragedy* (1872). The sympathetic accord between these two men, at opposite stages in their intellectual development, is in fact more compelling than it may seem at first glance.

Nietzsche, whose relationship with Richard Wagner and Cosima von Bülow began in the spring of 1869, started reading Semper during that summer. At the end of July (and apparently in response to conversations at Triebschen) he sent to Richard and Cosima the published version of Semper's lecture, "On Architectural Styles," delivered in Zurich the previous March.[70] Cosima was most thankful for the work, "which like everything that emanates from great artists both fascinates and instructs me to the greatest extent."[71] In August Cosima read the lecture to Richard, who in a rare moment of humanity regretted that they were no longer in contact with Semper. He attributed this breach of friendship, however, to Semper's "bad conscience," and he viewed the lecture itself as a sign of how far the star of Semper had fallen: when he "with all his magnificent thoughts, is obliged to submit to the circumstances (a lecture to a mixed public in Zurich about matters which would require a whole book)." He complained further that it was a great pity "that Semper is now writing instead of building."[72]

Another letter from Cosima to Nietzsche in the same month is also of some interest.[73] Cosima related ideas contained in Semper's lecture to some remarks made by Wagner, as well as to ideas she read in a lecture of Nietzsche, which he had sent to her. The basis for Cosima's connection is, unfortunately, not transparent from her comments but it is interesting that she understood the philosophical links between the three men.[74]

Nietzsche stayed with his absorption of Semper's ideas through the fall of 1869, at which time he read both *Der Stil* and – seemingly – Semper's pamphlet on Greek polychromy.[75] Semper and Nietzsche even exchanged letters shortly thereafter, although these related only to a subterfuge that Cosima was orchestrating. She had apparently been enamored with a silver bowl or vessel that she had seen in Dresden, which Semper had designed in the early 1840s for the Jewish synagogue there. She asked Nietzsche to write to Semper on behalf of an unnamed lady and ask him for a sketch of the piece so that it could be re-commissioned.

Nietzsche, in the midst of the deepest throes of his naive adulation for Richard and Cosima, was willing to perform any service at this time and dutifully complied. Semper responded with a half-scale drawing of the vessel and the name of the jewelry firm that executed the first piece.[76] Nietzsche sent the letter to Cosima, who was overjoyed at duping Semper out of the design. After sending Semper's letter back to Nietzsche in partial payment for his effort – "an autograph of S[emper]'s is always valuable" – she then asked Nietzsche to assist her further in writing to the firm of jewelers in Dresden.[77] She confessed to Nietzsche the fear that local newspapers might bring to light her order from a Jewish firm.

It is much to be regretted historically that the correspondence between Semper and Nietzsche – two minds that shared so many interests at this time – should have been concerned with such a petty matter. Nietzsche, for his part, could not have been proud of his deception and role as errand boy, even if he were only expressing loyalty to Richard and Cosima. But his respect and appreciation for the ideas of Semper seem not at all contaminated by the negative energy emanating from Triebschen. During these same weeks he was editing the galleys of Wagner's autobiography, which contained numerous positive reminiscences of the friendship of Semper and Wagner. One particular Zurich conversation related by Wagner – Semper's criticism of the libretto of *Tristan* for being too serious and straightforward in its artistic presentation – may even have formed the basis, as Nietzsche's annotators have surmised, of remarks Nietzsche made in the fourth of his *Untimely Meditations* – that concerning Richard Wagner in Bayreuth.[78]

Nietzsche's fascination with *Der Stil* is made even more evident by the various passages he recorded in the notes of his reading.[79] Certainly the most instructive of these citations is the sentence Nietzsche gleaned from Semper's already discussed footnote in *Der Stil* – that expressing his belief that "the haze of carnival candles is the true atmosphere of art."[80] The note was recorded in the fall of 1869, as Nietzsche was preparing his first public lecture in Basel, "The Greek Music Drama." Semper's passage, as we have seen, related to the great antiquity of the theatrical dressing or mask, to the universal joy shared by artists in denying or suspending reality in the practice of their craft. Semper argued that this denial or suspension of reality is essential if "form" (thematically and artistically in the sense used by Schiller) can emerge as a meaningful human symbol, and it was precisely this exalted masking of a noble piece of human history that underscored the classical Greek conception of art – from the "stone dramas" of Phidias to the choral masques of Aeschylus, Sophocles, Euripides, and Aristophanes. Such a veiling of reality also supplied the legacy, Semper felt, for the more recent dramatic efforts of German playwrights such as Goethe and Schiller.

Nietzsche's lecture on "The Greek Music Drama" falls in line with this theme. The leading idea is that the well known works of Aeschylus and Sophocles are, in effect, only stripped down librettos of far more complex choral works: emaciated readings of Greek art akin in contemporary German culture to the earlier erroneous view of Greek sculpture as white (certainly a Semperian allusion). If modern man were somehow transposed back into Attic times, Nietzsche argued, he would find these more satiric performances both foreign and barbaric in their emotional display. This primitive artistic instinct that earlier gave rise to Attic drama (the festive rituals enacting the seasonal return of spring and the spiritual ecstasy of Dionysian intoxication) indeed survived in some form down into high classical times, and it was precisely this choral frenzy, together with the evening haze and provocative masking of the actors, that combined and were specifically intended to release these primal urges. In making his case, Nietzsche actually recited a passage from *Der Stil* – now referring to Semper as "the most significant living architect" – in which Semper described the unfortunate artistic consequences (*ennui*) of adopting only the customary visual vantage point.[81] Nietzsche transposed this passage into theatrical terms to underscore his point that the pleasure gained in the choral song of ancient times rested on this forceful spiritual annihilation of the customary – of reality – by which the freedom of the human spirit then became exalted.

The lecture "The Greek Music Drama" became the basis for Nietzsche's book *The Birth of Tragedy from the Spirit of Music* in the following year; it abounds with similar sentiments. Two themes, if we follow one contemporary analysis, particularly inspire the work.[82] First is the argument that Greek tragedy was born out of the union of Apollonian and Dionysian elements – a union, however, in which the Dionysian tendency dominated. This union effectively ended at the height of classical Greek culture when the rational tendencies of Euripides and Socrates purged the Dionysian component. Such a condition, for Nietzsche, was similar to the rationalist predilection of modern culture in Germany, which once again denied these necessary Dionysian impulses to symbolic artistic expression. The second theme of the book is the belief of Schopenhauer that if life is both terrifying and brutal in its historical and existential underpinnings, art provides the means for the Greeks and for mankind in general to escape (albeit momentarily) from this primal condition of angst.

Thus this "narcotic draught" of Dionysus implied for Nietzsche not only "complete self-forgetfulness" (the annihilation of Schopenhauer's veil of Maya) but it was also the satiric chorus that provided the Greek person of culture with the means of ridding himself of his civilizing conceits and of recovering his primal unity (universal harmony) with nature. Yet this personal redemption, which was symbolically enacted on stage with the annihilation of the tragic hero, came about only with strenuous effort and by releasing these pent-up Dionysian urges. The satiric chorus was no arbitrary world placed somewhere between heaven and earth but formed in the Greek drama its own real world sanctified by myth and cult: "For this chorus the Greek built up the scaffolding of a fictitious *natural state* and on it placed fictitious *natural beings*. On this foundation tragedy developed and so, of course, it could dispense from the beginning with a painstaking portrayal of reality."[83]

These philosophical connections should not lead to an overstatement of the importance of Semper to Nietzsche's intellectual development, for the latter in this formative stage of his thinking was also explicitly drawing upon the ideas of Schiller, Schopenhauer, and Wagner. However, this relatively brief but nevertheless significant point of intellectual contact should not be overlooked as it has been up to now. Nietzsche found in his reading of Semper's "masking of reality" not only strong support for his thesis of a psychologically transcending choral wall as the necessary component of all monumental art but also an alternative vision to Wagner's view of a *Gesamtkunstwerk* – one in which music was not necessarily elevated above the other arts but rather one in which all of the arts, including architecture, emanated from or shared this very same theatrical impulse. This thesis also lends support to the recent argument that Nietzsche's book was not so much about Greek tragedy at all, but rather pondered an aesthetic for great art in general.[84]

The ideas of *Der Stil* at the same time may have reinforced for Nietzsche his aversion to the smug satisfaction of a bourgeois society that exalted its rationalist moderation and erudition – always at the expense of these more dissimulating (and sometimes terrifying) human instincts. Semper's illusional embrace of "unreality," like Nietzsche's, could not have been more antithetical to the growing realism of modernity, notwithstanding their shared "modern" perspectives. Those who today attempt to portray Semper as a proto-realist fundamentally misread this essential illusional veil of his aesthetics, which always pays homage, in essence, to the carnival mask.

It is also important to be very clear on why the iconography of the second Dresden Theater came to mirror *The Birth of Tragedy* in its exaltation of the Dionysian impulse. It may very well be that when Semper turned to a consideration of his iconographic themes around 1873 he had indeed read the published lecture on "The Greek Music Drama" or possibly *The Birth of Tragedy*, and therefore drew directly upon them. But this is unlikely and even unnecessary. The reason Semper's iconographic program resonated with these same themes is simply because Nietzsche's fascination with Greek drama brought to a conclusion an interest in theatricality that Semper himself had started in the 1830s: one that he had shared with Wagner in the 1840s, and one that was handed down from Wagner to Nietzsche in 1869. It was an intoxicating view of art that Nietzsche inherited, but it was a line of reasoning that was, at least in part, Semperian.

For Semper this reconstituted "choral wall" of his Dresden Theater also ended his search for an artistic means to articulate that "chameleonic color that sometimes laughs, sometimes cries, but that is always playful."[85] As he noted in his early pamphlet on polychromy, the monument is indeed the making permanent of the provisional theatrical scaffold, a giving of plastic form to this quintessence of the arts, to the place where

150 Portrait of Gottfried Semper, ca. 1878.

originally the arts were summoned collectively, "at times appearing individually in a splendid contest, at other times working together in various combinations as a chorus. The architect was the choragus, he led them – his name even says it."[86] This new and more expressive theater simply mirrored this vision and brought to fulfillment his earlier impulses – in the sense of a musical finale.

Thus the second Hoftheater is where Semper's theatricality concludes, and indeed it was a finale in one other respect. By 1876, when he found himself shunted aside in Vienna and forced into retirement, he effectively entered his second and final exile – this time the aged architect in search of his artistic homeland. His whereabouts for the first part of 1876 is unknown, although he most probably remained in Vienna and visited his theater under construction in Dresden. He spent the winter of 1876–77 in Venice, but his asthma grew more severe and, on his doctor's order, he traveled north to pass the summer in the Bavarian town of Reichenhall, known for its brine springs.

During these months he became familiar with the German historian Ferdinand Gregorovius, who had produced the first definitive history of Rome during the Middle Ages. Also in Reichenhall he followed with great interest the latest discoveries of Heinrich Schliemann. The latter's unearthing of Troy had taken place earlier in the decade and in 1877 Schliemann was excavating parts of the city of Mycenae, which Semper himself had visited in his youth. Semper felt that many of his earlier theories on Greek art had now found vindication.

Once he had recuperated, Semper returned in the fall of 1877 to Vienna via Dresden, where he viewed for the last time his nearly completed theater. Vienna again proved inhospitable. Friedrich Bruckmann was pressing him hard for the third volume of *Der Stil* and Semper responded with the threat of another lawsuit. The publisher only relented in the following year, when Semper agreed to a second (quite popular as it turned out) edition of the first two volumes. Also while in Vienna, his lung ailment returned and he went down to Venice to pass the winter of 1877–78 (Pl. 150). He was by then too weak to travel north for the successful opening of his Dresden Hoftheater in February, but he read the many newspaper reports with great satisfaction.

In the spring the migrant artist ventured north to the Como Sea, where he was often seen late at night on the balcony of the Hôtel d'Angleterre, smoking his pipe and listening to the songs of the nightingales. He spent the summer in northeastern Italy, where for the second time Franz Lenbach painted his portrait. In the fall Semper wanted to visit Genoa, which had always been his favorite Italian city. At Lenbach's urging, however, he decided to accompany the latter to Rome. There he passed the winter of 1879, taking excursions around the Roman *campagna* and re-living the artistic fire of his youth. In more ways than one, the artistic refugee had at last come home.

In early spring, while still in Rome, his asthma worsened and this time his kidneys too began to fail. First Emmanuel came to attend to his father on his deathbed, then Manfred made his frantic journey south. The architect died in the latter's arms on 15 May. Manfred, who brought to execution his father's last grand creation, pressed his eyes close in death.

Epilogue

The Semper Legacy: Semper and Riegl

When Semper arrived in Vienna in the fall of 1871 he had already ascended to the top of the European architectural profession and become the recognized master of German theory and practice. After his death in 1879, his stature continued to grow over the next two decades. Indeed, even a casual glance at the German literature on architectural theory and practice in the last decades of the nineteenth century reveals that Semper and his ideas dominated his professional culture in a way that few architects have done since – Gropius and Le Corbusier notwithstanding.

That an architect could have risen to such heights of fame only to become almost entirely forgotten ("repressed" by one account)[1] by early twentieth-century explanations of this period only underscores just how fragile and selective historical research can be. Even today many still labor under some of the historical prejudices and simplifications of this kind of historiography – chief of which perhaps was the denial that anything of architectural significance took place in the second half of the nineteenth century. Such an attitude, in the end, only makes it more difficult to understand modernism itself, not to mention its more recent permutations.

One measure of Semper's fame, certainly, was the large number of biographies and critical studies that appeared shortly after his death. The first hagiography was by Friedrich Pecht, a longtime friend from the early days in Dresden; it preceded Semper's passing by two years. Pecht sketched a glowing account of his friend's life and deeds in the fifth chapter of his *Deutsche Künstler des neunzehnten Jahrhunderts* (German Artists of the Nineteenth Century). In the months following Semper's death, in 1879, numerous personal profiles and artistic reviews appeared in the pages of almost every German-speaking newspaper and journal. Of these, Josef Bayer's lengthy necrology on the architect, which appeared in the journal *Zeitschrift für Bildende Kunst* in the summer of 1879, remains today one of the best analyses of Semper's theory and architecture ever written.

Semper's two sons, Hans and Manfred, also prepared a number of historical studies of their father's work, the first of which was Hans Semper's biographical study of 1880, *Gottfried Semper: Ein Bild seines Lebens und Wirkens* (Gottfried Semper: A Portrait of his Life and Work). Hans Semper, an art historian, also teamed up with his brother Manfred in assembling – and in some cases translating – their father's essays for *Kleine Schriften* (Short Writings), which appeared in 1884. Manfred also authored separate studies on the Munich Festspielhaus and his father's relationship with Hasenauer.

Another early biography that was excellent in its critical analysis was Constantin Lipsius's *Gottfried Semper in seiner Bedeutung als Architekt* (The Significance of Gottfried Semper as an Architect). It first appeared late in 1879 as a continuous necrology in the

Berlin journal *Deutsche Bauzeitung*, but shortly thereafter the text was printed separately as a 103-page pamphlet – by far the longest necrology that ever appeared in the pages of *Deutsche Bauzeitung*.

Also important from a biographical perspective are a number of analyses and doctoral dissertations that appeared later, most of which were devoted to aspects of Semper's thought and practice. Perhaps the starting point to this scholarly interest in Semper was the Festschrift prepared on the occasion of the unveiling of the Semper monument in Dresden in 1892.[2] The doctoral candidate Hans Prinzhorn followed this interest in 1908 with his *Gottfried Sempers aesthetische Grundanschauungen* (Gottfried Semper's Aesthetic Views). Five years later Max Georg Mütterlein presented to the Technische Hochschule in Dresden his informative history of Semper's monumental buildings on that city's main square, *Gottfried Semper und dessen Monumentalbauten am Dresdner Theaterplatz*.

World War I interrupted this work but even afterward Semper's name – now largely removed from mainstream historical consideration – was still held in high esteem by some architects. The Hamburg architect and noted modernist Fritz Schumacher, for example, was an informed Semper scholar and a great admirer of his ideas, and often invoked his name in glowing terms in his many writings.[3] And Wolfgang Herrmann's introductory chapters of *Deutsche Baukunst des 19. und 20. Jahrhunderts* (German Architecture of the 19th and 20th Centuries), written in 1932, gave much consideration to Semper and his legacy.[4]

Two doctoral studies from the 1930s devoted exclusively to Semper's theory continued this tendency: Leopold Ettlinger's *Gottfried Semper und die Antike: Beiträge zur Kunstanschauung des deutschen Klassizismus* (Gottfried Semper and Antiquity: Contributions to the Artistic Viewpoint of German Classicism) and Ernst Stockmeyer's *Gottfried Sempers Kunsttheorie* (Gottfried Semper's Theory of Art). Interest in Semper was (barely) kept alive after World War II through Claus Zoege von Manteuffel's informative doctoral study of 1952, "Die Baukunst Gottfried Sempers" (The Architecture of Gottfried Semper). A decade later Hans Quitzsch published his doctoral work, *Die ästhetischen Anschauungen Gottfried Sempers* (The Aesthetic Views of Gottfried Semper).

All of these efforts, however, were but a prelude to the cascade of studies that began to appear shortly after the symposium on Semper that took place in 1974, hosted by the Institut für Geschichte und Theorie der Architektur at the ETH-Hönggerberg.[5] This initiative, which coincided with the cataloging of the Semper archives in Zurich, was followed up by much activity around 1979, as various historians from in and around Dresden celebrated the centennial of Semper's death with a major exhibition and another colloquium.[6] Thus by the early 1980s this once nearly forgotten nineteenth-century architect had become, in effect, "rediscovered" in a very serious way.

Of course a better way to measure Semper's impact on the intellectual development of the nineteenth century is to gauge the extent to which his buildings and writings shifted the very foundations of theory and practice. Architecturally, his influence began to be felt long before his death, as the first Dresden theater of 1838–41 represented an early flowering of the Neorenaissance movement in Germany. Interest in the Renaissance on the Continent, as has already been noted, began in France several decades earlier, starting with Percier and Fontaine's pictorial study of Renaissance buildings, *Palais, maison et autres édifices modernes, dessinés à Rome* (1798). This interest, however, took another generation to filter down into practice, and thus Semper's first Dresden efforts were nearly contemporaneous with the early efforts of his French counterparts: Félix Duban's Palais des Beaux-Arts (1832–39) and Henri Labrouste's Bibliothèque Ste-Geneviève (1838–50).

Notwithstanding this convergence with French tendencies, the forms of the Renaissance were still regarded quite differently in Germany. For instance, Leo von Klenze, who was trained in France under Percier and Fontaine, employed this style in a very literal way in the design of several Munich works, such as the Leuchtenberg Palais (1816), and Royal Residence or Königsbau (1826–35). Klenze actually preferred Greek classicism to Renaissance forms but he was fluent in many styles. Outside Munich, interest in the Renaissance was more scattered. Schinkel in Berlin had little appreciation for the style and thus its forms rarely made an appearance in Prussia. Various architects in other parts of Germany practiced the style, but mostly on smaller works. Thus there arose in the 1820s Renaissance-inspired buildings in Weimar by Clemens Wenzeslaus Coudray, and in the 1830s in Leipzig by Woldemar Herrmann. In Dresden, Semper's preference for the Renaissance was preceded by various Italian-inspired works by Gottlob Friedrich Thormeyer.[7]

Semper, however, was the first German architect to draw upon Renaissance forms on a monumental scale, and his motifs were adapted in a much less literal way than had been done by Klenze and others. In the 1840s Semper virtually stood alone in Germany in his appreciation of the monumental possibilities of this style, as German practice had pretty much splintered into the *Rundbogenstil* (rounded-arch or Romanesque style) and Neogothic camps. The Renaissance was equally disdained by both parties, as well as by others. The late Neoclassicist Johann Heinrich Wolff, for example, would not recognize the Renaissance as a "true style" but only as an aberration of Roman classicism. And the champion of the *Rundbogen*, Heinrich Hübsch, referred to the Renaissance style as "sham architecture," which possessed the double infelicity of not only slavishly imitating the Roman style but also of leading architecture down the false path to the "Periwig style" (Baroque).[8]

Architectural historians of this period were scarcely any more enlightened. Franz Kugler in his *Handbuch der Kunstgeschichte* (Handbook of the History of Art) dismissed virtually the entire Renaissance period with a few condemning pages. Semper, by contrast, defended the style specifically because of its classical grounding, but more importantly (and here he was quite in advance of his time) for the emotive possibilities that this style and its creative development afforded. In one essay prepared in the 1840s for the Nicolaikirche competition, he reasoned that the Renaissance style "permits multiple characteristics of a building; as with human features, the finest variations of forms and proportions suffice to impress a building with a very different character. With it, as with the use of the Greek-Roman column element, architectural expression can be raised almost to a level of physiognomic refinement."[9]

Semper's opinion regarding the Renaissance remained a minority view throughout the 1850s, but by the 1860s the situation changed dramatically, in part due to the historical interest generated in the Renaissance by the studies of Jakob Burckhardt. Now this period and its motifs became very much in vogue, and Semper's lead was taken up by older practitioners as well as by the younger generation. This can be best seen in Vienna (geographically and culturally not very distant from Dresden), where Semper's Dresden works, as Renate Wagner-Rieger has pointed out, were widely studied and employed as models.[10]

Actually, Semper's influence had a longer history here. Ludwig Förster founded the architectural journal *Allgemeine Bauzeitung* in 1836 as a tool to advance Viennese architecture on a more progressive track, and in the 1840s he seems to have become particularly enamored with various of Semper's Dresden works, among them the Dresden Forum and Theater, the Villa Rosa, and the Synagogue. All were displayed in his journal, and Förster in his own practice adopted various Semperian motifs.

Even stronger, it seems, was Semper's influence on Förster's younger partner, Theophil von Hansen. He traveled to Berlin, Munich, and Dresden in 1858, and when he returned to Vienna his work now took on a Semperian flair, perhaps seen most clearly in his late work, the Academy of Fine Arts (1874–84). Semper's style also became an admired paradigm for the younger generation that first came on the scene in the 1860s; chief among them were Karl Hasenauer, August Weber, and Otto Wagner. It was no accident that Hasenauer actively sought out Semper's (and only Semper's) advice in 1869, as Hasenauer's first designs for the Art Museum and Natural History Museum owed much to Semper's Dresden Gallery. Semper's revised design and his later presence in the city only reinforced this tendency and even started a new phase of influence. His joint-designs for the two museums and theater, with their Baroque overtones, intensified interest in the late-Renaissance and early Baroque – tendencies that became quite popular in Vienna in the late 1870s.

Semper's architectural legacy after 1879 can be best seen by turning to the three urban centers in which he was active: Dresden, Zurich, and Vienna.

The first city built few monumental works between the time of his Art Gallery and the second Hoftheater, but his influence became manifest in other ways. The Villa Rosa (1838), for instance, was a much admired work and its Venetian features became a model for countless other villas built in the following decades. In all fairness to Georg Hermann Nicolai – the latter's contemporary Seebach residence formed the basis of the dispute between the two men, as to who was the first to introduce the villa style of the Veneto into the city. Yet Semper's Villa Rosa, with its Palladian lineaments, caryatids, tripartite central projection on the south, and nine-square plan with a two-story central rotunda, clearly set the tenor of later productions. By the 1860s these features were almost universally employed in the larger residential productions, as can be discerned in Karl Eberhard's Villa Häbler (1866–67) (Pl. 151), Bernhard Schreiber's Villa Pilz (1868–69), Karl Böttger's residence on Wienerstrasse (1870), Hermann August Richter's Villa Opitz (1873–74), and Hübner and Baron's Villa Hartmann and Villa Laubegaster, both built in 1874.[11] Few of these architects were actually schooled under Semper.

The rebuilding of the Dresden Hoftheater between 1871–77, however, reestablished Semper's force within the city, and achieved for him the featured spot within that city's pantheon of artists – a position that remains firm even today. After his departure from the city in 1849 his post at the Academy had been filled by Nicolai, who struggled hard to impress his own mark on both the curriculum and the students. He was less fortunate than his rival in his practice, however. In the absence of new monumental commissions, Nicolai specialized for the most part in residential architecture: commissions which he designed in a studied but nevertheless highly competent Renaissance manner. But this success was only transitory, as Semper's return to the city around 1869 had the result of eclipsing Nicolai's last years of practice. When the latter died in 1881 his position was

151 Karl Eberhard, Villa Häbler, Dresden, 1866–67. Courtesy of Heidrun Laudel.

filled by Constantin Lipsius, his former student but, more importantly, Semper's principal biographer and interpreter.

Lipsius, had he been born a decade or two earlier, might have been one of the most important architects of the nineteenth century. A native of Leipzig, he studied architecture in that city before enrolling in Nicolai's Dresden studio in 1851. After finishing his studies there, he traveled first to Italy and then to Paris, where he joined the studio of Hittorff. He greatly admired contemporary French architecture, but when he returned to Leipzig in 1856 he fell into an eclectic practice that was competent but not in any way exceptional. Still, by the late-1870s he had somewhat effortlessly moved to the forefront of the German architectural profession, in part because of his espousal of the use of iron.[12] Late in 1879 he wrote his biography of Semper, and in 1881, perhaps due in part to this study, he was called to Dresden with the promise of designing the new Academy of Fine Arts. His vast complex of pavilions (1883–94) exceeded all expectations, but this success, as it turns out, was somewhat ephemeral.

The Academy is a busy, Renaissance-inspired work along the fashionable Brühlischen Terrasse with its ground-story rustication at the opposite east facade of truly gargantuan proportions. As J. Duncan Berry has pointed out, Lipsius revealed much of his own design attitudes and intentions in the last pages of his biography of Semper.[13] The latter's principal historic breakthrough, Lipsius reasoned, was that he was the first to recognize the importance of Roman architecture: an architecture not based on the necessities of real construction but on functioning only apparently or symbolically, that is, through its artistic dressing. This Roman masking of constructional reality, Lipsius argued, was new to architectural history. Because of it, such Roman features as the combination of a column with an arch, far from being a sham architecture, were in fact well considered attempts to enliven architectural masses. In this system, the dressing of the column was justified purely on aesthetic grounds as a spatial motif and then brought together with the arch in a grand, unifying effect.

Semper, Lipsius argued further, had brought the same conception of symbolic architecture to his own Renaissance practice, but he did so with a profound realist undercurrent, that is, with a materiality that was expressed by his compositional massing and by his highly lithic manner of rustication. Semper's buildings functioned or evolved vertically in their underlying symbolism, said Lipsius – from the realist premises of the foundations to the symbolic attributes of the upper stories. Through such means, Lipsius argued, Semper was able to form buildings as "living organisms," to create buildings that "articulate their purpose in their whole and in their parts with physiognomic clarity, without a trace of arbitrariness; they carry the stamp of inner necessity and conscious restraint, yet with artistic freedom."[14]

This is also the reasoning behind the exaggerated rustication of the Dresden Academy of Fine Arts, which evolves tectonically – as Berry had analyzed it – into stories depicting the wall as a woven hanging, the invention of trabeation, and the invention of arcuation. Whatever similarity the terrace facade has to Félix Duban's Quai Malaquais facade of the Ecole des Beaux-Arts (1856–63) is almost coincidental, for Lipsius's masterpiece is one permeated with the spirit of Semper. It was only fitting that when Semper's statue was unveiled in 1892, it was placed on a pedestal adjacent to this building.

The one major drawback to Lipsius's homage to Gottfried Semper was, however, its timing; it was not finished until 1894 – that is, during the very months that Otto Wagner in Vienna was writing the first manifesto to modern architecture. This problem of Lipsius's historical incongruity is one that would haunt many of Semper's followers, especially those who tried to continue the master's plastic symbolism.

Semper's legacy in Zurich is slightly more difficult to define if only because of the scarcity of monumental commissions in Switzerland as a whole. Here it is necessary to look at the Polytechnikum itself, the school that Semper raised to become one of the leading programs in Europe, to find his continuing imprint. It was a very small school in its inception in 1855, but within a decade it had begun to compete successfully with its counterparts in Munich and Vienna. Even after Semper left for Vienna, the program he instituted continued in place for several years through his able assistants Georg Lasius and Julius Stadler. Two students of Semper who took their training there went on to achieve great success: Alfred Friedrich Bluntschli (1842–1920) and Hans Auer (1847–1930).

Bluntschli was born in Zurich but was raised and educated in Germany. In 1860 he enrolled at the Polytechnikum and soon became an assistant in Semper's office. After a tour of Italy he traveled to France, where he enrolled at the Ecole des Beaux-Arts and rounded out his architectural education by acquiring an exquisite skill in rendering. Semper admired his talent and tried to get him involved first with the design of the Festspielhaus and later with the rebuilding of his second Dresden Theater. Bluntschli, however, settled in Frankfurt, where he joined another Semper student, Karl Jonas Mylius, in a partnership. The office flourished almost at once and it was only a call to Zurich in 1881 – to assume Semper's old chair – that lured Bluntschli back to his native city. Here he ran the school up until the beginning of World War I.

Bluntschli built much throughout his Zurich years, including a large church in Enge (1888-94), but he is perhaps best known for his two additions to the Polytechnikum (now the ETH complex): the Chemistry Building (1886) and the Physics Building (1887–88). The earlier design drew upon Semper's fascination with rustication, but it was somewhat subdued in its detailing. The Physics Building, with its subterranean vaulted laboratories, sat high above the other buildings on a rusticated terrace, treated in a cyclopean manner. Berry also spoke of this building's textile-like surfaces and its "lithic evolution" from the stony base to the graceful refinement of its cornice line.[15]

Hans Auer (1847–1906) was perhaps Semper's most talented student from the Zurich years. He entered the Polytechnikum in 1864 and three years later walked away with the first prize. After working in Zurich for a while he moved to Vienna in 1869 and eventually took a position in Theophil Hansen's office, where he became the most trusted designer in the studio. His gifted hand, at least in part, can be found in the designs for the Stock Exchange, the Fine Arts Academy, and in the interiors of the Austrian Parliament Building. Auer was also active as a theorist; in the early 1880s he wrote several prominent essays that dealt with Semperian ideas, including the consideration of architecture as the creation of space.[16]

His career, however, jumped to an altogether different level in 1885, when he entered the competition for the new Swiss Parliament Building in Bern. The result was initially indecisive, but he was invited to the city to build one of the adjoining administrative buildings, which he modeled on the Zurich Polytechnikum. Through another limited competition in 1892 Auer won the Parliament commission outright, which he built between 1894 and 1902.

Like Lipsius's building in Dresden, this monumental work – had it been built a decade or two earlier – would certainly have become one of the most admired buildings of the nineteenth century. Gloriously situated on a bluff high above the river Aar, the segmental curve of the south front echoes the curved front of Semper's later theaters and indeed the work displays a tectonic and decorative detailing that even exceeds Semper's hand at times in its grandiloquence (Pl. 152). The two-story entrance hall and domed central hall are spatial extravaganzas, and the meeting chamber itself is one of the finest in Europe. Of all of Semper's many students, Auer is the one who best understood the master's penchant for theatricality and he imposed it here with gifted assurance.[17]

In Vienna, too, Semper left his mark and it was perhaps stronger here than in Dresden or Zurich. His reputation in the Habsburg capital, as we have seen, was well established prior to his arrival – with Hansen, Hasenauer, Eitelberger – but his infiuence lingered until the end of the century. The architect who appears most profoundly moved by his early and late presence in the city was Heinrich von Ferstl (1828–83), a participant in the 1866 and 1868 competitions for the two museums. Ferstl had studied at the Vienna Academy under Siccardsburg and van der Nüll in the 1840s and, after traveling extensively throughout Europe, he returned to Vienna and set up an architectural practice – only to win within a few years the competition for the Votivkirche in 1855. Although he was required by the program to submit a Gothic design, he much preferred the high Renaissance style of Semper, as seen in his competition design for the Art Museum and Natural History Museum of 1866. He declined to revise his entry in the second round of 1868 because the faulty program itself was not rewritten.

This cost him further consideration in this project but he subsequently received the commission for the Austrian Museum for Art and Industry (1868–71), on which he worked with Eitelberger in recreating the South Kensington model. Later in the decade he added an applied arts school, once again drawing closer to the London initiative. His best designs, however, were for the various buildings of the University of Vienna, another project whose planning started around 1868. Ferstl traveled to Italy at this time to seek out

152 Hans Auer, Swiss Parliament, Bern, 1894–1902. Institut für Geschichte und Theorie der Architectur, Semper Archiv, ETH-Zurich.

examples there, but Semper's influence was never far below the surface of the finished work. At one stage of the design in 1872, before construction had started, Semper was even asked by the Crown to review Ferstl's scheme, to which he gave his (rare) nod of approval. This allowed the government officials to begin the project, the construction of which continued down to 1884.

Ferstl's debt to Semper is clearest in an address he gave to the Technische Hochschule (now Technische Universität) in Vienna in 1880, on the occasion of his being appointed a rector. The theme of the address was the close relationship that architecture enjoyed with its encompassing social and political life. After citing Semper's definition of style and taking his listeners through a quick review of architectural history, Ferstl turned his attention to Schinkel and Semper – the two most important pioneers of the nineteenth century. Semper succeeded in difficult circumstances, he noted, because of his broad humanistic basis and because his ideas transcended the art of architecture proper. Ferstl then went on to outline in detail the main themes of *Der Stil*, including the notion of the "dressing" and its essential denial of reality. He concluded his talk by insisting that Semper's analyses had put artistic investigation on "a completely new footing," one that would make it far easier for the new generation "to fulfill the tasks that modern architecture has put forth in the higher sense of artistic design."[18]

Ferstl's respect and admiration for Semper in the early 1880s matched that of another prominent faculty member of the Technische Hochschule, the drama critic and aesthetician Josef Bayer (1827–1910). A close friend of Johannes Brahms, Bayer's intellectual "models were Burckhardt and G. Semper," as one of his biographers has noted.[19] He instilled his architectural analyses, like his mentors, with a broad range of interests, including a keen understanding of contemporary trends. His posthumously published (1919) writings on art, under the title *Baustudien und Baubilder* (Architectural Studies and Architectural Images), ranged studiously over a range of themes, sometimes only remotely related to architecture: Rome, Goethe, Schinkel, Richard Wagner as an architect, the history of the wreath as a symbol, architectural polychromy, and the importance of iron and glass for modern design.

His high regard for Semper in the 1870s no doubt led to the biographical sketch that he produced for the journal *Zeitschrift für bildende Kunst.* He began this piece with a string of epithets for this "great man" who was blessed with an unusual "Roman sensitivity." Bayer then proceeded to carry out one of the most thorough and learned explorations of Semper's contributions to architecture and theory. Bayer was the first critic to point out that the Wagnerian notion of a *Gesamtkunstwerk* for musical drama had its origins in Semper's early pamphlet on polychromy.[20] Bayer was also the first to focus attention on the symbolic and evolving importance of rustication for Semper throughout his work.[21]

Perhaps the strongest part of his biography, however, was his casting of Semper in the role of the archetypical hero: the forceful personality who prevailed in the face of numerous obstacles and the most troubling personal circumstances, "as in a Shakespearean story." Notwithstanding the "frequent change of scenery," Semper in his "life and work left behind the most distinct impression throughout the world, and the legacy of his day on earth will never go unrecognized in those places where he, for longer or shorter periods, tarried and worked."[22]

In the 1880s Bayer began to focus his Semperian perspective on various issues of contemporary architecture, chief and foremost was the issue of style. He defined the notion of style, however, in a much more deterministic manner than had Semper, as "a specific way of thinking and a formative expression of art deriving from the innermost foundation and essence of the age, which can have only *one* prescribed, main direction."[23] This direction was currently in the midst of a profound turn, he argued, in that the former monarchical, aristocratic, and religious impulses to architecture had given way to social concerns and higher needs. The new style taking shape could not be discerned, as before, in historicist details or stylistic dresses but rather in the underlying physiognomy of buildings, that is, in their horizontal prospect, rhythm of masses, and grouping with other buildings.

In another essay Bayer likened the modern style to a new cut of clothing fitted to new forms: here he indicated that the new style could also be seen in the new developments of the floor plan, and in architecture's truly new compositional forms.[24]

The Semperian tenor of Bayer's remarks in the 1880s was not unique to the architectural situation of Vienna, nor even new to artistic discussion in general. Bayer's friend and Viennese colleague, Carl von Lützow (the editor of the *Zeitschrift für Bildende Kunst*), had stressed the importance of Semper's ideas on style already in the first review of *Der Stil* in 1863. Lützow saw the breakthrough of this "epoch-making" book to be the fact that it provided a "scientifically grounded theory of style" to an age (the modern) that had lost its direction and artistic confession of faith. This lack of direction was due, Lützow reasoned, to the fact that contemporary artistic sensitivity had become subverted by novel materials and mushrooming technologies, and had thus fallen victim to the expanding lure of "fashion."[25]

The gist of Lützow's review came to be echoed again and again in the 1870s and 1880s, as the implications of the changing political, economic, and social conditions became more and more apparent. Semper's former colleague in Zurich, the historian Wilhelm Lübke, praised Semper and *Der Stil* in 1872 for showing modern architecture the correct path, that is, for underscoring the organic connection between the fine arts, as well as between architecture and the applied arts.[26] Another critic, Eduard Wulff, saw Semper's breakthrough in 1874 in more deterministic or materialistic terms; he argued that Semper had delineated each technical product as the result of the material used in its creation and in its purpose.[27]

This last interpretation fell in with another line of development taking place with respect to Semper's theory, as various architects and theorists in this decade and later attempted to develop the notion of a new or modern style strictly through such material parameters. The native Swiss architect Rudolf Redtenbacher, for instance, made a plea to architects in 1877 to become less historically biased and more scientific in their selection of forms.[28] Trained under both Bötticher and Nicolai, Redtenbacher sought to join Semper's theory with that of his first mentor in some sort of grand comparative method of style theory. In two works of 1881 and 1883 he produced something of a primer on the principles that should govern the design of form.[29] He rejected Semper's theory of dressing and countered instead (presaging Otto Wagner) with the premise that construction itself (not symbolism) was the starting point of design. He defined tectonics as the theory of shaping form consistent with purpose and material.

A similar argument was pursued by the Cologne architect Georg Heuser, who in numerous articles in the late 1880s and early 1890s, attempted to meld the ideas of Semper, Darwin, and Ernst Kapp into a technological theory of architecture, in which natural selection became the primary force of change.[30] Heuser's reasoning was that new materials and technologies are initially treated in ways learned from older materials and purposes, yet gradually new variations and new options appear. A new style is thus a crossbreeding of methods and techniques, which Heuser specifically argued for in the case of iron.

It must be said that this materialist path was but one interpretation or development of Semper's theory. The anonymous reviewer of Semper's *Kleinen Schriften* in 1884, for instance, was impressed by how aspects of Semper's overall theory became clarified by his shorter writings, chief of which was Semper's anti-Darwinism and his late espousal of the human free will as the most important factor in artistic design.[31] By the style and substance of this review, it is clear that the critic expected all of his readers to be familiar with the intricacies of Semper's theory.

This knowledge was even expected to some extent outside Germany and Austria. Ákos Moravánszky, for instance, has pointed out the profound influence Semper and his theory had in other parts of the former Habsburg empire, especially in Prague and Budapest, where its signs lingered down into the twentieth century.[32] Doctoral research in the past decade has also revealed Semper's somewhat surprising influence in France, England, and the United States.

The key figure in France was Paul Sédille, the highly respected architect of the Printemps department store in Paris and a brilliant polychromist in his own right. In 1884 Sédille wrote a review of the two museums in Vienna, in which he claimed, after praising these two works, that *Der Stil* had recently been translated into French. No translation has since surfaced, but – if untrue – this claim was certainly outdone by that of another French admirer of Semper, Louis Meslin, who in 1859 wrote a review of a completely non-existent book by Semper.[33]

In England Semper's thought was given much publicity in the 1880s by the writings of Lawrence Harvey, an Englishman who had studied under Semper in Zurich between 1864 and 1867. After Zurich, Harvey went to the Ecole des Beaux-Arts in Paris and then returned to London to set up his own practice. He first presented an address to the RIBA in December 1884, entitled "Semper's Theory of Evolution in Architectural Ornament," in which he laid out in a relatively accurate way (notwithstanding the Darwinian term evolution) the ideas to be gleaned from a reading of the first volume of *Der Stil*.[34] The talk, as he noted to Hans Semper in a letter the next day, was a "decided success," and therefore "called forth a great deal of opposition."[35] Harvey also mentioned in his letter that he had been asked by officials at South Kensington to prepare an English translation of *Der Stil*, yet he had declined on the basis that he was too busy with his practice.[36]

Harvey's remarks did indeed prompt a Semper debate, which continued for almost a year in the pages of *The Architect*. The discussion was somewhat uninformed, however, in that few of the protagonists, including Harvey himself, understood Semper's theory in much depth and the debate often turned on more parochial issues. Still, the most sensible Semper supporter, the art historian G. Baldwin Brown, later made extensive use of Semper in his later writings on English art and primitive art.[37]

Semper's popularity among architects in Chicago in the late-1880s might also seem inexplicable, except that, as Roula Geraniotis has noted, this community possessed one of the largest contingents of German émigrés in the United States.[38] Many had been trained in Germany but had left their homeland in the 1850s and 1860s for political, religious, or economic reasons. Certainly the leading Semper exponent in Chicago was Frederick Baumann, who between 1887 and 1897 enunciated Semperian themes again and again in lectures before various local and national architectural forums.[39] In the most informative of these papers, that given before the American Institute of Architects at their convention in Washington DC in 1889, he outlined Semper's four-motive theory and "dressing" thesis.

Baumann's almost unbounded enthusiasm for Semper also brought the latter's ideas into the circle of John Root, Denkmar Adler (another German émigré), W. W. Boyington, and Louis Sullivan. In one gathering of these men, a local discussion held early in 1889 and published in the March issue of *The Inland Architect and News Record*, Baumann presented a somewhat corrupted summary of Semper's definition of style, to which Sullivan responded by saying that style is not something outside but something within an individual, an inner impulse expressed in the character and quality of thought. It was, however, the enthusiasm of Baumann that prompted John Root's translation (with Fritz Wagner) of Semper's Zurich lecture, "On Architectural Styles," which appeared in the *Inland Architect* in 1889–90.[40]

Much has been made of this midwestern infatuation with Semper, including the suggestion that his theory of "dressing" had something to do with the development of the curtain wall. If such connections are difficult to make historically, it is at least interesting that the *Inland Architect* was the only American paper to publish an article on the unveiling of the Semper monument in Dresden in 1892, complete with a translation (made by Baumann) of Lipsius's formal remarks.[41] Incidentally, Root was not the only American architect to try his hand at translating Semper. The first issue of the San Francisco journal

Architectural News (January 1891) contained an announcement that Bernard Maybeck was planning a translation of *Der Stil*. Unfortunately, the work seems to have stalled.

This interest in Semper in the last decades of the nineteenth century was also reflected in many disciplines other than architecture. Archaeology was one area of research radically transformed by many of the suggestions contained in *Der Stil* – even if discoveries of Neolithic and Palaeolithic art in the caves of France and Spain had soon proved many of Semper's technical assumptions to be wrong. Semper's imprint was significant as well in aesthetics and art history – an impression that up to now has been little appreciated. One of the key figures in this regard was Friedrich Theodor Vischer.

When this fiery philosopher came to Zurich in the late 1850s, he brought with him a comprehensive aesthetic system (published in six volumes) that was idealist in its foundations and Hegelian in its particulars. Semper cared little for Hegel; he rejected the underlying historicism of Hegel's aesthetics and he found Hegel's penchant for abstract conceptualization entirely irrelevant to the practice of art. It was because of Hegel and the whole genre of German idealist philosophy that Semper subtitled his main work: "Practical Aesthetics." Notwithstanding these differences, Semper and Vischer became fast friends and it is certainly significant that shortly after he arrived in Zurich Vischer embarked on a thorough revision and repudiation of his earlier aesthetic system, which he published in six volumes between 1860 and 1873, under the title *Kritische Gänge* (Critical Proceedings).

Vischer's revision in part centered around the concept of the symbol, which in Hegel's aesthetics had been restricted to the earliest and lowest stage of art, the period (such as in ancient Egypt and India) when the desired harmony between spiritual content and its material representation had yet to be attained. Vischer's earlier aesthetics had followed Hegel in this regard, although there are passages in Vischer's discussion of architecture that forecast his later approach. Vischer had earlier spoken, for instance, of architecture as a "symbolic art" in which the architect sets for himself the task of rhythmically animating form, by inserting "buoyant life" into form through ornaments and the linear and planar play of suspended bodies. Hence, architectural masses appear to move, lines rise and fall, and circles flow in space; in the successful orchestration of this array of symbolic effects, architecture as a cultural art came "to express the whole outer and inner life of nations."[42]

In his important essay of 1866, "Kritik meiner Aesthetik" (Critique of my Aesthetics), Vischer expounded upon his earlier concept of the symbolism of architectural forms. Acknowledging that his earlier concept had, like Hegel's, been too narrowly conceived, Vischer now insisted that these animate readings of architectural forms were examples of a "higher" symbolic process, that is, higher than the presumed unconscious symbolism of Hindu or Egyptian art. In its effect, architecture composed an internal symbolism of form that was both conscious and voluntary, a symbolism that could not be aligned with any specific cultural stage. It was a symbolism also basic to human aesthetic behavior in general, in that mankind's relation to the world is defined at least in part through the symbolic transposition or reading of human emotions in worldly forms. Vischer referred to this animation of form as a "unifying and contractive feeling" (*Ineins- und Zusammenfühlung*), a pantheistic impulse to merge with the sensuous world.[43]

What made this quite Semperian formulation of architectural symbolism so important was that these passages became the basis for the aesthetics of Robert Vischer (1847–1933, Friedrich Theodor's son), which he codified in 1873 under the line of development known as "empathy theory" (*Einfühlungstheorie*).[44] The notion of empathy (our unconscious projection of emotions into the phenomena of visual perception) became, in fact, one of the most popular ideas of late nineteenth-century aesthetics. The theory was, at basis, an attempt to consider the subjective content that the viewer of works of art bring to the aesthetic process. In this sense it was a critique of the "empty" formalism of Johann Herbart and Robert Zimmermann, as well as of the "thematic" or absolute content of Hegelian metaphysics. Robert Vischer's ideas were disseminated in the late 1870s by a number of critics, chief of whom was the aesthetic philosopher Johannes Volkelt,[45] but it was not until the next decade that this conceptual line of development came to fruition. Heinrich Wöllflin (1864–1945), for instance, ran with the idea of empathy in his doctoral dissertation of 1886, *Prolegomena zu einer Psychologie der Architektur* (Prolegomena to a Psychology of Architecture).[46]

What is fascinating about Wölfflin's study is that this Swiss student of philosophy (following his doctoral studies at the universities of Basel, Berlin, and Munich) drew his ideas less from the writings of the two Vischers (he seems to have known of Robert Vischer's ideas only through his reading of Volkelt), and more directly from their sources. From both the text of his doctoral study and his preparatory notebooks, it is clear that Semper's text on style was indeed one of his principal sources (the writings of Bötticher and Burckhardt were two others).[47] Wölfflin studied both *Der Stil* and Semper's recently published *Kleine Schriften* (1884). The Semper passage referred to earlier on the "physiognomic refinement" that can be architecturally exploited became the leading theme of Wölffiin's analysis. Page after page of Wölfflin's text pays a discernible homage to Semper's ideas: from his criticism of Munich's Finance Ministry for its "furrowed brow" (rustication above) to his approbation of the "lacy ornament" that dresses the Doges' Palace in Venice.[48] Even seemingly unrelated comments – such as his reduction of the "moments" of pure form to two external moments (limitation, measure) and four internal moments (regularity, symmetry, proportion, and harmony) – find a line of development back through Friedrich Vischer (whom Wölfflin cites) to Semper's Prolegomena to *Der Stil*.

The dissertation, moreover, was not the last time Wölfflin drew upon Semper's thinking. In his first book *Renaissance and Baroque*, of 1888, Wölfflin converted his individual, physiognomically based psychology into a collective, cultural psychology, in which every period is invested with a vital feeling and every style with a mood. One of his starting examples is Semper's reading of the Greek and Egyptian cultural expressions, together with those peoples' physical demeanors, in their respective vessels for hauling water, the *hydria* and *situla*.[49] Another Semperian idea central to Wölfflin's thinking at this stage of his development was that the signs of formal or stylistic change first become manifested not in such high arts as architecture or painting but in the decorative or applied arts.[50] In these instances, Semper must be viewed as a prime source for Wölfflin's later formalism.

The young Wölfflin was not alone in his high regard for Semper in this decade. His mentor at the University of Berlin, Wilhelm Dilthey (1833–1911), referred to Semper a few years later as the "real successor to Goethe," because of his exploration of the "inner structure" of art: "The way he proceeded from the laws of spatial imagination, traced their effects in simple artistic achievements, and then moved up to the great creations is an enlightening model for how an important historical problem is to be solved in aesthetics."[51]

Another philosopher who was profoundly moved by what he termed Semper's "revelations" was Conrad Fiedler (1841–1895). His lone foray into architectural theory, "Observations on the Nature and History of Architecture" (1878), was nothing less than a commentary on the main themes of *Der Stil*.[52] Aside from praising Semper's "dressing" thesis – and the way in which it turns philosophically on a dematerialization of form, that is, on the animation of form with symbolic or ideal content – Fiedler focused on those passages of Semper's text that described the exploitation of space as holding the key to the future of architecture. He concluded that architecture might make a fresh start neither by following the formal possibilities of the Renaissance nor by observing the audacious spans of the Gothic, but by developing the notion of "a vaulted enclosure of space," as seen in the Romanesque style.[53] Fiedler, quite in contrast to such other theorists as Redtenbacher, viewed Semper as an idealist who successfully countered the materialist direction of contemporary aesthetics.

The same Semperian theme of space became the aesthetic starting point for yet another aesthetician, August Schmarsow (1853–1936). After beating Wölfflin for the chair in art history at the University of Leipzig in 1893, Schmarsow in his inaugural address, "The Essence of Architectural Creation," focused on defining architecture exclusively as the spatial art – in contrast to Wölfflin's formalism.[54] Schmarsow criticized the Semperians harshly, and somewhat unfairly, for reducing architecture to "the art of dressing," but then went on to employ not only Semper's suggestions of space but also the essential features of his directional axes to define his phenomenology of space, by which the human being knows space by virtue of his orientation and movement forward into it.

Schmarsow's model was developed further in a lecture of 1896, in which he expanded the idea of spatial creation to both painting and sculpture.[55] The same scheme underwent further elaboration in his *Grundbegriffe der Kunstwissenschaft am Übergang vom Altertum zum Mittelalter* (The Principles of the Science of Art at the Transition from Antiquity to the Middle Ages).[56] The axial dimension of Semper's three "moments of configuration" (symmetry, proportion, and direction) were now aligned with a single type of artistic expression as well as with a creative principle.

In another respect, Schmarsow's criticism of Semper in his address of 1893 was an indication that admiration for Semper was just now cresting and even beginning to wane in the 1890s. This was especially true in architecture, which, with the general dissatisfaction with historicism throughout Europe, was now in the midst of the most profound changes. Nowhere is this better seen than in the theory and practice of the Viennese architect Otto Wagner (1841–1918), one of the leading architects of Europe.

Wagner was an especially proficient designer and architectural thinker, always flexible to change. Born in Vienna in 1841, he studied architecture at the Academy of Fine Arts under Siccardsburgh and van der Nüll in the 1860s before settling down to a rather routine practice, designing mainly speculative apartment buildings in the vicinity of the Ringstrasse. He longed to become a monumental architect, however, and his adulation for the models of Semper (and Fischer von Erlach) is best seen in his palatial "Artibus" fantasy of 1880. Yet his career did not really gain international stature until around 1894, the year in which he was awarded both the commission for Vienna's local railway system and Hasenauer's old chair at the Vienna Academy of Fine Arts.

These new responsibilities encouraged a rethinking of his architectural outlook. Wagner quickly discarded the historicist curriculum at the Academy and substituted a new one predicated on architecture attending to the needs of modern life. In his practice he now gave up his adherence to "a certain free Renaissance" (a Semperian style of practice) and began to explore more revolutionary solutions.[57] The first result of his new consciousness was his brilliant polemical text of 1896, *Modern Architecture*, effectively the first architectural manifesto of the "Modern Movement."

Modern Architecture addressed itself to many of the issues of the looming modern debate. The starting point of Wagner's theoretical deliberations was his materialist criticism of Semper for preferring symbolic over material factors in the creation of a style – which, he felt, did not take into account the scientific bent of the time. Semper, he argued, simply "lacked the courage to complete his theories from above and below and had to make do with a symbolism of construction, instead of naming construction itself as the primitive cell of architecture."[58] Wagner's counter thesis, which he expressed in an unrelenting and uncompromising way throughout the text, can be summed up in the simple axiom: "The architect always has to develop the art-form [new style] out of construction."[59]

This criticism is quite enlightening of the modern architectural debate as it was shaping up in the mid-1890s. Three years after the publication of Wagner's book, the most percipient and thorough of its reviewers, the architect Richard Streiter, in turn criticized Wagner for vastly simplifying Semper's theory on the one hand, and for the materialist drift of his theory on the other hand. Streiter's contention was that Wagner's own practice did not match his theory: "Nowhere does one find that Wagner conceives the relation of construction and art-form differently than his modern architectural colleagues have become accustomed to conceiving it; in fact, it can even be asserted that a number of English, French, American, and German architects take far greater account of the principle – the architect always has to develop the art-form out of the construction – than Wagner does himself."[60]

Streiter actually saw quite clearly in 1898 what art historians have only recently come to see again – namely, that Wagner, notwithstanding his materialist polemics, adhered in his heart and in his practice to Semper's symbolic conception of architecture. It was Wagner who transplanted Semper's wreath-bearing angels from atop the Vienna Art Museum to the top of the "modern" Post Office Savings Bank, designed in 1903. It was Wagner again who created a frieze for his church Am Steinhof (also designed in 1903) with huge gilded wreaths (the wreath for Semper was the symbolic beginning of art).

Streiter's argument, in fact, was that Wagner – despite his avowed modernism – continued to view architecture almost exclusively in terms of its exterior and interior sheathings, that is, in a Semperian sense as symbolic dressings. The decorative boltheads (the Semperian concept of a rivet) that appear to nail the marble revetment panels to both his bank building and church Am Steinhof have less a constructional value and serve more the symbolic function of depicting the new technological direction of the profession: fitting the building with a new cut of clothing, as Josef Bayer would have termed it. It was a motif that Wagner began to play with as early as 1898, in his proposed renovation of the Capuchin church. One year later he applied this scarcely unworldly motif to his design of the Vienna Stadtmuseum.[61] On the Post Office Savings Bank, he even wanted these boltheads to be gilded, so as to be better seen from the Ringstrasse, one block away. Clearly they were more symbolic than real.

This interpretation of Semper on Wagner's part, in turn, leads to the problem that has plagued architectural history for some decades: the problem of correctly interpreting the so-called pioneers of the modern architecture in light of their often overlooked theoretical grounding. This problem can be seen, in particular, in the enigmatic figure of Adolf Loos (1870–1933), who also in more ways than one was influenced by Semper.

Loos – who not insignificantly was schooled in Dresden rather than in Vienna – followed Semper's theory quite closely in his essay of 1898, "Das Prinzip der Bekleidung" (The Principle of Dressing), by insisting that the architectural dressing (inherently ornamental in the primitive grass-woven mat) was older than the supporting structure. The implications of this fact, he noted further, is what separates "some architects" from "the architect." The former, the lesser category of designers, simply create walls then select an appropriate dressing; the artist-architect, however, moves in the opposite way by starting the creative process first with the consideration of the dressing. "He first senses the effect he intends to evoke and envisions the space he wishes to create. The effect he wishes to bring to bear on the spectator – be it fear or horror in a prison, reverence in a church, respect for the power of the state in a governmental palace, piety in a tomb, a sense of homeyness in a dwelling, gaiety in a tavern – this effect he evokes by the material and the form."[62]

Hence, the decorative wall dressing for Loos – far from being a criminal "ornament" to be dispensed with – becomes the essential motif by which the architect orchestrates or invokes his or her effects. The polychrome splendor of Loos's own dazzling interiors, which he achieved with the palette of brass, bronze, copper, and gold mosaics, colorful floor tiles, painted glass, decorative plaster, Oriental carpets, and above all by a truly Roman array of highly chromatic marble sheathings, demonstrates his essentially Semperian conception perfectly. The wall dressing now emerges as a haptic device: smooth surfaces that can be touched as much as seen. They are there to evoke that sense of "homeyness" that he found so important to this non-art of architecture. To view Loos, the sentimental ornamentalist, as the arch-opponent to ornament is to miscast him woefully.

A third modernist to draw inspiration from Semper was the Dutch architect Hendrik Berlage (1856–1934). After receiving his initial training at the Ryjksakademie von Beeldende Kunsten in Amsterdam, Berlage traveled to Zurich in 1875 to study at the Polytechnikum and partake of the Semper program. Berlage's writings, throughout his life, remained centered on Semper and Eugène Emmanuel Viollet-le-Duc – in his view the two great masters of modern theory. The uneasy juxtaposition of these two diverse thinkers was somewhat mitigated in Berlage's mind by his efforts to interpret Semper as a faithful rationalist. Nevertheless, Berlage also did not fail to laud Semper for his intentional symbolism, particularly for his advice to treat the constructional seam (the knot) decoratively.[63] Berlage's most important advancement of Semper's theory, however, was his definition of architecture in 1905 as the "art of spatial enclosure." It was this theme of space that was carried down through World War I and became such an important staple of the avant-garde modernism of the 1920s.[64] In this, it was Berlage's reflections on this theme – more so than those of Auer, Fiedler, or Schmarsow – which impressed itself into the architectural consciousness of the next generation.

Berlage's text of 1905, however, already reaches the point at which Semper's star was in rapid decline and countermovements were in formation. In 1902 the Berlin critic and architect Hermann Muthesius (1861–1927) published the second great manifesto of the modern movement, *Stilarchitektur und Baukunst* (Style-Architecture and Building-Art), which opened yet another front of modernist ideology with its criticism of both historicism and the symbolic infatuations of the *Jugendstil* movement. Muthesius also went after the Semperian grasp on theory in the last half of the nineteenth century, even though he could still praise "the brilliant Gottfried Semper" for being – after Schinkel – the most gifted German architect of his century. Semper's second Hoftheater, he felt, also displayed a "great mastery of every creative means of architecture;" his text on style had achieved "world renown" and made Semper "one of the most important writers on architecture of the century."[65]

In Muthesius's eyes, however, all of these accomplishments were insufficient to overcome Semper's one great failing, his inability to appreciate the "medieval building-art," that is, to participate in the theoretical line of modernism that Muthesius himself was mapping (ignoring comparable German sources) through William Morris. Actually, Semper's rejection of Gothicism, in Muthesius's eyes, reflected an even a more serious shortcoming in his character – his cosmopolitanism: "Semper also recognized and perceived no Nordic art; he perceived its every manifestation down to the present as only unwelcome deviations from his great world art – the antique. The whole tenor of Semper's work can be altogether understood as the outpouring of that cosmopolitan architecture that German Neoclassicism had created. A cosmopolitan architecture of the future, based on the antique, was its goal."[66]

Here, in this one incredible passage of 1902, Semper is criticized for precisely the same reasons that Walter Gropius, Mies van der Rohe, and others were criticized by the Nationalist Socialists in the early 1930s! Muthesius was also the first modern critic to hold the artistic efforts of the nineteenth century up to ridicule, to claim that there was little to be learned or remembered despite all the toil. This perceived "break" with the past became one of the most significant features of avant-gardism in the 1920s.

In any case it had by this later date little bearing on Semper's reputation, as he had now become largely irrelevant to the debate. From Peter Behrens' abrupt dismissal of Semper's theory in 1910 for its "mechanistic view of the nature of the work of art" (that is – strangely – for its inartistic values!), it is clear that few architects of this generation and the next were taking the time to read Semper firsthand.[67] And though Semper's name continued to be bandied about by various German architects in the 1920s and 1930s (Fritz Höber, Adolf Behne, and Fritz Schumacher, among others), Semper's theory had for the most part become incomprehensible, if not entirely forgotten by architects at this time.

This leads to what should certainly be one of the more interesting historiographic problems of the twentieth century – the problem of how major historical figures, such as Semper, can have their views falsely represented or effectively become lost to historical consciousness altogether. When Peter Behrens chastised Semper in 1910 for his "mechanistic view of the nature of a work of art," he was invoking not his own words but paraphrasing those of Alois Riegl, the famed Viennese art historian who had died in 1905 at the age of forty-seven. It was indeed Riegl's slowly evolving criticism of Semper's theory, unexpectedly erupting and terminating in 1901, that impressed itself within the art-historical consciousness of the twentieth century and became the colored lense through which many historians came to view Semper's thought – exclusively.

This historical ruse, if this is the correct word, becomes doubly interesting considering that Riegl himself can be counted among Semper's staunchest intellectual protégés, indeed as one of his greatest admirers. The relation of Riegl to Semper (the son intellectually devouring the historical reputation of his father) is indeed a fascinating one.

Riegl was born on 14 January 1858 in the Austrian town of Linz. His childhood, according to Max Dvorák, was an unhappy one.[68] He was forced by a strict father to labor from an early age over books, and thus was not able to enjoy the more normal pleasures of youth. At the age of sixteen, shortly after the death of his father, he entered the University of Vienna and enrolled in the department of humanities, not law, as is often said.[69] He attended lectures by such diverse thinkers as Robert Zimmermann and Franz Brentano and had an unusually rich education. In 1881 he was accepted into the Austrian Institute for Historical Research, run by Theodor von Sickel (Semper's son-in-law), where he learned many of the methodologies of the trade. There he also studied art history under Moritz Thausing. His early scholarly work, at least in part, was centered in architecture; in 1883 he prepared his doctoral dissertation on St. Jacob's church in Regensburg.

He was granted a fellowship to Rome for six months, then he returned to Vienna and joined the Austrian Museum for Art and Industry in 1884 as an apprentice in its textile department. The museum had been founded by Rudolf von Eitelberger in 1864, and its collections were arranged in part according to the ideas of Semper and the example of the museum in South Kensington. In one passage of *Der Stil* Semper had lamented the fact that whereas such fields as ceramics had many excellent collections throughout Europe (though he was thinking chiefly of Sèvres and the Zwinger), attention to textiles had been very slow in developing and few museums had realized the importance of assembling specimens in this field.[70]

The Austrian Museum for Art and Industry, specifically under Riegl's curatorship of this department in 1886, attempted to rectify this problem. Since the whole first volume of Semper's *Der Stil* was given over to the aesthetic and technical history of textiles, this book remained in 1886 one of the definitive texts in Riegl's new field of specialization. Riegl also shared with Semper a similar interest in the technical history of ornamental designs, even after he augmented his work at the Museum in 1889 with that of a *Privatdozent* at the University of Vienna (he gained the two stages of full professorship in 1895 and 1897). Riegl's first two books, *Altorientalische Teppiche* (Ancient Oriental Carpets; 1891) and *Stilfragen* (Questions of Style; 1893), were devoted, respectively, to textiles and textile ornament.

Margaret Olin's recently published analysis of Riegl's conceptual development allows us for the first time to understand and characterize much of Riegl's earlier scholarship.[71] It is an intellectual career that in its first stages was very much dependent on Semper's lead; it is not unfair to say that Riegl's cast of thought was essentially Semperian. Important intermediary figures in this regard are various interpreters of Semper in the 1870s and early 1880s, among them Alexander Conze.

This Austrian archaeologist, of the same generation as the German archaeologists Ernst Curtius and Heinrich Schliemann, made his mark in the mid-1870s with his excavations at Samothrace – diggings accompanied for the first time by precisely drawn plans and the first use of photographs for documentation. In his writings, Conze drew upon Semper's consideration of purpose, materials, and technical processes in the formation of certain ornamental patterns. Yet whereas Semper held such factors to be but a few of the variables influencing a style (there were also local, cultural, and personal factors), Conze – like so many of his contemporaries in archaeology and ethnology – employed these variables in a much more rigid manner, by interpreting ornamental motifs solely as patterns determined by the original materials and technical procedures used by a nation. Conze was interested in establishing early historical migration routes through the stylistic development of such motifs and argued, for instance, that Greek geometric vases could be traced back to Indo-Germanic models in northern Europe, thereby establishing a special affinity between the Greek and German peoples.

These were widely accepted paradigms when Riegl began his own study of ornamental designs. In one of his first historical writings of 1888, "Geschichte der textilen Kunst" (History of Textile Art), Riegl echoed Semper by insisting that many ornamental patterns found in other arts could be traced back to textiles, which he also characterized as one of the oldest arts. Riegl also placed great emphasis on materials in the development of a style.[72] Olin even goes so far as to define Riegl's historical premises at this juncture in his development as "mechanistic" in their structure.[73]

In his lectures given at the University of Vienna in 1890–91 on the history of ornament, Riegl continued to structure his stylistic analyses largely in Semperian terms, for instance, in his distinction between the ornamental "frame and filling," that is, the division Semper made between ornament that symbolizes the technically-functioning parts of a design and ornament (sometimes high art) intended simply to fill in the panels or spaces in between.[74]

The working hypotheses and language of Semper also inform Riegl's first book of 1891, *Altorientalische Teppiche*, in which Riegl attempted to prove that Saracenic principles of ornamentation descended from classical Greek and Roman models. This was a subject that had also fascinated Semper, beginning with the oriental tapestries he viewed at the Great Exhibition of 1851 and later at Henry Cole's Department of Practical Art. In section after section of his remarks on textiles in *Der Stil*, Semper lauded oriental carpets for their non-naturalistic or conventionalized designs as superb examples to study because of their ingenious decorative principles and color harmonies.

In his Preface to *Altorientalische Teppiche* Riegl lauded Semper, Richard Redgrave, and Owen Jones (and the arts and crafts reform movement in general) for first appreciating the stylistic merits of oriental carpets.[75] Another important source is Julius Lessing's book of 1877, *Altorientalischen Teppichmustern* (Ancient Oriental Carpet Patterns). This book, in Riegl's view, was not only the first study "to propose a reliable chronology of ancient oriental carpets," but also the work that set down the parameters in which "further research had to move." Moreover, in an interesting attribution, "it was Lessing who first brought to full light the fundamental importance of the factors of technical production for the judgment of oriental carpets."[76]

The high praise afforded Lessing in this book also sheds further light on the Semper-Riegl relationship. Lessing was the influential director of the Kunstgewerbemuseum or Berlin Museum of Applied Arts and was (like his colleague Eitelberger in Vienna) sufficiently moved by Semper's ideas to arrange his collections after Semper's four-motive thesis. The Berlin museum had been founded in 1867 and the first buildings, erected between 1877 and 1884, housed – as in Vienna – a museum, library, and school. Lessing's artistic views remained strongly influenced by Semper and by the mid-1890s Lessing became (as Riegl himself later became) a major protagonist in the debate on modernism.

But Lessing, like so many of his contemporaries in the related fields at this time, was interpreting Semper's theory in a highly deterministic and materialist way – far beyond the boundaries that Semper himself had established. In a very instructive essay of 1895, "Neue Wege" (New Paths), Lessing pondered the many changes that had overtaken the applied arts during the previous thirty years, chief of which was the infusion of naturalistic motifs. Yet these advances, he went on to argue, pulled up short of satisfying the needs of modern life, which should be shaped not by naturalism but by the criteria of appropriateness to purpose, material, and technologies. Lessing then posed two questions that Semper had also considered with respect to art. "Is it conceivable," Lessing asked, "that instead of a gradual development taking place from the historical tradition, these technical factors themselves will create completely new forms?" And "can we consider the recently invented, purely constructional form of a modern steel girder to be a creation similar to the Greek column, whose hallowed form has ruled all periods of art up to today?"[77]

Semper had specifically answered both questions in the negative, by arguing that the steel girder added nothing conceptually new to the structural principles of timber. But Lessing answered the same questions with an emphatic "yes," insisting that the modern steel girder, like the Greek column, was a product of structural calculation, just like the purely functional lines of an automobile or ship. "Like it or not," he concluded, "our work has to be based on the soil of the practical life of our time; it has to create those forms that correspond to our needs, our technology, and our materials."[78]

Lessing and Semper also shaped Riegl's book on ancient oriental carpets in other respects. Both are often cited and thus are obviously seen by Riegl as authorities in this field. Thematically, as Olin has constructed it, the book presents a developmental history of ornamental motifs in oriental carpets, passing through three stages of: 1) designs technically determined and geometric in style; 2) designs conventionalized, in which technical difficulties are avoided and replaced by pleasing stylization; and 3) designs in which the technical difficulties are fully overcome and the artist (and this is where Riegl differed from Semper) is free to disregard all stylistic limits.[79]

Echoes of Semper reverberate elsewhere. Carpets are first divided into those that are woven (wall hangings) and those that are knotted (floor mats); characteristics are determined by the necessities of technical production. Riegl also spoke of carpets through Semper's terminology – discussing their design, for instance, through the arrangement of their centers, seams, borders, and hems. Therefore he should be viewed as still a Semperian in 1891. (The ideas of the Semperians, however, should be distinguished from those of Semper himself, for whom these technical factors were but one aspect of a broader style theory.) Riegl, in short, was partaking of the same deterministic and materialist use of Semper's ideas that colored so much other artistic theory at this time.

Riegl himself came to recognize this fact by the time that he wrote his next book: *Stilfragen: Grundlegungen zu einer Geschichte der Ornamentik* (Questions of Style: Foundations for a History of Ornament; 1893). Much new intellectual terrain is won here in other respects. Notwithstanding the emphasis that is so often placed on Riegl's later writings, *Stilfragen* was an extremely important book; certainly his most scholarly contribution to this expansive theme of ornamentation. With it, as its title suggests, Riegl sought to carry on the encompassing intellectual tradition of his predecessor, even though the scope of the book is more limited. The theme is, however, more intensely and systematically pursued.

In amassing considerable ornamental material, Riegl attempted to demonstrate a continuous tradition in ornamental pattern development, from the lotus blossoms of the Egyptians down to the Islamic arabesques of the early Middle Ages.

The leitmotif of the book derives in part from Riegl's new campaign against those who attributed ornamental patterns solely to technical-material origins. This was not an entirely spontaneous realization on Riegl's part but rather a view that had been slowly forming in his lectures over the past three years. It is highlighted in the introduction by Riegl's now famous distinction between Semper and the "Semperians," in which Riegl, in essence, came to the defense of Semper against the overly deterministic and materialist reading of his theory by so many of his followers.

The argument is ingeniously constructed. Riegl starts by conceding that this technical-materialist interpretation of the origin of art for the most part developed in the 1860s and is a view "usually attributed to Gottfried Semper." Yet Riegl finds this association no more acceptable that the one made between contemporary Darwinism and Darwin. This comparison, as it turns out, was a far-reaching connection to make and it eventually led to much confusion. But this was not the case in 1893: "I find the analogy between Darwinism and artistic materialism especially appropriate," Riegl continued, "since there is unquestionably a close and causal relationship between the two: the materialist interpretation of the origin of art is nothing other than Darwinism imposed upon an intellectual discipline."[80]

Only after making this point did Riegl return to Semper's theory in very precise terms: "However, one must distinguish just as much and just as sharply between Semper and his followers as between Darwin and his adherents. Whereas Semper did suggest that material and technique play a role in the genesis of art forms, the Semperians jumped to the conclusion that all art forms were always the direct product of materials and techniques."[81]

Riegl's words in this passage are exceedingly clear, even if scores of later commentators have since confused them. Riegl declared his opposition to ascribing ornamental patterns solely to technical or material causes, and in doing so he defended Semper against the excesses of certain unnamed "Semperians," who misrepresented certain aspects of his theory. In the next paragraph he again drew upon Semper, this time in support of his thesis of *Kunstwollen* (artistic will): "It may seem paradoxical that so many practicing artists also joined the extreme faction of art materialism. They were, of course, not acting in the spirit of Gottfried Semper, who would never have agreed to exchanging free and creative artistic impulse [*Kunstwollen*] for an essentially mechanical and materialist drive to imitate."[82]

Once again his meaning is abundantly clear. Semper himself, as an artist who held nothing but the highest esteem for the creative aspects of his craft, was also in radical opposition to these lines of materialist thinking. If he had wanted, Riegl might have cited Semper's passage in his Zurich lecture on style, in which Semper – in censoring certain Darwinians of his own day who would impose "Darwin's theory on the origin of species" upon art – insisted that old monuments, or art works in general, "are the free creations of man, on which he employed his understanding, observation of nature, genius, will, knowledge, and power."[83] Instead, Riegl simply reproved those scholars, archaeologists, and art historians for invoking Semper for their own ends: "Their misinterpretation was taken to reflect the genuine thinking of the great artist and scholar."[84] Riegl's assessment of Semper in these passages was entirely accurate and fair. He wanted to align himself with

Semper against the excesses of the Semperians. His principal task was to disprove the assumption that all ornamental designs derive from technical-material causes.

But just who were these "Semperians" who had distorted their master's theory or falsely invoked Semper's name? Architects have sometimes been assumed to have been the primary culprits in this matter, and there were certainly various individuals who could have fallen into this category. Margaret Iversen, for instance, has recently hypothesized: "I want to argue that Otto Wagner must have been one of the people Riegl disparagingly referred to as the 'sub-Semperians,' or at the very least he represented the latest and most prominent exponent of a theoretical position to which Riegl was implacably opposed."[85]

The last part of her statement is undoubtedly true, but it is unlikely that Riegl could have had Wagner in mind in 1893. Wagner at this date was still relatively unknown and had published very little. He first gained prominence only in 1894 when he received the two separate appointments as the designer of Vienna's railway system and as a professor at the Academy of Fine Arts. His book *Modern Architetur,* in which he promulgated his materialist beliefs and criticized Semper for not doing away with his symbolism in favor of a more hard-line materialist approach, did not appear until 1896.

This is not to say that architects were not keenly aware of these issues. In addition to Wagner's coupling of Semper and Darwin in 1896, Hans Semper, in 1880, had already somewhat injudiciously characterized his father's theory as "only a step away" from that of Darwin.[86] The problem of technology and materialism in architecture (and its evolution) had been a constant of a vigorous Germanic debate since the 1840s, but was especially evident in the 1880s and 1890s.[87] It was so prominent by the end of the century that Richard Streiter, in his 1898 review of Wagner's book, could – after citing in full the above passages by Riegl – also confidently place Wagner in that category of "Semperians" who had misconstrued their master's thought.[88] But this was, of course, after the fact with regard to Riegl's comments in 1893.

If architects were not, or were only a few of the unnamed footsoldiers in this army of Semperians, then there were certainly other candidates. Julius Lessing, whose comments of 1895 have already been quoted, would certainly fall into this category, as would various other critics and curators connected with the technical arts. The trouble with building the case of the Semperians around these people, however, is that their names do not appear in *Stilfragen.* Riegl's focus at this time was rather narrowly centered on textile motifs.

It becomes clear, however, who some of these Semperians were from reading the first chapter of *Stilfragen.* The anti-materialist polemic weaves like a red thread through this chapter on "The Geometric Style," and always wherever Semper's name appears. Riegl in this chapter sought to knock down two propositions governing contemporary archaeological and ethnological studies: 1) that the geometric style of ornamentation was a spontaneous creation of various cultures; 2) that the geometric style originated from the technical processes of wickerwork and weaving. To do so, Riegl, in all cases, invoked Semper to support his own argument against the technical-material excesses of the Semperians.

Semper, Riegl wrote, was the first to trace certain designs of the geometric style back to weaving techniques, but he did so in conjunction with his theory of "dressing." "It is obvious in numerous passages in *Der Stil,*" Riegl continued, "that Semper originally conceived of the prototypes of the cover and the band primarily as abstractions and not really in a concrete materialist way, for Semper would surely have been the last person to discard thoughtlessly truly creative, artistic ideas in favor of the physical-materialist imitative impulse; it was his numerous followers who subsequently modified the theory into its crassly materialist form."[89]

Riegl next identified the first of these crass modifiers of Semper's theory – the archaeologist Alexander Conze. He did so at this point with some degree of restraint, as he was still at this time a relatively minor scholar on the European stage and his opposition to Conze may even have related to a contemporary political debate within Austrian academia.[90] Conze rigorously applied Semper's theory of the technical origin of certain motifs to the vases of the Greek geometric style, and his work was so distinguished in its scholarly detail that for the past twenty years no one has challenged this underlying premise. Riegl likened Conze's reading of Semper to the *Weltanschauung* propagated by Lamarck, Goethe, and Darwin, in which art was considered a higher intellectual activity and therefore could not have been practiced at the very earliest period of human evolution. In opposing this, Riegl argued that on the basis of recent ethnological evidence of Neolithic and Paleolithic cultures, art in many cases preceded the development of primitive technologies.

To oppose this Darwinian contention and to demonstrate "how far they [Conze and others] strayed from the ideas of the actual father of the theory," Riegl turned away from Conze and back to Semper. He cited a passage from the second volume of *Der Stil* in which Semper, in reflecting on the difficulty of tracing the origin of zigzag ornaments in ceramics, admitted it was impossible to determine if they preceded in time the engraved embellishments on the oldest bronze utensils or vice versa.[91] Riegl returned to a familiar theme: "This is the cautious wording of an author who, as both artist and scholar knew and understood better than most others of his century the technical procedures involved in the creation of art as a larger, mutually interactive process. According to Semper, as quoted above, technology played its formative role at a more advanced stage of artistic development and not at the very inception of artistic activity." He concluded this phase of his argument in forceful terms: "This is precisely my conviction."[92]

Riegl next cited another passage from *Der Stil*, in which Semper ruminated on the origin of weaving. Semper had pointed to the abundant ethnological evidence of so-called primitive societies, such as those in the South Pacific, in which crude fences or pens were made by interlacing sticks and branches. The transition from weaving branches to weaving grasses for primitive textile enclosures was an "easy and natural" maneuver, says Semper: "The variations in the natural colors of the blades soon led people to use them in alternating arrangements and thus arose the pattern."[93]

Riegl interpreted this passage – like a faithful exegesist interpreting an Old Testament verse – to mean that the pattern was produced not through some blind technical chance but through a conscious, creative instinct. Moreover, as Riegl finished his point, "the passages in *Der Stil* in which Semper stands in direct contradiction to the technical-materialist interpretation are, incidentally, not at all rare."[94]

Having defended Semper in a very cogent way, Riegl turned to another of the "crassly materialist" followers of Semper: the archaeologist Reinhard Kekulé. He also arrived at the heart of the issue he was pursuing. Riegl objected not to a published book but to a paper Kekulé read at the Berlin Archaeological Society in 1890, on the origin of the forms and ornaments of the oldest Greek and pre-Greek vases. Kekulé, it seems, had insisted that the zigzag patterns on these vases were derived from the forms and patterns of older basket prototypes, thereby (in Riegl's view) discounting creative or artistic activity altogether.

To counter this thesis, Riegl turned over his ace: the zigzag patterns found carved on reindeer bones in the Paleolithic caves of French Aquitaine. These discoveries made in the late-1870s and 1880s (and therefore unavailable to Semper but known to Kekulé) conclusively demonstrate, Riegl felt, that artistic essays preceded the invention of certain human technologies, such as weaving, by thousands of years. And to altogether dismantle Kekulé's contention, Riegl further cited Semper on the primacy of the decorative instinct, that is, Semper's view that the painting and tattooing of the body may have preceded the use of clothing.[95]

Riegl concluded this chapter with one final and spirited defense of Semper against the scourge of the Semperians: "In order to avoid any misunderstanding, I would like to stress once again that I consider Gottfried Semper in no way responsible for the subsequent interpretation and extension of his ideas as described above. He was not at all intent on finding the supreme materialist explanation for the earlier forms of human artistic expression."[96] Semper's only fault, and it was an exceedingly minor fault in Riegl's eyes at this time, was that he simply overestimated the importance of the textile arts in supplying decorative motifs.

To the archaeologists Conze and Kekulé, however, should be added one other Semperian whom Riegl was contesting in 1893 – Riegl himself, or rather his own earlier beliefs. This seems to be so obvious in view of the preceding passages that it scarcely needs an explanation. *Stilfragen* was that defining moment in Riegl's intellectual career (one that is a part of every creative scholar's life) at which he came to recognize the limitations of both his own earlier historical assumptions and – in this case – his own materialist tendencies. He saw not only the limitation of the premises by which archaeology was generally framed in the 1880s (that which is very apparent in his own earlier writings) but also the fact that Semper himself, who was writing not as an archaeologist but as an artist, never couched his theory in such terms. Semper's text could therefore be used as a forceful weapon in Riegl's assault on later developments. Why else would he focus so much time and effort on a book that was written thirty years earlier and had been completely superseded by the intervening and unprecedented historical research?

But what Riegl did not realize at this time was that his own theory had not fully evolved. I would suggest further that he was in only the first phase of a classic "love-hate" relationship toward his mentor Semper, one that was yet to play itself out. Riegl in 1893 truly admired the range of Semper's interests as well as his many original insights, and he no doubt saw himself as a worthy successor. This is the reason why, again and again in the first chapter of this book, Riegl felt compelled to defend Semper against the "misinterpretations" of his admirers.

He was also entirely correct that many passages of *Der Stil* supported Semper's long-standing opposition to material and technical explanations as having any genuine validity for architectural development. This is evident at the very beginning of the text, when Semper insisted that his consideration of material and technology should not be read in a materialist manner: "The constructional-technical understanding of the origin of basic architectural forms, alluded to above and pursued below, has nothing in common with the coarsely materialist view that suggests that an architecture's particular essence is nothing but constructional design – illustrated statics and mechanics, a mere demonstration of material."[97] In Semper's style theory – it must be underscored in view of what follows – these material and technical factors were but the internal factors conditioning (not determining) a style; among the outward factors were such things as the climate, geography, social-political conditions, and above all the personal influence and free will of the artist. Riegl in 1893 was fully in accord with Semper's theory.

But it is only by the analogy of a "love-hate" relationship that the second phase of Riegl's regard toward Semper can be explained, the stage Riegl had reached when he wrote the introduction to *Spätrömische Kunstindustrie* in 1901. Nothing, in fact, in Riegl's complex intellectual development during these eight years, would lead one to expect his extreme change of attitude toward one of the primary shapers of his own beliefs. Semper's name comes up in this lengthy book only in two places and the first passage – because it soon became of such paramount importance to the historical reputation of Semper – deserves to be quoted in full. Riegl approached the topic of Semper by criticizing those art historians of the 1890s who were unable to make a break with the "dominant" notion of the fine arts that had ruled artistic thinking for the previous thirty or forty years:

> This is that theory generally associated with the name of Gottfried Semper, according to which the work of art is nothing other than a mechanical product of purpose, raw material, and technique. When this theory appeared it was correctly seen as an essential advance over the altogether unclear notions of the previous romantic period; yet today it is long overdue that it finally be consigned to history. For as with so many other theories from the middle of the past century, which were originally presumed to be the greatest triumph of the exact natural sciences, Semper's theory on final review also turns out to be nothing more than a dogma of materialist metaphysics.
>
> In contrast to this mechanistic conception of the nature of the work of art, I presented in *Stilfragen* (as I see it, for the first time) a teleological theory, in which I viewed the work of art as a result of a specific and purposeful artistic will [*Kunstwollen*] that asserts itself in confiict with purpose, raw material, and techniques. Thus these last three factors no longer have that positive creative role attributed to them by so-called Semperian theory but rather a restraining negative one: they form, so to speak, the coefficients of friction within the total product.[98]

Even with such mitigating qualifiers as "generally associated" and "name of Gottfried Semper" (rather than denouncing Semper himself), one must ask why did Riegl completely reverse his own explanation of eight years earlier? Why did this notion of a *Kunstwollen*, which he introduced in 1893 by invoking Semper's support, become the issue with which he vehemently denounced Semper? Had he, in fact, made such a dramatic shift in his own art-historical thinking away from Semper's model?

This third question is highly debatable. Even if one grants the historical innovations of his analytical terms "tactile" and "optic" space, there is still the matter (though it is beyond the scope of this study to pursue it in detail) of the rich array of intellectual sources (few of whom Riegl credits) that lay behind Riegl's new-found perceptual and psychological aesthetics – illustrious names such as Adolf Hildebrand, August Schmarsow, Adolf Göller, Heinrich Wölfflin, Conrad Fiedler, and Robert Vischer. The problem is that many, if not all, of these thinkers contributing to Riegl's innovative treatment of space also drew upon aspects of Semper's theory. Thus the line of intellectual development between Semper and Riegl, it can be argued, is still intact. In addition, the very theme of Riegl's new analysis – the development of a spatial impulse in the plastic and technical arts of late Roman antiquity – certainly owes a direct obligation to Semper, even if the latter isolated the concept of space as an artistic urge in the architecture of late-Hellenic times.[99] What also should be figured into this discussion is the infatuation Riegl still had for certain Semperian concepts as late as the time of writing of his two unpublished "Grammars" of 1897–98 and 1899.[100]

The second issue of the *Kunstwollen* is equally problematic. In 1893, as noted above, he introduced this term and seized the artistic support of Semper, "who would never have agreed to exchanging free and creative artistic impulse for an essentially mechanical and materialist drive to imitate." In 1901 the term was used in a manner that directly opposed the theory of Semper. It is an "artistic will" acting in opposition to purpose, material, and techniques; the latter are merely "negative coefficients." The last phrase is an allusion to Semper's mathematical analogy, which was corrupted (although Riegl could not have known this) by Hans Semper in its German translation from English. This allusion presents, however, an especially cruel historical irony, as Riegl essentially used a mistranslation of Semper "as a crutch" not only for explicating the notion of *Kunstwollen* but also for reducing all of Semper's theory to the factors of purpose, material, and technique.

But something did indeed change with regard to the notion of *Kunstwollen* during those eight years – Riegl's understanding of the meaning of the term itself. Whereas earlier it was a notion to be associated with a personal artistic will or freedom, it clearly came to mean a teleological or controlling *Zeitgeist* that rules the artistic development of an epoch. Such a view has far more in common with Hegel (although the historical approach of Carl Schnaase is more frequently invoked)[101] than with Semper, and in fact this type of historical analysis bears no relation to any aspect of Semper's thought. Thus Riegl perhaps had some basis for discrediting Semper's theory by invoking the term in this case – as Semper with his exaltation of artistic free will would certainly have condemned Riegl for his mechanistic and deterministic historical understanding!

Riegl himself appears to have felt some remorse over this ploy, for on the second and last occasion that Semper's name appears in Riegl's text, in a footnote 142 pages later, its author again linked Semper to post-Semperian materialism, but with the parenthetical qualification, "yet partly in a misinterpretation of his statements."[102] This faint apology is, however, soon recanted, as at the end of his note Riegl equated Semper's uncritical attitude to that of the "dilettante modern artist." This note, incidentally, is instructive in other respects, as Riegl counts as disciples of materialism "modern architects," as well as "modern artists involved with aesthetics," such as Adolf Göller and Adolf Hildebrand. In essence, Riegl blames the phenomenon of historicism in the nineteenth century on the lack of imagination of those mechanically thinking architects who could do nothing other than imitate the past.

But this still leaves us with the first question as to why Riegl in 1901, at a time when Semper's thought had all but lost its relevance to the artistic debate, felt compelled once again to raise Semper's name and condemn his thought outright as a "dogma of materialist metaphysics," one "long overdue to be finally consigned to history." The operative term here seems to be the adverb "finally" (*endgültig*), as it demonstrates that Riegl was obviously growing impatient with how slowly the older biases employed in art history were being surrendered. If this is in part the case, then it is understandable that the demons of his own past had to be exorcised, that his intellectual father had to be carried to the sacrificial altar. This is at least suggested by Riegl's use here of the German verb *einverleiben*, which we have so innocuously translated as "consigned." When used reflexively and colloquially, it has the meaning of "to consume, to eat, to drink." Literally, it has the meaning of ingesting something into the body, similar to the English verb "to incorporate." And what better way to perform this sacrificial rite of art-historical cannibalism than to define Semper as the founding member of that cult Riegl so facetiously and disdainfully referred to in 1893 as the "Semperians!"

Whatever the explanation for this event, Riegl's characterization of Semper in 1901 (the only reference to Semper's thought that passed through the filter of the next generation of historians) had a devastating effect on Semper's historical reputation. This overtly "crass" misinterpretation became in fact yet another "dogma" of the art-historical literature of the twentieth century, as seen most cogently in Lionello Venturi's blistering attack on Semper's thought in 1936:

> It was Semper who gave general value and aesthetic pretension to technical motives. He is the adversary of all idealism and tends to natural science of the Darwinian type. He is not interested in the intimate life of art, but in the evolution of forms assumed as essential. He believes he is able to find in technique the origin of essential forms, of types and symbols in art. He occupies himself neither with painting nor sculpture, but with architecture and the decorative arts, textiles, ceramics, works in metal, and so on. Apart from the material of art he considers utilitarian character as the only aim of art. Even if repugnant, such a materialistic conception of art has, however, had its use: that of recalling the attention of the historian to the realisation of mind in matter, to the way in which matter had been sensibilised by art. Semper's culture was, however, too limited to enable him to draw from his own principles the stylistic conclusions in a historical sense, as they were later drawn by Robert Vischer and Alois Riegl.[103]

The interesting thing about this woeful miscasting of Semper's thought is that Venturi obviously formed his view of Semper not by reading his words directly but (like Behrens) by reading and paraphasing Riegl. Moreover, Venturi's terminology refers to both the 1893 and 1901 texts, but he fails to understand their fundamental contradiction. Did he miss altogether the point of Riegl's analogy of Semper with Darwin in 1893, as well as the crucial distinction between Semper and the Semperians?

Nevertheless, Venturi's summary analysis now "had its use": that of underscoring the very fragility of historical understanding itself. And Semper presents us with a model case in other respects as well, for it was not just his theory but also his practice that was miscast and displaced by the distillations of later ideologies. But it is unnecessary any longer to dwell on these issues. The importance that Semper holds for us today is really the depth and understanding that he brings to this particular historical period, to a time when architects had the courage to pose and attempt to answer the most difficult questions concerning the practice of their art. It is a period that for nearly a century has been undervalued for its accomplishments in practice and theory. It is a period that still has much to say with regard to our contemporary deliberations – now that Modernism itself is falling victim to the same process of historical simplification and distortion.

Notes

Prologue

1. The single, anonymous account of Semper's funeral appears in the *Neues Wiener Tagblatt*, 221, 12 August 1879, under the title "Gottfried Semper: als Mensch und Künstler." The author signed it "x. y. z" and indicates that he had direct access to some of the family papers held by Manfred Semper.
2. For a description of Schinkel's funeral, see Kugler, *Karl Friedrich Schinkel*, 21.
3. Semper's statue was privately commissioned and unveiled in Dresden during a formal ceremony on 1 September 1892. Earlier, in 1887, a bust of Semper had been set up in the stairhall of the Eidgenössische Polytechnikum (now Eidgenössische Technische Hochschule) in Zürich.
4. Muthesius, *Stilarchitektur und Baukunst*, 9; Eng. trans. by Stanford Anderson, *Style-Architecture and Building-Art* (Santa Monica: The Getty Center for the History of Art and the Humanities), 50.
5. See Karl Friedrich Schinkel's remarks in *Aus Schinkels Nachlass*, II, 211–12. Karl Bötticher struggled with this possibility in "Das Prinzip der hellenischen und germanischen Bauweise hinsichtlich der Übertragung in die Bauweise unserer Tage," *Allgemeine Bauzeitung* (1846), 111–25. This essay has recently been translated and published in Herrmann, *In What Style should we Build?*
6. Friedrich Nietzsche, *The Use and Abuse of History*, trans. Adrian Collins (Indianapolis: Bobbs-Merrill, 1957), 16.
7. The chief monographic studies in recent times focusing on Semper's built works are Manteuffel's "Die Baukunst Gottfried Sempers (1803–1879)"; Martin Fröhlich, *Gottfried Semper: Zeichnerischer Nachlass*; Staatliche Kunstsammlungen Dresden, *Gottfried Semper 1803–79: Baumeister zwischen Revolution und Historismus*; Magirius, *Gottfried Sempers zweites Dresdner Hoftheater*; Magirius, "Die Gemäldegalerie in Dresden"; Hänsch, *Die Semperoper*; Franck, *Die Nikolaikirche*. For Semper's theory, biographical details, and practice, see Herrmann, *In Search of Architecture*; Dresden Technischen Universität, *Gottfried Semper 1803–79*; Herrmann, *Theoretischer Nachlass*; Laudel, *Architektur und Stil*.
8. Duncan Berry, "From Historicism to Architectural Realism: On Some of Wagner's Sources," in Mallgrave (ed.), *Otto Wagner: Reflections on the Raiment of Modernity*, 247–48. See also Berry's doctoral study concerning this theme, "The Legacy of Gottfried Semper: Studies in Späthistorismus," 170–74. A similar approach has been taken by Peter Wegmann in his excellent study, *Gottfried Semper und das Winterthurer Stadthaus*.
9. *Die k. k. Hofmuseen in Wien und Gottfried Semper: Drei Denkschriften Gottfried Semper*. This text and a reading of Semper's buildings was also furthered by Lhotsky in *Die Baugeschichte der Museen*.
10. Heinrich Magirius has two highly instructive studies: *Gottfried Sempers zweites Dresdner Hoftheater*, 80–266, and his essay, "Die Gemäldegalerie in Dresden," in *Gemäldegalerie Dresden*, 29–61. See also Hänsch, *Die Semperoper*. One of the earliest and best of the past studies is Lübke, "Das Neue Museum zu Dresden".
11. See Benjamin's concept of a *flâneur*, as developed in his incomplete sketch, "Paris, Capital of the Nineteenth Century," in *Reflections: Essays, Aphorisms*.
12. The term "theatricality" has recently been applied to Semper's architecture in an essay by Magirius, "Das zweite Dresdner Hoftheater Gottfried Sempers". Although I developed this concept with regard to Semper through my own studies, I find support from this parallel line of reasoning by Professor Magirius.
13. See especially Michael Fried's notion of theatricality, beginning with his seminal essay on sculpture, "Art and Objecthood," in *Art Forum* (Summer 1967), and continuing down to *Absorption and Theatricality* and *Courbet's Realism*.
14. Charles Garnier, *Le Théâtre* (Paris: Librairie Hachette, 1871), 2. "Tout ce qui se passe au

monde n'est en somme que théâtre et représentation.... Voir et se faire voir, entendre et se faire entendre, c'est le cercle fatal de l'humanité; être acteur ou spectateur, c'est la condition vitale des êtres; c'est le but en même temps que le moyen."

15. Ibid., 8.
16. Richard Wagner, *Mein Leben*, I, 382.
17. See Constantin Lipsius, *Gottfried Semper*, 101. Lipsius's biography also appeared in the journal *Deutsche Bauzeitung*, running in installments from January to May 1880.
18. Ibid. "'Er besass,' schreibt mir Herr Professor Bursian, 'mehr als alle Menschen, die ich kennen gelernt habe, die grösste Unmittelbarkeit der künstlerischen Empfindung und das feinste künstlerische Urtheil.'" For other biographical accounts of Semper's personality, see Pecht, *Deutsche Kunstler*; Bayer, "Gottfried Semper," also published in *Josef Bayer: Baustudien und Baubilder*; Hans Semper, *Gottfried Semper*.

1 *Despondent Years*

1. Semper's baptismal certificate, which was issued in Altona, is preserved in the Semper Archives in Zürich, but his birth certificate is not. Other evidence is ambivalent. In enrolling at the Munich Academy of Fine Arts in 1825, Semper listed his place of birth as Altona. Yet some years later, in a fragment of an autobiographical statement, he wrote that he was born in Hamburg.
2. Hans Semper, *Gottfried Semper*; and Lipsius, *Gottfried Semper*. Their reports conform with Claus Zoege von Manteuffel's statement, based on other evidence, that the house in Altona was owned by Gottfried's maternal grandparents. This accounts for the baptism taking place there. See Manteuffel's "Die Baukunst Gottfried Sempers," 17.
3. For a brief history of the Semper family see Paul Hoffmann, *Neues Altona 1919–29: Zehn Jahre Aufbau einer Deutschen Großstadt* (Jena: Eugen Diedericks, 1929), 272–74.
4. See Pecht, *Deutsche Kunstler*, 154.
5. Gottfried to parents, 18 April 1818, 3 January 1819, and 7 March 1819, Semper Archiv, ETH-Hönggerberg.
6. Semper discussed Hipp's advice in a letter to his parents, dated 10 May 1824. Hipp later referred to his recommendation to study mathematics in a letter to Semper dated 12 August 1825, Semper Archiv.
7. Adolf Hertz to Gottfried, no date (fragment), Semper Archiv.
8. Eduard Sthamer to Gottfried, 20 June 1823, Semper Archiv.
9. Friedrich Heeren to Gottfried, 7 August 1823 and 29 August 1823, Semper Archiv.
10. Gottfried to father, 2 November 1823, Semper Archiv.
11. Gottfried to father, 10 May 1824, Semper Archiv.
12. Gottfried to parents, 19 August 1824, Semper Archiv.
13. Gottfried to Carl, 10 December 1823, Semper Archiv.
14. Elise to Gottfried, 24 February 1824, Semper Archiv.
15. Gottfried to father, 10 May 1824, Semper Archiv.
16. Gottfried to parents, 5 August 1824, Semper Archiv.
17. Gottfried to parents, 19 August 1824, Semper Archiv.
18. Gottfried to father, 25 March 1825, Semper Archiv.
19. Gottfried To Wilhelm, 29 April 1825, Semper Archiv.
20. For some comments on German university life in the early nineteenth century, see Berlin, "The Apotheosis of the Romantic Will," in *The Crooked Timber of Humanity*, 207–37. For the prevalence of dueling at this time, see Robinson, *The Birth of the Modern: World Society 1815–30*, 466.
21. Hipp to Gottfried, 12 August 1825, Semper Archiv.
22. Johann Carl to Gottfried, 6 September 1825, Semper Archiv.
23. Gottfried to Johann Carl, 5 September 1825, Semper Archiv.
24. Ibid.
25. See Herrmann, "Sempers Weg von der Mathematik zur vergleichenden Baulehre," 73–81.
26. Gottfried to Wilhelm, 20 October 1825, Semper Archiv.
27. Semper's enrollment number was 1073, but other school records that may have indicated what studio or courses he attended were destroyed in World War II. I would like to thank Regierungsamtsrat Hausner for supplying me with this information.
28. Father to Wilhelm, 15 November 1825, Semper Archiv.
29. Gottfried to Wilhelm, 18 November 1825, Semper Archiv.
30. Also speaking against extensive academic

instruction are the architectural drawings from Semper's training in Paris under Gau, now preserved in Zürich. The earliest of these drawings suggest little more than a beginning student in architecture rather than someone trained under Gärtner, who was noted for his delineatory emphasis.

31. Gottfried to August Wilhelm Döbner, 5 August 1827. A transcript of this letter is in the Semper Archiv. The original has apparently been lost.
32. Ibid.
33. The four letters are Caroline Marca to Gottfried, 30 October 1826; Johanna von Thon-Dittmar, 30 October 1826; Julie von Thon-Dittmar, 30 October 1826; Clara Scholler, 3 November 1826 – all in the Semper Archiv. Julie von Thon-Dittmar became a lifelong friend of Semper.
34. Gottfried to Johann Carl, 15 December 1826, Semper Archiv.
35. This is the explanation that Karl Hammer provides in his *Jakob Ignaz Hittorff: Ein Pariser Baumeister 1792–1867*, 73.
36. Gottfried to August Wilhelm Döbner, 5 August 1827, Semper Archiv.
37. Ibid.
38. Gottfried to father, 11 December 1827, Semper Archiv.
39. See von Manteuffel, "Die Baukunst Gottfried Sempers," 19.
40. Gottfried to Georg, 30 March 1829, Semper Archiv.
41. Gottfried to Herr von Zerzog, 30 March 1829, Semper Archiv.
42. Gottfried to mother, 4 July 1829, Semper Archiv. "Dich die zerknirschte Mutter, deren Thränen bei meinem Abschied strömen, die mich anfleht nur *ein* freundliches letztes Wort zu sagen, deren grosses Elend bisher nur noch durch *dies* vermehrt werden konnte, kalt von mir abzustossen keine Thränen, kein Händedruck für sie – mein Herz ist todt. Und doch konnte ich nicht anders – hätte ich freundliche Blicke gezeigt, es wären Heuchlerblicke gewesen. – Hätte ich geweint, es wären krokodilsthränen gewesen. – Hätte ich geküsst – es wäre ein Judaskuss gewesen."
43. Father to Gottfried, 22 July 1829, Semper Archiv.
44. Gottfried to father, 27 July 1829, Semper Archiv. The meeting in Rotterdam was with Herr Ronzelen, the father of Semper's employer in Bremerhaven. Ronzelen's son in Bremerhaven apparently did not give Gottfried the letter of recommendation he was led to expect.
45. Gottfried to mother, 25 August 1829, Semper Archiv.
46. Ibid.
47. Gottfried to father, 1 December 1829, Semper Archiv.
48. The veterinary school is illustrated in Fröhlich, *Gottfried Semper: Zeichnerischer Nachlass*, 18–19 (catalogue number 10-1-2, 10-1-3).
49. Gottfried to father, 1 December 1829, Semper Archiv. "Leider muss ich befürchten dass die hochmögenden Herren welche in Hamburg das gewichtige Ruder des Staates und der Verwaltung führen mich in der Ueberzeugung bestärken werden, dass es ein höchst undankbares Unternehmen sey für *Narren* Häuser bauen zu wollen."
50. For a history of the Hamburg exchange, see Gelder and Fischer, *"Nutzen und Zierde zugleich bieten dem Auge sich Dar,"* 30–33.
51. Gottfried to mother, 20 June 1830, Semper Archiv.
52. Father to Gottfried, 22 August 1829, Semper Archiv.
53. Gottfried to father, 1 December 1829, Semper Archiv.
54. Gottfried to Wilhelm, 19 March 1830, Semper Archiv.
55. Gottfried to father, 28 July 1830, Semper Archiv.
56. For one indication of the student interest in the events, see François Guizot's *The History of France from the Earliest Times to 1848*, VIII, 279.
57. Father, mother, and Elise to Gottfried, 6 August 1830, Semper Archiv.
58. Gottfried to father, 26 August 1830, Semper Archiv. "Welchem echten Sohn Holsteins würde es einfallen für die Freiheit der Presse in den Tod zu gehen. Das wäre je einfältige Faselei. Die Freiheit macht keinen Menschen satt und so lange der liebe Gott Buchweizen auf unsern Feldern fortkommen lässt sind wir zufrieden – vorausgesetzt das man uns nicht mehr als 3/4 des Ertags wieder abnimmt."
59. Ibid. "...und zugleich zu verdienen ich um einen nothwendigen Theil meiner Ausbildung zu erwerben, *muss* nach Italien und mein Alter *duldet* keinen Aufschub. In der sicheren Ueberzeugung dass ich hingehen würde habe ich nicht kopirt was andere gesammelt haben sondern lieber eigene Ideen hervorzubringen gesucht um später selbst an Ort und Stelle zu sammeln."
60. Gottfried to mother, 25 August 1829, Semper Archiv.

61. Middleton and Watkin, *Neoclassical and 19th Century Architecture*, 358. For a history of the church, see Falières-Lamy, "La Basilique Sainte-Clotilde," in *Paris et Ile-de-France, Mémoires*, vol. 40 (Paris, 1989), 207–55.
62. Gottfried to mother, 25 August 1829, Semper Archiv. We should also point out that Gau did not keep Semper employed throughout 1830. In a letter to his mother of 20 June 1830, Semper reported that he now only occasionally went to Gau's studio.
63. Forster, "Das Wachhaus des Bastille-Platzes."
64. Levine, "The Book and the Building: Hugo's Theory of Architecture and Labrouste's Bibliothèque Ste-Geneviève," in *The Beaux-Arts and Nineteenth-century French Architecture*, ed. Middleton, 146–47. See also his *Architectural Reasoning in the Age of Positivism.*
65. Barry Bergdoll points out that Vernet was appointed to his post during the (short) moderate ministry of Martinac in 1828. Vernet was also close to Guizot and Chateaubriand, both vehement anti-royalists. See Bergdoll's *Léon Vaudoyer: Historicism in the Age of Industry*, 90–91.
66. Van Zanten, *Designing Paris*, 13. See also *The Architectural Polychromy of the 1830s.*
67. Letter of Vaudoyer to Lebas, 22 March 1830. Quoted from Van Zanten, *Designing Paris*, 18.
68. Chief among these was Jules Goury, with whom he remained almost twelve months, traveling from Rome to Naples, to Sicily, and to Greece. In Sicily Semper also traveled with Mathieu Prosper Morey, the *grand-prix* winner of 1831.
69. In addition to various comments from Gau, Eduard Rastoin-Brémond appraised Gottfried on several occasions of the artistic developments in Paris. See in particular the latter's undated letter of 1832–33, and the letter of 15 July 1834, Semper Archiv. Semper was also a regular reader of César Daly's *Revue générale de l'architecture* and returned to Paris periodically over the course of his career.
70. Winckelmann, *Geschichte der Kunst des Alterthums*, 147–48. "Da nun die weisse Farbe diejenige ist, welche die mehresten Lichtstrahlen zurückschicket, sogleich sich empfindlicher macht, so wird auch ein schöner Körper desto schöner seyn, je weisser er ist, ja er wird nackend dadurch grösser, als er in der That ist, erscheinen, so wie wir sehen, dass alle neu in Gips geformte Figuren grösser, als die Statuen, von welchen jene genommen sind, sich vorstellen."
71. Stieglitz, *Archäologie der Baukunst der Griechen und Römer*, I, 258–59.
72. Stuart and Revett, *The Antiquities of Athens*, I, 10 (plate VIII). Stuart and Revett described the fascia as "enriched with painted ornament, which appears to be as ancient as the Building itself."
73. See Vitruvius, *De Architectura,* Book IV, ch. 2; Pausanias, *Guide to Greece*, I, 28.
74. Pliny had argued in two places in his *Natural History* (Book 35, I.3, and XXXVII.118) that painting directly on the wall was not practiced in Greek times, but was a sympton of later Roman decadence. Winckelmann responded in his *Geschichte der Kunst des Alterthusm* (page 264) with a litany of famed Greek painters who executed paintings on walls, and even traced the practice of wall painting back to the Chaldeans.
75. The architect and historian Alois Hirt supported Winckelmann's view by arguing that the Greek artists practiced fresco painting with a technique similar to that used at Pompeii. See his *Die Baukunst nach den Grundsätzen der Alten*, 234–35. Böttiger replied in *Ideen zur Archäologie der Malerie*, 211, that the pictures were rather painted on larch or some other hardwood panels, and therefore were true *tabulae.*
76. Wilkins, *Atheniensia*, 86–88.
77. Leake, *The Topography of Athens*, 335.
78. Dodwell, *A Classical and Topographical Tour Through Greece*, 342–43. See also 320–42, 365–67.
79. A few of the chryselephantine works mentioned by Pausanias in his *Guide to Greece* are the horses and tritons of the Temple of Poseidon in Cornith, the statues of Pan and Aphrodite at Sikyon, the statue of Asklepios at Epidauros, Polykleitos's work at the Hearion at Mycenae, the numerous works at the Elean Temple of Hera, the statues in the Temple of Patrai, and Athena's statue at Pellene.
80. Quatremère de Quincy, *Le Jupiter olympien*, 389–91.
81. Ibid., 17–18. "Il suffit d'avoir vu que le bois fut une des matières que la sculpture grecque exploita le plus anciennement et le plus constamment; que l'emploi de cette matière, après être trouvé d'accord avec le goût que fut celui de l'enfance de l'art dans les *statues-mannequins,* seconda puissamment le développement de la sculpture polychrome, et fut l'apprentissage de la statuaire en ivoire."
82. Ibid., 36.
83. Cockerell, "On the Aegina Marbles," in *Journal of Science and the Arts*, 340–41. For Cockerell's

account of his findings, see his *Travels in Southern Europe and the Levant.* Cockerell was joined at Aegina by Carl Haller von Hallerstein.

84. Leo von Klenze, *Versuch einer Wiederherstellung des toskanischen Tempels nach seinen historischen und technischen Analogien,* 9 and 77.

85. Stackelberg, *De Apollotempel zu Bassae in Arcadien,* 33. "Die Farbe, noch jetzt bey allen südlichen Völkern zur Belebung von Architekturmassen unentbehrlich, wandten die Griechen in der höchsten Meisterwerke der Baukunst aus dem Periklerschen Zeitalter, sowohl Dorischer als Ionischer Bauart, noch bezeugen: das Theseium, der Parthenon, der Tempel der Minerva Polias, die Propyläen, wo selbst äussere Bauverzierungen mit Farben aufgetragen waren. Das milde Clima begünstigte diesen Gebrauch und Dorische Tempel erscheinen hiedurch viel reicher geschmückt, als man sich denkt." Stackelberg originally accompanied P. O. Brønsted to Greece in 1810, working as his secretary.

86. William Kinnaird, in James Stuart and Nicholas Revett, *The Antiquities of Athens,* 2nd ed., 44–45n. Kinnaird first gained architectural attention by opposing the projection in the facade of John Soane's house at Lincoln's Inn Fields in 1812. He traveled with Charles Barry and Charles Eastlake to Greece in 1817–19, edited the second edition of the *Antiquities of Athens* (1825–30), then began a small architectural practice.

87. Brønsted, *Reisen und Untersuchungen,* 145.

88. Ibid., 147.

89. Several studies have been devoted to Hittorff and his role in the polychrome controversy. See Hammer, *Jakob Ignaz Hittorff;* Van Zanten, *The Architectural Polychromy of the 1830s;* Schneider, *The Works and Doctrines of Jacques Ignace Hittorff (1792–1867);* Middleton, "Hittorff's Polychrome Campaign," in *The Beaux-Arts and Nineteenth-century French Architecture,* 174–95; Musée Carnavalet, *Hittorff: un Architecte du XIXème.*

90. Gau, on several occasions in letters to Semper, went out of his way to criticize Hittorff. In one letter dated 18 February 1833, he accused Hittorff of practicing "charlatanism" for his attempt to produce an annotated French edition of Stuart and Revett's work without knowledge of Latin or Greek. In another letter to Semper, dated 22 February 1835, Gau referred to Hittorff as a "dammed braggart!"

91. Hittorff first informed the painter François Gérard of his discoveries in Agrigento in a letter of 14 December 1823. On 30 December he wrote to Ludwig von Schorn from Selinunte. The art historian Schorn, a protégé of Boisserée, was also a close friend of Carl Haller von Hallerstein and C. O. Müller. Schorn became very influential during the 1820s in Germany after starting the journal *Kunstblatt,* which often reported the latest antiquarian research.

92. The atlas to *L'Architecture antique de la Sicile, ou Recueil des plus intéressants monuments d'architecture des villes et des lieux,* consisting of forty-nine engravings, was issued in parts between 1827 and 1830. The later publication of the work carried out by his son (expanded to eighty-nine engravings and a 655-page text) did not appear until 1870.

93. Hittorff in his text of 1851, *Restitution du temple D'Empédocle à Selinonte, ou Architecture polychrome chez les grecs,* refers to the fact (pp. 33–40) that Semper in his pamphlet of 1834 had made mention only of the plates from Hittorff's earlier text of 1827, and not his drawings exhibited at the Louvre. Semper may, however, have been familiar with the contents of Hittorff's lecture.

94. J.I. Hittorff, "De l'architecture polychrôme chez les Grecs," in *Annales de l'Institut de Correspondance archéologique* (Paris, 1830), II, 264.

95. The first appraisal of Hittorff's restoration is from Raoul Rochette's review of *L'Architecture Antique de la Sicile* in the *Journal des Savants,* July 1829. The second is from the article "De la peinture sur mur chez les anciens," in *Journal des Savants,* June–August, 1833. Raoul Rochette, however, first changed his mind with regard to Hittorff's accuracy in an address to the Académie in July 1830.

96. Gottfried to Betty, 27 October 1830, Semper Archiv.

97. Gottfried to Elise, 3 December 1830, Semper Archiv.

98. Semper's father, in a letter to his son while still in Paris (18 May 1830), indicated that he could provide him with a letter of introduction to Thorwaldsen. Bertel Thorwaldsen's father was a noted carver of ships' figureheads and it is possible that Semper's father may have had contact with him through his shipping interests.

99. Gottfried to father, 1 February 1831, Semper Archiv.

100. Ibid.

101. Gottfried to mother, 18 March 1831, Semper Archiv.

102. Ibid.
103. Gottfried to father, 17 May 1831, Semper Archiv.
104. Ibid.
105. G. Semper, "Reiseerinnerungen aus Griechenland," Erster Brief: "Die Ueberfahrt von Unteritalien aus," in *Kleine Schriften*, 431.
106. Ibid., 432.
107. Ibid., 435. See also Gottfried to brother (unspecified), 9 October 1831, Semper Archiv.
108. See Ettlinger, *Gottfried Semper und die Antike*, 46.
109. Gottfried to brother, 11 April 1832, Semper Archiv. For another account of Thiersch's activities, see the biographical notice by Friedrich Baumeister, in *Allgemeine Deutsche Biographie* (Leipzig: Duncker & Humblot, 1894), XVIII, 7–17.
110. Ettlinger, *Gottfried Semper und die Antike*, 47.
111. Gottfried to brother (unspecified), 11 April 1832, Semper Archiv.
112. Gottfried to brother (unspecified), 17 July 1832, Semper Archiv.
113. Ibid. "Du keinen Begriff von der Pracht u. dem Reichthum d. Alten machen."
114. Gottfried to Wilhelm, 24 September 1832, Semper Archiv. "Wie grau wird mir die Welt erscheinen bin ich erst hier fern von diesem Farbenschimmer."
115. Gottfried to mother, 9 January 1833, Semper Archiv.
116. Gau to Gottfried, 18 February 1833, Semper Archiv. "Ich predige, lieber Semper, und gebe selbst schlechtes Beispiel; aber eben darum weil ich meine Schuld erkenne und tief dafür büsse, nenne ich andere."
117. Gottfried to brother, 9 March 1833, Semper Archiv. "Ich habe versucht es in ein System zu bringen und um den Effect zu zeigen jetzt eine kolorirte Restauration der sich auf der Akropolis befindenden Gebäude angefertigt."
118. Gau to Gottfried, 18 February 1833, Semper Archiv.
119. Gottfried to Carl, 1 June 1833, Semper Archiv.
120. G. Semper, "Entdeckung alter Farbenreste an der Trajanssäule in Rom," *Kleine Schriften*, 107–8. "Hiernach drängt sich der schluss auf, dass ursprünglich die ganze Säule mit lebhaften Farben bedeckt war, welche die schönen Skulpturen trotz der grossen Höhe vortrefflich zu Geltung bringen mussten."
121. Teresa to Gottfried, 25 July 1834, Semper Archiv.
122. Gottfried to Wilhelm, 4 September 1833, Semper Archiv.
123. Gau to Gottfried, 15 November 1833, Semper Archiv. Gau at first was disparaging about Gärtner's standing in Munich in relation to Klenze. Then he related the story of Gärtner sending him a "sketch of his church" for his appraisal. After Gau responded "candidly," he had not since heard from Gärtner. Gau's contempt for Gärtner is seen in another letter to Semper, dated 22 February 1835, in which Gau noted that Gärtner had twice written to him to nominate him for the Munich Academy, but Gau rudely left the letters unanswered.
124. Pecht, *Deutsche Künstler*, 156–57. There may indeed be something to this claim, as Kugler, in his "Über die Polychromie der griechischen Architektur und Sculptur und ihre Grenzen," in *Kleine Schriften* (page 267), also remarked on the excitement Semper stirred when he came to Berlin and presented to various circles his "highly imaginative" restorations.
125. Gottfried to Elise, 26 December 1833, Semper Archiv.
126. Schinkel to Gottfried, 19 June 1834, Semper Archiv. Semper published Schinkel's letter in his "Schlussbemerkungen" to *Der Stil*, I, 523–24.
127. Pecht, *Deutsche Künstler*, 157.
128. In the edition of these plates in the Victoria and Albert Museum, the alternative title for the work is *Ueber Anwendung der Farben in der Baukunst*. The six plates have French titles: 1) *Temple de Thésée Athènes, détails de l'ordre extérieur*; 2) *Détails de l'intéreur du peristil du Temple de Thésée à Athènes*; 3) *Du Temple de Thésée. D'un Tombeau Etrusque, Fragmens Divers*; 4) *Détails du Plafonds du Temple de Thésée*; 5) *Etablement Restauré du Parthenon d'Athènes*; 6) *Sarcapage trouvé à Girgenti, Piedestal trouvé à Salamis, Sarcapage trouvé à Girgenti*. The Hamburg Museum für Kunstgewerbe also has an edition of these plates.
129. These have been meticulously studied, arranged, and annotated by Herrmann in *Gottfried Semper theoretischer Nachlass*. Other notes by Herrmann are preserved in the Semper archives in Zürich as well as in the Getty Center for the History of Arts and the Humanities in Santa Monica.
130. Semper, *Vorläufige Bemerkungen*, viii; Eng. trans., 47. "So lange wir nach jedem alten Fetzen haschen und unsere Künstler sich in den Winkeln verkriechen, um aus dem Moose der Vergangenheit sich dürftige Nahrung zo holen, so lange is keine Aussicht auf ein wirksames Künstlerleben."

131. Ibid., viii–ix; Eng. trans., 47. "... es gedeiht nur auf dem Boden des Bedürfnisses und unter der Sonne der Freiheit."
132. Ms. 3, fol. 9, Semper Archiv. "Unser Privatbedürfnis hat sich vereinfacht. Zweckmässigkeit, Bequemlichkeit und Anmuth sind die Erfordernisse des Bürgerhauses." For a similar viewpoint in the 1880s, see Robert Dohme, *Das englische Haus: Eine kultur- und baugeschichtliche Skizze* (Braunschweig: G. Westermann, 1888).
133. See Bergdoll, *Léon Vaudoyer*, 101–2.
134. Barrault, *Aux Artistes, du passé et de l'avenir des Beaux-Arts*, 9.
135. Ibid., 73.
136. Semper to Gau, undated 1833, Semper Archiv.
137. Ms. 3, fol. 8, Semper Archiv.
138. Gau to Semper, 15 November 1833, Semper Archiv.
139. Ibid. Gau's sentence reads: "Die Wuth fing an mit dem Romantischen und mit dem Styl der Renaissance und jetzt sind wir schon in dem Rococo von Ludwig dem 15t und 16ten. Das schnelle Vorschreiten gibt Hoffnung dass der Unfug nun bald zu Ende geth." Herrmann also notes that in the printed version of Semper's text the phrase "romantischen Zeit der Renaissance" is actually a printing error to the manuscript version "romantischen Zeit und der Renaissance." See Herrmann, *Gottfried Semper theoretischer Nachlass*, 70 (Ms. 3).
140. Metzger reported this in a letter to Semper, dated 14 June 1834, Semper Archiv.
141. See Wolfgang Herrmann, "Probleme zeitgenössischer Architektur," in *Gottfried Semper Theoretischer Nachlass*, 45–46; Eng. trans. in Herrmann, *Gottfried Semper: In Search of Architecture*, 158.
142. See Otto Wagner, *Moderne Architektur*, 55. Wagner, of course, accused Semper of not living up to this motto in his own designs.
143. See, in particular, Pevsner's chapter on Semper in his *Some Architectural Writers*, 252–68.
144. For various remarks on the lectures of Huyot, which survive only in manuscript pages from the 1830s, see Bergdoll, *Léon Vaudoyer*, 41–48, and Middleton, "Rationalist Interpretations," 33.
145. Semper, *Vorläufige Bemerkungen*, 11; Eng. trans., 54. "Das Magere, Trockne, Scharfe, Charakterlose der neueren Erzeugnisse der Architektur lässt sich ganz einfach aus dieser unverständigen Nachäfferei antiker Bruchstücke erklären."
146. Semper, *Vorläufige Bemerkungen*, 29–30; Eng. trans., 63–64.
147. Ettlinger, *Gottfried Semper und die Antike*, 56.
148. Semper, *Vorläufige Bemerkungen*, 33–34; Eng. trans., 65. "Dabei darf neben der Malerei der metallene Zierrath, die Vergoldung, die Drapperie von Teppichen, Baldachinen und Vorhängen und das bewegliche Geräthe nicht ausser Augen gelassen werden. Auf alles dieses und mehr noch auf die mitwirkende Umgebung und Staffage von Volk, Priestern und Festzügen waren die Monumente beim Entstehen berechnet. Sie waren das Gerüste, bestimmt, allen diesen Kräften einen gemeinsamen Wirkungspunkt zu gewähren. Der Glanz, der die Einbildungskraft ausfüllt, denkt man sich lebhaft in jene Zeiten zurück, macht die Nachahmungen aus denselben, wie man sich seither gefallen hat, sie den unsrigen aufzudringen, erbleichen und erstarren."
149. Ibid., 6; Eng. trans., 52. "Der Architekt war Chorage, er führte sie an; sein Name schon sagt es."
150. Ibid., 5; Eng. trans., 52. "Unter seiner Leitung bildete sich das Monument zu einem Inbegriff der Künste aus, das, als einiges zusammenhängendes Kunstwerk, sich in seinen Einzelnheiten erklärte, entfaltete, bestätigte. Und es entwickelte sich von selbst das Verhältniss der Architectur als besondere Kunst betrachtet, zu den übrigen Schwestern." It should be pointed out that Klaus Eggert in his essay "Der Begriff des Gesamtkunstwerks in Sempers Theorie," was the first to develop the notion of *Gesamtkunstwerk* with respect to Semper – although our two interpretations of this concept within the framework of Semper's theory, as will become apparent, are somewhat different. See his important essay in *Gottfried Semper und die Mitte des 19 Jahrhunderts*, ed. Vogt, 121–28.
151. Ibid., 6; Eng. trans., 52. "Er ward gewählt aus der Mitte der Künstler, weniger wegen durchgreifender Meisterschaft in all künstlerischen Vorzügen, sondern vielmehr wegen der besonderen Gabe des Ueberblicks, des Vertheilens der Kräfte, des richtigen Auges für Verhältniss und Oeconomie der Mittel."
152. Implied here is a critique of Ettlinger's view (*Gottfried Semper und die Antike*, 47) that Semper, after returning from his tour of the south, was "ebensogut Architekt wie Archäologe."
153. Semper, *Vorläufige Bemerkungen*, 14, 37, 19n., 22–23, 38.
154. Serradifalco not only enlarged the size of Hittorff's plan but also changed the temple type from an Ionic tetrastyle to a Doric in antis. In his review of this book, Raoul Rochette raised the pitch of his dispute with Hittorff to a new level, comparing Serradifalco's "travail exact et sévère" with Hittorff's "oeuvre d'imagination et de fantasie, plutôt que critique et de vérité"

(*Journal des Savants,* January 1835, 14–18). Hittorff responded to Raoul Rochette in the same issue; Raoul Rochette, in turn, answered Hittorff's response, somewhat gleefully, by noting Semper's comments at the end of *Preliminary Remarks* on Hittorff's "liberties."

155. Schinkel to Gottfried, 19 June 1834, Semper Archiv.
156. Gau to Gottfried, 19 August 1834 & 23 December 1834, Semper Archiv.
157. Raoul Rochette to Gottfried, 1 November 1834, Semper Archiv.
158. Raoul Rochette's review of *Preliminary Remarks* appeared in the *Journal des Savants,* 1 November 1836, 668–84.
159. Semper had defended Müller in his dispute with Raoul Rochette over whether the Greeks painted wall murals or made paintings on panels, which were then attached to the wall. This was the issue that C. A. Böttiger had raised at the beginning of the century.
160. Müller, *Göttingische gelehrte Anzeigen,* 1 (1834), 1391.
161. See "Briefe Rumohrs an Otfried Müller und andere Freunde," ed. Stock, *Jahrbuch der Pruszischen Kunstsammlungen,* 54, 20 June 1835.
162. Kugler's essay first appeared in March 1835. It was republished in his *Kleine Schriften,* vol. 1, 265–327. It was also translated in part into English by W. R. Hamilton, "On the Polychromy of Greek Architecture," in *Transactions of the Institute of British Architects of London,* Sessions 1835–56 (London, 1836), vol. 1, 73–99.
163. Carl Schnaase, *Geschichte der bildenden Künste,* vol. 2, 144.
164. Gottfried to mother, 9 January 1833, Semper Archiv.
165. Elise to Gottfried, 30 December 1833, Semper Archiv.
166. When Semper left Altona in the late summer for his new position in Dresden, he turned over the supervision of the project to his friend Franz Georg Stammann, who carried out sketches Semper sent from Dresden and kept him regularly informed of the progress of the work. In a letter from Stammann to Gottfried of 25 February 1835, he informed Semper that Donner was upset about the cost of the work and would not finish all the interior decoration. In another letter of 16 March 1835, he mentioned that Donner had engaged a second architect for advice.
167. Stammann noted Semper's seeming lack of interest in his letter to Gottfried, dated 25 February 1835.
168. For Soller's work see Grundmann, *August Soller 1805–53.*
169. Gau to Graf Vitzthum, 22 December 1833, Dresden Staatarchiv, "Kunstakademie," 40, 139–40.
170. Manfred Kobuch chronicles Semper's appointment in "Gottfried Sempers Berufung nach Dresden," in Dresden Technische Universität, *Gottfried Semper 1803–1879,* 97–115.
171. Wulsten to Heinrich Schütze, 11 February 1834, Dresden Staatarchiv, "Kunstakademie," 40, 141–42, reproduced in Kobuch's article (note 75) as appendix 2.
172. Pehmöller to Heinrich Schütze, 24 February 1834, Dresden Staatarchiv, "Kunstakademie, 40, 40; reproduced in Kobuch's article (note 75) as appendix 3.
173. Report of 5 March 1834, Dresden Staatarchiv, "Kunstakademie," 40, 72–87.
174. Gottfried to Graf Vitzthum, 6 June 1834, Dresden Staatarchiv, "Kunstakademie," 40, 182.

2 *Royal Success in Dresden*

1. Gottfried to mother, 30 September 1834, Semper Archiv. Semper also expressed his misgivings to Gau, who responded (on 22 February 1835) with a pep talk concerning his various talents.
2. On the necessity of visiting Dresden to obtain an artistic education, see Johann Wolfgang von Goethe's comments in *Dichtung und Wahrheit,* Book 8.
3. Semper's lecture was given on 13 January 1838, and was entitled "Über die Anwendung der Farben in der Baukunst." This was also the projected title for his proposed folio volume on polychromy.
4. See Pecht's remarks in *Das alte Dresden,* ed. Haenel and Kalkschmidt, 335–41.
5. Gottfried to mother, 1 November 1834, Semper Archiv.
6. Gottfried to Wilhelm, 3 August 1835, Semper Archiv.
7. Semper's proposals are preserved in the Dresden Staatsarchiv: "Kunstakademie," 17, 39–42.
8. Gottfried to mother, 1 July 1835, Semper Archiv.
9. The children were Johanna Elisabeth (1836–1872), Carl Manfred (1838–1913), Conrad Julius (1843–1925), Anna Catarina (1843–1926), Hans Semper (1845–1920), and Gottfried Emanuel (1848–1911).
10. Gottfried to Bertha, 16 October 1836; Bertha to Gottfried, 18 October 1836, Semper Archiv.

11. See, for instance, Gottfried to Bertha, 14 January 1839, Semper Archiv.
12. Mother to Gottfried, 12 May 1838, Semper Archiv.
13. Pecht, *Deutsche Künstler*, 169–70. "Als ich ihn damals in Dresden zuerst sah, fand ich mich vor einem mittelgroßen Manne mit gedrungenem Körperbau, einem mißtrauisch messended, durchdringenden Blick, der doch zugleich fast mehr der inneren Eingebung zu lauschen, als die äußeren Erscheinungen zu beobachten schien."
14. Ibid., 170. "Den Freuden der Geselligkeit, besonders in der Form eines heiteren Bachusopfers . . .".
15. *Briefwechsel zwischen Rauch und Rietschel,* ed. Eggers, Rauch to Rietschel, 28 August 1834, I, 262; Rietschel to Rauch, 1 September 1834, I, 36–64.
16. Ibid., Rietschel to Rauch, 2 January 1836, I, 326.
17. Ibid.
18. Pecht, *Deutsche Künstler*, 168.
19. *Briefwechsel zwischen Rauch und Rietschel,* ed. Karl Eggers (note 15), Rietschel to Rauch, 14 April 1839, I, 484.
20. Ibid., Rietschel to Rauch, 4 September 1839, I, 495.
21. Ibid., Rietschel to Rauch, 1 January 1844, II, 130.
22. Ibid., Rietschel to Rauch, 23 April 1843, II, 104.
23. Pecht, *Deutsche Künstler*, 176.
24. Richard Wagner, *Mein Leben*, I, 373. "Mit ihm hatte ich mich kurz zuvor bei der Besprechung dieses Stoffes auf das heftigste ereifert; er wollte nämlich von dem minnesängerlichen und pilgerfahrtbereiten Mittelalter für die Kunst durchaus nichts wissen, und gab mir zu verstehen, dass er mich um der Wahl eines solchen Stoffes willen geradeswegs verachte."
25. Ibid., I, 382. "Er hielt mich beständig für den Repräsentanten einer mittelalterlich katholicisirenden Richtung, die er oft mit wahrer Wuth bekämpfte."
26. Ibid. "Unmöglich ging es jedoch je ohne lebhaften Streit ab, und hieran mochte nicht nur Semper's wunderliche und krampfhafte Neigung zum absoluten Widerspruch, sondern auch diess der Grund sein, dass er sich von der ganzen Gesellschaft gänzlich verschieden erkannte. Seine paradoxesten Behauptungen, die offenbar nur auf Streiterregung abgesehen waren, liessen mich jedoch bald mit Bestimmtheit erkennen, dass er mit mir unter allen Anwesenden der Einzige war, der es mit dem, was er sagte, bis zur Leidenschaftlichkeit ernst nahm, während allen Andern es gern recht war, zur gelegenen Zeit die Sache auf sich beruhen zu lassen."
27. See Meissner's remarks in *Das alte Dresden*, ed. Haenel and Kalkschmidt, 330. "Die Debatte über diesen Bau und was damit zusammenhing, füllte den ganzen Abend aus. Ich hörte von nichts als Einkehlungen und Lisenen, von selbständig und organisch gegliederten Bogen, von Friesen, Pilastern, Füllungen und Gurtbändern, bis mir der Kopf zu wirbeln anfing."
28. Caroline Bauer, "Der Tieck-Kreis," in *Dresden zwischen Wiener Kongress und Maiaufstand*, ed. Jäckel, 174–76. "Selbst ihre früheren Gönnerinnen und Anbeter mieden sie und bekamen fast Verlegenheitskrämpfe, wenn ihr Name nur genannt wurde. Nur in Gesellschaft einiger kühner Herren, darunter der junge Architekt Gottfried Semper, wurde die schöne Abenteuerin noch gesehen."
29. Pecht, *Deutsche Künstler*, 177. "Beide Frauen trugen das Banner der Empörung gegen die gesellschaftlichen Satzungen nicht nur in die artistisch-literarischen, sondern sogar in die altaristokratischen Kreise. Auch dort spielte man mit dem Feuer, das bald Alles in helle Flammen setzen sollte."
30. See Friedrich August Krubsacius, *Betrachtungen über den Geschmack der Alten in der Baukunst* (Observations on the Architectural Taste of the Ancients; 1745) and *Ursprung, Wachstum und Verfall der Verzierungen in den schönen Künsten* (Origin, Development, and Decline of Decoration in the Fine Arts; 1759). Winckelmann's one architectural essay, *Anmerkungen über die Baukunst der Alten* (Remarks on Ancient Architecture; 1762), is said to have been modeled on the first treatise by Krubsacius. See Carl Justi, *Winckelmann und seine Zeitgenossen*, 3 vols. (Leipzig: Vogel, 1866–72), I, 308.
31. See Watkin and Mellinghoff, *German Architecture and the Classical Ideal*, 51.
32. For a discussion of the architecture of Schuricht, Thormeyer, and Thürmer, see Löffler, *Das alte Dresden*, and Helas, *Architektur in Dresden 1800–1900*.
33. See Gottfried to August Wilhelm Döbner, 5 August 1827, Semper Archiv. Semper's words were: "His other students are not friendly toward me and soon go to Italy. They are all from the Weinbrenner school, only Germans"; "Seine übrigen Schüler sind wenig vertraut mit mir and gehen nächstens nach Italien. Sie sind alle aus der Weinbrennerschen Schule, lauter Deutsche."

34. Semper, *Vorläufige Bemerkungen*, vii; Eng. trans., 46.
35. Hübsch, *In welchem Style sollen wir bauen?* Preface; Eng. trans., Herrmann, *In What Style Should We Build?*
36. For an excellent summary of this debate, see Herrmann's introduction to *In What Style Should We Build?* Herrmann also translates the mentioned essays by Hübsch, Rosenthal, Wiegmann, in addition to other writings by Johann Heinrich Wolff, and Carl Gottlieb Wilhelm Bötticher. Certainly one of the best expositions of the *Rundbogenstil* is Kathleen Curran's "The German Rundbogenstil and Reflections on the American Round-Arched Style," in *Journal of the Society of Architectural Historians*, XLVII, 4, 351–73.
37. Klenze, *Architektur des christlichen Cultus*, 9.
38. Rudolf Wiegmann, "Bemerkungen über die Schrift *In welchem Style sollen wir bauen?* von H. Hübsch," *Kunst-Blatt* 10 (1829), 44, 173–74; 45, 177–79; 46, 181–83.
39. Carl Albert Rosenthal, "In welchem Style sollen wir bauen? Eine Frage für die Mitglieder des deutschen Architektenvereins," *Zeitschrift für praktische Baukunst* 4 (1844), 23–27.
40. Franz Kugler, "Über den Kirchenbau und seine Bedeutung für unsere Zeit," *Museum: Blätter für bildende Kunst* 2 (1834), 5.
41. Karl Friedrich Schinkel, *Sammlung architektonischer Entwurfe* (Berlin: Ernst & Korn, 1866; New York: Princeton Univ. Press, 1989), 36.
42. See especially his remarks in *Karl Friedrich Schinkel: Briefe, Tagebücher, Gedanken*, 194.
43. Karl Friedrich Schinkel, *Aus Schinkel's Nachlass* (Berlin: Könlichen Geheimen Ober-Hofbuchdruckerei, 1862; reprint Mittenwald: Mäander, 1981), III, 373–74. "Ich bemerkte, dass in den Formen der Baukunst alles auf drei Grundlagen beruhe: 1. auf den Formen der Construction, 2. auf den Formen, welche durch herkömmliche geschichtliche Wirklichkeit erzeugt werden, und 3. auf Formen, die, an sich bedeutsam, ihr Vorbild aus der Natur entlehnen. Ich bemerkte ferner einen grossen Schatz von Formen, der bereits in der Welt durch viele Jahrhunderte der Entwickelung und bei sehr verschiedenen Völkern in Ausführung von Bauwerken entstanden war und niedergelegt ist. Aber ich sah zugleich, dass unser Gebrauch von diesem angehäuften Schatz oft sehr heterogener Gegenstände willkührlich sei, weil jede einzelne Form einen eigenthümlichen Reiz an sich trägt, der durch eine dunkele Ahnung eines nothwendigen Motivs, sei es geschichtlich, oder constructiv, noch erhöht wird und verführt, davon Anwendung zu machen, indem man seinem Werke durch einen solchen Gegenstand einen besonderen Reiz zu verleihen glaubt. Ich bemerkte also, dass was mir in seinem primitiven Erscheinen an alten Werken eine höchst erfreuliche Wirkung erzeugte, bei seiner neuen Anwendung an Werken unserer Tage oft durchaus widerstand. Besonders ward mir klar, dass in dieser Willkührlichkeit des Gebrauches der Grund grosser Charakterlosigkeit und Styllosigkeit zu finden sei, woran so viele neue Gebäude zu leiden schienen. Es ward mir eine Lebensaufgabe, hierin volle Klarheit zu gewinnen. Aber je tiefer ich den Gegenstand durchdrang, je grösser sah ich die Schwierigkeiten, die sich meinem Bestreben entgegenstellten. Sehr bald gerieth ich in den Fehler der rein radicalen Abstraction, wo ich die ganze Conception für ein bestimmtes Werk der Baukunst aus seinem nächsten trivialen Zweck allein und aus der Construction entwickelte; in diesem Falle entstand etwas Trockenes, Starres, das der Freiheit ermangelte und zwei wesentliche Elemente, das Historische und das Poetische, ganz auschloss."
44. Kugler, *Karl Friedrich Schinkel*, 110–20. See also the DDR museum catalogue *Karl Friedrich Schinkel, 1781–1841* (Berlin: Verlag das europäische Buch, 1981), 147–52.
45. See Kurt W. Forster's enormously instructive essay, "'Only things that Stir the Imagination': Schinkel as a Scenographer," in *Karl Friedrich Schinkel: The Drama of Architecture*, ed. John Zukowsky, 18–35, and Bergdoll, *Karl Friedrich Schinkel*, 14–15 and 48.
46. Bergdoll, *Karl Friedrich Schinkel*, 51.
47. The description for the most part derives from the exhibition catalogue *Karl Friedrich Schinkel: Architektur Malerie Kunstgewerbe*, ed. Börsch-Supan and Griesebach, 190–91.
48. See Rave, *Karl Friedrich Schinkel*, 76–77.
49. Gottfried to mother, 1 November 1834, Semper Archiv.
50. Hans Semper reported that his father was given complete control of the layout, without any intervention on Böttiger's part. See *Gottfried Semper*, 13.
51. Letter of Caroline von Humboldt to G. Welcker, 9 October 1835. Quoted from Ettlinger, *Gottfried Semper und die Antike*, 68.
52. Manteuffel, "Die Baukunst Gottfried Sempers," 197.
53. Franz Georg Stammann, who completed the Donner Museum for Semper, ordered the slate in February 1837, and sent Semper a sketch of how to lay it. The shipment was delayed and the building stood for some time without a

finished roof, much to the embarassment of Semper.

54. Gottfried to Wilhelm, 3 August 1835, Semper Archiv.
55. Gottfried to city officials, 19 April 1838. Published by H. A. Richter, in "Gottfried Semper und das Dresdener Materni-Hospital," *Deutsche Bauzeitung*, 22, 1888.
56. Gottfried to Stadtrath Rachel, Ibid.
57. Gottfried to city officials, 19 April 1838, Ibid.
58. Rietschel to Christian Rauch, 23 April 1843, in *Briefwechsel zwischen Rauch und Rietschel*, ed. Eggers, II, 104.
59. For a description of the proceedings, see Dietrich, *Das Friedrich August-Monument in Dresden und seine feierliche Enthüllung am 7 June 1843.*
60. Gottfried to mother, 22 April 1835, Semper Archiv.
61. See Herrmann, *In Search of Architecture*, 4–5.
62. Much of this history has been taken from Max Georg Mütterlein's published dissertation, *Gottfried Semper und dessen Monumentalbauten am Dresdner Theaterplatz*, 1–22. See illustrations of Herrmann's and Thormeyer's projects in Volker Helas, *Architektur in Dresden 1800–1900*, 16, 24–25.
63. Gottfried to Wilhelm, 3 August 1835, Semper Archiv.
64. Ms. 43, fol. 1, Semper Archiv.
65. Heidrun Laudel reconstructs this scenario in "Sempers Planungen für ein Zwingerforum in Dresden," in Dresden Techische Universität, *Gottfried Semper 1803–79*, 116, 120, n. 4.
66. Ibid., 116.
67. Gottfried to Carl (from Berlin), 21 October 1836, and Gottfried to Bertha (from Berlin), 15 and 16 October 1836. Semper had forgotten to bring along a part of his presentation and in a frantic state wrote to Bertha in Dresden and asked her to forward the material to him immediately.
68. For Schinkel's design of 1835, see Goerd Poeschken, *Das architektonische Lehrbuch*, 152 and illus. 255–56; for Schinkel's 1813 design proposal, see Bergdoll, *Karl Friedrich Schinkel*, 16.
69. Gottfried to brother, 17 July 1837, Semper Archiv.
70. This is the explanation of Mütterlein in *Gottfried Semper und dessen Monumentalbauten am Dresdner Theaterplatz*, 23.
71. For a sketch of Ida Lüttichau, see Meffert, *Carl Gustav Carus*, 42.
72. Gottfried to Wolframsdorf, 2 January 1839, Semper Archiv.
73. Gottfried to Carl, 3 April 1839, Semper Archiv.
74. See Gottfried to Ottoman Glöckner, 27 September 1840, Semper Archiv. The *Allgemeine Bauzeitung* in 1845 published an extremely laudatory review of the work and called it Semper's best work after his theater.
75. "Villa des Banquiers Herrn Oppenheim bei Dresden," *Allgemeine Bauzeitung* 10, 1845, 5.
76. See Milde, *Neorenaissance in der deutschen Architektur des 19 Jahrhunderts*, 133–41.
77. For some remarks on Nicolai see Berry, "The Legacy of Gottfried Semper", 125–33.
78. See Gottfried to Nicolai, 30 June 1839 and Nicolai to Gottfried, 1 July 1839, Semper Archiv. The actual point of contention is not clear from what is said in the two letters, but it is clear that both men were extremely annoyed with each other.
79. See Manteuffel, "Die Baukunst Gottfried Sempers," 168.
80. Lipsius, *Gottfried Semper*, 46.
81. Pecht, "Die Geselligkeit der Fremdenstadt," in *Das Alte Dresden*, ed. Haenel and Kalkschmidt, 340.
82. Gottfried to Bertha, 16 December 1843, Semper Archiv.
83. For remarks on the competition, see Serafim Polenz, "Sempers Konkurrenzentwurf für den Umbau des Schlosses Schwerin"; Manfred Franz, "Die architektonischen Vorstellungen in den Schweriner Schloßbauentwürfen Demmlers, Sempers und Stülers als Ausdruck unterschiedlicher politisch-weltanschaulicher Indealvorstellungen und gesellschaftlicher Widersprüche," both in Dresden Techische Universität, *Gottfried Semper 1803–1879*, 141–44.
84. Lipsius, *Gottfried Semper*, 31–32.
85. The dates of much of the narrative below are taken from two essays in the proceedings of the 1879 colloquium at the Technischen Universität Dresden (note 65), Walter May's "Gottfried Sempers Entwürfe für das Dresdner Museum," and Heidrun Laudel's "Semper Planungen für ein Zwingerforum in Dresden." Some material has been taken from Max Georg Mütterlein's older but less accurate account, *Gottfried Semper und dessen Monumentalbauten am Dresdner Theaterplatz*. (see note 62). Another, more recent account is presented in Magirius (with Harald Marx), *Gemäldegalerie Dresden*, 29–62.
86. Gottfried to mother, 25 December 1839, Semper Archiv.
87. Gottfried to Ottomar Glöckner, 27 September 1840, Semper Archiv.
88. "Denkmal für Friedrich August den Gerechten zu Dresden," *Allgemeine Bauzeitung*, 1844, 8.

89. See Romberg's footnote to "Das neue Orangeriehaus in dem sogenannten herzogliche Garten in der Osteraallee zu Dresden," *Zeitschrift für praktische Baukunst*, 1846, 463.

90. Bayer, "Gottfried Semper," in *Baustudien und Baubilder*, 118–19. "Kein neuerer Architekt hat diese echte Stein-Idee, dies Kunstmotiv, aus dem sich eine so wirksame Steigerung des Baues vom elementar Derben ins Mannigfache und Prächtige nach aufwärts ergibt, mit gleicher Gründlichkeit durchdacht und mit ebenso vielseitigem Verständnis angewendet."

91. Semper, *Der Stil*, II, 365. "Desgleichen erhalten die Fugenbänder zwischen den Höckern einen regelmässigen 'Schlag,' der durch seine Rhythmik dekorativ wirkt und die anders behandelte Spiegelfläche kontrastlich hervorhebt, oder man erreicht das Gleiche durch sorgfältiges Glätten der Fugenflächen. So lässt sich die rustike Derbheit in eine gewisse männliche Eleganz kleiden und ein Ausdruck gewinnen, der dem Dorischen in der Symbolik der Säulenordnungen entspricht."

92. Lübke, "Das Neue Museum zu Dresden," 25, 32. The allegorical treatment of this facade has also recently been discussed in detail by Magirius in *Gemäldegallerie Dresden*, 46–52.

93. Ibid., 31. "In Dresden hat man dagegen Bedeutung und Zwecke eines Museumbaues klar und fest vor Augen gehalten, wie. u. A. Schinkel in dem älteren Berliner Museum so trefflich es vorgezeichnet: dass nämlich am Aeusseren durch monumentale Behandlung die idealen Zwecke des Baues sich weithin aussprechen, das Innere dagegen, möglichst einfach gehalten, in den zur Betrachtung aufzustellenden Kunstschätzen seinen einzigen, zugleich kostbarsten Schmuck habe."

94. Victor Helas has pointed out (*Architektur in Dresden 1800–1900*, 31) that the figurative encrustation of the building's facade presages Semper's later theme of "dressing." I prefer to see the notion of "dressing" as Semper's attempted elucidation of his theme of theatricality.

95. *Hannoversche Zeitung* 90, 16 April 1841. Cited from Harold Hammer-Schenk, introduction to Semper's *Das königliche Hoftheater zu Dresden*, 5. "Jedermann war von der Pracht und dem Glanze desselben überrascht. So reich geschmückt, so königlich verziert und doch nicht überladen hatte man es nicht erwartet. Man staunte; und als der König eintrat, da wurde ihm mit unbeschreiblichem Jubel ein Hoch gebracht, und er mit tausendfältigen Beifallszeichen und Dank dafür bestürmt, dass Dresden durch ihn ein solch prachtvolles Theater besitzt, welches nur wenige seines Gleichen in Deutschland haben möchte."

96. Semper, *Das königliche Hoftheater zu Dresden*, 27.

97. Francesco Milizia's *Trattato complete, formale e materiale del Teatro*, as Hammer Schenk indicated, was written in the early 1770s, but its press edition was confiscated by the censors. Thus it did not appear until 1785.

98. Friedrich Gilly's drawings for the Berlin theater, after his death, passed into the hands of Schinkel. Ludwig Catel published his theater plan in 1818, under the title *Darstellung eines Schauspielhauses in Ansicht, Grundriß und Durchschnitten.* See also Jean-Nicolas-Louis Durand, *Précis des leçons d'architecture* (Paris, 1802–5), vol. II, plate 16.

99. Diary remark recorded by C. Schneemann, *C. W. Coudray: Goethes Baumeister* (Weimar, 1945), 121.

100. See Peschken, *Das Architektonische Lehrbuch*, 152 and illus. 255–56.

101. A fact already pointed out by Eva Börsch-Supan, "Der Renaissancebegriff der Berliner Schule im Vergleich zu Semper," in *Gottfried Semper und die Mitte des 19. Jahrhunderts*, ed. Vogt, 162.

102. This was an idea actually first voiced by Schinkel in a letter from Naples to Johann Friedrich Unger, July 1804. See *Karl Friedrich Schinkel: Briefe, Tagebücher, Gedanken*, 73.

103. G. Semper, Ms. 178, fol. 16, Semper Archiv.

104. See especially Percier and Fontaine, *Palais, maisons.*

105. Semper, *Das königliche Hoftheater*, 27. "...und weil ein gewisses Spielen mit den Formen bei einem Gebäude, welches eine so chamäleontische Färbung hat, in welchem bald gelacht, bald geweint, aber immer gespielt wird, ihm um so mehr gerechtfertigt schien, als damit (bezeichnend für die Richtung unserer Bühnenkunst) an das Jahrhundert erinnert wird, in welchem die Grundsätze antiker Baukunst ziemlich freie und willkürliche Anwendung fanden, und durch Shakespeare und Andere auch das Schauspiel ein neues Leben erhielt, welches durch die grossen Dichter und Kunstrichter der letztern Zeit bei uns in zweiter Jugend erblühte."

106. Edouard Conte, "Charles Garnier," *L'Echo de Paris* 6, August 1898. Cited from Mead, *Charles Garnier's Paris Opera*, 258.

107. See Semper's description in *Das königliche Hoftheater*, 22–24.

108. For a discussion of Schinkel's proposed reforms in 1813 and in his built playhouse, see Bergdoll, *Karl Friedrich Schinkel*, 26–31 & 58–63.

109. Semper, *Das königliche Hoftheater*, 24. This idea may stem from Goethe.
110. Gas lighting appears to have made its first entrance in theater design in London in 1817.
111. Semper, *Das königliche Hoftheater*, 26.
112. Pecht, *Deutsche Künstler*, 172.
113. Lipsius, *Gottfried Semper*, 36. "Es giebt Theatersäle, die einen imposanteren, weiträumigeren, großartigeren, packenderen Eindruck hervor bringen, als dies bei dem Dresdener Theater der Fall war: in seiner liebenswürdigen, harmonischen, fein empfundenen, anmuthigen, edlen Wirkung ist es bisher nicht erreicht, geschweige denn übertroffen worden."
114. See Friedrich Schiller, *On the Aesthetic Education of Man*, 105, letter 22.
115. Semper, *Der Stil*, I, 231n.2.
116. Ibid., I, 232n. "Aus demselben Grunde konnte auch das Drama nur im Beginnen und auf dem höchsten Gipfel der steigenden Bildung eines Volks Bedeutung haben. Die ältesten Vasenbilder geben uns Begriffe von den frühen materiellen Maskenspielen der Hellenen – in vergeistigter Weise, gleich jenen steinernen Dramen des Phidias, wird durch Aeschylos, Sophokles, Euripides, gleichzeitig durch Aristophanes und die übrigen Komiker das uralte Maskenspiel wieder aufgenommen, wird das Proskenion zum Rahmen des Bildes eines grossartigen Stückes Menschengeschichte, die nicht irgendwo einmal passirt ist, sondern die überall sich ereignet, so lange Menschenherzen schlagen. 'Was war ihnen Hekuba?' Maskenlaune atmet in Shakespears Dramen; Maskenlaune und Kerzenduft, Karnevalstimmung (die wahrlich nicht immer lustig ist), tritt uns in Mozarts Don Juan entgegen; denn auch die Musik bedarf dieses Wirklichkeit vernichtenden Mittels..."
117. Cited from David Van Zanten, "Architectural Composition at the Ecole des Beaux-Arts from Charles Percier to Charles Garnier," in *The Architecture of the Ecole des Beaux-Arts*, ed. Arthur Drexler (New York: The Museum of Modern Art, 1977), 162.
118. See Percier and Fontaine, *Palais, maisons et autres édifices modernes*, plates 43 & 61.
119. For a discussion of these graphic innovations, see Mead, *Charles Garnier's Paris Opera*, see especially 120–27.
120. Brance (bookdealer) to Gottfried, 31 January 1839. Semper Archiv. Semper purchased altogether seven books. In addition to those of Gauthier and Letarouilly, he bought one on the public buildings of London, studies of the Palazzo Massimi and Villa Pia, one by Serrurerie, and another by Kauffmann, entitled *Architectonographie*. The Gauthier text was by far the most expensive at 160 francs; the first volume of Letarouilly's work was 90 francs.
121. See especially Wagner's remarks concerning Paris in *Mein Leben*, I, 512–13.
122. Richard Wagner, "Das Kunstwerk der Zukunft," in *Gesammelte Schriften*, 124–25. "Vor der Göttereiche zu Dodona neigte sich der des Naturorakels bedürfstige *Urhellene*; unter dem schattigen Laubdach und umgeben von den grünenden Baumsäulen des *Götterhaines* erhob der *Orphiker* seine Stimme: unter dem schön gefügten Giebeldache und zwichen den sinnig gereihten Marmorsäulen des *Göttertempels* ordnete aber der kunstfreudige *Lyriker* seine Tänze nach dem tönenden Hymnos, – und in dem *Theater*, das von dem Götteraltere – als seinem Mittelpunkte – aus sich zu der verständnisgebenden Bühne, wie zu den weiten Räumen für die nach Verständnis verlangenden zuschauer erhob, führte der *Tragöde* das lebendigste Werk vollendester Kunst aus.
123. Ibid., 129. "Nur mit der Erlösung der egoistisch getrennten, reinmenschlichen Kunstarten in das gemeinsame Kunstwerk der Zukunft, mit der Erlösung des *Nützlichkeitsmenschen* überhaupt in den *künstlerischen Menschen* der Zukunft, wird auch die Baukunst aus den Banden der Knechtschaft, aus dem Fluche der Zeugungsunfähigkeit zur freiesten, unerschöpflich fruchtbarsten Kunsttätigkeit erlöst werden."
124. Ibid., 150. "Nur dasjenige Bauwerk ist nach Notwendigkeit errichtet, das einem Zwecke des Menschen am dienlichsten entspricht: der höchste Zweck des Menschen ist der künstlerische, der höchste künstlerische das Drama."
125. Ibid., 151. "Alles, was auf der Bühne atmet und sich bewegt, atmet und bewegt sich durch ausdrucksvolles Verlangen nach Mitteilung, nach Angeschaut-Angehörtwerden in jenem Raume, der bei immer nur verhältnismässigem Umfange vom scenischen Standpunkte aus dem Darsteller doch die gesamte Menschheit zu enthalten dünkt..."
126. Ibid., 152. "Solche Wunder entblühen dem Bauwerke des Architekten, solchen Zaubern vermag er realen Grund und Boden zu geben, wenn er die Absicht des höchsten menschlichen Kunstwerkes zu der seinigen macht, wenn er die Bedingungen ihres Lebendigwerdens aus seinem eigentümlichen künstlerischen Vermögen heraus in das Dasein ruft."
127. The other members of the committee were Ascan Wilhelm Lutteroth-Legat, Georg Nicolaus Mohr, J. N. C. Brandenburg, Franz Matth-

ias Mutzenbecher, Christian Jacob Johns, Franz Ferdinand Eiffe, Carl Wilhelm Schröder, Georg Friedrich Vorwerk, Georg Hinrich Büsch, A. E. Vidal, Johann Siemsen, Adolf Jencquel, A. L. Goetze.

128. F. Georg Stammann to Gottfried, 3 and 8 February 1837, Semper Archiv.
129. F. Georg Stammann to Gottfried, 14 May 1837, Semper Archiv.
130. Sthamer to Gottfried, 7 February 1837, Semper Archiv.
131. See Sthamer to Gottfried, 28 April 1837 and 5 May 1837, Semper Archiv.
132. Sthamer to Gottfried, 17 June 1837, Semper Archiv.
133. Gottfried to Sthamer, 2 July 1837, Semper Archiv.
134. Sthamer to Gottfried, 17 July 1837, Semper Archiv.
135. See Gelder and Fischer, *"Nutzen und Zierde,"* 41–42.
136. Sthamer to Gottfried, 10 August 1837, Semper Archiv.
137. The Hamburg fire and the city's reconstruction has been the subject of three major studies. See Faulwasser, *Der Große Brand*, and Schumacher, *Das Kunstwerk Hamburg*. More recently Franck has considered the problem in even greater detail and specifically with regard to Semper, in *Die Nikolaikirche*. Much of the chronology of events depicted here is derived from Schumacher's and Franck's research.
138. See Schumacher, *Das Kunstwerk Hamburg*, 50–54n.4.
139. See Franck, *Die Nikolaikirche*, 230 (Text 3).
140. See Schumacher, *Das Kunstwerk Hamburg*, 57–58n.6.
141. See Franck, *Die Nikolaikirche*, 41–42, 233–34 (Text 10).
142. *Allgemeine Bauzeitung,* 1848, 279–82.
143. Gottfried to Sthamer, 30 December 1842, Semper Archiv.
144. Semper, "Unmaßgebliche Vorschläge." The report was presented 22 January 1843.
145. Herrmann, "Semper's Position on the Gothic," *In Search of Architecture*, 124–38.
146. Châteauneuf to Gottfried, 12 January 1843, in Franck, *Die Nikolaikirche*, 62.
147. Franck, *Die Nikolaikirche*, 66–68.
148. Ibid., 248–51 (text 27).
149. Ibid., 95.
150. Ibid., 261–62 (text 38).
151. Gottfried to Wilhelm, 1 November 1844, Semper Archiv.
152. See Lewis, *The German Gothic Revival.*
153. Gottfried Semper, Dresden Academy lecture, Ms. 25, 213. Semper Archiv. "In größerer Entfernung erscheinen die Strebepfeiler, die Thürmchen auf den Widerlagern, die durchbrochenen Fenster und Giebel, wie ein mit Baugerüsten umgebenes Gebäude, wobei noch hinzukommt, dass selten die Massen so malerisch gruppirt sind, als man dies bei den byzantinischen Kirchen findet."
154. Ibid. "...die Äussere einer gothischen Kirche doch immer einen Anschein behält als wäre sie nicht fertig, oder als sollte sie noch eine Umkleidung erhalten." See also Herrmann, "Semper's Position on the Gothic," *In Search of Architecture*, 133.
155. G. Semper, Remarks to "Andeutungen," Ms.13, fol. 5, Semper Archiv. See also Herrmann, "Semper's Position on the Gothic," *In Search of Architecture*, 135. "Ein goth. Bau von ferne ist zu durchbrochen, die Massen verschwinden, so wie das Einzelne. Es sieht aus wie ein Werk im Bau begriffen, mit Gerüsten umgeben."
156. G. Semper, Explanatory Report for the Competition, in Franck, *Die Nikolaikirche*, 266 (text 42). "Ein Schauspielhaus muß durchaus an ein römisches Theater erinnern, wenn es Charakter haben soll. Ein gothisches Theater ist unkenntlich. Kirchen in altdorischem oder selbst in dem Renaissancestyl des 16[n] Jahrhunderts haben für uns nichts Kirchliches. Auf diesem Standpunkte stehen wir einmal. Auch wenn es nich so wäre, würde es doch unmöglich seyn, einen nagelneuen Styl zu erfinden; nur der allmähliche Gang der Zeiten bringt unmerklich nach langem Uebergange ganz unähnliche Resultate hervor."
157. The line of reasoning was mapped out by Semper in "Ueber den Bau evangelischer Kirchen," in *Kleine Schriften*, 443–67.
158. Porth to Gottfried, 7 January 1845, Semper Archiv. See also Franck, *Die Nikolaikirche*, 111.
159. Porth to Gottfried, 7 February 1845, Semper Archiv. See also Franck, *Die Nikolaikirche*, 262–63 (text 39).
160. See Franck, *Die Nikolaikirche*, 146–47.
161. Ibid., 153–68.
162. Ibid., 168–69.
163. Gottfried to Porth, 10 February 1845, Semper Archiv. See also Franck, *Die Nikolaikirche*, 264–66 (text 41).
164. Gottfried to Speckter, ca. 10 February 1845, Semper Archiv. See also Franck, *Die Nikolaikirche*, 281 (text 45).
165. G. Semper, "Noch etwas über den St. Nikolai-Kirchenbau," in *Neue hamburgische Blätter*, 12. Also in *Kleine Schriften*, 468–73.

166. See Gottfried to Wilhelm, 8 April 1845, Semper Archiv, and "Ueber den Bau evangelischer Kirchen," in *Kleine Schriften*, 443–67.
167. Bülau to Gottfried, 10 May 1845, Semper Archiv. See also Franck, *Die Nikolaikirche*, 194–95.
168. Bülau to Gottfried, 1 March, Semper Archiv. See Franck, *Die Nikolaikirche*, 152.
169. See Franck, *Die Nikolaikirche*, 183.
170. Bülau to Gottfried, 10 May 1845, Semper Archiv. See also Franck, *Die Nikolaikirche*, 194–95.
171. Schaumann, "Die drei gekrönten Pläne," 28.
172. See Franck, *Die Nikolaikirche*, 190–94.
173. Gottfried to mother, 26 November 1845, Semper Archiv.
174. Extractus protocolli der Rath- und Bürger-Deputation to Gottfried, 13 December 1845, Semper Archiv.
175. G. Semper, Ms. 19, fol. 6, Semper Archiv.
176. Müller, *Handbuch der Archäologie der Kunst*, section 39.
177. Ibid., sections 1–6.
178. See, among others, A. W. Schlegel, "Vorlesungen über schöne Litteratur und Kunst," in *Deutsche Litteraturdenkmale des 18. und 19. Jahrhunderts* (Nendeln, 1968), 160–61.
179. Müller, *Handbuch der Archäologie der Kunst*, section 12. "Schön nennen wir diejenigen Formen, welche die Seele auf eine ihrer Natur durchaus angemessene, wohlthätige, wahrhaft gesunde Weise zu empfinden vernalassen, gleichsam in Schwingungen setzen, die ihrer innersten Struktur gemäß sind."
180. Ibid., para. 13. "Daher der tiefe Ausspruch Winckelmann's (VII. S. 76), daß die völlige Schönheit unbezeichnend sein müsse, gleich dem reinsten Wasser."
181. G. Semper, Ms. 19, fol. 20. "Wer den Herrn v. Rumohr aus seinen Schriften und persönlich genauer kennt, wird Gelegenheit gehabt haben, an ihm gerade die architectonische Richtung und Ausbildung seines forschenden und ordnenden Geistes zu bewundern. Als feinfühlender Baumeister weiß er seinen Stoff zu behandeln, als solcher tritt er auf in dem geselligen Verkehr mit Menschen, stets wohl geordnet und mit feinem Takt."
182. Waetzoldt, *Deutsche Kunsthistoriker*, I, 292.
183. Rumohr, *Italienische Forschungen*, I, iv.
184. W. Dilthey, "The Three Epochs of Modern Aesthetics and its Present Task," in *Selected Works*, V, 204.
185. Rumohr, *Italienische Forschungen*, III, 160. "...so werden wir mehr und mehr einsehen lernen, dass in Bezug auf Schönheit keine Linie, keine Form, kein Verhältniss in einer neuen Verbindung noch ganz dieselben sind."
186. Ibid., III, 193. "...der umsichtvollen Auswahl des Materials, aus welchem die Kuppel construirt worden, erkennt man die römische, in der Verarbeitung des Backsteins unerreichte Bauschule."
187. Ibid., III, 200. "Was den nun hätten die Bewohner Italiens vom sechsten zum achten Jahrhunderte aus der Baukunst des östlichen Reiches entlehnen sollen? Das Technische? Keineswegs; denn, wie ich gezeigt habe, beruhete dieses in beiden Bauschulen auf römischen Traditionen, ist kein Grund vorhanden, bey den Italienern des gothischen und langobardischen Zeiten gänzliche Ausrottung römischer Baukunde anzunehmen, was zwar dem Ghiberti und Vasari, doch unseren Zeitgenossen gewiss nicht zu verzeihen wäre. Nun gar das Beyspiel, welches man dafür anführt! Die Kirche S. Vitale zu Ravenna! Als wenn es nicht längst erwiesen wäre, dass sie ein Werk der letzten gothischen Regierung ist, welches Justinian nur musivisch ausgeziert, und mit einer Vorhalle versehehen hat." Rumohr used the term "gothischen" to refer to the Visigothic and Ostogothic intrusions of the fifth and sixth centuries. Construction of S. Vitale did begin under Ostogothic rule, and the mosaics of the Justinian era were added in AD 546–48.
188. Ibid., III, 228. "Durch die Entwicklung ihres geschichtlichen und gleichsam organischen Zusammenhanges beyweckte ich, Ansichten zu verdrängen welche einem blödsinnigen Nachahmungstriebe beymesssen, was nur aus Nothwendigkeiten, Absichten und Zwecken abzuleiten ist."
189. F. W. Schelling, "Über das Verhaltniss der bildenden Künsten zu der Natur," *Sämmtliche Werke* (Stuttgart: Cotta, 1860), VIII, 305.
190. Ibid. "Nur durch die Vollendung der Form kann die Form vernichtet werden, und dieses ist allerdings im Charakteristischen das letzte Ziel der Kunst."
191. Rumohr, *Italienische Forschungen*, I, 15. "Ja in gewisser Beziehung der einzige Bürge für die Güte oder Schwäche der Auffassung selbst."
192. Ibid., I, 45–35.
193. Ibid., I, 60. "...die typen der Natur in ihrem ursprünglichen und eigenen Sinne in Anwendung zu bringen."
194. Ibid., I, 87. "...wir den Styl als ein zu Gewohnheit gediehenes sich Fügen in die inneren Forderungen des Stoffes erklären, in

welchem der Bildner seine Gestalten wirklich bildet, der Maler sie erscheinen macht."

195. See Hegel, *Philosophy of Fine Art*, 399. Hegel preferred not to limit the meaning of style to its sensuous material.
196. An inventory of nearly 200 books (Ms. 148) passed through English Customs in 1850, giving a fairly good indication of Semper's reading habits in the 1840s. The two largest sections of his library were given to classical works and to architectural/technical texts. The library contained numerous historical works, relatively few works devoted to aesthetics, and none to philosophy proper. Rumohr and Müller's *Handbuch* were listed, as were Winckelmann's *Geschichte der Kunst* and Lessing's *Laocoön*. Semper's interest in aesthetics and philosophy – in the ideas of Schiller, Schopenauer, Hegel, and Schelling – seems to have originated in the 1850s, particularly during the writing of *Der Stil*.
197. G. Semper, Ms. 19, fol. 17. "...wie Winckelmann unbeschadet ihrer Kennerschaft in den Werken der Plastik und Malerei, dennoch deutlich ihre Inkompetenz in Beurtheilung der Werke der Baukunst darlegen."
198. Ibid., fol. 34. "...einen allgemeinen Vortheil in der Handhabung des Kunstmaterials, sowie eine Unterordnung der Darstellung unter bestimmte Gesetzlichkeiten darunter versteht."
199. Ibid., fol. 35. "...den positiveren Gesetzen der Convention und der besonderen Bildungsrichtung eines Volkes und eines Zeitalters entsprechen."
200. Ibid., fol. 36. "Die Künste entwicklen sich erst dann in ihrer schönsten Reife, wenn der freie Sinn sich die allgemein verständliche Sprache des Naturausdrucks aneignet, die Mystik sich zur Symbolik erhebt und Geschmack und Achtung des Herkömmlichen der ausschweifenden Entartung Schranken setzt."
201. See Mss. 20–23, Semper Archiv.
202. The inventory of the Semper library (Ms. 148) lists four separate works by Heeren, including five volumes of his *Ideen über die Politik, den Verkehr und den Handel der vornehmsten Völker der alten Welt*. Other likely sources from his library are Alois Hirt's *Die Geschichte der Baukunst bei den Alten* (1822), C. A. Böttiger's *Ideen zur Archäologie der Malerei* (1811), and C. L. Stieglitz's *Geschichte der Baukunst vom frühesten Alterthume bis in die neuern Zeiten* (1827).
203. Herrmann, *Gottfried Semper theoretischer Nachlass*, notes to Ms. 25, 79.
204. G. Semper, Ms. 25, fols. 315–19, Semper Archiv.
205. Vieweg to Gottfried, 30 July and 12 September 1843, Semper Archiv. For the history of this relationship see W. Herrmann, "Semper und Eduard Vieweg," in *Gottfried Semper und die Mitte des 19. Jahrhunderts*, ed. Vogt, 199–237. See also Herrmann *In Search of Architecture*, 89–114.
206. Gottfried to Vieweg, 26 September 1843, Semper Archiv, ETH-Hönggerberg. "Man nennt die Gebilde der Baukunst organisch, wenn sie aus einer wahren Grundidee hervorgehen, und bei ihren Formation die Gesetzlichkeit und innere geistige Nothwendigkeit hervortritt, durch welche die Natur schafft, nur Gutes und Schönes schafft, und das Hässliche selbst als nothwendiges Element zur Harmonie des Ganzen verwendet."
207. Ibid. "Man wird dabei zu der Anschauung kommen, dass, so wie die Natur bei ihrer Mannichfaltigkeit in den Grundideen doch nur einfach, und sparsam ist, wie sich in ihr eine stete Wiedererneuerung derselben Grundformen zeigt, die nach dem Stufengang der Ausbildung der Geschöpfe und nach ihren Daseynbedingungen tausendfältig modificiert, in Theilen anders ausgebildet, in Theilen verkürzt und verlängert erscheinen, dass, sage ich, eben so auch der Baukunst gewisse Normalformen zum Grunde liegen, die durch eine ursprüngliche Idee bedungen, in steter Wiedererscheinung doch eine, durch spezielle Zwecke und durch näher bestimmende Umstände bedungene unendliche Mannichfaltigkeit gestatten."
208. Ms. 122, fol. 6, Semper Archiv.
209. Ibid., fol. 3.
210. Cuvier, *The Animal Kingdom*, 3.
211. J. W. von Goethe, *Gedenkausgabe der Werke, Briefe und Gespräche*, XVII, 381. "...hegt das Ganze im innern Sinne und lebt in der Überzeugung fort, das Einzelne könne daraus nach und nach entwickelt werden."
212. Ibid., XVII, 415. "Die Gestalt ist ein Bewegliches, ein Werdendes, ein Vergehendes. Gestaltenlehre ist Verwandlungslehre. Die Lehre der Metamorphose ist der Schlüssel zu allen Zeichen der Natur."
213. Ibid., XVII, 420. "Funktion und Gestalt notwendig verbunden. Die Funktion ist das Dasein in Tätigkeit gedacht."
214. See Bruhns, *Alexander von Humboldt*, II, 178.
215. See Kellner, *Alexander von Humboldt*, 199.
216. Humboldt, *Cosmos*, I, Preface.
217. Ibid., 22. Semper eventually owned a copy of Humboldt's book, but in a later exchange of letters with Bertha it seems he purchased it in 1849, just a few months before he fled Dresden.

Bertha was thinking of returning it to the publisher, since it was unopened and unread.

218. Quatremère de Quincy, *De l'architecture égyptienne*, 15–19.
219. Lavin, *Quatremère de Quincy*, 65–74.
220. R. Rochette's review of *Preliminary Remarks* was published in the *Journal des Savants*, 1 November 1836, 671.
221. Bopp, *A Comparative Grammar*, vi.
222. Prichard, *Natural History of Man*, 123.
223. Ibid., 170.
224. See Klemm, "Fantasie über ein Museum für die Culturgeschichte der Menschkeit" (Fantasy for a Museum for the Cultural History of Mankind), published as an appendix to the first volume of *Cultur-Geschichte*. Klemm made his case by providing a full agenda for the museum, which would start with rooms devoted to geology, botany, and zoology, before proceeding to human culture. In Klemm's later description of his collection, in the tenth volume, he indicated that a building the size of the Munich Glyptothek would be adequate. Klemm's description of his contents formed the Preface to the tenth volume of the *Cultur-Geschichte*. Klemm's collection was reassembled in 1870 and formed the basis for the city's Museum für Völkerkunde.
225. Klemm, *Cultur-Geschichte*, I, 22.
226. See Mallgrave, "Gustav Klemm and Gottfried Semper."
227. Robert Ker Porter, *Travels in Georgia, Persia, Armenia, Ancient Babylonia*, 2 vols. (London, 1821–22). Herodotus wrote a book on Assyria, but this was lost.
228. See Layard, *Nineveh and its Remains*.
229. Botta, *Monument de Ninive*; reprint, V, 174–76.
230. Ms. 31, fols. 10–17, Semper Archiv.
231. Ms. 33, fols. 3–5, Semper Archiv. "...ebenso bildeten sich nach seinem Vorbild Flecken & Städte aus, bei denen ebenfalls die Mauern das Erste waren, innerhalb welcher sich ein gemeinschaftliche Forum (agora) die Wohnungen der einzelnen Familien ordneten. Eine Gottheit bewohnte als Schutzpatron die Stadt. Ihr ward eine besondere Herd am Markte geweiht, & ein Stelle hinter diesem, diente ihr zur Wohnung. Liess der Kultus mehrere Gottheiten zu, so musste jeder ein besonderer Bezirk geheiligt seyn, in dem ihr Altar & Tempelhaus stand."
232. Gottfried to Vieweg, 27 November 1845, Semper Archiv.
233. Gottfried to Vieweg, 21 January 1848, Semper Archiv.
234. Gottfried to Vieweg, 3 December 1848, Semper Archiv.
235. Gottfried to Vieweg, 24 February 1850, Semper Archiv. "Glauben Sie ja nicht, dass meine Sorgfalt für die Entwicklung der Anfänge der Kunst überflüssig ist. Auf ihnen basirt der Gedanke, den ich durch das ganze Werk durchzuführen gedenke."

3 Refugee in Paris and London

1. Gottfried to Carl, 25 March 1848, Semper Archiv.
2. Richard Wagner, *My Life*, 478–79.
3. Gottfried to Bertha, 22 May 1849, Semper Archiv.
4. Waldersee, *Der Kampf in Dresden*, 25–26.
5. Richard Wagner, *My Life*, 479.
6. Gottfried to Carl, 15 May 1849, Semper Archiv. "Jeder muss wissen, was sein Pflichtgefühl von ihm fordert und darnach handeln. Halbheit ist ohnedies nur zu sehr bei uns gebildeteren Ständen zu finden, die, wenn schon Parthei nehmend, doch nichts für ihre Parthei opfern mögen. Kurz ich fühle mich frei von Vorwurf."
7. Gottfried to Carl, 28 May 1849, Semper Archiv. "Wäre ich 20 Jahre jünger, hätte kein Weib und keine Kinder und hätte Reichthum, dann würdet ihr mehr von mir hören."
8. Gottfried to Bertha, 17 May 1849, Semper Archiv. "Also fort von hier und frisch die Segel nach Amerika gespannt! Doch vorher noch abwarten, vielleicht ist der Tag der Vergeltung näher als wir glauben."
9. Gottfried to Carl, 28 May 1849, Semper Archiv. "Ich bin kein Repitant und werde gerne Rede and Antwort stehen für meine Thaten und Worte...Büssen denn!"
10. Gottfried to Bertha, 21 June 1849, Semper Archiv. "Überhaput bereue ich es fast, geflohen zu seyn...Ausserdem ist die Welt nur ein grosses Gefängnis für mich."
11. See J. Sheehan, *German History*, 708.
12. Quandt to Gau, 7 July 1849, Semper Archiv.
13. H. W. Schulz to Gottfried, 8 August 1849, Semper Archiv.
14. Gottfried to Krüger, 26 June 1849, Semper Archiv.
15. For Semper's hesitation about the letter, see Herrmann, *In Search of Architecture*, 13.
16. Cole, "Journey to Vienna."
17. He recounts their conversations in his letter to Bertha of 19 June 1849, Semper Archiv.
18. Gottfried to Krüger, 9 June 1849, Semper Archiv.
19. Gottfried to Vieweg, 15 June 1849; Vieweg to Gottfried, 20 June 1849. Semper Archiv.

20. Heine to Gottfried, 24 September 1849, Semper Archiv.
21. See undated letter to "Herr Legationsrath," Semper Archiv.
22. Gottfried to Lindenau, 10 April 1850, Semper Archiv.
23. Lindenau to Gottfried, 16 April 1850, Semper Archiv.
24. Gottfried to Bertha, 16 November 1849, Semper Archiv. "O Bertha, wenn du wüsstest, wie das alles weh thut, wie mir zuweilen hier ums Herz ist – doch Muth!"
25. See Semper's articles in *Zeitschrift für praktische Baukunst,* 9 (Leipzig, 1849), 502–28 (with plates); 10 (Leipzig, 1850), 3 (with plates).
26. Lindley to Gottfried, 2 April 1850, Semper Archiv.
27. Two bank receipts for Semper's loan are preserved in the Semper Archiv in Hönggerberg. The first, dated 20 July 1850, is for the sum of 2000 francs. The second, dated 13 August, is for the sum of $869.57.
28. Braun to Gottfried, 16 September 1850, Semper Archiv. "Ich glaube im Stande zu sein Ihnen ein Feld für Ihre künstlerische Thätigkeit darzubieten oder wenigstens nachzuweisen, welches nicht weniger ruhmreich zu werden verspricht als das welches Sie verlassen haben."
29. Gottfried to brother, 30 September 1850, Semper Archiv. "Du wirst erstaunen, einen Brief datiert aus London von mir zu erhalten. In der That gleicht das Ganze ziemlich einer Shakespearische Bühne...etwa dem letzten Akt im Hamlet".
30. Vieweg to Gottfried, 20 June 1849, Semper Archiv.
31. Gottfried to Vieweg, 24 February 1850, published in W. Herrmann, "Semper und Eduard Vieweg," *Gottfried Semper und die Mitte des 19. Jahrhunderts*, ed. Vogt, 223–25, letter no. 6.
32. Gottfried to Bertha, 21 March 1850, Semper Archiv.
33. Ms. 55, fol. 8. Semper Archiv. Trans. Herrmann, in *In Search of Architecture*, 193. "Indem man so die Construction als das Wesen der Baukunst ansah, verirrte man sich fest eben so weit vom Ziele, wie andere, die in der Baukunst eine Art von plastischer und malerischer Dekoration für Häuser sehen."
34. Ibid., fol. 10. See Herrmann, ibid., 193–94. "Der Baukünstler, welcher diese herkömmlichen Formen verschmäht, gleicht dem Autor, der für die Behandlung seines Themas seiner Sprache Zwang anthut, und eine veraltete, fremde oder selbstgeschaffene Wortstellung und Ausdrucksweise dafür annimmt. Er wird nur mühsam verstanden werden und, als Schriftsteller wenigstens kein Glück machen, während er an Originalität des Gedankens nichts einbüsste, wenn er sich zu ihrer Darstellung gereinigter aber verständlicher Formen bediente."
35. Ibid., fol. 11. See Herrmann, 194. "Aber es darf Aufgabe des denkenden Architecten seyn, die der Baukunst innewohnenden Grundideen in ihrem Entstehen aufzusuchen, auf ihrem Entwickelungsgange zu verfolgen, und das Gesetz, welches in der künstlerischen Verhüllung derselben verborgen liegt, auf seinen einfachsten Ausdruck zurückzuführen."
36. Ms. 58, fol. 98. Semper Archiv. See Herrmann, ibid., 205. "Es blieb der Teppich die eigentliche Wand, die sichtbare Raumbegränzung. Die dahinter befindlichen, oft sehr starken Mauern wurden wegen anderer, das Räumliche nicht betreffender Zwecke nothwendig, zur Sicherheit, zum Tragen, zu grösserer Dauer u.s.w."
37. Ibid., fol. 99. See Herrmann, ibid., 206. "Der Charakter des Neuen folgte lange dem des Urbildes. Malerei und Plastik auf Holz, Stuck, Stein oder Metall war und blieb in später kaum mehr bewusster Überlieferung eine Nachahmung der bunten Stickereien der uralten Teppichwände. Das ganze System der Orientalischen Polychromie in folgedessen auch die Kunst des Malens und die Basrelief-Sculptur überhaupt ist hervorgegangen aus den Webstühlen und Kesseln der betriebsamen Assyrer oder ihrer Vorgänger in den Erfindungen der Vorzeit."
38. Gottfried to Vieweg, 19 January 1850. See Herrmann, "Semper und Eduard Vieweg," *Gottfried Semper und die Mitte des 19. Jahrhunderts*, ed. Vogt, 228–30, letter no. 9.
39. See "Report of the Committee Appointed to Examine the Elgin Marbles, in order to Ascertain Whether any Evidence Remains as to the Employment of Colour in the Decoration of the Architecture or Sculpture," in Royal Institute of British Architects, *Transactions of the Royal Institute of British Architects of London*, vol. I, part II, 101–8.
40. Mathew Digby Wyatt, "Mediaeval Polychromatic Decoration," 37–41.
41. Jones, "Internal Decoration," 32–34. On Jones's color theories see Van Zanten, *Architectural Polychromy.*
42. For a summary of Semper's remarks, see Donaldson, "Polychromatic Embellishments," 42–50.
43. Semper, *Die Vier Elemente*, 1; Eng. trans., 75. "...war eine der wichtigsten Erscheinungen der

Kunstlitteratur und ein Triumph unseres Jahrhunderts."

44. Herodotus, III, 57. Loeb translation by A. D. Godley. Semper even sought out the advice of a noted philologist on this passage, see Gottfried to O. Klepperbein, 26 December 1850, Semper Archiv.
45. Semper, *Die Vier Elemente*, 45; Eng. trans., 98.
46. Ibid., 8; Eng. trans., 78. "Kann er den Chorus wieder aus dem Orcus zusammenrufen, dem sich das Drama entwand, bei welchem alle Künste, und die hellenische Erde und das Meer und der Himmel und das ganze Volk selbst zu gemeinsamer Verherrlichung zusammenwirkten? Und Alles bleibt doch nur eine unheimliche Phantasmagorie, ehe sich unser Volksleben nicht zu harmonischem Kunstwerke, analog dem Griechischen in seiner kurzen Blüthezeit, nur reicher noch, gestaltet. Wenn dies geschieht, dann lösen sich alle Räthsel!"
47. Ibid., 52; Eng. trans., 101. "Hellenische Bildung konnte nur auf dem Humus vieler längst erstorbener und verwitterter früherer Zustände und fremder von Aussen herübergetragener, in ihrer ursprünglichen Bedeutung nich mehr verstandener Motive entstehen."
48. See Hope, *Essay on Architecture*.
49. Semper, *Die Vier Elemente*, 97; Eng. trans., 125. "Es ist nämlich wohl mehr als blosse Muthmassung, dass der Dorismus, wie in der Musik, so auch in der Ausübung der beiden genannten Künste, und hauptsächlich in ihrer Anwendung auf den Tempelbau, sich principiell von dem Ionismus unterschied, dass eine dorische Farbentonart bestand, wie es eine dorische Tonart in der Musik gab."
50. Ibid., 100; Eng. trans., 127. "Zuerst darf die Wand niemals durch das darauf Dargestellte ihre ursprüngliche Bedeutung als Raumabschluss verlieren, es ist vielmehr immer noch rathsam, bei der Verzierung der Wände durch Malerei des Teppichs, als frühesten Raumabschlusses, eingedenk zu bleiben. Ausnahme machen nur solche Fälle, wo der Raumabschluss wohl materiell, aber nicht der Idee nach vorhanden ist. Dann tritt die Malerei in das Gebiet der Theaterdecoration ein, was sie öfters mit gutem Erfolge thun mag."
51. Ibid., 103; Eng. trans., 128. "Wie grosses Unrecht thut man uns Architekten mit dem Vorwurfe der Armuth an Erfindung, während sich nirgend eine neue weltgeschlichtliche, mit Nachdruck und Kraft verfolgte Idee kund giebt. Vorher sorgt für einen neuen Gedanken, dann wollen wir schon den architektonischen Ausdruck dafür finden. Bis dahin begnüge man sich mit dem Alten."
52. Semper's mention of Schaubert in his text is in response to Kugler's coupling of Schaubert's report of finding a patch of yellow paint, on one anta of the Theseum, with Semper's report of finding blue samples. Semper denies that Schaubert was present when he and Goury did their investigation and insists that Schaubert only retraced the drawings he and Goury had already done. Schaubert's drawings were published by Quast in *Museum. Blätter für bildende Kunst*, 32, 1833, under the title "Nachrichten aus Griechenland, nach mündlichen Nachrichten des Hrn. Schaubert." See Quast's defense of himself against Semper's charge, "Entgegnung," in *Deutsches Kunstblatt*, 11, 13 March 1852, 97–98.
53. Franz Kugler, "Antique Polychromie," *Deutsches Kunstblatt*, 15, 10 April 1852, 131. "Der Verf. geht auf die Urzustände der ältesten Völker zurück und entwickelt aus diesen und aus der verschiedenartigen geschichtlichen Stellung der Völker die Grundelemente der Architektur und die verschiedenartige Richtung, welche die letztere nehmen musste.... Es ist ein anziehendes Gefühl, an der Hand, eines geistvollen Mannes in jene dunkeln Regionen der Weltgeschichte hinabzusteigen; mag die Ausdeutung der Nebelbilder auch ein gut Theil individueller Phantasie nötig machen, so empfangen wir doch immer die schätzbarsten Anregungen zu eigner Gedankenarbeit."
54. "On the Study of Polychromy and its Revival," *The Museum of Classical Antiquity*, I (1851), 228–48.
55. Braun to Gottfried, 22 September 1850, Semper Archiv.
56. Gottfried to Braun, undated draft, late September 1850, Semper Archiv.
57. See Herrmann, *In Search of Architecture*, 3–83.
58. *Eidgenössische Zeitung*, Morgenausgabe, 87, 28 March 1851, 347–48.
59. See especially Gottfried to Julia Becher, July 1851, Semper Archiv. The same sentiment is expressed in various other letters from this period.
60. Gottfried to Carl, 30 September 1850, Semper Archiv. "Von den Fürsten und Aristokraten kann nicht die Rede seyn, denn sie sind unsere offenen Feinde, – sie thun was sie können sich zu erhalten und haben Recht daran es zu thun, denn es geht ihnen ans Leben. Sie sind nicht minder Eure Feinde als die unsrigen, und alle Eure Bemühungen Euch ihre Gunst zu erhalten, sind vergeblich. Eben so Euer Rechtsboden und der passive Widerstand. Endlich muss doch wieder das Pulver und das Blei entscheiden."

61. See Reiner Gross, "Gottfried Semper in seinen Beziehungen zu Sachsen vom Juni 1849 bis Ende 1870," in Dresden Technische Universität, *Gottfried Semper 1803–1879*, 1980, 13, 152.
62. Karl Marx/Friedrich Engels, *Briefwechsel* (Berlin, 1949), I, 309. Cited from Quitzsch, *Die ästhetischen Anschauungen*, 12. "Es wurde ein neues provisorisches Kommitee gewählt, bestehend aus den Herren Kinkel, Graf Reichenbach, Bucher und dem Sachsen Semper. Du siehst hieraus, dass man in eine neue Phase getreten ist. Man hat sich in die Arme des respektablen 'homme d'état' geworfen, da die bisherigen 'Führer' als bürgerliche Lumpen kompromittiert sind."
63. Cited from Bonython, *King Cole*, 2. See also Quentin Bell's *The Schools of Design* (London: Routledge & Kegan Paul, 1963), 211–15.
64. Bell, *Schools of Design* (note 63), 1.
65. For more on William Dyce, see Quentin Bell, *Victorian Artists* (London, 1967), 23ff.
66. Pugin made know his views in a letter to the *Builder*, 2 August 1845. His complaint was that the Schools had become "mere drawing" schools.
67. The letter, written in September 1846, was published as an appendix to Redgrave's *Manual of Design*.
68. *Journal of Design and Manufactures*, March, 1849, I, 3.
69. Ibid., I, 4.
70. Ibid., October, 1849, II, 72.
71. Mrs. Merrifield, "The Harmony of Colours as exemplified in the Exhibition," *The Crystal Palace Exhibition: Illustration Catalogue* (London, 1851; reprint: New York, 1970), appendix, page II. On the Exhibition see also Beaver, *The Crystal Palace*.
72. Cited from Beaver, *The Crystal Palace*, 41–42.
73. Whewell, "On the General Bearing," 12.
74. Cole, "On the International Results of the Exhibition of 1851," in *Fifty Years of Public Work*, II, 240.
75. Friedrich Wetzler noted that Semper would "probably" also obtain the commissions of Greece and a part of that of the United States, see Wetzler to Wiegand, 12 April 1851, Semper Archiv.
76. G. Semper, Ms. 129, fol. 1, Semper Archiv.
77. G. Semper, Ms. 97, fol. 27, Semper Archiv. "Es ist allgemein anerkannt, dass die Erzeugnisse des naivesten Verfahrens in der Stofffabrikation sowohl in den Mustern wie in den Farben die raffinirten Werke der civilisirten Völker in dem was man Styl nennt weit übertroffen haben."
78. Robert Kerr, Preface to the third edition of James Fergusson's *History of the Modern Styles of Architecture* (New York, 1891), vi.
79. Wornum, "The Exhibition as a Lesson," Appendix, vi***.
80. Ibid., vii***.
81. Ibid., xxi***.
82. Ibid., xxii***.
83. Redgrave, "Supplementary Report," 708.
84. Ibid., 710.
85. Ibid., 710–11.
86. Ibid., 713.
87. Ibid.
88. Wyatt discussed Redgrave's and Jones's remarks in "On the Principles of Design applicable to Textile Art," extracted from J. B. Waring's *Art Treasures of the United Kingdom* (London, 1858), 73.
89. O. Jones, "Gleanings from the Great Exhibition of 1851," *Journal of Design and Manufactures*, June 1851, V, 93.
90. On Jones's two lectures, see his "Colour in the Decorative Arts," 255–99; and *The True and the False*, 4–68.
91. Wyatt, "Form in the Decorative Arts," 215–51.
92. Wyatt, *The Industrial Arts*, I, vii.
93. M. D. Wyatt, "The Exhibition under its Commercial Aspects," *Journal of Design and Manufactures,* August 1851, V, 157.
94. Jones, "Colour in the Decorative Arts," 290.
95. Ibid., 292.
96. O. Jones, "Plan of Decorating the Interior of the Exhibition Building," *The Civil Engineer and Architect's Journal*, 14, 21 December 1851, 33.
97. M. D. Wyatt, "Iron Work and the Principles of its Treatment," *Journal of Design and Manufactures*, IV, September 1850, 78.
98. Semper, *Wissenschaft, Industrie und Kunst,* 4; Eng. trans., 130.
99. Ibid., 12; Eng. trans., 135. "Die Praxis müht sich vergeblich ab, Herr ihres Stoffes zu werden, vornehmlich in geistiger Beziehung. Sie erhält ihn zu beliebiger weiterer Verwerthung von der Wissenschaft ausgeliefert, ohne dass durch vielhundertjährigen Volksgebrauch sein Styl sich entwickeln konnte."
100. Ibid., 10; Eng. trans., 134. "Die Machine näht, strickt, stickt, schnitzt, malt, greift tief ein in das Gebiet der menschlichen Kunst und beschämt jede menschliche Geschicklichkeit."
101. Ibid., 20; Eng. trans., 139. "Dort ist man doppelt abhängig; Sklave des Brotherrn und der Mode des Tage, die Letzterem Absatz für seine Waaren verschafft. Man opfert seine Individualität, seine 'Erstgeburt' für ein Linsengericht."

102. Ibid., 24; Eng. trans., 141. "...Alles ist auf den Markt berechnet und zugeschnitten."
103. Ibid., 27; Eng. trans., 142. "Während aber unsere Kunstindustrie richtungslos forwirthschaften wird, erfüllt sie unbewusst ein hehres Werk, das der *Zersetzung traditioneller Typen* durch ihre ornamentale Behandlung."
104. Ibid., 28; Eng. trans., 142–43. "Täusche man sich nicht! Jene Zustände haben allerdings die Gewissheit künftiger allgemeiner Geltung für sich, weil sie Verhältnissen entsprechen, die in allen Ländern Gültigkeit haben, und zweitens empfinden wir nur zu schmerzlich, dass gerade die höhere Kunst dabei am tödtlichsten getroffen wird."
105. Ibid., 31; Eng. trans., 144. "*Diesen Process der Zersetzung der vorhandenen Kunsttypen muss die Industrie, die Speculation und die auf das Leben angewendete Wissenschaft vorher vollenden, ehe etwas Gutes und Neues erfolgen kann.*"
106. Ibid., 15; Eng. trans., 136. "Styl ist das zu künstlerischer Bedeutung erhobene Hervortreten der Grundidee und aller inneren und äusseren Coefficienten, die bei der Verkörperung derselben in einem Kunstwerke modificirend einwirkten. – Styllosigkeit ist dann nach dieser Definition der Ausdruck für die Mängel eines Werkes, welche aus Nichtberücksichtigung der ihm zuhehörigen Grundidee und aus der Unbeholfenheit in ästhetischer verwerthung der gebotenen Mittel zu seiner Vollendung entstehen."
107. For details of the political controversy surrounding Pugin's liturgical motifs, see Alexandra Wedgwood, "The Mediæval Court," in *Pugin: A Gothic Passion*, ed. Atterbury and Wainwright, 237–45. Wedgwood also points out that the reference to the exhibition as a "Great Babel" was bandied about as early as March 1851, and therefore was not an analogy original to Semper.
108. See Ettlinger, "Science, Industry and Art," 63.
109. These meetings are recorded in various entries in Cole's diaries, beginning 19 August 1851. London, Victoria and Albert Museum, 55.AA.14.
110. Cole met with Prince Albert on 15 November and again on 5 January and 19 February. Regarding the second meeting, Cole noted in his diary that it was the Prince's plan "to buy plenty of ground at Kensington, to provide a Collection of History of Manufacturers, lectures, etc." Cole also noted that the Prince would reform the London School of Design into a College of Applied Art.
111. Henry Cole to J. W. Henley, 10 March 1852. London, Victoria and Albert Museum Library, Ms. Box 1, 83.xx, 5.
112. See Cole's diary, 19 November 1851. London, Victoria and Albert Museum Library (note 32).
113. Gottfried to Henry Cole, 29 January 1852, Semper Archiv.
114. See Cole, "Journey to Vienna," 101.A.72. On the theater Cole noted: "After dinner we went to the theatre which belongs to the King. It is very striking and its architecture differs from that of any other theatre I know – so far as relates to the arrangement of the boxes. Each one accommodates two persons in front and each has a sort of canopy above and between the width, a curtain which makes it both public and private. It is said that these semicircular canopies add to the acoustic property of the theatre. It is very plainly coloured inside so that the audience constitute the chief coloured attraction."
115. Henry Cole to Gottfried, 10 February 1852, Semper Archiv.
116. Jones's lectures were published under the title, *On the True and the False in the Decorative Arts*.
117. Herbert Minton to Henry Cole, 23 March 1852, Herrmann Archive, The Getty Center for the History of Art and the Humanities.
118. Gottfried to Henry Cole, 9 April 1952, Herrmann Archive, The Getty Center for the History of Art and the Humanities.
119. In addition to extensive notes on this manuscript, given by Wolfgang Herrmann to The Getty Center for the History of Art and the Humanities, two copies of Semper's metals catalogues are preserved: one at the Victoria and Albert Museum in London, the other at the Österreichisches Museum für Kunst und Industrie in Vienna.
120. W. R. Deverell to Gottfried, 11 September 1952, Herrmann Archive, The Getty Center for the History of Art and the Humanities.
121. Gottfried to Bertha, 13 September 1852, Semper Archiv.
122. Richard Redgrave to Henry Cole, 21 September 1852. London, Victoria and Albert Museum, Box 14, Correspondence.
123. See Gottfried to Henry Cole, 11 October 1852, Semper Archiv. See also Mss. 112 & 113, Semper Archiv.
124. See Herrmann, *In Search of Architecture*, 77.
125. C. R. Cockerell to Gottfried, 11 March 1853, Semper Archiv.
126. See Cole, *First Report of the Department of Practical Art*; *First Report of the Department of Science*

and Art; and *Second Report of the Department of Science and Art.*

127. Ms. 114. Semper Archiv.
128. G. Semper, in Cole, *First Report of the Department of Science and Art*, 211.
129. The Crystal Palace Company to Gottfried, 22 March 1854, Semper Archiv.
130. The Crystal Palace Company to Gottfried, 25 April 1854, Semper Archiv.
131. The Crystal Palace Company to Gottfried, 16 May 1854, Semper Archiv.
132. Henry Cole, 20 May 1853. London, Victoria and Albert Museum, 55.AA.16.
133. See Herrmann, *Gottfried Semper theoretischer Nachlass*, 153–77.
134. Ms. 122, fol. 15, Semper Archiv.
135. Ms. 179, fol. 46, Semper Archiv. "Es ist daher der Styl *das zu künstlerischer Bedeutung erhobene Hervortreten des Grundthema, und aller inneren und äusseren Coefficienten, die bei der Verkörperung desselben in einem Kunstwerke modificirend einwirkten.*"
136. See Streiter, *Karl Böttichers Tektonik der Hellenen.* Streiter argued that Bötticher's views in general had, by 1899, been superseded by the new direction of psychological aesthetics.
137. Herrmann uncovered the date of Semper's first reading of Bötticher 13 December 1852. See also his important essay on these two men, "Semper and the Archeologist Bötticher," in *In Search of Architecture*, 139–52.
138. Bötticher, *Die Tektonik der Hellenen*, xv. "Die Kernform jedes Glieders ist das mechanisch nothwendige, das statisch fungirende Schema...".
139. Ibid., xv and 8.
140. Ms. 142, Semper Archiv. Published in *RES: Journal of Anthropology and Aesthetics* 9, Spring 1985, 61–67,
141. Quoted from Herrmann's essay "Semper and the Archeologist Bötticher" (note 60), 141. Semper's remarks (contained in Ms. 101, fol. 16, Semper Archiv) were apparently deleted from the published text by the editor in order not to embarass either the journal or Semper.
142. See Semper, *Der Stil*, I, 444.
143. Gottfried to Friedrich Krause, 14 January 1854, Semper Archiv.
144. Semper, *Ueber die bleiernen Schleudergeschosse der Alten*, 5. "...bloss Gerüste oder sogenannte 'Strukturschemen,' die mittels äusserer Anheftung von Symbolen aus der animalischen und vegetabilischen Welt verziert sind, wozu Professor Karl Bötticher in Berlin sie machen will..."
145. Ibid. "Denn das geheimnissvolle organische Gesetz, das auch in der Kunst ewig waltet, muss, wo es in Perioden hoher künstlerischer Entwicklung als Prinzip klar aufgefasst werden wird, immer wieder auf Formen und Analogieen führen, die denjenigen sehr nahe stehen, welche schon einmal in so herrlicher Blüthe aus diesem geistigen Keime hervorgingen."
146. Ibid., 60. "...soll nicht behauptet sein, dass die Griechen ihre Formen nach mathematischen Formeln construirten, welches in der Kunst anzunehmen absurd wäre, sondern dass sie das Gesetz der Natur, wonach diese bei ihren Formengebungen die extremen Grenzen beobachtet und überall Spannung herrschen lässt, nicht bloss dunkel ahnten, sondern klar erkannten."
147. For an excerpt of Wagner's earlier letter on Semper's behalf to Jakob Sulzer, 22 February 1850, see Erismann, *Richard Wagner in Zürich*, 108–9.
148. Richard Wagner to Gottfried, 4 August 1854, Semper Archiv.
149. Gottfried to Bertha, n.d. (probably March 1855), Semper Archiv.
150. Ibid.

4 *The Zurich Years*

1. The role of Semper in Vischer's re-evaluation of his earlier aesthetics has not been discussed so far by German biographers, but it certainly deserves some scrutiny. For a more general overview of the Semperian backdrop to German aesthetics of the second half of the nineteenth century see my introduction to *Empathy, Form, and Space.*
2. Burckhardt to Gottfried, 20 September 1862, in Jakob Burckhardt, *Briefe*, ed. Max Burckhardt, (Basel, 1961), cited from Albert Knoepfli, "Zu Tische in der Aula des Semperschen Polytechnikumgebäudes, Zu den Zürcher Kreisen der frühen Semperzeit," in *Gottfried Semper und die Mitte des 19. Jahrhunderts*, ed. Vogt, 257.
3. See Keller to Hermann Hettner, 21 February 1856 and 11 November 1857, in Keller, *Leben, Briefe und Tagebücher.*
4. Keller to Marie von Frisch, Christmas Eve, 1879, in Keller, *Leben, Briefe und Tagebücher.* Keller's dream is depicted in his biography, presented in volume one (page 375).
5. Richard Wagner, *My Life*, 651.
6. Ibid.
7. The drawing in the Semper Archiv listed as the baton derives from another publication of 1841–43. Semper's design of 1858 may, however, have been based on this drawing. See

Kötzsche, "Ein Takstock für Richard Wagner?", 289–95.
8. Richard Wagner, *My Life*, 670.
9. Gottfried to mother, 27 December 1855, Semper Archiv.
10. Cole to Gottfried, 4 July 1857, Semper Archiv.
11. Cole to Gottfried, 1 August 1857, Semper Archiv.
12. Gottfried To Wilhelm, 1 November 1857, Semper Archiv.
13. Carolyne Sayn-Wittgenstein to Gottfried, 17 January 1857, Semper Archiv. Three letters between Sayn-Wittgenstein and Semper were published in Sayn-Wittgenstein, *Aus der Glanzzeit der Weimarer Altenburg*, although – as Wolfgang Herrmann has pointed out – with many important passages written by Semper deleted.
14. Gottfried to Sayn-Wittgenstein, 8 December 1857, Semper Archiv. "Meine Verhältnisse gestalten sich hier sehr unangenehm. Ich komme immer mehr zu der Uberzeugung – kein Republikaner zu seyn. Aber vielmehr: das Grundprinzip meiner Republik ist ein anderes als das der Schweiz oder irgend welcher anderen bestehenden. *Mein* Gemeinwesen ist eine Gemeinde des Vertrauens die demjenigen der seiner Lache gewachsen ist Vollmacht des Wirkens ertheilt ihr dann in dem was er am besten verstehen muss frei halten lässt und ihm die ganze Verantwortung seines Amtes übergiebt; – hier ist die Republik der Vielregiererei die dem Wichte eine erwünschte Gewissheit verschafft, dass er seiner Nullität zum Trotze doch eben so viel gelte und eben so viel wirke als ein andrer."
15. Gottfried to Professor Ludwig Eckhardt, quoted from "Gottfried Semper, Semper als Politiker," signed x. y. z., in *Neues Wiener Tagblatt*, 19 August 1879, 228, 1. "Republiken haben kein Geld für die Kunst...der schlimmste despotischeste Fürst und der fanatischeste Papst thut mehr für die Kunst und Künstler als ein Freistaat."
16. Gottfried to Sayn-Wittgenstein, 8 December 1857, Semper Archiv. "Man muthet mir zu mich als Michconcurrent zu stellen obschon man offen bekennt das Ganze sey nur pro forma und der Bau schon vergeben. Meine Erfahrungen sind nicht der Art mich zu verlocken auf diese Leimruthe zu gehen."
17. Among Semper's papers in his archives in Zurich is his letter of commission for the design of the Polytechnikum, at the bottom of which is his handwritten "Notiz für die Nachwelt" (Notice for Posterity), dated January 1867. In it Semper complains that he was not treated as an equal partner by Wolff in the execution of the work and of the great injury he has suffered "in money and influence" as a result of the cost reductions applied to the school during construction.
18. See *Konkurs-Program zur Einreichung von Bauplänen für die eidgenössische polytechnische Schule und die zürcherische Hochschule* (Zurich: Zürcher und Furrer, 1857).
19. See "Dekoration der Aula: Plan der Composition," Semper Archiv. Nearly all of the text was published in Martin Fröhlich, *Schweizerische Kunstführer: Sempers Hauptgebäude der ETH Zürich* (Bern: Gesellschaft für Schweizerische Kunstgeschichte, n.d.). See also Fröhlich's analysis of the building in *Zeichnerischer Nachlass* and *Gottfried Semper.*
20. For an account of the villa in Nagyhörcsök, together with correspondence, see József Sisa, "Gottfried Semper és Magyarország," in *Múvészettörténeti Értesító*, 1985, vol. I, 2, 1–10.
21. Pevsner, *A History of Building Types*, 228. Pevsner terms the lunette window of François Duquesney's Gare de l'Est "the most functional façade motif."
22. Lasius, "Die Sternwarte," 74–75.
23. The Winterthur Town Hall has been the subject of a comprehensive study by Wegmann, *Gottfried Semper und das Winterthurer Stadthaus.* See also Fröhlich's discussion of the work in his *Zeichnerischer Nachlass.*
24. See "Abdruck der Weisung des Stadtrathes [Heller] an die E. Bürgergemeinde Winterthur," 25 April 1865, Semper Archiv. "Im Unterschied von dieser Arbeit hat Herr Professor Dr. Semper in seinen Plänen ein monumentales Kunstwerk im vollsten Sinne des Wortes entworfen, ohne dass die praktischen Bedürfnisse irgendwie beeinträchtigt wären. Durch die Ausführung seines Planes würde die Stadt in den Besitz einer Kunstbaute gelangen, die in Bezug auf Kunstwerth und ungesuchte Schönheit von keinem andern in der Schweiz übertroffen wurde..."
25. Semper, *Der Stil*, II, 364. "Der Quader bekommt den Ausdruck von Rusticität und fortifikorischer Derbheit, wenn die rohe Bruchfläche, wie sie ist, oder die mit dem Spitzeisen splittricht rauh vorgerichtete Bank mit tiefen rechteckig eingesenkten Falzen oder Rändern umgeben wird. Aehnliches erricht man durch das sog. schräge Abfasen der Kanten des Steins, wodurch dreieckige Fugen entstehen. Hier is die Bossage mit dem Falz mehr in Eins verschmolzen."

26. See Wegmann, *Gottfried Semper und das Winterthurer Stadthaus*, 78–81.
27. The collaboration was for the Théâtre de la Monnaie, which burned in a fire on 21 January 1855. The competition for a new building was won by Joseph Poelart, although it is unknown if Semper and Séchan's drawings, which still survive, were officially entered.
28. The competition for a new theater in Rio de Janeiro was announced on 28 November 1857 and the designs were due at the beginning of July, 1858. Little is known of Semper's expectations regarding the project but his brilliantly rendered design drawings show that he invested much effort in the work.
29. Richard Wagner to Gottfried, 13 December 1864, Semper Archiv.
30. Gottfried to Richard Wagner, 16 December 1864, Semper Archiv. "Wenn ich zwei Tage vorübergehen liess, ehe ich zu der Beantwortung deines bereits seit vorgestern in meinen Händen befindlichen Schreibens schritt, so möge mich dafür die Gemüthserregung, in die ich mich durch dasselbe versetzt fühle, entschuldigen. In Wahrheit ist seitdem mein ganzes Sinnen und Sein durch dessen Inhalt erfüllt und ganz und gar in Anspruch genommen."
31. By far the best account with regard to Semper is Manfred Semper's early account, *Das Münchener Festspielhaus*, which relates the story mainly through his father's correspondence with Wagner. A more recent study – from a Wagnerian perspective – is that presented by Habel, *Festspielhaus und Wahnfried*. There is also Habler's essay, "Sempers städtebauliche Planungen im Zusammenhang mit dem Richard-Wagner-Festspielhaus in München," in *Gottfried Semper und die Mitte des 19. Jahrhunderts*, ed. Vogt, 129–52. Sophie Gobran has recently chronicled important aspects of the story, in "The Munich Festival Theater Letters," *Perspecta 26: The Yale Architecture Journal* (New York: Rizzoli, 1990). See also Eckhardt's excellent essay, "Gottfried Semper's Planungen für ein Richard Wagner-Festtheater". Another surprisingly good account of the matter in English is contained in Newman's classic biography, *The Life of Richard Wagner*, III, 409–37. Another short account that has recently appeared is contained in Spotts's *Bayreuth*.
32. In a letter of 15 February 1865 (Semper Archiv), Wagner insisted that Semper had been personally authorized and should accept the oral commission as firm.
33. See Friedrich Pecht to Gottfried, 26 February 1846, 9 March 1865, and 17 March 1865, Semper Archiv. Pecht's observations proved to be very sound.
34. Pfistermeister to Gottfried, 8 April 1865 and 27 April 1865, Semper Archiv.
35. See Semper's letter to Richard Wagner, 10 May 1865, in Manfred Semper, *Das Münchener Festspielhaus*, 27–32.
36. See Leinfelder to Gottfried, 24 July 1865, and Pfistermeister to Gottfried, 28 August 1865, Semper Archiv.
37. Richard Wagner, *Diary*, 9 September 1865, 71.
38. King Ludwig to Gottfried, 6 November 1865, Semper Archiv.
39. Pfistermeister to Gottfried, 16 December 1865, Semper Archiv.
40. Gottfried to Neureuther, 8 March 1866, in Manfred Semper, *Das Münchener Festspielhaus*, 51.
41. Gottfried to Frau Wesendonck, 28 May 1866, in Manfred Semper, *Das Münchener Festspielhaus*, 56.
42. Wagner to Ludwig, 2 January 1867, cited in Habel's *Festspielhaus und Wahnfried*, 61–62.
43. Wagner to Ludwig, 11 January 1867, cited in Habel's *Festspielhaus und Wahnfried*, 63.
44. This aspect is one of the most confusing of the whole affair. On 30 January 1867, Wagner, now through Cosima, passed on a copy of a letter sent to him by August Röckel (who had recently been released from prison for his part in the Dresden uprising), which reported the negative gossip in Munich surrounding the theater and the new street. Semper responded harshly that Röckel should have nothing to do with the matter and he explained to Wagner the benefits of the new street. Wagner soon responded with his undated letter of recrimination, almost certainly prepared sometime in February.
45. Düfflipp to Gottfried, 4 September 1867, Semper Archiv.
46. Semper's invoice in his legal dispute was for 37,305 florins, of which he received 30,543 florins.
47. Gottfried Semper, "Aus dem Erläuterungsberichte zu den Hauptplänen für das monumentale Festspielhaus," in Manfred Semper, *Das Münchener Festspielhaus*, 109. "Die Dekoration dieses vorderen Bühnenprosceniums ist in den Motiven, Ordonnanzen und Verhältnissen derjenigen des hinteren Bühnenprosceniums vollkommen gleich, aber in den wirklichen Grössenverhältnessen davon verschieden, woraus eine perspectivische Täuschung entsteht, weil das Auge die thatsächlichen Grössenverschiedenheiten nicht von den perspektivischen

zu unterscheiden vermag. Eine Illusion, die nach Befinden und nach Umständen durch alle erdenklichen Beleuchtungskünste noch gehoben und modifiziert werden kann."

48. See Habel, *Festspielhaus und Wahnfried*, 59.
49. See Manfred Semper, *Das Münchener Festspielhaus*, 91. "Diesen Brief, aus dem ich nicht klug werden konnte, liess ich unbeantwortet."
50. See *Cosima Wagner's Diaries*, 6 May 1875.
51. Wagner to Gottfried, 13 June 1877. Cited from Habel's *Festspielhaus und Wahnfried*, 91.
52. See Newman's account, for instance, in *The Life of Richard Wagner*, IV, 440.
53. Gottfried to Vieweg, 25 July 1855, Semper Archiv. "Mein Sehnen nach derjenigen äusseren Ruhe und Musse, die es mir allein möglich machen wird, den lang gehegten Plan der Herausgabe meiner vergleichenden Baukunde zur Ausführung zu bringen, war ein Hauptmotiv zu der Annahme einer Professor und des Directoriums der Bauabtheilung an dem hiesigen eigenössischen Polytechnicum."
54. Herrmann has presented us with a comprehensive history of the details of the relationship of Semper and Vieweg, in his chapter "The Genesis of *Der Stil*, 1840–77," in *In Search of Architecture*, 88–117. See also his essay, "Semper and Eduard Vieweg," in *Gottfried Semper und die Mitte des 19. Jahrhunderts*, ed. Vogt, 199–237.
55. Gottfried to Vieweg, 13 October 1856, Semper Archiv.
56. Gottfried to Suchsland, n.d., draft, Semper Archiv.
57. In Semper's letter to Suchsland of 8 December 1856, he noted that he had sent Vieweg four letters without a response, the first of which was dated 27 October 1856. In the Semper Archiv there is also a draft of a letter to Vieweg's son, probably written around this time.
58. Gottfried to Suchsland, 27 October 1855, Semper Archiv.
59. See Gottfried to Suchsland, 29 October 1855, Semper Archiv, and Semper, "Ueber die formelle Gesetzmässigkeit des Schmuckes und dessen Bedeutung als Kunstsymbolik." Also published in the *Monatsschrift des wissenschaftliche Vereins*, vol. I.
60. Keller to Hermann Hettner, 21 February 1856, in Keller, *Leben, Briefe und Tagebücher*, II, 398.
61. Ibid.
62. G. Semper, "Ueber die formelle Gesetzmässigkeit des Schmuckes und dessen Bedeutung als Kunstsymbol," 6. "Wo der Mensch schmückt, hebt er nur mit mehr oder weniger bewußtem Tun eine Naturgesetzlichkeit an dem Gegenstand, den er ziert, deutlicher hervor." A recent discussion of the Greek word *Kosmos* and its architectural implications (in the B1 fragment of Anaximander) can be read in Indra Kagis McEwen's *Socrates' Ancestor: An Essay on Architectural Beginnings* (Cambridge, MA: MIT Press, 1993), 41–47.
63. Ibid., 5. "Die Ästhetik der Hellenen, soweit sie das Gesetzliche des formell-Schönen betrifft, fusst auf den einfachen Grundsätzen, die beim Schmücken des Körpers in ursprünglichster Klarheit und Fasslichkeit hervortreten."
64. Ibid., 7. "Die Maske war schon lange in den bildenden Künsten ein bedeutsames Symbol, bevor die dramatische Kunst sich desselben bemächtigte."
65. Ibid., 9. "...so dass es nicht zu paradox wäre, den Ursprung gewisser überlieferter Flächenornamente in der Tätowierungskunst zu suchen."
66. For Zeising's influence on Semper, in particular on his terminology, see Laudel's remarks in his *Architektur und Stil*, 168–73.
67. Zeising, *Aesthetische Forschungen*, section 156. "Da es die Aesthetik nur mit der Anschauung der Dinge, nicht mit den Dingen als solchen zu thun hat, so hat sie sich nur auf die planimetrischen Figuren einzulassen und auf diese wird daher auch im Folgenden hauptsächlich Rücksicht genommen werden."
68. G. Semper, *Über die formelle Gesetzmäßigkeit des Schmuckes* (note 59), 41. "...als das zu künstlerischer Bedeutung erhobene Hervortreten des Grundthemas und aller inneren und äußeren Koeffizienten, die bei der Verkörperung desselben in einem Kunstwerke modifizierend einwirkten."
69. See Gottfried to Suchsland, 29 October 1856, Semper Archiv.
70. See Hegel, *Philosophy of Fine Art*, I, 399–400.
71. See Herrmann, *In Search of Architecture*, 122.
72. See Herrmann, *Theoretischer Nachlass*, 118–25.
73. I am not convinced that all of these manuscripts fall under the heading "Attributes of Formal Beauty," as several of them cannot easily be divorced from other efforts during this time. The two earliest outlines (Mss. 168, 169), for instance, might have been earlier drafts of Semper's work on artistic forms, as they develop familiar themes from his London period and conclude with his new scheme of formal beauty. The proposed critique of Zeising – and even of Kant, Schelling, and Hegel – suggest that this draft arose late in 1855 or early 1856, when Semper was preoccupied with similar ideas in preparing his inaugural lecture. Moreover, I think Semper would have read Zeising (whose

relevant work appeared in 1855) after he arrived in Zurich. Zeising's ideas were to some extent built upon those of Friedrich Theodor Vischer and the latter would have been more than willing to raise the various issues. Other manuscripts of this series (Mss. 170, 171, 174, 178–80) are so close to the published version of his Prolegomena to *Der Stil* that they can rather be seen as preliminary drafts to this work.

74. G. Semper, *Der Stil*, I, vi; Eng. trans., 182. "...die bei dem Prozess des Werdens und Entstehens von Kunsterscheinungen hervortretende Gesetzlichkeit und Ordnung im Einzelnen aufzusuchen, aus dem Gefundenen allgemeine Prinzipien, die Grundzüge einer empirischen Kunstlehre, abzuleiten."
75. Ibid., vii; Eng. trans., 183. "Sie sucht die Bestandtheile der Form die nicht selbst Form sind, sondern Idee, Kraft, Stoff und Mittel; gleichsam die Vorbestandtheile und Grundbedingungen der Form."
76. Rumohr, *Italienische Forschungen*, I, 1–133.
77. G. Semper, *Der Stil*, I, xv; Eng. trans., 190. "...da doch vielmehr der Stoff der Idee dienstbar, und keineswegs für das sinnliche Hervortreten der letztern in der Erscheinungswelt alleinig massgebend ist."
78. Ibid. "Die historische Schule...ist bestrebt gewisse Vorbilder der Kunst längst vergangener Zeiten oder fremder Völker mit möglichst kritischer Stiltreue nachzubilden...wie Anforderungen der Gegenwart nach ihnen zu modeln anstatt, wie es natürlicher scheint, die Lösung der Aufgabe aus ihren Prämissen, wie sie die Gegenwart gibt, frei heraus zu entwickeln..."
79. Ms. 178, fol. 25, Semper Archiv. In Herrmann, *Theoretischer Nachlass*, 247.
80. G. Semper, *Der Stil*, I, xviii; Eng. trans., 193.
81. Ibid., xviii–xix; Eng. trans., 193. "Ihm ist der Kunstgenuss Verstandesübung, philosophisches Ergötzen, bestehend in dem Zurücktragen des Schönen aus der Erscheinungswelt in die Idee, in dem Zergliedern desselben und dem Herauspräpariren des Begriffskerns aus ihm."
82. Ibid., xx; Eng. trans., 195. "Unter ihnen sind in der That älteste Ueberlieferungen der Baukunst, welche durchaus der Logik des Bauens, allgemein der des Kunstschaffens, entsprechen, und die ihren symbolischen Werth haben, der älter als die Geschichte und durch Neues gar nicht ausdrückbar ist."
83. Ibid. "...die Kunst auf ihrer höchsten Erhebung hasst die Exegese, sie vermeidet daher aus Ueberlegung das Hervortreten derartigen Wollens..."
84. Ibid., xxii; Eng. trans., 196. "Diesen Anfängen sind die Musik und die *Baukunst* entwachsen, die beiden höchsten rein kosmischen (nicht imitativen) Künste, deren legislatorischen Rückhalt keine andre Kunst entbehren kann."
85. Ibid., "Das Einzelne ist geschaffen nur um dem Ganzen als Nahrung zu dienen."
86. Ibid.
87. See especially Ms. 179. In Herrmann, *Theoretischer Nachlass*, 217–21. Eng. trans., 219–23.
88. G. Semper, *Der Stil*, I, xxxviii; Eng. trans., 209. "...*nämlich* das Hervortreten gewisser formaler Bestandtheile einer Erscheinung aus der Reihe der übigen, wodurch sie innerhalb ihres Bereiches gleichsam zu Chorführern und sichtbaren Repräsentanten eines einigenden Prinzip werden."
89. See Herrmann, *In Search of Architecture*, 115–16.
90. Baljon, *The Structure of Architectural Theory*, 104.
91. Ms. 205, 6, Semper Archiv; "Prospectus, Style in the Technical and Tectonic Arts or Practical Aesthetics," in *Gottfried Semper: The Four Elements*, 179.
92. Georges Cuvier and Alexandre Brongniart, *Essai sur la Géographie minéralogique des environs de Paris* (Paris, 1811). For Cuvier's *Dictionnaire des sciences naturelles*, Brongniart wrote all the articles on geology and mineralogy.
93. Gottfried Semper, *Der Stil*, II, 119n.1.
94. See Ziegler's remarks in *Etudes céramiques*, 42.
95. Ibid., 15–16. "Reconnaissons qu'ils sont mis en évidence par un potier cent fois dans un jour...par conséquent l'on peut trouver les rudiments, les bases d'une architecture nationale et nouvelle."
96. The only historian, to my knowledge, to have discussed Semper's use of Ziegler is Forty, in "Of Cars, Clothes and Carpets." This effort by Ziegler to understand the beauty of ceramic forms in terms of their profiles was not the first, as it was attempted in the eighteenth century by William Hamilton, J. J. Winckelmann, and others. See Oechslin, "Die Vase als ästhetisches Ideal."
97. G. Semper, *Der Stil*, II, 81n.
98. Ibid., II, 118. "Nicht nur sind die allgemeinen Grundsätze formaler Gliederung, und die Gegensätze zwischen den Theilen, die diese Gliederung ausmachen, in der Baukunst ganz die gleichen mit den so eben entwickelten, auch einen grossen Theil der herkömmlichen Zeichen und Termen ihrer formalen Kunstsprache hat die genannte Kunst offenbar von der ursprünglicheren Gefässkunst entlehnt."
99. G. Semper, Ms. 122, fol. 10–11, Semper Archiv. This English lecture was published in

RES: Journal of Aesthetics and Anthropology, 6, Autumn 1983, 8–22.

100. See Wölfflin's remarks on Semper's comparison in *Renaissance and Baroque*, 167n.5. Wölfflin's connection with this aspect of Semper's theory is more complex than first appears, see my introduction to Wölfflin's earlier dissertation, "Prolegomena zur ein Psychologie der Form" (1886), in *Empathy, Form, and Space*, 39–52. It was, of course, not just Wölfflin's generation that was fascinated by these formal and cultural suggestions. Such a historical perspective carried down well into the twentieth century, see for instance, Irving K. Pond, *The Meaning of Architecture* (Boston: Marshall Jones, 1918). As late as 1957 Zevi felt it was important to refute this approach. See *Architecture as Space*, 172, 185.
101. G. Semper, *Der Stil*, II, 6. "Noch mehr! – die Grundzüge der gesammten ägyptischen Architektur scheinen in dem Mileimer gleich wie im Embryo enthalten zu sein, und nicht minder auffallend ist die Verwandtschaft der Form der Hydria mit gewissen Typen des dorischen Baustils!"
102. For details of the Moleschott-Liebig conflict, see Wittich's introduction to *Vogt, Moleschott, Büchen*, XXIVff.
103. G. Semper, *Der Stil*, II, 210. Semper's opposition to Bötticher's contention that Greek stone architecture and its development was solely the product of the Greek mind was longstanding.
104. Ibid., II, 210n1. Viollet-le-Duc's explanation is in the first of his *Lectures on Architecture*, 4–46.
105. G. Semper, Ms. 7, fol. 9f. Semper Archiv. See Herrmann, *In Search of Architecture*, 176. See also Semper's published article, "Der Wintergarten zu Paris," in *Zeitschrift zur praktische Aesthetik* (Leipzig, 1849), 515–26.
106. See Herrmann, *In Search of Architecture*, 179.
107. G. Semper, *Der Stil*, II, 263–64. "Von einem eigenen monumentalen Stab-und Gussmetallstil kann nicht die Rede sein; das Ideal desselben ist unsichtbare Architektur! Denn je dünner das Metallgespinnst, desto vollkommener in seiner Art."
108. Ibid., II, 265. For Herrmann's remarks, see *In Search of Architecture*, 17–79.
109. Sigfried Giedion in his text of 1928, *Bauen im Frankreich, Bauen in Eisen, Bauen in Eisenbeton*, attempted to cast the development of modern architecture solely through the French development of iron. For an excellent summary of the German theoretical debate concerning iron, see Sokratis Georgiadis's introduction to Giedion's *Building in France, Building in Iron, Building in Reinforced Concrete* (Santa Monica: Getty Center for the History of Art and the Humanities, 1995).
110. G. Semper, *Der Stil*, II, 394. "Wir halten die Römer keineswegs für die Erfinder dieser grossartigen Raumeskunst, die etwa zu der Architektur der Griechen sich verhalten würde wie symphonisches Instrumentalkonzert zum lyabegleiten Hymnus, wäre sie in gleichem Grade wie diese in sich vollendet."
111. G. Semper, *Ueber Baustyle*, 28. "Hierin liegt ihre Zukunft und die Zukunft der Baukunst überhaupt."
112. The idea of architecture as a spatial art is certainly suggested in Bötticher's address of 1846, "Das Prinzip der hellenischen und germanischen Bauweise," 111–25. Eng. trans. by Herrmann, in *In What Style Should We Build?*, 147–67.
113. See Conrad Fiedler, "Bemerkungen über Wesen und Geschichte der Baukunst," *Deutsche Rundschau* 15 (1878): 361–83. Eng. trans. in *Empathy, Form, and Space*, ed. Mallgrave and Ikonomou, 125–46.
114. Lucae, "Über die æsthetische Ausbildung der Eisen-Konstruktionen," 9–12. See Auer, "Die Entwickelung des Raumes," 65–74.
115. Schmarsow, *Das Wesen der architektonischen Schöpfung*. Eng. trans. in *Empathy, Form, and Space*, ed. Mallgrave and Ikonomou, 281–96.
116. Gottfried to Lothar Bucher, 28 August 1855, Semper Archiv.
117. J. C. Robinson to Gottfried, 23 September 1855, Semper Archiv.
118. For Hudson's study, see "A list of Additions to the Museum of Art during the year 1853," appendix G, in Cole, *First Report of Department of Science and Art*.
119. G. Semper, *Der Stil*, I, 32.
120. Ibid., I, 227. "... *dass die Anfänge des Bauens mit den Anfängen der Textrin zusammenfallen*."
121. Ibid., I, 214. "... das Gewand als ein Schmuck der alle drei Schönheitsmomente, nämlich Proportion, Symmetrie und Richtung..."
122. Ibid., I, 385.
123. For an excellent discussion of Semper's concept of structural symbolism, see Olin, *Forms of Representation*, 39–66.
124. G. Semper, *Der Stil*, I, 444. "Es handelte sich nur, die mechanischen Bedürfnissformen der asiatischen Bekleidungskonstruktion in dynamische, ja in organische Formen zu verwandeln, sie zu beseelen, und alles was keinen morphologischen Zweck hat, wohl sogar der

rein formalen Idee fremd und ihr entgegen ist, auszustossen, oder auf neutralen Boden zu verweisen."

125. Ibid., I, 445. "Bei dieser Tendenz musste das hellenische Bauprinzip vornehmlich die *Farbe* als die subtilste körperloseste Bekleidung, für sich vindiciren und pflegen. Sie ist das vollkommenste Mittel die Realität zu beseitigen, denn sie ist selbst, indem sie den Stoff bekleidet, unstofflich; auch entspricht sie in sonstigen Beziehungen den freieren Tendenzen der hellenischen Kunst. Die Polychromie ersetzt die barbarische Bekleidung mit edlen Metallen, die Inkrustationen, die eingelegten Edelsteine, die Getäfel und sonstigen Parerga, womit das asiatische Werk so verschwenderisch ausgestattet ist."

126. Ibid., I, 220. Eng. trans. in *The Four Elements of Architecture*, 248. "...ihre Mission bestand in anderem, darin nämlich, diese, fertig wie sie dem Stofflichen nach bereits fixirt waren, ihren nächsten gleichsam tellurischen Ausdruck und Gedanken in *höherem Sinne* aufzufassen, in einer Symbolik der Form, in welcher Gegensätze und Prinzipe, die in Barbarenthum einander ausschliessen und bekämpfen, in freistem Zusammenwirken und zu schönster reichster Harmonie sich verbinden."

127. Ibid., I, 229–30; Eng. trans. in *The Four Elements of Architecture*, 255–56. "Der Festapparatus, das improvisirte Gerüst, mit allem Gepränge und Beiwerke welches den Anlass der Feier näher bezeichnet und die Verherrlichung des Festes erhöht geschmückt und ausgestattet, mit Teppichen verhangen, mit Reisern und Blumen bekleidet, mit Festons und Kränzen, flatternden Bändern und Tropäen geziert, diess ist das *Motiv* des *bleibenden* Denkmals, das den feierlichen Akt und das Ereigniss das in ihm gefestet ward den kommenden Generationen fortverkünden soll."

128. Bötticher, *Der Baumkultus der Hellenen*.

129. G. Semper, *Der Stil*, I, 231; Eng. trans. in *The Four Elements of Architecture*, 257. "Es war mir bei der Aufführung dieser Beispiele vorzüglich darum zu thun, auf das Prinzip der *äusserlichen Ausschmückung und Bekleidung* des structiven Gerüstes hinzuweisen, das bei improvisirten Festbauten nothwendig wird und die Natur der Sache stets und überall mit sich führt, um daran die Folgerung zu knüpfen dass dasselbe Prinzip der Verhüllung der structiven Theile, verbunden mit der monumentalen Behandlung der Zeltdecken und Teppiche welche zwischen den structiven Theilen des motivgebenden Gerüstes aufgespannt waren, auch ebenso natürlich erscheinen muss wo es sich an frühen Denkmälern der Baukunst kund gibt."

130. Wigley's dicussion of Semper's "dressing" thesis is invaluable in other respects, see "Untitled: The Housing of Gender," 368. He argued that Semper's theory was really an attempt to displace the institutional location of architecture, that is, the academic tradition emanating from Winckelmann.

131. G. Semper, *Der Stil*, I, 231n.2; Eng. trans. in *The Four Elements of Architecture*, 257n. "Ich meine das *Bekleiden* und *Maskiren* sei so alt wie die menschliche Civilisation und die Freude an beidem sei mit der Freude an demjenigen Thun, was die Menschen zu Bildern, Malern, Architekten, Dichtern, Musikern, Dramatikern, kurz zu Künstlern machte identisch. Jedes Kunstschaffen einerseits, jeder Kunstgenuss anderseits, setzt eine gewisse Faschingslaune voraus, um mich modern auszudrücken, – der Karnevalkerzendunst ist die wahre Atmosphäre der Kunst. Vernichtung der Realität, des Stofflichen, ist nothwendig, wo die Form als bedeutungsvolles symbol als selbstständige Schöpfung des Menschen hervortreten soll."

132. For a slightly different interpretation of this phrase, and the whole of this passage, see Baljon's published dissertation, *The Structure of Architectural Theory*, 134–38. It is certainly possible that Semper's reference in this passage to the "denial of reality" (*Vernichtung der Realität*) may very well have been to Schiller's twenty-second letter in *On the Aesthetic Education of Man*. The passage of Schiller reads: "In a truly beautiful work of art the content should do nothing, the form everything; for the wholeness of Man is affected by the form alone, and only individual powers by the content. However sublime and comprehensive it may be, the content always has a restrictive action upon the spirit, and only from the form is true aesthetic freedom to be expected. Therefore, the real artistic secret of the master consists in his *annihilating the material by means of the form* [*daß er den Stoff durch die Form vertilgt*] and the more imposing, arrogant and alluring the material is in itself, the more autocratically it obtrudes itself in its operation, and the more inclined the beholder is to engage immediately with the material, the more triumphant is the art which forces back material and asserts its mastery over form."

I am, however, less convinced of Baljon's contention that Semper's theory can be read almost exclusively in terms of Schiller's "play" theory. Such a reading really removes Semper's theory from its legitimate architectural context and ignores the thrust of the entire excursus on the dressing, in which Semper repeatedly and almost exclusively refers to the architectural material in its physical sense.

133. G. Semper, *Der Stil*, I, 231–2n.2.; Eng. trans. in *The Four Elements of Architecture*, 257n. "Vergessen machen sollen wir die Mittel, die zu dem erstrebten Kunsteindruck gebraucht werden müssen und nicht mit ihnen herausplatzen und elendiglich aus der Rolle fallen. Dahin leitet das unverdorbene Gefühl bei allen früheren Kunstversuchen die Naturmenschen, dahin kehrten die grossen wahren Meister der Kunst in allen Fächern derselben zurück, nur dass diese in den Zeiten hoher Kunstentwicklung auch von der *Maske das Stoffliche maskirten.* Diess fürhte Phidias zu jener Auffassung der beiden Tympanonsüjets an dem Parthenon; offenbar war ihm die Aufgabe, d.h. der dargestellte doppelte Mythos, waren ihm die darin handelnd auftretenden Gottheiten zu *behandelnder Stoff* (wie der Stein, worin er sie bildete), den er möglichst verhüllte, d.h. von aller materiellen und äusserlich demonstrativen Kundgebung seines ausserbildlichen religiös-symbolischen Wesens befreite. Daher treten seiner Götter uns entgegen, begeistern sie uns, einzeln und im Zusammenwirken, zunächst und vor allen Dingen als Ausdrücke des rein menschlich Schönen und Grossen. 'Was war ihm Hekuba?' "

134. Richard Wagner, *My Life*, 670.

135. G. Semper, *Der Stil*, I, 232n; Eng. trans. in *The Four Elements of Architecture*, 257n. "Aus demselben Grunde konnte auch das Drama nur im Beginnen und auf dem höchsten Gipfel der steigenden Bildung eines Volks Bedeutung haben. Die ältesten Vasenbilder geben uns Begriffe von den frühen materiellen Maskenspielen der Hellenen – in vergeistigter Weise, gleich jenen steineren Dramen des Phidias, wird durch Aeschylos, Sophokles, Euripides, gleichzeitig durch Aristophanes und die übrigen Komiker das uralte Maskenspiel wieder aufgenommen, wird das Proskenion zum Rahmen des Bildes eines grossartigen Stückes Menschengeschichte, die nicht irgendwo einmal passirt ist, sondern die überall sich ereignet, so lange Menschenherzen schlagen. 'Was war ihnen Hekuba?' Maskenlaune athmet in Shakespears Dramen; Maskenlaune und Kerzenduft, Karnevalsstimmung, (die währlich nicht immer lustig ist,) tritt uns in Mozarts Don Juan entgegen; den auch die Musik bedarf dieses Wirklichkeit vernichtenden Mittels, auch dem Musiker ist Hekuba nichts, – oder sollte sie es sein."

136. The phrase "What's Hecuba to him?" is from the second scene, act 2, of *Hamlet*, in which Hamlet, after watching a performance of the fall of Troy and the fate of the Queen Hecuba, questions the reason for the actor's emotion.

137. G. Semper, *Der Stil*, I, 232n; Eng. trans. in *The Four Elements of Architecture*, 258n. "Wie auch die griechische Baukunst das Gesagte rechtfertige, wie in ihr das Prinzip vorwalte das ich anzudeuten versuchte, wonach das Kunstwerk in der Anschauung die Mittel und den Stoff vergessen macht womit und wodurch es erscheint und wirkt, und sich selbst als Form genügt, dieses nachzuweisen ist die schwierigste Aufgabe der Stillehre."

138. Ibid., Eng. trans. in *The Four Elements of Architecture*, 258n. "Nur vollkommen technische Vollendung, wohl verstandene richtige Behandlung des Stoffs nach seinen Eigenschaften, vor allem aber Berücksichtigung dieser letzteren bei der Formengebung selbst, können den Stoff vergessen machen, können das Kunstgebilde von ihm ganz befreien, können sogar ein einfaches Naturgemälde zum hohen Kunstwerk erheben."

139. See Herrmann, *In Search of Architecture*, 100.

140. Ms. 205, Semper Archiv. For Eng. trans., see *The Four Elements of Architecture*, 174–80.

141. Ibid., 7; Eng. trans., 179. "So eröffnet sich ein weites Gebiet der Erfindung, indem wir unsere socialen Bedürfnisse als Momente des Stils *unserer* Baukunst in analoger Weise, wie es die Geschichte zeigt, künstlerisch zu verwerthen trachten. Wogegen schwerlich je durch neue Stoffe und neue Methoden ihrer konstruktiven Verwerthung, noch weniger durch die blosse Kraft des Genius, der seinen angeblichen Stil aus der Luft greift, ein nachhaltiger neuer Umschwung in der Baukunst herbeigeführt werden wird."

142. G. Semper, "Science, Industry, and Art," in *The Four Elements of Architecture*, 139.

143. Ms. 205, Semper Archiv, 8; Eng. trans. in *The Four Elements of Architecture*, 180. "Hat sie ihre Aufgabe gelöst, fängt schon wieder eine neue Aera für uns an oder sind wir erst in den Anfängen der Renaissance? Wie erkennen und verwerthen wir die socialen Motive und alles Neue, was unsere Zeit bietet, mit wahrem stilgeschichtlichem Geiste? Welche Aufgaben der Gegenwart sind in dieser Beziehung die wichtigsten? In welchem Sinne wurden sie bis jetzt gelöst?"

144. Ms. 283, Semper Archiv. The manuscript has

been published in Herrmann, *Theoretischer Nachlass*, 250–60.

145. G. Semper, *Ueber Baustyle*; see Eng. trans. in *The Four Elements of Architecture*, 164–84.

146. Ibid., 11; Eng. trans. in *The Four Elements of Architecture*, 269. "Styl ist die Uebereinstimmung einer Kunsterscheinung mit ihrer Entstehungsgeschichte, mit allen Vorbedingungen und Umständen ihres Werdens."

147. Ms. 283, fol. 12. See Herrmann, *Theoretischer Nachlass*, 252. "...diese Harmonie der Form mit der ihr inneliegenden Idee..."

148. Ibid., 11–12. See Herrmann, *Theoretischer Nachlass*, 252. "Aber unter Stoff versteht man, ausser dem Materiale der Kunstform noch etwas Höheres, nämlich die *Aufgabe*, das zu künstlerischen Verwethung, aufgegebene *Problem* oder *Thema. Dieses inhaltliche Moment der Kunstgestaltung ist jedenfalls* das vor allen vorgenannten überwiegend wichtigste, weil es die Form zum absoluten Ausdrucke ihres Inhalts macht."

149. Ms. 282, fol. 2, Semper Archiv.

150. G. Semper, *Ueber Baustyle*, 10; Eng. trans. in *The Four Elements of Architecture*, 268. "Man bezeichnet sehr richtig die alten Monumente als die fossilen Gehäuse ausgestorbener Gesellschaftsorganismen, aber diese sind letzteren, wie sie lebten, nicht wie Schneckenhäuser auf den Rücken gewachsen, noch sind sie nach einem blinden Naturprozesse wie Korallenriffe aufgeschossen, sondern freie Gebilde des Menschen, der dazu Verstand, Naturbeobachtung, Genie, Willen, Wissen und Macht in Bewegung setzte."

151. The characterization of Semper as a Darwinian, which has been almost a fixture of twentieth-century historiography, seems to derive from Leonello Venturi's somewhat crude characterization of Semper as "the adversary of all idealism who tends to natural science of the Darwinian type." See his *History of Art Criticism*, 226, and the epilogue below.

152. G. Semper, *Ueber Baustyle*, 28; Eng. trans. in *The Four Elements of Architecture*, 281. "Er repräsentirt die Synthesis der beiden scheinbar einander ausschliessenden Kulturmomente, nämlich des individuellen Strebens und des Aufgehens in die gesammtheit."

153. See Herrmann, *In Search of Architecture*, 114–15.

154. See Bruckmann to Gottfried, 7 November 1861, Semper Archiv.

155. Gottfried to Bruckmann, 10 April 1873; trans. by Herrmann in *In Search of Architecture*, 113–14.

156. G. Semper, *Ueber Baustyle*, 31; Eng. trans. in *The Four Elements of Architecture*, 284. "Man ist gegen uns Architekten mit dem Vorwurfe der Armuth an Erfindung zu hart, da sich nirgend eine neue welthistorische, mit Kraft und Bewusstsein verfolgte Idee kundgibt. Wir sind überzeugt, dass sich schon dieser oder jener unter unseren jüngeren Collegen befähigt zeigen würde, einer solchen Idee, wo sie sich wirklich Bahn bräche, das geeignete architektonische Kleid zu verleihen. Bis es dahin kommt, muss man sich, so gut es gehen will, in das Alte hineinschicken."

5 *The Monumental Builder*

1. Gurlitt, *Das neue königliche Hoftheater*, 9.
2. Wilhelm Lübke to Gottfried, 31 January 1867, Semper Archiv.
3. J. Leliman to Gottfried, 29 June 1863, Semper Archiv.
4. Koeniglich Bayerische Akademie der Wissenschaften to Gottfried, 25 July 1866, Semper Archiv.
5. Charles Nelson to Gottfried, 25 May 1863, Semper Archiv. Nelson noted that previous medal winners were Hittorff, Stüler, and Jean-Baptiste-Ciceron Lesueur.
6. Rudolf von Eitelberger to Gottfried, 25 November 1867 and 20 December 1867, Semper Archiv.
7. For Semper's influence in both the industrial museums of Vienna and Hamburg, see Richards, *Industrial Art and the Museum*.
8. Semper's connections with Vienna were long-standing and Viennese architects seem from an early date to have taken an interest in his architecture. See Renate Wagner-Rieger, "Semper und die Wiener Architektur," in *Gottfried Semper und die Mitte des 19. Jahrhunderts*, ed. Vogt, 275–89.
9. For an account of Semper's dealings with the Saxon authorities, see Reiner Gross, "Gottfried Semper in seinen Beziehungen zu Sachsen vom Juni 1849 bis Ende 1870," in Dresden Technische Universität, *Gottfried Semper 1803–1879*, 151–58.
10. Dr. Abendroth to Gottfried, 4 March 1863, Semper Archiv. A follow-up letter by Emil Lehmann with the official invitation was dated 23 May 1863.
11. Gottfried to Manfred, 6 December 1864, Semper Archiv.
12. Victoria & Albert Museum, "Commissioners of the Exhibition of 1851," XXI, 45–50 (notes taken by Wolfgang Herrmann). See Charles Grey to Mr. Fisher (11 January 1866) and to Lord Derby (12 January 1866).

13. Ibid., Henry Cole to Charles Grey, 13 January 1866.
14. Ibid., Mr. Fisher to Charles Grey, 17 January 1866.
15. Ibid., Lord Derby to Prince of Wales (17 January 1866) and Lord Derby to Charles Grey (17 January 1866).
16. See Semper's argument in "Zum florentiner Domfacade," *Kleine Schriften*, 496–507.
17. G. Semper, *Ueber Baustyle*, 31; "On Architectural Styles," in *The Four Elements of Architecture*, 283.
18. Ibid., 31; Eng. trans., 283–84. "Wenn Graf Bismark (sic) sich um das Baudepartement bekümmerte, wir glauben, er würde lieber zu *seinem* Ideal eines Nationalmonumentes sich an der vorhinerwähnten grossartigen Bauunternehmungen des kaiserlichen Fürstendepossedirers Tschin-Tschi-Huan-Ti inspiriren oder dazu den labyrinthischen Bundespalast der ägyptischen Dodekarchie zum Vorbild nehmen, als beim heiligen Petrus desshalb anfragen."
19. Hasenauer to Gottfried, 7 August 1868, Semper Archiv. This and several other letters from Hasenauer to Semper were published by Semper's son Manfred in his extensive, correctional account of their relationship, *Hasenauer und Semper*. For more on their relationship, see also Eggert, "Gottfried Semper, Carl von Hausenauer," 73–223.
20. Aside from Manfred Semper's and Eggert's account of the competition, as mentioned in the previous note, see also Lhotsky's excellent study, *Die Baugeschichte der Museen*.
21. Hasenauer to Gottfried, 23 November 1868, Semper Archiv (for this and parts of other letters published by Manfred Semper, see note 19).
22. Karl Tietz to Gottfried, 22 November 1868, Semper Archiv.
23. Lhotsky cites this meeting in *Die Baugeschichte der Museen*, 70.
24. Hasenauer to Gottfried, 19 December 1868, Semper Archiv.
25. Baron von Türckheim to Gottfried, 15 January 1869, Semper Archiv.
26. An excerpt of this competition report was published by Manfred Semper, in *Hasenauer und Semper*, 6. The full report was published by Edlinger, in *Die k. k. Hof-Museen in Wien*.
27. Gottfried to Manfred, 9 April 1869, Semper Archiv.
28. Hasenauer to Gottfried, 21 July 1869, Semper Archiv.
29. Gottfried to Prince Hohenlohe, 12 August 1869, draft in Semper Archiv.
30. Two different newspaper clippings of this event are found in the Semper Archives in Zurich; both carry the handwritten date of 1904 in the margin. It is apparent from the start of the article that the onlooker was F. Boscovits, who published his memoirs, "Thirty Years Ago," in the journal *Der Nebelspalter*. Manfred Semper, in *Hasenauer und Semper*, wrote that Semper left for Vienna on 21 September, and thus could not have been in Zurich. Yet he provided no documentation. It seems unlikely, however, that this account by Boscovits, so concrete in its details, could have been manufactured in his memoirs.
31. Gurlitt, *Das neue königliche Hoftheater*, 7.
32. The account that follows derives in large part from the reports contemporaneously published in the *Deutsche Bauzeitung*, and in the three studies that have since been devoted to these events: Mütterlein's *Gottfried Semper und dessen Monumentalbauten*; Hänsch's *Die Semperoper*; Magirius's *Gottfried Sempers zweites Dresdner Hoftheater*.
33. *Deutsche Bauzeitung* 52, 23 December 1869, 646. "Das Manöver, mich bei einer Ausschreibung in erster Linie in Betracht ziehen zu wollen, ist sehr pfiffig erfunden, um die öffentliche Meinung zu beschwichtigen und meiner sich mit bester Manier zu entledigen; denn man weiss sehr wohl, das ich mich auf keine Konkurrenz einlassen kann."
34. Ibid.
35. *Deutsche Bauzeitung* 53, 30 December 1869, 656.
36. Magirius, *Gottfried Sempers zweites Dresdner Hoftheater*, 11.
37. Parts of Pecht's article on Semper are reprinted by Manfred Semper and published in *Hasenauer und Semper*, 26.
38. Gottfried to Prince Hohenlohe, 19 January 1870 (draft), Semper Archiv.
39. Hasenauer to Gottfried, 22 July 1970, Semper Archiv.
40. Prince Hohenlohe to Gottfried, 20 July 1870, Semper Archiv.
41. Prince Hohenlohe to Gottfried, 13 May 1871, Semper Archiv.
42. Gottfried to Manfred, 19 May 1871, Semper Archiv.
43. Gottfried to Prince Hohenlohe, 20 May 1871, (draft), Semper Archiv.
44. Gottfried to Manfred, 5 June 1871, Semper Archiv. "Grosse Sorgen machen mir auch die Verhältnisse zu Hasenauer, dem zwar der Fürst und auch die Anderen (wie mir scheint) nicht sonderliches Ansehen schenken, der aber, wie ich fürchte, dieses nicht einsieht, sondern mich

mehr nur als ein Symbol, als eine beengende und seinen Gewinn schmälernde Konzession an die öffentliche Meinung betrachtet und danach möglicherweise handeln wird."

45. Eggert, "Gottfried Semper, Carl von Hasenauer," vol. 8, 185.
46. Semper, *Die k. k. Hofmuseen in Wien*, ed. by his sons. The three writings consist of Semper's report to Franz Josef of 1869, and his thematic programs for the two museums.
47. G. Semper, "Entwurf eines Programmes für die bildernische Decoration der Facaden des k. k. Museums für Kunst und Alterthum," *Die k. k. Hofmuseen in Wien*, 51. "Wenn eine Kunstform in ihrem Erscheinen mit den Vorbedingungen ihres Entstehens im Einklange steht... dieses mit dem Ausdrucke Stil, welcher also nichts anderes, als die Uebereinstimmung eines Werkes der Kunst mit der Geschichte seines Werdens bezeichnet."
48. G. Semper, "Programm-Entwurf für die bildnerische Auschmückung des neuen k. k. naturhistorischen Museums in Wien," *Die k. k. Hofmuseen in Wien*, 38. The sentence Semper cites from Humboldt's *Kosmos* (II, 138) reads, "Die Behandlungsweise der Geschichte der physischen Weltanschauung kann nur in der Aufzählung dessen bestehen, wodurch der Begriff von der Einheit der Erscheinungen sich allmählig ausgebildet hat."
49. See Eggert, "Gottfried Semper, Carl von Hasenauer," vol. 8, 213–14. Eggert is the only historian thus far to consider Semper's Vienna works in detail.
50. One newspaper, the *Deutsche Zeitung*, even published a rather lengthy biography of his life. The newspaper drawing of Semper's bust on a pedestal is in the Semper Archiv in Zurich, but the paper carries no identification, only the date 17 January 1874; the drawing of Semper within the laurel is in the *Illustrirte Zeitung* of the same date, published in Leipzig.
51. Gottfried to Hasenauer, 19 January 1875, published by Manfred Semper in *Hasenauer und Semper*, 17. "Sollten Sie jedoch wider mein Erwarten meiner Auffassung und Formulirung ihrer Forderungen nicht beipflichten, diese Forderungen anders verstanden, oder auch noch weitergehende Forderungen an mich stellen wollen, so bitte ich Sie, zur Vermeidung weiterer unliebsamer, mündlicher Diskussionen, sich gleichfalls schriftlich zu äussern und Ihr diesbezügliches Verlangen zugleich zu begründen."
52. See Cosima Wagner, *Diaries*, 6 May 1875.
53. B. R. Schembera, "Austellungen und Austellungen," *Neues Wiener Tagblatt*, 11 August 1880, front page.
54. Em. Ranzoni, "Professor Baron Hasenauer," Kunstblatt, *Neue Freie Presse*, Abendblatt, 2 September 1884, 4.
55. Arnold Cattani, Albert Müller, Hans Pestalozzi, "Professor Semper's Antheil an den Wiener Monumental-Bauten," *Deutsche Bauzeitung* 63, 8 August 1885, 379–80.
56. Manfred republished it in *Hasenauer und Semper*, 2. He gives the citation, Vienna, Saturday, 6 January, 1894, 5.
57. Ibid. "Er war somit vier Jahre und zwei Monate nominativ mein Kompagnon, während ich seit 1866, somit 24 Jahre, an diesen Arbeiten unausgesetzt thätig gewesen war."
58. "Das neue Hoftheater zu Dresden," *Deutsche Bauzeitung* 34, 1878, 167.
59. Lipsius, *Gottfried Semper in seiner Bedeutung als Architekt*, 90. "...dass das Dresdener Theater unter allen Bauten Semper's empor ragt durch die Grossartigkeit und Kühnheit, mit welcher der Meister, indem er dem Bedürfniss und der Nützlichkeit nach jeder Richtung hin rücksichtslos Ausdruck und Befriedigung giebt, die innerste Wesenheit des ganzen Baues im Aeussern zum wahrhaftigen Ausdruck bringt und ihm eine Physiognomie von sprechender Klarheit und siegreicher Schönheit verleiht..."
60. Gurlitt, *Das neue königliche Hoftheater*, 8–9.
61. Ibid., 15. "Die Kurven der Exedra sammeln sich in der höchst wirkungsvollen Nische, die mit lauter Sprache verkündet, dass hier ein Haus sei, welches dem gastlichen Einkehren sich willig öffnet."
62. Ibid., 22. "Deutlich erkennt man als Grundidee ein mit Konsequenz und weiser Mässigung durchgeführtes Anwachsen von würdiger Einfachheit bis zu reichen Entfaltung aller dekorativen Mittel, aber auch in den letzen Steigerungen der Pracht liegt noch ein gewisser Ernst der Stimmung, der unserer Auffassung eines Theaters sehr wohl angepasst ist."
63. Ibid., 41. "Nur eine gleich begabte Natur konnte mit Glück sich ihren Gebilden einreihen, nur ein Künstler von der umfassenden Stilkenntnis Sempers die so heterogenen Werke zu glücklichem Zusammenklingen verschmelzen.... Er wusste die Errungenschaften der modernen Kunstphilosophie praktisch zu verwerten..."
64. Friedrich Schiller, Explanatory Preface to *Bride of Messina*.
65. Nietzsche, *The Birth of Tragedy*, 62.
66. The iconography for the Theater has been extensively studied by Magirius, *Gottfried*

Sempers zweites Dresdner Hoftheater. Much of what follows is based upon his identifications.

67. Ibid., 141–44. The two proposals were dated 28 March and 2 April 1874.
68. Ibid., 144.
69. Ibid., 67.
70. Gottfried Semper, *Ueber Baustyle.*
71. Cosima to Nietzsche, 5 August 1869, *Nietzsche Briefwechsel,* II.2, 29. "Besten Dank für die freundliche Zusendung der Semperschen Schrift welche, gleich allem was von dem grossen Künstler stammt, mich in höchsten Grade gefesselt und belehrt hat." Nietzsche's letter has not survived. In her diaries, Cosima did not record receiving the package until 19 August.
72. See Cosima Wagner, *Diaries,* 19 August 1869.
73. Cosima to Nietzsche, 26 August 1869, *Nietzsche Briefwechsel,* II, 34–36.
74. Cosima related Semper's description of the idea of Roman architecture as a continuation of Alexander's political and military ideals to Nietzsche's coupling of August Wolf to Greek research, and to Wagner's comments on the flowering of the Reformation within Germanic culture under Goethe and Schiller.
75. That Nietzsche read *Preliminary Remarks on Polychrome Architecture* (1834) is apparent in his comments on Greek polychromy in his lecture "Greek Music Drama" (see below). See Nietzsche, *Sämtliche Werke,* I, 519.
76. Gottfried Semper to Nietzsche, 23 January 1870, *Nietzsche Briefwechsel,* II.2, 121–22. Nietzsche's letter to Semper has not survived.
77. Ibid., II.2, 123–24. Cosima to Nietzsche, 27 January 1870.
78. It is remarkable that Giorgio Colli and Mazzino Montinari made the connection of this diary entry to a passage in Nietzsche's *Unzeitgemässe Betrachtungen.* See Nietzsche, *Sämtliche Werke,* 14, 90. See also Richard Wagner, *My Life,* 670.
79. In addition to the two passages discussed in this text, Nietzsche also recorded passages by Semper on the perception of color and made reference to Semper's view of Rococo architecture. See Nietzsche, *Sämtliche Werke,* 9, 123 & 11, 255–56. I am most indebted to J. Duncan Berry for pointing out to me the existence of these passages.
80. See Nietzsche, *Sämtliche Werke,* 7, 16. "Der Karnevalskerzendunst ist die wahre Atmosphäre der Kunst." See Gottfried Semper, *Der Stil,* I, 231–32n. Eng. trans., 257–58.
81. Nietzsche, *Sämtliche Werke,* "Das griechische Musikdrama," I, 522.
82. See Young, *Nietzsche's Philosophy of Art,* 30.
83. Nietzsche, *The Birth of Tragedy,* 58.
84. See Young, *Nietzsche's Philosophy of Art,* 31.
85. Gottfried Semper, *Das königliche Hoftheater zu Dresden,* 27.
86. Gottfried Semper, *Vorläufige Bemerkungen,* 5–6. Eng. trans., 52. "Auf Monumenten waren die Künste berufen, bald in schönen Wettstreit sich einzeln zu zeigen, bald in mannifgaltigen Verbindungen gemeinsam im Chor zu wirken. Der Architekt war Chorage, er führte sie an; sein Name schon sagt es."

Epilogue

1. See Wigley, "Untitled: The Housing of Gender," 375.
2. *Festschrift zur Erinnerung an die Enthüllungsfeier des Semper-Denkmals in Dresden am 1 September 1892* (Dresden: Verlag des Gesammtausschusses für Enthüllung des Semper-Denkmals, 1892). The keynote address was given by Constantin Lipsius.
3. These references vary from the heroic portrait of Semper in Schumacher's account of the Hamburg fire, *Wie das Kunstwerk Hamburg,* to his edifying regard for Semper in his relatively late study, *Der Geist der Baukunst.*
4. Only the first section of Herrmann's book, "Von 1770 bis 1840" (From 1770 to 1840) appeared in 1932, before Herrmann was forced to flee Germany. The second part, "Von 1840 bis zu Gegenwart" (From 1840 to the Present), although written in 1932, was suppressed by the German government and did not appear until 1977. See *Deutsche Baukunst des 19. und 20. Jahrhunderts,* ed. Vogt.
5. The papers given at the symposium were published in *Gottfried Semper und die Mitte des 19. Jahrhunderts,* ed. Vogt.
6. See the exhibition catalogue, Staatliche Kunstsammlungen Dresden, *Gottfried Semper 1803–79: Baumeister zwischen Revolution und Historismus;* The colloquium papers were presented in Dresden Technische Universität, *Gottfried Semper 1803–79.*
7. See Milde, *Neorenaissance in der deutschen Architektur.*
8. J. H. Wolff, "Polemisches: Berichtigung," *Allgemeine Bauzeitung* 12 (1847), 180; Heinrich Hübsch, *Die Architektur und ihr Verhältniss zur heutigen Malerei und Skulptur* (Stuttgart: J. G. Cotta, 1847), 168–85. Both cited by Herrmann in his introduction to *In What Style Should We Build?*
9. G. Semper, "Über den Bau evangelischer Kirchen," *Kleine Schriften,* 461. "Er gewährt eine mannigfaltigere Charakteristik der

Gebäude; die feinsten Abweichungen der Formen und Verhältnisse, wie bei der menschlichen Gesichtsbildung, sind hinreichend, dem Bauwerke in ganz anderes Gepräge aufzudrücken. Durch ihn, wie durch das griechisch-römische Säulenelement, kann der Ausdruck in der Baukunst fast zu physiognomischer Feinheit erhoben werden."

10. See Renate Wagner-Rieger, "Semper und die Wiener Architektur," *Gottfried Semper und die Mitte des 19. Jahrhunderts*, ed. Vogt, 275–88.
11. See the recent study by Helas, *Villenarchitektur/Villa Architecture in Dresden*; text in English, French, and German.
12. See Lipsius, "Über die ästhetische Behandlung des Eisen im Hochbau."
13. See J. Duncan Berry, "From Historicism to Architectural Realism: On Some of Wagner's Sources," in *Otto Wagner: Reflections on the Raiment of Modernity*, ed. Mallgrave, 248. See also his "The Legacy of Gottfried Semper." Berry is the only scholar in recent times to have looked critically at Lipsius's work.
14. Lipsius, *Gottfried Semper*, 100. "...lebendige Organismen, die im ganzen und einzelnen ihre Bestimmung mit physiognomischer Schärfe aussprechen, die nicht die Spur der Willkür, sondern den Stempel der inneren Nothwendigkeit und selbstgewollten Beschränkung, darum aber der künstlerischen Freiheit tragen."
15. Berry, "The Legacy of Gottfried Semper," 253–54.
16. See H. Auer, "Der Einfluss der Construction auf die Entwicklung der Baustile," *Zeitschrift des österreichischen Ingenieur- und Architekten-Vereins*, XXXIII (1881), 8–18; and "Die Entwickelung des Raumes in der Baukunst," (with plates).
17. An excellent description (with photographs) of the building just after its completion is given in *Das neue schweizerische Bundeshaus: Festschrift anlässlich dessen Vollendung und Einweihung* (Bern: Büchler, 1902).
18. Heinrich von Ferstl, address of 9 October 1880, "Rede des neu antretenden Rectors," in *Reden gehalten bei der feierlichen Inauguration des für das Studienjahr 1880/81*, 51. "Auf solchen Grundlagen wird es der neuen Generation weit leichter, als den vorangegangenen werden, die Aufgaben, welche der modernen Baukunst im höheren kunstgestaltendem Sinne gestellt sind, zu vollführen."
19. See Robert Stiassny (ed.) in Bayer, *Baustudien und Baubilder*, VII.
20. Ibid., 98.
21. Ibid., 118–22.
22. Ibid., 128. "So hat sein Leben und Wirken auch in der Breite der Welt die deutlichsten Eindrücke zurückgelassen, und die Spur seiner Erdentage wird an keiner Stätte jemals unkenntlich werden, wo er länger oder kürzer verweilte und wirkte."
23. Ibid., 280. "Der Stil ist eine bestimmte, aus dem innersten Grund und Wesen des Zeitalters stammende Denkweise und Gestaltungs-Äußerung der Kunst, die nur *eine* obligatorisch vorgezeichnete Hauptrichtung haben kann."
24. Bayer, "Stilkrisen unserer Zeit," in *Baustudien und Baubilder*, 295.
25. Carl von Lützow, review of *Der Stil*, in *Recensionen und Mittheilungen über bildende Kunst* (Vienna), II, 5 (June 1863), 85–86. I thank Duncan Berry for sending me a copy of this review.
26. Wilhelm Lübke, "Die Kunstgewerbe und die Architektur," *Blätter für Kunstgewerbe* 1 (1872), 18. Cited in Mitchell Schwarzer's forthcoming book, *German Architectural Theory and the Search for Modern Identity*.
27. Eduard Wulff, *Architectonische Harmonielehre* (Vienna: Waldheim, 1874), 63. Mitchell Schwarzer's book, which I have seen only in manuscript, discusses Wulff together with the ideas of Egon Zöller, who also stressed the role of technology in the development of a culture.
28. Rudolf Redtenbacher, "Die Baubestrebungen der Gegenwart," *Allgemeine Bauzeitung*, 1877, 61–63, 77–80.
29. Redtenbacher, *Tectonik*; and *Die Architektonik der modernen Baukunst*.
30. For some of Heuser's writings, see "Über Pfeiler von verschiedenseitiger Struktur," *Deutsche Bauzeitung*, 30 July 1881, 344–45; "Über Pfeiler von verschiedenseitiger Struktur II," *Deutsche Bauzeitung*, 7 October 1882, 468–69; "Über Pfeiler von verschiedenseitiger Struktur III," *Deutsche Bauzeitung*, 17 November 1883, 546–50; "Die Stabilrahmen, Strukturformen der Metall- Tektonik und ihre Nachbildung in anderem Rohstoffe," *Allgemeine Bauzeitung*, 1884, 97–103; "Die Stabilrahmen, Strukturformen der Metall-Tektonik und ihre Nachbildung in anderem Rohstoffe," *Deutsche Bauzeitung*, 10 February 1886, 73–76; "Die Stabilrahmen," *Allgemeine Bauzeitung*, 1887, 1–5; "Der Gefachstil," *Deutsche Bauzeitung*, 25 March 1893, 149–54; "Das Werden von Stylformen," *Allgemeine Bauzeitung*, 1894, 53–54, 63–69.
31. The author is only identified by the initials "E.E.E." See "Gottfried Sempers 'Kleine Schriften'," *Deutsche Bauzeitung*, 31 January 1885, 50–53; 14 February 1885, 74–78. I thank

Duncan Berry for sharing this review with me.

32. See Moravánszky, *Die Architektur der Donaumonarchie*, 23–28, 37–38, 51–54. See also Moravánszky's essay, "The Aesthetics of the Mask: The Criticial Reception of Wagner's *Modern Architektur* and Architectural Theory in Central Europe," in *Otto Wagner: The Raiment of Modernity*, ed. Mallgrave, 203, 208–9, 222–29.
33. See Duncan Berry on Semper and Sédille in "From Historicism to Architectural Realism," in *Otto Wagner: Reflections on the Raiment of Modernity*, ed. Mallgrave, 274n.50.
34. Lawrence Harvey, "Semper's theory of Evolution in Architectural Ornament," *Transactions of the RIBA*, New Series, I (1885), 29–54.
35. Lawrence Harvey to Hans Semper, 16 December 1884, Semper Archiv.
36. Ibid.
37. See Berry, "The Legacy of Gottfried Semper," 196.
38. See Geraniotis's dissertation, "German Architects in Nineteenth-Century Chicago." See also her articles, "German Architectural Theory and Practice in Chicago," and "The University of Illinois and German Architectural Education."
39. See Frederick Baumann's remarks to the question, "To what extent is it necessary in design to emphasize the essentially structural elements of a building?" in *Inland Architect & News Record*, May 1887, IX, 6, 59–62; "Thoughts on Architecture" (address to the AIA in Washington D.C.), in *Inland Architect & News Record*, November 1890, CVI, 5, 59–60; "Thoughts on Style" (address to the AIA convention in Chicago, 1892), in *Inland Architect & News Record*, November 1892, XX, 4, 34–37; and his remarks to "Two Questions Considered" (talk to the Illinois chapter of the AIA), in *Inland Architect & News Record*, April 1897, XXIX, 3, 23–26.
40. Root's translation, which appeared under the title "Development of Architectural Style," has some translation problems. It appeared in the *Inland Architect & News Record*, December 1889, 76–78; January 1890, 92–94; February 1890, 5–6, March 1890, 32–33.
41. See *Inland Architect & News Record*, XX, 6, January 1893, 62–63.
42. Vischer, *Aesthetik*, 3: sec. 559, 228.
43. Vischer, "Kritik meiner Ästhetik," in *Kritische Gänge*, 4: 316–22.
44. Robert Vischer, *Über das optische Formgefühl: Ein Beitrag zur Aesthetik* (Leipzig: Hermann Credner, 1873). Vischer's essay has recently appeared in English translation under the title "On the Optical Sense of Form: A Contribution to Aesthetics," in *Empathy, Form, and Space*, ed. Mallgrave and Ikonomou.
45. Volkelt, *Der Symbol-Begriff*.
46. Wölfflin, *Prolegomena*. The dissertation also appears in English translation in *Empathy, Form, and Space*.
47. See the introductory remarks to *Empathy, Form, and Space* (note 56), 45.
48. Ibid., 176.
49. Wölfflin, *Renaissance and Baroque*, 77, 167n. 5.
50. Ibid., 78–79.
51. Dilthey, "The Three Epochs of Modern Aesthetics," 204.
52. Conrad Fiedler, "Bemerkungen über Wesen und Geschichte der Baukunst," *Deutsche Rundschau* 15 (1878). English translation, "Observations on the Nature and History of Architecture," in *Empathy, Form, and Space*, ed. Mallgrave and Ikonomou. Fiedler used the term "revelations" when referring to Semper in a letter to Adolf Hildebrand, in *Adolf von Hildebrands Briefwechsel mit Conrad Fiedler* (Dresden: Wolfgang Jess, 1927), 54–55.
53. Fiedler, "Observations on the Nature and History of Architecture" in *Empathy, Form, and Space*, 142.
54. August Schmarsow, *Das Wesen der architektonischen Schöpfung* (Leipzig: Karl W. Hiersemann, 1894), inaugural address given at the University of Leipzig on 8 November 1893. Eng. trans. in *Empathy, Form, and Space*, 281–97.
55. August Schmarsow, "Über den Werth der Dimensionen im menschlichen Raumgebilde," *Berichte über die Verhandlungen der königlich Sächsischen Gesellschaft der Wissenschaften zu Leipzig*. Philologisch-historische Klasse 48 (1896), 44–61.
56. August Schmarsow, *Grundbegriffe der Kunstwissenschaft am Übergang vom Altertum zum Mittelalter, kritisch erörtert und in systematischem Zusammenhange dargestellt* (Leipzig: B. G. Teubner, 1905).
57. Wagner never gave up his hope of being appointed an Imperial architect, which would have carried his designs in an entirely different direction. See Renate Kassal-Mikula's essay, "Otto Wagner's Unsuccessful *Parallel-Aktion*," in *Otto Wagner: Reflections on the Raiment of Modernity*, ed. Mallgrave, 21–51.
58. Wagner, *Moderne Architektur*, 58; Eng. trans. by H. Mallgrave, *Modern Architecture* (Santa Monica: The Getty Center for the History of Art and the Humanities, 1988). "...hatte er nicht den Muth, seine Theorien nach oben und unten zu vollenden und hat sich mit einer Symbolik der Construction beholfen, statt die Con-

struction selbst als die Urzelle der Baukunst zu bezeichnen."

59. Ibid. "Der Architekt hat immer aus der Construction die Kunstform zu entwickeln."
60. Richard Streiter, "Architektonische Zeitfragen," in *Ausgewählte Schriften zur Aesthetik und Kunst-Geschichte* (Munich: Delphin, 1913), 105. "Nirgends ist zu entdecken, dass Wagner das Verhältnis von Konstruktion und Kunstform anders auffasst, als es sonst von der moderen Architektenschaft ausgefasst zu werden pflegt; ja es kann vielmehr behauptet werden, dass eine Reihe englischer, französischer, amerikanischer und detuscher Architekten dem Satz: 'Der Architekt hat immer aus der Konstruktion die Kunstform zu entwickeln,' weit mehr Rechnung trägt, als Wagner selbst."
61. See Peter Haiko's essay, "The Franz Josef-Stadtmuseum: The Attempt to Implement a Theory of Modern Architecture," in *Otto Wagner: Reflections on the Raiment of Modernity*, ed. Mallgrave, 52–83.
62. Loos, "Das Prinzip der Bekleidung," 140. "...fühlt zuerst die wirkung, die er hervorzubringen gedenkt, und sieht dann mit seinem geistigen auge die räume, die er schaffen will. Die wirkung, die er auf den beschauer ausüben will, sei es nun angst oder schrecken wie beim kerker; gottesfurcht wie bei der kirche; ehrfurcht vor der staatsgewalt wie beim regierungspalast; pietät wie beim grabmal; heimgefühl wie beim wohnhause; fröhlichkeit wie in der trinkstube; diese wirkung wird hervorgerufen durch das material und durch die form."
63. See Berlage, *Gedanken über Stil in der Baukunst*, 28. Berlage's text will shortly be released in English translation in the Getty Center's Texts and Documents series.
64. Ibid., 52. "...Architektur ist die Kunst der Raumumschliessung..." Aside from such major figures as Sigfried Giedion and Fritz Schumacher who appealed to a new aesthetic based on space, there were also a number of other, lesser known developers of this theme, among them Herman Sörgel, Paul Klopfer, Otto Schubert, and Leo Adler.
65. Muthesius, *Stil-Architektur und Baukunst*, 34. Eng. trans. by Stanford Anderson, *Style-Architecture and the Building-Art* (Santa Monica: The Getty Center for the History of Art and the Humanities, 1994), 68.
66. Ibid., 35. "Auch Semper kannte und sah noch keine nordische Kunst, er erblickt in allen ihren bisherigen Aeusserungen nur unwillkommene Abweichungen von seiner grossen Weltkunst Antike. Die ganze Richtung, die sich in dem Schaffen Sempers verkörpert, ist eben durchaus noch als der Ausläufer jener weltbürgerlichen Architektur aufzufassen, die der Neuklassicismus in Deutschland geschaffen hatte. Eine auf der Antike fussende kosmopolitische Zukunstsarchitektur war ihr Ziel."
67. Behrens, "Art and Technology," 214.
68. See Max Dvorák's sketch of Riegl in *Gesammelte Aufsätze zur Kunstgeschcihte*, ed. J. Wilde and K. M. Swoboda (Munich, 1929), 279–99.
69. See Olin, "Alois Riegl," 113.
70. G. Semper, *Der Stil*, I, 90–91.
71. See Olin, *Forms of Representation.*
72. Ibid., 206n.60.
73. Ibid., 54.
74. Ibid., 65.
75. Riegl, *Altorientalische Teppiche*, v. Interestingly, Riegl cites Owen Jones by his first name only.
76. Ibid., v–vi. "...Julius Lessing in seinen *Altorientalischen Teppichmustern* nicht nur den ersten Versuch gemacht hat, Kritieren für eine verlässliche Zeitbestimmung älterer orientalischer Teppische aufzustellen, sondern auch die Grundlinien gezogen hat, innherhalb deren sich die weitere Forschung zu bewegen hatte. Lessing war es, der die fundamentale Wichtigkeit der auf die technische Herstellung bezüzglichen Momente für die Beurteilung orientalischer Teppiche zuerst ins volle Licht gesetz hat."
77. Julius Lessing, "Neue Wege," *Kunstgewerbeblatt*, 1895, 3. "Ist es nun denkbar, dass an Stelle historischer Überlieferung und allmählicher Weiterbildung diese technischen Fakoren durchaus neue Formen schaffen? Können wir die neu gefundene, rein konstruktive Form eines modernen eisernen Trägers als eineSchöpfung betrachten wie die griechische Säule, deren geheiligte Form bis heute alle Kunstperioden beherrscht?"
78. Ibid., 5. "Bequem oder nicht: unsere Arbeit hat einzusetzen auf dem Boden des praktischen Lebens unserer Zeit, hat diejenigen Formen zu schaffen, welche unseren Bedürfnissen, unserer Technik, unserem Material entsprechen."
79. Olin, *Forms of Representation*, 55.
80. Riegl, *Problems of Style*, 4; *Stilfragen*, vi–vii. "Es geschieht dies mit demselben, oder besser gesagt, mit ebensowenig Recht, als die Identificirung des modernen Darwinismus mit Darwin; die Parallele – Darwinismus und Kunstmaterialismus – scheint mir um so zutreffender, als zwischen diesen beiden Erscheinungen zweifellos ein inniger kausaler Zusammenhang existirt, die in Rede stehende

materialische Strömung in der Auffassung der Kunstanfänge nichts Anderes ist, als so zu sagen die Uebertragung des Darwinismus auf ein Gebiet des Geisteslebens."

81. Ibid., vii. "So wie aber zwischen Darwinisten und Darwin, ist auch zwischen Semperianern und Semper scharf und streng zu unterscheiden. Wenn Semper sagte: beim Werden einer Kunstform kämen auch Stoff und Technik in Betracht, so meinten die Semperianer sofort schlechtweg: die Kunstform wäre eine Produkt aus Stoff und Technik."
82. Ibid. "Es mag paradox erscheinen, dass die extreme Partei der Kunstmaterialisten auch unter den ausübenden Künstlern zahlreich Anhänger gefunden hat. Dies geschah gewiss nicht im Geiste Gottfried Sempers, der wohl der Letzte gewesen wäre, der an Stelle des frei schöpferischen Kunstwollens einen wesentlich mechanisch-materiellen Nachahmungstrieb hätte gesetz wissen wollen."
83. G. Semper, "On Architectural Styles," in *The Four Elements of Architecture*, 268.
84. Riegl, *Problems of Style*, 4; *Stilfragen*, vii. "Aber das Missverständniss, als handelte es sich hiebei um die reine Idee des grossen Künstler-Gelehrte Semper, war einmal vorhanden. . . ."
85. Iversen, *Alois Riegl*, 25.
86. Hans Semper, *Ein Bild seines Lebens und Wirkens*, 4.
87. See Duncan Berry's essay, "From Historicism to Architectural Realism: On Some of Wagner's Sources," and my essay, "From Realism to Sachlichkeit: The Polemics of Architectural Modernity in the 1890s," in *Otto Wagner: Reflections on the Raiment of Modernity*, ed. Mallgrave, 242–360.
88. See Richard Streiter, "Architektonische Zeitgfragen," in *Richard Streiter: Ausgewählte Schriften* (Munich: Delphin, 1913), 98–99.
89. Riegl, *Problems of Style*, 4; *Stilfragen*, 6. "Es geht nun aus zahlreichen Stellen im *Stil* hervor, dass Semper sich diese Vorbildlichkeit von Decke und Band ursprünglich und überwiegend nich so sehr in stofflich-materiellem, als in ideellem Sinne gedacht hat, wie denn auch Semper gewiss der Letzte gewesen wäre, der den frei schöpferischen Kunstgedanken gegenüber dem sinnlich-materiallen Nachahmungstriebe nicht gebührend berücksichtigt hätte; die Ausbildung dieser seiner Theorie in grob materialistischem Sinne ist erst durch seine zahllosen Nachfolger erfolgt."
90. This is a hypothesis Margaret Olin has discussed with me in correspondence and it relates to Riegl's personal feud with his rival historian Josef Strzygowski. See her essay, "Alois Riegl," 107–20.
91. G. Semper, *Der Stil*, II, 90.
92. Riegl, *Problems of Style*, 23; *Stilfragen*, 12. "So vorsichtig drückte sich der Autor aus, der, Künstler und Gelehrter zugleich, in höherem Masse als irgend Einer seines Jahrhunderts die technischen Proceduren des Kunstschaffens in ihrer Gesammtheit und ihren Wechselbeziehungen überblickte und umfasste. Es geht auch aus seinen obcitirten Worten hervor, dass er sich die formenbildende Thätigkeit der "Technik" im Wesentlichen erst in vorgerücktere Zeiten der Kunstentwicklung verlegt denkt, und nicht in die ersten Anfänge des Kunstschaffens überhaupt. Und dies ist auch meine Überzeugung."
93. G. Semper, *Der Stil*, I, 228. "Die Verschiedenheiten der natürlichen Farben der Halme veranlassten bald ihre Benützung nach abwechselnder Ordnung und so entstand das Muster."
94. Riegl, *Problems of Style*, 24; *Stilfragen*, 13. "Die Stellen in denen sich Semper zu technisch-materiellen Auffassung in direkten Widerspruch setzt, sind übrigens im *Stil* gar nicht so selten."
95. G. Semper, *Der Stil*, I, 227.
96. Riegl, *Problems of Style*, 40; *Stilfragen*, 32. "Noch drängt es mich, um jedwedes Missverständniss zu vermeiden, ausdrücklich zu widerholen, was ich schon mehrfach angedeutet habe: dass ich Gottfried Semper keineswegs dafür verantwortlich machen möchte, dass man seine Worte in der erörterten Richtung interpretirt und weiter entwickelt hat. Semper handelte es sich keineswegs darum, eine möglichst materielle Erklärung fur die frühesten Kunstäusserungen des Menschen zu finden . . ."
97. G. Semper, *Der Stil*, I, 7. "Die oben angedeutete und in dem Folgenden durchzuführende konstructiv-technische Auffassung des Ursprungs der Grundformen der Baukunst hat nichts gemein mit der grob-materialistischen Anschauung, wonach das eigene Wesen der Baukunst nichts sein soll als durchgebildete Construction, gleichsam illustrirte und illuminirte Statik und Mechanik, reine Stoffkundgebung." For other responses of Semper to materialist tendencies of his day, see Herrmann's essay, "Was Semper a Materialist?," in *In Search of Architecture*, 121–23.
98. Riegl, *Spätrömische Kunstindustrie*, 8–9. "Es ist dies jene Theorie, die in der Regel mit dem Namen *Gottfried Sempers* in Verbindung gebracht wird und derzufolge das Kunstwerk nichts anderes sein soll als ein mechanisches Produkt aus Gebrauchszweck, Rohstoff und

Technik. Diese Theorie wurde zu Zeit ihres Aufkommens mit Recht als ein wesentlicher Forschritt gegenüber den völlig unklaren Vorstellungen der unmittelbar vorangegangenen Zeit der Romantik angesehen; heute ist sie aber längst reif dazu, endgültig der Geschichte einverleibt zu werden, denn wie so viele andere Theorien aus der Mitte des abgelaufenen Jahrhunderts, in denen man ursprünglich den höchsten Triumph exakter Naturforschung vermutete, hat sich auch die *Sempersche* Kunsttheorie schliesslich als ein Dogma der materialistischen Metaphysik herausgestellt.

Im Gegensatze zu dieser mechanistischen Auffassung vom Wesen des Kunstwerkes habe ich – soviel ich sehe, als Erster – in den "Stilfragen" eine teleologische vertreten, indem ich im Kunstwerke das Resultat eines bestimmten und zweckbewussten Kunstwollens erblickte, das sich im Kampfe mit Gebrauchszweck, Rohstoff und Technik durchsetzt. Diesen drei letzteren Faktoren kommt somit nicht mehr jene positiv-schöpferische Rolle zu, die ihnen die sogenannte *Sempersche* Theorie zugedacht hatte, sondern vielmehr eine hemmende, negative: sie bilden gleichsam die Reibungskoeffizienten innerhalb des Gesamtprodukts."

99. See G. Semper, *Der Stil*, II, 389–90.
100. See Olin, "Grammars of Truth and Volition," in *Forms of Representation*, 113–27. The two manuscripts of Riegl were published as *Historische Grammatik der bildenden Künste*, ed. Karl M. Swoboda and Otto Pächt (Graz, 1966).
101. See Podro, *The Critical Historians of Art*, 72 & 96.
102. Riegl, *Spätrömische Kunstindustrie*, 151n.1. "Das ebenerwährnte Bestreben, die künstlerische Eigenart einzelner dekorativer Formen auf die Nachahmung bestimmter Pflanzenspezies in der Natur zurückzuführen, ist die jüngste (und wohl auch letzte?) Phase des seit Semper (jedoch zum Teile in missverständlicher Auslegung seiner Äusserungen) beliebten Kunstmaterialismus."
103. Venturi, *History of Art Criticism*, 226–27.

Bibliography

Writings by Semper

1833 "Scoprimento d'antichi colori sulla colonna di Trajano," *Bulletino dell'Istituto di corrispondenza archaeologica*, 1833, 92–93 ("Entdeckung alter Farbenreste an der Trajanssäule in Rom," in *Gottfried Semper: Kleine Schriften*).

1834 *Vorläufige Bemerkungen über bemalte Architectur und Plastik bei den Alten*. Altona: Johann Friedrich Hammerich (Eng. trans. by H. Mallgrave and Wolfgang Herrmann, in *Gottfried Semper: The Four Elements of Architecture and other Writings*. New York: Cambridge Univ. Press, 1988).

1843 "Unmassgebliche Vorschläge zur Erhaltung und Wiederherstellung des Domes in Meissen," *Zentralblatt der Bauverwaltung* 36, 1904, 229–30.

1845 *Über den Bau evangelischer Kirchen*. Leipzig: B. G. Teubner.

1845 "Noch etwas über den St. Nikolai-Kirchenbau," *Neue Hamburgische Blätter*, 12 March.

1849 *Das königliche Hoftheater zu Dresden*. Brunswick: Vieweg & Sohn; reprint Brunswick: Vieweg & Sohn, 1986.

1849 "Die Kunst unter der französischen Republik," *Zeitschrift für praktische Baukunst* 9, 481–82.

1849 "Reise nach Belgien im Monat Oktober 1849," *Zeitschrift für praktisches Baukunst* 9, 501–14.

1849 "Der Wintergarten zu Paris," *Zeitschrift für praktisches Baukunst* 9, 516–26.

1849 "Farbiges Erdpech," *Zeitschrift für praktisches Baukunst* 9, 526–28.

1850 "Wohnhaus in Paris in der Rue St. George," *Zeitschrift für praktische Baukunst* 10, 13.

1851 *Die Vier Elemente der Baukunst: Ein beitrag zur vergleichenden Baukunde*. Brunswick: Vieweg und Sohn (Eng. trans. by H. Mallgrave and Wolfgang Herrmann, in *Gottfried Semper: The Four Elements of Architecture and other Writings*, New York: Cambridge Univ. Press, 1988).

1851 "On the Study of Polychromy and its Revival," *The Museum of Classical Antiquity*, I, London.

1852 *Wissenschaft, Industrie und Kunst: Vorschläge zur Anregung nationalen Kunstgefühles*. Brunswick: Vieweg und Sohn (Eng. trans. by H. Mallgrave and Wolfgang Herrmann, in *Gottfried Semper: The Four Elements of Architecture and other Writings*, New York: Cambridge Univ. Press, 1988).

1852 "Practical Art in Metals and Hard Materials; Its Technology, History and Styles" (manuscript), Victoria and Albert Museum Library.

1853 "Outline for a System of Comparative Style-Theory," *RES: Journal of Anthropology and Aesthetics* 6, 1983, 8–22. (London lecture, 11 Nov. 1853.)

1853 "On the Origin of Some Architectural Styles," *RES: Journal of Anthropology and Aesthetics* 9, Spring 1985, 53–60. (London lecture.)

1853 "The Development of the Wall and Wall Construction in Antiquity," *RES: Journal of Anthropology and Aesthetics* 11, Spring 1986, 33–41. (London lecture.)

1854 "On Architectural Symbols," *RES: Journal of Anthropology and Aesthetics* 9, Spring 1985, 61–67. (London lecture.)

1854 "On the Relations of Architectural Systems with the General Cultural Conditions," *RES: Journal of Anthropology and Aesthetics* 11, Spring 1986, 42–53. (London lecture.)

1856 *Ueber die formelle Gesetzmässigkeit des Schmuckes und dessen Bedeutung als Kunstsymbolik.* Zurich: Meyer & Zeller, 1856.

1859 *Ueber die bleiernen Schleudergeschosse der Alten und zweckmässige Gestaltung der Wurfkörper im Allgemeinen: Ein Versuch die dynamische Entstehung gewisser Formen in der Natur und in der Kunst nachzuweisen.* Frankfurt: Verlag für Kunst und Wissenschaft, 1859.

1860–63 *Der Stil in den technischen und tektonischen Künsten oder praktische Ästhetik: Ein Handbook für Techniker, Künstler und Kunstfreunde.* 2 vols. Frankfurt: Verlage für Kunst und Wissenschaft (reprint Mittenwald: Mäander Kunstverlag, 1977); 2nd edition, Munich: Friedrich Bruckmann, 1878 (partial Eng. trans. by H. Mallgrave and Wolfgang Herrmann, in *Gottfried Semper: The Four Elements of Architecture and other Writings.* New York: Cambridge Univ. Press, 1988).

1869 *Ueber Baustyle: Ein Vortrag gehalten auf dem Rathhaus in Zürich am 4 Marz 1869.* Zürich: Friedrich Schulthess (Eng. trans. by H. Mallgrave and Wolfgang Herrmann, in *Gottfried Semper: The Four Elements of Architecture and other Writings*, New York: Cambridge Univ. Press, 1988).

1884 *Gottfried Semper: Kleine Schriften.* Berlin and Stuttgart, 1884 (reprint Mittenwald: Mäander Kunstverlag, 1977).

1892 *Die k. k. Hofmuseen in Wien und Gottfried Semper: Drei Denkschriften Gottfried Semper's.* Innsbruck: A. Edlinger, 1892.

Selected Secondary Sources

Anthony, John. *Joseph Paxton: An Illustrated Life of Sir Joseph Paxton, 1803–1865.* London: Shire Publications, 1973.

Atterbury, Paul, and Clive Wainwright (eds). *Pugin: A Gothic Passion.* New Haven: Yale Univ. Press, 1994.

Auer, Hans. "Die Entwickelung des Raumes in der Baukunst," *Allgemeine Bauzeitung* 48, 1883, 65–74.

Baljon, Cornelis J. *The Structure of Architectural Theory: A Study of Some Writings by Gottfried Semper, John Ruskin, and Christopher Alexander.* Diss. pub. by author, Technische Universiteit Delft, 1993.

Barrault, Emile. *Aux Artistes, du passé et de l'avenir des Beaux-Arts.* Paris, 1830.

Bauer, Oswald Georg. "Utopie als Aufgabe: Aus der hundertjährigen Geschichte der Bayreuther Festspiele," in *100 Jahre Richard-Wagner-Festspiele.* Munich: Bayerische Vereinsbank, 1976.

Baumann, Frederick. "To what extent is it necessary in design to emphasize the essentially structural elements of a building," *Inland Architect & News Record*, vol. IX, 6, 59-62.

——. "Thoughts on Architecture," *Inland Architect & News Record*, vol. CVI, 5, 59–60.

——. "Thoughts on Style," *Inland Architect & News Record*, vol. XX, 4, 34-37.

——. "Two Questions Considered," *Inland Architect & News Record*, vol. XXIX, 3, 23–26.

Baumann, Walter. *Gottfried Keller: Leben, Werk, Zeit.* Zurich: Artemis, 1986.

Bayer, Josef. "Gottfried Semper," in *Zeitschrift für Bildende Kunst*, ed. Carl von Lützow. Vol. 14, Leipzig, 1879.

——. *Baustudien und Baubilder: Schriften zur Kunst*, ed. Robert Stiassny. Jena: Eugen Diederichs, 1919.

Beaver, Patrick. *The Crystal Palace: 1851–1936, A Portrait of Victorian Enterprise*. London: Hugh Evelyn, 1970.

Behrens, Peter. "Art and Technology" (1910), in *Industriekultur: Peter Behrens and the AEG, 1907–14*, trans. Iain Boyd Whyte. Cambridge, MA: MIT Press, 1984.

Benjamin, Walter. *Reflections: Essays, Aphorisms, Autobiographical Writings*, ed. Peter Demetz. New York: Harcourt Brace Jovanovich, 1978.

Bergdoll, Barry. *Léon Vaudoyer: Historicism in the Age of Industry*. Cambridge, MA: MIT Press, 1994.

——. *Karl Friedrich Schinkel: An Architecture for Prussia*. New York: Rizzoli, 1994.

Berlage, H. P. *Gedanken über Stil in der Baukunst*. Leipzig: Julius Zeitler, 1905.

Berlin, Isaiah. *The Crooked Timber of Humanity*. New York: Vintage, 1992.

Berry, J. Duncan. "The Legacy of Gottfried Semper: Studies in Späthistorismus," Ph.D. diss., Brown Univ., 1991.

Bluntschli, Alfred Friedrich. *Der neue Physikbau für das Eidgenössische Polytechnikum zu Zürich*. Zurich: Meyer & Zeller, 1887.

Bonython, Elizabeth. *King Cole: A Picture Portrait of Sir Henry Cole, KCB 1808–1882*. London: Victoria and Albert Museum, 1992.

Bopp, Franz. *A Comparative Grammar of the Sanscrit, Zend, Greek, Latin, Lithuanian, Gothic, German, and Sclavonic Languages*. London, 1845.

Börsch-Supan, Helmut, and Lucius Griesebach (eds). *Karl Friedrich Schinkel: Architektur Malerie Kunstgewerbe*. Berlin: Schloß Charlottenburg, 1981.

Botta, P. E. *Monument de Ninive*. 5 vols. Paris: Imprimerie Nationale, 1846–50 (reprint Osnabrück: Biblio Verlag, 1972).

Bötticher, Karl. *Die Tektonik der Hellenen*. Potsdam: Ferdinand Riegel, 1844-52.

——. "Das Prinzip der hellenischen und germanischen Bauweise hinsichtlich der Übertragung in die Bauweise unserer Tage," *Allgemeine Bauzeitung* 11, 1846, 111–25.

——. *Der Baumkultus der Hellenen nach den gottesdienstlichen Gebräuchen und den überlieferten Bildwerken*. Berlin: Weidmannsche Buchhandlung, 1856.

Böttiger, C. A. *Ideen zur Archäologie der Malerie*. Dresden, 1811.

Brønsted, P. O. *Reisen und Untersuchungen in Griechenland*. Paris, 1825–30.

Bruhns, K. (ed.). *Life of Alexander von Humboldt*. London, 1873.

Casteras, Susan P., and Ronald Parkinson. *Richard Redgrave: 1804–88*. New Haven: Yale Univ. Press, 1988.

Clogg, Richard. *A Short History of Modern Greece*. Cambridge: Cambridge Univ. Press, 1990.

Cockerell, C. R. "On the Aegina Marbles," *Journal of Science and the Arts* 12, London, 1819.

——. *Travels in Southern Europe and the Levant*. London, 1903.

Cole, Henry. "Notes of a Journey to Vienna and Back in November and December" (manuscript). London, Victoria and Albert Museum Library.

——. Diaries. London, Victoria and Albert Museum Library, Box 101.A.72.

Cole, Henry (ed.). *The Journal of Design and Manufactures*. London: Chapman & Hall, 1849–52.

Cole, Henry. "An Introductory Lecture on the Facilities Afforded by the Department of Practical Art to all Classes of the Community for Obtaining Education in Art," in *Addresses of the Superintendents of the Department of Practical Art*. London: Chapman & Hall, 1853.

——. *First Report of the Department of Practical Art.* London: George E. Eyre & William Spottiswoode, 1853.

——. *First Report of the Department of Science and Art.* London: George E. Eyre & William Spottiswoode, 1854.

——. *Second Report of the Department of Science and Art.* London: George E. Eyre & William Spottiswoode, 1855.

——. *Fifty Years of Public Work of Sir Henry Cole, K.C.B. Accounted for in his Deeds, Speeches and Writings.* 2 vols. London: George Bell & Sons, 1884.

Curran, Kathleen. "The German Rundbogenstil and Reflections on the American Round-Arched Style," *Journal of the Society of Architectural Historians*, vol. XLVII, 4, 351-73.

Cuvier, Georg. *The Animal Kingdom, Arranged after its Organization; forming a Natural History of Animals, and an Introduction to Comparative Anatomy.* London: Henry G. Bohn, 1863; New York: Kraus Reprint, 1969.

Davitz, Jürg. *Die Rathäuser des Landes Glarus.* Glarnerland/Walensee, 1985.

Dietrich, D. Wald Victorin. *Das Friedrich August-Monument in Dresden und seine feierliche Enthüllung am 7 June 1843.* Dresden, 1843.

Dilthey, Wilhelm. "The Three Epochs of Modern Aesthetics and its Present Task," in *Selected Works: Poetry and Experience*, ed. Makkreel and Rodi, trans. Michael Neville. Princeton: Princeton Univ. Press, 1985.

Dodwell, Edward. *A Classical and Topographical Tour Through Greece, during the Years 1801, 1805, and 1806.* 2 vols. London, 1819.

Dohme, Robert. *Das englische Haus: Eine kultur- und baugeschichtliche Skizze.* Brunswick: G. Westermann, 1888.

Donaldson, Thomas L. "Polychromatic Embellishments in Greek Architecture," *Civil Engineer and Architect's Journal*, vol. XV (London: R. Groombridge, 1852), 42–50.

Dresden Technische Universität. *Gottfried Semper 1803–1879: Sein Wirken als Architekt, Theoretiker und revolutionärer Demokrat und die schöpferische Aneignung seines progressiven Erbes.* Dresden: Technische Universität Dresden, 1980, no. 13.

Eckhardt, Wolfgang. "Gottfried Semper's Planungen für ein Richard Wagner-Festtheater in München," *Jahrbuch des Museum für Kunst und Gewebe Hamburg*, vol. 2, 1983, 41–72.

Edlinger, A. *Die k. k. Hof-Museen in Wien.* Innsbruck, 1892.

Eggert, Klaus von. "Gottfried Semper, Carl von Hausenauer," in *Die Wiener Ringstrasse: Bild einer Epoch*, ed. Renate Wagner-Rieger. Wiesbaden: Franz Steiner, 1978.

Eggers, Karl (ed.). *Briefwechsel zwischen Rauch und Rietschel.* Berlin: F. Fontane, 1890.

1848 Augenzeugen der Revolution: Briefe, Tagebücher, Reden, Berichte. Berlin: Rütten & Loening, 1973.

Erismann, Hans. *Richard Wagner in Zürich.* Zürich: Verlag neue Zürcher Zeitung, 1987.

Ettlinger, Leopold. *Gottfried Semper und die Antike: Beiträge zur Kunstanschauung des deutschen Klassizismus.* Halle: Carl Nieft, 1937.

——. "On Science, Industry and Art: Some Theories of Gottfried Semper," *Architectural Review*, vol. 136, July 1964.

Falières-Lamy, Adeline. "La Basilique Sainte-Clotilde," in *Paris et Ile-de-France: Mémoires publiés par la Fédération des Sociétés historiques et archéologiques de Paris de de l'Ile-de France*, vol. 40, Paris, 1989, 207–55.

Faulwasser, Julius. *Der Große Brand und der Wiederaufbau von Hamburg.* Hamburg: Otto Meissner, 1892.

Fausch, Deborah (ed. with others). *Architecture in Fashion.* New York: Princeton Architectural Press, 1994.

Ferstel, Heinrich. "Rede des neu antretenden Rectors," in *Reden gehalten bei der Feierlichen Inauguration des für das Studienjahr 1880/81.* Vienna: k. k. Technischen Hoschschule, 1881.

Forster, Edward S. *A Short History of Modern Greece: 1821-1945.* London: Methuen, 2nd ed. n.d.

Forster, Kurt W. "'Vento preistorico dalle montagne gelate . . .' Vorzeitiges und Zukünftiges im Werk Karl Friedrich Schinkels," in *Bildfälle: Die Moderne im Zwielicht,* ed. Beat Wyss. Zurich: Artemis, 1990.

Forster, Ludwig. "Das Wachhaus des Bastille-Platzes zu Paris," *Allgemeine Bauzeitung* 8, 1843, 45-47.

Forty, Adrian. "Of Cars, Clothes and Carpets: Design Metaphors in Architectural Thought," *Journal of Design History,* vol. 2, 1, 1989.

Franck, Bernd. *Die Nikolaikirche nach dem Hamburger Großen Band: Gottfried Semper und die Entwurfsgeschichte für den Hopfenmarkt mit dem Kirchenbau 1842–45.* Hamburg: Friedrich Wittig, 1989.

Fried, Michael. *Absorption and Theatricality: Painting and Beholder in the Age of Diderot.* Chicago: Univ. of Chicago Press, 1988.

——. *Courbet's Realism.* Chicago: Univ. of Chicago Press, 1990.

Fritsch, K. E. O. "Zur Erinnerung an Constantin Lipsius," *Deutsche Bauzeitung* 39, 10 April 1895, 181–205.

Fröhlich, Marie, and Hans-Günther Sperlich. *Georg Moller: Baumeister, Der Romantik.* Darmstadt: Eduard Roether, 1959.

Fröhlich, Martin. *Gottfried Semper: Zeichnerischer Nachlass an der ETH Zürich.* Basel: Birkhäuser, 1974.

——. *Gottfried Semper.* Zürich: Verlag für Architektur, 1991.

——. *Sempers Hauptgebäude der ETH Zürich.* Bern: Gesellschaft für Schweizerische Kunstgeschichte, n.d.

Garnier, Charles. *Le Théâtre.* Paris: Librairie Hachette, 1871.

Gelder, Ludwig, and Manfred F. Fischer. *"Nutzen und Zierde zugleich bieten dem Auge sich dar": 1841 Hamburgs neue Börse 1991.* Hamburg: Handelskammer Hamburg, 1991.

Geraniotis, Roula. "German Architects in Nineteenth-Century Chicago." Ph.D. diss., Univ. of Illinois, 1985.

——. "The University of Illinois and German Architectural Education," *Journal of Architectural Education* 38, 4, 1985, 15–21.

——. "German Architectural Theory and Practice in Chicago, 1850–1900," *Winthur Portfolio* 21, 4, 1986, 293–306.

Gobran, Sophie. "The Munich Festival Theater Letters," in *Perspecta 26: The Yale Architecture Journal.* New York: Rizzoli, 1990.

Goethe, Johann Wolfgang von. *Goethes Werke.* 8 vols. Berlin: Deutsches Verlagshaus Bong & Co., n.d.

——. *Gedenkausgabe der Werke, Briefe und Gespräche.* Zurich, 1949.

Grundmann, Günther. *August Soller 1805–53: Ein Berliner Architekt im Geiste Schinkels.* Munich: Prestel, 1973.

Guizot, François. *The History of France from the Earliest Times to 1848.* New York: A. L. Burt, n.d.

Gurlitt, Cornelius. *Das neue königliche Hoftheater zu Dresden.* Dresden, 1878 (reprint Hellerau: Verlag Dresden, 1990).

——. *Die deutsche Kunst des XIX. Jahrhunderts.* Berlin: Georg Bondi, 1899.

——. *Zur Befreiung der Baukunst: Ziele und Taten deutscher Architekten im 19. Jahrhundert.* Berlin: Ullstein, 1900.

Gutman, Robert W. *Richard Wagner: The Man, His Mind, and His Music.* New York: Harcourt Brace Jovanovich, 1968.

Haag Bletter, Rosemarie. "On Martin Fröhlich's Gottfried Semper," *Oppositions* 4, October 1974, 146–53.

——. "Gottfried Semper," in *Macmillan Encyclopedia of Architects.* vol. 4. London: The Free Press, 1982, 25–33.

Habel, Heinrich. *Festspielhaus und Wahnfried: Geplante und ausgeführte Bauten Richard Wagners.* Munich: Prestel, 1985.

Haenel, Erich. *Hundert Jahre sächsischer Kunstverein: Jubiläums Festschrift.* Dresden: Wilhelm Limpert, 1928.

Haenel, Erich, and Eugen Kalkschmidt (eds). *Das alte Dresden.* Dresden: H. Schmidt & C. Günther, 1934 (reprint Frankfurt: Wolfgang Weidlich, 1977).

Hammer, Karl. *Jakob Ignaz Hittorff: Ein Pariser Baumeister 1792–1867.* Stuttgart: Anton Hiersemann, 1968.

Hänsch, Wolfgang. *Die Semperoper: Geschichte und Wiederaufbau der Dresdner Staatsoper.* Stuttgart: Deutsche Verlags-Anstalt, 1986.

Hare, Augustus J. C. *The Life and Letters of Frances Baroness Bunsen.* New York: George Routledge, n.d.

Harries, Karsten. "Theatricality and Re-presentation," in *Perspecta 26: The Yale Architecture Journal.* New York: Rizzoli, 1990.

Harvey, Lawrence. "Semper's Theory of Evolution in Architectural Ornament," *Transactions of the RIBA*, new series, I, 1885, 29–54.

Hederer, Oswald. *Friedrich von Gärtner 1792–1847.* Munich: Prestel-Verlag, 1976.

Hegel, G. W. F. *The Philosophy of Fine Art.* 4 vols. London: George Bell & Sons, 1920.

Helas, Volker. "Einige unbekannte Zeichnungen Gottfried Sempers," *Jahrbuch des Museums für Kunst und Gewerbe Hamburg*, vol. I, 1982, 31–38.

——. *Architektur in Dresden 1800–1900.* Dresden: Verlag der Kunst Dresden, 1991.

——. *Villenarchitektur/Villa Architecture in Dresden.* Cologne: Benedikt Taschen, 1991.

Herrmann, Wolfgang. *Deutsche Baukunst des 19. und 20. Jahrhunderts.* Basel: Birkhäuser, 1977.

——. *Gottfried Semper theoretischer Nachlass an der ETH Zürich: Katalog und Kommentare.* Basel: Birkhäuser, 1981.

——. *Gottfried Semper: In Search of Architecture.* Cambridge, MA: MIT Press, 1984.

——. "Sempers Weg von der Mathematik zur vergleichenden Baulehre," in *Bildfälle: Die Moderne im Zwielicht*, ed. Beat Wyss. Zurich: Artemis, 1990.

——. *In What Style Should We Build? The German Debate on Architectural Style.* Santa Monica: The Getty Center for the History of Art and the Humanities, 1992.

Hirt, Alois. *Die Baukunst nach den Grundsätzen der Alten.* Berlin, 1809.

Hittorff, J. I. *L'Architecture antique de la Sicile, ou Recueil des plus intéressants monuments d'architecture des villes et des lieux*. Paris, 1827–30.

——. "De l'architecture polychrôme chez les Grecs," in *Annales de l'Institut de Correspondance Archéologique*. Paris, 1830.

——. *Restitution du temple D'Empédocle à Selinonte, ou Architecture polychrome chez les grecs*. Paris, 1851.

Hope, Thomas. *An Historical Essay on Architecture*. London, 1835.

Hübsch, Heinrich. *In welchem Style sollen wir bauen?* Karlsruhe: Müller'schen Hofbuchhandlung, 1828.

Humboldt, Alexander. *Cosmos: Sketch of a Physical Description of the Universe*, trans. Edward Sabine. London: Longman, Brown, Green, and Longmans, 1850.

Iversen, Margaret. *Alois Riegl: Art History and Theory*. Cambridge, MA: MIT Press, 1993.

Jäckel, Günther (ed.). *Dresden zwischen Wiener Kongress und Maiaufstand: Die Elbestadt von 1815 bis 1850*. Berlin: Verlag der Nation, 1990.

Jones, Owen. *Plans, Elevations, Sections, and Details of the Alhambra*. London, 1842.

——. "Internal Decoration of the Great Exhibition Building," *Civil Engineer and Architect's Journal* (London: R. Groombridge, 1851), vol. XIV, 32–34.

——. "An Attempt to Define the Principles which should Regulate the Employment of Colour in the Decorative Arts," in *Lectures on the Results of the Great Exhibition of 1851: Second Series*. London, 1853.

——. *Principles of Decorative Art*. London: Chapman & Hall, 1853.

——. *On the True and the False in the Decorative Arts: Lectures delivered at Marlborough House, June 1852*. London: Chapman & Hall, 1853.

——. *Description of the Egyptian Court: Erected in the Crystal Palace by Owen Jones & Joseph Bonomi*. London, 1854.

——. *The Grammar of Ornament*. London, 1856. (Plates by F. Bedford.)

Keller, Gottfried. *Gottfried Kellers Leben, Briefe und Tagebücher*. 3 vols. Stuttgart: Cotta'sche Buchhandlung, 1919.

Kellner, L. *Alexander von Humboldt*. London, 1963.

Klemm, Gustav. *Allgemeine Cultur-Geschichte der Menschheit*. Leipzig: Teubner, 1843–52.

Klenze, Leo von. *Versuch einer Wiederherstellung des toskanischen Tempels nach seinen historischen und technischen Analogien*. Munich, 1822.

——. *Der Tempel des olympischen Jupiter zu Agrigent*. Stuttgart, 1827.

——. *Anweisung zur Architektur des christlichen Cultus*. Munich: In der liter. artist. Anstalt, 1833.

Kötzsche, Dietrich. "Ein Takstock für Richard Wagner?", in *Studien zum europäischen Kunsthandwerk: Festschrift Yvonne Hackenbroch*, ed. Jörg Rasmussen. Munich, 1981.

Kugler, Franz. "Über den Kirchenbau und seine Bedeutung für unsere Zeit," *Museum: Blätter für bildende Kunst* 2, 1834.

——. "On the Polychromy of Greek Architecture," in *Transactions of the Institute of British Architects of London*, sessions 1835–56. London, 1836, vol. 1.

——. *Karl Friedrich Schinkel: Eine Charakteristik seiner künstlerischen Wirksamkeit*. Berlin: George Gropius, 1842.

——. "Antique Polychromie," *Deutsches Kunstblatt* 15, 10 April 1852, 129–39.

——. *Kleine Schriften und Studien zur Kunstgeschichte.* Stuttgart, 1853.

Lasius, Georg. "Die Sternwarte in Zürich – ein Bau Gottfried Semper's," in *Die Eisenbahn*, vol. 12, 13, 1880, 74–75.

Laudel, Heidrun, "Gottfried Semper (1803–1879) – Architekt, Theoretiker und revolutionärer Demokrat," *Wissenschaftliche Zeitschrift der Technischen Universität Dresden* 29, 1980, 569–76.

——. "Gottfried Sempers Position im Streit um den richtigen Stil," *Wissenschaftliche Zeitschrift der Technischen Universität* 34, 1985.

——. *Gottfried Semper: Architektur und Stil.* Dresden: Verlag der Kunst, 1991.

Laudel, Heidrun, and Franke Ronald (eds). *Bauen in Dresden im 19. und 20. Jahrhundert.* Dresden: Eigenverlag, 1991.

Launay, Louis de. *Les Brongniart.* Paris: G. Rapilly et Fils, 1940.

Lavin, Sylvia. *Quatremère de Quincy and the Invention of a Modern Language of Architecture.* Cambridge, MA: MIT Press, 1992.

Layard, Austen Henry. *Nineveh and its Remains: with an Account of a Visit to the Chaldaean Christians of Kurdistan, and the Yezidis, or Devil-Worshippers; and an Inquiry into the Manners and Arts of the Ancient Assyrians.* London: John Murray, 1848–49.

Leake, William Martin. *The Topography of Athens, with some Remarks on its Antiquities.* 2nd edition, London, 1841.

Leppmann, Wolfgang. *Winckelmann.* New York: Alfred A. Knopf, 1970.

Letronne, M. *Lettres d'un Antiquaire à un Artiste sur l'emploi de la Peinture Historique murale dans la décoration des Temples et des autres Edifices publics ou particuliers chez les Grecs et les Romans.* Paris, 1835.

Levine, Neil. *Architectural Reasoning in the age of Positivism: Henri Labrouste and the Néo-Grec Idea of the Bibliothèque Sainte-Geneviève.* New York: Garland, 1975.

——. "The Book and the Building: Hugo's Theory of Architecture and Labrouste's Bibliothèque Ste-Geneviève," in *The Beaux-Arts and nineteenth-century French Architecture*, ed. Robin Middleton. Cambridge, Mass: MIT Press, 1982.

Lewis, Michael J. *The Politics of the German Gothic Revival: August Reichensperger.* Cambridge, MA: MIT Press, 1993.

Lhotsky, Alphons. *Die Baugeschichte der Museen und der neuen Burg.* Vienna: Ferdinand Berger, Horn, 1941.

Lipsius, Constantin. "Über die ästhetische Behandlung des Eisen im Hochbau," *Deutsche Bauzeitung* 12, 4 September 1878, 363–66.

——. *Gottfried Semper in seiner Bedeutung als Architekt.* Berlin: Verlage der Deutschen Bauzeitung, 1880. Also published in *Deutsche Bauzeitung* 14, 1880.

——. *Festschrift zur Erinnerung and die Enthüllungsfeier des Semper-Denkmals in Dresden am 1 September 1892.* Dresden: Verlag des Gesammtausschusses für Enthüllung des Semper-Denkmals, 1892.

——. "To the Memory of Gottfried Semper," *The Inland Architect and News Record*, vol. XX, 6, 62–63.

Löffler, Fritz. *Das Alte Dresden: Geschichte seiner Bauten.* Leipzig: E. A. Seemann, 1987.

Loos, Adolf. "Das Prinzip der Bekleidung," in *Ins leere gesprochen.* Zurich: Georges Crèt, 1931 (reprint Vienna: Prachner, 1987).

Lübke, Wilhelm. "Das Neue Museum zu Dresden," *Deutsches Kunstblatt* 4, 1855, 29–32, 41–42.

Lucae, Richard. "Über die aesthetische Ausbildung der Eisen-Konstruktionen, besonders in ihrer Anwendung bei Räumen von bedeutender Spannweite," *Deutsche Bauzeitung* 4, 13 January 1870, 9–12.

Lützow, Carl von. Review of Semper's *Der Stil, Recensionen und Mittheilungen über bildende Kunst*, vol. II, 5, 85–86.

Magirius, Heinrich. *Gottfried Sempers zweites Dresdner Hoftheater: Entstehung, Künstlerische Ausstattung, Ikonographie.* Vienna: Hermann Böhlaus, 1985.

——. "Das zweite Dresdner Hoftheater Gottfried Sempers und die theatralisierung von Architektur und Bildenden Künsten des späten Historismus in Dresden," *Dresdner Hefte*, vol. 27, 9, March 1991.

——. "Die Gemäldegalerie in Dresden: Ein Bau von Gottfried Semper," in *Gemäldegalerie Dresden.* Leipzig: E. A. Seemann, 1992.

Mallgrave, H. F. "The Idea of Style: Gottfried Semper in London." Ph.D. diss., Univ. of Pennsylvania, 1983.

——. "A Commentary on Semper's November Lecture," *RES: Journal of Anthropology and Aesthetics* 6, Spring 1983, 23–31.

——. "Gustav Klemm and Gottfried Semper: The Meeting of Ethnological and Architectural Theory," *RES: Journal of Anthropology and Aesthetics* 9, Spring 1985, 68–79.

Mallgrave, H. F. (with Eleftherios Ikonomou). *Empathy, Form, and Space: Problems in German Aesthetics 1873–93.* Santa Monica: The Getty Center for the History of Art and the Humanities, 1993.

Mallgrave, H. F. (ed.). *Otto Wagner: Reflections on the Raiment of Modernity.* Santa Monica: The Getty Center for the History of Art and the Humanities, 1993.

Manteuffel, Claus Zoege von. "Die Baukunst Gottfried Sempers (1803–79)." Ph.D. diss., Univ. of Freiburg, 1952.

Marx, Karl, and Friedrich Engels. *Briefwechsel.* Berlin, 1949.

Mead, Christopher Curtis. *Charles Garnier's Paris Opera: Architectural Empathy and the Renaissance of French Classicism.* Cambridge, MA: MIT Press, 1991.

Meffert, Ekkehard. *Carl Gustav Carus: Sein Leben – seine Anschauung von der Erde.* Stuttgart: Freies Geistesleben, 1986.

Middleton, Robin (ed.). *The Beaux-Arts and Nineteenth-century French Architecture*, Cambridge, MA: MIT Press, 1982.

Middleton, Robin, and David Watkin. *Neoclassical and 19th Century Architecture.* New York: Harry N. Abrams, 1980.

Middleton, Robin. "The Rationalist Interpretations of Leonce Reynaud and Viollet-de-Duc," *AA Files*, II, Spring 1986.

Milde, Kurt. *Neorenaissance in der deutschen Architektur des 19. Jahrhunderts: Grundlagen, Wesen und Gültigkeit.* Dresden: Verlag der Kunst Dresden, 1981.

Minikan, Janet. *The Nationalization of Culture: The Development of State Subsidies to the Arts in Great Britain.* London: Hamish Hamilton, 1977.

Moleschott, Jacob. *Physiologie des Stoffwechsels in Pflanzen und Thieren.* Erlangen: Ferdinand Enke, 1851.

Moller, Georg. *Das neue Schauspielhaus zu Mainz.* Darmstadt, Carl Wilhelm Leeke, n.d.

Moravánszky, Ákos. *Die Architektur der Donaumonarchie 1867–1918.* Berlin: Ernst & Sohn, 1988; Orig. Corvina Kiadó, 1988.

Müller, C. O. Review of *Vorläufige Bemerkungen über bemalte Architectur und Plastik bei den Alten*, in *Göttingische gelehrte Anzeigen* 2, 1834, 1389–94.

——. *Handbuch der Archäologie der Kunst.* 2nd edition, Breslau: Josef Max, 1835.

Musée Carnavalet. *Hittorff: un Architecte du XIX*[ème]. Alençon: Alençonnaise, 1986.

Muthesius, Hermann. *Stilarchitektur und Baukunst: Wandlungen der Architektur im XIX. Jahrhundert und ihr heutiger Standpunkt.* Mülheim-Ruhr: Schimmelpfeng, 1902.

Mütterlein, Max Georg. *Gottfried Semper und dessen Monumentalbauten am Dresdner Theaterplatz.* Dresden: Wilhelm u. Bertha v. Baensch Stiftung, 1913.

Newman Ernest. *The Life of Richard Wagner.* 4 vols. Cambridge: Cambridge Univ. Press, 1968.

Nietzsche, Friedrich. *Nietzsche Briefwechsel: Kritische Gesamtausgabe*, ed. Giorgio Colli and Mazzino Montinari. Berlin: Walter de Gruyter, 1977.

——. *Friedrich Nietzsche: Sämtliche Werke: Kritische Studienausgabe in 15 Einzelbänden*, ed. Giorgio Colli und Mazzino Montinari. Berlin: Walter de Gruyter, 1988.

——. *The Birth of Tragedy* (1872), trans. Walter Kaufmann. New York: Vintage, 1967.

Noach, Friedrich. *Deutsches Leben in Rom 1700–1900.* Stuttgart, 1907.

Oechslin, Werner. "Die Vase als ästhetisches Ideal," *Neue Züricher Zeitung* 223, 25/26 September 1982.

Olin, Margaret. *Forms of Representation in Alois Riegl's Theory of Art.* University Park: Penn State Univ. Press, 1992.

——. "Alois Riegl: The Late Roman Empire in the Late Habsburg Empire," in *The Habsburg Legacy: National Identity in Historical Perspective*, ed. Ritchie Robertson and Edward Timms. Edinburgh: Edinburgh Univ. Press, 1992.

Pallottino, Massimo. *The Etruscans.* Harmondsworth: Penguin, 1978.

Pecht, Friedrich. "Gottfried Semper," in *Deutsche Künstler des neunzehnten Jahrhunderts: Studien und Erinnerungen.* Nördlingen: C. H. Beck'ischen Buchhandlung, 1877.

Percier, C., and P. Fontaine. *Palais, maisons, et autres édifices modernes, dessinés à Rome.* Paris: Chez les auteurs, 1798.

Peschken, Goerd. *Das Architektonische Lehrbuch.* Munich: Deutscher Kunstverlag, 1979.

Pevsner, Nikolaus. *Some Architectural Writers of the Nineteenth Century.* Oxford: Clarendon Press, 1972.

——. *A History of Building Types.* Princeton: Princeton Univ. Press, 1976.

Plagemann, Volker. *Das deutsche Kunstmuseum 1790–1870.* Munich: Prestel, 1967.

Podro, Michael. *The Critical Historians of Art.* New Haven: Yale Univ. Press, 1982.

Prichard, James. *The Natural History of Man; comprising Inquiries into the modifying influence of Physical and Moral Agencies on the different Tribes of the Human Family.* London, 1855.

Prinzhorn, Hans. *Gottfried Sempers aesthetische Grundanschauungen.* Stuttgart: Union Deutsche Verlagsgesellschaft, 1909.

Quast, Alexander Ferdinand von. "Entgegnung," *Deutsches Kunstblatt*, 11, 13 March 1852, 97–98.

Quatremère de Quincy, A. C. *De l'architecture égyptienne, considérée dans son origine ses principes et son goût, et comparée sous les mêmes rapports à l'architecture grecque.* Paris: Barrois l'aîné et Fils, 1803.

——. *Le Jupiter olympien, ou l'art de la sculpture antique considéré sous un nouveau point de vue.* Paris, 1815.

Quitzsch, Heinz. *Die ästhetischen Anschauungen Gottfried Sempers.* Berlin: Akademie Verlag, 1962.

Raoul-Rochette, Désiré. Review of Semper's *Vorläufige Bemerkungen über bemalte Architectur und Plastik bei den Alten*, *Journal des Savants*, November 1836, 668–84.

Rave, Paul Ortwin. *Karl Friedrich Schinkel*, ed. Eva Börsch-Supan. Munich: Deutscher Kunstverlag, 1981.

Redgrave, F. M. *Richard Redgrave: A Memoir compiled from his Diary*. London, 1891.

Redgrave, Richard. "Supplementary Report on Design," in *Reports by the Juries*. London: William Clowes & Sons, 1852.

——. "An Introductory Address on the Methods Adopted by the Department of Practical Art," in *Addresses of the Superintendents of the Department of Practical Art*. London: Chapman & Hall, 1853.

——. *An Elementary Manual of Colour*. London: Chapman & Hall, 1859.

——. *Manual of Design: Compiled from the Writings and Addresses of Richard Redgrave*. London, 1876.

Redtenbacher, Rudolf. *Tectonik, Principien der künstlerischen Gestaltung der Gefüge und Gebilde von Menschenhand, welche den Gebieten er Architektur, der Ingenieurfächer und der Kunstindustrie angehören*. Vienna, 1881.

——. *Die Architektonik der modernen Baukunst*. Berlin, 1883.

Reidelbach, Hans. *König Ludwig I. von Bayern und seine Kunstschöpfungen*. Munich: Jos. Roth, 1988.

Richards, Charles R. *Industrial Art and the Museum*. New York: Macmillan, 1927.

Richter, H. A. "Gottfried Semper und das Dresdener Materni-Hospital," *Deutsche Bauzeitung* 22, 1888.

Riegl, Alois. *Altorientalische Teppiche*. Leipzig: T. O. Weigel Nachfolger, 1891.

——. *Stilfragen: Grundlegungen zu einer Geschichte der Ornamentik*. Berlin: Georg Siemens, 1893.

——. *Spätrömische Kunstindustrie*. 2nd edition, Darmstadt: Wissenschaftliche Bachgesellschaft, 1927 (reprint, 1987 (orig. 1901)).

——. *Problems of Style: Foundations for a History of Ornament*, trans. Evelyn Kain. Princeton: Princeton Univ. Press, 1992.

Robertson, Priscilla. *Revolutions of 1848: A Social History*. Princeton: Princeton Univ. Press, 1971.

Robinson, Michael. *The Birth of the Modern: World Society 1815–30*. New York: Harper Collins, 1991.

Röckel, August. *Aus dem Grabe eines 48er Revolutionärs*. Leipzig: Gustav Gohike, 1912.

Root, John. "Development of Architectural Style" (translation of Semper's *Ueber Baustyle*), *Inland Architect & News Record*, December 1889, 76–78; January 1890, 92–94; February 1890, 5–6; March 1890, 32–33.

Royal Institute of British Architects. "Report of the Committee Appointed to Examine the Elgin Marbles, in order to Ascertain Whether any Evidence Remains as to the Employment of Color in the Decoration of the Architecture or Sculpture," in *Transactions of the Royal Institute of British Architects of London*. vol. I, part II. London: Longman, Brown, Green, and Longmans, 1842.

Rumohr, Carl F. *Italienische Forschungen*. 3 vols. Berlin, 1827–31.

Sayn-Wittgenstein, Carolyne. *Aus der Glanzzeit der Wiemarer Altenburg*. Leipzig, 1906.

Schaumann, C. "Die drei gekrönten Pläne zur Nikolaikirche in Hamburg," *Allgemeine Bauzeitung* 13, 1848, 20–29.

Schelling, F. W. "Über das Verhaltniss der bildenden Künste zu der Natur," in *Sämmtliche Werke*. Stuttgart: Cotta, 1860.

Schiller, Friedrich. *On the Aesthetic Education of Man*, trans. Reginald Snell. New York: Frederick Ungar, 1977.

Schinkel, Karl Friedrich. *Aus Schinkel's Nachlass*. Berlin: Könlichen Geheimen Ober-Hofbuchdruckerei, 1862 (reprint Mittenwald: Mäander, 1981).

——. *Karl Friedrich Schinkel, 1781–1841*. Exhibition catalogue. Berlin: Verlag das europäische Buch, 1981.

——. *Karl Friedrich Schinkel: Briefe, Tagebücher, Gedanken*, ed. Hans Mackowsky. Berlin: Propyläen, 1921 (reprint Frankfurt: Ullstein, 1981).

——. *Sammlung architektonischer Entwurfe*. Berlin: Ernst & Korn, 1866; New York: Princeton Architectural Press, 1989.

Schmarsow, August. *Das Wesen der architektonischen Schöpfung*. Leipzig: Karl W. Hiersemann, 1894.

Schmidt, Eva. "Ernst Rietschel – Ein bildhauer des 19. Jahrhunderts," *Bildende Kunst*, vol. 4, 1954, 19–24.

Schmitz, Hermann. "Hauptströmungen der deutschen Architektur während der letzten sechzig Jahre," *Deutsche Bauzeitung*, January 1926, 3–16.

Schnaase, Carl. *Geschichte der bildenden Künste bei den Alten*. 2 vols. Dusseldorf: Julius Buddeus, 1843.

Schneider, Donald David. *The Works and Doctrines of Jacques Ignace Hittorff (1792–1867): Structural Innovation and Formal Expression in French Architecture, 1810–67*. 2 vols. New York: Garland, 1977.

Schumacher, Fritz. *Wie das Kunstwerk Hamburg nach dem grossen Brande entstand: Ein Beitrage zur Geschichte des Städtebaus*. Hamburg: Hans Christians, 1969.

Semper, Hans. *Gottfried Semper: Ein Bild seines Lebens und Wirkens*. Berlin: S. Calvary, 1880.

Semper, Manfred. *Hasenauer und Semper: Eine Erwiderung und Richtigstellung*. Hamburg: Boysen & Maasch, 1895.

——. *Das Münchener Festspielhaus: Gottfried Semper und Richard Wagner*. Hamburg: Conrad H. U. Klotz, 1906.

Sheehan, James J. *German History: 1770–1866*. Oxford: Clarendon Press, 1989.

Sisa, József. "Gottfried Semper és Magyarország," *Művészettörténeti Értesítő*, vol. I, 2, 1–10.

Spotts, Frederic. *Bayreuth: A History of the Wagner Festival*. New Haven: Yale Univ. Press, 1994.

Staatliche Kunstsammlungen Dresden. *Gottfried Semper 1803–1879: Baumeister zwischen Revolution und Historismus*. Dresden: Staatliche Kunstsammlungen Dresden, 1979; Munich: Georg D. W. Callwey, 1980.

Stackelberg, Baron O. M. von. *De Apollotempel zu Bassae in Arcadien und die Daselbst ausgegrabenen Bildwerke*. Rome, 1826.

Stieglitz, C. L. *Archäologie der Baukunst der Griechen und Römer*. Weimar, 1801.

Stier, Hubert. *Vergleichende zusammenstellung der Grundrisse der wichtigsten Entwürfe für die Dombau-Konkurrenz in Berlin*. Berlin: Deutschen Bauzeitung, 1869.

Stock, Friedrich. "Briefe Rumohrs an Otfried Müller und andere Freunde," in *Jahrbuch der Preussischen Kunstsammlungen* 54. Berlin: Jahrbuch der Preussischen Kunstsammlungen, 1933.

Stockmeyer, Ernst. *Gottfried Sempers Kunsttheorie*. Zurich: Rascher, 1939.

Streiter, Richard. *Karl Böttichers Tektonik der Hellen als ästhetische und kunstgeschichtliche Theorie: Eine Kritik*. Hamburg: Leopold Voss, 1896.

Stuart, James, and Nicholas Revett. *The Antiquities of Athens*. 2nd edition, London, 1825–30.

Switzerland, Department of Interior. *Das neue Schweizerische Bundeshaus*. Bern: Büchler & Co., 1902.

Taylor, A. J. P. *The Course of German History*. New York: Paragon, 1979.

Technische Universität Dresden. *Gottfried Semper 1803–1879: Sein Wirken als Architekt, Theoretiker und revolutionärer Demokrat und die schöpferische Aneignung seines progressiven Erbes*. Dresden: Technische Universität, 1979.

Tieck, Ludwig. *Letters of Ludwig Tieck: Hitherto Unpublished, 1792–1853*, ed. Zeydel, Matenko, and Fife. New York: Oxford Univ. Press, 1937.

Van Zanten, David. *The Architectural Polychromy of the 1830s*. New York: Garland, 1977.

——. *Designing Paris: The Architecture of Duban, Labrouste, Duc, and Vaudoyer*. Cambridge, MA: MIT Press, 1987.

Venturi, Lionello. *History of Art Criticism*, trans. Charles Marriott. New York: E. P. Dutton & Co., 1936.

Viollet-le-Duc, Eugène-Emmanuel. *Lectures on Architecture*, trans. Benjamin Bucknall. New York: Dover, 1987 (orig. Eng. trans. 1877).

Vischer, F. T. *Aesthetik oder Wissenschaft des Schönen*, ed. Robert Vischer. 2nd edition, Munich: Meyer & Jessen, 1922–23.

——. *Kritische Gänge*, ed. Robert Vischer. 2nd edition, Munich: Meyer & Jessen, 1922.

Vogt, Adolf Max, Christina Reble, and Martin Fröhlich (eds). *Gottfried Semper und die Mitte des 19. Jahrhunderts*. Basel: Birkhäuser, 1976.

Volkelt, Johannes. *Der Symbol-Begriff in der neuesten Aesthetik*. Jena: Hermann Dufft, 1876.

Waetzoldt, W. *Deutsche Kunsthistoriker*. Berlin, 1921.

Wagner, Cosima. *Cosima Wagner's Diaries, 1869–77*. New York: Harcourt Brace Javonovich, 1978.

Wagner, Otto. *Moderne Architektur*. Vienna: Anton Schroll, 1896.

Wagner, Richard. *Mein Leben*. 2 vols. Munich: F. Bruckmann, 1911.

——. *My Life*. New York: Dodd, Mead & Co., 1939.

——. *The Diary of Richard Wagner: The Brown Book 1865–82*, ed. Joachim Bergfeld, trans. George Bird. Cambridge: Cambridge Univ. Press, 1980.

——. *Richard Wagner: Gesammelte Schriften und Dichtungen*, ed. Wolfgang Golther. Berlin: Bong & Co., n.d.

Waldersee, Graf Friedrich von. *Der Kampf in Dresden: Mit besonderer Rücksicht auf die Mitwirkung der Preussischen Truppen*. Berlin: E. S. Mittler & Sohn, 1849.

Wallot, Paul. *Das Reichstagsgebäude in Berlin*. Leipzig: Cosmos, n.d.

Watkin, David, and Mellinghoff, Tilman. *German Architecture and the Classical Ideal*. Cambridge, MA: MIT Press, 1987.

Watson, Derek. *Richard Wagner: A Biography*. New York: Schirmer Books, 1979.

Weber, Rolf. *Die Revolution in Sachsen 1848/49*. Berlin: Akademie Verlag, 1970.

Wegmann, Peter. *Gottfried Semper und das Stadthaus: Sempers Architektur im Spiegel seiner Kunsttheorie*. Winterthur: Stadtbibliothek Winterthur, 1985.

Whewell, W. "On the General Bearing of the Great Exhibition," in *Lectures on the Progress of Arts and Science*. New York, 1856.

Wibiral, Norbert, and Mikula, Renata. *Heinrich von Ferstel*. Wiesbaden: Franz Steiner, 1974.

Wiese, Benno von. *Deutsche Dichter der Romantik: Ihr Leben und Werk*. Berlin: Erich Schmidt, 1983.

Wigley, Mark. "Untitled: The Housing of Gender," in *Sexuality & Space*. New York: Princeton Architectural Press, 1992.

——. "White-Out: Fashioning the Modern [Part 2]," *Assemblage: A Critical Journal of Architecture and Design Culture* 22, December 1993, 6–49.

Wilkins, William. *Atheniensia; or Remarks on the Topography and Buildings of Athens*. London, 1816.

Winckelmann, J. J. *Geschichte der Kunst des Alterthums*. Dresden: Waltherischen Hof-Buchhandlung, 1764.

Wittich, Dieter (ed.). *Vogt, Moleschott, Bücher: Schriften zum kleinbürgerlichen Materialismus in Deutschland*. Berlin: Akademie Verlag, 1971.

Wölfflin, Heinrich. *Prolegomena zu einer Psychologie der Architektur*. Inaugural-Dissertation der hohen philosophischen Fakultät der Universität München. Munich: Kgl. Hof- & Universitäts-Buchdruckerei, 1886.

——. *Renaissance and Baroque*, trans. Kathrin Simon. Ithaca: Cornell, 1963 (orig. 1888).

Wornum, Ralph. "The Exhibition as a Lesson in Taste," in *The Crystal Palace Exhibition Illustrated Catalogue*. London, 1851 (reprint New York, 1970).

Wyatt, Matthew Digby. *Specimens of Geometrical Mosaic of the Middle Ages*. London, 1848.

——. "Mediaeval Polychromatic Decoration of Italy," in *Civil Engineer and Architect's Journal*, vol. XIV. London: R. Groombridge, 1851.

——. *The Industrial Arts of the Nineteenth Century: A Series of Illustrations of the Choicest Specimens Produced by Every Nation at the Great Exhibition of Works of Industry, 1851*. London, 1851.

——. "Observations on Polychromatic Decoration in Italy from the 12th to the 16th Century," *The Civil Engineer and Architect's Journal*, vol. XIV. London, 1851.

——. *Metal-Work and its Artistic Design*. London: Day & Son, 1852.

——. "An Attempt to define the Principles which determine Form in the Decorative Arts," in *Lectures on the Results of the Great Exhibition of 1851: Second Series*. London, 1853.

——. *The Byzantine and Romanesque Court in the Crystal Palace*. London, 1854.

——. "On the Principles of Design applicable to Textile Art," in J. B. Waring, *The Art Treasures of the United Kingdom*. London, 1858.

——. *Fine Art: A Sketch of its History, Theory, Practice, and Application to Industry*. London, 1870. (Lectures delivered at Cambridge 1870.)

x.y.z. "Gottfried Semper: Als Mensch und Künstler," *Neues Wiener Tagblatt* 221, 12 August, 1879.

Young, Julian. *Nietzsche's Philosophy of Art*. New York: Cambridge Univ. Press, 1992.

Zaddach, Carl. *Lothar Bucher bis zum Ende seines Londoner Exils (1817–61)*. Heidelberg: Carl Winters Universitätsbuchhandlung, 1915.

Zeising, Adolf. *Aesthetische Forschungen*. Frankfurt: Meidinger, 1855.

Zevi, Bruno. *Architecture as Space*, trans. Milton Gendel. New York: Horizon, 1957.

Ziegler, Jules. *Etudes céramiques: recherche des principes de beau dans l'architecture, l'art céramique et la forme en Général*. Paris: Mathias, 1850.

Zukowsky, John (ed.). *Karl Friedrich Schinkel: The Drama of Architecture*. Wasmuth: The Art Institute of Chicago, 1994.

Index

Abendroth, Dr. 311
Adler, Denkmar 365
Adler, Friedrich 313
Aegina: Temple of Aphaia 33, 34, 45
Aeschylus 60, 121, 125, 296, 301, 347, 350
Affoltern am Albis: church tower 245
Alavoine, Jean-Antoine 26
Albert, Prince Consort 193, 194, 195, 196, 209, 215, 226, 312
Alberti, Leon Battista 120
Alexander the Great 116, 289, 330
Algarotti, Francesco 69
Ali, Muhammad 43
Altona: Donner Pavilion 62–63, 64, 94, 130; railway station 311
Angell, Samuel 35, 41
Anton, King of Saxony 67–68, 75, 76, 94
Antwerp: Cathedral 21; theater 118
Apollo 6, 86, 90, 116, 336, 346, 347
Ariadne 139, 264, 336, 346, 347
Aristophanes 125, 301, 350
Aristotle 157, 331
Assyrian excavations 162–63
Astor, John Jacob 173
Athene, Pallas 31, 238, 251, 270, 287, 327, 331
Athens: Choragic Monument of Lysicrates 45, 54; Erechtheum 45, 54, 182; Parthenon 31, 34, 35, 45, 48, 50, 54, 59, 60, 62, 155, 182, 182, 183, 301; Propylaea 31, 45, 34, 48; statue of Athena 31; Temple on the Ilussus 30; Temple of Theseus 30, 31, 34, 45, 50, 54, 183; Tower of Winds 45
Auer, Hans 290, 360, 361, 370
Augustus, Emperor of Rome 330
Augustus III 67–68, 69
Augustus the Strong 67–68, 69

Bad Ragas: hotel project 240
Baden: Casino 240
Bähr, Georg 68, 95
Ballu, Théordore 26
Bareiss, Wilhelm 246
Barrault, Emile 56
Barry, Charles 34
Barthélemy, Jean-Jacques 42
Basile, Giovanni Battista Filippo 313
Bassae: Temple at 34
Bauer, Caroline 72, 78
Baumann, Frederick 365
Baumann, Ludwig 332
Baumgartner, Anton 333
Bayreuth: Festival theater 262, 265–67, 339
Bautzen: military barracks 105
Bayer, Josef 112, 355, 362–63, 369
Beethoven 61, 171, 330
Behne, Adolf 371
Behrens, Peter 371, 381
Bélanger, François-Joseph 35
Bell, Quentin 194
Bendemann, Eduard Friedrich 71, 77, 107
Benjamin, Walter 7
Bergdoll, Barry 56, 89
Berlage, Hendrik P. 229, 290, 370
Berlin: Altes Museum 6, 87–89, 91, 92, 117, 132, 238, 313, 348; Bauakademie 89–91, 92; Cathedral 87, 313; Neue Wache 86; Neues Museum 105, 107, 117; Residence for Count Redern 120; Royal Palace 313; Schauspielhaus 86, 122–23
Berlioz, Hector 72
Bern: Swiss Parliament 361
Berry, J. Duncan 359, 360, 361
Bibiena, Guiseppe Galli 97
Bismarck, Otto von 82, 192, 267, 310, 311, 313, 323
Blanc, Charles 174
Blanc, Louis 165
Blanqui, Auguste 165
Blouet, Abel 27, 50
Blum, Robert 166
Bluntschli, Alfred Friedrich 359
Boisserée, Sulpiz 144, 145, 147, 148
Bonaparte, Jérôme 83
Bonaparte, Lucien, King of Etruria 50
Bonaparte, Napoleon, Emperor of France 11, 14, 50, 68, 86, 97, 323
Bopp, Franz 160, 292
Boston: Trinity Church 140
Botta Paul Emile 161–62, 163, 164, 177, 187, 298
Böttger, Johann Friedrich 69
Böttger, Karl 357
Bötticher, Karl 4, 219–22, 224, 225, 271, 287, 289, 297, 299, 306, 364, 367
Böttiger, Carl August 30, 34, 44, 92
Bourla, Pierre Bruno 118

Boyington, W.W. 365
Brahms, Johannes 362
Bramante 3, 84, 120, 245, 340
Brandt, Carl 266
Braun, Emil 176, 189–90, 192, 210
Brentano, Franz 371
Brongniart, Alexandre 217, 279–81, 282
Brongniart, Théodore 27
Brønsted, Peter Oluf 31, 34, 36, 61
Brown, G. Baldwin 364
Bruckmann, Friedrich 268, 302, 306, 353
Brückwald, Otto 266
Brühl, Karl Graf von 97, 98
Brunelleschi, Filippo 140, 312
Brunnen: villa project 241
Brunswick: Brunswick Castle 244; railway station 244
Brussels: theater 251
Bucher, Lothar 192, 213, 290
Bularchus 331
Bülau, Theodor 17, 137, 139, 145, 146, 147, 148, 149, 210
Bülow, Cosima von 257, 258, 259, 337–38, 348–49
Bülow, Hans von 257, 259
Bundsen, Axel 22, 130
Bunsen, Christian 50, 147
Burckhardt, Jakob 151, 230, 231, 270, 312, 357, 362, 367
Bürcklein, Friedrich 263
Burmester, Heinrich Wilhelm 139, 140, 147, 148
Butterfield, William 188
Byron, Lord 42

Caesar 12
Canachus 331
Canova, Antonio 327, 332
Capodistrias, Agostino 43–45
Capodistrias, John 43–44, 52
Castasegna: Villa Garbald 241
Cartensen, Georg 176
Carus, Charlotte 71, 159
Carus, Carl Gustav 70–71, 159, 163
Caserta: Royal Palace 329
Catel, Ludwig 118
Cattini, Arnold 338
Caylus, Comte de 34
Cendrier, Alexis 56
Chadwick, Edwin 190, 193, 197, 200, 209
Charles X, King of France 23–24, 35
Châteauneuf, Alexis de 130, 136, 139, 148
Chevreul, Michel 183, 203
Chiaveri, Gaëtano 68, 340
Cicero 12
Cockerell, C.R. 31, 33, 34, 182, 213
Codrington, Admiral 43
Coe, Henry Edward 145
Cole, Henry 173, 193–97, 207–13, 214, 217, 226, 232–33, 290, 291, 310, 312, 373
Cologne: Cathedral 143, 146, 148
Constantinople: Hagia Sophia 152
Conte, Edouard 121
Conze, Alexander 372–373, 377, 378
Cook, James 161
Coquirole, Dr. 26
Cornelius, Peter von 50, 89, 116
Corneto: Painted tombs 31, 50, 183
Correggio, Antonio Allegri 69
Coste, P. 177
Cotta, J.F. 52
Coudray, Clemens Wenzeslaus 118, 356
Curtius, Ernst 371
Cuvier, Georges 157–59, 159, 160, 161, 163, 179, 279, 332

Dahl, Johann Christian 70
Dante 116
Darmstadt: theater 333
Darwin, Charles 157, 160, 276, 278, 305, 364, 375, 376, 377
Davout, Louis Nicolas 12
Davy, Humphry 61
Debret, François 18, 120
Demmler, Georg Adolf 105
Democritus 296
Derby, Lord 193, 312
Despléchin, Edouard 100, 124, 171, 174
Devéria, Achille 21
Devéria, Eugène 21
Devrient, Gustav Emil 70
Devrient, Karl August 70
Devrient, Phillip Eduard 70, 76
Dickens, Charles 213
Diefenbach, L. 292
Dieterle, Jules 100, 124, 174, 175, 215, 279
Dilthey, Wilhelm 152, 367
Diodorus Siculus 163
Dionysian over Apollonian 6, 121, 346–51
Dionysus 6, 121, 264, 336, 346, 348, 350–51
Döbner, August Wilhelm 17, 19
Dodwell, Edward 31
Dom Pedro II, Emperor of Brazil 252
Donaldson, T.L. 34, 100, 164, 182, 183, 184, 182, 183, 184, 213
Donner, C.H. 62–63, 130
Dresden: Academy of Fine Arts 359–60; Antonplatz 80, 81; Art Gallery 6, 76, 78, 107–17, 121, 126, 225, 230, 233, 237, 250, 309, 311, 321, 326, 358; Comedy House 97, 99; cholera memorial 105, 107; Dresden Forum 96–99, 107–11, 357; Dresden Landhaus 80; Elimayer Shop 105; festival designs for King Anton 75–76, 94; Frauenkirche 68; guardhouse 81, 109, 340; Hofkirche 68, 96, 340; Hoftheater (1st) 9, 76–77, 96–100, 106, 117–29, 210, 309, 320–21, 341, 356, 358; Hoftheater (2nd) 6, 321-22, 336, 339–52, 353, 358, 371; Houpe residence 105; Japanese Palace, Antiquity Rooms 92–94; Leipziger Tor 80; Lüttichau Villa 82; maternity hospital 92, 94–95; old Opera 97,

170; Oppenheim Palais 103–05, 112; orangerie 96, 98, 110, 120; pedestal for statue of Friedrich August I 76, 92, 95; provisional triumphal arch 105; Seebach villa 103, 358; Stallgebäude 107; synagogue 100, 107, 349, 358; Third Belvedere 80; Villa Häbler 358; Villa Hartmann 358; Villa Laubegaster 358; Villa Opitz 358; Villa Pilz 358; Villa Rosa 100–03, 358; Zwinger 68, 96–99, 108–12, 117, 118, 170, 321, 340, 372
Duban, Félix 27, 82, 100, 120, 236, 357, 360
Duc, Joseph-Louis 26, 304
Düfflipp, Lorenz von 259, 260
Dumas, Alexandre 21
Durand, Jean-Nicolas-Louis 25, 55, 83, 118, 179
Dürer, Albrecht 116
Dusquesney, François 242
Dvorák, Max 372
Dyce, William 194, 210

Eastlake, Charles 34
Eberhard, Karl 358
Eggert, Klaus 329
Eiffel, Gustave 4
Eitelberger, Rudolf von 310, 315, 361, 372, 373
Elgin, Lord 31
Elmes, Harvey Lonsdale 213
Empathy, theory of 367
Enfantin, Père 56
Engels, Friedrich 165, 192
Epidaurus 45
Ettlinger, Leopold 208, 356
Euripides 60, 121, 125, 301, 350

Fabris, Emilio de 312
Falkener, Edward 189, 190
Faraday, Michael 182, 184
Ferstel, Heinrich von 314–16, 361–62
Fichte, J.G. 82
Fiedler, Conrad 289, 368, 370, 379
Field, George 183
Fischer, Karl 82, 83
Fischer von Erlach 368
Flandin, M.E. 177
Florence: Santa Maria del Fiori 140, 312, 314; Palazzo Pandolfini 105, 112
Forsmann, Franz 131, 132, 146
Forster, Kurt W. 89
Förster, Ludwig 110, 357
Fox Henderson and Co. 196
Fowke, Captain Francis 226, 312
Franck, Bernd 140, 148
Frankfurt: Exchange 106
Franz Josef, Emperor of Austria-Hungary 311, 314, 315, 317, 318, 320, 322, 323, 324, 329, 332, 334
Friedrich August I, King of Saxony 76, 92, 95
Friedrich August II, King of Saxony 68, 95, 98, 107–08, 110, 167, 172, 173, 311
Friedrich, Caspar David 70, 71
Friedrich Franz II, Grand Duke of Mecklenburg 105
Friedrich Wilhelm IV, King of Prussia 1, 50, 97, 143, 166
Fritsch, K. E. O. 339

Garnier, Charles 7, 121, 304, 343
Garnier, Tony 4
Gärtner, Friedrich von 16, 17, 27, 52, 71, 83, 85, 103, 130
Gau, Franz Christian 18–19, 21, 25–27, 28, 29, 35, 36, 38, 47–48, 50, 52, 53, 54, 57, 61, 63, 64, 73, 75, 79, 83, 103, 155, 164, 172, 174, 190, 298
Gauss, Carl Friedrich 12, 13, 14
Gautier, Pierre 126, 155
Gell, William 42
Gensler, Martin 137
Gentz, Heinrich 82, 86
Geraniotis, Roula 365
Gérard, François 36
Gesamtkunstwerk 8, 59–60, 125–29, 184–85, 264–65, 274, 351–52, 363
Geutebrück, Albert 101
Geyer, Ludwig 71
Ghiberti, Lorenzo 152
Giedion, Sigfried 3, 288
Gildemeister, Charles 176
Gilly, David 82, 86, 156
Gilly, Friedrich 82, 86, 118, 122
Giotto 116
Girard & Rehlender 326
Giska, Karl 323
Glarus: Town Hall 240
Glöckner, Ottomar 67
Goethe, Johann Wolfgang von 53, 69, 70, 71 82, 116, 117, 118, 121, 122, 124, 144, 158–59, 272, 274, 322, 347, 350, 363, 377
Göller, Adolf 379, 380
Goury, Jules 40–42, 45–46, 54, 183, 195
Grahl, August 101
Granada: Alhambra 183, 195
Great Exhibition of 1851 192–209
Gregorovius, Ferdinand 353
Grey, Charles 312
Grimm, Hermann 305
Grimm, Jakob 292
Grimm, Wilhelm 292
Gropius, Walter 355, 371
Guizot, François 23, 24, 165
Gurlitt, Cornelius 321, 339–40

Haenel, Karl Moritz 322
Haerdtl, Dr. 337
Hahn-Hahn, Ida 72, 78
Hähnel, Ernst Julius 71, 76, 77, 78, 121, 311, 321, 332
Haller von Hallerstein, Carl 31, 33, 34
Hamburg: City Hall 106, 136–37; Exchange 21–23, 129–33, 134, 136; Kunsthalle 311; Nikolaikirche 133, 134, 137–49, 156, 274, 357;

rebuilding plan (Lindley Plan) 133–37; Wilhelm Semper Pharmacy 134, 137, 139
Hansen, Theophil von 314–18, 333, 336, 358, 361
Harris, William 35, 41
Harvey, Lawrence 365
Hasenauer, Carl von 314–20, 322–26, 329, 332–39, 354, 358, 361, 368
Heeren, Arnold H.L. 13, 155
Heeren, Friedrich 12–13, 18, 130
Hegel, G. W. F. 152, 271, 272, 274, 285, 366, 380
Heidecker, General 47
Heine, Heinrich 44
Heine, Wilhelm 173, 176
Herbart, Friedrich 271, 367
Herbert, J.R. 194
Herodotus 163, 183, 184, 189
Herrmann, Wolfgang 57, 139, 155, 190, 217, 268, 273, 306, 356
Herrmann, Woldemar 97, 103, 357
Herwegh, Georg 231–32
Hesiod 58, 116
Hessemer, Friedrich 63
Hettner, Hermann 231
Heuchler, Eduard 287
Heuser, Georg 364
Hildebrand, Adolf 379, 380
Hiller, Ferdinand 72, 77
Hipp, Karl Heinrich 12, 13–14, 15–16
Hirt, Alois 30, 34, 85, 306
Hittorff, Jacques Ignace 18, 35–38, 48, 58, 61, 62, 103, 155, 182, 183, 190, 242, 359
Höber, Fritz 371
Höfer, Karl Gustav Albert 292
Hohenlohe, Prince 320, 322, 323
Holbein, Hans 116
Holmes, W.D. 136
Homer 58, 116, 121, 128, 237
Hope, Thomas 185
Hörnig, Gustav 101
Horsley, John 193, 194
Hübbe, Heinrich 134, 139
Hübner, Julius 71, 77, 78, 124
Hübner (Max) and Baron (Rudolf) 358
Hübsch, Heinrich 83, 85, 307, 357
Hude, Hermann von der 311
Hudson, Octavius 216, 290, 291
Hugo, Victor 21
Humboldt, Alexander von 15, 71, 157, 158, 161, 179, 332
Humboldt, Caroline von 94
Humboldt, Wilhelm von 44, 94, 158, 292
Huvé, Jean-Jacques-Marie 27
Huyot, Jean-Nicolas 25, 58

Iktinos 34, 90
Ingres, Jean-Auguste-Dominique 281
Iverson, Margaret 376

Jenkins, William 34
Jochmus, General 174
Johann, Prince of Saxony (later King) 97, 321, 322
Jones, Owen 183, 191, 194, 195, 196, 203, 204, 205, 206, 209, 210, 212, 213, 216, 217, 373

Kant, Immanuel 82, 211
Kapp, Ernst 364
Karl August, Grand Duke of Saxe-Weimar 118
Karlsruhe: Finance Ministry 85; Technische Hochschule 85
Kauffmann, Johann Christian 130
Kekulé, Reinhard 377–78
Keller, Ferdinand 347
Keller, Gottfried 231, 232, 270, 320
Kellermann, Olaf 51
Ker Porter 161, 163
Kerr, Robert 200
Kestner, August 50
Kinnaird, William 34, 36
Klemm, Gustav 161, 163, 186
Klenze, Leo von 27, 33–34, 36, 39, 44, 52, 57, 83–85, 103, 107, 120, 357
Klimpt brothers 332
Klingenberg, E. 313
Knöffel, Johann Christoph 107
Kobuch, Manfred 63
Köchly, Professor 232
Koes, Georg 34
Kolettis, John 43, 45
Kolokotronis, Theodor 43
Krause, Friedrich 175
Krubsacius, Friedrich August 80
Kruger, Bernhard 173
Kugler, Franz 53, 62, 85, 89, 120, 184, 189, 303, 306, 357

Labrouste, Henri 3, 27, 28, 120, 287, 357
Lamarck, Jean Baptiste 157, 377
Lange, Ludwig 148
Langhans, Carl Gotthard 82, 122
La Pérose, Jean-Francois de 161
Laplace, Pierre Simon 179, 237
Larochfoucault-Liancourt, Count 175
Laugier, Marc-Antoine 80
Lasius, Georg 230, 245, 359
Lassaulx, Johann Claudius 146
Lassen, Christian 177
Lassus, Jean-Baptiste-Antoine 144
Layard, Henry 161–62, 298
Leake, William 31
Lebas, Louis-Hippolyte 18
Leclère, Achille 40
Lecointe, Joseph 35
Le Corbusier 4, 355
Ledoux, Claude-Nicolas 80
Lenbach, Franz 354
Lenoir, Albert 56
Leonardo da Vinci 170
Lesueur, Jean Baptiste 100
Lessing, Gotthold, Ephraim 124, 150, 151, 153

Lessing, Julius 373–74, 376
Letarouilly, Paul-Marie 126, 155, 214
Letronne, J.-A. 61, 298
Liebig, Justus von 284, 285
Lindenau, Bernhard August 67, 68, 71, 72, 109, 174, 176
Lindley, William 134–36, 148, 175–76
Linnaeus 157
Lipsius, Constantin 105, 107, 124, 339, 355–56, 359–60, 361, 365
Liszt, Franz 72, 174, 229, 232, 257
Liverpool: Lime Street Station 242; St. George's Hall 213
Löhr, Moritz 314–18
London: British Museum 193, 223, 292, 299; Buckingham Palace 212; cemetery project 190; Duke of Wellington's hearse 214–15; Elgin Marbles 182; Great Exhibition building 183, 190–91, 197, 205, 288; King's Cross Station 242; Marlborough House 209, 212, 217, 226; St. Pancras Station 242; competition design for Whitehall 233; Royal Albert Hall 226, 312; Somerset House 209; South Kensington complex 209, 226–27, 233, 310; Windsor Castle 100
Loos, Adolf 370
Louis XVIII, King of France 35
Louis-Philippe, King of France 24, 165, 166
Lübke, Wilhelm 116–17, 230, 233, 305, 306, 309, 316, 364
Lucae, Richard 290
Lucerne: Hotel Schweizerhof 240; Palais Segesser 241
Ludwig I, King of Bavaria 39, 44, 45, 78, 83, 257, 264
Ludwig II, King of Bavaria 252–60, 265, 266
Lüttichau, August von 70, 82, 98, 99, 100, 172
Lützow, Carl von 363–64
Lyell, Charles 160
Lysippus 116

Magarius, Heinrich 347
Mahmud II, Sultan 43
Mainz: theater 118, 119
Makart, Hans 267, 332, 338
Malthus, Thomas 276
Manteuffel, Claus, Zoege von 94, 103, 356
Marchard, Etienne 161
Marx, Karl 165, 192, 278
Maximilian II, King of Bavaria 16, 39, 85, 253, 263, 264
Maybeck, Bernard 366
Mazois, François 18, 173, 298
Mengs, Anton Raphael 69
Meissner, Alfred 72, 78
Meslin, Louis 365
Messina: Cathedral 41
Metzger, Eduard 17, 45, 54, 57, 63, 64, 79
Michelangelo 3, 90, 116, 170, 237, 267, 306, 330
Middleton, Robin 26
Mies van der Rohe, Ludwig 371
Milan: Cathedral 59
Milde, Kurt 101
Milizia, Francesco 118
Mill, John Stuart 193
Minton, Herbert 193, 207, 210
Moleschott, Jakob 1, 230, 232, 268, 284–85
Molière 121, 124
Moller, Georg 63, 79, 118, 119, 147, 333
Montez, Lola 78, 257
Montigny, Gradjean de 155
Moravánszky, Ákos 364
Moretti, Pietro 97
Morris, William 371
Morey, Mathieu Prosper 40, 41
Mozart, Wolfgang Amadeus 121, 124, 125, 232, 301, 330, 347
Müller, Albert 338
Müller, Carl Otfried 13, 61, 150–51, 155, 184, 219
Munich: Alte Pinokothek 84, 107; Bavarian Nationalmuseum 310; Church of All Saints 84; Festspielhaus 3, 252–67, 306, 307, 311, 322, 333, 340, 341, 343, 355; Finance Ministry 366; Glass Palace 254; Glyptothek 33, 83; Leuctenberg Palais 84, 357; Ludwigskirche 83; Maximilianeum 254, 256–57, 263, 264; Königsbau 84, 357; provisional theater (in Glass Palace) 252, 254–56; State Library 85
Muthesius, Hermann 3, 370–71
Mütterlein, Max Georg 356
Mycenae: Treasury of Atreus 31
Mylius, Karl Jonas 360

Nagyhörcsök: Scholss Zichy 241–42
Nelson, Charles 309
Neureuther, Gottfried 255, 257
Newton, Issac 13, 179, 237
Nicolai, Georg Hermann 103, 176, 210, 321, 358, 364
Niebuhr, Barthold 18, 44, 50
Nietzsche, Friedrich 5, 6, 9, 346, 347–51
Nuremberg 310

Ohmann, Friedrich 332
Oken, Lorenz 159
Olin, Margaret 372, 373
Olympia: Statue of Zeus 31
Onatus 30
Oppenheim, Martin Wilhelm 100, 103, 175
Orvieto: Cathedral 51
Ottmer, Carl Theodor 97, 243–44
Otto, Prince of Bavaria (King of Greece) 44, 45, 47
Overbeck, Friedrich 50, 71
Ovid 12

Paestum: temples 28, 40, 41
Palermo: Theater Massimo 312–13
Palm, Georg 147

Papworth, John 194
Paris: Beaux-Arts addition (Quai Malaquais) 359; Bibliothèque Ste-Geneviève 120, 287, 357; Gare de l'Est 242; Gare du Nord 242; guardhouse 26; Hôtel de Ville 100; Jardin d'Hiver 175, 287; Jardin des Plantes 21, 156, 157, 279; July Column 26; Madeleine 27; Notre-Dame 144; Opéra 265, 304, 336, 339, 340, 343; Palais des Beaux-Arts 82, 100, 120, 236, 357; Palais de Justice 304; Ste Clotilde 25; St. Julien-le-Pauve 19; St. Severin 19, 25; Sèvres Porcelain Manufactury 279, 371; Stock Exchange 27; Synagogue project 175, 176
Paul, Jean 44
Pausanias 30, 31, 42, 184
Pausias 30
Pauw, Cornelius de 159
Paxton, Joseph 183, 190, 196, 205, 215, 216, 288
Pecht, Friedrich 53, 71, 75, 76, 78, 105, 124, 255, 323, 355
Pehmöller, Christian 63
Percier, Charles 35, 36
Percier (Charles) and Fontaine (Pierre) 80, 83, 120, 126, 156, 356
Pericles 33, 116, 330
Perret, Auguste 4
Pestalozzi, Hans 338
Pevsner, Nikolaus 57, 243
Pfistermeister, Franz Seraph von 256, 258
Phidias 31, 33, 116, 125, 301, 331, 350
Pillnitz: Neues Palais 80
Pistratus 330
Playfair, Lyon 208
Pliny the Elder 30, 184, 292
Plutarch 12, 292
Polycrates 330
Polycritus 331
Polygnotus 30, 331
Pompeii: wall paintings 19, 31, 39–40, 59, 183, 298
Popp, Justus 17
Pöppelmann, Matthäus Daniel 68, 69, 80, 92, 98, 112, 114, 340
Porta, Count della 312
Porth, Hans 145–46, 147, 148
Prince of Wales 312
Prichard, James 160, 163
Prinzhorn, Hans 356
Pugin, Augustus Welby 144, 194, 201, 204, 207, 208, 209
Pythagoras 221, 331

Quandt, Johann Gottlob 70–71, 78, 107, 172
Quast, Alexander Ferdinand von 189
Quatremère de Quincy, Antoine-Chrysostome 27, 28, 31–33, 34, 35, 36, 58, 155, 159, 183, 185, 284, 298
Quitzsch, Hans 356

Raoul-Rochette, Désiré 30, 38, 61, 62, 159, 298
Raphael 69, 112, 116, 154, 330
Rauch, Christian 71, 75, 76, 79
Ravenna: San Vitale 152
Redgrave, Richard 193, 194–95, 196, 201–03, 204, 206, 209, 212, 213, 214, 215, 216, 217, 290, 291, 373
Redgrave, Samuel 194
Redtenbacher, Rudolf 364, 368
Regensburg: Cathedral 17; Church of St. Jacob 372; Walhalla 57, 84
Reichenbach, Graf 192
Reichensperger, August 144, 274
Reissiger, Karl 71
Revett, Nicholas 30, 34, 58, 60, 204
Richardson, H.H. 140
Richter, Hermann August 358
Richter, Ludwig 71
Riechardt, Charl Friedrich 136
Rietschel, Ernst Wilhelm 71, 75–76, 77, 78, 95, 107, 121, 159, 169
Riegl, Alois 5, 152, 371–81
Rimini: San Francesco 120
Riocreux, M. 279
Rio de Janeiro: theater project 251–52, 322, 340, 341
Robinson, John Charles 212, 213, 216, 290
Röckel, August 167, 311
Rolle, Karl 121
Romberg, J. Andreas 110, 130, 131, 132, 175
Rome: Belvedere 84, 340; Cancelleria 84; Coliseum 60; Palazzo Massimi 126; Palazzo Farnese 84, 126; St. Peter's 306; Trajan's Column 50–51, 61
Rondelet, Jean-Baptiste 179
Root, John 365
Rosenthal, Carl Albert 85
Rösner, Johann 316
Rothschild, Baron de 175
Rubens, Peter Paul 15, 69
Ruge, Arnold 167, 192
Rumohr, Carl Friedrich 61, 105, 150, 151–55, 272, 274, 304
Runge, Philipp Otto 70
Ruskin, John 188, 195
Russell, John 194

Sack, Baron von 18
Saint-Hilaire, Geoffroy 158
Saint-Simon, Claude Henri de 56
Sangiorgio, Pietro di 118
Sansovino, Andrea 114
Sayn-Wittgenstein, Carolyne 229, 232, 233–34, 235
Schadow, Wilhelm von 71
Schaubert, Eduard 189
Schauss, Friedrich 260, 265
Schelling, F. W. 151, 153–54, 159, 274
Schiller, Friedrich 82, 121, 124, 125, 158, 272, 276, 346, 347, 350, 351
Schilling, Johannes 346

Schinkel, Karl Friedrich 1–2, 4, 6, 7, 27, 53, 61, 62, 63, 79, 81, 83, 86–92, 94, 95, 98, 105, 116, 117, 118–19, 120, 121, 122–23, 131, 143, 145, 179, 238, 275, 313, 331, 340, 347, 357, 363, 371
Schirrmacher, Georg Theodor 311
Schlegel, Friedrich 144, 274
Schliemann, Heinrich 353, 372
Schmarsow, August 290, 368, 370, 379
Schmidt, Friedrich von 314, 336
Schnaase, Carl 62, 306, 380
Schnorr von Carolsfeld, Julius 71, 72, 76, 78, 112, 321
Schnorr von Carolsfeld, Ludwig 257
Schönauer, Alexander 215
Schopenhauer, Arthur 70, 271, 272, 276, 350, 351
Schorn, Ludwig von 36, 44
Schreiber, Bernhard 358
Schröder, Christian Matthias 130, 132
Schröder-Devrient, Wilhelmine 70, 71, 78, 170
Schubert, Andreas 68, 75
Schülter, Andreas 90
Schulz, H. W. 172
Schumacher, Fritz 356, 371
Schumann, Clara 72
Schumann, Robert 72, 77
Schuricht, Christian Friedrich 80, 97
Schwerin: Castle 105
Scott, George Gilbert 141, 145, 146, 148, 149
Scott, Major-General Henry 312
Séchan, Charles 100, 174, 175, 210, 215, 251
Sédille, Paul 364
Selinunte: Temple of Empedocles 36
Semper, Anna Catharina (daughter) 336
Semper, Bertha, née Thimmig (wife) 73–75, 97, 165, 170, 171, 172, 174, 176, 178, 192, 199–200, 211, 212, 213, 226, 234
Semper, Christian Gottfried Emmanuel (father) 11, 13, 14, 16, 19, 20, 21, 23, 24, 25, 39, 42, 45
Semper, Conrad (son) 200, 311, 336, 355
Semper, Elise (sister) 11, 13, 14, 53, 176
Semper, Emmanuel (son) 336, 341, 353
Semper, Georg (brother) 11, 20, 52
SEMPER, GOTTFRIED
Life: Early years and schooling 11–16; in Munich 16–17; first stay in Paris 18–19; second stay in Paris 21–25; Gau's influence on 25–27; in Italy and Sicily 38–42; in Greece 42–46; meets Schinkel 53; appointment to Dresden chair 63–64; reorganization of Academy 72–73; marriage 73–75; early projects 92–129; Hamburg projects 129–49; inaugural address 150–55; Academy lectures 155–64; flight from Dresden 167–71; third stay in Paris 171–76; settles in London 176, 189–90; involvement with Great Exhibition of 1851 192–99; at Department of Practical Art 209–18; relocation to Zurich 225–27; resumption of architectural practice 234–51; Semper and Nietzsche 348–52
Architectural Drawings, Designs, and Buildings: student designs in Paris 21–23; sketches in Italy 40, 47; polychrome drawings of Athens 48; tomb for Georg Semper 52; Donner Pavilion 62–63, 65, 94, 130; festival designs for King Anton 75–76, 94; stage designs for *Antigone* 76; pedestal for statue of Friedrich August I 76, 92, 95; first Hoftheater 9, 76–77, 96–100, 106, 117–129, 210, 225, 309, 320–21, 341, 355, 357; Japanese Palace (Antiquity Rooms) 92–94; maternity hospital 92, 94–95; Dresden Forum 96–99, 105, 107–12, 357; Dresden Synagogue 100, 106, 349, 358; Villa Rosa 100–03, 358; Oppenheim Palais 103–05, 112; Elimayer shop 105; Houpe residence 105; military barracks in Bautzen 105; cholera memorial 105, 106; provisional triumphal arch 105; vase designs for Meissen 105; tomb for Carl Friedrich von Rumohr 105; tomb for Charl Maria von Weber 105; tomb for Oppenheim 105; Leipzig Railway Station (design) 105; Blasewitz School (design) 105; Oschatz City Hall (design) 105, 106; Freemasonry Lodge (design) 105; hospital in Bucharest (design) 105; Schwerin Castle (design) 105; Dresden Art Gallery 6, 78, 107–17, 121, 126, 230, 233, 236, 250, 305, 309, 311, 321, 326, 358; Hamburg Exchange (design) 21–23, 129–32, 136; rebuilding plan for Hamburg 133–36; Hamburg City Hall (design) 106, 136–37; Wilhelm Semper Pharmacy 134, 137, 139; Nikolaikirche (Church of St. Nicholas, design) 134, 136, 137–49, 156, 274, 356; Paris Synagogue (design) 175, 176; cemetery project for Woolrich 190; layouts of Great Exhibition 197; hearse for Duke of Wellington 214–15; ebony sideboard for Sir James Emerson 215; exhibition for Gore House 215; telegraph kiosk (design) 215; Department certificate 215; Punchbowl 215; hostel (design) 215; pottery school (design) 215; bath and laundry (design) 215, 225, 251; addition to Woolrich Royal Arsenal (design) 215; Mixed Fabric Court 215; Roman Ampitheater for Crystal Palace (design) 215–16, 251, 254, 256; layouts for Paris World Exposition of 1855 213, 226; design for South Kensington complex 209, 226–27, 233, 310; ivory baton for Richard Wagner 232; competition design for Whitehall 233; Zurich Polytechnikum 234, 235–40, 250, 309, 360; department store in Zurich (design) 235; Zurich City Hall and Kranz Quarter (design) 234; Glarus Town Hall (design) 240; Hotel in Bad Ragas (design) 240; Hotel Schweizerhof (design) 240; casino in Baden (design) 240;

villa in Brunnen (design) 241; Villa Garbald 241; Palais von Segesser (design) 241; Villa Rieter-Rothpletz (design) 241; Schloss Zichy (design) 241–42; Zurich Hauptbahnhof (design) 242–44; floating laundry 244–45; Polytechnikum Observatory 245; Fierz textile concern 246; apartments in Winterthur (design) 246; catholic church in Winterthur (design) 246; Winterthur Town Hall 246–51, 264, 306, 309, 313; theater in Brussels 251; theater for Rio de Janeiro 251–52, 322, 340, 341; Munich Provisional Theater 252, 254–56; Munich Festspielhaus 3, 252–67, 306, 307, 311, 322, 333, 340, 341, 343, 355; Kunsthalle (design) 311; Altona Railway Station (design) 311; Hofburg Forum 317–20, 323, 326, 332, 338; Vienna Art History Museum 6, 7, 314–20, 323–32, 338, 358, 361, 369; Vienna Natural History Museum 6, 314–20, 323–27, 338, 358, 361; Hofburg Theater 320, 322, 323–24, 333–36, 343; second Dresden Hoftheater 6, 321–22, 336, 339–52, 353, 358, 371; Hofburg Palace 314, 317, 318, 323, 332, 333; Hofburg administration 318, 332; Vienna Stock Exhange (design) 333; apartment complex on Löwelstrasse (design) 333; Hofburg Theater warehouse 333; theater in Darmstadt (design) 333

Writings and Theory: theatricality 7–8, 59–60, 87–92, 116–17, 125–29, 237–40, 260–65, 299–302, 326–32, 339–52, 361; report on Trajan's Column 50–51, "Die Anwendung der Farben in der Architectur und Plastik" 53–54; *Preliminary Remarks on Polychrome Architecture* 53–62, 125, 221; notion of *Gesamtkunstwerk* 8, 60, 125–29, 184, 185, 264–65, 274, 351–52, 361; monograph on first Dresden Hoftheater 129, 177; views on classical polychromy 48–51, 53–54, 58–61, 63, 92–94, 180–81, 182–85, 188, 294, 298–301; views on contemporary architecture 55–57, 274–75, 304; meaning of "organic" 56, 224–25; use of Renaissance style 119–21, 125–26, 307, 339, 357; on Medieval architecture 137–45; inaugural address at Dresden Academy 150–55; style theory 154–55, 206–07, 217–18, 272–73, 277, 304, 329–30, 362; "Comparative Building Theory" 156–64, 177–82, 267–68, 306; use of biological analogy 157–59; use of anthropology and ethnology 159–63; articles of *Zeitschrift für praktische Baukunst* 175; *Four Elements of Architecture* 182–89, 304; theory of dressing (*Bekleidung*) 180–81, 290–302, 362, 368, 370, 376; *Science, Industry and Art* 200, 205–08, 209, 218, 274; on industrialization 205–06; "Practical Art in Metal and Hard Materials" 210–11; London lectures 216–18; critique of Bötticher's theory 219–22, 224, 225, 271, 287, 297, 299; *On the Leaden Slingshot Missiles of the Ancients* 222–25, 268; *Der Stil in den tectonischen und tektonischen Künsten* 268–308, 361, 363, 364, 365, 366, 376, 377, 378; "On the Formal Lawfulness of Ornament" 270–73; Prolegomena to *Der Stil* 273–77; notion of ornament 270–73, 291–300, 370, 377–78; notion of *Stoffwechsel* 284–85; spatial motive 288–90, 368, 370, 379–80; theory of masking 299–302, 350–53; Dionysian over Apollonian 6, 121, 346–51; *On Architectural Styles* 303–08, 348–49, 365; critique of Darwinism 305; Riegl's interpretation of 371–81

Semper, Hans (son) 16, 217, 218, 219, 336, 353, 354, 365, 376, 380
Semper, Johann Carl (brother) 11, 16, 18, 20, 47, 133, 166, 171, 176, 192, 311
Semper, Johanna Elisabeth (daughter) 336
Semper, Johanna Marie, née Papp (mother) 11, 14, 15, 20, 23, 38, 52, 53, 74, 75 96, 149, 212
Semper, Manfred (son) 1, 200, 214, 226, 233, 241, 260, 267, 309, 311, 320, 322, 333, 336, 337, 339, 353, 355
Semper, Wilhelm (brother) 11, 15, 20, 50, 134, 137, 139, 140, 147, 233
Seneca 184
Serradifalco, Domenico 61
Seyn-Wittgenstein, Princess Carolyne 233–34, 235
Shakespeare 121, 124, 126, 176, 301, 363
Siccardsburgh (August Siccard von) and van der Nüll (Eduard) 314, 361, 368
Sickel, Theodor von 336, 337, 372
Sieveking, Karl 64
Siemens, Ernst Werner 213
Siemens, Karl Wilhelm 213–14, 232
Simpson, J. 210
Socrates 350
Soller, August 63
Sophocles 60, 121, 125, 301, 348, 350
Soufflot, Jacques-Germain 80
Speckter, Otto 137
Stackelberg, Baron von 31, 34, 36, 50, 58
Stadler, Ferdinand 225, 246
Stadler, Julius 230, 360
Stahmer, Eduard 12, 131–32, 134, 136–37, 149
Stammann, Franz Georg 64, 130, 136
Stammann, Friedrich 136
Stephenson, George 68
Stieglitz, Christian Ludwig 29, 269, 306
Stier, Wilhelm 313
Stockmeyer, Ernst 356
Stöter, Ferdinand 147
Strack, Johann Heinrich 145, 147, 148
Street, George Edmund 145
Streiter, Richard 369, 376
Stuart, James 30, 34, 58, 60, 61, 204
Stüler, Friedrich August 105–06, 109, 311, 313
Suchsland, Friedrich 268–69

Sullivan, Louis 365
Sulzer, Johann Jakob 175, 231, 232, 246
Sydenham: Roman Ampitheater for Crystal Palace 215–16, 251, 254, 256; Crystal Palace 210, 213, 215; Mixed Fabrics Court in Crystal Palace 215, 225, 251

Tennant, James Emerson 215
Thausing, Moritz 372
Theatricality 7–8, 59–60, 87–92, 116–17, 125–29, 237–40, 260–65, 299–302, 326–32, 339–52, 361
Thibaut, Bernhard Friedrich 12, 13, 14
Thiersch, Friedrich Theodor 43–45, 48, 52, 61, 155
Thormeyer, Gottlob Friedrich 80, 81, 97, 357
Thömig (painter) 47
Thorwaldsen, Bertel 33, 35, 39, 44, 50, 62, 71, 83
Thron-Dittmar, Herr von 17
Thürmer, Joseph 63, 81, 97, 103
Tieck, Ludwig 70, 100, 121–22, 124, 144
Tietz, Karl 316, 333
Titian 69
Townsend, H. J. 194

Uprising in Dresden 165–70

Valentin, Madame 21, 27
Van der Nüll, Eduard 314, 316
Vanvitelli, Luigi 329
Van Zanten, David 28, 125
Vasari, Giorgio 152, 154, 156
Vaudoyer, A.-L.-T. 125
Vaudoyer, Léon 27, 28
Vernet, Horace 28
Venice: Doge's Palace 367; Library 114
Venturi, Lionello 381
Vermeer, Jan 69
Veronese, Paolo 69
Vicenza: Villa Rotunda 101
Viel de Saint-Maux, Charles 59
Vienna: Academy of Fine Arts 338, 358, 361; Art History Museum 6, 7, 314–20, 323–32, 338, 358, 361, 369; Burgtor 314, 318; Church of Am Steinhof 369; City Hall 314, 336; Hofburg Forum 317–20, 323, 326, 332, 338; Hofburg Palace 314, 317, 318, 323, 332, 333; Hofburg Theater 320, 322, 323–24, 333–36, 343; Hofburg Theater warehouse 333; Museum for Art and Industry 310, 315, 360; Natural History Museum 6, 314–20, 323–27, 338, 358, 361; Opera House 314, 340; Parliament 314, 361; Post Office Savings Bank 331, 369; Stock Exchange 333, 361; University of Vienna 314, 361–62; Votivkirche 314, 361; World Exhibition 324
Vieweg, Eduard 156, 164, 173, 177, 178, 179, 182, 200, 210, 224, 267–69, 272, 277, 278, 279, 290
Vignon, Alexandre-Pierre 27
Viollet-le-Duc, Eugène-Emmanuel 144, 269, 287, 312, 370
Virgil 153
Vischer, Friedrich Theodor 230–31, 270, 272–73, 316, 366, 367, 379
Vischer, Robert 366, 367, 381
Viterbo: rock tomb 50
Vitruvius 90, 250, 276
Vitzthum, Prince 63–64, 67
Vogel von Vogelstein, Carl Christian 107
Voigt, August von 254
Volkelt, Johannes 367
Vulci: painted tombs 31

Waagen, Gustav 194, 311
Wackenroder, Wilhelm Heinrich 70
Waetzoldt, Wilhelm 151
Wagner, Fritz 365
Wagner, Otto 57, 331, 358, 360, 364, 368–69, 376
Wagner, Minna 253, 311
Wagner, Richard 7–9, 60, 71–72, 76–78, 95, 126–29, 169, 170, 174, 175, 185, 191, 225, 231, 232, 234, 252–67, 271, 301, 309, 311, 337–38, 347–48, 351, 363; Semper's influence on 77–78, 128–29, 174, 232
Wagner-Rieger, Renate 357
Wanner, Jakob Friedrich 244
Weber, August 358
Weber, Carl Maria 70, 71, 105, 124, 347
Wegmann, Albert 225
Wegmann, Peter 250
Weinbrenner, Friedrich 19, 83, 275
Wellington, Duke of 214–15
Wesendonck, Mathilde 232, 242, 258
Whewell, William 197
Wiebeking, Carl Friedrich 16
Wiegmann, Rudolf 63, 64, 85
Wigley, Mark 300
Wilhelm, King of Prussia 310
Wilkins, William 31
Wilson, Charles 194
Wimmel, Carl Ludwig 130–32, 134, 136, 139, 140, 146, 147
Winckelmann, J. J. 29, 30, 34, 44, 58, 62, 69, 80, 83, 150, 151, 153, 154, 272
Winterthur: apartments (project) 246; Catholic church (project) 246; Town Hall 246–51, 264, 306, 309, 313
Wolff, Johann Heinrich 357
Wolff, Johann Kaspar 225, 236, 246
Wölfflin, Heinrich 283, 367, 368, 379
Wolframsdorf, Otto 98, 100, 109, 110
Woods, Joseph 34
Wornum, Ralph 201, 206, 210, 212, 216
Wulff, Eduard 364
Wulsten, Johann 63
Wyatt, Matthew Digby 182–83, 195, 196, 197, 203–05, 210, 213, 215

Ypsilanti, Alexander 42

Zeising, Adolf 271, 273, 276
Zerzog, Julia von 210
Zeus 31, 238, 270, 346
Zevi, Bruno 290
Zichy, Princess 242
Ziegler, Jules 217, 279, 281–82
Zimmermann, Robert 271, 367, 372
Zucci, Andrea 97
Zurich: church in Enge 360; chemistry building (ETH) 360; Fierz textile concern 246; floating laundry 244–45; Hauptbahnhof 242–44; physics building (ETH) 360–61; Polytechnikum (ETH) 234, 235–40, 250, 309, 361; Polytechnikum Observatory 245
Zwirner, Ernst 143, 145, 147, 148, 149